New Revised Edition

Webster's
Classic
Reference
Library

Over 6 million in print!

THESAURUS

McGraw-Hill
Children's Publishing

A Division of The McGraw-Hill Companies

Copyright © 2001 McGraw-Hill Children's Publishing.
Published by Landoll, an imprint of McGraw-Hill Children's Publishing, a division of The McGraw-Hill Companies.
Made in Canada.

Send all inquiries to:
McGraw-Hill Children's Publishing
8787 Orion Place
Columbus, Ohio 43240-4027

00730-1589

The thesaurus is a useful tool for expanding vocabulary, which adds variety to speech and writing.

A thesaurus is a compilation of words and phrases that are similar in meaning. The name for these like words is synonyms; words that are opposite in meaning are called antonyms.

This Webster's thesaurus from Landoll is organized alphabetically, using a base of common words and their variants. Synonyms *(SYN.)* are listed first, followed by antonyms *(ANT.)* when applicable. We believe you will find this to be a handy and reliable reference book.

a *(SYN.)* any, one.

abandon *(SYN.)* relinquish, resign, surrender, leave, give up, cease, forsake, desert, quit, vacate, abjure, discard, evacuate, withdraw. *(ANT.)* keep, stay, maintain, embrace, adopt, join, engage, retain.

abandoned *(SYN.)* depraved, wicked, deserted, desolate, forsaken, rejected, cast off, degraded, loose, unrestrained, marooned, immoral, evil. *(ANT.)* befriended, cherished, chaste, moral, respectable, virtuous, righteous.

abase *(SYN.)* humble, reduce, bring down, degrade, demote, mock, scorn, belittle, shame. *(ANT.)* exalt, cherish, elevate, uplift, dignify.

abash *(SYN.)* disconcert, bewilder, confuse, put off. *(ANT.)* comfort, relax, hearten.

abashed *(SYN.)* confused, ashamed, embarrassed, mortified, humiliated.

abate *(SYN.)* lessen, curtail, reduce, decrease, restrain, decline, stop, moderate, subside, slow, diminish, slacken. *(ANT.)* grow, prolong, increase, extend, intensify, quicken, enhance, accelerate.

abbey *(SYN.)* nunnery, convent, cloister.

abbot *(SYN.)* friar, monk.

abbreviate *(SYN.)* shorten, lessen, abridge, condense, curtail, reduce, cut, trim, restrict, clip, contract. *(ANT.)* lengthen, increase, expand, extend, prolong, enlarge.

abbreviation *(SYN.)* abridgment, reduction, shortening, condensation. *(ANT.)* expansion, extension, amplification, lengthening dilation.

abdicate *(SYN.)* relinquish, renounce, vacate, waive, desert, forsake, abolish, quit, abandon, surrender, resign. *(ANT.)* maintain, stay, retain, uphold.

abdomen *(SYN.)* paunch, belly, stomach.

abduct *(SYN.)* carry off, take, kidnap.

aberrant *(SYN.)* capricious, devious, irregular, unnatural, abnormal. *(ANT.)* regular, usual, fixed, ordinary.

aberration *(SYN.)* oddity, abnormality, irregularity, deviation, monster, abortion, eccentricity. *(ANT.)* conformity, normality.

abet *(SYN.)* support, connive, encourage, conspire, help, incite, aid, assist. *(ANT.)* deter, check, hinder, frustrate, oppose, discourage, resist.

abettor *(SYN.)* accomplice, ally, confederate, associate, accessory. *(ANT.)* opponent, enemy.

abeyance *(SYN.)* cessation, pause, inactivity, rest, suspension, recess, dormancy, remission. *(ANT.)* ceaseless, continuation.

abhor *(SYN.)* hate, loathe, execrate, avoid, scorn, detest, despise.

abhorrent *(SYN.)* loathsome, horrible, detestable, nauseating, hateful, despicable, disgusting, foul, offensive, terrible, revolting.

abide *(SYN.)* obey, accept, tolerate, endure, dwell, stay, reside.

ability *(SYN.)* aptness, capability, skill, faculty, talent. *(ANT.)* incapacity, incompetency, weakness, ineptitude, inability.

abject *(SYN.)* sordid, infamous, miserable, wretched, mean, base, contempt.

abjure *(SYN.)* relinquish, renounce, vacate, waive, desert, quit, leave, forsake, foreswear, abdicate, resign, surrender. *(ANT.)* maintain, uphold, stay.

able *(SYN.)* qualified, competent, fit, capable, skilled, efficient, clever, talented, adequate, skillful. *(ANT.)* inadequate, trained, incapable, weak, incompetent, unable.

abnegation *(SYN.)* rejection, renunciation, self-denial, abandonment, refusal, relinquishment, abjuration.

abnormal *(SYN.)* uncommon, unnatural, odd, irregular, monstrous. *(ANT.)* natural, usual, normal, average.

aboard *(SYN.)* on board.

abode *(SYN.)* dwelling, habitat, home, residence, address, quarters, lodging place, domicile.

abolish *(SYN.)* end, eradicate, annul, cancel, revoke, destroy, invalidate, overthrow, obliterate, abrogate, erase, exterminate, wipe out, eliminate. *(ANT.)* promote, restore, continue, establish, sustain.

abominable

abominable *(SYN.)* foul, dreadful, hateful, revolting, vile, odious, loathsome, detestable, bad, horrible, terrible, awful, disgusting. *(ANT.)* delightful, pleasant, agreeable, commendable, admirable, noble.

abominate *(SYN.)* despise, detest, hate, dislike, abhor, loathe. *(ANT.)* like, cherish, approve, admire.

abomination *(SYN.)* freak, detestation, hatred, disgust, revulsion, horror.

abort *(SYN.)* flop, fizzle, miscarry, abandon, cancel.

abortion *(SYN.)* miscarriage, fiasco, disaster, failure, defeat.

abortive *(SYN.)* unproductive, vain, unsuccessful, useless, failed, futile. *(ANT.)* rewarding, effective, profitable, successful.

abound *(SYN.)* swarm, plentiful, filled, overflow, teem. *(ANT.)* scarce, lack.

about *(SYN.)* relating to, involving, concerning, near, around, upon, almost, approximately, of, nearby, ready to, nearly.

about-face *(SYN.)* reversal, backing out, shift, switch.

above *(SYN.)* higher than, overhead, on, upon, over, superior to. *(ANT.)* under, beneath, below.

aboveboard *(SYN.)* forthright, open, frank, honest, overt, plain, straightforward, guileless, trustworthy. *(ANT.)* sneaky, wily.

abracadabra *(SYN.)* voodoo, magic, charm, spell.

abrasion *(SYN.)* rubbing, roughness, scratching, scraping, friction, chap, chafe, chapping, scrape.

abrasive *(SYN.)* rough, hurtful, sharp, galling, annoying, grating, cutting, irritating, caustic. *(ANT.)* pleasant, soothing, comforting, agreeable, smooth.

abreast *(SYN.)* beside, side by side, alongside.

abridge *(SYN.)* condense, cut, abbreviate, make shorter, contract, shorten, reduce, summarize, curtail. *(ANT.)* increase, lengthen, expand, extend.

abridgment *(SYN.)* digest, condensation, summary, abbreviation, shortening.

(ANT.) lengthening, expansion, enlargement.

abroad *(SYN.)* away, overseas, broadly, widely. *(ANT.)* at home, privately, secretly.

abrogate *(SYN.)* rescind, withdraw, revoke, annul, cancel, abolish, repeal.

abrupt *(SYN.)* sudden, unexpected, blunt, curt, precipitous, sharp, hasty, unannounced, harsh, precipitate, brusque, rude, rough, short, steep. *(ANT.)* foreseen, smooth, warm, courteous, gradual, smooth, expected, anticipated.

abscess *(SYN.)* pustule, sore, wound, inflammation.

absence *(SYN.)* nonexistence, deficiency, lack, need, shortcoming. *(ANT.)* attendance, completeness, existence, presence.

absent *(SYN.)* gone, away, truant, departed, inattentive, lacking, not present, out, off. *(ANT.)* attending, attentive, present.

absent-minded *(SYN.)* inattentive, daydreaming, preoccupied, absorbed, bemused, dreaming, forgetful. *(ANT.)* observant, attentive, alert.

absolute *(SYN.)* unconditional, entire, actual, complete, thorough, total, perfect, essential, supreme, ultimate, unrestricted, positive, unqualified, whole. *(ANT.)* partial, conditional, dependent, accountable, restricted, qualified, limited, fragmentary.

absolutely *(SYN.)* positively, really, doubtlessly. *(ANT.)* doubtfully, uncertainly.

absolution *(SYN.)* pardon, forgiveness, acquittal, mercy, amnesty, remission.

absolutism *(SYN.)* autarchy, dictatorship, authoritarianism.

absolve *(SYN.)* exonerate, discharge, acquit, pardon, forgive, clear, excuse. *(ANT.)* blame, convict, charge, accuse.

absorb *(SYN.)* consume, swallow up, engulf, assimilate, imbibe, engage, engross, take in, integrate, incorporate, occupy. *(ANT.)* discharge, dispense, emit, exude, leak, eliminate, bore, tire, weary, drain.

absorbent *(SYN.)* permeable, spongy, pervious, porous. *(ANT.)* waterproof, impervious.

absorbing *(SYN.)* interesting, engaging, exciting, engrossing, entertaining, thrilling, intriguing, pleasing, fascinating. (*ANT.*) *dull, boring, tedious, tiresome.*

abstain (*SYN.*) forbear, forego, decline, resist, withhold, refrain. (*ANT.*) *pursue.*

abstemious (*SYN.*) abstinent, sparing, cautious, temperate, ascetic, self-disciplined, continent, sober. (*ANT.*) *uncontrolled, indulgent, abandoned, excessive.*

abstinence (*SYN.*) fasting, self-denial, continence, forbearance, sobriety, refrain. (*ANT.*) *gluttony, greed, excess, self-indulgence.*

abstract (*SYN.*) theoretical, ideal, part, appropriate, steal, separate, purloin, nonconcrete, summarize. (*ANT.*) *return, concrete, unite, add, replace, specific, clear, particular, restore.*

abstracted (*SYN.*) preoccupied, absent-minded, parted, removed, stolen, abridged, taken away. (*ANT.*) *replaced, returned, alert, united, added.*

abstraction (*SYN.*) idea, image, generalization, thought, opinion, impression, notion. (*ANT.*) *matter, object, substance.*

abstruse (*SYN.*) arcane, obscure, complicated, abstract, esoteric, metaphysical. (*ANT.*) *uncomplicated, direct, obvious, simple.*

absurd (*SYN.*) ridiculous, silly, unreasonable, foolish, irrational, nonsensical, impossible, inconsistent, preposterous, self-contradictory, unbelievable. (*ANT.*) *rational, sensible, sound, meaningful, consistent, reasonable.*

absurdity (*SYN.*) foolishness, nonsense, farce, drivel, joke, senselessness, folly.

abundance (*SYN.*) ampleness, profusion, copiousness, plenty. (*ANT.*) *insufficiency, want, absence, dearth, scarcity.*

abundant (*SYN.*) ample, overflowing, plentiful, rich, teeming, profuse, abounding. (*ANT.*) *insufficient, scant, not enough, scarce, deficient, rare, uncommon, absent.*

abuse (*SYN.*) maltreatment, misuse, reproach, defamation, dishonor, mistreat, damage, ill-use, reviling, aspersion, desecration, invective, insult, outrage, profanation, perversion, disparagement, misem-

ploy, misapply, hurt, harm, injure, scold, berate. (*ANT.*) *plaudit, respect, appreciate, commendation, protect, praise, cherish.*

abusive (*SYN.*) harmful, insulting, libelous, hurtful, slanderous, nasty, defamatory, injurious, scathing, derogatory. (*ANT.*) *helpful, laudatory.*

abut (*SYN.*) touch, border, meet, join, connect with.

abutment (*SYN.*) pier, buttress, bulwark, brace, support.

abysmal (*SYN.*) bottomless, unfathomable, yawning, overwhelming.

abyss (*SYN.*) depth, chasm, void, infinitude, limbo, unknowable.

academic (*SYN.*) learned, scholarly, theoretical, erudite, bookish, formal, pedantic. (*ANT.*) *ignorant, practical, simple, uneducated.*

academy (*SYN.*) college, school.

accede (*SYN.*) grant, agree, comply, consent, yield, endorse, accept, admit. (*ANT.*) *dissent, disagree, differ, oppose.*

accelerate (*SYN.*) quicken, dispatch, facilitate, hurry, rush, speed up, forward, hasten, push, expedite. (*ANT.*) *hinder, retard, slow, delay.*

accent (*SYN.*) tone, emphasis, inflection, stress, consent.

accept (*SYN.*) take, approve, receive, allow, consent to, believe, adopt, admit. (*ANT.*) *ignore, reject, refuse.*

acceptable (*SYN.*) passable, satisfactory, fair, adequate, standard, par, tolerable. (*ANT.*) *poor, substandard.*

access (*SYN.*) entrance, approach, course, gateway, door, avenue, gain, enter.

accessible (*SYN.*) nearby, attainable, achievable, affable, accommodating. (*ANT.*) *remote, unobtainable, unachievable, standoffish, forbidding, unfriendly.*

accessory (*SYN.*) extra, addition, assistant, supplement, contributory, accomplice.

accident (*SYN.*) casualty, disaster, misfortune, mishap, chance, calamity, contingency, fortuity, misadventure, mischance, injury, catastrophe. (*ANT.*) *purpose, intention, calculation.*

accidental *(SYN.)* unintended, chance, casual, fortuitous, contingent, unplanned, unexpected, unforeseen. *(ANT.)* calculated, planned, willed, intended, intentional, deliberate.

acclaim *(SYN.)* eminence, fame, glory, honor, reputation, credit, applaud, distinction, approve, notoriety. *(ANT.)* infamy, obscurity, disapprove, reject, disrepute.

acclimated *(SYN.)* adapted, habituated, acclimatized, accommodated, seasoned, inured, used to, weathered, reconciled.

accolade *(SYN.)* praise, honor, acclaim, recognition, applause, kudos, bouquet, crown, testimonial, acclamation, salute.

accommodate *(SYN.)* help, assist, aid, provide for, serve, oblige, hold, house. *(ANT.)* inconvenience.

accommodating *(SYN.)* obliging, helpful, willing, kind, cooperative, gracious, cordial, sympathetic, unselfish. *(ANT.)* unfriendly, selfish, hostile.

accommodation *(SYN.)* change, alteration, adaptation, convenience, adjustment, acclimatization, aid, help, boon, kindness, service, courtesy. *(ANT.)* inflexibility, rigidity, disservice, stubbornness, disadvantage.

accommodations *(SYN.)* housing, lodgings, room, place, quarters, board.

accompany *(SYN.)* chaperon, consort with, escort, go with, associate with, attend, join. *(ANT.)* abandon, quit, leave, desert, avoid, forsake.

accomplice *(SYN.)* accessory, ally, associate, partner in crime, assistant, sidekick, confederate. *(ANT.)* opponent, rival, enemy, adversary.

accomplish *(SYN.)* attain, consummate, achieve, do, execute, carry out, fulfill, complete, effect, perform, finish. *(ANT.)* fail, frustrate, spoil, neglect, defeat.

accomplished *(SYN.)* proficient, skilled, finished, well-trained, gifted, masterly, polished, able. *(ANT.)* unskilled, amateurish, crude.

accomplishment *(SYN.)* deed, feat, statute, operation, performance, action, achievement, transaction. *(ANT.)* cessation, inhibition, intention, deliberation.

accord *(SYN.)* concur, agree, award, harmony, conformity, agreement, give, tale, sum, statement, record, grant.

accordingly *(SYN.)* consequently, therefore, whereupon, hence, so, thus.

accost *(SYN.)* approach, greet, speak to, address. *(ANT.)* avoid, shun.

account *(SYN.)* description, chronicle, history, narration, reckoning, rate, computation, detail, narrative, relation, recital, consider, believe, deem, record, explanation, report, tale, story, anecdote, reason, statement, tale, ledger.

accountable *(SYN.)* chargeable, answerable, beholden, responsible, obliged, liable.

account for *(SYN.)* justify, explain, substantiate, illuminate, clarify, elucidate.

accredited *(SYN.)* qualified, licensed, deputized, certified, commissioned, vouched for, empowered. *(ANT.)* illicit, unofficial, unauthorized.

accrue *(SYN.)* amass, collect, heap, increase, accumulate, gather, hoard. *(ANT.)* disperse, dissipate, waste, diminish.

accrued *(SYN.)* accumulated, totaled, increased, added, enlarged, amassed.

accumulate *(SYN.)* gather, collect, heap, increase, accrue, assemble, compile, hoard, amass. *(ANT.)* spend, give away, diminish, dissipate.

accumulation *(SYN.)* heap, collection, pile, store, hoard, stack, aggregation.

accurate *(SYN.)* perfect, just, truthful, unerring, meticulous, correct. *(ANT.)* incorrect, mistaken, false, wrong, inaccurate.

accursed *(SYN.)* ill-fated, cursed, condemned, doomed, bedeviled, ruined. *(ANT.)* fortunate, hopeful.

accusation *(SYN.)* charge, incrimination, indictment, arraignment. *(ANT.)* pardon, exoneration, absolve.

accuse *(SYN.)* incriminate, indict, censure, tattle, denounce, charge, arraign, impeach, blame. *(ANT.)* release, vindicate, exonerate, acquit, absolve, clear.

accustom *(SYN.)* addict, familiarize, condition.

accustomed *(SYN.)* familiar with, used to, comfortable with. *(ANT.)* *strange, unusual, rare, unfamiliar.*

ace *(SYN.)* champion, hotshot, pip, one, secret, fighter pilot.

acerbity *(SYN.)* bitterness, harshness, unkindness, sourness, acidity, unfriendliness, acrimony, coldness, sharpness. *(ANT.)* *sweetness, gentleness, kindness, tenderness.*

ache *(SYN.)* hurt, pain, throb.

achieve *(SYN.)* do, execute, gain, obtain, acquire, accomplish, realize, perform, complete, accomplish, finish, fulfill, reach, attain, secure, procure. *(ANT.)* *fail, lose, fall short.*

achievement *(SYN.)* feat, accomplishment, attainment, exploit, realization, performance, completion, deed. *(ANT.)* *botch, dud, mess, omission, defeat, failure.*

acid *(SYN.)* tart, sour, bitter, mordant, biting. *(ANT.)* *base, pleasant, friendly, bland, mild, sweet.*

acknowledge *(SYN.)* allow, admit, concede, recognize, answer, grant, accept, receive. *(ANT.)* *reject, refuse, disavow, refute, deny.*

acme *(SYN.)* summit, top, zenith, peak, crown. *(ANT.)* *bottom.*

acquaint *(SYN.)* inform, teach, enlighten, notify, tell.

acquaintance *(SYN.)* fellowship, friendship, cognizance, knowledge, intimacy, familiarity, companionship, associate, colleague, companion. *(ANT.)* *inexperience, unfamiliarity, ignorance.*

acquiesce *(SYN.)* submit, agree, concur, assent, comply, consent, succumb. *(ANT.)* *refuse, disagree, rebel, argue.*

acquire *(SYN.)* amass, attain, earn, get, procure, assimilate, obtain, secure, gain, appropriate. *(ANT.)* *surrender, lose, forego, forfeit.*

acquirement *(SYN.)* training, skill, learning, achievement, attainment, education, information.

acquisition *(SYN.)* procurement, gain, gift, purchase, proceeds, possession, grant.

acquisitive *(SYN.)* greedy, avid, hoarding, covetous.

acquit *(SYN.)* forgive, exonerate, absolve, cleanse, pardon, excuse, discharge, found not guilty. *(ANT.)* *doom, saddle, sentence, condemn.*

acrid *(SYN.)* bitter, sharp, nasty, stinging, harsh. *(ANT.)* *pleasant, sweet.*

acrimonious *(SYN.)* sharp, sarcastic, acerb, waspish, cutting, stinging, testy. *(ANT.)* *soft, kind, sweet, pleasant, soothing.*

acrobat *(SYN.)* athlete, gymnast.

act *(SYN.)* deed, doing, feat, execution, accomplishment, performance, action, operation, transaction, law, decree, statute, edict, achievement, exploit, statute, judgment, routine, pretense. *(ANT.)* *inactivity, deliberation, cessation.*

acting *(SYN.)* behaving, performing, pretending, officiating, substituting, surrogate, temporary, delegated.

action *(SYN.)* deed, achievement, feat, activity, exploit, movement, motion, behavior, battle, performance, exercise. *(ANT.)* *idleness, inertia, repose, inactivity, rest.*

activate *(SYN.)* mobilize, energize, start, propel. *(ANT.)* *paralyze, immobilize, stop, deaden.*

active *(SYN.)* working, operative, alert, agile, nimble, supple, sprightly, busy, brisk, lively, quick, industrious, energetic, vigorous, industrious, occupied, vivacious, dynamic, engaged. *(ANT.)* *passive, inactive, idle, dormant, lazy, lethargic.*

activism *(SYN.)* engagement, confrontation, agitation, commitment, aggression, fervor, zeal. *(ANT.)* *detachment, lethargy, disengagement.*

activist *(SYN.)* militant, doer, enthusiast.

activity *(SYN.)* action, liveliness, motion, vigor, agility, exercise, energy, quickness, enterprise, movement, briskness. *(ANT.)* *idleness, inactivity, dullness, sloth.*

actor *(SYN.)* performer, trouper, entertainer, thespian.

actual *(SYN.)* true, genuine, certain, factual, authentic, concrete, real. *(ANT.)* *unreal, fake, bogus, nonexistent, false.*

actuality

actuality *(SYN.)* reality, truth, deed, occurrence, fact, certainty. *(ANT.)* theory, fiction, falsehood, supposition.

acute *(SYN.)* piercing, severe, sudden, keen, sharp, perceptive, discerning, shrewd, astute, smart, intelligent. *(ANT.)* bland, mild, dull, obtuse, insensitive.

adamant *(SYN.)* unyielding, firm, obstinate. *(ANT.)* yielding.

adapt *(SYN.)* adjust, conform, accommodate, change, fit, alter, vary, modify. *(ANT.)* misapply, disturb.

add *(SYN.)* attach, increase, total, append, sum, affix, augment, adjoin, put together, unite, supplement. *(ANT.)* remove, reduce, deduct, subtract, detach, withdraw.

address *(SYN.)* greet, hail, accost, speak to, location, residence, home, abode, dwelling, speech, lecture, greeting, oration, presentation. *(ANT.)* avoid, pass by.

adept *(SYN.)* expert, skillful, proficient. *(ANT.)* unskillful.

adequate *(SYN.)* capable, commensurate, fitting, suitable, satisfactory, sufficient, enough, ample, suitable, plenty, fit. *(ANT.)* lacking, scant, insufficient, inadequate.

adhere *(SYN.)* stick fast, grasp, hold, keep, retain, cling, stick to, keep, cleave. *(ANT.)* surrender, abandon, release, separate, loosen.

adherent *(SYN.)* follower, supporter. *(ANT.)* renegade, dropout, defector.

adjacent *(SYN.)* next to, near, bordering, adjoining, touching, neighboring. *(ANT.)* separate, distant, apart.

adjoin *(SYN.)* connect, be close to, affix, attach. *(ANT.)* detach, remove.

adjoining *(SYN.)* touching, bordering, next to, close to. *(ANT.)* distant, remote, separate.

adjourn *(SYN.)* postpone, defer, delay, suspend, discontinue, put off. *(ANT.)* begin, convene, assemble.

adjust *(SYN.)* repair, fix, change, set, regulate, settle, arrange, adapt, suit, accommodate, modify, vary, alter, fit.

administer *(SYN.)* supervise, oversee, direct, manage, rule, govern, control, conduct, provide, give, execute, preside, apply,

contribute, help.

administration *(SYN.)* conduct, direction, management, supervision.

admirable *(SYN.)* worthy, fine, praiseworthy, commendable, excellent.

admiration *(SYN.)* pleasure, wonder, esteem, approval. *(ANT.)* disdain, disrespect, contempt.

admire *(SYN.)* approve, venerate, appreciate, respect, revere, esteem, like. *(ANT.)* abhor, dislike, despise, loathe, detest, hate.

admissible *(SYN.)* fair, justifiable, tolerable, allowable, permissible. *(ANT.)* unsuitable, unfair, inadmissible.

admission *(SYN.)* access, admittance, entrance, pass, ticket. *(ANT.)* denial.

admit *(SYN.)* allow, assent, permit, acknowledge, welcome, concede, agree, confess, accept, grant. *(ANT.)* deny, dismiss, shun, obstruct.

admittance *(SYN.)* access, entry, entrance. *(ANT.)* refusal.

admonish *(SYN.)* caution, advise against, warn, rebuke, reprove, censure. *(ANT.)* glorify, praise.

admonition *(SYN.)* advice, warning, caution, reminder, tip.

ado *(SYN.)* trouble, other, fuss, bustle, activity, excitement, commotion, action, upset, confusion, turmoil. *(ANT.)* tranquillity.

adolescent *(SYN.)* young, youthful, immature, teenage. *(ANT.)* grown, mature, adult.

adoration *(SYN.)* veneration, reverence, glorification, worship, homage.

adore *(SYN.)* revere, venerate, idolize, respect, love, cherish, esteem, honor. *(ANT.)* loathe, hate, despise.

adorn *(SYN.)* trim, bedeck, decorate, ornament, beautify, embellish, glamorize, enhance, garnish. *(ANT.)* mar, deform, deface, strip, bare.

adrift *(SYN.)* floating, afloat, drifting, aimless, purposeless, unsettled. *(ANT.)* purposeful, stable, secure, well organized.

adroit *(SYN.)* adept, apt, dexterous, skillful,

clever, ingenious, expert. *(ANT.) awkward, clumsy, graceless, unskillful, oafish.*

adult *(SYN.)* full-grown, mature, grown-up. *(ANT.) infantile, immature, baby, child.*

advance *(SYN.)* further, promote, bring forward, propound, proceed, aggrandize, elevate, improve, adduce, propose, progress, move, advancement, improvement, promotion, upgrade. *(ANT.) retard, retreat, hinder, revert, withdraw, flee, retardation.*

advantage *(SYN.)* edge, profit, superiority, benefit, leverage, favor, vantage, gain. *(ANT.) handicap, impediment, obstruction, disadvantage, detriment, hindrance, loss.*

adventure *(SYN.)* undertaking, occurrence, enterprise, happening, event, project, incident, exploit.

adventurous *(SYN.)* daring, enterprising, rash, bold, chivalrous. *(ANT.) cautious, timid, hesitating.*

adversary *(SYN.)* foe, enemy, contestant, opponent, antagonist. *(ANT.) ally, friend.*

adverse *(SYN.)* hostile, counteractive, unfavorable, opposed, disastrous, contrary, antagonistic, opposite, unlucky, unfriendly, unfortunate. *(ANT.) favorable, propitious, fortunate, friendly, beneficial.*

adversity *(SYN.)* misfortune, trouble, calamity, distress, hardship, disaster. *(ANT.) benefit, happiness.*

advertise *(SYN.)* promote, publicize, make known, announce, promulgate.

advertisement *(SYN.)* commercial, billboard, want ad, handbill, flyer, poster, brochure, blurb.

advice *(SYN.)* counsel, instruction, suggestion, warning, information, caution, exhortation, admonition, recommendation, plan, tip, guidance, opinion.

advisable *(SYN.)* wise, sensible, prudent, suitable, fit, proper, fitting. *(ANT.) ill-considered, imprudent, inadvisable.*

advise *(SYN.)* recommend, suggest, counsel, caution, warn, admonish.

adviser *(SYN.)* coach, guide, mentor, counselor.

advocate *(SYN.)* defend, recommend, support, defender, proponent, lawyer. *(ANT.)* opponent, adversary, oppose.

aesthetic *(SYN.)* literary, artistic, sensitive, tasteful, well-composed. *(ANT.) tasteless, crude, barbaric.*

affable *(SYN.)* pleasant, courteous, sociable, friendly, amiable, gracious, approachable, communicative. *(ANT.) unfriendly, unsociable.*

affair *(SYN.)* event, occasion, happening, party, occurrence, matter, festivity, business, concern, liaison, infidelity.

affect *(SYN.)* alter, modify, concern, regard, move, touch, feign, pretend, influence, sway, transform, change, impress.

affected *(SYN.)* pretended, fake, sham, false, pretentious.

affection *(SYN.)* fondness, kindness, emotion, love, feeling, tenderness, attachment, endearment, liking, friendliness, warmth. *(ANT.) aversion, indifference, repulsion, hatred, repugnance, dislike, antipathy.*

affectionate *(SYN.)* warm, loving, tender, fond, attached. *(ANT.) distant, unfeeling, cold.*

affirm *(SYN.)* assert, aver, declare, swear, maintain, endorse, certify, state, ratify, pronounce, say, confirm, establish. *(ANT.) deny, dispute, oppose, contradict, demur, disclaim.*

afflict *(SYN.)* trouble, disturb, bother, agitate, perturb. *(ANT.) soothe.*

affliction *(SYN.)* distress, grief, misfortune, trouble, illness. *(ANT.) relief, benefit, easement.*

affluent *(SYN.)* wealthy, prosperous, rich, abundant, ample, plentiful, bountiful, well-to-do. *(ANT.) poor, destitute.*

afford *(SYN.)* provide, supply, yield, furnish, manage to buy.

affront *(SYN.)* offense, slur, slight, provocation, insult. *(ANT.) compliment.*

afraid *(SYN.)* scared, faint-hearted, frightened, timid, fearful, apprehensive, cowardly, terrified. *(ANT.) assured, composed, courageous, bold, confident.*

after *(SYN.)* following, subsequently, behind, next. *(ANT.) before.*

again *(SYN.)* anew, repeatedly, afresh.

against *(SYN.)* versus, hostile, opposed to, in disagreement, touching. *(ANT.)* pro, with, for, promoting.

age *(SYN.)* antiquity, date, period, generation, time, senility, grow old, senescence, mature, dotage, ripen, mature, era, epoch. *(ANT.)* youth, childhood.

aged *(SYN.)* ancient, elderly, old. *(ANT.)* youthful, young.

agency *(SYN.)* office, operation.

agent *(SYN.)* performer, doer, worker, operator, instrument, manager.

aggravate *(SYN.)* intensify, magnify, annoy, irritate, increase, nettle, irk, vex, provoke, embitter, worsen. *(ANT.)* soften, sooth, appease, pacify, mitigate, ease, relieve.

aggregate *(SYN.)* collection, entirety, sum, accumulate, total, compile, conglomeration. *(ANT.)* part, unit, ingredient, element.

aggression *(SYN.)* anger, assault, attack, invasion, offense. *(ANT.)* defense.

aggressive *(SYN.)* hostile, offensive, belligerent, attacking, militant, pugnacious. *(ANT.)* timid, withdrawn, passive, peaceful.

aghast *(SYN.)* surprised, astonished, astounded, awed, thunderstruck, flabbergasted, bewildered.

agile *(SYN.)* nimble, graceful, lively, active, alert, fast, quick, athletic, spry. *(ANT.)* inept, awkward, clumsy.

agility *(SYN.)* quickness, vigor, liveliness, energy, activity, motion. *(ANT.)* dullness, inertia, idleness, inactivity.

agitate *(SYN.)* disturb, excite, perturb, rouse, shake, arouse, disconcert, instigate, inflame, provoke, jar, incite, shake, stir up, toss. *(ANT.)* calm, placate, quiet, ease, soothe, steady.

agitated *(SYN.)* jumpy, jittery, nervous, restless, restive, upset, disturbed, ruffled.

agony *(SYN.)* anguish, misery, pain, suffering, torture, ache, distress, throe, woe, torment, grief. *(ANT.)* relief, ease, comfort.

agree *(SYN.)* comply, coincide, conform, concur, assent, accede, tally, settle, harmonize, unite, yield, consent. *(ANT.)* differ, disagree, protest, contradict, argue, refuse.

agreeable *(SYN.)* amiable, charming, gratifying, pleasant, suitable, pleasurable, welcome, pleasing, acceptable, friendly, cooperative.

agreement *(SYN.)* harmony, understanding, unison, contract, pact, stipulation, alliance, deal, bargain, treaty, contract, arrangement, settlement, accord, concord. *(ANT.)* variance, dissension, discord, disagreement, difference.

agriculture *(SYN.)* farming, gardening, tillage, husbandry, cultivation, agronomy.

ahead *(SYN.)* before, leading, forward, winning, advanced. *(ANT.)* behind.

aid *(SYN.)* help, remedy, assist, helper, service, support, assistant, relief. *(ANT.)* obstruct, hinder, obstacle, impede, hindrance.

ail *(SYN.)* bother, trouble, perturb, disturb, suffer.

ailing *(SYN.)* sick, ill. *(ANT.)* hearty, hale, well.

ailment *(SYN.)* illness, disease, affliction, sickness.

aim *(SYN.)* direction, point, goal, object, target, direct, try, intend, intention, end, objective.

aimless *(SYN.)* directionless, adrift, purposeless.

air *(SYN.)* atmosphere, oxygen, display, reveal, expose, publicize. *(ANT.)* conceal, hide.

airy *(SYN.)* breezy, light, gay, lighthearted, graceful, fanciful, exposed.

aisle *(SYN.)* corridor, passageway, lane, alley, opening.

ajar *(SYN.)* slightly open.

akin *(SYN.)* alike, related, connected, similar, affiliated, allied.

alarm *(SYN.)* frighten, signal, warning, terror, apprehension, affright, consternation, fear, siren, arouse, startle, bell. *(ANT.)* tranquility, composure, security, quiet, calm, soothe, comfort.

alarming *(SYN.)* shocking, appalling, daunting. *(ANT.)* comforting, calming, soothing.

alcoholic *(SYN.)* sot, drunkard, tippler, inebriate.

alert *(SYN.)* attentive, keen, clear-witted,

ready, nimble, vigilant, watchful, observant. *(ANT.)* *logy, sluggish, dulled, listless.*

alias *(SYN.)* anonym, assumed name.

alibi *(SYN.)* story, excuse.

alien *(SYN.)* foreigner, stranger, remote, strange, different, extraneous. *(ANT.)* *germane, kindred, relevant, akin, familiar, accustomed.*

alight *(SYN.)* land, debark, disembark. *(ANT.)* *embark, board.*

alive *(SYN.)* living, existing, breathing, live, lively, vivacious, animated. *(ANT.)* *inactive, dead, moribund.*

allay *(SYN.)* soothe, check, lessen, calm, lighten, relieve, soften, moderate, quiet. *(ANT.)* *intensify, worsen, arouse.*

allege *(SYN.)* testify, affirm, cite, claim, declare, maintain, state, assert. *(ANT.)* *deny, disprove, refute, contradict, gainsay.*

allegiance *(SYN.)* faithfulness, duty.

allegory *(SYN.)* fable, fiction, myth, saga, parable, legend. *(ANT.)* *history, fact.*

alleviate *(SYN.)* diminish, soothe, solace, abate, assuage, allay, soften, mitigate, extenuate, relieve, case, slacken, relax, weaken. *(ANT.)* *increase, aggravate, augment, irritate.*

alley *(SYN.)* footway, byway, path, passageway, aisle, corridor, opening, lane.

alliance *(SYN.)* combination, partnership, union, treaty, coalition, association, confederacy, marriage, pact, agreement, relation, interrelation, understanding, relationship. *(ANT.)* *separation, divorce, schism.*

allot *(SYN.)* divide, mete, assign, give, measure, distribute, allocate, share, grant, dispense, deal, apportion. *(ANT.)* *withhold, retain, keep, confiscate, refuse.*

allow *(SYN.)* authorize, grant, acknowledge, admit, let, permit, sanction, consent, concede, mete, allocate. *(ANT.)* *resist, refuse, forbid, object, prohibit.*

allowance *(SYN.)* grant, fee, portion, ration, allotment.

allude *(SYN.)* intimate, refer, insinuate, hint, advert, suggest, imply, mention. *(ANT.)* *demonstrate, specify, state, declare.*

allure *(SYN.)* attract, fascinate, tempt, charm, infatuate, captivate. *(ANT.)* *repulse.*

ally *(SYN.)* accomplice, associate, confederate, abettor, assistant, friend, partner. *(ANT.)* *rival, enemy, opponent, foe, adversary.*

almighty *(SYN.)* omnipotent, powerful.

almost *(SYN.)* somewhat, nearly. *(ANT.)* *completely, absolutely.*

alms *(SYN.)* dole, charity, donation, contribution.

aloft *(SYN.)* overhead.

alone *(SYN.)* desolate, unaided, only, isolated, lone, secluded, lonely, deserted, solitary, single, apart, solo, separate. *(ANT.)* *surrounded, attended, accompanied, together.*

aloof *(SYN.)* uninterested, uninvolved, apart, away, remote, unsociable, standoffish, separate, distant. *(ANT.)* *warm, outgoing, friendly, cordial.*

also *(SYN.)* in addition, likewise, too, besides, furthermore, moreover, further.

alter *(SYN.)* adjust, vary, deviate, modify, change. *(ANT.)* *maintain, preserve, keep.*

alteration *(SYN.)* difference, adjustment, change, modification. *(ANT.)* *maintenance, preservation.*

altercation *(SYN.)* controversy, dispute, argument, quarrel.

alternate *(SYN.)* rotate, switch, spell, interchange. *(ANT.)* *fix.*

alternative *(SYN.)* substitute, selection, option, choice, replacement, possibility.

although *(SYN.)* though, even if, even though, despite.

altitude *(SYN.)* elevation, height. *(ANT.)* *depth.*

altogether *(SYN.)* totally, wholly, quite, entirely, thoroughly, completely. *(ANT.)* *partly.*

altruism *(SYN.)* benevolence, philanthropy, kindness, tenderness, generosity, charity, liberality. *(ANT.)* *selfishness, unkindness, cruelty.*

always *(SYN.)* evermore, forever, perpetually, ever, unceasingly, continually, constantly, eternally, everlastingly. *(ANT.)* *never, rarely, sometimes, occasionally.*

amalgamate *(SYN.)* fuse, unify, unite,

commingle, merge, blend, combine, consolidate. *(ANT.) decompose, disintegrate, separate.*

amass *(SYN.)* collect, accumulate, heap up, gather, increase, compile, assemble, store up. *(ANT.) disperse, dissipate, spend.*

amateur *(SYN.)* beginner, dilettante, learner, dabbler, neophyte, apprentice, novice, nonprofessional, tyro. *(ANT.) expert, master, adept, professional, authority.*

amaze *(SYN.)* surprise, flabbergast, stun, dumb-found, astound, bewilder, aghast, thunderstruck, astonish. *(ANT.) bore, disinterest, tire.*

ambiguous *(SYN.)* vague, uncertain, obscure, dubious, equivocal, unclear, deceptive. *(ANT.) plain, clear, explicit, obvious, unequivocal, unmistakable, certain.*

ambition *(SYN.)* eagerness, goal, incentive, aspiration, yearning, longing, desire. *(ANT.) indifference, satisfaction, indolence, resignation.*

ambitious *(SYN.)* aspiring, intent upon. *(ANT.) indifferent, content.*

amble *(SYN.)* saunter, stroll.

ambush *(SYN.)* trap, surprise, hiding place.

amend *(SYN.)* change, mend, better, correct, improve. *(ANT.) worsen.*

amends *(SYN.)* compensation, restitution, payment, reparation, remedy, redress.

amiable *(SYN.)* friendly, good-natured, gracious, pleasing, agreeable, outgoing, pleasant. *(ANT.) surly, hateful, churlish, disagreeable, ill-natured, ill-tempered, cross, captious, touchy.*

amid *(SYN.)* among, amidst, surrounded by.

amiss *(SYN.)* wrongly, improperly, astray, awry. *(ANT.) properly, rightly, correct.*

ammunition *(SYN.)* shot, powder, shells, bullets.

among *(SYN.)* between, mingled, amidst, amid, betwixt, surrounded by. *(ANT.) separate, apart.*

amorous *(SYN.)* amatory, affectionate, romantic.

amount *(SYN.)* sum, total, quantity, number, price, value, measure.

ample *(SYN.)* plentiful, large, profuse, spacious, copious, liberal, full, bountiful, abundant, great, extensive, generous, wide, enough, sufficient, roomy. *(ANT.) limited, insufficient, meager, small, lacking, cramped, confined, inadequate.*

amplification *(SYN.)* magnification, growth, waxing, accrual, enhancement, enlargement, heightening, increase. *(ANT.) decrease, diminishing, reduction, contraction.*

amplify *(SYN.)* make louder, broaden, develop, expand, enlarge, extend. *(ANT.) confine, restrict, abridge, narrow.*

amuse *(SYN.)* divert, please, delight, entertain, charm. *(ANT.) tire, bore.*

amusement *(SYN.)* diversion, pastime, entertainment, pleasure, enjoyment, recreation. *(ANT.) tedium, boredom.*

amusing *(SYN.)* pleasant, funny, pleasing, entertaining, comical. *(ANT.) tiring, tedious, boring.*

analogous *(SYN.)* comparable, corresponding, like, similar, correspondent, alike, correlative, parallel, allied, akin. *(ANT.) different, opposed, incongruous.*

analysis *(SYN.)* examination, separation, investigation.

analyze *(SYN.)* examine, explain, investigate, separate.

ancestral *(SYN.)* hereditary, inherited.

ancestry *(SYN.)* family, line, descent, lineage. *(ANT.) posterity.*

anchor *(SYN.)* fix, attach, secure, fasten. *(ANT.) detach, free, loosen.*

ancient *(SYN.)* aged, old-fashioned, archaic, elderly, antique, old, primitive. *(ANT.) new, recent, current, fresh.*

anecdote *(SYN.)* account, narrative, story, tale.

anesthetic *(SYN.)* opiate, narcotic, sedative, painkiller, analgesic.

angel *(SYN.)* cherub, archangel, seraph. *(ANT.) demon, devil.*

angelic *(SYN.)* pure, lovely, heavenly, good, virtuous, innocent, godly, saintly. *(ANT.) devilish.*

anger *(SYN.)* exasperation, fury, ire,

passion, rage, resentment, temper, indignation, animosity, irritation, wrath, displeasure, infuriate, arouse, nettle, annoyance, exasperate. *(ANT.) forbearance, patience, peace, self-control.*

angry *(SYN.)* provoked, wrathful, furious, enraged, incensed, exasperated, maddened, indignant, irate, mad, inflamed. *(ANT.) pleased, calm, satisfied, content, tranquil.*

anguish *(SYN.)* suffering, torment, torture, distress, pain, heartache, grief, agony, misery. *(ANT.) solace, relief, joy, comfort, peace, ecstasy, pleasure.*

animal *(SYN.)* beast, creature.

animate *(SYN.)* vitalize, invigorate, stimulate, enliven, alive, vital, vigorous. *(ANT.) dead, inanimate.*

animated *(SYN.)* gay, lively, spry, vivacious, active, vigorous, chipper, snappy. *(ANT.) inactive.*

animosity *(SYN.)* grudge, hatred, rancor, spite, bitterness, enmity, opposition, dislike, hostility, antipathy. *(ANT.) goodwill, love, friendliness, kindliness.*

annex *(SYN.)* join, attach, add, addition, wing, append.

annihilate *(SYN.)* destroy, demolish, end, wreck, abolish, erase.

announce *(SYN.)* proclaim, give out, make known, notify, publish, report, herald, promulgate, advertise, broadcast, state, tell, declare, publicize. *(ANT.) conceal, withhold, suppress, bury, stifle.*

announcement *(SYN.)* notification, report, declaration, bulletin, advertisement, broadcast, message.

annoy *(SYN.)* bother, irk, pester, tease, trouble, vex, disturb, inconvenience, molest, irritate, harry, harass. *(ANT.) console, gratify, soothe, accommodate, please, calm, comfort.*

annually *(SYN.)* yearly.

anoint *(SYN.)* baptize, besprinkle, purify.

answer *(SYN.)* reply, rejoinder, response, retort, rebuttal, respond. *(ANT.) summoning, argument, questioning, inquiry, query, ask, inquire.*

antagonism *(SYN.)* opposition, conflict, enmity, hostility, animosity. *(ANT.) geniality, cordiality, friendliness.*

antagonist *(SYN.)* adversary, rival, enemy, foe, opponent. *(ANT.) ally, friend.*

antagonize *(SYN.)* provoke, counter, oppose, embitter. *(ANT.) soothe.*

anthology *(SYN.)* treasury, collection.

anticipate *(SYN.)* await, foresee, forecast, hope for, expect.

anticipated *(SYN.)* expected, foresight, hoped, preconceived. *(ANT.) dreaded, reared, worried, doubted.*

antics *(SYN.)* horseplay, fun, merrymaking, pranks, capers, tricks, clowning.

antipathy *(SYN.)* hatred. *(ANT.) sympathy.*

antiquated *(SYN.)* old, out-dated, old-fashioned.

antique *(SYN.)* rarity, curio, old, ancient, old-fashioned, archaic, out-of-date. *(ANT.) new, recent, fresh.*

anxiety *(SYN.)* care, disquiet, fear, concern, solicitude, trouble, worry, apprehension, uneasiness, distress, foreboding. *(ANT.) nonchalance, assurance, confidence, contentment, peacefulness, placidity, tranquillity.*

anxious *(SYN.)* troubled, uneasy, perturbed, apprehensive, worried, concerned, desirous, bothered, agitated, eager, fearful. *(ANT.) tranquil, calm, peaceful.*

anyway *(SYN.)* nevertheless, anyhow.

apartment *(SYN.)* suite, flat, dormitory.

apathy *(SYN.)* unconcern, indifference, lethargy. *(ANT.) interest, feeling.*

aperture *(SYN.)* opening, gap, pore, cavity, chasm, abyss, hole, void. *(ANT.) connection, bridge, link.*

apex *(SYN.)* acme, peak, tip, summit, crown, top.

apologize *(SYN.)* ask forgiveness.

apology *(SYN.)* defense, excuse, confession, justification, alibi, explanation, plea. *(ANT.) denial, complaint, dissimulation, accusation.*

apostate *(SYN.)* unbeliever, nonconformist, dissenter, heretic, schismatic. *(ANT.) saint, conformist, believer.*

appall *(SYN.)* shock, stun, dismay, frighten,

terrify, horrify. (*ANT.*) *edify, please.*

appalling (*SYN.*) fearful, frightful, ghastly, horrid, repulsive, terrible, dire, awful. (*ANT.*) *fascinating, beautiful, enchanting, enjoyable.*

apparatus (*SYN.*) rig, equipment, furnishings, gear, tackle.

apparel (*SYN.*) clothing, attire, garb, garments, dress, robes.

apparent (*SYN.*) obvious, plain, self-evident, clear, manifest, transparent, unmistakable, palpable, unambiguous, ostensible, visible, seeming, evident, understandable, illusory. (*ANT.*) *uncertain, indistinct, dubious, hidden, mysterious.*

apparition (*SYN.*) illusion, ghost, phantom, vision, fantasy, dream.

appeal (*SYN.*) plea, petition, request, entreaty, plead, beseech, beg, attract. (*ANT.*) *repulse, repel.*

appear (*SYN.*) look, arrive, emanate, emerge, arise, seem, turn up. (*ANT.*) *vanish, withdraw, exist, disappear, evaporate.*

appearance (*SYN.*) advent, arrival, aspect, demeanor, fashion, guise, apparition, manner, mien, look, presence. (*ANT.*) *disappearance, reality, departure, vanishing.*

appease (*SYN.*) calm, compose, lull, quiet, relieve, assuage, pacify, satisfy, restraint, lessen, soothe, check, ease, alleviate, still, allay, tranquilize. (*ANT.*) *excite, amuse, incense, irritate, inflame.*

append (*SYN.*) supplement, attach, add.

appendage (*SYN.*) addition, tail, supplement.

appetite (*SYN.*) zest, craving, desire, liking, longing, stomach, inclination, hunger, thirst, relish, passion. (*ANT.*) *satiety, disgust, distaste, repugnance.*

appetizer (*SYN.*) hors d'oeuvre.

applaud (*SYN.*) cheer, clap, hail, approve, praise, acclaim. (*ANT.*) *disapprove, denounce, reject, criticize, condemn.*

appliance (*SYN.*) machine, tool, instrument, device, utensil, implement.

applicable (*SYN.*) fitting, suitable, proper, fit, usable, appropriate, suited. (*ANT.*) *inappropriate, inapplicable.*

apply (*SYN.*) affix, allot, appropriate, use, employ, petition, request, devote, avail, pertain, attach, ask, administer, petition, assign, relate, utilize. (*ANT.*) *give away, demand, detach, neglect, ignore.*

appoint (*SYN.*) name, choose, nominate, designate, elect, establish, assign, place. (*ANT.*) *discharge, fire, dismiss.*

appointment (*SYN.*) rendezvous, meeting, designation, position, engagement, assignment. (*ANT.*) *discharge, dismissal.*

appraise (*SYN.*) value, evaluate, place a value on.

appreciate (*SYN.*) enjoy, regard, value, prize, cherish, admire, go up, improve, rise, respect, esteem, appraise. (*ANT.*) *belittle, misunderstand, apprehend, degrade, scorn, depreciate, undervalue.*

apprehend (*SYN.*) seize, capture, arrest, understand, dread, fear, grasp, perceive. (*ANT.*) *release, lose.*

apprehension (*SYN.*) misgiving, fear, dread, uneasiness, worry, fearfulness, anticipation, capture, seizure. (*ANT.*) *confidence, composure, self-assuredness.*

apprehensive (*SYN.*) worried, afraid, uneasy, bothered, anxious, concerned, perturbed, troubled, fearful. (*ANT.*) *relaxed.*

apprentice (*SYN.*) amateur, recruit, novice, learner, beginner. (*ANT.*) *experienced, professional, master.*

approach (*SYN.*) greet, inlet, come near, advance, access, passageway. (*ANT.*) *avoid, pass by, retreat.*

appropriate (*SYN.*) apt, particular, proper, fitting, suitable, applicable, loot, pillage, purloin, rob, steal, embezzle, assign, becoming, apportion, authorize. (*ANT.*) *improper, contrary, inappropriate, buy, repay, restore, return, unfit, inapt.*

approval (*SYN.*) commendation, consent, praise, approbation, sanction, assent, endorsement, support. (*ANT.*) *reproach, censure, reprimand, disapprove.*

approve (*SYN.*) like, praise, authorize, confirm, endorse, appreciate, ratify, commend, sanction. (*ANT.*) *criticize, nullify, disparage, frown on, disapprove, deny.*

approximate *(SYN.)* near, approach, roughly, close. *(ANT.)* absolute.

apt *(SYN.)* suitable, proper, appropriate, fit, suited, disposed, liable, inclined, prone, clever, bright, alert, intelligent, receptive. *(ANT.)* ill-becoming, unsuitable, unlikely, slow, retarded, dense.

aptitude *(SYN.)* knack, talent, gift, ability.

aptness *(SYN.)* capability, dexterity, qualification, skill, ability, aptitude. *(ANT.)* incompetence, unreadiness, incapacity.

aqueduct *(SYN.)* gully, pipe, canal, waterway, channel.

arbitrary *(SYN.)* unrestricted, absolute, despotic, willful, unreasonable, unconditional, authoritative. *(ANT.)* contingent, qualified, fair, reasonable, dependent, accountable.

arbitrate *(SYN.)* referee, settle, mediate, umpire, negotiate.

architecture *(SYN.)* structure, building, construction.

ardent *(SYN.)* fervent, fiery, glowing, intense, keen, impassioned, fervid, hot, passionate, earnest, eager, zealous, enthusiastic. *(ANT.)* cool, indifferent, nonchalant, apathetic.

ardor *(SYN.)* enthusiasm, rapture, spirit, zeal, fervent, eager, glowing, eagerness. *(ANT.)* unconcern, apathy, disinterest, indifference.

arduous *(SYN.)* laborious, hard, difficult, burdensome, strenuous, strained. *(ANT.)* easy.

area *(SYN.)* space, extent, region, zone, section, expanse, district, neighborhood, size.

argue *(SYN.)* plead, reason, wrangle, indicate, prove, show, dispute, denote, imply, object, bicker, discuss, debate, disagree. *(ANT.)* reject, spurn, ignore, overlook, agree, concur.

argument *(SYN.)* debate, dispute, discussion, controversy. *(ANT.)* harmony, accord, agreement.

arid *(SYN.)* waterless, dry, flat, dull, unimaginative, stuffy. *(ANT.)* fertile, wet, colorful.

arise *(SYN.)* enter, institute, originate, start, open, commence, emerge, appear. *(ANT.)* terminate, end, finish, complete, close.

aristocrat *(SYN.)* noble, gentleman, peer, lord, nobleman, bourgeoisie. *(ANT.)* peasant, commoner, proletariat.

arm *(SYN.)* weapon, defend, equip, empower, fortify.

armistice *(SYN.)* truce, pact, deal, understanding, peace, treaty, contract, alliance, agreement.

army *(SYN.)* troops, legion, military, forces, militia.

aroma *(SYN.)* smell, odor, fragrance, perfume, scent.

arouse *(SYN.)* stir, animate, move, pique, provoke, kindle, disturb, excite, foment, stimulate, awaken. *(ANT.)* settle, soothe, calm.

arraign *(SYN.)* charge, censure, incriminate, indict, accuse. *(ANT.)* acquit, release, vindicate, exonerate, absolve.

arraignment *(SYN.)* imputation, charge, accusation, incrimination. *(ANT.)* pardon, exonerate, exculpation.

arrange *(SYN.)* classify, assort, organize, place, plan, prepare, devise, adjust, dispose, regulate, order, group, settle, adapt, catalog, systematize, distribute, prepare. *(ANT.)* jumble, scatter, disorder, confuse, disturb, disarrange.

arrangement *(SYN.)* display, grouping, order, array, deal.

array *(SYN.)* dress, adorn, attire, clothe, arrange, order, distribute, display, exhibit. *(ANT.)* disorder, disorganization, disarray.

arrest *(SYN.)* detain, hinder, restrain, seize, withhold, stop, check, obstruct, apprehend, interrupt, catch, capture. *(ANT.)* free, release, discharge, liberate.

arrival *(SYN.)* advent, coming. *(ANT.)* leaving, departure.

arrive *(SYN.)* come, emerge, reach, visit, land, appear. *(ANT.)* exit, leave, depart, go.

arrogance *(SYN.)* pride, insolence. *(ANT.)* humbleness, modest, humility.

arrogant *(SYN.)* insolent, prideful, scornful, haughty, cavalier, proud. *(ANT.)* modest, humble.

art *(SYN.)* cunning, tact, artifice, skill,

aptitude, adroitness, painting, drawing, design, craft, dexterity, composition, ingenuity. (*ANT.*) *clumsiness, innocence, unskillfulness, honesty.*

artery *(SYN.)* aqueduct, pipe, channel.

artful *(SYN.)* clever, sly, skillful, knowing, deceitful, tricky, crafty, cunning. (*ANT.*) *artless.*

article *(SYN.)* story, composition, treatise, essay, thing, report, object.

artifice *(SYN.)* trick, clever, scheme, device.

artificial *(SYN.)* bogus, fake, affected, feigned, phony, sham, unreal, synthetic, assumed, counterfeit, unnatural, manmade, unreal, manufactured, false, feigned, pretended. (*ANT.*) *genuine, natural, true, real, authentic.*

artisan *(SYN.)* worker, craftsman, mechanic.

artist *(SYN.)* actor, actress, painter, sculptor, singer, designer.

artless *(SYN.)* innocent, open, frank, simple, honest, candid, natural, unskilled, ignorant, truthful, sincere. (*ANT.*) *artful.*

ascend *(SYN.)* rise, scale, tower, mount, go up. (*ANT.*) *fall, sink, descend, go down.*

ascertain *(SYN.)* solve, learn, clear up, answer.

ascribe *(SYN.)* attribute, assign.

ashamed *(SYN.)* shamefaced, humiliated, abashed, mortified, embarrassed. (*ANT.*) *proud.*

ask *(SYN.)* invite, request, inquire, query, question, beg, solicit, demand, entreat, claim, interrogate, charge, expect. (*ANT.*) *order, reply, insist, answer.*

askance *(SYN.)* sideways.

askew *(SYN.)* disorderly, crooked, awry, twisted. (*ANT.*) *straight.*

asleep *(SYN.)* inactive, sleeping, dormant. (*ANT.*) *alert, awake.*

aspect *(SYN.)* appearance, look, view, outlook, attitude, viewpoint, phase, part, feature, side.

aspersion *(SYN.)* dishonor, insult, misuse, outrage, reproach, defamation, abuse, disparagement. (*ANT.*) *plaudit, respect, approval.*

asphyxiate *(SYN.)* suffocate, stifle, smother, choke, strangle, throttle.

aspiration *(SYN.)* craving, desire, hope, longing, objective, passion, ambition.

aspire *(SYN.)* seek, aim, wish for, strive, desire, yearn for.

ass *(SYN.)* mule, donkey, burro, silly, dunce, stubborn, stupid, fool.

assail *(SYN.)* assault, attack.

assassinate *(SYN.)* purge, kill, murder.

assault *(SYN.)* invade, strike, attack, assail, charge, bombard, onslaught. (*ANT.*) *protect, defend.*

assemble *(SYN.)* collect, gather, meet, congregate, connect, manufacture. (*ANT.*) *disperse, disassemble, scatter.*

assembly *(SYN.)* legislature, congress, council, parliament.

assent *(SYN.)* consent to, concede, agree, approval, accept, comply, permission. (*ANT.*) *deny, dissent, refusal, denial, refuse.*

assert *(SYN.)* declare, maintain, state, claim, express, defend, press, support, aver, uphold, consent, accept, comply, affirm, allege, emphasize. (*ANT.*) *deny, refute, contradict, decline.*

assertion *(SYN.)* statement, affirmation, declaration. (*ANT.*) *contradiction, denial.*

assess *(SYN.)* calculate, compute, estimate, levy, reckon, tax, appraise.

asset *(SYN.)* property, wealth, capitol, resources, goods.

assign *(SYN.)* apportion, ascribe, attribute, cast, allot, chose, appropriate, name, elect, appoint, distribute, designate, specify. (*ANT.*) *release, relieve, unburden, discharge.*

assignment *(SYN.)* task, job, responsibility, duty.

assimilate *(SYN.)* digest, absorb, blot up.

assist *(SYN.)* help, promote, serve, support, sustain, abet, aid, back. (*ANT.*) *prevent, impede, hamper.*

assistance *(SYN.)* backing, help, patronage, relief, succor, support. (*ANT.*) *hostility, resistance, antagonism, counteraction.*

assistant *(SYN.)* accomplice, ally, associate, confederate, abettor. (*ANT.*) *rival, enemy, adversary.*

associate *(SYN.)* affiliate, ally, join, connect, unite, combine, link, mingle, partner, mix. *(ANT.)* separate, disconnect, divide, disrupt, estrange.

association *(SYN.)* organization, club, union, society, fraternity, sorority, companionship, fellowship.

assorted *(SYN.)* varied, miscellaneous, classified, different, several, grouped, various. *(ANT.)* alike, same.

assortment *(SYN.)* collection, variety, mixture, conglomeration.

assuage *(SYN.)* calm, quiet, lessen, relieve, ease, allay, moderate, alleviate, restrain.

assume *(SYN.)* arrogate, affect, suspect, believe, appropriate, take, pretend, usurp, simulate, understand, postulate, presume, suppose. *(ANT.)* doff, demonstrate, prove, grant, concede.

assumption *(SYN.)* presumption, guess, supposition, conjecture, postulate.

assure *(SYN.)* promise, convince, warrant, guarantee, pledge. *(ANT.)* equivocate, deny.

astonish *(SYN.)* astound, amaze, surprise, shock. *(ANT.)* tire, bore.

astound *(SYN.)* shock, amaze, astonish, stun, surprise, floor.

asunder *(SYN.)* divided, separate, apart. *(ANT.)* together.

asylum *(SYN.)* shelter, refuge, home, madhouse, institution.

athletic *(SYN.)* strong, active, able-bodied, gymnastic, muscular, well-built.

atone *(SYN.)* repay, make up.

atrocious *(SYN.)* horrible, savage, brutal, ruthless, dreadful, awful, horrifying. *(ANT.)* good, kind.

attach *(SYN.)* connect, adjoin, annex, join, append, stick, unite, affix. *(ANT.)* unfasten, separate, disengage.

attack *(SYN.)* raid, assault, besiege, abuse, censure, offense, siege, denunciation, aggression, push, criticism, invade. *(ANT.)* surrender, defense, opposition, aid, defend, protect, repel.

attain *(SYN.)* achieve, acquire, accomplish, gain, get, reach, win. *(ANT.)* discard, abandon, desert.

attainment *(SYN.)* exploit, feat, accomplishment, realization, performance. *(ANT.)* omission, defeat, failure, neglect.

attempt *(SYN.)* essay, experiment, trial, try, undertaking, endeavor, effort. *(ANT.)* laziness, neglect, inaction.

attend *(SYN.)* accompany, escort, watch, serve, care for, follow, lackey, present, frequent, protect, guard. *(ANT.)* desert, abandon, avoid.

attendant *(SYN.)* waiter, servant, valet.

attention *(SYN.)* consideration, heed, circumspection, notice, watchfulness, observance, application, reflection, study, care, alertness, mindfulness. *(ANT.)* negligence, indifference, omission, oversight, disregard.

attentive *(SYN.)* careful, awake, alive, considerate, heedful, mindful, wary. *(ANT.)* unaware, oblivious, apathetic.

attest *(SYN.)* testify, swear, vouch, certify.

attire *(SYN.)* apparel, dress, clothe.

attitude *(SYN.)* standpoint, viewpoint, stand, pose, aspect, position, posture.

attract *(SYN.)* enchant, interest, pull, fascinate, draw, tempt, infatuate, entice. *(ANT.)* deter, repel, repulse, alienate.

attractive *(SYN.)* enchanting, winning, engaging, pleasant, pleasing, seductive. *(ANT.)* unattractive, obnoxious, repellent, repulsive, forbidding.

attribute *(SYN.)* give, apply, place, trait, characteristic, feature, nature, credit.

audacious *(SYN.)* daring, bold, arrogant, foolhardy, cavalier, haughty, insolent. *(ANT.)* humble, shy.

audacity *(SYN.)* effrontery, fearlessness, temerity, boldness. *(ANT.)* humility, meekness, circumspection, fearfulness.

audible *(SYN.)* distinct, plain, clear. *(ANT.)* inaudible.

augment *(SYN.)* enlarge, increase, raise, expand, broaden, extend.

auspicious *(SYN.)* lucky, timely, favorable, promising, fortunate. *(ANT.)* untimely, unfortunate.

austere *(SYN.)* stern, severe, harsh, strict. *(ANT.)* lenient, soft.

authentic *(SYN.)* real, true, genuine, pure,

authenticate

accurate, reliable, legitimate, factual. (*ANT.*) *false, spurious, artificial, counterfeit, erroneous.*

authenticate *(SYN.)* validate, warrant, guarantee, verify, certify.

author *(SYN.)* father, inventor, maker, originator, writer, composer.

authoritative *(SYN.)* certain, secure, commanding, sure, tried, trustworthy, safe, influential, dependable. (*ANT.*) *uncertain, unreliable, dubious, fallible, questionable.*

authority *(SYN.)* dominion, justification, power, permission, authorization, importance, domination, supremacy. (*ANT.*) *incapacity, denial, prohibition, weakness, impotence.*

autocrat *(SYN.)* monarch, ruler, tyrant.

autograph *(SYN.)* endorse, sign, approve.

automatic *(SYN.)* self-acting, mechanical, spontaneous, uncontrolled, involuntary. (*ANT.*) *hand-operated, intentional, deliberate, manual.*

automobile *(SYN.)* auto, car.

auxiliary *(SYN.)* assisting, helping, aiding.

avail *(SYN.)* help, profit, use, value, benefit, serve, advantage.

available *(SYN.)* obtainable, convenient, ready, handy, accessible, prepared. (*ANT.*) *unavailable, out of reach, inaccessible, unobtainable.*

avarice *(SYN.)* lust, greed.

average *(SYN.)* moderate, ordinary, usual, passable, fair, intermediate, medium. (*ANT.*) *outstanding, exceptional, extraordinary, unusual.*

averse *(SYN.)* unwilling, opposed, forced, against, involuntary. (*ANT.*) *willing.*

avert *(SYN.)* avoid, prevent, prohibit. (*ANT.*) *invite.*

avid *(SYN.)* greedy, eager.

avoid *(SYN.)* elude, forestall, evade, escape, dodge, avert, forbear, eschew. (*ANT.*) *oppose, meet, confront, encounter, seek.*

award *(SYN.)* reward, prize, medal, gift, trophy.

aware *(SYN.)* mindful, perceptive, formed, apprised, realizing, conscious. (*ANT.*) *unaware, ignorant, oblivious.*

away *(SYN.)* absent, departed, distracted, gone, not at home. (*ANT.*) *present, attentive, attending.*

awe *(SYN.)* surprise, respect, dread, astonishment, alarm.

awful *(SYN.)* frightful, horrible, awe-inspiring, dire, terrible, unpleasant. (*ANT.*) *humble, pleasant, wonderful, commonplace.*

awkward *(SYN.)* inept, unpolished, clumsy, gauche, rough, ungraceful. (*ANT.*) *adroit, graceful, polished, skillful.*

awry *(SYN.)* askew, wrong, twisted, crooked, disorderly. (*ANT.*) *straight, right.*

axiom *(SYN.)* fundamental, maxim, principle, theorem, adage, apothegm, byword, aphorism.

B

babble *(SYN.)* twaddle, nonsense, gibberish, prattle, balderdash, rubbish, chatter, baby talk, poppycock, jabber, maunder, piffle.

baby *(SYN.)* newborn, infant, neonate, babe, teeny, small, wee, little, undersized, midget, papoose, protect, cosset, pamper.

babyish *(SYN.)* infantile, childish, whiny, unreasonable, immature, puerile, foolish, dependent. (*ANT.*) *mature, adult, sensible, reasonable, grown-up.*

back *(SYN.)* help, assist, endorse, support, second, ratify, approve, stand by, posterior, rear. (*ANT.*) *anterior, front, face, undercut, veto, undermine.*

backbiting *(SYN.)* gossip, slander, abuse, malice, cattiness, aspersion, derogation, belittling, badmouthing. (*ANT.*) *compliments, praise, loyalty, friendliness, approval.*

backbone *(SYN.)* vertebrae, spine, pillar, support, staff, mainstay, basis, courage, determination, toughness, character. (*ANT.*) *timidity, weakness, cowardice, spinelessness.*

backbreaking *(SYN.)* exhausting, fatiguing, tough, tiring, demanding, wearying, wearing, difficult. (*ANT.*) *light, relating,* *undemanding, slight.*

back down *(SYN.)* accede, concede, acquiesce, yield, withdraw, renege. *(ANT.) persevere, insist.*

backer *(SYN.)* underwriter, benefactor, investor, patron, sponsor, supporter.

backfire *(SYN.)* flop, boomerang, fail, founder, disappoint. *(ANT.) succeed.*

background *(SYN.)* training, practice, knowledge, experience.

backing *(SYN.)* help, support, funds, money, assistance, grant, advocacy, subsidy, sympathy, endorsement. *(ANT.) criticism, detraction, faultfinding.*

backlog *(SYN.)* inventory, reserve, hoard, amassment, accumulation.

backslide *(SYN.)* relapse, revert, return, weaken, regress, renege.

backward *(SYN.)* dull, sluggish, stupid, loath, regressive, rearward, underdeveloped, slow, retarded. *(ANT.) progressive, precocious, civilized, advanced, forward.*

bad *(SYN.)* unfavorable, wrong, evil, immoral, sinful, faulty, improper, unwholesome, wicked, corrupt, tainted. *(ANT.) good, honorable, reputable, moral, excellent.*

badger *(SYN.)* tease, question, annoy, pester, bother, taunt, bait, provoke, torment, harass, hector.

baffle *(SYN.)* confound, bewilder, perplex, puzzle, mystify, confuse, frustrate. *(ANT.) inform, enlighten.*

bag *(SYN.)* catch, snare, poke, sack.

bait *(SYN.)* enticement, captivate, ensnare, tease, torment, pester, worry, entrap, question, entice, lure, trap, harass, tempt, badger.

balance *(SYN.)* poise, stability, composure, remains, residue, equilibrium, compare, weigh, equalize. *(ANT.) unsteadiness, instability.*

bald *(SYN.)* bare, hairless, nude, open, uncovered, simple. *(ANT.) covered, hairy.*

balk *(SYN.)* unwilling, obstinate, stubborn, hesitate, check, stop. *(ANT.) willing.*

ball *(SYN.)* cotillion, dance, globe, sphere, spheroid.

ballad *(SYN.)* poem, song, ditty.

balloon *(SYN.)* puff up, enlarge, swell. *(ANT.) shrivel, shrink.*

ballot *(SYN.)* choice, vote, poll.

balmy *(SYN.)* soft, gentle, soothing, fragrant, mild. *(ANT.) tempestuous, stormy.*

ban *(SYN.)* prohibit, outlaw, disallow, block, bar, exclude, obstruct, prohibition, taboo, forbid. *(ANT.) allow, permit.*

banal *(SYN.)* hackneyed, corny, vapid, trite, overused, humdrum. *(ANT.) striking, original, fresh, stimulating, novel.*

band *(SYN.)* company, association, crew, group, society, belt, strip, unite, gang.

bandit *(SYN.)* thief, robber, highwayman, outlaw, marauder.

bang *(SYN.)* hit, strike, slam.

banish *(SYN.)* drive away, eject, exile, oust, deport, dismiss, expel. *(ANT.) receive, accept, shelter, admit, harbor, embrace, welcome.*

bank *(SYN.)* barrier, slope, storage, treasury, row, series, string, shore.

banner *(SYN.)* colors, standard, pennant, flag.

banquet *(SYN.)* feast, celebration, festival, dinner, regalement, affair.

banter *(SYN.)* joke, tease, jest.

bar *(SYN.)* counter, impediment, saloon, exclude, obstacle, barricade, obstruct, shut out, hindrance, forbid, block, barrier, obstruction. *(ANT.) allow, permit, aid, encouragement.*

barbarian *(SYN.)* brute, savage, boor, ruffian, rude, uncivilized, primitive, uncultured, coarse, cruel, barbaric, crude. *(ANT.) cultured, civilized.*

barbarous *(SYN.)* savage, remorseless, cruel, uncivilized, rude, unrelenting, merciless, crude, ruthless, inhuman. *(ANT.) kind, civilized, humane, refined, tasteful.*

barber *(SYN.)* coiffeur, hairdresser.

bare *(SYN.)* naked, nude, uncovered, undressed, unclothed, unfurnished, plain, barren, empty, disclose, reveal, publicize, bald, expose, scarce, mere. *(ANT.) dressed, garbed, conceal, covered, hide, clothed.*

barefaced *(SYN.)* impudent, bold,

insolent, brazen, shameless, audacious, impertinent, rude.

barely *(SYN.)* hardly, scarcely, just.

bargain *(SYN.)* agreement, arrangement, deal, contract, arrange, sale.

baroque *(SYN.)* ornamented, elaborate, embellished, ornate.

barren *(SYN.)* unproductive, bare, unfruitful, infertile, sterile, childless. *(ANT.) productive, fruitful, fertile.*

barricade *(SYN.)* fence, obstruction, shut in, fortification, barrier. *(ANT.) free, open, release.*

barrier *(SYN.)* fence, wall, bar, railing, obstacle, hindrance, fortification, restraint, impediment, limit, barricade.

barter *(SYN.)* exchange, deal, trade.

base *(SYN.)* bottom, rest, foundation, establish, found, immoral, evil, bad, wicked, depraved, selfish, worthless, cheap, debased, poor, support, stand, low, abject, menial. *(ANT.) exalted, righteous, lofty, esteemed, noble, honored, refined, valuable.*

bashful *(SYN.)* timorous, abashed, shy, coy, timid, diffident, modest, sheepish, embarrassed, shame-faced, humble, recoiling, uneasy, awkward, ashamed. *(ANT.) fearless, outgoing, adventurous, gregarious, aggressive, daring.*

basic *(SYN.)* underlying, chief, essential, main, fundamental. *(ANT.) subsidiary, subordinate.*

basis *(SYN.)* presumption, support, base, principle, groundwork, presupposition, foundation, postulate, ground, assumption, premise, essential. *(ANT.) implication, trimming, derivative, superstructure.*

basket *(SYN.)* hamper, creel, dossier, bassinet.

bastion *(SYN.)* mainstay, support, staff, tower, stronghold.

bat *(SYN.)* strike, hit, clout, stick, club, knock, crack.

batch *(SYN.)* group, set, collection, lot, cluster, bunch, mass, combination.

bath *(SYN.)* washing, shower, tub, wash, dip, soaping.

bathe *(SYN.)* launder, drench, swim, cover, medicate, immerse, wet, dip, soak, suffuse, rinse, saturate.

bathing suit *(SYN.)* maillot, swimsuit, trunks.

bathos *(SYN.)* mawkishness, soppiness, slush, sentimentality.

bathroom *(SYN.)* powder room, toilet, bath, lavatory.

baton *(SYN.)* mace, rod, staff, billy club, crook, stick, caduceus, fasces.

battalion *(SYN.)* mass, army, swarm, mob, drove, horde, gang, legion, regiment.

batten *(SYN.)* thrive, flourish, fatten, wax, expand, bloom, boom, grow. *(ANT.) decrease, weaken, fail.*

batter *(SYN.)* pound, beat, hit, pommel, wallop, bash, smash, mixture, strike.

battery *(SYN.)* series, troop, force, rally, muster, set.

battle *(SYN.)* strife, fray, combat, struggle, contest, skirmish, conflict, fight, war, flight, warfare, action, campaign, strive against. *(ANT.) truce, concord, agreement, settlement, harmony, accept, concur, peace.*

battlement *(SYN.)* parapet, crenelation, rampart, fort, bastion, stronghold, escarpment.

bauble *(SYN.)* plaything, toy, trinket.

bawd *(SYN.)* procuress, prostitute.

bawdy *(SYN.)* vulgar, smutty, filthy, dirty, obscene, pornographic.

bawl *(SYN.)* sob, shout, wail, cry loudly, bellow, weep, cry.

bawl out *(SYN.)* scold, upbraid, censure, berate, reprove, reprimand.

bay *(SYN.)* inlet, bayou, harbor, lagoon, cove, sound, gulf.

bazaar *(SYN.)* fair, market, marketplace.

beach *(SYN.)* sands, seashore, waterfront, seaside, strand, coast, shore.

beacon *(SYN.)* light, signal, watchtower, guide, flare, warning, alarm.

bead *(SYN.)* globule, drop, pill, blob.

beak *(SYN.)* nose, bill, proboscis.

beam *(SYN.)* gleam, ray, girder, cross-member, pencil, shine, glisten, smile, glitter, gleam.

beaming *(SYN.)* joyful, bright, happy, radiant, grinning. *(ANT.) sullen, gloomy, threatening, scowling.*

bear *(SYN.)* carry, support, take, uphold, suffer, convey, allow, stand, yield, endure, tolerate, produce, sustain, brook, transport, undergo, permit, suffer, abide, tolerate. *(ANT.) evade, shun, avoid, refuse, dodge.*

bearable *(SYN.)* sufferable, supportable, manageable, tolerable. *(ANT.) terrible, painful, unbearable, awful, intolerable.*

bearing *(SYN.)* course, direction, position, posture, behavior, manner, carriage, relation, reference, connection, application, deportment, air, way, conduct.

bearings *(SYN.)* orientation, whereabouts, location, direction, position, reading, course.

bear on *(SYN.)* affect, relate to.

bear out *(SYN.)* confirm, substantiate, justify, verify, prove.

bear up *(SYN.)* carry on, endure.

bear with *(SYN.)* tolerate, forbear.

beast *(SYN.)* monster, savage, brute, creature, animal.

beastly *(SYN.)* detestable, mean, low, hateful, loathsome, nasty, unpleasant, despicable, obnoxious, brutal, brutish, offensive. *(ANT.) considerate, sympathetic, refined, humane, fine, pleasant.*

beat *(SYN.)* pulse, buffet, pound, defeat, palpitate, hit, thump, belabor, knock, overthrow, thrash, pummel, rout, smite, throb, punch, subdue, pulsate, dash, strike, overpower, vanquish, conquer, batter, overcome, blow. *(ANT.) stroke, fail, defend, surrender, shield.*

beaten *(SYN.)* disheartened, dejected, licked, discouraged, hopeless, downcast, down, depressed. *(ANT.) eager, hopeful, cheerful.*

beatific *(SYN.)* uplifted, blissful, elated, happy, wonderful, joyful, divine. *(ANT.) awful, hellish, ill-fated, accursed.*

beating *(SYN.)* whipping, drubbing, flogging, lashing, scourging, walloping.

beau *(SYN.)* lover, suitor, swain, admirer.

beautiful *(SYN.)* pretty, fair, lovely, charming, comely, handsome, elegant, attractive. *(ANT.) repulsive, hideous, unsightly, foul, homely, plainness, unattractive, ugly.*

beauty *(SYN.)* handsomeness, fairness, charm, pulchritude, attractiveness, loveliness, comeliness, grace, allegiance. *(ANT.) ugliness, disfigurement, homeliness, plainness, deformity, eyesore.*

becalm *(SYN.)* calm, quiet, smooth, still, hush, repose, settle.

because *(SYN.)* inasmuch as, as, since, for.

because of *(SYN.)* as a result of, as a consequence of.

beckon *(SYN.)* call, signal, summon, motion, gesture, wave.

becloud *(SYN.)* obfuscate, confuse, befog, confound, obscure, muddle. *(ANT.) illuminate, clarify, solve.*

become *(SYN.)* change, grow, suit, be appropriate, befit.

becoming *(SYN.)* suitable, meet, befitting, appropriate, fitting, seemly, enhancing, attractive, pleasing, flattering, tasteful, smart, adorning, ornamental. *(ANT.) unsuitable, inappropriate, incongruent, ugly, unattractive, improper.*

bed *(SYN.)* layer, cot, vein, berth, stratum, couch, accumulation, bunk, cradle.

bedazzle *(SYN.)* glare, blind, dumbfound, flabbergast, bewilder, furbish, festoon.

bedeck *(SYN.)* deck, adorn, beautify, smarten, festoon, garnish.

bedevil *(SYN.)* worry, fret, irk, torment, harass, pester, nettle, tease, vex, plague. *(ANT.) soothe, calm, delight, please.*

bedlam *(SYN.)* tumult, uproar, madhouse, commotion, confusion, racket, rumpus, pandemonium. *(ANT.) calm, peace.*

bedraggled *(SYN.)* shabby, muddy, sodden, messy, sloppy. *(ANT.) dry, neat, clean, well-groomed.*

bedrock *(SYN.)* basis, foundation, roots, basics, essentials, fundamentals, bottom, bed, substratum, core. *(ANT.) top, dome, apex, nonessentials.*

bedroom *(SYN.)* chamber, bedchamber.

beef *(SYN.)* brawn, strength, heft, gripe,

sinew, fitness, huskiness, might.

beef up *(SYN.)* reinforce, vitalize, nerve, buttress, strengthen. *(ANT.)* sap, weaken, enervate, drain.

beefy *(SYN.)* solid, strong, muscular, heavy, stocky.

befall *(SYN.)* occur, come about, happen.

before *(SYN.)* prior, earlier, in advance, formerly. *(ANT.)* behind, following, afterward, latterly, after.

befriend *(SYN.)* welcome, encourage, aid, stand by. *(ANT.)* dislike, shun, desert, avoid.

befuddle *(SYN.)* stupefy, addle, confuse, rattle, disorient.

beg *(SYN.)* solicit, ask, implore, supplicate, entreat, adjure, petition, beseech, request, importune, entreat, implore. *(ANT.)* grant, cede, give, bestow, favor.

beget *(SYN.)* sire, engender, produce, create, propagate, originate, breed, generate, procreate, father. *(ANT.)* murder, destroy, kill, abort, prevent, extinguish.

beggar *(SYN.)* scrub, tatterdemalion, pauper, wretch, ragamuffin, vagabond, starveling.

begin *(SYN.)* open, enter, arise, initiate, commence, start, inaugurate, originate, institute, create. *(ANT.)* terminate, complete, finish, close, end, stop.

beginner *(SYN.)* nonprofessional, amateur, apprentice. *(ANT.)* veteran, professional.

beginning *(SYN.)* outset, inception, origin, source, commencement, start, opening, initiation, inauguration. *(ANT.)* termination, completion, end, close, consumption, closing, ending, finish.

begrime *(SYN.)* soil, dirty, smear, muddy, splotch, tarnish. *(ANT.)* wash, clean, freshen, launder.

begrudge *(SYN.)* resent, envy, stint, withhold, grudge.

begrudging *(SYN.)* hesitant, reluctant, resentful, unwilling, forced. *(ANT.)* willing, eager, quick, spontaneous.

beguiling *(SYN.)* enchanting, interesting, delightful, intriguing, engaging, bewitching, attractive, enthralling, captivating. *(ANT.)* boring, dull, tedious.

behalf *(SYN.)* benefit, welfare, support, aid, part, interest.

behave *(SYN.)* deport, comport, manage, act, demean, bear, interact, carry, operate, conduct.

behavior *(SYN.)* manners, carriage, disposition, action, deed, bearing, deportment, conduct, demeanor. *(ANT.)* rebelliousness, misbehavior.

behead *(SYN.)* decapitate, guillotine, decollate.

behest *(SYN.)* order, command, decree, mandate, bidding.

behind *(SYN.)* after, backward, at the back, in back of. *(ANT.)* frontward, ahead, before.

behold *(SYN.)* look, see, view, notice, observe, perceive, sight. *(ANT.)* overlook, ignore.

being *(SYN.)* life, existing, existence, living, actuality, organism, individual. *(ANT.)* death, nonexistence, expiration.

belabor *(SYN.)* repeat, reiterate, pound, explain, expatiate, din.

belated *(SYN.)* late, delayed, overdue, tardy. *(ANT.)* well-timed, early.

belch *(SYN.)* emit, erupt, gush, disgorge, bubble, eructation, burp.

beleaguered *(SYN.)* bothered, annoyed, beset, harassed, badgered, vexed, plagued, victimized.

belie *(SYN.)* distort, misrepresent, twist, disappoint.

belief *(SYN.)* trust, feeling, certitude, opinion, conviction, persuasion, credence, confidence, reliance, faith, view, creed, assurance. *(ANT.)* heresy, denial, incredulity, distrust, skepticism, doubt.

believe *(SYN.)* hold, apprehend, fancy, support, accept, conceive, suppose, imagine, trust, credit. *(ANT.)* doubt, reject, distrust, disbelieve, question.

believer *(SYN.)* adherent, follower, devotee, convert, zealot. *(ANT.)* doubter, critic, scoffer, skeptic.

belittle *(SYN.)* underrate, depreciate, minimize, decry, disparage, diminish, demean, slight, discredit, militant, depreciate, humiliate. *(ANT.)* esteem, admire, flatter, *overrate, commend.*

bell *(SYN.)* pealing, ringing, signal, tolling, buzzer, chime.

belligerent *(SYN.)* aggressive, warlike, hostile, offensive, combative, militant. *(ANT.) easygoing, compromising, peaceful.*

bellow *(SYN.)* thunder, roar, scream, shout, yell, howl.

bellwether *(SYN.)* leader, pilot, guide, ringleader, boss, shepherd.

belly *(SYN.)* stomach, abdomen, paunch.

belonging *(SYN.)* loyalty, relationship, kinship, acceptance, rapport.

belongings *(SYN.)* property, effects, possessions.

beloved *(SYN.)* adored, sweet, loved, cherished, prized, esteemed, valued, darling.

below *(SYN.)* under, less, beneath, underneath, lower. *(ANT.) aloft, overhead, above, over.*

belt *(SYN.)* girdle, sash, strap, cummerbund, band, waistband, whack, hit, wallop, punch.

bemoan *(SYN.)* mourn, lament, grieve, sorrow, regret, deplore.

bend *(SYN.)* turn, curve, incline, submit, bow, lean, crook, twist, yield, stoop, crouch, agree, suppress, oppress, mold, kneel, deflect, subdue, influence. *(ANT.) resist, straighten, break, stiffen.*

beneath *(SYN.)* under, below. *(ANT.) above, over.*

benediction *(SYN.)* thanks, blessing, prayer.

beneficial *(SYN.)* salutary, good, wholesome, advantageous, useful, helpful, serviceable, profitable. *(ANT.) harmful, destructive, injurious, disadvantageous, unwholesome, deleterious, detrimental.*

benefit *(SYN.)* support, help, gain, avail, profit, account, favor, aid, good, advantage, serve, interest, behalf, service. *(ANT.) handicap, calamity, trouble, disadvantage, distress.*

benevolence *(SYN.)* magnanimity, charity, tenderness, altruism, humanity, philanthropy, generosity, liberality, beneficence, goodwill. *(ANT.) malevolence, unkindness,*

cruelty, selfishness, inhumanity.

benevolent *(SYN.)* kindhearted, tender, merciful, generous, altruistic, obliging, kind, good, well-wishing, philanthropy, liberal, unselfish, kindly, disposed, open-hearted, humane, benign, friendly. *(ANT.) malevolent, greedy, wicked, harsh.*

bent *(SYN.)* curved, crooked, resolved, determined, set, inclined, firm, decided. *(ANT.) straight.*

berate *(SYN.)* scold.

beseech *(SYN.)* appeal, entreat, plead, ask, beg, implore.

beset *(SYN.)* surround, attack.

besides *(SYN.)* moreover, further, except for, also, as well, furthermore.

besiege *(SYN.)* assault, attack, siege, bombard, raid, charge.

bespeak *(SYN.)* engage, reserve, indicate, show, signify, express.

best *(SYN.)* choice, prime, select. *(ANT.) worst.*

bestial *(SYN.)* brutal, beastly, savage, cruel.

bestow *(SYN.)* confer, place, put, award, give, present. *(ANT.) withdraw, withhold.*

bet *(SYN.)* gamble, give, stake, wager, pledge, ante.

betray *(SYN.)* reveal, deliver, expose, mislead, trick, deceive, exhibit, show. *(ANT.) shelter, protect, safeguard.*

betrothal *(SYN.)* marriage, engagement, contract.

better *(SYN.)* superior, preferable, improve. *(ANT.) worsen.*

between *(SYN.)* among, betwixt.

beware *(SYN.)* take care, watch out, look sharp, be careful.

bewilder *(SYN.)* perplex, confuse, mystify, baffle, puzzle, overwhelm. *(ANT.) clarify, enlighten.*

bewitch *(SYN.)* captivate, charm, delight, enchant.

beyond *(SYN.)* past, farther, exceeding.

bias *(SYN.)* slant, inclination, proneness, turn, bent, penchant, tendency, disposition, propensity, partiality, predisposition, leaning, proclivity, prejudice, influence, warp, slanting, predilection. *(ANT.)*

fairness, justice, even-handedness, equity, detachment, impartiality.

bible *(SYN.)* guide, handbook, gospel, manual, sourcebook, guidebook.

bibulous *(SYN.)* guzzling, intemperate, winebibbing, sottish, alcoholic. *(ANT.) sober, moderate.*

bicker *(SYN.)* dispute, argue, wrangle, quarrel. *(ANT.) go along with, agree.*

bid *(SYN.)* order, command, direct, wish, greet, say, offer, instruct, invite, purpose, tender, proposal.

bidding *(SYN.)* behest, request, decree, call, charge, beck, summons, solicitation, invitation, instruction, mandate.

bide *(SYN.)* stay, tarry, delay, wait, remain.

big *(SYN.)* large, huge, bulky, immense, colossal, majestic, august, monstrous, hulking, gigantic, massive, great, enormous, tremendous, outgoing, important, kind, big-hearted, considerable, generous, grand. *(ANT.) small, little, tiny, immature, petite.*

big-hearted *(SYN.)* good-natured, liberal, generous, unselfish, open-handed, unstinting, charitable, magnanimous. *(ANT.) cold, selfish, mean, uncharitable.*

bigoted *(SYN.)* intolerant, partial, prejudiced, biased, unfair, chauvinist.

bigotry *(SYN.)* bias, blindness, intolerance, unfairness, prejudice, ignorance, passion, sectarianism. *(ANT.) acceptance, open-mindedness.*

big-shot *(SYN.)* somebody, brass hat, big gun. *(ANT.) underling, nobody, cipher.*

bijou *(SYN.)* gem, bauble, jewel, ornament.

bile *(SYN.)* spleen, rancor, anger, bitterness, peevishness, ill-humor, resentment, discontent, irascibility. *(ANT.) cheerfulness, affability, pleasantness.*

bilge *(SYN.)* hogwash, drivel, gibberish, rubbish, bosh, foolishness, twaddle.

bilious *(SYN.)* petulant, crabby, ill-natured, cross, peevish, crotchety, cranky. *(ANT.) happy, agreeable, pleasant, good-natured.*

bilk *(SYN.)* defraud, trick, cheat, hoodwink, deceive, fleece, rook, bamboozle.

bill *(SYN.)* charge, invoice, account, statement, beak.

billet *(SYN.)* housing, quarters, berth, shelter, barrack, installation.

billingsgate *(SYN.)* swearing, scurrility, cursing, abuse, vulgarity, gutter, profanity.

billow *(SYN.)* surge, swell, rise, rush, peaking, magnification, amplification, augmentation, increase, intensification. *(ANT.) lowering, decrease.*

bin *(SYN.)* cubbyhole, box, container, chest, cubicle, crib, receptacle, can.

bind *(SYN.)* connect, restrain, band, fasten, oblige, obligate, engage, wrap, connect, weld, attach, tie, require, restrict. *(ANT.) unlace, loose, unfasten, untie, free.*

binding *(SYN.)* compulsory, obligatory, mandatory, compelling, unalterable, imperative, indissoluble, unconditional, unchangeable, hard-and-fast. *(ANT.) adjustable, flexible, elastic, changeable.*

binge *(SYN.)* fling, spree, carousal, toot.

birth *(SYN.)* origin, beginning, infancy, inception. *(ANT.) decline, death, disappearance, end.*

biscuit *(SYN.)* bun, roll, cake, muffin, bread, rusk, scone.

bit *(SYN.)* fraction, portion, scrap, fragment, particle, drop, speck, harness, small amount, restraint, morsel.

bite *(SYN.)* gnaw, chew, nip, sting, pierce, mouthful, snack, morsel.

biting *(SYN.)* cutting, sharp, acid, sneering, sarcastic. *(ANT.) soothing, kind, gentle, agreeable.*

bitter *(SYN.)* distasteful, sour, acrid, pungent, piercing, vicious, severe, biting, distressful, stinging, distressing, ruthless, hostile, grievous, harsh, painful, tart. *(ANT.) sweet, mellow, pleasant, delicious.*

bizarre *(SYN.)* peculiar, strange, odd, uncommon, queer, unusual. *(ANT.) usual, everyday, ordinary, inconspicuous.*

black *(SYN.)* sooty, dark, ebony, inky, swarthy, soiled, filthy, dirty, stained, somber, depressing, sad, dismal, gloomy. *(ANT.) white, clean, pristine, glowing, pure, cheerful, light-skinned, sunny, bright.*

blackball *(SYN.)* turn down, ban, blacklist,

exclude, snub, reject, debar. *(ANT.) accept, include, invite, ask, bid.*

blacken *(SYN.)* tar, ink, black, darken, besoot, smudge, begrime, discredit, defile, dull, dim, tarnish, ebonize, denounce, sully, libel, blemish, defame. *(ANT.) exalt, honor, whiten, brighten, shine, bleach.*

blackmail *(SYN.)* bribe, payment, bribery, extortion, shakedown, coercion.

blackout *(SYN.)* faint, coma, unconsciousness, oblivion, amnesia, stupor, swoon.

bladder *(SYN.)* saccule, sac, vesicle, pouch, pod, cell, blister, container, cyst.

blade *(SYN.)* cutter, lancet, knife, sword.

blame *(SYN.)* upbraid, criticize, fault, guilt, accuse, rebuke, charge, implicate, impeach, tattle, condemn, indict, responsibility, censure, denounce, reproach. *(ANT.) exonerate, credit, honor, absolve.*

blameless *(SYN.)* moral, innocent, worthy, faultless. *(ANT.) blameworthy, culpable, guilty.*

blanch *(SYN.)* whiten, bleach, decolorize, peroxide, fade, wash out, dim, dull.

bland *(SYN.)* soft, smooth, gentle, agreeable, vapid, insipid, mild, polite. *(ANT.) harsh, outspoken, disagreeable.*

blandish *(SYN.)* praise, compliment, overpraise, cajole, puff, adulate, salve, fawn, court, toady, butter up, please, jolly. *(ANT.) insult, deride, criticize, belittle.*

blandisher *(SYN.)* adulator, booster, sycophant, eulogist, flunky. *(ANT.) knocker, faultfinder, belittler.*

blandishment *(SYN.)* applause, cajolery, honor, adulation, plaudits, acclaim, fawning, compliments. *(ANT.) criticism, deprecation.*

blank *(SYN.)* unmarked, expressionless, uninterested, form, area, void, vacant, empty. *(ANT.) marked, filled, alert, animated.*

blanket *(SYN.)* quilt, coverlet, cover, comforter, robe, padding, carpet, wrapper, mantle, envelope, housing, coat, comprehensive, universal, across-the-board, panoramic, omnibus. *(ANT.) limited, detailed, restricted, precise.*

blare *(SYN.)* roar, blast, resound, jar, scream, clang, peal, trumpet, toot, hoot.

blasphemous *(SYN.)* profane, irreverent, impious, godless, ungodly, sacrilegious, irreligious. *(ANT.) reverent, reverential, religious, pious.*

blasphemy *(SYN.)* profanation, impiousness, cursing, irreverence, sacrilege, abuse, swearing, contempt. *(ANT.) respect, piety, reverence, devotion.*

blast *(SYN.)* burst, explosion, discharge, blow-out.

blasted *(SYN.)* blighted, withered, ravaged, decomposed, spoiled, destroyed.

blastoff *(SYN.)* launching, expulsion, launch, shot, projection.

blatant *(SYN.)* shameless, notorious, brazen, flagrant, glaring, bold, obvious. *(ANT.) deft, subtle, insidious, devious.*

blaze *(SYN.)* inferno, shine, flare, marking, fire, outburst, holocaust, notch, flame. *(ANT.) die, dwindle.*

bleach *(SYN.)* pale, whiten, blanch, whitener. *(ANT.) darken, blacken.*

bleak *(SYN.)* dreary, barren, cheerless, depressing, gloomy, windswept, bare, cold, dismal, desolate, raw, chilly. *(ANT.) lush, hopeful, promising, cheerful.*

bleary *(SYN.)* hazy, blurry, fuzzy, misty, clouded, overcast, dim. *(ANT.) clear, vivid, precise, clear-cut.*

bleed *(SYN.)* pity, lose blood, grieve, sorrow.

blemish *(SYN.)* injury, speck, flaw, scar, disgrace, imperfection, stain, fault, blot. *(ANT.) purity, embellishment, adornment, perfection.*

blend *(SYN.)* beat, intermingle, combine, fuse, unite, consolidate, amalgamate, conjoin, mix, coalesce, intermix, join, merge, compound, combination, stir, mixture, mingle. *(ANT.) separate, decompose, analyze, disintegrate.*

bless *(SYN.)* thank, celebrate, extol, glorify, adore, delight, praise, gladden, exalt. *(ANT.) denounce, blaspheme, slander, curse.*

blessed *(SYN.)* sacred, holy, consecrated, dedicated, hallowed, sacrosanct, beatified, joyful, delighted, joyous, sainted, canonized, blissful. *(ANT.)* *miserable, sad, dispirited, cheerless.*

blessing *(SYN.)* sanction, favor, grace, benediction, invocation, approbation, approval, compliment, bounty, windfall, gift, benefit, advantage, kindness, felicitation, invocation. *(ANT.)* *disapproval, execration, curse, denunciation, malediction, rebuke, displeasure, condemnation, adversity, misfortune, mishap, calamity.*

blight *(SYN.)* decay, disease, spoil, sickness, wither, ruin, damage, harm, decaying, epidemic, affliction, destroy.

blind *(SYN.)* sightless, unmindful, rash, visionless, ignorant, unsighted, unconscious, discerning, heedless, oblivious, purblind, unknowing, screen, unaware, thoughtless, shade, unthinking, cover, curtain, without thought, headlong. *(ANT.)* *discerning, sensible, calculated, perceiving, perceptive, aware.*

blink *(SYN.)* bat, glance, flicker, wink, twinkle.

bliss *(SYN.)* ecstasy, rapture, glee, elation, joy, blessedness, gladness, happiness, delight, felicity, blissfulness. *(ANT.)* *woe, sadness, sorrow, grief, unhappiness, torment, wretchedness, misery.*

blissful *(SYN.)* happy, elated, rapturous, ecstatic, paradisiacal, joyous, enraptured.

blister *(SYN.)* swelling, welt, sore, blob, bubble, inflammation, boil, canker.

blithe *(SYN.)* breezy, merry, airy, lighthearted, light, gay, fanciful, graceful. *(ANT.)* *morose, grouchy, low-spirited, gloomy.*

blitz *(SYN.)* strike, onslaught, thrust, raid, lunge, drive, incursion, assault, sally.

blizzard *(SYN.)* storm, snowfall, gale, tempest, blast, blow, swirl.

bloat *(SYN.)* distend, puff up, inflate, swell. *(ANT.)* *deflate.*

blob *(SYN.)* bubble, blister, pellet, globule.

block *(SYN.)* clog, hinder, bar, impede, close, obstruct, barricade, blockade, obstruction, hindrance, obstacle, impediment, retard, check, stop. *(ANT.)* *forward,*

promote, aid, clear, advance, advantage, assist, further, open.

blockade *(SYN.)* barrier, fortification, obstruction, barricade.

blockhead *(SYN.)* dunce, dolt, fool, sap, idiot, simpleton, chump, booby, bonehead, woodenhead.

blood *(SYN.)* murder, gore, slaughter, bloodshed, ancestry, lineage, heritage.

bloodcurdling *(SYN.)* hair-raising, terrifying, alarming, chilling, stunning, scary.

bloodless *(SYN.)* dead, torpid, dull, drab, cold, colorless, passionless, lackluster. *(ANT.)* *passionate, vital, ebullient, animated, vivacious.*

bloodshed *(SYN.)* murder, killing, slaying, blood bath, massacre, carnage.

bloodthirsty *(SYN.)* murderous, cruel.

bloody *(SYN.)* cruel, pitiless, bloodthirsty, inhuman, ruthless, ferocious, murderous. *(ANT.)* *kind, gentle.*

bloom *(SYN.)* thrive, glow, flourish, blossom, flower. *(ANT.)* *wane, decay, dwindle, shrivel, wither.*

blooming *(SYN.)* flush, vigorous, thriving, vital, abloom, healthy, fresh, booming. *(ANT.)* *flagging, declining, withering.*

blooper *(SYN.)* muff, fluff, error, bungle, botch, blunder, fumble, howler, indiscretion.

blossom *(SYN.)* bloom, flower, flourish. *(ANT.)* *shrink, wither, dwindle, fade.*

blot *(SYN.)* stain, inkblot, spot, ink-stain, blemish, dishonor, disgrace, spatter, obliterate, soil, dry.

blot out *(SYN.)* wipe out, destroy, obliterate, abolish, annihilate, cancel, expunge, strike out, shade, darken, shadow, overshadow, obfuscate, cloud, eclipse.

blow *(SYN.)* hit, thump, slap, cuff, box, shock, move, drive, spread, breeze, puff, whistle, inflate, enlarge.

blowout *(SYN.)* blast, explosion, burst.

blue *(SYN.)* sapphire, azure, gloomy, sad, unhappy, depressed, dejected, melancholy. *(ANT.)* *cheerful, optimistic, happy.*

blueprint *(SYN.)* design, plan, scheme, chart, draft, prospectus, outline, proposal, conception, project, layout.

blues *(SYN.)* dumps, melancholy, depression, doldrums, despondency, gloominess, moroseness.

bluff *(SYN.)* steep, perpendicular, vertical, abrupt, precipitous, rough, open, frank, hearty, blunt, foot, mislead, pretend, deceive, fraud, lie, fake, deceit.

blunder *(SYN.)* error, flounder, mistake, stumble.

blunt *(SYN.)* solid, abrupt, rough, dull, pointless, plain, bluff, edgeless, unceremonious, obtuse, rude, outspoken, unsharpened, rounded, worn, crude, direct, impolite, short, curt, gruff. *(ANT.) tactful, polite, subtle, polished, suave, sharp, keen, pointed, diplomatic.*

blur *(SYN.)* sully, dim, obscure, stain, dull, confuse, cloud, smear, stain, smudge. *(ANT.) clear, clarify.*

blush *(SYN.)* redden.

board *(SYN.)* embark, committee, wood, mount, cabinet, food, get on, lumber.

boast *(SYN.)* vaunt, flaunt, brag, glory, crow, exaggerate. *(ANT.) humble, apologize, minimize, deprecate.*

body *(SYN.)* remains, bulk, mass, carcass, form, company, corpus, society, firmness, group, torso, substance, collection, cadaver, trunk, group, throng, company, crowd, band. *(ANT.) spirit, intellect, soul.*

bogus *(SYN.)* counterfeit, false, pretend, fake, phony. *(ANT.) genuine.*

boil *(SYN.)* seethe, bubble, pimple, fume, cook, swelling, rage, foam, simmer, stew.

boisterous *(SYN.)* rough, violent, rowdy, noisy, tumultuous. *(ANT.) serene.*

bold *(SYN.)* daring, forward, pushy, striking, brave, dauntless, rude, prominent, adventurous, fearless, insolent, conspicuous, defiant, arrogant, cavalier, brazen, unafraid, intrepid, courageous, valiant, heroic, gallant, disrespectful, impudent, shameless. *(ANT.) modest, bashful, cowardly, timid, retiring, flinching, fearful, timorous, polite, courteous, deferential.*

bolt *(SYN.)* break away, fastener, floe, take flight, lock.

bombard *(SYN.)* shell, open fire, bomb, rake, assail, attack.

bond *(SYN.)* fastener, rope, tie, cord, connection, attachment, link, tie, promise. *(ANT.) sever, separate, untie, disconnect.*

bondage *(SYN.)* slavery, thralldom, captivity, imprisonment, servitude, confinement, vassalage, enslavement. *(ANT.) liberation, emancipation, free, independence, freedom.*

bonds *(SYN.)* chains, cuffs, fetters, shackles, irons, bracelets.

bone up *(SYN.)* learn, master, study, relearn.

bonus *(SYN.)* more, extra, premium, gift, reward, bounty.

bony *(SYN.)* lean, lank, thin, lanky, rawboned, fleshless, skinny, gangling, weight. *(ANT.) plump, fleshy, stout.*

book *(SYN.)* manual, textbook, work, booklet, monograph, brochure, tract, volume, pamphlet, treatise, publication, hardcover, paperback, novel, workbook, text.

bookish *(SYN.)* formal, scholarly, theoretical, academic, learned, scholastic, erudite. *(ANT.) ignorant.*

boom *(SYN.)* advance, grow, flourish, progress, gain, roar, beam, rumble, reverberate, thunder, prosper, swell, thrive, pole, rush. *(ANT.) decline, fail, recession.*

booming *(SYN.)* flourishing, blooming, thriving, vigorous, prospering, exuberant. *(ANT.) waning, dying, failing, declining.*

boon *(SYN.)* gift, jolly, blessing, pleasant, godsend, windfall.

boondocks *(SYN.)* sticks, backwoods.

boor *(SYN.)* lout, clown, oaf, yokel, rustic, vulgarian, ruffian.

boorish *(SYN.)* coarse, churlish, uncivil, ill-mannered, ill-bred, uncivilized, crude, uncouth. *(ANT.) polite, cultivated, well-mannered.*

boost *(SYN.)* push, lift, help, hoist, shove. *(ANT.) depress, lower, belittle, disparage, decrease, decline, reduction, down turn.*

booster *(SYN.)* supporter, fan, rooter, plugger, follower.

boot *(SYN.)* shoe, kick.

booth

booth *(SYN.)* enclosure, cubicle, stand, compartment, box.

bootless *(SYN.)* purposeless, ineffective, profitless, useless. *(ANT.) favorable, successful, useful.*

bootlicker *(SYN.)* flunky, fawner, toady, sycophant.

booty *(SYN.)* prize, plunder, loot.

booze *(SYN.)* spirits, drink, liquor, alcohol.

border *(SYN.)* fringe, rim, verge, boundary, edge, termination, brink, limit, brim, outskirts, frontier, margin. *(ANT.) interior, center, mainland, core, middle.*

borderline *(SYN.)* unclassifiable, indeterminate, halfway, obscure, inexact, indefinite, unclear. *(ANT.) precise, absolute, definite.*

border on *(SYN.)* approximate, approach, resemble, echo, parallel, connect.

bore *(SYN.)* tire, weary, hole, perforate, pierce, drill. *(ANT.) arouse, captivate, excite, interest.*

boredom *(SYN.)* ennui, doldrums, weariness, dullness, tedium. *(ANT.) stimulation, motive, activity, stimulus, excitement.*

boring *(SYN.)* monotonous, dull, dead, flat, tedious, wearisome, trite, prosaic, humdrum, long-winded.

born *(SYN.)* hatched, produced.

borrow *(SYN.)* copy, adopt, simulate, mirror, assume, usurp, plagiarize, take. *(ANT.) allow, advance, invent, originate, credit, lend.*

bosom *(SYN.)* chest, breast, feelings, thoughts, mind, interior, marrow, heart.

boss *(SYN.)* director, employer, oversee, direct, foreman, supervisor, manager.

bossy *(SYN.)* overbearing, arrogant, domineering, lordly, tyrannical. *(ANT.) flexible, easygoing, cooperative.*

botch *(SYN.)* blunder, bungle, fumble, goof, muff, mishandle, mismanage. *(ANT.) perform, realize.*

bother *(SYN.)* haunt, molest, trouble, annoy, upset, fleeting, transient, harass, inconvenience, momentary, disturb, passing, pester, tease, irritate, worry, vex. *(ANT.) prolonged, extended, long, protracted,* lengthy, comfort, solace.

bothersome *(SYN.)* irritating, vexatious, worrisome, annoying, distressing, troublesome, disturbing.

bottle *(SYN.)* container, flask, vessel, decanter, vial, ewer, jar.

bottleneck *(SYN.)* obstacle, obstruction, barrier, block, blockage, detour.

bottom *(SYN.)* basis, fundament, base, groundwork, foot, depths, lowest part, underside, foundation, seat, buttocks, rear, behind. *(ANT.) top, peak, apex, summit, topside.*

bough *(SYN.)* branch, arm, limb.

bounce *(SYN.)* recoil, ricochet, rebound.

bound *(SYN.)* spring, vault, hop, leap, start, surrounded, jump, limit, jerk, boundary, bounce, skip, tied, shackled, trussed, fettered, certain, sure, destined, compelled, required. *(ANT.) unfettered, free.*

boundary *(SYN.)* bound, limit, border, margin, outline, circumference, perimeter, division, frontier, edge.

boundless *(SYN.)* limitless, endless, inexhaustible, unlimited, eternal, infinite. *(ANT.) restricted, limited.*

bounteous *(SYN.)* plentiful, generous, liberal, abundant. *(ANT.) scarce, rare.*

bountiful *(SYN.)* bounteous, fertile, plentiful, generous, abundant. *(ANT.) sparing, infertile, scarce.*

bounty *(SYN.)* generosity, gift, award, bonus, reward, prize, premium.

bourgeois *(SYN.)* common, ordinary, commonplace, middle-class, conventional. *(ANT.) upper-class, unconventional, loose, aristocratic.*

bout *(SYN.)* round, contest, conflict, test, struggle, match, spell, fight.

bow *(SYN.)* bend, yield, kneel, submit, stoop.

bowels *(SYN.)* entrails, intestines, innards, guts, stomach.

bowl *(SYN.)* container, dish, pot, pottery, crock, jug, vase.

bowl over *(SYN.)* fell, floor, overturn, astound, nonplus, stagger, jar.

bow out *(SYN.)* give up, withdraw, retire,

resign, abandon.

box *(SYN.)* hit, fight, crate, case, container.

boxer *(SYN.)* prizefighter, fighter.

boy *(SYN.)* male, youngster, lad, kid, fellow, buddy, youth. *(ANT.)* girl, man.

boycott *(SYN.)* picket, strike, ban, revolt, blackball.

boyfriend *(SYN.)* date, young man, sweetheart, courtier, beau.

brace *(SYN.)* strengthen, tie, prop, support, tighten, stay, strut, bind, truss, crutch.

bracelet *(SYN.)* armband, bangle, circlet.

bracing *(SYN.)* stimulating, refreshing, restorative, fortifying, invigorating.

bracket *(SYN.)* join, couple, enclose, relate, brace, support.

brag *(SYN.)* boast, flaunt, vaunt, bluster, swagger. *(ANT.)* demean, debase, denigrate, degrade, depreciate, deprecate.

braid *(SYN.)* weave, twine, wreath, plait.

brain *(SYN.)* sense, intelligence, intellect, common sense, understanding, reason. *(ANT.)* stupid, stupidity.

brake *(SYN.)* decelerate, stop, curb. *(ANT.)* accelerate.

branch *(SYN.)* shoot, limb, bough, tributary, offshoot, part, division, expand, department, divide, spread, subdivision.

brand *(SYN.)* make, trademark, label, kind, burn, trade name, mark, stamp, blaze.

brave *(SYN.)* bold, daring, gallant, valorous, adventurous, heroic, magnanimous, chivalrous, audacious, valiant, courageous, fearless, intrepid, unafraid. *(ANT.)* weak, cringing, timid, cowardly, fearful, craven.

brawl *(SYN.)* racket, quarrel, fracas, riot, fight, melee, fray, disturbance, dispute, disagreement.

brawn *(SYN.)* strength, muscle. *(ANT.)* weakness.

brazen *(SYN.)* immodest, forward, shameless, bold, brassy, impudent, insolent, rude. *(ANT.)* retiring, self-effacing, modest, shy.

breach *(SYN.)* rupture, fracture, rift, break, crack, gap, opening, breaking, quarrel, violation.

break *(SYN.)* demolish, pound, rack, smash, burst, rupture, disobey, violate, crack, infringe, crush, squeeze, transgress, fracture, shatter, wreck, crash, atomize, disintegrate, collapse, splinter, gap, breach, opening. *(ANT.)* restore, heal, join, renovate, mend, repair.

breed *(SYN.)* engender, bear, propagate, father, beget, rear, conceive, train, generate, raise, procreate, nurture, create, mother, produce, originate. *(ANT.)* murder, abort, kill.

breeze *(SYN.)* air, wind, zephyr, breath. *(ANT.)* calm.

breezy *(SYN.)* jolly, spry, active, brisk, energetic, lively, carefree, spirited.

brevity *(SYN.)* briefness, conciseness. *(ANT.)* length.

brew *(SYN.)* plot, plan, cook, ferment, prepare, scheme.

bribe *(SYN.)* buy off.

bridle *(SYN.)* control, hold, restrain, check, harness, curb, restraint, halter. *(ANT.)* release, free, loose.

brief *(SYN.)* curt, short, fleeting, passing, compendious, terse, laconic, succinct, momentary, transient, temporary, concise, compact, condensed. *(ANT.)* long, extended, prolonged, lengthy, protracted, comprehensive, extensive, exhaustive.

brigand *(SYN.)* bandit, robber, thief.

bright *(SYN.)* luminous, gleaming, clever, witty, brilliant, lucid, vivid, clear, smart, intelligent, lustrous, clever, shining, shiny, sparkling, shimmering, radiant, cheerful, lively, gay, happy, lighthearted, keen, promising, favorable, encouraging. *(ANT.)* sullen, dull, murky, dark, gloomy, dim, lusterless, boring, colorless, stupid, backward, slow.

brilliant *(SYN.)* bright, clear, smart, intelligent, sparkling, shining, alert, vivid, splendid, radiant, glittering, talented, ingenious, gifted. *(ANT.)* mediocre, dull, lusterless, second-rate.

brim *(SYN.)* border, margin, lip, rim, edge. *(ANT.)* middle, center.

bring *(SYN.)* fetch, take, carry, raise, introduce, propose. *(ANT.)* remove, withdraw.

brink *(SYN.)* limit, verge, rim, margin, edge.

brisk

brisk *(SYN.)* fresh, breezy, cool, lively, refreshing, spirited, jolly, energetic, quick, active, animated, nimble, spry, agile, sharp, keen, stimulating, invigorating. *(ANT.) musty, faded, stagnant, decayed, hackneyed, slow, lethargic, sluggish, still, dull, oppressive.*

briskness *(SYN.)* energy, exercise, motion, rapidity, agility, action, quickness, activity, vigor, liveliness, movement. *(ANT.) inertia, idleness, sloth, dullness, inactivity.*

bristle *(SYN.)* flare up, anger, rage, seethe, get mad.

brittle *(SYN.)* crumbling, frail, breakable, delicate, splintery, crisp, fragile, weak. *(ANT.) tough, enduring, unbreakable, thick, strong, sturdy, flexible, elastic, supple.*

broach *(SYN.)* set afoot, introduce, inaugurate, start, mention, launch, advance.

broad *(SYN.)* large, wide, tolerant, expanded, vast, liberal, sweeping, roomy, expansive, extended, general, extensive, full. *(ANT.) restricted, confined, narrow, constricted, slim, tight, limited, negligible.*

broadcast *(SYN.)* distribute, announce, publish, scatter, circulate, spread, send, transmit, relay.

broaden *(SYN.)* spread, widen, amplify, enlarge, extend, increase, add to, expand, stretch, deepen, magnify. *(ANT.) tighten, narrow, constrict, straiten.*

broad-minded *(SYN.)* unprejudiced, tolerant, liberal, unbigoted. *(ANT.) prejudiced, petty, narrow-minded.*

brochure *(SYN.)* booklet, pamphlet, leaflet, mailing, circular, tract, flier.

broil *(SYN.)* cook, burn, beat, roast, bake, scorch, fire, grill, singe, sear, toast.

broken *(SYN.)* flattened, rent, shattered, wrecked, destroyed, reduced, smashed, crushed, fractured, ruptured, interrupted, burst, separated. *(ANT.) whole, integral, united, repaired.*

brokenhearted *(SYN.)* disconsolate, forlorn, heartbroken, sad, grieving.

bromide *(SYN.)* banality, platitude, stereotype, commonplace, slogan, proverb.

brooch *(SYN.)* clasp, pin, breast-pin.

brood *(SYN.)* study, consider, ponder, reflect, contemplate, meditate, young, litter, offspring, think, muse, deliberate.

brook *(SYN.)* rivulet, run, branch, stream, creek.

brother *(SYN.)* comrade, man, kinsman, sibling. *(ANT.) sister.*

brotherhood *(SYN.)* kinship, kindness, fraternity, fellowship, clan, society, brotherliness, bond, association, relationship, solidarity. *(ANT.) strife, discard, acrimony, opposition.*

brotherly *(SYN.)* affectionate, fraternal, cordial, sympathetic, benevolent, philanthropic, humane, kindred, communal, altruistic.

brow *(SYN.)* forehead, eyebrow.

browbeat *(SYN.)* bully, domineer, bulldoze, intimidate, henpeck, oppress, grind.

brown study *(SYN.)* contemplation, reflection, reverie, musing, thoughtfulness, deliberation, rumination, self-communion.

browse *(SYN.)* scan, graze, read, feed.

bruise *(SYN.)* hurt, injure, wound, damage, abrasion, injury, contusion, mark, harm, wound.

brunt *(SYN.)* force, impact, shock, strain, oppression, severity.

brush *(SYN.)* rub, wipe, clean, bushes, remove, shrubs, broom, whisk, paintbrush, hairbrush, underbrush, thicket.

brush-off *(SYN.)* dismissal, snub, sight, rebuff, turndown.

brusque *(SYN.)* sudden, curt, hasty, blunt, rough, steep, precipitate, rugged, craggy, gruff, surly, abrupt, short, bluff. *(ANT.) smooth, anticipated, courteous, expected, gradual, personable.*

brutal *(SYN.)* brute, cruel, inhuman, rude, barbarous, gross, sensual, ferocious, brutish, coarse, bestial, carnal, remorseless, ruthless, savage, mean, pitiless, barbaric. *(ANT.) kind, courteous, humane, civilized, gentle, kindhearted, mild.*

brute *(SYN.)* monster, barbarian, beast, animal, wild, savage.

bubble *(SYN.)* boil, foam, seethe, froth.

buccaneer *(SYN.)* sea robber, privateer, pirate.

buck *(SYN.)* spring, jump, vault, leap.

bucket *(SYN.)* pot, pail, canister, can.

buckle *(SYN.)* hook, fastening, fastener, bend, wrinkle, clip, clasp, distort, catch, strap, fasten, collapse, yield, warp.

bud *(SYN.)* develop, sprout.

buddy *(SYN.)* companion, comrade, friend, partner, pal.

budge *(SYN.)* stir, move.

budget *(SYN.)* schedule, ration.

buff *(SYN.)* shine, polish, burnish, rub, wax.

buffet *(SYN.)* bat, strike, clout, blow, knock, beat, crack, hit, slap, cabinet, counter, server.

buffoon *(SYN.)* jester, fool, clown, jokester, zany, comedian, chump, boor, dolt.

bug *(SYN.)* fault, hitch, defect, catch, snag, failing, rub, flaw, snarl, weakness, annoy, pester, hector, vex, nag, nettle.

bugbear *(SYN.)* bogy, specter, demon, devil, fiend.

build *(SYN.)* found, rear, establish, constructed, raise, set up, erect, assemble. *(ANT.)* raze, destroy, overthrow, demolish, undermine.

building *(SYN.)* residence, structure, house, edifice.

buildup *(SYN.)* gain, enlargement, increase, praise, commendation, promotion, jump, expansion, uptrend, testimonial, plug, puff, blurb, endorsement, compliment. *(ANT.)* reduction, decrease, decline.

bulge *(SYN.)* lump, protuberance, bump, swelling, protrusion, extend, protrude. *(ANT.)* hollow, shrink, contract, depression.

bulk *(SYN.)* lump, magnitude, volume, size, mass, most, majority.

bulky *(SYN.)* great, big, huge, large, enormous, massive, immense, clumsy, cumbersome, unwieldy. *(ANT.)* tiny, little, small, petite, handy, delicate.

bull *(SYN.)* push, force, press, drive, thrust, bump.

bulldoze *(SYN.)* cow, bully, coerce, thrust, push.

bulletin *(SYN.)* news, flash, message, statement, newsletter, circular.

bullheaded *(SYN.)* dogged, stiff-necked, stubborn, mulish, rigid, pigheaded, willful, tenacious, unyielding. *(ANT.)* flexible, submissive, compliant.

bully *(SYN.)* pester, tease, intimidate, harass, domineer.

bulwark *(SYN.)* wall, bastion, abutment, bank, dam, rampart, shoulder, parapet, backing, maintainer, embankment, safeguard, reinforcement, sustainer.

bum *(SYN.)* idler, loafer, drifter, hobo, wretch, dawdler, beggar, vagrant.

bumbling *(SYN.)* bungling, inept, blundering, clumsy, incompetent, awkward, maladroit, lumbering, ungainly. *(ANT.)* facile, handy, dexterous, proficient.

bump *(SYN.)* shake, push, hit, shove, prod, collide, knock, bang, strike.

bumpkin *(SYN.)* hick, yokel, rustic, yahoo.

bumptious *(SYN.)* arrogant, self-assertive, conceited, forward, overbearing, pushy, boastful, obtrusive. *(ANT.)* sheepish, self-effacing, retiring, shrinking, unobtrusive, diffident.

bumpy *(SYN.)* uneven, jolting, rough, jarring, rocky, coarse, irregular. *(ANT.)* flat, smooth, flush, polished, level.

bunch *(SYN.)* batch, bundle, cluster, company, collection, flock, group.

bundle *(SYN.)* package, mass, collection, batch, parcel, packet, box, carton, bunch.

bungalow *(SYN.)* ranch house, cabana, cabin, cottage, lodge, summer house, villa.

bungle *(SYN.)* fumble, botch, foul up, boggle, mess up, louse up, blunder.

bunk *(SYN.)* berth, rubbish, nonsense, couch, bed, cot.

buoyant *(SYN.)* light, jolly, spirited, effervescent, blithe, sprightly, lively, resilient. *(ANT.)* hopeless, dejected, sullen, depressed, heavy, despondent, sinking, low, pessimistic, downcast, glum.

burden *(SYN.)* oppress, afflict, trouble, encumber, tax, weight, load, worry, contents, trial, lade, overload. *(ANT.)* lighten, alleviate, ease, mitigate, console, disburden.

bureau *(SYN.)* office, division, department, unit, commission, chest, dresser.

bureaucrat *(SYN.)* clerk, official,

burglar

functionary, servant, politician.

burglar *(SYN.)* thief, robber.

burial *(SYN.)* interment, funeral.

burn *(SYN.)* scorch, blaze, scald, sear, char, incinerate, fire, flare, combust. *(ANT.)* quench, extinguish.

burrow *(SYN.)* tunnel, search, seek, dig, excavate, hunt, den, hole.

burst *(SYN.)* exploded, broken, erupt.

bury *(SYN.)* hide, inhume, conceal, immure, cover, inter, entomb, secrete. *(ANT.)* reveal, display, open, raise, disinter.

business *(SYN.)* employment, profession, trade, work, art, vocation, occupation, company, concern, firm. *(ANT.)* hobby, avocation, pastime.

bustle *(SYN.)* noise, flurry, action, fuss, ado, stir, excitement, commotion. *(ANT.)* calmness, composure, serenity, peacefulness.

busy *(SYN.)* careful, industrious, active, patient, assiduous, diligent, perseverant. *(ANT.)* unconcerned, indifferent, careless, inactive, unemployed, lazy, indolent.

busybody *(SYN.)* gossip, tattletale, pry, meddler, snoop.

but *(SYN.)* nevertheless, yet, however, though, although, still.

butcher *(SYN.)* kill, murder, slaughter, assassinate, slay, massacre. *(ANT.)* save, protect, vivify, animate, resuscitate.

butt *(SYN.)* bump, ram, bunt, shove, jam, drive, blow, push, thrust, propulsion.

buttocks *(SYN.)* hind end, rump, posterior, behind, bottom, rear, butt.

button *(SYN.)* clasp, close, fasten, hook, buttress, support, brace, stay, frame, prop, reinforcement, bulwark.

buy *(SYN.)* procure, get, purchase, acquire, obtain. *(ANT.)* vend, sell.

buzz *(SYN.)* whir, hum, drone, burr.

by *(SYN.)* near, through, beside, with, from, at, close to.

bygone *(SYN.)* bypast, former, earlier, past, onetime, forgotten. *(ANT.)* present, current, modern.

bypass *(SYN.)* deviate from, go around, detour around.

bystander *(SYN.)* onlooker, watcher, viewer, observer, witness, kibitzer.

byway *(SYN.)* passage, detour, path.

byword *(SYN.)* adage, proverb, axiom, shibboleth, apothegm, motto, slogan.

C

cab *(SYN.)* coach, taxi, car, hack, taxicab, carriage.

cabin *(SYN.)* cottage, shack, shanty, hut, dwelling, house.

cabinet *(SYN.)* ministry, council, committee, case, cupboard.

cable *(SYN.)* wire, cord, rope, telegraph.

cache *(SYN.)* bury, hide, cover, store.

cad *(SYN.)* knave, rascal, scoundrel, rogue.

cafe *(SYN.)* coffeehouse.

cafeteria *(SYN.)* cafe, diner, restaurant.

cagey *(SYN.)* cunning, wary, clever, tricky, cautious, shrewd, evasive. *(ANT.)* innocent, straightforward, guileless, naive.

calamity *(SYN.)* ruin, disaster, casualty, distress, hardship, trouble, misfortune, bad luck, catastrophe. *(ANT.)* blessing, fortune, welfare.

calculate *(SYN.)* count, compute, figure, estimate, consider, tally, determine, measure, subtract, add, divide, multiply, judge, reckon. *(ANT.)* guess, miscalculate, assume, conjecture.

calculating *(SYN.)* crafty, shrewd, scheming, cunning. *(ANT.)* simple, guileless, direct, ingenuous.

calculation *(SYN.)* figuring, reckoning, computation, estimation. *(ANT.)* guess, assumption.

calendar *(SYN.)* timetable, schedule, diary.

call *(SYN.)* designate, name, yell, cry, ask, shout, speak, cry out, call out, exclaim, command, term, label, phone, ring up, collect, waken, awaken, ring, wake, arouse, rouse, outcry, need, demand, claim, assemble, telephone, occasion, invite.

calling *(SYN.)* occupation, profession, trade.

callous *(SYN.)* insensitive, impenitent, obdurate, unfeeling, indurate, hard, insensible, heartless. *(ANT.) soft, compassionate, tender.*

calm *(SYN.)* appease, lull, quiet, soothe, alloy, assuage, unruffled, mild, tranquil, smooth, serene, cool, level-headed, unexcited, aloof, detached, stillness, calmness, serenity, composure. *(ANT.) tempestuous, disturbed, emotional, turmoil, incite, inflame, roiled, incense, upheaval, excite, upset, disturb, arouse.*

campaign *(SYN.)* movement, cause, crusade.

can *(SYN.)* tin, container.

canal *(SYN.)* gully, tube, duct, waterway.

cancel *(SYN.)* eliminate, obliterate, erase, delete, nullify, repeal, revoke, cross out, expunge, void, recall, set aside, abolish, rescind. *(ANT.) perpetuate, confirm, ratify, enforce, enact.*

candid *(SYN.)* free, blunt, frank, plain, open, sincere, honest, straightforward, direct, outspoken. *(ANT.) sly, contrived, wily, scheming.*

candidate *(SYN.)* applicant, aspirant, nominee.

canine *(SYN.)* pooch, dog, puppy.

canny *(SYN.)* artful, skillful, shrewd, clever, cautious, cunning, careful.

canopy *(SYN.)* awning, screen, shelter, cover.

cant *(SYN.)* dissimulation, patois, jargon, shoptalk, deceit, argot, pretense. *(ANT.) honesty, candor, frankness, truth.*

cantankerous *(SYN.)* crabby, grouchy, irritable, surly, grumpy, irascible.

canyon *(SYN.)* gulch, gully, arroyo, ravine, gorge.

cap *(SYN.)* top, cover, crown, beat, lid, excel.

capability *(SYN.)* aptness, ability, capacity, aptitude, dexterity, power, efficiency, qualification. *(ANT.) incapacity, disability, incompetency.*

capable *(SYN.)* clever, qualified, able, efficient, competent, skilled, fit, skillful, accomplished, fitted. *(ANT.) unfitted, incapable, incompetent, unskilled, inept, inadequate.*

capacity *(SYN.)* capability, power, ability, talent, content, skill, volume, size. *(ANT.) inability, stupidity, incapacity, impotence.*

cape *(SYN.)* pelisse, cloak, mantle, neck, point, headland, peninsula.

caper *(SYN.)* romp, frisk, cavort, frolic, gambol.

capital *(SYN.)* leading, chief, important, property, wealth, money, city, cash, assets, principal, resources, major, primary, first, funds. *(ANT.) unimportant, trivial, secondary.*

capricious *(SYN.)* undependable, erratic, inconstant, fickle, changeable, irregular, inconsistent, unstable.

captain *(SYN.)* commander, authority, supervisor, leader, skipper, master, officer.

caption *(SYN.)* heading, title, headline.

captivate *(SYN.)* fascinate, charm, delight.

captive *(SYN.)* convict, prisoner, hostage.

captivity *(SYN.)* detention, imprisonment, custody, confinement, bondage, slavery. *(ANT.) liberty, freedom.*

capture *(SYN.)* catch, grip, apprehend, clutch, arrest, snare, seize, nab, seizure, catching, grasp, take prisoner, grab, recovery, trap. *(ANT.) set free, lose, liberate, throw, free, release.*

car *(SYN.)* auto, automobile, motorcar, vehicle.

carcass *(SYN.)* remains, frame, corpse, form, bulk, mass, corpus, association, body, cadaver. *(ANT.) mind, intellect, soul.*

cardinal *(SYN.)* chief, primary, important, prime, leading, major, essential. *(ANT.) subordinate, secondary, auxiliary.*

care *(SYN.)* concern, anxiety, worry, caution, solicitude, charge, ward, attention, regard, supervision, consider, consideration, keeping, protection, attend, watch, supervise, keep, guardianship, custody. *(ANT.) neglect, disregard, indifference, unconcern, negligence.*

career *(SYN.)* occupation, profession, job, calling, vocation, trade.

carefree *(SYN.)* lighthearted, happy, unconcerned, breezy, jolly, uneasy, nonchalant, happy-go-lucky, lively.

careful *(SYN.)* prudent, thoughtful, attentive, cautious, painstaking, scrupulous, heedful, circumspect, vigilant, guarded, discreet, watchful, wary, concerned, meticulous, thorough. *(ANT.)* nice, careful, heedless, messy, careless, sloppy.

careless *(SYN.)* imprudent, heedless, unconcerned, inattentive, lax, indiscreet, desultory, reckless, negligent. *(ANT.)* careful, nice, cautious, painstaking, prudent, accurate.

caress *(SYN.)* hug, fondle, embrace, pet, pat, stroke, kiss, cuddle. *(ANT.)* spurn, vex, buffet, annoy, tease.

cargo *(SYN.)* freight, load, freight-load, shipment.

caricature *(SYN.)* exaggeration, parody, spoof, takeoff, lampoon, satire, burlesque.

carnage *(SYN.)* massacre, liquidation, slaughter, genocide, butchery, extermination, annihilation.

carnal *(SYN.)* base, corporeal, animal, lustful, worldly, sensual, bodily, gross, fleshy, voluptuous. *(ANT.)* intellectual, spiritual, exalted, temperate.

carnival *(SYN.)* fete, fair, jamboree, festival.

carol *(SYN.)* hymn, song, ballad.

carp *(SYN.)* pick, praise, complain.

carpet *(SYN.)* mat, rug.

carping *(SYN.)* discerning, exact, captions, accurate, fastidious, important, hazardous. *(ANT.)* superficial, cursory, approving, encouraging, unimportant, insignificant.

carriage *(SYN.)* bearing, conduct, action, deed, behavior, demeanor, disposition, deportment.

carry *(SYN.)* convey, transport, support, bring, sustain, bear, hold, move, transfer, take. *(ANT.)* drop, abandon.

carry off *(SYN.)* seize, abduct, capture, kidnap. *(ANT.)* set free, let go, liberate.

carry on *(SYN.)* go on, continue, proceed, misbehave. *(ANT.)* stop.

carry out *(SYN.)* succeed, complete, fulfill, win, accomplish, effect.

carve *(SYN.)* hew, shape, cut, whittle, chisel, sculpt.

case *(SYN.)* state, covering, receptacle, condition, instance, example, occurrence, happening, illustration, sample, suit, action, claim, lawsuit, crate, container, carton, box.

cash *(SYN.)* currency, money.

casket *(SYN.)* coffin, box, crate.

cast *(SYN.)* fling, toss, throw, pitch, form, company, shape, sort, mold, hurl, sling, shed, direct, impart, turn, actors, players, type, variety.

caste *(SYN.)* class, grade, order, category, status, elegance, set, rank, station, social standing, denomination, excellence, genre.

castle *(SYN.)* mansion, palace, chateau.

casual *(SYN.)* chance, unexpected, informal, accidental, incidental, offhand, unplanned, relaxed, fortuitous, unintentional, spontaneous. *(ANT.)* planned, expected, calculated, formal, deliberate, dressy, premeditated, pretentious.

casualty *(SYN.)* calamity, fortuity, mishap, loss, injured, dead, wounded, accident, contingency, victim, sufferer, misfortune. *(ANT.)* design, purpose, intention, calculation.

catalog *(SYN.)* classify, roll, group, list, inventory, directory, index, record, file.

catastrophe *(SYN.)* mishap, calamity, disaster, adversity, accident, ruin. *(ANT.)* fortune, boon, triumph, blessing, advantage.

catch *(SYN.)* hook, snare, entrap, ensnare, capture, grip, apprehend, grasp, take, grab, nab, arrest, contract, seize, apprehension, latch, bolt, pin, clasp, trap. *(ANT.)* lose, free, liberate, throw, release.

catching *(SYN.)* contagious, pestilential, communicable, infectious, virulent. *(ANT.)* non-communicable, healthful.

catchy *(SYN.)* tricky, misleading, attractive.

category *(SYN.)* class, caste, kind, order, genre, rank, classification, sort, elegance, type, set, excellence.

cater *(SYN.)* coddle, oblige, serve, humor, baby, mollycoddle, pamper, spoil, indulge, provide.

cause *(SYN.)* effect, incite, create, induce, inducement, occasion, incentive, prompt, principle, determinant, reason, origin, motive.

caustic *(SYN.)* bitter, disagreeable, distasteful, acrid, sour, spiteful, pungent, tart, painful, cruel, insulting, peevish, mean, ruthless, malicious, hateful, harsh. *(ANT.) mellow, sweet, delicious, pleasant.*

caution *(SYN.)* heed, vigilance, care, prudence, counsel, warning, wariness, advice, warn, injunction, admonish, watchfulness. *(ANT.) carelessness, heedlessness, incaution, abandon, recklessness.*

cautious *(SYN.)* heedful, scrupulous, attentive, prudent, thoughtful, discreet, guarded, circumspect, vigilant, watchful, wary, careful. *(ANT.) improvident, headstrong, heedless, foolish, forgetful, indifferent.*

cavalcade *(SYN.)* column, procession, parade.

cavalier *(SYN.)* contemptuous, insolent, haughty, arrogant.

cave *(SYN.)* grotto, hole, shelter, lair, den, cavern.

cave in *(SYN.)* fall in, collapse.

cavity *(SYN.)* pit, hole, crater.

cavort *(SYN.)* caper, leap, frolic, hop, prance.

cease *(SYN.)* desist, stop, abandon, discontinue, relinquish, end, terminate, leave, surrender, resign. *(ANT.) occupy, continue, persist, begin, endure, stay.*

cede *(SYN.)* surrender, relinquish, yield.

celebrate *(SYN.)* honor, glorify, commemorate, keep, solemnize, extol, observe, commend, praise. *(ANT.) decry, overlook, profane, disregard, disgrace.*

celebrated *(SYN.)* eminent, glorious, distinguished, noted, illustrious, famed, well-known, popular, renowned, famous. *(ANT.) obscure, hidden, anonymous, infamous, unknown.*

celebrity *(SYN.)* somebody, personage, heroine, hero, dignitary, notable.

celestial *(SYN.)* godlike, holy, supernatural, divine, paradisiacal, utopian, transcendent, superhuman. *(ANT.) diabolical, profane, mundane, wicked.*

cement *(SYN.)* solidify, weld, fasten, secure.

cemetery *(SYN.)* graveyard.

censure *(SYN.)* denounce, reproach, upbraid, blame, disapproval, reprehend, condemn, criticism, disapprove, criticize, reprove. *(ANT.) commend, approval, forgive, approve, praise, applaud, condone.*

center *(SYN.)* heart, core, midpoint, middle, nucleus, inside, hub, focus. *(ANT.) rim, boundary, edge, border, periphery, outskirts.*

central *(SYN.)* chief, necessary, main, halfway, dominant, mid, middle, inner, focal, leading, fundamental, principal. *(ANT.) side, secondary, incidental, auxiliary.*

ceremonious *(SYN.)* correct, exact, precise, stiff, outward, external, solemn, formal. *(ANT.) material, unconventional, easy, heartfelt.*

ceremony *(SYN.)* observance, rite, parade, formality, pomp, ritual, protocol, solemnity. *(ANT.) informality, casualness.*

certain *(SYN.)* definite, assured, fixed, inevitable, sure, undeniable, positive, confident, particular, special, indubitable, secure, unquestionable. *(ANT.) probable, uncertain, doubtful, questionable.*

certainly *(SYN.)* absolutely, surely, definitely. *(ANT.) dubiously, doubtfully, questionably.*

certainty *(SYN.)* confidence, courage, security, assuredness, firmness, assertion, statement. *(ANT.) humility, bashfulness, modest, shyness.*

certificate *(SYN.)* affidavit, document.

certify *(SYN.)* validate, affirm, verify, confirm, authenticate, substantiate.

certitude *(SYN.)* confidence, belief, conviction, feeling, faith, persuasion, trust. *(ANT.) doubt, incredulity, denial, heresy.*

cessation *(SYN.)* ending, finish, stoppage, termination, conclusion, end.

chafe *(SYN.)* heat, rub, warm, annoy, disturb.

chagrin *(SYN.)* irritation, mortification, embarrassment, annoyance, vexation, worry, bother, shame, annoy, irk, humiliation, irritate, vex, frustrate, humiliate, embarrass, mortify, exasperate, disappoint, disappointment.

35

chain

chain *(SYN.)* fasten, bind, shackle, restrain.

chairman *(SYN.)* speaker.

challenge *(SYN.)* question, dare, call, summon, threat, invite, threaten, demand.

chamber *(SYN.)* cell, salon, room.

champion *(SYN.)* victor, winner, choice, best, conqueror, hero, support, select.

chance *(SYN.)* befall, accident, betide, disaster, opportunity, calamity, occur, possibility, prospect, happen, luck, fate, take place. *(ANT.)* design, purpose, inevitability, calculation, certainty, intention.

change *(SYN.)* modification, alternation, alteration, mutation, variety, exchange, shift, alter, transfigure, veer, vary, variation, substitution, substitute, vicissitude. *(ANT.)* uniformity, monotony, settle, remain, endure, retain, preserve, steadfastness, endurance, immutability, stability.

changeable *(SYN.)* fitful, fickle, inconstant, unstable, shifting, wavering. *(ANT.)* stable, uniform, constant, unchanging.

channel *(SYN.)* strait, corridor, waterway, artery, duct, canal, way, trough, groove, passageway.

chant *(SYN.)* singing, incantation, hymn, intone, sing, carol, psalm, song, ballad.

chaos *(SYN.)* confusion, jumble, turmoil, anarchy, disorder, muddle. *(ANT.)* organization, order, tranquility, tidiness, system.

chaotic *(SYN.)* confused, disorganized, disordered, messy. *(ANT.)* neat, ordered, systematic, organized.

chap *(SYN.)* break, fellow, person, crack, split, man, rough, individual, boy.

chaperon *(SYN.)* associate with, escort, convoy, accompany, consort with. *(ANT.)* avoid, desert, leave, abandon, quit.

chapter *(SYN.)* part, section, division.

char *(SYN.)* scorch, singe, burn, sear.

character *(SYN.)* description, class, kind, repute, mark, individuality, disposition, traits, personality, reputation, symbol, features, quality, eccentric, nature.

characteristic *(SYN.)* exclusive, distinctive, special, mark, feature, property, typical, unique, attribute, distinguishing, trait, quality.

charge *(SYN.)* arraignment, indictment, accusation, sell for, attack, assail, assault, indict, blame, allegation, care, custody, imputation. *(ANT.)* pardon, flee, exculpation, excuse, absolve, retreat, exoneration.

charitable *(SYN.)* benevolent, generous, liberal, altruistic, kind, obliging, considerate, unselfish. *(ANT.)* petty, mean, harsh, wicked, greedy, narrow-minded, stingy, malevolent.

charity *(SYN.)* benevolence, kindness, magnanimity, altruism, generosity. *(ANT.)* malevolence, cruelty, selfishness.

charm *(SYN.)* allure, spell, enchantment, attractiveness, magic, witchery, amulet, talisman, lure, enchant, bewitch, fascinate, captivate.

charmer *(SYN.)* siren, temptress, enchantress, vamp, seductress, seducer, enchanter.

charming *(SYN.)* attractive, enchanting, fascinating, alluring, appealing, winsome, agreeable, bewitching, winning. *(ANT.)* revolting, repugnant, repulsive.

chart *(SYN.)* design, plan, cabal, plot, sketch, stratagem, map, diagram, conspiracy, graph, intrigue.

charter *(SYN.)* lease, hire, rent, alliance.

chase *(SYN.)* hunt, run after, pursue, trail, follow, persist, scheme. *(ANT.)* escape, flee, abandon, elude, evade.

chasm *(SYN.)* ravine, abyss, canyon, gorge.

chaste *(SYN.)* clear, immaculate, innocent, sincere, bare, clean, modest, pure, decent, virtuous, virginal, sheer, absolute, spotless. *(ANT.)* polluted, tainted, foul, impure, sinful, worldly, sullied, defiled.

chasten *(SYN.)* chastise, restrain, punish, discipline.

chastise *(SYN.)* punish, castigate, correct. *(ANT.)* release, acquit, free, exonerate.

chat *(SYN.)* argue, jabber, blab, plead, consult, converse, lecture, discuss, talk, conversation, tattle.

chatter *(SYN.)* dialogue, lecture, speech, conference, talk, discourse. *(ANT.)* silence, correspondence, writing.

cheap *(SYN.)* poor, common, inexpensive,

shabby, low-priced, beggary, low-cost, shoddy, mean, inferior. (*ANT.*) *honorable, dear, noble, expensive, costly, well-made, elegant, dignified.*

cheat (*SYN.*) deceive, fool, bilk, outwit, victimize, dupe, gull, hoodwink, circumvent, swindler, cheater, trickster, phony, fraud, defraud, charlatan, crook, chiseler, con artist, hoax, swindle.

check (*SYN.*) dissect, interrogate, analyze, contemplate, inquire, question, scrutinize, arrest, stop, halt, block, curb, control, investigate, review, examine, test, counterfoil, stub, barrier, watch. (*ANT.*) *overlook, disregard, advance, foster, continue, promote, omit, neglect.*

checkup (*SYN.*) medical examination, physical.

cheek (*SYN.*) nerve, effrontery, impudence, gall, impertinence.

cheer (*SYN.*) console, gladden, comfort, encourage, applause, encouragement, joy, glee, gaiety, mirth, soothe, sympathize, approval, solace. (*ANT.*) *depress, sadden, discourage, derision, dishearten, discouragement, antagonize.*

cheerful (*SYN.*) glad, jolly, joyful, gay, happy, cherry, merry, joyous, lighthearted. (*ANT.*) *mournful, sad, glum, depressed, gloomy, sullen.*

cherish (*SYN.*) prize, treasure, appreciate, nurse, value, comfort, hold dear, foster, nurture, sustain. (*ANT.*) *disregard, neglect, deprecate, scorn, reject, undervalue, abandon.*

chest (*SYN.*) bosom, breast, coffer, box, case, trunk, casket, dresser, commode, cabinet, chiffonier.

chew (*SYN.*) gnaw, munch, bite, nibble.

chic (*SYN.*) fashionable, modish, smart, stylish, trendy.

chide (*SYN.*) admonish, rebuke, scold, reprimand, criticize, reprove. (*ANT.*) *extol, praise, commend.*

chief (*SYN.*) chieftain, head, commander, captain, leader, principal, master, boss, leading, ruler. (*ANT.*) *servant, subordinate, secondary, follower, incidental, accidental, auxiliary, attendant.*

chiefly (*SYN.*) mainly, especially, mostly.

childish (*SYN.*) immature, childlike, infantile, babyish. (*ANT.*) *mature, grownup.*

chill (*SYN.*) coolness, cold, cool, coldness, brisk, frosty. (*ANT.*) *hot, warm, heat, heated, warmth.*

chilly (*SYN.*) cold, frigid, freezing, arctic, cool, icy, passionless, wintry, unfeeling. (*ANT.*) *fiery, heated, passionate, ardent.*

chirp (*SYN.*) peep, cheep, twitter, tweet, chirrup.

chivalrous (*SYN.*) noble, brave, polite, valorous, gallant, gentlemanly, courteous. (*ANT.*) *crude, rude, impolite, uncivil.*

chivalry (*SYN.*) courtesy, nobility, gallantry, knighthood.

choice (*SYN.*) delicate, elegant, file, dainty, exquisite, pure, refined, subtle, splendid, handsome, option, selection, beautiful, minute, pretty, pick, select, uncommon, rare, precious, valuable, thin, small. (*ANT.*) *coarse, rough, thick, blunt, large.*

choke (*SYN.*) throttle, gag, strangle.

choose (*SYN.*) elect, decide between, pick, select, cull, opt. (*ANT.*) *reject, refuse.*

chop (*SYN.*) hew, cut, fell, mince.

chore (*SYN.*) routine, task, job, duty, work.

chronic (*SYN.*) persistent, constant, lingering, continuing, perennial, unending, sustained, permanent. (*ANT.*) *fleeting, acute, temporary.*

chronicle (*SYN.*) detail, history, narrative, account, description, narration. (*ANT.*) *misrepresentation, confusion, distortion.*

chuckle (*SYN.*) titter, laugh, giggle.

chum (*SYN.*) friend, pal, buddy, companion.

cinema (*SYN.*) effigy, film, etching, appearance, drawing, engraving, illustration, likeness, image, panorama, picture.

circle (*SYN.*) disk, ring, set, group, class, club, surround, encircle, enclose, round.

circuit (*SYN.*) circle, course, journey, orbit, revolution, tour.

circuitous (*SYN.*) distorted, devious, indirect, roundabout, swerving, crooked, tortuous. (*ANT.*) *straightforward, straight, direct, honest.*

circular *(SYN.)* complete, curved, bulbous, cylindrical, round, ring-like, globular, entire, rotund. *(ANT.)* straight.

circumference *(SYN.)* border, perimeter, periphery, edge.

circumspection *(SYN.)* care, worry, solicitude, anxiety, concern, caution, attention, vigilance. *(ANT.)* neglect, negligence, indifference.

circumstance *(SYN.)* fact, event, incident, condition, happening, position, occurrence, situation.

circumstances *(SYN.)* facts, conditions, factors, situation, background, grounds, means, capital, assets, rank, class.

cite *(SYN.)* affirm, assign, allege, advance, quote, mention, declare, claim, maintain. *(ANT.)* refute, gainsay, deny, contradict.

citizen *(SYN.)* native, inhabitant, national, denizen, subject, dweller, resident.

city *(SYN.)* metropolis, municipality, town.

civil *(SYN.)* courteous, cultivated, accomplished, public, municipal, respectful, genteel, polite, considerate, gracious, urban. *(ANT.)* uncouth, uncivil, impertinent, impolite, boorish.

civilization *(SYN.)* cultivation, culture, education, breeding, enlightenment, society, refinement. *(ANT.)* ignorance, vulgarity.

civilize *(SYN.)* refine, tame, polish, cultivate, instruct, teach.

claim *(SYN.)* aver, declare, allege, assert, affirm, express, state, demand, maintain, defend, uphold. *(ANT.)* refute, deny, contradict.

clamor *(SYN.)* cry, din, babble, noise, racket, outcry, row, sound, tumult, shouting, shout, uproar. *(ANT.)* hush, serenity, silence, tranquility, stillness, quiet.

clan *(SYN.)* fellowship, kindness, solidarity, family, brotherhood, association, fraternity. *(ANT.)* discord, strife, opposition, acrimony.

clandestine *(SYN.)* covert, hidden, latent, private, concealed, secret, unknown. *(ANT.)* exposed, known, conspicuous, obvious.

clarify *(SYN.)* educate, explain, expound, decipher, illustrate, clear, resolve, define, interpret, unfold. *(ANT.)* darken, obscure, baffle, confuse.

clash *(SYN.)* clank, crash, clang, conflict, disagreement, opposition, collision, struggle, mismatch, contrast, disagree, collide, interfere. *(ANT.)* accord, agreement, harmony, blend, harmonize, match, agree.

clasp *(SYN.)* grip, hold, grasp, adhere, clutch, keep, have, maintain, possess, occupy, retain, support, confine, embrace, fastening, check, detain, curb, receive. *(ANT.)* relinquish, vacate, surrender, abandon.

class *(SYN.)* category, denomination, caste, kind, genre, grade, rank, order, elegance, classification, division, sort, family, species, set, excellence.

classic *(SYN.)* masterpiece.

classification *(SYN.)* order, category, class, arrangement, ordering, grouping, organization.

classify *(SYN.)* arrange, class, order, sort, grade, group, index.

clause *(SYN.)* condition, paragraph, limitation, article.

claw *(SYN.)* hook, talon, nail, scratch.

clean *(SYN.)* mop, tidy, neat, dustless, clear, unsoiled, immaculate, unstained, untainted, pure, dust, vacuum, scour, decontaminate, wipe, sterilize, cleanse, scrub, purify, wash, sweep. *(ANT.)* stain, soil, pollute, soiled, impure, dirty.

cleanse *(SYN.)* mop, purify, wash, sweep. *(ANT.)* stain, soil, dirty, pollute.

clear *(SYN.)* fair, sunny, cloudless, transparent, apparent, limpid, distinct, intelligible, evident, unmistakable, understandable, unclouded, light, bright, certain, manifest, lucid, plain, obvious, unobstructed. *(ANT.)* obscure, unclear, muddled, confused, dark, cloudy, blocked, obstructed, questionable, dubious, blockaded, foul, overcast.

clearly *(SYN.)* plainly, obviously, evidently, definitely, surely, certainly. *(ANT.)* questionably, dubiously.

clemency *(SYN.)* forgiveness, charity, compassion, grace, mercy, leniency, pity, mildness. *(ANT.)* punishment, *vengeance, retribution.*

clerical *(SYN.)* ministerial, pastoral, priestly, celestial, holy, sacred, secretarial.

clerk *(SYN.)* typist, office worker, salesperson, salesclerk.

clever *(SYN.)* apt, dexterous, quick, adroit, quick-witted, talented, bright, skillful, witty, ingenious, smart, intelligent, shrewd, gifted, expert, sharp. *(ANT.) unskilled, slow, stupid, backward, maladroit, bungling, dull, clumsy.*

cleverness *(SYN.)* intellect, intelligence, comprehension, mind, perspicacity, sagacity, fun. *(ANT.) sobriety, stupidity, solemnity, commonplace, platitude.*

client *(SYN.)* patron, customer.

cliff *(SYN.)* scar, tor, bluff, crag, precipice, escarpment.

climate *(SYN.)* aura, atmosphere, air, ambience.

climax *(SYN.)* apex, culmination, peak, summit, consummation, height, acme, zenith. *(ANT.) depth, base, anticlimax, floor.*

climb *(SYN.)* mount, scale, ascend. *(ANT.) descend.*

clip *(SYN.)* snip, crop, cut, mow, clasp.

cloak *(SYN.)* conceal, cover, disguise, clothe, cape, guard, envelop, hide, mask, protect, shield. *(ANT.) divulge, expose, reveal, bare, unveil.*

clod *(SYN.)* wad, hunk, gobbet, lump, chunk, clot, gob, dunce, dolt, oaf, fool.

clog *(SYN.)* crowd, congest, cram, overfill, stuff.

cloister *(SYN.)* monastery, priory, hermitage, abbey, convent.

close *(SYN.)* adjacent, adjoining, immediate, unventilated, stuffy, abutting, neighboring, dear, oppressive, mean, impending, nearby, near, devoted. *(ANT.) afar, faraway, removed, distant.*

close *(SYN.)* seal, shut, clog, stop, obstruct, cease, conclude, complete, end, terminate, occlude, finish. *(ANT.) unlock, begin, open, unbar, inaugurate, commence, start.*

closet *(SYN.)* cabinet, locker, wardrobe, cupboard.

cloth *(SYN.)* fabric, goods, material, textile.

clothe *(SYN.)* garb, dress, apparel. *(ANT.) strip, undress.*

clothes *(SYN.)* array, attire, apparel, clothing, garb, dress, garments, raiment, drapery, vestments. *(ANT.) nudity, nakedness.*

clothing *(SYN.)* attire, clothes, apparel, array, dress, drapery, garments, garb, vestments. *(ANT.) nudity, nakedness.*

cloud *(SYN.)* fog, mist, haze, mass, collection, obscure, dim, shadow.

cloudy *(SYN.)* dim, dark, indistinct, murky, mysterious, indefinite, vague, sunless, clouded, obscure, overcast, shadowy. *(ANT.) sunny, clear, distinct, limpid, lucid, clarified, cloudless, brilliant, bright.*

club *(SYN.)* society, association, set, circle, organization, bat, cudgel, stick, blackjack.

clue *(SYN.)* sign, trace, hint, suggestion.

clumsy *(SYN.)* bungling, inept, rough, unpolished, bumbling, awkward, ungraceful, gauche, ungainly, unskillful, untoward. *(ANT.) polished, skillful, neat, graceful, dexterous, adroit.*

cluster *(SYN.)* batch, clutch, group, bunch, gather, pack, assemble, crowd.

clutch *(SYN.)* grip, grab, seize, hold.

coalition *(SYN.)* combination, association, alliance, confederacy, entente, league, treaty. *(ANT.) schism, separation, divorce.*

coarse *(SYN.)* unpolished, vulgar, rough, impure, rude, crude, gruff, gross. *(ANT.) delicate, smooth, refined, polished, genteel, cultivated, suave, fine, cultured.*

coast *(SYN.)* seaboard, seashore, beach, shore, drift, glide, ride.

coax *(SYN.)* urge, persuade, wheedle, cajole. *(ANT.) force, bully, coerce.*

coddle *(SYN.)* pamper, baby, spoil, indulge.

coerce *(SYN.)* constrain, compel, enforce, force, drive, oblige, impel. *(ANT.) prevent, persuade, convince, induce.*

coercion *(SYN.)* emphasis, intensity, energy, dint, might, potency, power, vigor, strength, compulsion, force, constraint, violence. *(ANT.) impotence, frailty, feebleness, weakness, persuasion.*

cognizance *(SYN.)* apprehension,

erudition, acquaintance, information, learning, knowledge, lore, science, scholarship, understanding. (ANT.) illiteracy, misunderstanding, ignorance.

cognizant (SYN.) conscious, aware, apprised, informed, mindful, observant, perceptive. (ANT.) unaware, ignorant, oblivious, insensible.

coherent (SYN.) logical, intelligible, sensible, rational, commonsensical, reasonable.

coiffeur (SYN.) hairdresser.

coiffure (SYN.) haircut, hairdo.

coincide (SYN.) acquiesce, agree, accede, assent, consent, comply, correspond, concur, match, tally, harmonize, conform. (ANT.) differ, disagree, protest, contradict.

coincidence (SYN.) accident, chance. (ANT.) plot, plan, prearrangement, scheme.

coincident (SYN.) identical, equal, equivalent, distinguishable, same, like. (ANT.) distinct, contrary, disparate, opposed.

coincidental (SYN.) unpredicted, unexpected, chance, unforeseen, accidental, fortuitous.

cold (SYN.) cool, freezing, chilly, frigid, icy, frozen, wintry, arctic, unfriendly, indifferent, phlegmatic, stoical, passionless, chill, unemotional, heartless, unfeeling. (ANT.) hot, torrid, fiery, burning, ardent, friendly, temperate, warm, passionate.

collapse (SYN.) descend, decrease, diminish, fail, downfall, failure, decline, fall, drop, sink, subside, topple. (ANT.) soar, steady, limb, mount, arise.

colleague (SYN.) companion, attendant, comrade, associate, crony, mate, friend, partner. (ANT.) enemy, stranger, adversary.

collect (SYN.) assemble, amass, concentrate, pile, accumulate, congregate, obtain, heap, gather, solicit, secure, procure, raise, get, mass, hoard, consolidate. (ANT.) divide, dole, assort, dispel, distribute, disperse.

collected (SYN.) cool, calm, composed, imperturbable, placid, sedate, quiet. (ANT.) excited, violent, aroused, agitated.

collection (SYN.) amount, conglomeration, sum, entirety, aggregation, hoard, accumulation, pile, store, aggregate, total, whole. (ANT.) part, unit, particular, element, ingredient.

collide (SYN.) hit, smash, crash, strike.

collision (SYN.) conflict, combat, duel, battle, encounter, crash, smash, fight, contention, struggle, discord. (ANT.) concord, amity, harmony, consonance.

collusion (SYN.) combination, cabal, intrigue, conspiracy, plot, treachery.

color (SYN.) hue, paint, pigment, complexion, dye, shade, tone, tincture, stain, tint, tinge. (ANT.) paleness, transparency, achromatism.

colorful (SYN.) impressive, vivid, striking, full-color, multicolored, offbeat, weird, unusual. (ANT.) flat, dull, uninteresting.

colossal (SYN.) enormous, elephantine, gargantuan, huge, immense, gigantic, prodigious. (ANT.) little, minute, small, miniature, diminutive, microscopic, tiny.

combat (SYN.) conflict, duel, battle, collision, encounter, fight, contest, oppose, war, contention, struggle, discord. (ANT.) consonance, harmony, concord, yield, surrender, succumb, amity.

combination (SYN.) association, confederacy, alliance, entente, league, compounding, mixture, blend, composite, federation, mixing, compound, blending, union. (ANT.) separation, division, schism.

combine (SYN.) adjoin, associate, accompany, conjoin, connect, link, mix, blend, couple, unite, join. (ANT.) detach, disjoin, divide, separate, disconnect.

come (SYN.) near, approach, reach, arrive, advance. (ANT.) depart, leave, go.

comedian (SYN.) comic, wit, humorist, gagman, wag.

comely (SYN.) charming, elegant, beauteous, beautiful, fine, lovely, pretty, handsome. (ANT.) hideous, repulsive, foul, unsightly.

come-on (SYN.) lure, inducement, enticement, temptation, premium.

comfort (SYN.) contentment, ease, enjoyment, relieve, consolation, relief, cheer, console, calm, satisfaction, soothe, encourage, succor, luxury, solace. (*ANT.*) *depress, torture, discomfort, upset, misery, disturb, agitate, affliction, discompose, uncertainty, suffering.*

comfortable (*SYN.*) pleasing, agreeable, convenient, cozy, welcome, acceptable, relaxed, restful, cozy, gratifying, easy, contented, rested, satisfying, pleasurable. (*ANT.*) *miserable, distressing, tense, strained, troubling, edgy, uncomfortable.*

comical (*SYN.*) droll, funny, humorous, amusing, ludicrous, witty, ridiculous, odd, queer. (*ANT.*) *sober, solemn, sad, serious, melancholy.*

command (*SYN.*) class, method, rank, arrangement, series, sequence, point, aim, conduct, manage, guide, bid, system, succession, bidding, direct, order, demand, direction, rule, dictate, decree. (*ANT.*) *consent, obey, misdirect, distract, deceive, misguide, license, confusion.*

commandeer (*SYN.*) take possession, seize, confiscate, appropriate.

commanding (*SYN.*) imposing, masterful, assertive, authoritative, positive.

commence (*SYN.*) open, start. (*ANT.*) *stop, end, terminate, finish.*

commend (*SYN.*) laud, praise, applaud, recommend. (*ANT.*) *censure, criticize.*

commendable (*SYN.*) deserving, praiseworthy. (*ANT.*) *bad, deplorable, lamentable.*

commendation (*SYN.*) approval, applause, praise, recommendation, honor, medal. (*ANT.*) *criticism, condemnation, censure.*

commensurate (*SYN.*) keep, celebrate, observe, honor, commend, extol, glorify, laud, praise, honor. (*ANT.*) *decry, disgrace, disregard, overlook, profane, dishonor.*

comment (*SYN.*) assertion, declaration, annotation, explanation, review, commentary, report, remark, observation, utterance, criticism, statement.

commerce (*SYN.*) business, engagement, employment, art, trade, marketing, enterprise, occupation. (*ANT.*) *hobby, pastime, avocation.*

commiseration (*SYN.*) condolence, empathy, pity. (*ANT.*) *hardness, brutality, inhumanity, cruelty.*

commission (*SYN.*) board, committee, command, permit, order, permission, delegate, authorize, deputize, entrust.

commit (*SYN.*) perpetrate, perform, obligate, do, commend, consign, relegate, bind, delegate, empower, pledge, entrust, authorize, trust. (*ANT.*) *neglect, mistrust, release, free, miscarry, fail.*

commitment (*SYN.*) duty, promise, responsibility, pledge.

committee (*SYN.*) commission, bureau, board, delegate, council.

commodious (*SYN.*) appropriate, accessible, adapted, favorable, handy, fitting, timely. (*ANT.*) *inconvenient, troublesome, awkward.*

commodity (*SYN.*) article, merchandise, wares, goods.

common (*SYN.*) ordinary, popular, familiar, mean, low, general, vulgar, communal, mutual, shared, natural, frequent, prevalent, joint, conventional, plain, usual, universal. (*ANT.*) *odd, exceptional, scarce, noble, extraordinary, different, separate, outstanding, rare, unusual, distinctive, refined.*

commonplace (*SYN.*) common, usual, frequent, ordinary, everyday. (*ANT.*) *distinctive, unusual, original.*

commonsense (*SYN.*) perceptible, alive, apprehensible, aware, awake, cognizant, conscious, comprehending, perceptible. (*ANT.*) *unaware, impalpable, imperceptible.*

commotion (*SYN.*) confusion, chaos, disarray, ferment, disorder, stir, tumult, agitation. (*ANT.*) *tranquillity, peace, order.*

communicable (*SYN.*) infectious, virulent, catching, transferable, contagious. (*ANT.*) *hygienic, non-communicable.*

communicate (*SYN.*) convey, impart, inform, confer, disclose, reveal, relate, tell, advertise, publish, transmit, publicize, divulge. (*ANT.*) *withhold, hide, conceal.*

communication (*SYN.*) disclosure, transmission, declaration, announcement, notification, publication, message, report,

communicative

news, information.

communicative *(SYN.)* unreserved, open, frank, free, straightforward, unrestrained. *(ANT.) close-mouthed, secretive.*

communion *(SYN.)* intercourse, fellowship, participation, association, sacrament, union. *(ANT.) nonparticipation, alienation.*

community *(SYN.)* public, society, city, town, village, township.

compact *(SYN.)* contracted, firm, narrow, snug, close, constricted, packed, vanity, treaty, agreement, tense, taut, tight, niggardly, close-fisted, parsimonious, compressed, stingy. *(ANT.) slack, open, loose, relaxed, unconfined, unfretted, sprawling, lax.*

companion *(SYN.)* attendant, comrade, consort, friend, colleague, partner, crony, mate, associate. *(ANT.) stranger, enemy, adversary.*

companionship *(SYN.)* familiarity, cognizance, acquaintance, fellowship, knowledge, intimacy. *(ANT.) unfamiliarity, inexperience, ignorance.*

company *(SYN.)* crew, group, band, party, throng, house, assemblage, troop, fellowship, association, business, concern, partnership, corporation, companionship, firm. *(ANT.) seclusion, individual, solitude.*

comparable *(SYN.)* allied, analogous, alike, akin, like, correspondent, correlative, parallel. *(ANT.) opposed, incongruous, dissimilar, unalike, different, divergent.*

compare *(SYN.)* discriminate, match, differentiate, contrast, oppose.

comparison *(SYN.)* likening, contrasting, judgment.

compartment *(SYN.)* division, section.

compassion *(SYN.)* mercy, sympathy, pity.

compassionate *(SYN.)* sympathizing, benign, forbearing, good, tender, affable, humane, indulgent, kind, sympathetic, kindly. *(ANT.) inhuman, merciless, unkind, cold-hearted, unsympathetic, cruel.*

compatible *(SYN.)* consistent, agreeing, conforming, accordant, congruous, harmonious, cooperative, agreeable, constant, consonant, correspondent. *(ANT.) discrepant, paradoxical, disagreeable, contradictory.*

compel *(SYN.)* drive, enforce, coerce, constrain, force, oblige, impel. *(ANT.) induce, coax, wheedle, persuade, cajole, convince.*

compensate *(SYN.)* remunerate, repay, reimburse, recompense, balance.

compensation *(SYN.)* fee, earnings, pay, payment, recompense, allowance, remuneration, remittance, settlement, stipend, repayment, salary, wages. *(ANT.) present, gratuity, gift.*

compete *(SYN.)* rival, contest, oppose, vie. *(ANT.) reconcile, accord.*

competence *(SYN.)* skill, ability, capability.

competent *(SYN.)* efficient, clever, capable, able, apt, proficient, skillful, fitted, qualified. *(ANT.) inept, incapable, unfitted, awkward, incompetent, inadequate.*

competition *(SYN.)* contest, match, rivalry, tournament.

competitor *(SYN.)* rival, contestant, opponent. *(ANT.) ally, friend, colleague.*

complain *(SYN.)* lament, murmur, protest, grouch, grumble, regret, moan, remonstrate, whine, repine. *(ANT.) rejoice, praise, applaud, approve.*

complaint *(SYN.)* protest, objection, grievance.

complement *(SYN.)* supplement, complete. *(ANT.) clash, conflict.*

complete *(SYN.)* consummate, entire, ended, thorough, finished, full, whole, concluded, over, done, terminate, unbroken, total, undivided. *(ANT.) unfinished, imperfect, incomplete, start, partial, begin, commence, lacking.*

completion *(SYN.)* achievement, attainment, end, conclusion, close, finish, windup, accomplishment, realization. *(ANT.) omission, neglect, failure, defeat.*

complex *(SYN.)* sophisticated, compound, intricate, involved, perplexing, elaborate, complicated. *(ANT.) basic, simple, rudimentary, uncompounded, uncomplicated, plain.*

complexion *(SYN.)* paint, pigment, hue, color, dye, stain, tincture, tinge, tint, shade. *(ANT.) paleness, transparency.*

compliant *(SYN.)* meek, modest, lowly, plain, submissive, simple, unostentatious, unassuming, unpretentious. *(ANT.)* proud, vain, arrogant, haughty, boastful.

complicated *(SYN.)* intricate, involved, complex, compound, perplexing. *(ANT.)* simple, plain, uncompounded.

compliment *(SYN.)* eulogy, flattery, praise, admiration, honor, adulation, flatter, commendation, tribute. *(ANT.)* taunt, affront, aspersion, insult, disparage, criticism.

complimentary *(SYN.)* gratis, free.

comply *(SYN.)* assent, consent, accede, acquiesce, coincide, conform, concur, tally. *(ANT.)* differ, dissent, protest, disagree.

component *(SYN.)* division, fragment, allotment, moiety, apportionment, scrap, portion, section, share, segment, ingredient, organ. *(ANT.)* whole, entirety.

comport *(SYN.)* carry, conduct, behave, act, deport, interact, operate, manage.

compose *(SYN.)* forge, fashion, mold, make, construct, create, produce, shape, form, constitute, arrange, organize, make up, write, invent, devise, frame. *(ANT.)* misshape, dismantle, disfigure, destroy.

composed *(SYN.)* calm, cool, imperturbable, placid, quiet, unmoved, sedate, peaceful, collected, tranquil. *(ANT.)* aroused, violent, nervous, agitated, perturbed, excited.

composer *(SYN.)* author, inventor, creator, maker, originator.

composition *(SYN.)* paper, theme, work, essay, compound, mixture, mix.

composure *(SYN.)* calmness, poise, control, self-control, self-possession. *(ANT.)* anger, rage, turbulence, agitation.

compound *(SYN.)* blend, confound, jumble, consort, aggregate, complicated, combination, combined, mixture, complex, join. *(ANT.)* segregate, separate, divide, simple, sort.

comprehend *(SYN.)* apprehend, discern, learn, perceive, see, grasp, understand. *(ANT.)* mistake, misunderstand, ignore.

comprehension *(SYN.)* insight, perception, understanding, awareness, discernment. *(ANT.)* misconception, insensibility.

comprehensive *(SYN.)* wide, inclusive, complete, broad, full. *(ANT.)* fragmentary, partial, limited, incomplete.

compress *(SYN.)* press, compact, squeeze, pack, crowd. *(ANT.)* spread, stretch, expand.

comprise *(SYN.)* contain, hold, embrace. *(ANT.)* emit, encourage, yield, discharge.

compulsion *(SYN.)* might, energy, potency, strength, vigor. *(ANT.)* persuasion, impotence, frailty.

compulsory *(SYN.)* required, obligatory, necessary, unavoidable. *(ANT.)* elective, optional, free, unrestricted.

computation *(SYN.)* reckoning, record. *(ANT.)* misrepresentation.

compute *(SYN.)* count, calculate, determine, figure, reckon. *(ANT.)* conjecture, guess, miscalculate.

comrade *(SYN.)* attendant, companion, colleague, associate, friend. *(ANT.)* stranger, enemy, adversary.

conceal *(SYN.)* disguise, cover, hide, mask, screen, secrete, veil, withhold. *(ANT.)* reveal, show, disclose, expose.

concede *(SYN.)* permit, suffer, tolerate, grant, give, admit, acknowledge, allow, yield. *(ANT.)* forbid, contradict, protest, refuse, deny, negate, resist.

conceit *(SYN.)* pride, vanity, complacency, conception, idea, egotism, self-esteem, caprice, fancy, whim. *(ANT.)* humility, meekness, humbleness, modesty.

conceited *(SYN.)* proud, arrogant, vain, smug, egotistical. *(ANT.)* humble, modest, self-effacing.

conceive *(SYN.)* design, create, imagine, understand, devise, concoct, perceive, frame, grasp, invent. *(ANT.)* imitate, reproduce, copy.

concentrate *(SYN.)* localize, focus, condense, ponder, meditate, center, scrutinize. *(ANT.)* scatter, diffuse, dissipate, disperse.

concentrated *(SYN.)* compressed, thick, dense. *(ANT.)* sparse, quick, dispersed.

concept *(SYN.)* fancy, conception, image,

notion, idea, sentiment, thought. *(ANT.)* thing, matter, substance, entity.

conception *(SYN.)* consideration, deliberation, fancy, idea, notion, regard, thought, view.

concern *(SYN.)* matter, anxiety, affair, disturb, care, business, solicitude, interest, affect, involve, touch, trouble, worry. *(ANT.)* unconcern, negligence, disinterest, tire, bore, calm, indifference.

concerning *(SYN.)* regarding, about, respecting.

concerted *(SYN.)* united, joint, combined. *(ANT.)* individual, unorganized, separate.

concession *(SYN.)* admission, yielding, granting. *(ANT.)* insistence, demand.

concise *(SYN.)* pity, neat, brief, compact, succinct, terse. *(ANT.)* wordy, lengthy, verbose, prolix.

conclude *(SYN.)* decide, achieve, close, end, finish, terminate, complete, arrange, determine, settle, perfect, perform. *(ANT.)* start, begin, commence.

concluding *(SYN.)* extreme, final, last, terminal, utmost. *(ANT.)* first, foremost, opening, initial.

conclusion *(SYN.)* end, finale, termination, deduction, close, settlement, decision, finish, resolution, determination, completion, issue, judgment. *(ANT.)* commencement, inception, opening, start, beginning.

conclusive *(SYN.)* decisive, eventual, final, terminal, ultimate. *(ANT.)* original, first, inaugural.

concord *(SYN.)* agreement, unison, understanding, accordance, stipulation. *(ANT.)* disagreement, discord, dissension.

concrete *(SYN.)* solid, firm, precise, definite, specific. *(ANT.)* undetermined, vague, general.

concur *(SYN.)* agree, assent, consent, accede. *(ANT.)* dissent, protest, differ.

condemn *(SYN.)* denounce, reproach, blame, upbraid, convict, rebuke, doom, judge, censure, reprehend, punish, reprobate, sentence. *(ANT.)* condone, forgive, absolve, praise, applaud, extol, approve, par-

don, laud, excuse, commend.

condense *(SYN.)* shorten, reduce, abridge, abbreviate, concentrate, digest, compress, diminish. *(ANT.)* enlarge, increase, swell, expand.

condition *(SYN.)* circumstance, state, situation, case, plight, requirement, position, necessity, stipulation, predicament, provision, term.

conditional *(SYN.)* dependent, relying. *(ANT.)* casual, original, absolute.

condolence *(SYN.)* commiseration, concord, harmony, pity, sympathy, warmth. *(ANT.)* harshness, indifference, unconcern.

conduct *(SYN.)* control, supervise, manage, behavior, deed, actions, act, behave, manners, deportment.

confederate *(SYN.)* ally, abettor, assistant. *(ANT.)* enemy, rival, opponent, adversary.

confederation *(SYN.)* combination, league, union, marriage, treaty. *(ANT.)* separation, divorce.

confer *(SYN.)* gossip, grant, speak, tattle, blab, chat, deliberate, consult, award, give, bestow, talk. *(ANT.)* retrieve, withdraw.

confess *(SYN.)* avow, acknowledge, admit, concede, grant, divulge, reveal. *(ANT.)* disown, renounce, deny, conceal.

confession *(SYN.)* defense, justification, excuse, apology. *(ANT.)* dissimulation, denial, complaint.

confidence *(SYN.)* firmness, self-reliance, assurance, faith, trust, pledge, declaration, self-confidence, reliance, self-assurance, courage, statement. *(ANT.)* distrust, shyness, mistrust, bashfulness, diffidence, doubt, modesty, suspicion.

confident *(SYN.)* certain, sure, dauntless, self-assured. *(ANT.)* uncertain, timid, shy.

confine *(SYN.)* enclose, restrict, hinder, fence, limit, bound. *(ANT.)* release, expose, free, expand, open.

confirm *(SYN.)* acknowledge, establish, settle, substantiate, approve, fix, verify, assure, validate, ratify, corroborate, strengthen. *(ANT.)* disclaim, deny, disavow.

confirmation *(SYN.)* demonstration, experiment, test, trial, verification. *(ANT.)*

fallacy, invalidity.

confirmed *(SYN.)* regular, established, habitual. *(ANT.) occasional, infrequent.*

confiscate *(SYN.)* capture, catch, gain, purloin, steal, take, clutch, grip, seize, get, obtain, bear.

conflagration *(SYN.)* flame, glow, heat, warmth, fervor, passion, vigor. *(ANT.) apathy, cold, quiescence.*

conflict *(SYN.)* duel, combat, fight, collision, discord, encounter, interference, inconsistency, contention, struggle, opposition, clash, oppose, battle, controversy, contend, engagement, contest, variance. *(ANT.) consonance, harmony, amity.*

conform *(SYN.)* adapt, comply, yield, submit, obey, adjust, agree, fit, suit. *(ANT.) misapply, misfit, rebel, vary.*

conformity *(SYN.)* congruence, accord, agreement, correspondence.

confound *(SYN.)* confuse, baffle, perplex, puzzle, bewilder.

confront *(SYN.)* defy, hinder, resist, thwart, withstand, bar. *(ANT.) submit, agree, support, succumb.*

confuse *(SYN.)* confound, perplex, mystify, dumbfound, baffle, puzzle, jumble, mislead, mix up, mistake, bewilder. *(ANT.) explain, instruct, edify, illumine, enlighten, illuminate, solve.*

confused *(SYN.)* deranged, indistinct, disordered, muddled, bewildered, disconcerted, disorganized, perplexed. *(ANT.) organized, plain, clear, obvious.*

confusion *(SYN.)* commotion, disarray, agitation, disorder, chaos, ferment, stir, perplexity, tumult, bewilderment, disarrangement, uncertainty, muss, mess, turmoil. *(ANT.) order, tranquility, enlightenment, comprehension, understanding, tidiness, organization, peace.*

congregate *(SYN.)* gather, foregather, meet, convene. *(ANT.) scatter, dispel, disperse, dissipate.*

congress *(SYN.)* parliament, legislature, assembly.

congruous *(SYN.)* agreeing, conforming, constant, correspondent. *(ANT.) incongru-*

ous, inconsistent, discrepant.

conjecture *(SYN.)* law, supposition, theory. *(ANT.) proof, fact, certainty.*

conjunction *(SYN.)* combination, junction, connection, link. *(ANT.) separation, disconnection, diversion.*

connect *(SYN.)* adjoin, link, combine, relate, join, attach, unite, associate, attribute, affix. *(ANT.) detach, separate, disjoin, untie, dissociation, disconnect, disassociation, unfasten.*

connection *(SYN.)* conjunction, alliance, link, affinity, bond, tie, association, relationship, union. *(ANT.) isolation, dissociation, separation, disassociation, disunion.*

conquer *(SYN.)* master, beat, humble, defeat, overcome, rout, win, succeed, achieve, gain, overpower, quell, subdue, crush, vanquish. *(ANT.) cede, yield, retreat, surrender.*

conquest *(SYN.)* triumph, victory, achievement. *(ANT.) surrender, failure, defeat.*

conscientious *(SYN.)* upright, straight, honest, incorruptible, scrupulous. *(ANT.) careless, irresponsible, slovenly.*

conscious *(SYN.)* cognizant, informed, perceptive, aware, intentional, sensible, awake, purposeful, deliberate. *(ANT.) unaware, insensible, asleep, comatose, ignorant.*

consecrate *(SYN.)* exalt, extol, hallow, honor. *(ANT.) mock, degrade, debase, abuse.*

consecrated *(SYN.)* holy, divine, devout, spiritual. *(ANT.) evil, worldly, secular.*

consent *(SYN.)* permission, leave, agree, let, assent, agreement, license, permit. *(ANT.) refusal, opposition, denial, dissent, prohibition.*

consequence *(SYN.)* outcome, issue, result, effect, significance, importance. *(ANT.) impetus, cause.*

consequential *(SYN.)* significant, important, weighty. *(ANT.) trivial, unimportant, minor, insignificant.*

consequently *(SYN.)* hence, thence, therefore.

conservative *(SYN.)* conventional,

reactionary, cautious, moderate, careful. (ANT.) radical, liberal, foolhardy, reckless.

conserve (SYN.) save, retain, reserve, guard, keep, support, sustain. (ANT.) dismiss, neglect, waste, reject, discard.

consider (SYN.) heed, ponder, contemplate, examine, study, weigh, reflect, think about, regard, deliberate, respect. (ANT.) ignore, overlook, disdain, disregard, neglect.

considerable (SYN.) much, noteworthy, worthwhile, significant, important.

considerate (SYN.) careful, heedful, prudent, kind, thoughtful, polite, introspective, reflective. (ANT.) thoughtless, heedless, inconsiderate, selfish, rash.

consideration (SYN.) kindness, care, heed, politeness, empathy, notice, watchfulness, kindliness, thoughtfulness, courtesy, concern, sympathy, thought, attention, reflection, fee, pay, study. (ANT.) omission, oversight, negligence.

consistent (SYN.) conforming, accordant, compatible, agreeing, faithful, constant, harmonious, expected, regular, congruous, correspondent. (ANT.) paradoxical, discrepant, contrary, antagonistic, opposed, eccentric, inconsistent, incongruous.

consolation (SYN.) enjoyment, sympathy, relief, ease, contentment, comfort, solace. (ANT.) discomfort, suffering, discouragement, torture, burden, misery.

console (SYN.) solace, comfort, sympathize with, assuage, soothe. (ANT.) worry, annoy, upset, disturb, distress.

consolidate (SYN.) blend, combine, conjoin, fuse, mix, merge, unite. (ANT.) decompose, separate, analyze, disintegrate.

consort (SYN.) companion, comrade, friend. (ANT.) stranger, enemy, adversary.

conspicuous (SYN.) distinguished, clear, manifest, salient, noticeable, striking, obvious, prominent, visible. (ANT.) hidden, obscure, neutral, common, inconspicuous.

conspiracy (SYN.) machination, combination, treason, intrigue, cabal, treachery, plot, collusion.

conspire (SYN.) plan, plot, scheme.

constancy (SYN.) devotion, faithfulness, accuracy, precision, exactness. (ANT.) faithlessness, treachery, perfidy.

constant (SYN.) continual, invariable, abiding, permanent, faithful, invariant, true, ceaseless, enduring, unchanging, steadfast, unchangeable, loyal, stable, immutable, staunch, steady, fixed. (ANT.) fickle, irregular, wavering, off-and-on, infrequent, occasional, mutable.

constantly (SYN.) eternally, ever, evermore, forever, unceasingly. (ANT.) rarely, sometimes, never, occasionally.

consternation (SYN.) apprehension, dismay, alarm, fear, fright, dread, horror, terror. (ANT.) bravery, courage, boldness, assurance.

constitute (SYN.) compose, found, form, establish, organize, create, appoint, delegate, authorize, commission.

constitution (SYN.) law, code, physique, health, vitality.

constrain (SYN.) necessity, indigence, need, want, poverty. (ANT.) luxury, freedom, uncertainty.

construct (SYN.) build, form, erect, make, fabricate, raise, frame. (ANT.) raze, demolish, destroy.

constructive (SYN.) useful, helpful, valuable. (ANT.) ruinous, destructive.

construe (SYN.) explain, interpret, solve, render, translate. (ANT.) distort, confuse, misconstrue.

consult (SYN.) discuss, chatter, discourse, gossip, confer, report, rumor, deliberate, speech, talk. (ANT.) writing, correspondence, silence.

consume (SYN.) engulf, absorb, use up, use, expend, exhaust, devour, devastate, destroy, engross. (ANT.) emit, expel, exude, discharge.

consumer (SYN.) user, buyer, purchaser.

consummate (SYN.) close, conclude, do, finish, perfect, terminate.

consummation (SYN.) climax, apex, culmination, peak. (ANT.) depth, base, floor.

contact (SYN.) meeting, touching.

contrition

contagious *(SYN.)* infectious, virulent, communicable, catching. *(ANT.)* noncommunicable, healthful, hygienic.

contain *(SYN.)* embody, hold, embrace, include, accommodate, repress, restrain. *(ANT.)* emit, encourage, yield, discharge.

contaminate *(SYN.)* corrupt, sully, taint, defile, soil, pollute, dirty, infect, poison. *(ANT.)* purify.

contemplate *(SYN.)* imagine, recollect, consider, study, reflect upon, observe, deliberate, muse, ponder, plan, intend, view, regard, think about, reflect, think, mean. *(ANT.)* forget, guess, conjecture.

contemplative *(SYN.)* meditative, thoughtful, pensive, studious. *(ANT.)* inattentive, indifferent, thoughtless.

contemporary *(SYN.)* modern, present, simultaneous, fashionable, coexisting, contemporaneous, up-to-date. *(ANT.)* old, antecedent, past, ancient, succeeding, bygone.

contempt *(SYN.)* detestation, malice, contumely, disdain, derision, scorn. *(ANT.)* respect, reverence, admiration, esteem, awe.

contemptible *(SYN.)* base, mean, vile, vulgar, nasty, low, detestable, selfish, miserable, offensive. *(ANT.)* generous, honorable, noble, exalted, admirable.

contemptuous *(SYN.)* disdainful, sneering, scornful, insolent. *(ANT.)* modest, humble.

contend *(SYN.)* dispute, combat, contest, assert, claim, argue, maintain.

content *(SYN.)* pleased, happy, contented, satisfied. *(ANT.)* restless, dissatisfied, discontented.

contented *(SYN.)* delighted, fortunate, gay, happy, joyous, lucky, merry. *(ANT.)* gloomy, blue, depressed.

contention *(SYN.)* combat, duel, struggle, discord, battle, variance. *(ANT.)* concord, harmony, amity, consonance.

contentment *(SYN.)* delight, happiness, gladness, pleasure, satisfaction. *(ANT.)* misery, sorrow, grief, sadness, despair.

contest *(SYN.)* dispute, debate, competition, tournament, oppose, discuss, quarrel, squabble. *(ANT.)* allow, concede, agree, assent.

continence *(SYN.)* forbearance, temperance. *(ANT.)* self-indulgence, excess, intoxication.

contingency *(SYN.)* likelihood, possibility, occasion, circumstance.

contingent *(SYN.)* depending, subject. *(ANT.)* independent, original, casual.

continual *(SYN.)* constant, unceasing, everlasting, unremitting, endless, continuous, uninterrupted, regular, connected, consecutive, ceaseless. *(ANT.)* periodic, rare, irregular.

continue *(SYN.)* proceed, extend, endure, persist, resume, renew, recommence, last, remain, prolong, pursue. *(ANT.)* check, cease, discontinue, stop, suspend.

continuous *(SYN.)* continuing, uninterrupted, ceaseless, unceasing, incessant, constant. *(ANT.)* intermittent, irregular, sporadic.

contract *(SYN.)* condense, diminish, reduce, bargain, restrict, agreement, compact, pact, shrink, get, treaty, shorten. *(ANT.)* lengthen, extend, swell, expand.

contraction *(SYN.)* reduction, shortening. *(ANT.)* enlargement, expansion, extension.

contradict *(SYN.)* gainsay, counter, oppose, confute, dispute. *(ANT.)* verify, confirm, agree, support.

contradictory *(SYN.)* inconsistent, conflicting, incompatible, paradoxical, unsteady. *(ANT.)* congruous, consistent, correspondent.

contrary *(SYN.)* disagreeable, perverse, hostile, stubborn, opposite, opposing, opposed, disagreeing, disastrous, conflicting, headstrong, unlucky. *(ANT.)* lucky, agreeable, propitious, favorable, like, obliging, similar, complementary, tractable.

contrast *(SYN.)* differentiate, compare, distinction, disagreement, distinguish, differ, discriminate, difference, oppose. *(ANT.)* agreement, similarity, likeness.

contribute *(SYN.)* grant, give, donate, bestow, provide, offer. *(ANT.)* deny, withhold.

contribution *(SYN.)* grant, gift, offering, donation.

contrition *(SYN.)* grief, regret,

contrive

self-reproach. *(ANT.) self-satisfaction, complacency.*

contrive *(SYN.)* devise, intend, plan, make, invent, plot, hatch, form, project, arrange, manage, maneuver, scheme, sketch.

control *(SYN.)* govern, regulate, rule, command, dominate, direct, manage, check, repress, curb, management, mastery, direction, restraint, superintend. *(ANT.) ignore, forsake, follow, submit, abandon.*

controversy *(SYN.)* disagreement, dispute, debate. *(ANT.) agreement, harmony, accord, concord, decision.*

convenience *(SYN.)* accessibility, aid, benefit, help, service, availability. *(ANT.) inconvenience.*

convenient *(SYN.)* adapted, appropriate, fitting, favorable, handy, suitable, accessible, nearby, ready, available, advantageous, timely. *(ANT.) inconvenient, troublesome, awkward.*

convention *(SYN.)* meeting, conference, assembly, practice, custom, rule.

conventional *(SYN.)* common, regular, usual, everyday, habitual, routine, accustomed. *(ANT.) exotic, unusual, bizarre, extraordinary.*

conversant *(SYN.)* aware, intimate, familiar, versed, close, friendly, sociable. *(ANT.) affected, distant, cold, reserved.*

conversation *(SYN.)* colloquy, dialogue, chat, parley, discussion, talk.

converse *(SYN.)* jabber, talk, argue, comment, harangue, plead, rant, spout, discuss, chat, speak, reason.

conversion *(SYN.)* alteration, change, mutation, modification, metamorphosis.

convert *(SYN.)* change, alter, turn, transform, shift, modify, exchange, win over, vary, veer. *(ANT.) establish, settle, retain.*

convey *(SYN.)* carry, bear, communicate, transport, transmit, support, sustain. *(ANT.) drop, abandon.*

conveyance *(SYN.)* van, car, train, truck, plane.

convict *(SYN.)* felon, offender, criminal.

conviction *(SYN.)* opinion, position, view, faith, belief, confidence, feeling, reliance,

trust. *(ANT.) doubt, incredulity, denial.*

convince *(SYN.)* persuade, assure, exhort, induce, influence. *(ANT.) deter, compel, restrain, dissuade.*

convivial *(SYN.)* jolly, social, jovial, gregarious. *(ANT.) solemn, stern, unsociable.*

convoy *(SYN.)* with, attend, chaperone. *(ANT.) avoid, desert, quit, leave.*

cool *(SYN.)* frosty, chilly, icy, cold, wintry, quiet, composed, collected, distant, unfriendly, quiet, moderate. *(ANT.) hot, warm, heated, overwrought, excited, hysterical, friendly, outgoing.*

cooperate *(SYN.)* unite, combine, help, contribute, support.

coordinate *(SYN.)* attune, harmonize, adapt, match, balance.

copious *(SYN.)* ample, abundant, bountiful, overflowing, plentiful, profuse, rich. *(ANT.) scant, scarce, insufficient, meager, deficient.*

copy *(SYN.)* facsimile, exemplar, imitation, duplicate, reproduction, likeness, print, carbon, transcript. *(ANT.) prototype, original.*

cordial *(SYN.)* polite, friendly, affable, genial, earnest, gracious, warm, ardent, warmhearted, hearty, sincere. *(ANT.) unfriendly, cool, aloof, hostile, reserved.*

core *(SYN.)* midpoint, heart, kernel, center, middle. *(ANT.) outskirts, border, surface, outside, boundary, rim.*

corporation *(SYN.)* business, organization, crew, group, troop, society, company, conglomerate, firm. *(ANT.) individual, dispersion, seclusion.*

corpse *(SYN.)* cadaver, carcass, remains, body, form. *(ANT.) spirit, soul, mind, intellect.*

corpulent *(SYN.)* obese, portly, chubby, stout. *(ANT.) slim, thin, slender, lean.*

correct *(SYN.)* true, set right, faultless, impeccable, proper, accurate, precise, mend, right, rebuke, punish, amend, rectify, better, emend, caution, discipline, exact, strict. *(ANT.) condone, aggravate, false, inaccurate, wrong, untrue, faulty.*

correction *(SYN.)* order, improvement,

cowardly

regulation, instruction, amendment, emendation, remedy, rectification, repair, training, punishment. *(ANT.) confusion, turbulence, chaos.*

correlative *(SYN.)* allied, correspondent, like, similar, parallel. *(ANT.) different, opposed, divergent.*

correspond *(SYN.)* compare, coincide, match, agree, suit, fit, write. *(ANT.) differ, diverge, vary.*

correspondent *(SYN.)* allied, alike, comparable, like, parallel, similar. *(ANT.) different, opposed, divergent, dissimilar.*

corridor *(SYN.)* hallway, hall, foyer, passage, lobby, passageway.

corrode *(SYN.)* erode.

corrupt *(SYN.)* crooked, untrustworthy, treacherous, debased, unscrupulous, wicked, evil, low, contaminated, perverted, bribe, depraved, corrupted, demoralize, degrade, venal, putrid, tainted, dishonest, impure. *(ANT.) upright, honest, pure, sanctify, edify, purify, sanctified, scrupulous.*

corrupted *(SYN.)* crooked, dishonest, impure, spoiled, unsound.

cost *(SYN.)* price, value, damage, charge, loss, sacrifice, penalty, worth.

costly *(SYN.)* dear, expensive. *(ANT.) cheap, inexpensive.*

costume *(SYN.)* dress, clothes, apparel, clothing, garb.

couch *(SYN.)* davenport, sofa, loveseat.

council *(SYN.)* caution, instruction, committee, cabinet, board, suggestion.

counsel *(SYN.)* guidance, attorney, lawyer, counselor, hint, imply, opinion, advice, offer, advise. *(ANT.) declare, dictate, insist.*

count *(SYN.)* consider, number, enumerate, total, figure, compute, tally, estimate. *(ANT.) conjecture, guess, miscalculate.*

countenance *(SYN.)* visage, face, aspect, support, appearance, approval, encouragement, favor. *(ANT.) forbid, prohibit.*

counteract *(SYN.)* thwart, neutralize, offset, counterbalance, defeat.

counterfeit *(SYN.)* false, fraudulent, pretended, pretend, sham, imitate, forgery, artificial, bogus, fake, spurious, imitation, unreal. *(ANT.) authentic, natural, real, genuine, true.*

country *(SYN.)* state, nation, forest, farmland. *(ANT.) city.*

couple *(SYN.)* team, pair, accompany, associate, attach, combine, connect, brace, join, link, unite. *(ANT.) detach, separate, disjoin, disconnect.*

courage *(SYN.)* fearlessness, boldness, chivalry, fortitude, mettle, spirit, daring, bravery, prowess, intrepidity, valor, resolution. *(ANT.) fear, timidity, cowardice.*

courageous *(SYN.)* bold, dauntless, brave, daring, intrepid, valorous, plucky, fearless, heroic, valiant. *(ANT.) fearful, weak, timid, cowardly.*

course *(SYN.)* passage, advance, path, road, progress, way, direction, bearing, route, street, track, trail, way.

courteous *(SYN.)* civil, respectful, polite, genteel, well-mannered, gracious, refined. *(ANT.) discourteous, rude, uncivil, impolite.*

courtesy *(SYN.)* graciousness, politeness, respect. *(ANT.) discourtesy, rudeness.*

covenant *(SYN.)* agreement, concord, harmony, unison, compact, stipulation. *(ANT.) variance, discord, dissension, difference.*

cover *(SYN.)* clothe, conceal, disguise, curtain, guard, envelop, mask, cloak, shield, hide, screen, protect, embrace, top, lid, covering, stopper, protection, refuge, spread, overlay, include, veil. *(ANT.) bare, expose, reveal.*

covert *(SYN.)* potential, undeveloped, concealed, dormant. *(ANT.) explicit, visible, manifest.*

covetous *(SYN.)* grasping, greedy, acquisitive, avaricious. *(ANT.) generous.*

coward *(SYN.)* dastard, milquetoast, cad. *(ANT.) hero.*

cowardice *(SYN.)* dread, dismay, fright, dismay, panic, terror, timidity. *(ANT.) fearlessness, courage, bravery.*

cowardly *(SYN.)* fearful, timorous, afraid, faint-hearted, yellow, pusillanimous, spineless.

49

cower *(SYN.)* wince, flinch, cringe, quail, tremble.

coy *(SYN.)* embarrassed, sheepish, shy, timid. *(ANT.) fearless, outgoing, bold, adventurous, daring.*

crack *(SYN.)* snap, break, split.

cracker *(SYN.)* wafer, biscuit, saltine.

craft *(SYN.)* talent, skill, expertness, ability, cunning, guile, deceit, trade, profession, occupation.

crafty *(SYN.)* covert, clever, cunning, skillful, foxy, tricky, sly, underhand, shrewd. *(ANT.) frank, sincere, gullible, open, guileless, ingenuous.*

craggy *(SYN.)* rough, rugged, irregular, uneven. *(ANT.) level, sleek, smooth, fine, polished.*

crank *(SYN.)* cross, irritable, bad tempered, testy. *(ANT.) cheerful, happy.*

crash *(SYN.)* smash, shatter, dash.

crave *(SYN.)* want, desire, hunger for. *(ANT.) relinquish, renounce.*

craving *(SYN.)* relish, appetite, desire, liking, longing, passion. *(ANT.) renunciation, distaste, disgust.*

crazy *(SYN.)* delirious, deranged, idiotic, mad, insane, imbecilic, demented, foolish, maniacal. *(ANT.) sane, sensible, sound, rational, reasonable.*

creak *(SYN.)* squeak.

create *(SYN.)* fashion, form, generate, engender, formulate, make, originate, produce, cause, ordain, invent, beget, design, construct, constitute. *(ANT.) disband, abolish, terminate, destroy, demolish.*

creative *(SYN.)* imaginative, ingenious, original, resourceful, clever, inventive, innovative, mystical. *(ANT.) unromantic, dull, literal.*

credence *(SYN.)* confidence, faith, feeling, opinion, trust. *(ANT.) doubt, incredulity, denial.*

credible *(SYN.)* conceivable, believable. *(ANT.) inconceivable, unbelievable.*

credit *(SYN.)* believe, accept, belief, trust, faith, merit, honor, apprehend, fancy, hold, support. *(ANT.) doubt, reject, question, distrust, debt.*

creditable *(SYN.)* worthy, praiseworthy. *(ANT.) dishonorable, discreditable, shameful.*

credulous *(SYN.)* trusting, naive, believing, gullible. *(ANT.) suspicious.*

creed *(SYN.)* belief, precept, credo, faith, teaching. *(ANT.) practice, deed, conduct, performance.*

creek *(SYN.)* brook, spring, stream, rivulet.

crime *(SYN.)* offense, insult, aggression, wrongdoing, wrong, misdeed. *(ANT.) right, gentleness, innocence, morality.*

criminal *(SYN.)* unlawful, crook, gangster, outlaw, illegal, convict, delinquent, offender, malefactor, culprit, felonious, felon, transgressor.

cripple *(SYN.)* hurt, maim, damage, injure.

crippled *(SYN.)* deformed, disabled, maimed, hobbling, limping, unconvincing, unsatisfactory. *(ANT.) robust, sound, vigorous, athletic.*

crisis *(SYN.)* conjuncture, emergency, pass, pinch, acme, climax, contingency, juncture, exigency, strait. *(ANT.) calm, normality, stability, equilibrium.*

crisp *(SYN.)* crumbling, delicate, frail, brittle. *(ANT.) calm, normality, stability.*

criterion *(SYN.)* measure, law, rule, principle, gauge, proof. *(ANT.) fancy, guess, chance, supposition.*

critic *(SYN.)* reviewer, judge, commentator, censor, defamer, slanderer, faultfinder.

critical *(SYN.)* exact, fastidious, faultfinding, accurate, condemning, reproachful, risky, dangerous, momentous, carping, acute, hazardous, hypercritical, perilous, decisive, important. *(ANT.) shallow, uncritical, approving, insignificant, trivial, unimportant.*

criticize *(SYN.)* examine, analyze, inspect, blame, censure, appraise, evaluate, scrutinize, reprehend. *(ANT.) neglect, overlook, approve.*

critique *(SYN.)* criticism, inspection, review.

crony *(SYN.)* colleague, companion, chum, buddy, comrade, friend, mate. *(ANT.) stranger, enemy, adversary.*

crooked *(SYN.)* twisted, corrupt, hooked,

curved, criminal, dishonest, degraded, bent, zigzag, impaired. *(ANT.) improved, raised, straight, honest, vitalized, upright, enhanced.*

crop *(SYN.)* fruit, produce, harvest, cut, mow, reaping, result, yield.

cross *(SYN.)* mix, mingle, traverse, interbreed, annoyed, irritable, cranky, testy, angry, mean, ill-natured. *(ANT.) cheerful.*

crouch *(SYN.)* duck, stoop.

crow *(SYN.)* boast, brag.

crowd *(SYN.)* masses, flock, host, squeeze, mob, multitude, populace, press, cramp, throng, swarm.

crown *(SYN.)* coronet, apex, crest, circlet, pinnacle, tiara, skull, head, top, zenith. *(ANT.) base, bottom, foundation, foot.*

crude *(SYN.)* rude, graceless, unpolished, green, harsh, rough, coarse, ill-prepared, unfinished, raw, boorish, unrefined, uncouth. *(ANT.) finished, refined, polished, cultured, genteel, cultivated.*

cruel *(SYN.)* ferocious, mean, heartless, unmerciful, malignant, savage, brutal, pitiless, inhuman, ruthless, merciless. *(ANT.) humane, forbearing, kind, compassionate, merciful, benevolent, kindhearted, gentle.*

cruelty *(SYN.)* harshness, meanness, savagery, brutality. *(ANT.) compassion, kindness.*

crumb *(SYN.)* jot, grain, mite, particle, shred. *(ANT.) mass, bulk, quantity.*

crunch *(SYN.)* champ, gnaw, nibble, pierce.

crush *(SYN.)* smash, break, crash.

cry *(SYN.)* yowl, yell, roar, shout, bellow, scream, wail, weep, bawl, sob.

cryptic *(SYN.)* puzzling, mysterious, enigmatic, hidden, secret, vague, obscure, occult, unclear.

cull *(SYN.)* elect, choose, pick, select. *(ANT.) reject, refuse.*

culpable *(SYN.)* guilty, blameworthy. *(ANT.) innocent.*

cultivate *(SYN.)* plant, seed, farm, till, refine, educate, teach.

cultivation *(SYN.)* farming, horticulture, tillage, agriculture.

cultural *(SYN.)* civilizing, educational, elevating, instructive.

cumbersome *(SYN.)* bulky, clumsy, awkward, unmanageable. *(ANT.) handy.*

cunning *(SYN.)* clever, wily, crafty, foxy, skillful, tricky, ingenious, foxiness, ability, skill, wiliness, devious. *(ANT.) gullible, honest, naive, openness, straightforward, simple, direct.*

curb *(SYN.)* check, restraint, hinder, hold, limit, control, stop, suppress. *(ANT.) aid, loosen, incite, encourage.*

cure *(SYN.)* help, treatment, heal, medicine, restorative, relief, remedy.

curiosity *(SYN.)* marvel, rarity, phenomenon, admiration, amazement. *(ANT.) apathy, indifference, expectation.*

curious *(SYN.)* interrogative, interested, peculiar, queer, nosy, peeping, prying, inquisitive, snoopy, inquiring, unusual. *(ANT.) unconcerned, ordinary, indifferent, uninterested, common.*

current *(SYN.)* up-to-date, contemporary, present, new, tide, stream, modern. *(ANT.) antiquated, old, bygone, ancient, past.*

curse *(SYN.)* ban, oath, denounce, swear, condemn. *(ANT.) boon, blessing.*

cursory *(SYN.)* frivolous, shallow, slight. *(ANT.) complete, deep, profound, thorough.*

curt *(SYN.)* hasty, short, abrupt, brusque, brief, blunt, rude, harsh. *(ANT.) friendly, smooth, gradual, polite, courteous, generous.*

curtail *(SYN.)* condense, contract, diminish, reduce, limit, abbreviate. *(ANT.) lengthen, extend.*

curtain *(SYN.)* blind, drapery, drape, shade.

curve *(SYN.)* crook, deflect, bend, bow, incline, turn, twist. *(ANT.) resist, stiffen, straighten.*

cushion *(SYN.)* pillow, pad, absorb.

custodian *(SYN.)* guard, keeper, guardian, watchman.

custody *(SYN.)* guardianship, care. *(ANT.) neglect, disregard, indifference.*

custom *(SYN.)* fashion, rule, routine.

customary *(SYN.)* common, usual, regular, everyday, general. *(ANT.) exceptional, irregular, rare, unusual, abnormal.*

customer *(SYN.)* patron, client, buyer.

cut

cut *(SYN.)* slash, gash, prick, slit, sever, cleave, mow, incision, chop, lop, slice.

cutting *(SYN.)* bitter, stern, caustic, scathing, harsh, acerbic.

cylindrical *(SYN.)* circular, curved, plump, rotund, spherical, round.

D

dab *(SYN.)* coat, pat, smear.

dabble *(SYN.)* splatter, toy, splash, fiddle, putter.

dabbler *(SYN.)* amateur, dilettante, tinkerer, trifler. *(ANT.)* master, expert, scholar, specialist, authority.

daft *(SYN.)* crazy, foolish, insane.

dagger *(SYN.)* knife, dirk, blade.

daily *(SYN.)* every day, diurnal, regularly.

daily *(SYN.)* dawdle, linger, lag, delay. *(ANT.)* rush, hurry, dash, bustle.

dam *(SYN.)* dike, levee, barrier, slow, stop, check, obstruct, block. *(ANT.)* free, release, loose, unleash.

damage *(SYN.)* spoil, deface, impair, mar, hurt, injury, impairment, destruction. *(ANT.)* repair, benefit, mend, rebuild, improve, ameliorate.

dame *(SYN.)* woman, lady.

damn *(SYN.)* denounce, doom, curse, reprove, blame. *(ANT.)* bless, honor, glorify, praise, accept, applaud, commend, consecrate.

damp *(SYN.)* humid, dank, moisture, wetness, humidity. *(ANT.)* arid, dry.

dampen *(SYN.)* wet, depressed, moisten, dull, suppress, sprinkle, discouraged, retard, slow, inhibit, deaden, muffle. *(ANT.)* dehumidify, increase, encourage.

dance *(SYN.)* bounce, flit, skip, sway, prance, bob, glide, caper, cavort, frisk.

dandle *(SYN.)* jounce, joggle, bounce, jiggle, nestle, cuddle, caress.

dandy *(SYN.)* coxcomb, fop, swell, great, fine, wonderful, excellent. *(ANT.)* rotten, terrible, awful, miserable, slob.

danger *(SYN.)* jeopardy, risk, threat, hazard, uncertainty, peril. *(ANT.)* safety, immunity, security, defense.

dangerous *(SYN.)* risky, insecure, threatening, critical, perilous, unsafe, uncertain, hazardous. *(ANT.)* secure, protected, safe.

dangle *(SYN.)* swing, flap, hang, sag.

dank *(SYN.)* moist, muggy, wet. *(ANT.)* dry.

dapper *(SYN.)* spruce, trim, natty, smart, well-tailored, dashing, neat. *(ANT.)* untidy, shabby, messy, unkempt.

dappled *(SYN.)* spotted, flecked, brindled, variegated, piebald, pied. *(ANT.)* uniform, solid, unvaried.

dare *(SYN.)* brave, call, question, defy, risk, challenge, summon.

daredevil *(SYN.)* lunatic, thrill-seeker, madcap, adventurer.

daring *(SYN.)* foolhardy, chivalrous, rash, fearless, courageous, intrepid, valiant, courage, bravery, brave, precipitate, bold. *(ANT.)* timid, cowardice, timidity, cautious.

dark *(SYN.)* somber, obscure, gloomy, black, unilluminated, dim, evil, hidden, secret, swarthy, murky, opaque, dismal, mournful, sable, sullen, shadowy, sinister, dusky, mystic, shadowy, unlit, sunless, shaded, wicked, occult. *(ANT.)* lucid, light, happy, cheerful, illuminated, pleasant.

darling *(SYN.)* dear, adored, sweetheart, favorite, cherished. *(ANT.)* uncherished, unlovable, disagreeable, rejected, forlorn.

darn *(SYN.)* repair, mend.

dart *(SYN.)* scurry, arrow, barb, hurry, dash, throw, missile, run, hasten, scamper, toss, rush, cast.

dash *(SYN.)* pound, thump, beat, smite, buffet, thrash, smash, break, scurry, run, dart, rush, scamper, hint, pinch, hit, strike. *(ANT.)* stroke, hearten, encourage, defend.

dashing *(SYN.)* swashbuckling, dapper, flamboyant, handsome. *(ANT.)* dull, colorless, shabby, lifeless.

dastardly *(SYN.)* mean-spirited, craven, cowardly, mean, rotten, villainous, dishonorable. *(ANT.)* heroic, brave, high-minded, courageous.

data *(SYN.)* information, statistics, proof, facts, evidence.

date *(SYN.)* interview, appointment,

commitment, engagement, meeting, rendezvous, regale, entertain.

dated *(SYN.)* out-of-date, old-fashioned, outmoded. *(ANT.) latest, now, current, fashionable, hot.*

daub *(SYN.)* coat, grease, soil, scribble, cover, stain, smear, scrawl.

daunt *(SYN.)* discourage, dishearten, intimidate, frighten, deter. *(ANT.) enspirit, encourage.*

dauntless *(SYN.)* fearless, brave, bold, courageous, intrepid, valiant. *(ANT.) fearful, timid, cowardly.*

dawn *(SYN.)* sunrise, start, outset, daybreak, origin, commencement. *(ANT.) dusk, sunset, nightfall, end, conclusion, finish.*

daydream *(SYN.)* woolgather, muse.

daze *(SYN.)* perplex, stun, puzzle, bewilder, upset, confuse, ruffle, confusion, stupor, bewilderment.

dazzle *(SYN.)* surprise, stun, astonish, impress, bewilder, stupefy.

dead *(SYN.)* departed, lifeless, deceased, insensible, inanimate, dull, defunct, gone, lifeless, unconscious, inoperative, inactive, inert, motionless, spiritless. *(ANT.) animate, functioning, active, living, alive, stirring.*

deaden *(SYN.)* anesthetize, numb, paralyze.

deadlock *(SYN.)* standstill, impasse, stalemate.

deadly *(SYN.)* lethal, mortal, fatal, deathly.

deaf *(SYN.)* unhearing, unheeding, unaware, unheedful, stubborn, oblivious, inattentive. *(ANT.) aware, conscious.*

deafening *(SYN.)* vociferous, noisy, stentorian, resounding, loud. *(ANT.) soft, inaudible, subdued.*

deal *(SYN.)* act, treat, attend, cope, barter, trade, bargain, apportion, give, distribute, deliver.

dear *(SYN.)* valued, esteemed, expensive, beloved, costly, darling, high-priced, loved, precious. *(ANT.) hateful, reasonable, inexpensive, cheap, unwanted.*

dearth *(SYN.)* shortage, lack, scarcity.

death *(SYN.)* decease, extinction, demise,

passing. *(ANT.) life.*

debase *(SYN.)* lower, degrade, alloy, adulterate, defile, humiliate, depress, abase, pervert, corrupt. *(ANT.) restore, improve, vitalize, enhance.*

debate *(SYN.)* wrangle, discuss, plead, argue, discussion, contend, argument, controversy, dispute. *(ANT.) agreement, accord, ignore, spurn.*

debonair *(SYN.)* urbane, sophisticated, refined, dapper, well-bred.

debris *(SYN.)* rubbish, litter, junk, wreckage, refuse, detritus, ruins, trash, residue.

debt *(SYN.)* amount due, liability, obligation.

decay *(SYN.)* decrease, spoil, ebb, decline, waste, disintegrate, wane, dwindle, molder, deteriorate, perish, wither, rot, collapse, rottenness, putrefy, decompose. *(ANT.) progress, rise, increase, grow, flourish.*

deceased *(SYN.)* lifeless, departed, dead, insensible, defunct. *(ANT.) living, alive.*

deceit *(SYN.)* duplicity, cheat, fraud, chicanery, trick, cunning, deception, guile, beguilement, deceitfulness, dishonesty, wiliness. *(ANT.) truthfulness, openness, forthrightness, honesty, candor.*

deceitful *(SYN.)* false, fraudulent, insincere, dishonest, deceptive. *(ANT.) sincere, honest.*

deceive *(SYN.)* cheat, defraud, hoodwink, mislead, swindle.

decency *(SYN.)* decorum, dignity, propriety, respectability.

decent *(SYN.)* befitting, fit, suitable, becoming, respectable, adequate, seemly, fitting, comely, appropriate, proper, tolerable, decorous. *(ANT.) vulgar, gross, improper, unsuitable, indecorous, reprehensible, indecent, coarse.*

deception *(SYN.)* trick, cheat, sham, deceit, trickery, craftiness, treachery, beguilement, cunning. *(ANT.) openness, frankness, candor, probity, truthfulness, honesty.*

deceptive *(SYN.)* specious, fallacious, deceitful, false, delusive, unreliable, illusive, tricky, dishonest, deceiving,

decide

misleading, delusory. (*ANT.*) *honest, real, genuine, true, truthful, authentic.*

decide *(SYN.)* resolve, determine, terminate, conclude, close, settle, adjudicate, choose, end. (*ANT.*) *waver, hesitate, vacillate, doubt, suspend.*

decipher *(SYN.)* render, unravel, construe, solve, decode, translate, elucidate, determine. (*ANT.*) *misconstrue, distort, misinterpret, confuse.*

decision *(SYN.)* resolution, determination, settlement.

decisive *(SYN.)* determined, firm, decided, unhesitating, resolute.

declaration *(SYN.)* pronouncement, notice, affirmation, statement, announcement, assertion.

declare *(SYN.)* assert, promulgate, affirm, tell, broadcast, express, proclaim, aver, say, pronounce, profess, announce. (*ANT.*) *deny, withhold, conceal, suppress.*

decline *(SYN.)* descend, decay, dwindle, refuse, incline, wane, sink, depreciate, deny, diminish, weaken. (*ANT.*) *accept, ascend, ameliorate, increase.*

decompose *(SYN.)* rot, disintegrate, molder, decay, crumble.

decorate *(SYN.)* trim, paint, deck, enrich, color, beautify, enhance, furbish, furnish, adorn, ornament. (*ANT.*) *uncover, mar, deface, defame, debase.*

decoration *(SYN.)* ornamentation, embellishment, adornment, furnishing, award, citation, medal.

decoy *(SYN.)* lure, bait.

decrease *(SYN.)* lessen, wane, deduct, diminish, curtail, remove, lessening, decline. (*ANT.*) *expansion, increase, enlarge, expand, grow.*

decree *(SYN.)* order, edict, statute, declaration, announce, act.

decrepit *(SYN.)* feeble, puny, weakened, infirm, enfeebled, languid, rickety, weak, run-down, tumble-down, dilapidated, faint. (*ANT.*) *strong, forceful, vigorous, energetic, lusty.*

decry *(SYN.)* lower, belittle, derogate, minimize, undervalue. (*ANT.*) *praise, commend, magnify, aggrandize.*

dedicate *(SYN.)* sanctify, consecrate, hallow, devote, assign.

dedicated *(SYN.)* disposed, true, affectionate, fond, wedded. (*ANT.*) *indisposed, detached, untrammeled, disinclined.*

deduct *(SYN.)* lessen, shorten, abate, remove, eliminate, curtail, subtract. (*ANT.*) *grow, enlarge, add, increase, amplify, expand.*

deed *(SYN.)* feat, transaction, action, performance, act, operation, achievement, document, certificate, title, accomplishment. (*ANT.*) *intention, cessation, inactivity, deliberation.*

deem *(SYN.)* hold, determine, believe, regard, reckon, judge, consider, account, expound, view.

deep *(SYN.)* bottomless, low, unplumbed, acute, obscure, involved, absorbed. (*ANT.*) *shallow.*

deface *(SYN.)* spoil, impair, damage, mar, hurt, scratch, mutilate, disfigure, injure, harm. (*ANT.*) *mend, benefit, repair.*

defamation *(SYN.)* invective, reproach, upbraiding, abuse, insult, outrage, reviling, desecration. (*ANT.*) *respect, approval, laudation, commendation.*

default *(SYN.)* loss, omission, lack, failure, want, dereliction. (*ANT.*) *victory, achievement, sufficiency, success.*

defeat *(SYN.)* quell, vanquish, beat, overcome, overthrow, subdue, frustrate, spoil, conquest. (*ANT.*) *submit, retreat, cede, yield, surrender, capitulate, lose.*

defect *(SYN.)* shortcoming, fault, omission, blemish, imperfection, forsake, leave, weakness, failure. (*ANT.*) *perfection, flawlessness, support, join, completeness.*

defective *(SYN.)* faulty, imperfect, inoperative, flawed, inoperable. (*ANT.*) *flawless, perfect, faultless.*

defend *(SYN.)* screen, espouse, justify, protect, vindicate, fortify, assert, guard, safeguard, shield. (*ANT.*) *oppose, assault, submit, attack, deny.*

defense *(SYN.)* resistance, protection, bulwark, fort, barricade, trench, rampart, fortress.

defer *(SYN.)* postpone, delay. *(ANT.)* speed, hurry, expedite.

deference *(SYN.)* fame, worship, adoration, reverence, admiration, respect, fame, dignity, homage. *(ANT.)* dishonor, derision, reproach, contempt.

defiant *(SYN.)* rebellious, antagonistic, obstinate. *(ANT.)* yielding, submissive.

deficient *(SYN.)* lacking, short, incomplete, defective, scanty, insufficient, inadequate. *(ANT.)* enough, ample, sufficient, adequate.

defile *(SYN.)* pollute, corrupt, dirty, debase, contaminate. *(ANT.)* purify.

define *(SYN.)* describe, fix, establish, label, designate, set, name, explain.

definite *(SYN.)* fixed, prescribed, certain, specific, exact, determined, distinct, explicit, correct. *(ANT.)* indefinite, confused, undetermined, equivocal.

definitely *(SYN.)* certainly, assuredly, absolutely, positively, surely.

definition *(SYN.)* sense, interpretation, meaning, explanation.

deft *(SYN.)* handy, adroit, clever, adept, dexterous, skillful, skilled. *(ANT.)* inept, clumsy, maladroit, awkward.

defunct *(SYN.)* lifeless, dead, departed, expired, extinct, spiritless, inanimate. *(ANT.)* living, alive, stirring.

defy *(SYN.)* hinder, oppose, withstand, attack, resist, confront, challenge, flout, dare, thwart. *(ANT.)* yield, allow, relent, surrender, submit, accede.

degenerate *(SYN.)* dwindle, decline, weaken, deteriorate, decrease. *(ANT.)* ascend, ameliorate, increase, appreciate.

degrade *(SYN.)* crush, reduce, subdue, abash, humble, lower, shame, demote, downgrade, abase, mortify. *(ANT.)* praise, elevate, honor.

degree *(SYN.)* grade, amount, step, measure, rank, honor, extent.

deign *(SYN.)* condescend, stoop.

dejected *(SYN.)* depressed, downcast, sad, disheartened, blue, discouraged. *(ANT.)* cheerful, happy, optimistic.

delectable *(SYN.)* tasty, delicious, savory, delightful, sweet, luscious. *(ANT.)* unsavory, distasteful, unpalatable, acrid.

delegate *(SYN.)* emissary, envoy, ambassador, representative, commission, deputize, authorize.

delete *(SYN.)* erase, cancel, remove. *(ANT.)* add.

deleterious *(SYN.)* evil, unwholesome, base, sinful, bad, wicked, immoral, destructive, injurious, hurtful, damaging, detrimental, unsound. *(ANT.)* moral, excellent, reputable, healthful, healthy, helpful, constructive, good.

deliberate *(SYN.)* studied, willful, intended, contemplated, premeditated, planned, methodical, designed. *(ANT.)* fortuitous, hasty, accidental.

delicate *(SYN.)* frail, critical, slender, dainty, pleasing, fastidious, exquisite, precarious, demanding, sensitive, savory, fragile, weak. *(ANT.)* tough, strong, coarse, clumsy, hearty, hale, vulgar, rude.

delicious *(SYN.)* tasty, luscious, delectable, sweet, savory. *(ANT.)* unsavory, distasteful, unpalatable, unpleasant, acrid.

delight *(SYN.)* joy, bliss, gladness, pleasure, ecstasy, happiness, rapture. *(ANT.)* revolt, sorrow, annoyance, displeasure, disgust, displease, revulsion, misery.

delightful *(SYN.)* pleasing, pleasant, charming, refreshing, pleasurable. *(ANT.)* nasty, disagreeable, unpleasant.

delirious *(SYN.)* raving, mad, giddy, frantic, hysterical, violent.

deliver *(SYN.)* impart, publish, rescue, commit, communicate, free, address, offer, save, give, liberate. *(ANT.)* restrict, confine, capture, enslave, withhold, imprison.

deluge *(SYN.)* overflow, flood.

delusion *(SYN.)* mirage, fantasy, phantasm, vision, dream, illusion, phantom, hallucination. *(ANT.)* substance, actuality.

delve *(SYN.)* dig, look, search, scoop, explore, hunt.

demand *(SYN.)* claim, inquire, ask, need, require, obligation, requirement, ask for, necessitate. *(ANT.)* tender, give, present,

demean

waive, relinquish, offer.

demean *(SYN.)* comport, bear, operate, carry, act, manage, deport.

demeanor *(SYN.)* manner, way, conduct, actions, behavior.

demented *(SYN.)* insane, crazy, mad, mental, psychotic, lunatic.

demolish *(SYN.)* ruin, devastate, ravage, annihilate, wreck, destroy, raze, exterminate, obliterate. *(ANT.) erect, make, save, construct, preserve, build, establish.*

demolition *(SYN.)* wrecking, destruction. *(ANT.) erection, construction.*

demon *(SYN.)* fiend, devil, ogre, spirit.

demonstrate *(SYN.)* evince, show, prove, display, illustrate, describe, explain, manifest, exhibit. *(ANT.) hide, conceal.*

demonstration *(SYN.)* exhibit, show, presentation, exhibition, display, rally.

demur *(SYN.)* waver, falter, delay, stutter, doubt, vacillate, hesitate, scruple. *(ANT.) proceed, decide, resolve, continue.*

demure *(SYN.)* meek, shy, modest, diffident, retiring, bashful, coy.

den *(SYN.)* cave, lair, cavern.

denial *(SYN.)* disallowance, proscription, refusal, prohibition.

denounce *(SYN.)* condemn, blame, reprove, reprehend, censure, reproach, upbraid, reprobate. *(ANT.) condone, approve, forgive, commend, praise.*

dense *(SYN.)* crowded, slow, close, obtuse, compact, dull, stupid, compressed, thick, concentrated, packed, solid. *(ANT.) sparse, quick, dispersed, clever, dissipated, empty, smart, bright.*

dent *(SYN.)* notch, impress, pit, nick.

deny *(SYN.)* refuse, withhold, dispute, disavow, forbid, refute, contradict, abjure, confute, gainsay. *(ANT.) confirm, affirm, admit, confess, permit, allow, concede, assert.*

depart *(SYN.)* quit, forsake, withdraw, renounce, desert, relinquish, die, perish, decease. *(ANT.) tarry, remain, come, abide, stay, arrive.*

departure *(SYN.)* valediction, farewell.

depend *(SYN.)* trust, rely, confide.

dependable *(SYN.)* secure, trustworthy, certain, safe, trusty, reliable, tried. *(ANT.) unreliable, fallible, dubious, uncertain.*

dependent *(SYN.)* relying, contingent, subordinate, conditional. *(ANT.) original, casual, absolute, independent.*

depict *(SYN.)* explain, recount, describe, portray, characterize, relate, narrate.

deplore *(SYN.)* repine, lament, bemoan, wail, bewail, weep, grieve, regret.

deport *(SYN.)* exile, eject, oust, banish, expel, dismiss, ostracize, dispel, exclude. *(ANT.) receive, admit, shelter, accept, harbor.*

deportment *(SYN.)* deed, behavior, manner, action, carriage, disposition, bearing, demeanor.

deposit *(SYN.)* place, put, bank, save, store, sediment, dregs, addition, entry. *(ANT.) withdraw, withdrawal.*

depreciate *(SYN.)* dwindle, decrease, belittle, disparage, weaken, minimize, descend, deteriorate. *(ANT.) ascend, ameliorate, praise, increase, applaud, appreciate.*

depress *(SYN.)* deject, dishearten, sadden, dampen, devaluate, devalue, lessen, lower, cheapen, reduce, dispirit, discourage, sink. *(ANT.) exalt, cheer, exhilarate.*

depression *(SYN.)* hopelessness, despondency, pessimism, dip, cavity, pothole, hole, despair, gloom, melancholy, sadness, sorrow, recession, decline, desperation, discouragement. *(ANT.) elation, optimism, happiness, confidence, elevation, hope.*

deprive *(SYN.)* bereave, deny, strip. *(ANT.) provision, supply, provide.*

derelict *(SYN.)* decrepit, shabby, dilapidated, neglected, forsaken, deserted, remiss, abandoned, lax.

dereliction *(SYN.)* want, lack, failure, miscarriage, loss, default, deficiency, omission, fiasco. *(ANT.) sufficiency, success, achievement, victory.*

derision *(SYN.)* irony, satire, banter, raillery, sneering, gibe, ridicule.

derivation *(SYN.)* source, birth, inception, start, beginning, spring, commencement, foundation, origin. *(ANT.) issue, end, outcome, harvest, product.*

derive *(SYN.)* obtain, acquire, get, receive.

destroyed

descend *(SYN.)* wane, lower, move, slope, incline, decline, slant, sink. *(ANT.)* increase, appreciate, ameliorate, ascend.

descendant *(SYN.)* child, issue, progeny, offspring.

describe *(SYN.)* portray, picture, recount, depict, relate, characterize, represent.

description *(SYN.)* history, record, recital, account, computation, chronicle, reckoning, narration, detail, narrative. *(ANT.)* misrepresentation, confusion, caricature.

desecration *(SYN.)* profanation, insult, defamation, reviling, abuse, maltreatment, aspersion, perversion, dishonor. *(ANT.)* respect, commendation, approval, laudation.

desert *(SYN.)* forsake, wilderness, resign, abjure, abandon, wasteland, waste, leave, surrender, abdicate, quit, barren, uninhabited. *(ANT.)* uphold, defend, stay, maintain, accompany, join, support.

deserter *(SYN.)* runaway, renegade, fugitive, defector.

deserts *(SYN.)* right, compensation, due, reward, requital, condign.

deserve *(SYN.)* earn, warrant, merit.

design *(SYN.)* drawing, purpose, outline, devise, intend, draw, contrive, draft, cunning, plan, artfulness, delineation, scheming, sketch, intent, invent, objective, mean, contrivance, plotting, intention, create. *(ANT.)* candor, accident, result, chance.

designate *(SYN.)* manifest, indicate, show, specify, denote, reveal, name, appoint, select, assign, disclose, signify, imply, nominate, intimate. *(ANT.)* divert, mislead, conceal, falsify, distract.

desirable *(SYN.)* coveted, wanted.

desire *(SYN.)* longing, craving, yearning, appetite, lust, long for, crave, covet, want, request, ask, need, wish, aspiration, urge. *(ANT.)* hate, aversion, loathing, abomination, detest, loathe, abhor, distaste.

desist *(SYN.)* cork, stop, cease, hinder, terminate, abstain, halt, interrupt, seal, arrest, plug, bar. *(ANT.)* promote, begin, speed, proceed, start.

desolate *(SYN.)* forlorn, waste, bare, lonely, abandoned, wild, deserted, uninhabited, empty, sad, miserable, wretched, unhappy, bleak, forsaken. *(ANT.)* crowded, teeming, populous, happy, cheerful, fertile.

despair *(SYN.)* discouragement, pessimism, depression, hopelessness, despondency, desperation. *(ANT.)* elation, optimism, hope, joy, confidence.

desperado *(SYN.)* criminal, crook, thug, gangster, hoodlum.

desperate *(SYN.)* reckless, determined, despairing, wild, daring, hopeless, despondent, audacious. *(ANT.)* optimistic, composed, hopeful, collected, calm, assured.

despicable *(SYN.)* vulgar, offensive, base, vile, contemptible, selfish, low, mean, worthless, nasty. *(ANT.)* noble, exalted, admirable, generous, worthy, dignified.

despise *(SYN.)* hate, scorn, detest, loath, disdain, abhor, condemn, dislike, abominate. *(ANT.)* love, approve, like, admire.

despite *(SYN.)* notwithstanding.

despoil *(SYN.)* plunder, rob, loot.

despondent *(SYN.)* sad, dismal, depressed, somber, dejected, melancholy, doleful, sorrowful. *(ANT.)* joyous, cheerful, merry, happy.

despot *(SYN.)* tyrant, ruler, oppressor, dictator.

despotic *(SYN.)* authoritative, unconditional, absolute, tyrannous, entire, unrestricted. *(ANT.)* dependent, conditional, qualified, accountable.

destiny *(SYN.)* fate, portion, outcome, consequence, result, fortune, doom, lot.

destitute *(SYN.)* poor, penurious, needy, impecunious, poverty-stricken, impoverished, indigent. *(ANT.)* opulent, wealthy, affluent, rich.

destroy *(SYN.)* raze, devastate, ruin, end, demolish, wreck, extinguish, annihilate, exterminate, obliterate, waste, slay, kill, eradicate. *(ANT.)* make, construct, start, create, save, establish.

destroyed *(SYN.)* rent, smashed, interrupted, flattened, wrecked, broken, ruptured, crushed. *(ANT.)* whole, repaired, integral, united.

destruction

destruction *(SYN.)* ruin, devastation, extinction, demolition. *(ANT.) beginning, creation.*

destructive *(SYN.)* deadly, baneful, noxious, deleterious, injurious, pernicious, fatal, detrimental. *(ANT.) salutary, beneficial, creative.*

detach *(SYN.)* deduct, remove, subtract, curtail, divide, shorten, decrease, disengage, reduce, separate, diminish. *(ANT.) hitch, grow, enlarge, increase, connect, amplify, attack, expand.*

detail *(SYN.)* elaborate, commission, part, itemize, portion, division, fragment, assign, circumstance, segment.

detain *(SYN.)* impede, delay, hold back, retard, arrest, restrain, stay. *(ANT.) quicken, hasten, expedite, forward, precipitate.*

detect *(SYN.)* discover, reveal, find, ascertain, determine, learn, originate, devise. *(ANT.) hide, screen, lose, cover, mask.*

determinant *(SYN.)* reason, incentive, source, agent, principle, inducement. *(ANT.) result, effect, consequence, end.*

determine *(SYN.)* decide, settle, end, conclude, ascertain, induce, fix, verify, resolve, establish, necessitate.

detest *(SYN.)* loathe, hate, despise. *(ANT.) savor, appreciate, like, love.*

detriment *(SYN.)* injury, harm, disadvantage, damage. *(ANT.) benefit.*

detrimental *(SYN.)* hurtful, mischievous, damaging, harmful. *(ANT.) salutary, advantageous, profitable, beneficial.*

develop *(SYN.)* evolve, unfold, enlarge, amplify, expand, create, grow, advance, reveal, unfold, mature, elaborate. *(ANT.) wither, contract, degenerate, stunt, deteriorate, compress.*

development *(SYN.)* growth, expansion, progress, unraveling, elaboration, evolution, maturing, unfolding. *(ANT.) compression, abbreviation, curtailment.*

deviate *(SYN.)* deflect, stray, divert, diverge, wander, sidetrack, digress. *(ANT.) preserve, follow, remain, continue, persist.*

device *(SYN.)* tool, utensil, means, channel, machine, agent, vehicle, gadget, apparatus, instrument, contrivance.

devilish *(SYN.)* diabolical, fiendish, diabolic, satanic, demonic.

devious *(SYN.)* tortuous, winding, distorted, circuitous, tricky, crooked, roundabout, cunning, erratic, indirect. *(ANT.) straight, direct, straightforward, honest.*

devise *(SYN.)* create, concoct, invent, originate.

devote *(SYN.)* assign, dedicate, give, apply. *(ANT.) withhold, relinquish, ignore, withdraw.*

devoted *(SYN.)* attached, dedicated, prone, wedded, addicted, ardent, earnest, loyal, disposed, inclined, fond, affectionate, faithful. *(ANT.) untrammeled, disinclined, detached, indisposed.*

devotion *(SYN.)* piety, zeal, ardor, loyalty, dedication, religiousness, consecration, affection, love, devoutness, fidelity, attachment. *(ANT.) unfaithfulness, aversion, alienation, indifference.*

devour *(SYN.)* consume, gulp, gorge, waste, eat, ruin, swallow, destroy.

devout *(SYN.)* sacred, religious, spiritual, holy, theological, pietistic, pious, sanctimonious, reverent. *(ANT.) profane, skeptical, atheistic, secular, impious.*

dexterity *(SYN.)* talent, capability, qualification, aptness, skill, ability. *(ANT.) unreadiness, incapacity, disability, incompetency.*

dexterous *(SYN.)* clever, adroit, handy, deft, facile, skillful, skilled, proficient. *(ANT.) awkward, clumsy.*

dialed *(SYN.)* slang, jargon, cant, speech, idiom, tongue, diction, vernacular. *(ANT.) nonsense, drivel, babble, gibberish.*

dialogue *(SYN.)* interview, chat, discussion, conference, exchange, talk, conversation.

diary *(SYN.)* memo, account, journal.

dicker *(SYN.)* haggle, bargain, negotiate.

dictate *(SYN.)* deliver, speak, record, command, order, direct.

dictator *(SYN.)* oppressor, tyrant, despot, persecutor, overlord, autocrat.

die *(SYN.)* fade, wane, cease, depart, wither,

directly

decay, decline, sink, expire, perish, decease, go, diminish, fail, languish, decrease. (*ANT.*) live, begin, grow, survive, flourish.

difference (*SYN.*) inequality, variety, disparity, discord, distinction, dissension, dissimilarity, disagreement, contrast, separation. (*ANT.*) harmony, similarity, identity, agreement, likeness, compatibility, kinship, resemblance.

different (*SYN.*) unlike, various, distinct, miscellaneous, divergent, contrary, differing, diverse, variant, incongruous, unalike, changed, dissimilar, opposite. (*ANT.*) similar, congruous, alike, identical.

differentiate (*SYN.*) separate, discriminate, distinguish, perceive, detect, recognize, discern. (*ANT.*) confuse, omit, mingle, confound, overlook.

difficult (*SYN.*) involved, demanding, arduous, trying, complicated, hard, laborious, perplexing, hard, intricate. (*ANT.*) simple, easy, facile, effortless.

difficulty (*SYN.*) trouble, hardship, fix, predicament, trouble. (*ANT.*) ease.

diffuse (*SYN.*) spread, sparse, scattered, scanty, dispersed, thin, rare. (*ANT.*) concentrated.

dig (*SYN.*) burrow, excavate, appreciate, understand.

digest (*SYN.*) consume, eat, reflect on, study, shorten, consider, summarize, abridge, abstract, abridgment, synopsis.

dignified (*SYN.*) serious, solemn, noble, stately, elegant.

dignify (*SYN.*) honor, elevate. (*ANT.*) shame, degrade, humiliate.

dignity (*SYN.*) stateliness, distinction, bearing.

digress (*SYN.*) divert, wander, bend, stray, deflect, sidetrack, crook. (*ANT.*) preserve, continue, remain, follow, persist.

dilate (*SYN.*) increase, widen, amplify, enlarge, augment, expand. (*ANT.*) shrink, contract, restrict, abridge.

dilemma (*SYN.*) fix, strait, condition, scrape, difficulty, plight. (*ANT.*) ease, calmness, satisfaction, comfort.

diligent (*SYN.*) patient, busy, hardworking, active, perseverant, assiduous, industrious, careful. (*ANT.*) unconcerned, indifferent, apathetic, lethargic, careless.

dim (*SYN.*) pale, shadowy, faint, faded, unclear, vague, darken, dull, indistinct. (*ANT.*) brighten, brilliant, bright, illuminate, glaring.

dimension (*SYN.*) size, importance, measure, extent.

diminish (*SYN.*) suppress, lower, decrease, shrink, wane, abate, reduce, lessen, assuage. (*ANT.*) enlarge, revive, amplify, increase.

diminutive (*SYN.*) small, wee, tiny, little, minute. (*ANT.*) large, big, gigantic, huge.

din (*SYN.*) tumult, clamor, sound, babble, outcry, row, noise, racket. (*ANT.*) quiet, stillness, hush.

dine (*SYN.*) lunch, eat, sup, feed.

dingy (*SYN.*) dull, dark, dismal, dirty, drab, murky, gray. (*ANT.*) cheerful, bright.

dip (*SYN.*) immerse, plunge, submerge, wet, swim.

diplomacy (*SYN.*) knack, dexterity, skill, address, poise, tact, finesse. (*ANT.*) vulgarity, blunder, awkwardness, incompetence.

diplomatic (*SYN.*) politic, adroit, tactful, discreet, judicious, gracious, polite, discriminating. (*ANT.*) rude, churlish, gruff, boorish, impolite, coarse.

dire (*SYN.*) horrible, terrible, appalling, fearful, harrowing, grievous, ghastly, awful, horrid, terrifying, dreadful, frightful, horrifying, monstrous, horrendous, repulsive. (*ANT.*) lovely, enchanting, fascinating, beautiful, enjoyable.

direct (*SYN.*) rule, manage, bid, order, level, command, conduct, regulate, point, indicate, show, aim, control, sight, guide, instruct, train, govern. (*ANT.*) swerving, untruthful, misguide, distract, indirect, crooked, deceive.

direction (*SYN.*) way, order, course, instruction, tendency, management, route, trend, guidance, administration, supervision, inclination.

directly (*SYN.*) immediately, straight.

dirt *(SYN.)* pollution, soil, filthiness, filth. *(ANT.)* cleanliness.

dirty *(SYN.)* muddy, base, pitiful, filthy, shabby, foul, soiled, nasty, mean, grimy, low, obscene, untidy, indecent, unclean, messy, squalid, contemptible, sloppy. *(ANT.)* pure, neat, wholesome, clean, presentable.

disability *(SYN.)* inability, weakness, handicap, incapacity, injury, unfitness, incompetence, impotence. *(ANT.)* power, ability, strength, capability.

disable *(SYN.)* weaken, incapacitate, cripple. *(ANT.)* strengthen.

disabled *(SYN.)* deformed, limping, weak, crippled, maimed, defective, unsatisfactory, halt, feeble. *(ANT.)* vigorous, athletic, sound, agile, robust.

disadvantage *(SYN.)* drawback, hindrance, handicap, inconvenience, obstacle. *(ANT.)* advantage, benefit, convenience.

disagree *(SYN.)* quarrel, dispute, differ, conflict. *(ANT.)* agree.

disagreement *(SYN.)* nonconformity, variance, difference, objection, challenge, remonstrance, dissent. *(ANT.)* assent, acceptance, compliance, agreement.

disappear *(SYN.)* end, fade out, vanish. *(ANT.)* emerge, appear.

disappoint *(SYN.)* fail, displease, mislead, dissatisfy. *(ANT.)* please, satisfy, gratify.

disappointment *(SYN.)* dissatisfaction, defeat, discouragement, failure. *(ANT.)* pleasure, satisfaction, gratification.

disapprove *(SYN.)* object to, disfavor, oppose. *(ANT.)* approve.

disarm *(SYN.)* paralyze, demilitarize.

disaster *(SYN.)* casualty, mishap, misfortune, catastrophe, accident, adversity, ruin, calamity. *(ANT.)* fortune, advantage.

disavow *(SYN.)* reject, revoke, disclaim, retract, disown. *(ANT.)* recognize, acknowledge.

disband *(SYN.)* scatter, split, dismiss, separate.

disbelief *(SYN.)* doubt, incredulity, skepticism. *(ANT.)* certainty, credulity.

discard *(SYN.)* scrap, reject.

discern *(SYN.)* distinguish, see, descry, separate, differentiate, perceive, discriminate, detect, observe, recognize. *(ANT.)* omit, confuse, overlook, mingle, confound.

discernment *(SYN.)* perception, sharpness, intelligence, perspicacity, acuity, keenness. *(ANT.)* dullness, stupidity.

discharge *(SYN.)* remove, relieve, dismiss, banish, unburden, shoot, fire, explosion, eject, detonation, liberation, release, unload, discard, send. *(ANT.)* retain, employ, enlist, hire, accept, recall, detain.

disciple *(SYN.)* learner, follower, student, adherent, supporter, scholar, pupil, votary, devotee. *(ANT.)* guide, leader.

discipline *(SYN.)* training, order, instruction, drill, restraint, regulation, practice, correction, control, self-control, train, teach, exercise. *(ANT.)* carelessness, sloppiness, confusion, negligence, messiness, chaos, turbulence.

disclaim *(SYN.)* retract, reject, deny, renounce, disavow, revoke. *(ANT.)* recognize, acknowledge.

disclose *(SYN.)* show, divulge, betray, uncover, discover, reveal, expose. *(ANT.)* hide, cloak, mask, cover, obscure, conceal.

discomfit *(SYN.)* malaise, concern, confuse, baffle, perplex, disconcert.

discomfort *(SYN.)* malaise, concern, anxiety, uneasiness.

disconcerted *(SYN.)* disturbed, agitated, upset.

disconnect *(SYN.)* divide, separate, unhook, disengage, detach. *(ANT.)* connect, bind, attach, unify, engage.

disconsolate *(SYN.)* depressed, downcast, sorrowful, dejected, dismal, sad, unhappy, wretched, somber, cheerless, morose, lugubrious, miserable, mournful. *(ANT.)* delightful, merry, glad, cheerful, happy.

discontent *(SYN.)* displeased, disgruntled, unhappy, dissatisfied, vexed.

discontinue *(SYN.)* postpone, delay, adjourn, stay, stop, defer, suspend, end, cease, interrupt. *(ANT.)* prolong, persist, continue, start, begin, proceed, maintain.

discord *(SYN.)* disagreement, conflict.

(ANT.) concord, accord, agreement.

discourage *(SYN.)* hamper, obstruct, restrain, block, dishearten, retard, check, dispirit, thwart, depress, hinder, stop. *(ANT.)* expedite, inspire, encourage, promote, inspirit, assist, further.

discourteous *(SYN.)* gruff, rude, vulgar, blunt, impolite, saucy, uncivil, boorish, rough. *(ANT.)* stately, courtly, civil, dignified, genteel.

discover *(SYN.)* find out, invent, expose, ascertain, devise, reveal, learn, determine, detect. *(ANT.)* hide, screen, cover, conceal, lose.

discredit *(SYN.)* disbelieve, dishonor, doubt, disgrace, shame.

discreet *(SYN.)* politic, discriminating, judicious, adroit, prudent, cautious, wise, tactful, careful, diplomatic. *(ANT.)* incautious, rude, coarse, boorish, tactless, imprudent, indiscreet, careless, gruff.

discrepant *(SYN.)* incompatible, wavering, contrary, irreconcilable, unsteady, illogical, contradictory. *(ANT.)* correspondent, compatible, consistent.

discriminating *(SYN.)* exact, particular, critical, accurate, discerning. *(ANT.)* unimportant, shallow, insignificant, superficial.

discrimination *(SYN.)* perspicacity, discernment, racism, wisdom, bias, sagacity, intolerance, prejudice, intelligence, understanding. *(ANT.)* thoughtlessness, senselessness, arbitrariness.

discuss *(SYN.)* gossip, plead, discourse, blab, lecture, talk, chat, spout, mutter, deliberate, consider, reason, comment.

discussion *(SYN.)* speech, chatter, lecture, conference, talk, dialogue, conversation, rumor. *(ANT.)* silence, correspondence, writing.

disdain *(SYN.)* derision, hatred, contempt, scorn, contumely, reject, haughtiness, detestation. *(ANT.)* respect, esteem, reverence, admire, prize, honor, admiration, awe, regard.

disdainful *(SYN.)* haughty, scornful, arrogant, contemptuous. *(ANT.)* awed,

admiring, regardful.

disease *(SYN.)* malady, disorder, ailment, illness, affliction, infirmity, complaint, sickness. *(ANT.)* soundness, health, vigor.

disentangle *(SYN.)* unwind, untie, clear, unravel, unknot, unsnarl, untangle.

disfigured *(SYN.)* deformed, marred, defaced, scarred.

disgrace *(SYN.)* odium, chagrin, shame, mortification, embarrassment, humiliate, scandal, dishonor, mortification. *(ANT.)* renown, glory, respect, praise, dignity, honor.

disgraceful *(SYN.)* ignominious, shameful, discreditable, disreputable, scandalous, dishonorable. *(ANT.)* renowned, esteemed, respectable, honorable.

disguise *(SYN.)* excuse, simulation, pretension, hide, camouflage, make-up, cover-up, mask, conceal, screen, affectation, pretext. *(ANT.)* show, reality, actuality, display, reveal, sincerity, fact.

disgust *(SYN.)* offend, repulse, nauseate, revolt, sicken. *(ANT.)* admiration, liking.

disgusting *(SYN.)* repulsive, nauseating, revolting, nauseous, repugnant.

dish *(SYN.)* serve, container, give, receptacle.

dishearten *(SYN.)* depress, sadden, discourage.

disheveled *(SYN.)* mussed, sloppy, rumpled, untidy.

dishonest *(SYN.)* crooked, impure, unsound, false, contaminated, venal, corrupt, putrid, thievish, vitiated, tainted. *(ANT.)* upright, honest, straightforward.

dishonor *(SYN.)* disrepute, scandal, indignity, chagrin, mortification, shame, obloquy, defamation, humiliation, disgrace, scandal. *(ANT.)* renown, glory, praise, honor, dignify.

disinclined *(SYN.)* unwilling, reluctant, loath.

disingenuous *(SYN.)* tricky, deceitful, scheming, dishonest, underhanded, cunning, artful, crafty, insidious.

disintegrate *(SYN.)* decompose, dwindle, spoil, decay, wane, ebb, decline, rot. *(ANT.)* increase, flourish, rise, grow.

disinterested

disinterested *(SYN.)* unbiased, open-minded, neutral, impartial, unprejudiced.

dislike *(SYN.)* aversion, dread, reluctance, abhorrence, disinclination, hatred, repugnance. *(ANT.)* devotion, affection, enthusiasm, attachment.

disloyal *(SYN.)* false, treasonable, apostate, unfaithful, recreant, treacherous, untrue, traitorous, faithless. *(ANT.)* true, devoted, constant, loyal.

dismal *(SYN.)* dark, lonesome, somber, bleak, dull, sad, doleful, sorrowful, cheerless, depressing, dreary, funeral, gloomy, melancholy. *(ANT.)* lively, gay, happy, lighthearted, charming, cheerful.

dismantle *(SYN.)* take apart, wreck, disassemble.

dismay *(SYN.)* disturb, bother, dishearten, horror, alarm, bewilder, frighten, scare, discourage, confuse. *(ANT.)* encourage, hearten.

dismiss *(SYN.)* remove, discharge, discard, release, liberate, exile, banish, eject, oust. *(ANT.)* retain, detain, engage, hire, accept.

disobedient *(SYN.)* refractory, forward, unruly, insubordinate, defiant, rebellious, undutiful. *(ANT.)* submissive, complaint, obedient.

disobey *(SYN.)* invade, break, violate, infringe, defile.

disorder *(SYN.)* tumult, chaos, jumble, confusion, muddle, turmoil, anarchy. *(ANT.)* organization, neatness, system, order.

disorganization *(SYN.)* jumble, confusion, muddle, anarchy. *(ANT.)* system, order.

disorganized *(SYN.)* muddled, confused, indistinct, bewildered, mixed. *(ANT.)* organized, lucid, clear, plain.

disown *(SYN.)* deny, renounce, reject, repudiate, forsake, disinherit.

disparage *(SYN.)* undervalue, depreciate, lower, belittle, derogate, minimize, decry, discredit. *(ANT.)* exalting, praise, aggrandize, magnify, commend.

disparagement *(SYN.)* lowering, decrying, undervaluing, belittling, minimizing. *(ANT.)* praise, exalting, aggrandizement, magnification.

disparaging *(SYN.)* belittling, deprecatory, discrediting, deprecating.

dispassionate *(SYN.)* calm, cool, composed, controlled, unemotional, imperturbable.

dispatch *(SYN.)* throw, impel, transmit, emit, cast, finish, report, message, send, speed, achieve, conclude, communication, promptness, discharge. *(ANT.)* reluctance, get, redeem, bring, slowness, hold.

dispel *(SYN.)* disseminate, scatter, disperse, separate, diffuse. *(ANT.)* collect, accumulate, gather.

dispense *(SYN.)* deal, give, allot, assign, apportion, mete, distribute, grant, allocate, measure. *(ANT.)* refuse, withhold, confiscate, retain, keep.

disperse *(SYN.)* dissipate, scatter, disseminate, diffuse, separate, dispel. *(ANT.)* collect, amass, gather, assemble, accumulate.

dispirited *(SYN.)* downhearted, unhappy, dejected, disheartened, sad, depressed, melancholy. *(ANT.)* cheerful, happy, optimistic.

displace *(SYN.)* remove, transport, lodge, shift, move. *(ANT.)* retain, leave, stay, remain.

display *(SYN.)* parade, exhibit, show, cover, flaunt. *(ANT.)* hide, cover, conceal.

displeasure *(SYN.)* dislike, disapproval, dissatisfaction, distaste, discontentment.

disposal *(SYN.)* elimination, adjustment, removal, release, arrangement, administration, settlement.

dispose *(SYN.)* settle, adjust, arrange.

disposition *(SYN.)* behavior, character, deed, deportment, action, manner, bearing, temperament, nature, demeanor, personality, carriage.

dispossess *(SYN.)* eject, expel, evict, oust, dislodge.

disprove *(SYN.)* refute, deny, invalidate, controvert.

dispute *(SYN.)* squabble, debate, argument, controversy, contention, disagreement, bicker, contest, argue, contend, quarrel, contradict, discuss, deny, oppose, altercate. *(ANT.)* harmony, concord, *agreement, allow, concur, agree, concede, decision.*

disregard *(SYN.)* slight, omit, ignore, inattention, oversight, skip, neglect, overlook. *(ANT.) regard, include.*

disrepair *(SYN.)* ruin, decay, dilapidation, destruction.

disreputable *(SYN.)* dishonored, notorious, dishonorable, disgraced.

disrespectful *(SYN.)* fresh, impertinent, rude, impolite, impudent. *(ANT.) polite, respectful, courteous.*

dissect *(SYN.)* examine, cut, analyze.

disseminate *(SYN.)* publish, circulate, spread, publish, broadcast.

dissent *(SYN.)* objection, challenge, disagreement, protest, remonstrance, difference, nonconformity, variance, noncompliance. *(ANT.) assent, acceptance, compliance, agreement.*

dissertation *(SYN.)* thesis, treatise, disquisition.

dissimilar *(SYN.)* diverse, unlike, various, distinct, contrary, sundry, different, miscellaneous. *(ANT.) same, alike, similar, congruous.*

dissimulation *(SYN.)* pretense, deceit, sanctimony, hypocrisy, cant. *(ANT.) honesty, condone, openness, frankness, truth.*

dissipate *(SYN.)* misuse, squander, dwindle, consume, waste, lavish, diminish. *(ANT.) save, conserve, preserve, accumulate, economize.*

dissolve *(SYN.)* liquefy, end, cease, melt, fade, disappear.

distant *(SYN.)* stiff, cold, removed, far, afar, unfriendly, remote, faraway, separated, aloof, reserved. *(ANT.) nigh, friendly, close, cordial, near.*

distasteful *(SYN.)* disagreeable, unpleasant, objectionable.

distend *(SYN.)* swell, widen, magnify, expand, enlarge.

distinct *(SYN.)* plain, evident, lucid, visible, apparent, different, separate, individual, obvious, manifest, clear. *(ANT.) vague, indistinct, uncertain, obscure, ambiguous.*

distinction *(SYN.)* importance, peculiarity, trait, honor, fame, characteristic, repute, quality, renown, prominence, attribute, property. *(ANT.) nature, substance, essence, being.*

distinctive *(SYN.)* odd, exceptional, rare, individual, eccentric, special, strange. *(ANT.) ordinary, general, common, normal.*

distinguish *(SYN.)* recognize, differentiate, divide, classify, descry, discern, separate, perceive, detect. *(ANT.) mingle, conjoin, blend, found, omit, confuse, overlook.*

distinguished *(SYN.)* eminent, illustrious, renowned, celebrated, elevated, noted, important, famous, prominent. *(ANT.) ordinary, common, obscure, unimportant.*

distort *(SYN.)* contort, falsify, twist, misrepresent.

distract *(SYN.)* occupy, bewilder, disturb, divert, confuse. *(ANT.) focus, concentrate.*

distracted *(SYN.)* abstracted, preoccupied, absent. *(ANT.) attentive, attending, watchful, present.*

distraction *(SYN.)* entertainment, confusion, amusement, diversion.

distress *(SYN.)* torment, misery, trouble, worry, pain, agony, torture, anguish, anxiety, disaster, wretchedness, peril, danger, suffering. *(ANT.) joy, solace, comfort, relief.*

distribute *(SYN.)* deal, sort, allot, mete, classify, share, issue, dole, apportion, allocate, dispense, group.

district *(SYN.)* domain, place, territory, country, region, division, neighborhood, section, area, land.

distrust *(SYN.)* scruple, unbelief, suspect, mistrust, hesitation, suspense, uncertainty, doubt, suspicion, ambiguity. *(ANT.) faith, conviction, trust, belief, determination.*

disturb *(SYN.)* perturb, vex, confuse, worry, agitate, derange, unsettle, perplex, rouse, bother, trouble, annoy, interrupt, discompose. *(ANT.) quiet, order, calm, settle, pacify, soothe.*

disturbance *(SYN.)* disorder, commotion, confusion, riot, light, brawl. *(ANT.) calm, tranquility, serenity.*

disturbed *(SYN.)* neurotic, psychopathic, psychotic. *(ANT.) normal.*

diverge

diverge *(SYN.)* fork, separate. *(ANT.)* converge, join, merge.

diverse *(SYN.)* unlike, various, different, several.

diversify *(SYN.)* change, modify, alter.

diversion *(SYN.)* entertainment, sport, distraction, amusement, recreation.

divert *(SYN.)* detract, amuse, confuse, distract, deflect, entertain, tickle. *(ANT.)* tire, bore, weary.

divide *(SYN.)* share, split, detach, cleave, apportion, sunder, part, distribute, allocate, disunite, estrange, separate, allot, sever. *(ANT.)* merge, unite, convene, join, gather, combine.

divine *(SYN.)* holy, supernatural, godlike, transcendent, celestial, heavenly. *(ANT.)* mundane, wicked, blasphemous, profane.

division *(SYN.)* partition, separation, sharing, section, segment, part, portion. *(ANT.)* union, agreement.

divorce *(SYN.)* disjoin, disconnect, separate, divide.

divulge *(SYN.)* discover, release, expose, show, betray, reveal, admit, disclose, uncover. *(ANT.)* hide, conceal, cloak, cover.

dizzy *(SYN.)* staggering, unsteady, giddy, light-headed, confused. *(ANT.)* rational, clearheaded, unconfused.

do *(SYN.)* effect, conduct, perform, work, suffice, accomplish, finish, transact, serve, discharge, execute, complete, carry on, make, settle, conclude, fulfill, consummate, produce, terminate, practice.

docile *(SYN.)* pliant, tame, complaint, teachable, obedient, submissive, yielding. *(ANT.)* unruly, obstinate, ungovernable, mulish.

dock *(SYN.)* moor, clip, anchor, tie.

doctor *(SYN.)* heal, treat, medic, remedy, cure.

doctrinaire *(SYN.)* formal, dogmatic, overbearing, authoritarian, formal, arrogant, magisterial. *(ANT.)* skeptical, indecisive, fluctuating.

doctrine *(SYN.)* tenet, precept, belief, dogma, teaching, principle, creed. *(ANT.)* deed, practice, conduct, perform.

document *(SYN.)* report, minute, memorial, vestige, account, note, trace.

dodge *(SYN.)* equivocate, recoil, elude, evade, avoid, duck.

dogma *(SYN.)* tenet, doctrine, belief, teaching, creed. *(ANT.)* deed, practice, conduct, performance.

dogmatic *(SYN.)* formal, domineering, authoritarian, doctrinaire, opinionated, dictatorial, positive, arrogant, authoritative, overbearing, doctrinal, magisterial. *(ANT.)* skeptical, indecisive, fluctuating.

doing *(SYN.)* feat, performance, act, deed, action, accomplishment, transaction. *(ANT.)* intention, inactivity, cessation.

dole *(SYN.)* deal, spread, allot, relief, divide, apportion, alms, welfare, distribute, dispense.

doleful *(SYN.)* dark, depressed, sad, dismal, dejected, bleak, dull, blue, sorrowful, unhappy, morose, lonesome, mournful, somber. *(ANT.)* gay, lively, cheerful, joyous.

dolt *(SYN.)* blockhead, dunce.

domain *(SYN.)* place, division, region, territory, empire, country, charge, kingdom, realm, quarter, dominion, bailiwick, jurisdiction, land.

domestic *(SYN.)* family, tame, native, servant, homemade, household, internal. *(ANT.)* alien, foreign, outside.

domesticate *(SYN.)* train, tame, housebreak, teach.

domicile *(SYN.)* dwelling, residence, home, abode.

dominate *(SYN.)* control, manage, rule, influence, subjugate, command, govern, tyrannize, direct, regulate. *(ANT.)* follow, ignore, abandon, submit, forsake.

domination *(SYN.)* mastery, sway, ascendancy, transcendence.

don *(SYN.)* wear, slip on.

donation *(SYN.)* gift, bequest, present, benefaction, grant, contribution, offering, largess, boon. *(ANT.)* earnings, purchase, deprivation, loss.

done *(SYN.)* complete, concluded, finished, over, terminated.

doom *(SYN.)* fortune, issue, result,

destruction, destiny, consequence, fate, outcome, destine, ruin, death, lot.

doomed *(SYN.)* fated, predestined, destined, foreordained.

dormant *(SYN.)* unemployed, inert, lazy, unoccupied, idle, indolent. *(ANT.)* working, employed, occupied, active, industrious.

dose *(SYN.)* quantity, amount, portion.

dote *(SYN.)* indulge, treasure, coddle, pamper, spoil. *(ANT.)* ignore.

double *(SYN.)* copy, fold, duplicate.

doubt *(SYN.)* distrust, incredulity, suspicion, hesitation, uncertainty, question, scruple, ambiguity, skepticism, suspect, mistrust, unbelief. *(ANT.)* conviction, belief, determination, trust, certainty.

doubtful *(SYN.)* uncertain, unsettled, dubious, questionable, unsure.

doubtless *(SYN.)* certainly, undoubtedly, assuredly, positively, unquestionably.

dour *(SYN.)* gloomy, sulky, crabbed, morose, fretful. *(ANT.)* joyous, pleasant, amiable, merry.

douse *(SYN.)* immerse, quench, dip, dunk, extinguish.

dowdy *(SYN.)* messy, unkempt, untidy, sloppy, shabby, frowzy.

downcast *(SYN.)* sad, disheartened, unhappy, downhearted, dejected, dispirited, discourage, depressed, glum.

downfall *(SYN.)* destruction, comedown.

downgrade *(SYN.)* reduce, lower, diminish, decrease, depreciate. *(ANT.)* improve, upgrade, appreciate.

downhearted *(SYN.)* glum, discouraged, depressed, gloomy, downcast, sad, dejected. *(ANT.)* enthusiastic, cheerful, happy.

downpour *(SYN.)* cloudburst, deluge, flood.

downright *(SYN.)* totally, positively, completely, definitely.

dowry *(SYN.)* endowment, gift, settlement, talent, ability.

drab *(SYN.)* flat, dull, lifeless, unattractive.

draft *(SYN.)* air, induction, wind, enrollment, drawing, outline.

drag *(SYN.)* heave, pull, tug, crawl, draw, tarry, tow, haul, delay.

drain *(SYN.)* empty, deprive, dry, filter, spend, tap, exhaust, waste, sap, use. *(ANT.)* fulfill, fill.

drama *(SYN.)* show, play, production, piece.

dramatist *(SYN.)* playwright.

drape *(SYN.)* flow, cover, hang.

drastic *(SYN.)* severe, rough, extreme, violent, tough, intense.

draw *(SYN.)* tug, obtain, trace, lure, drag, attract, persuade, induce, haul, write, remove, extend, stretch, take out, allure, pull, prolong, extract, tow, draft, delineate, unsheathe, lure, depict, entice, sketch, infer. *(ANT.)* shorten, contract, propel, alienate, drive.

drawback *(SYN.)* snag, hitch, disadvantage, handicap, deficiency, difficulty, check, obstacle, hindrance, impediment. *(ANT.)* gain, benefit, windfall, advantage.

drawing *(SYN.)* likeness, print, view, engraving, portrait, sketch, illustration, picture, resemblance, scene.

drawn *(SYN.)* tired, haggard, taut, strained, harrowed, weary, tense, sapped, spent. *(ANT.)* rested, relaxed, energetic, fresh.

draw out *(SYN.)* protract, extend, persist, prolong, lengthen, sustain, continue. *(ANT.)* reduce, curtail, shorten, abridge.

draw up *(SYN.)* draft, write out, prepare, compose, indite, formulate, wait, stay.

dread *(SYN.)* awe, horror, fear, terror, alarm, apprehension, foreboding. *(ANT.)* courage, boldness, assurance, confidence.

dreadful *(SYN.)* dire, inspiring, ghastly, appalling, horrid, impressive, terrible, awful, frightful, horrible, bad, hideous, outrageous, repulsive. *(ANT.)* fascinating, beautiful, enjoyable, enchanting, lovely.

dream *(SYN.)* fantasy, wish, hope, vision, daydream, reverie, imagine, fantasize, fancy, invent, muse.

dream up *(SYN.)* cook up, create, think up, concoct, contrive, originate, imagine, devise.

dreary *(SYN.)* dull, sad, bleak, lonesome, gloomy, chilling, somber, depressing, dismal, cheerless, dark. *(ANT.)* lively, hopeful,

dregs

gay, *cheerful, bright, joyous.*

dregs *(SYN.)* riffraff, scum, outcasts, dross, leftovers, flotsam.

drench *(SYN.)* wet, bathe, flood, soak, saturate.

dress *(SYN.)* garb, frock, gown, clothing, costume, apparel, attire, wardrobe, garments, vesture, clothes, habit, wear, don, robe, raiment. *(ANT.) undress, strip, divest, disrobe.*

dresser *(SYN.)* dude, clotherhorse, fop, dandy.

dressing *(SYN.)* bandage, seasoning, medicine, sauce.

dressy *(SYN.)* flashy, swank, showy, dapper. *(ANT.) dowdy, drab, frumpy, shabby, tacky.*

dribble *(SYN.)* fall, drip, leak, slaver, slobber.

drift *(SYN.)* roam, tendency, meander, sail, float, direction, wander, intention, stray.

drifter *(SYN.)* hobo, tramp, vagabond.

drill *(SYN.)* employment, lesson, task, use, activity, operation, training. *(ANT.) relaxation, indolence, rest, idleness, repose.*

drink *(SYN.)* gulp, swallow, imbibe, beverage, refreshment, potion.

drip *(SYN.)* dribble, drop, trickle.

drive *(SYN.)* impel, coerce, oblige, force, push, direct, constrain, journey, urge, enforce, trip, handle, ride, propel, control, run, compel.

drivel *(SYN.)* slaver, drool, spit, spittle, dribble, slobber, saliva, nonsense, twaddle, rubbish, babble, gibberish.

driver *(SYN.)* motorist, operator, teamster, trucker, motorman, pilot, coachman.

droll *(SYN.)* laughable, funny, amusing, witty, comical. *(ANT.) sober, sad, solemn, melancholy.*

drone *(SYN.)* buzz, hum, loafer, idler, nonworker.

drool *(SYN.)* drivel, slaver, dribble, spit, gibber, jabber, twaddle, trickle, salivate.

droop *(SYN.)* dangle, weaken, hang, sink, fail, settle, sag, weary, languish, despond. *(ANT.) stand, tower, extend, rise, straighten.*

drop *(SYN.)* droop, dribble, topple, collapse, downward, drip, trickle, tumble, gob, droplet, reduction, slump, slip, decrease, fall, dismiss, decline. *(ANT.) ascend, mount, steady, arise, soar.*

drop out *(SYN.)* back out, withdraw, stop, forsake, abandon, give up, leave, quit.

droppings *(SYN.)* feces, dung, waste, manure, excrement, ordure, guano.

dross *(SYN.)* dregs, impurity, leftovers, residue, debris, leavings, remains.

drove *(SYN.)* flock, herd.

drown *(SYN.)* sink, inundate, submerge, immerse.

drowse *(SYN.)* nap, doze, catnap, snooze, sleep, slumber, rest, drop off, repose.

drowsy *(SYN.)* dozing, torpid, soothing, dreamy, sleepy, comatose, sluggish, lulling, dull, calming, restful, lethargic. *(ANT.) alert, awake, sharp, keen, acute.*

drub *(SYN.)* wallop, thrash, beat, thump, cane, flog, rout, outclass, overcome, belabor, pummel, defeat, outplay.

drubbing *(SYN.)* walloping, flogging, beating, pounding, pummeling, thwacking, thrashing, rout, licking, clobbering.

drudge *(SYN.)* work, labor, hack, slave, toil, grub, grind, toiler, flunky, menial, servant.

drudgery *(SYN.)* toil, travail, effort, task, work, endeavor, labor. *(ANT.) recreation, indolence, leisure.*

drug *(SYN.)* remedy, medicine, stupefy, anesthetize, numb, benumb.

drugged *(SYN.)* numb, doped, numbed, stupefied, dazed, groggy, benumbed.

druggist *(SYN.)* apothecary, chemist, pharmacist.

drunk *(SYN.)* tight, intoxicated, soused, drunken, inebriated, alcoholic, sozzled, besotted, sot, toper, boozer, wino, rummy, dipsomaniac, lush, tipsy.

drunkard *(SYN.)* sot, drunk, alcoholic, lush.

dry *(SYN.)* thirsty, dehydrated, vapid, plain and uninteresting, drained, parched, barren, waterless, dull, tedious, boring, desiccated, tiresome. *(ANT.) fresh, wet, soaked, fascinating, attractive, lively, moist, interesting.*

dub *(SYN.)* nickname, name, christen, call,

• •

style, term, confer, bestow, denominate, entitle, characterize, tag, label.

dubious *(SYN.)* unsure, uncertain, undecided, hesitant, spurious, unreliable, puzzling, untrustworthy, questionable, ambiguous. *(ANT.)* decided, fired, *irrefutable, definite, genuine, unquestionable, sound, authentic, trustworthy.*

duct *(SYN.)* pipe, tube, passage, vein, funnel, gutter, main, trough, artery.

due *(SYN.)* payable, unpaid, owing, owed, imminent, expected.

duel *(SYN.)* competition, contest, engagement, rivalry, combat, strife, encounter.

dues *(SYN.)* assessment, fees, cost, levy, admission, fare, toll, contribution.

duffer *(SYN.)* bungler, slouch, blunderer, novice, incompetent, fumbler, lummox. *(ANT.) master, expert, pro.*

dull *(SYN.)* commonplace, slow, sad, dreary, boring, stupid, uninteresting. *(ANT.) clear, animated, interesting, lively.*

dullard *(SYN.)* dolt, dunce, moron, clod, blockhead, numskull.

dumb *(SYN.)* dull, witless, ignorant, mute, speechless, brainless, dense. *(ANT.) bright, alert, clever, intelligent.*

dump *(SYN.)* heap, fling down, drop, empty, unload, clear out, dispose of. *(ANT.) store, fill, load, hoard, pack.*

dunce *(SYN.)* deadhead, nitwit, booby, idiot, ignoramus, numskull, noddy, fool.

dungeon *(SYN.)* jail, prison, keep, cell.

dunk *(SYN.)* plunge, submerge, dip. *(ANT.) uplift, elevate, recover.*

dupe *(SYN.)* sucker, victim, gull, pushover, fool, cheat, deceive, defraud.

duplicate *(SYN.)* replica, replicate, facsimile, copy, reproduce, clone, double, twin, transcript. *(ANT.) prototype.*

duplicity *(SYN.)* dissimulation, deception, hypocrisy, deceitfulness, insincerity, artifice, cant, guile. *(ANT.) openness, artlessness, candor, straightforwardness, genuineness.*

durability *(SYN.)* might, strength, force, sturdiness, intensity, potency, vigor. *(ANT.) weakness, frailty, feebleness.*

durable *(SYN.)* constant, firm, fixed, unchangeable, enduring, abiding, lasting. *(ANT.) unstable, temporary, perishable, transitory.*

duration *(SYN.)* time, term, period, while, stage, era, epoch, interim.

duress *(SYN.)* force, demand, compulsion, emergency, pressure.

dusky *(SYN.)* sable, black, dark, darkish, swarthy, tawny, gloomy, overcast, misty, obscure, opaque, shadowy. *(ANT.) light, fair, white, pale, shining, clear, bright.*

dutiful *(SYN.)* docile, faithful, obedient. *(ANT.) disobedient, willful, unruly.*

duty *(SYN.)* bond, responsibility, accountability, faithfulness, function, obligation, assignment, engagement. *(ANT.) freedom, choice.*

dwarf *(SYN.)* midget, runt, reduce, stunt, minimize, tiny. *(ANT.) mammoth, colossus, monster, giant.*

dwell *(SYN.)* inhabit, roost, settle, abide, live, reside.

dwindle *(SYN.)* wane, decrease, diminish, fade, subside, ebb, shrivel, lessen. *(ANT.) enlarge, increase, grow, gain.*

dynamic *(SYN.)* active, forceful, kinetic, energetic, motive, mighty, vigorous. *(ANT.) sleepy, stable, inert, fixed, dead, still, uninspiring, ineffectual, listless.*

E

eager *(SYN.)* avid, hot, anxious, fervent, enthusiastic, impatient, ardent, impassioned, yearning. *(ANT.) unconcerned, apathetic, dull, uninterested, indifferent.*

early *(SYN.)* betimes, opportune, first, beforehand, advanced, soon, shortly. *(ANT.) retarded, late, tardy, belated, overdue.*

earmark *(SYN.)* peculiarity, characteristic, brand, sign, stamp, trademark.

earn *(SYN.)* attain, win, get, achieve, obtain, gain, deserve, realize, collect, net, acquire, merit. *(ANT.) lose, waste, forfeit.*

earnest *(SYN.)* sincere, decided, determined, intent, serious, eager, resolute.

(*ANT.*) *indifferent, frivolous, insincere.*

earnings (*SYN.*) wages, pay, salary, income.

earth (*SYN.*) globe, dirt, land, world, turf, soil, sod, ground.

earthly (*SYN.*) mundane, everyday, worldly. (*ANT.*) *heavenly.*

earthy (*SYN.*) earthlike, coarse, earthen, crude, unrefined, vulgar. (*ANT.*) *tasteful, elegant, polished, refined.*

ease (*SYN.*) lighten, alleviate, pacify, soothe, allay, comfort, contentedness. (*ANT.*) *worry, disturb, confound, trouble, intensify, distress.*

easily (*SYN.*) readily, effortlessly, smoothly, naturally, facilely. (*ANT.*) *hardly, arduously, painfully, laboriously.*

easiness (*SYN.*) repose, comfort, satisfaction, contentment, liberty, leisure, facility, simplicity. (*ANT.*) *unrest, torment, arduousness, difficulty, discomfort.*

easy (*SYN.*) light, simple, facile, gentle, effortless, unhurried, comfortable. (*ANT.*) *hard, demanding, awkward, strict, difficult, formal.*

eat (*SYN.*) consume, swallow, dine, corrode, chew, lunch, devour, feast.

eavesdrop (*SYN.*) spy, listen, snoop, overhear.

ebb (*SYN.*) diminish, recede, decline, decrease, retreat, lessen. (*ANT.*) *wax, grow, thrive, increase, swell.*

ebullient (*SYN.*) vivacious, buoyant, exuberant. (*ANT.*) *lethargic, sad, gloomy, depressed.*

eccentric (*SYN.*) odd, irregular, unusual, abnormal, peculiar. (*ANT.*) *ordinary, conventional, normal.*

eccentricity (*SYN.*) kink, idiosyncrasy, whim, freak, caprice, foible, quirk, oddness, strangeness, aberration. (*ANT.*) *conventionality, ordinariness.*

ecclesiastical (*SYN.*) religious, churchly, clerical.

echelon (*SYN.*) rank, level, grade, status.

echo (*SYN.*) response, imitation, suggestion, trace, reaction, imitate, repeat.

eclectic (*SYN.*) selective, diverse, broad, liberal, comprehensive. (*ANT.*) *limited,*

narrow, rigid, confined.

eclipse (*SYN.*) conceal, screen, hide, cover, obscure, overcast, veil.

economical (*SYN.*) saving, thrifty, careful, frugal, provident, sparing. (*ANT.*) *wasteful, extravagant, lavish, improvident.*

economy (*SYN.*) saving, thrift.

ecstasy (*SYN.*) frenzy, gladness, delight, madness, joy, glee, exaltation, pleasure, trance, rapture. (*ANT.*) *misery, melancholy, sadness.*

ecstatic (*SYN.*) overjoyed, thrilled, delighted, happy, elated.

edge (*SYN.*) margin, brim, verge, brink, border, keenness, extremity, boundary, trim, periphery, hem, rim, sting. (*ANT.*) *dullness, center, bluntness.*

edgy (*SYN.*) tense, touchy, nervous, irritable.

edict (*SYN.*) declaration, order, ruling, decree, pronouncement, command, law, proclamation.

edifice (*SYN.*) construction, building, establishment.

edit (*SYN.*) check, revise, correct, amend.

educate (*SYN.*) instruct, teach, school, train.

education (*SYN.*) training, development, knowledge, learning, cultivation, schooling, instruction, study.

eerie (*SYN.*) weird, fearful, ghastly, spooky, strange.

efface (*SYN.*) obliterate, erase.

effect (*SYN.*) produce, consequence, evoke, cause, make, complete, outcome, result, determine.

effective (*SYN.*) efficient, practical, productive. (*ANT.*) *useless, wasteful, ineffective.*

efficiency (*SYN.*) efficacy, capability, effectiveness, competency, ability. (*ANT.*) *wastefulness, inability.*

efficient (*SYN.*) efficacious, skillful, capable, adept, competent, useful, effectual, effective, apt, proficient. (*ANT.*) *inefficient, unskilled, ineffectual, incompetent.*

effort (*SYN.*) labor, endeavor, pains, essay, trial, exertion, struggle, strain.

egg (*SYN.*) stir, ovum, incite, urge, arouse

embryo, provoke.

egghead *(SYN.)* scholar, intellectual, pedant.

egoism *(SYN.)* self-interest, conceit, pride, selfishness, egotism. *(ANT.) modesty, generosity, selflessness.*

eject *(SYN.)* expel, remove, oust, eliminate. *(ANT.) include.*

elaborate *(SYN.)* detail, develop, decorated, decorative, ornate, complex. *(ANT.) simplify, simple, unadorned.*

elapse *(SYN.)* expire.

elastic *(SYN.)* yielding, flexible, adaptable, pliable.

elated *(SYN.)* delighted, rejoicing, overjoyed, jubilant. *(ANT.) sad, unhappy.*

elder *(SYN.)* senior. *(ANT.) younger.*

elderly *(SYN.)* aged, old. *(ANT.) young, youthful.*

elect *(SYN.)* pick, appoint, choose.

electrify *(SYN.)* shock, charge, stir, upset, generate, agitate.

elegant *(SYN.)* tasteful, refined, cultivated, choice, polished, superior, fine. *(ANT.) crude, coarse, unpolished, tasteless.*

elementary *(SYN.)* simple, primary, basic, uncomplicated, initial, beginning, fundamental. *(ANT.) involved, complex, sophisticated, complicated.*

elevate *(SYN.)* raise, lift. *(ANT.) lower, drop.*

elf *(SYN.)* devil, fairy, imp.

elicit *(SYN.)* summon.

eligible *(SYN.)* fit, suitable, qualified.

eliminate *(SYN.)* expel, eject, remove, dislodge, extirpate, erase, oust. *(ANT.) admit, involve.*

elite *(SYN.)* nobility, upper-class, aristocracy, gentry. *(ANT.) mob, proletariat.*

elongate *(SYN.)* extend, prolong, lengthen.

elope *(SYN.)* escape, flee.

eloquent *(SYN.)* expressive, fluent, articulate, glib, meaningful. *(ANT.) inarticulate.*

else *(SYN.)* different, another, other.

elude *(SYN.)* escape, miss, avoid, dodge. *(ANT.) odd, include.*

emaciated *(SYN.)* wasted, thin, starved, withered, shriveled, gaunt, shrunken, drawn, undernourished.

emancipate *(SYN.)* liberate, free, deliver, save. *(ANT.) restrain.*

embankment *(SYN.)* shore, dam, bank, fortification, buttress.

embargo *(SYN.)* prohibition, restriction, restraint.

embark *(SYN.)* board, depart.

embarrass *(SYN.)* discomfit, rattle, distress, hamper, fluster, entangle, abash, mortify, hinder, perplex, confuse, shame, trouble. *(ANT.) relieve, encourage, help.*

embassy *(SYN.)* ministry, legation, consulate.

embed *(SYN.)* root, inset, enclose, plant.

embellish *(SYN.)* adorn, decorate, ornament.

embezzle *(SYN.)* pilfer, misuse, rob, misappropriate, steal, take.

embitter *(SYN.)* provoke, arouse, alienate, anger, inflame.

emblem *(SYN.)* token, mark, symbol, badge.

embody *(SYN.)* comprise, cover, embrace, include.

embrace *(SYN.)* espouse, accept, receive, comprehend, contain, welcome, comprise, cover, clasp, include, adopt, hug. *(ANT.) spurn, reject, bar, exclude, repudiate.*

embroider *(SYN.)* decorate, adorn, stitch, trim, overstate, embellish, ornament, exaggerate, magnify.

emerge *(SYN.)* surface, show, appear.

emergency *(SYN.)* strait, pass, crisis, urgency, predicament, pinch.

eminent *(SYN.)* renowned, glorious, important, conspicuous, prominent, famous. *(ANT.) ordinary, commonplace, unknown, undistinguished, common.*

emissary *(SYN.)* envoy, minister, delegate, agent, spy.

emit *(SYN.)* expel, breathe, shoot, hurl, ooze, vent, belch, discharge.

emotion *(SYN.)* passion, turmoil, perturbation, affection, sentiment, feeling, trepidation, agitation. *(ANT.) dispassion,*

emotional

indifference, tranquillity, calm, restraint.

emotional *(SYN.)* ardent, passionate, stirring, zealous, impetuous, overwrought, enthusiastic. *(ANT.) tranquil, calm, placid.*

emphasis *(SYN.)* accent, stress, insistence.

emphatic *(SYN.)* positive, definite, forceful, energetic, strong. *(ANT.) lax, quiet, unforceful.*

employ *(SYN.)* avail, use, devote, apply, utilize, engage, sign, hire, retain, service, contract. *(ANT.) reject, discard.*

employee *(SYN.)* laborer, worker, servant. *(ANT.) boss, employer.*

employer *(SYN.)* owner, boss, management, proprietor, manager, superintendent, supervisor. *(ANT.) employee, worker.*

employment *(SYN.)* occupation, work, business, position, job, service, engagement. *(ANT.) leisure, idleness, slothfulness.*

empower *(SYN.)* enable, sanction, permit, warrant.

empty *(SYN.)* void, devoid, unfilled, barren, senseless, unoccupied, unfurnished, vacant, blank, evacuate, unload, hollow. *(ANT.) supplied, full, occupied.*

emulate *(SYN.)* follow, imitate, copy.

enable *(SYN.)* authorize, empower, sanction, qualify.

enact *(SYN.)* legislate, portray, pass, stage.

enchant *(SYN.)* charm, titillate, fascinate, bewitch, delight, thrill, captivate. *(ANT.) tire, bore.*

encircle *(SYN.)* comprise, include, bound, encompass.

enclose *(SYN.)* envelop, confine, bound, surround, encompass, encircle, circumscribe. *(ANT.) open, exclude, distend, expose, develop.*

encompass *(SYN.)* include, surround, encircle.

encore *(SYN.)* repetition, repeat, again.

encounter *(SYN.)* battle, meet, oppose, run into, face, collide.

encourage *(SYN.)* incite, favor, cheer, impel, countenance, inspirit, exhilarate, animate, hearten, embolden, support. *(ANT.) deter, dispirit, deject, dissuade.*

encroach *(SYN.)* interfere, trespass, intrude, infringe.

encumber *(SYN.)* hamper, load, burden.

end *(SYN.)* completion, object, close, aim, result, conclusion, finish, extremity, intent, halt, stop, limit, purpose, cessation, expiration, termination. *(ANT.) opening, start, introduction, beginning, launch, inception.*

endanger *(SYN.)* imperil, hazard, risk. *(ANT.) secure.*

endear *(SYN.)* allure, charm.

endeavor *(SYN.)* strive, struggle, exertion, attempt, try, labor.

endless *(SYN.)* constant, nonstop, continuous, incessant, everlasting.

endorse *(SYN.)* approve, accept, sign, confirm, pass.

endow *(SYN.)* provide, furnish, bestow, give, contribute. *(ANT.) divest.*

endure *(SYN.)* experience, undergo, sustain, last, bear, continue, remain, undergo, persist, brook, tolerate, suffer. *(ANT.) wane, perish, succumb, fail.*

enemy *(SYN.)* foe, antagonist, rival, opponent, competitor, adversary, opposition. *(ANT.) colleague, ally, friend, accomplice.*

energy *(SYN.)* strength, vim, force, power, stamina, vigor, might. *(ANT.) feebleness, lethargy.*

enervate *(SYN.)* enfeeble, weaken, debilitate, exhaust, devitalize. *(ANT.) invigorate.*

enfold *(SYN.)* clasp, surround, wrap, embrace, hug.

enforce *(SYN.)* make, drive, compel, execute, force.

engage *(SYN.)* absorb, occupy, employ, hold, involve, hire, agree, engross, retain, promise, commit, entangle. *(ANT.) fire, disengage, discharge, dismiss.*

engaged *(SYN.)* affianced, betrothed, busy, occupied.

engaging *(SYN.)* fascinating, appealing, enticing, interesting, tempting, lovely, beguiling, charming, enchanting, engrossing, delightful, exquisite. *(ANT.) ordinary, boring.*

engender *(SYN.)* develop, breed, cause, generate, produce.

engineer *(SYN.)* direct, conduct, guide,

lead, manage.

engrave *(SYN.)* print, cut, impress, inscribe, carve, sketch.

engross *(SYN.)* engage, enthrall, occupy, fascinate, absorb.

engulf *(SYN.)* flood, swallow.

enhance *(SYN.)* better, uplift, improve.

enigma *(SYN.)* mystery, stumper, riddle.

enigmatic *(SYN.)* perplexing, confusing, puzzling, baffling, mystifying.

enjoy *(SYN.)* savor, like, relish.

enjoyment *(SYN.)* pleasure, delight, gratification. *(ANT.)* abhorrence, displeasure.

enlarge *(SYN.)* widen, distend, amplify, broaden, extend, increase, augment, expand, dilate. *(ANT.)* diminish, shrink, contract, decrease, wane, restrict.

enlighten *(SYN.)* inform, illuminate, clarify, teach, instruct. *(ANT.)* confuse.

enlist *(SYN.)* enroll, prompt, join, induce, enter, register, persuade. *(ANT.)* quit, leave, abandon.

enliven *(SYN.)* inspire, brighten, stimulate.

enmity *(SYN.)* antagonism, hatred, animosity, malignity, ill-will, antipathy, hostility, unfriendliness. *(ANT.)* love, like, friendliness.

enormity *(SYN.)* heinousness, wickedness, barbarity, atrociousness.

enormous *(SYN.)* vast, huge, colossal, immense, gargantuan, elephantine, gigantic, stupendous, large. *(ANT.)* small, slight, tiny, minute, infinitesimal, diminutive, little.

enough *(SYN.)* ample, adequate, sufficient, plenty. *(ANT.)* inadequate, insufficient.

enrage *(SYN.)* anger, provoke, madden, inflame. *(ANT.)* appease, soothe, calm.

enrich *(SYN.)* better, improve.

enroll *(SYN.)* record, list, recruit, register, enlist, write, induct. *(ANT.)* quit, leave, abandon.

enshrine *(SYN.)* bury, entomb.

ensign *(SYN.)* banner, colors, flag, officer.

enslave *(SYN.)* keep, hold, capture.

ensue *(SYN.)* arise, succeed, follow.

ensure *(SYN.)* guarantee, assure, protect, defend, cover.

entangle *(SYN.)* confuse, snare, involve, ravel, snarl, tangle, trap.

enter *(SYN.)* join, go inside.

enterprise *(SYN.)* fete, deed, venture, project, adventure, undertaking, ambition, business, exploit.

enterprising *(SYN.)* energetic, resourceful. *(ANT.)* lazy, indolent, sluggish, unresourceful.

entertain *(SYN.)* cheer, gladden, hold, consider, please, contemplate, divert, amuse, harbor, fascinate, interest. *(ANT.)* repulse, tire, bore, disgust, annoy.

enthrall *(SYN.)* captivate, fascinate, enchant, charm, thrill.

enthusiasm *(SYN.)* fervor, fanaticism, zeal, ardor, intensity, devotion, excitement, eagerness, fervency, earnestness. *(ANT.)* indifference, ennui, apathy, unconcern, detachment.

enthusiastic *(SYN.)* earnest, zealous, eager. *(ANT.)* aloof, indifferent, unconcerned.

entice *(SYN.)* lure, attract, seduce.

entire *(SYN.)* complete, intact, whole, undivided. *(ANT.)* divided, separated, incomplete, partial.

entirely *(SYN.)* altogether, thoroughly, wholly, solely.

entitle *(SYN.)* call, label, name, empower, allow, authorize, license, title.

entourage *(SYN.)* train, company, retinue, escort.

entrance *(SYN.)* inlet, portal, doorway, fascinate, entry, intrigue, door, thrill.

entreat *(SYN.)* implore, beg, plead.

entreaty *(SYN.)* plea, appeal.

entrust *(SYN.)* commit, charge, assign, delegate, consign, commission.

enumerate *(SYN.)* count, tally, list, number.

enunciate *(SYN.)* announce, express, speak, state.

envelop *(SYN.)* embrace, cover, conceal, surround, wrap.

environment *(SYN.)* neighborhood, habitat, surroundings, setting.

envision *(SYN.)* picture, imagine, visualize.

envoy *(SYN.)* delegate, emissary,

representative, agent, messenger.

envy *(SYN.)* covetousness, jealousy, spitefulness, covet. *(ANT.)* indifference, generosity.

epicure *(SYN.)* gourmand, gourmet, connoisseur, gastronome, Epicurean, aesthete.

epidemic *(SYN.)* prevalent, scourge, plague, catching, widespread, pestilence, infectious.

episode *(SYN.)* happening, affair, occurrence, event, experience.

epoch *(SYN.)* age, era, period, time.

equal *(SYN.)* even, uniform, like, alike, equitable, same, identical, commensurate, equivalent, regular, parallel. *(ANT.)* different, unequal, irregular, uneven.

equilibrium *(SYN.)* stability, steadiness, balance, firmness.

equip *(SYN.)* fit, rig, provide, outfit, prepare, furnish.

equipment *(SYN.)* utensils, material, apparatus.

equitable *(SYN.)* square, rightful, fair, due, just, fit. *(ANT.)* partial, biased, unjust, uneven.

equity *(SYN.)* impartiality, fairness, justness, justice, fair-mindedness, evenhandedness.

equivalent *(SYN.)* match, rival, equal, like, replacement.

equivocal *(SYN.)* oblique, ambiguous, vague, indeterminate, uncertain, obscure. *(ANT.)* clear, precise, explicit, certain, clearcut, definite.

equivocate *(SYN.)* temporize, evade, hedge, quibble, fudge, waffle, straddle.

era *(SYN.)* epoch, cycle, age, time, period.

eradicate *(SYN.)* remove, demolish, eliminate.

erase *(SYN.)* obliterate, remove, cancel. *(ANT.)* add, include.

erect *(SYN.)* upright, build, straight, raise, construct, vertical. *(ANT.)* flat, horizontal, raze, flatten, demolish.

erection *(SYN.)* building, construction, raising, fabrication.

erode *(SYN.)* rust, consume, disintegrate.

erotic *(SYN.)* carnal, sensual, amatory, prurient, lewd, wanton, passionate, lecherous.

err *(SYN.)* slip, misjudge.

errand *(SYN.)* chore, duty, task, exercise.

errant *(SYN.)* roving, rambling, wandering, vagrant.

erratic *(SYN.)* irregular, abnormal, uneven, occasional, sporadic, changeable, unsteady, odd, eccentric, strange, extraordinary, unconventional, bizarre, peculiar, uncertain, unusual, unstable. *(ANT.)* regular, steady, normal, ordinary.

erroneous *(SYN.)* wrong, mistaken, incorrect, inaccurate, false, untrue. *(ANT.)* true, right, correct, accurate.

error *(SYN.)* inaccuracy, fault, slip, oversight, fallacy, mistake, blunder.

erudite *(SYN.)* sage, wise, learned, deep, profound.

erupt *(SYN.)* vomit.

escapade *(SYN.)* caper, antic, stunt, trick, prank.

escape *(SYN.)* shun, avoid, flee, decamp, elude, flight, avert, departure, abscond, fly, evade. *(ANT.)* meet, confront, invite, catch.

escort *(SYN.)* conduct, lead, attend, accompany, protection, guard, guide, convoy, usher, squire.

especially *(SYN.)* unusually, principally, mainly, particularly, primarily.

essay *(SYN.)* test, thesis, undertake, paper, try.

essence *(SYN.)* substance, character, nature, principle, odor, meaning, basis, smell, perfume.

essential *(SYN.)* vital, intrinsic, basic, requisite, fundamental, indispensable, critical, requirement, necessity, necessary, important. *(ANT.)* dispensable, unimportant, inessential.

establish *(SYN.)* prove, fix, found, settle, institute, raise, verify, conform, form, sanction, ordain, begin, organize. *(ANT.)* upset, discontinue, scatter, disperse, refute, abolish, unsettle.

esteem *(SYN.)* revere, deem, appreciate, honor, value, think, admire, respect, hold, prize, reverence, regard. *(ANT.)* scorn, *disdain, depreciate, disregard, contempt, abhor.*

estimate *(SYN.)* calculate, gauge, judge, rate, evaluate, compute, value, figure.

estimation *(SYN.)* judgment, viewpoint, opinion.

etch *(SYN.)* stamp, engrave, impress.

eternal *(SYN.)* undying, immortal, ceaseless, infinite, everlasting, deathless, perpetual, endless, timeless. *(ANT.) mortal, transient, finite, brief, temporary, passing.*

etiquette *(SYN.)* decorum, formality.

evacuate *(SYN.)* withdraw, depart, leave, vacate.

evade *(SYN.)* miss, avoid, bypass. *(ANT.) confront, meet, face.*

evaluate *(SYN.)* value, appraise, assay.

evaporate *(SYN.)* disappear, vanish. *(ANT.) condense, appear.*

even *(SYN.)* smooth, level, still, square, same, flat, balanced, equal, parallel, identical. *(ANT.) irregular, bumpy, unbalanced, unequal, divergent.*

evening *(SYN.)* twilight, dusk, sunset. *(ANT.) sunrise, dawn.*

event *(SYN.)* issue, end, result, circumstance, occurrence, incident, consequence, happening, episode, outcome.

even-tempered *(SYN.)* composed, calm, cool. *(ANT.) hotheaded.*

eventual *(SYN.)* consequent, ultimate. *(ANT.) present, current.*

eventually *(SYN.)* ultimately.

ever *(SYN.)* continuously, always, constantly. *(ANT.) never.*

everlasting *(SYN.)* permanent, ceaseless, endless, continual.

evermore *(SYN.)* always.

everyday *(SYN.)* commonplace, common, usual, ordinary, customary. *(ANT.) rare.*

evict *(SYN.)* oust, put out, expel.

evidence *(SYN.)* grounds, clue, facts, testimony, data, sign, proof.

evident *(SYN.)* apparent, clear, obvious, indubitable, plain, conspicuous, patent, manifest, open, unmistakable. *(ANT.) hidden, unclear, uncertain, obscure, concealed.*

evil *(SYN.)* immoral, harmful, badness, sinful, injurious, woe, bad, wicked. *(ANT.) goodness, moral, useful, upright, virtuous, beneficial, virtue, advantageous.*

evoke *(SYN.)* summon, prompt.

evolve *(SYN.)* grow, advance, develop, result, emerge, unfold.

exact *(SYN.)* correct, faultless, errorless, detailed, accurate. *(ANT.) inaccurate, inexact, faulty.*

exaggerate *(SYN.)* stretch, expand, amplify, embroider, heighten, overstate, caricature, magnify, enlarge. *(ANT.) understate, minimize, diminish, depreciate.*

exalt *(SYN.)* erect, consecrate, raise, elevate, extol, dignify. *(ANT.) humble, degrade, humiliate.*

examination *(SYN.)* investigation, inspection, test, scrutiny.

examine *(SYN.)* assess, contemplate, question, review, audit, notice, inquire, analyze, check, investigate, dissect, inspect, survey. *(ANT.) omit, disregard, overlook.*

example *(SYN.)* pattern, archetype, specimen, illustration, model, instance, prototype, sample. *(ANT.) rule, principle.*

exasperate *(SYN.)* aggravate, anger, madden, irritate.

excavate *(SYN.)* unearth, dig, burrow.

exceed *(SYN.)* excel, beat, surpass, top.

exceedingly *(SYN.)* extremely, very, especially, unusually, surprisingly.

excel *(SYN.)* better, beat, surpass.

excellence *(SYN.)* distinction, superiority. *(ANT.) poorness, inferiority, badness.*

excellent *(SYN.)* wonderful, fine, marvelous, superior. *(ANT.) poor, terrible, bad, inferior.*

except *(SYN.)* omitting, but, reject, excluding, save, exclude.

exception *(SYN.)* affront, offense, exclusion, deviation, omission, anomaly.

exceptional *(SYN.)* different, irregular, strange, unusual, abnormal.

excerpt *(SYN.)* abstract, extract.

excess *(SYN.)* surplus, intemperance, extravagance, immoderation, profusion, abundant, profuse, superfluity. *(ANT.) want, sparse, lack, dearth.*

exchange

exchange *(SYN.)* barter, interchange, substitute, trade, change, swap.

excite *(SYN.)* arouse, incite, agitate, stimulate, awaken, disquiet. *(ANT.)* lull, quiet, bore, pacify.

exclaim *(SYN.)* vociferate, cry, call out, cry out, ejaculate, shout.

exclamation *(SYN.)* shout, outcry, clamor.

exclude *(SYN.)* omit, restrain, hinder, bar, except, prevent. *(ANT.)* welcome, involve, embrace, admit, accept, include.

exclusion *(SYN.)* exception, bar, rejection. *(ANT.)* inclusion.

exclusive *(SYN.)* restricted, limited, restrictive, choice, selective, fashionable. *(ANT.)* common, general, ordinary, unrestricted, unfashionable.

excursion *(SYN.)* voyage, tour, trip.

excuse *(SYN.)* exculpate, forgive, remit, acquit, free, pardon, condone, explanation, overlook, exempt, reason, justify, absolve. *(ANT.)* revenge, punish, convict.

execute *(SYN.)* complete, accomplish, do, achieve, kill, perform.

exemplify *(SYN.)* show, illustrate.

exempt *(SYN.)* excuse, free, except, release.

exercise *(SYN.)* drill, task, use, activity, lesson, training, exertion, application, gymnastics, operation, practice. *(ANT.)* rest, indolence, repose.

exertion *(SYN.)* attempt, effort, strain, endeavor.

exhale *(SYN.)* blow, breathe out.

exhaust *(SYN.)* drain, tire, empty, wear out, use, finish, fatigue. *(ANT.)* renew, refresh, replace.

exhaustive *(SYN.)* comprehensive, thorough, extensive, complete. *(ANT.)* incomplete.

exhibit *(SYN.)* demonstrate, display, present, reveal, betray, show, flaunt. *(ANT.)* hide, conceal, disguise.

exhilarate *(SYN.)* gladden, refresh, cheer, excite, stimulate.

exhort *(SYN.)* advise, coax, press, urge.

exile *(SYN.)* expulsion, proscription, deportation, ostracism, expatriation, deport, extradition, expel, banishment. *(ANT.)*

retrieval, welcome, recall, admittance.

exist *(SYN.)* stand, live, occur, be.

exit *(SYN.)* leave, depart.

exodus *(SYN.)* leaving, exit, parting, departure.

exonerate *(SYN.)* acquit, clear.

exorbitant *(SYN.)* unreasonable, outrageous, overpriced, preposterous, excessive. *(ANT.)* normal, reasonable.

exotic *(SYN.)* strange, vivid, foreign, gay. *(ANT.)* dull, normal.

expand *(SYN.)* unfold, enlarge, broaden, spread, inflate, swell, grow. *(ANT.)* contract, shrivel, shrink.

expect *(SYN.)* await, think, hope, anticipate.

expedient *(SYN.)* helpful, desirable, rush, hasten, useful, fitting, sensible.

expedition *(SYN.)* trek, speed, trip, haste, voyage, journey, hurry.

expel *(SYN.)* exile, dislodge, discharge, excommunicate, oust, eject, dismiss, banish, disown. *(ANT.)* recall, invite, admit.

expend *(SYN.)* consume, waste, spend, exhaust. *(ANT.)* ration, reserve, conserve.

expense *(SYN.)* charge, cost, payment, price.

expensive *(SYN.)* costly, dear. *(ANT.)* modest, inexpensive, cheap.

experience *(SYN.)* occurrence, episode, sensation, happening, existence, background, feeling, living, encountering, knowledge.

experienced *(SYN.)* expert, qualified, accomplished, skilled, practiced. *(ANT.)* untutored, inexperienced, naive.

experiment *(SYN.)* trial, test, prove, research, examine, try, verify.

expert *(SYN.)* adept, handy, skillful, clever, specialist, authority, skilled, knowledgeable, ingenious. *(ANT.)* untrained, unskilled, inexperienced.

expire *(SYN.)* terminate, die, cease, perish, pass, end, disappear. *(ANT.)* commence, continue.

explain *(SYN.)* illustrate, decipher, expound, clarify, resolve, define, unravel, elucidate, unfold, justify, interpret. *(ANT.)*

darken, baffle, obscure.

explanation *(SYN.)* definition, description, interpretation, account, reason, justification, excuse.

explicit *(SYN.)* lucid, definitive, specific, express, clear, manifest. *(ANT.)* vague, implicit, ambiguous.

exploit *(SYN.)* feat, deed, accomplishment, adventure.

explore *(SYN.)* research, hunt, probe, search, investigate, look, examine.

explosion *(SYN.)* bang, boom, blowup, flare-up, blast, detonation, outbreak, convulsion, furor, tantrum, paroxysm.

explosive *(SYN.)* fiery, rabid, eruptive, volcanic, fulminatory, inflammatory. *(ANT.)* stable, inert, peaceful, calm.

exponent *(SYN.)* explicator, spokesman, supporter, expounder, interpreter.

expose *(SYN.)* uncover, display, bare, open, unmask, reveal. *(ANT.)* hide, conceal, mask, covered.

exposition *(SYN.)* fair, bazaar, show, expo, exhibition.

expound *(SYN.)* clarify, present, explain, lecture, demonstrate.

express *(SYN.)* voice, tell, send, say, ship, declare, stale, precise, specific, swift, describe.

expression *(SYN.)* declaration, statement, look.

expressive *(SYN.)* suggestive, meaningful, telling, significant, thoughtful. *(ANT.)* unthinking, meaningless, nondescript.

expressly *(SYN.)* precisely, exactly, definitely, clearly. *(ANT.)* tentatively, vaguely, ambiguously.

expulsion *(SYN.)* ejection, discharge, removal, elimination.

expunge *(SYN.)* blot out, erase, cancel, obliterate, delete, efface, remove.

expurgate *(SYN.)* cleanse, purge, censor, edit, emasculate, abridge, blip.

exquisite *(SYN.)* delicate, delightful, attractive, dainty, beautiful, elegant, fine, superb, lovely, excellent, perfect. *(ANT.)* vulgar, dull, ugly, unattractive.

extant *(SYN.)* subsisting, remaining, surviving, present, existing. *(ANT.)* lost, defunct, extinct, vanished.

extemporize *(SYN.)* improvise, devise.

extend *(SYN.)* lengthen, stretch, increase, offer, give, grant, magnify, expand. *(ANT.)* abbreviate, shorten, curtail.

extension *(SYN.)* expansion, increase, stretching, enlargement.

extensive *(SYN.)* vast, wide, spacious. *(ANT.)* cramped, confined, restricted.

extent *(SYN.)* length, degree, range, amount, measure, size, compass, reach, magnitude, scope, expanse, area.

extenuating *(SYN.)* exculpating, excusable, qualifying, justifying, softening.

exterior *(SYN.)* surface, face, outside, covering, outer, external. *(ANT.)* inside, interior, inner, internal.

exterminate *(SYN.)* slay, kill, destroy.

external *(SYN.)* outer, exterior, outside. *(ANT.)* inner, internal, inside, interior.

externals *(SYN.)* images, effects, look, appearance, veneer, aspect.

extinct *(SYN.)* lost, dead, gone, vanished. *(ANT.)* present, flourishing, alive, extant.

extinction *(SYN.)* eclipse, annihilation, obliteration, death, extirpation.

extol *(SYN.)* laud, eulogize, exalt, praise. *(ANT.)* denounce, discredit, disparage.

extra *(SYN.)* surplus, spare, additional.

extract *(SYN.)* remove, essence. *(ANT.)* penetrate, introduce.

extraordinary *(SYN.)* unusual, wonderful, marvelous, peculiar, noteworthy. *(ANT.)* commonplace, ordinary, usual.

extravagant *(SYN.)* excessive, exaggerated, lavish, wasteful, extreme. *(ANT.)* prudent, frugal, thrifty, economical.

extreme *(SYN.)* excessive, overdone, outermost, limit, greatest, utmost, furthest. *(ANT.)* reasonable, modest, moderate.

extricate *(SYN.)* rescue, free, clear, release, liberate.

exuberant *(SYN.)* buoyant, ebullient, vivacious. *(ANT.)* sad, depressed.

exult *(SYN.)* rejoice, delight.

eye *(SYN.)* watch, view, stare, look, inspect, glance.

fable

F

fable *(SYN.)* legend, parable, myth, fib, falsehood, fiction, tale, story.

fabled *(SYN.)* legendary, famous, tamed, historic.

fabric *(SYN.)* goods, textile, material, cloth, yard goods.

fabricate *(SYN.)* assemble, make, construct, produce, create, manufacture, form. *(ANT.)* raze, destroy, demolish.

fabrication *(SYN.)* deceit, lie, falsehood, untruth, forgery, prevarication, deception. *(ANT.)* verity, reality, actuality, truth, fact.

fabulous *(SYN.)* amazing, marvelous, unbelievable, fantastic, astounding, astonishing, striking. *(ANT.)* ordinary, commonplace, credible, proven, factual.

facade *(SYN.)* deception, mask, front, show, pose, veneer, guise, affectation.

face *(SYN.)* cover, mug, front, assurance, countenance, audacity, visage, expression, look, features, facade, encounter, meet, surface. *(ANT.)* rear, shun, avoid, evade, back, timidity.

facet *(SYN.)* perspective, view, side, phase.

facetious *(SYN.)* jocular, pungent, humorous, funny, clever, droll, witty, playful, jesting. *(ANT.)* sober, serious, grave, weighty.

face to face *(SYN.)* opposing, nose to nose, confronting.

facile *(SYN.)* simple, easy, quick, uncomplicated, clever, fluent, skillful. *(ANT.)* complex, difficult, complicated, laborious, hard, ponderous, painstaking, arduous.

facilitate *(SYN.)* help, speed, ease, promote, accelerate, expedite.

facilities *(SYN.)* aid, means, resources, conveniences.

facility *(SYN.)* ability, skill, ease, skillfulness, material. *(ANT.)* effort, difficulty.

facsimile *(SYN.)* reproduction, likeness, replica.

fact *(SYN.)* reality, deed, certainty, act, incident, circumstance, occurrence, event, truth, actuality. *(ANT.)* falsehood, fiction, delusion.

faction *(SYN.)* clique, party, sect.

factitious *(SYN.)* false, sham, artificial, spurious, unnatural, affected. *(ANT.)* natural, real, genuine, artless.

factor *(SYN.)* part, element, basis, cause.

factory *(SYN.)* installation, plant, mill, works.

factual *(SYN.)* true, correct, accurate, sure, genuine, authentic. *(ANT.)* incorrect, erroneous, fabricated, invented.

faculty *(SYN.)* power, capacity, talent, staff, gift, ability, qualification, ability, skill.

fad *(SYN.)* fashion, vogue, mania, rage.

faddish *(SYN.)* ephemeral, modish, temporary, passing, fleeting. *(ANT.)* lasting, permanent, enduring, classic.

fade *(SYN.)* pale, bleach, weaken, dim, decline, sink, discolor, fail, diminish, droop.

fagged *(SYN.)* exhausted, tired, weary, jaded, pooped, worn.

fail *(SYN.)* neglect, weaken, flunk, miss, decline, disappoint, fade. *(ANT.)* succeed, achieve, accomplish.

failing *(SYN.)* fault, foible, imperfection, frailty, defect, peccadillo, shortcoming. *(ANT.)* steadiness, strength, integrity.

failure *(SYN.)* miscarriage, omission, decline, deficiency, fiasco, lack, dereliction, failing, unsuccessfulness, loss, default, want, insufficiency, decay. *(ANT.)* conquest, accomplishment, success, triumph, victory, hit, luck, achievement.

faint *(SYN.)* timid, faded, languid, half-hearted, dim, pale, wearied, feeble, indistinct, weak. *(ANT.)* strong, sharp, forceful, glaring, clear, distinct, conspicuous.

fainthearted *(SYN.)* shy, cowardly, timid, bashful. *(ANT.)* fearless, brave, stouthearted, courageous.

fair *(SYN.)* pale, average, light, sunny, mediocre, just, clear, lovely, market, blond, honest, equitable, impartial, reasonable, comely, exposition. *(ANT.)* ugly, fraudulent, foul, outstanding, dishonorable, unfair.

fairly *(SYN.)* equally, evenly, rather, impartially, passably, justly, squarely, somewhat.

farewell

fair-minded *(SYN.)* reasonable, just, open-minded, honest, unprejudiced, impartial, evenhanded. *(ANT.)* bigoted, narrow-minded, unjust, close-minded, partisan.

fairness *(SYN.)* equity, justice, evenhandedness, honesty. *(ANT.)* favoritism, partiality, bias, one-sidedness.

fairy *(SYN.)* leprechaun, gnome, elf, pixie, sprite.

faith *(SYN.)* dependence, trust, reliance, creed, loyalty, doctrine, confidence, dogma, tenet, persuasion, constancy, credence, fidelity, religion, belief. *(ANT.)* mistrust, disbelief, doubt, infidelity.

faithful *(SYN.)* staunch, true, devoted, trusty, loyal, constant, credible, steadfast, strict, trust-worthy, accurate. *(ANT.)* untrustworthy, faithless, inaccurate, wrong, false, disloyal, erroneous, treacherous.

faithless *(SYN.)* treacherous, unfaithful, disloyal, perfidious, untrue. *(ANT.)* loyal, true, unwavering, constant, faithful.

fake *(SYN.)* falsify, distort, pretend, feign, fraud, counterfeit, cheat, false, artificial, phony, imitation, forgery, mock. *(ANT.)* honest, pure, real, genuine, authentic.

falderol *(SYN.)* foolery, jargon, nonsense, gibberish, blather, balderdash.

fall *(SYN.)* drop, decline, diminish, droop, topple, decrease, sink, hang, descend, subside, plunge, collapse. *(ANT.)* soar, climb, steady, rise, ascend.

fallacious *(SYN.)* untrue, false, wrong, erroneous, deceptive, illusory, delusive. *(ANT.)* accurate, true, exact, real, factual.

fallacy *(SYN.)* mistake, error, illusion, sophism, misconception, deception.

fall back *(SYN.)* retreat, recede, retire, withdraw, concede. *(ANT.)* progress, advance, gain, prosper, proceed.

fallow *(SYN.)* idle, unprepared, unproductive, inactive. *(ANT.)* prepared, productive, cultivated.

false *(SYN.)* incorrect, wrong, deceitful, fake, imitation, counterfeit. *(ANT.)* genuine, loyal, true, honest.

falsehood *(SYN.)* untruth, lie, fib, story. *(ANT.)* truth.

falsify *(SYN.)* misquote, distort, misstate, mislead, adulterate.

falter *(SYN.)* stumble, tremble, waver, hesitate, flounder.

fame *(SYN.)* distinction, glory, mane, eminence, credit, reputation, renown, acclaim, notoriety. *(ANT.)* infamy, obscurity, anonymity, disrepute.

famed *(SYN.)* known, renowned, famous. *(ANT.)* obscure, unknown, anonymous.

familiar *(SYN.)* informal, intimate, close, acquainted, amicable, knowing, cognizant, well-acquainted, versed, unreserved, friendly, sociable, affable, aware, known, courteous, intimate. *(ANT.)* unfamiliar, distant, affected, reserved.

familiarity *(SYN.)* sociability, acquaintance, awareness, frankness, intimacy, understanding, knowledge, fellowship. *(ANT.)* distance, ignorance, reserve, presumption, constraint, haughtiness.

family *(SYN.)* kin, tribe, folks, group, relatives.

famine *(SYN.)* want, deficiency, starvation, need. *(ANT.)* excess, plenty.

famous *(SYN.)* distinguished, noted, illustrious, famed, celebrated, well-known, eminent, renowned, prominent, esteemed. *(ANT.)* obscure, hidden, unknown.

fan *(SYN.)* arouse, spread, admirer, enthusiast, devotee, stir, whip, follower.

fanatic *(SYN.)* bigot, enthusiast, zealot.

fancy *(SYN.)* love, dream, ornate, imagine, suppose, imagination, taste, fantasy, ornamented, elaborate, think. *(ANT.)* plain, undecorated, simple, unadorned.

fantastic *(SYN.)* strange, unusual, odd, wild, unimaginable, incredible, unbelievable, unreal, bizarre, capricious. *(ANT.)* mundane, ordinary, staid, humdrum.

fantasy *(SYN.)* illusion, dream, whim, hallucination, delusion, caprice, mirage, daydream, fancy. *(ANT.)* bore.

far *(SYN.)* removed, much, distant, remote, estranged, alienated. *(ANT.)* close, near.

fare *(SYN.)* prosper, eat, passenger, thrive, toll, progress, succeed.

farewell *(SYN.)* good-by, valediction,

farm

departure, leaving. (ANT.) welcome, greeting.

farm (SYN.) grow, harvest, cultivate, ranch, hire, charter, plantation.

fascinate (SYN.) charm, enchant, bewitch, attract, enthrall.

fashion (SYN.) create, shape, style, mode, make, custom, form, manner, method, way, vogue.

fashionable (SYN.) chic, smart, stylish, modish, elegant, voguish. (ANT.) dowdy, unfashionable.

fast (SYN.) fleet, firm, quick, swift, inflexible, stable, secure, expeditious, rapid, steady, solid, constant, speedy. (ANT.) insecure, sluggish, unstable, loose, slow, unsteady.

fasten (SYN.) secure, bind, tie, join, fix, connect, attach, unite. (ANT.) open, loose, free, loosen, release, separate.

fastidious (SYN.) choosy, selective, discriminating, picky, meticulous.

fat (SYN.) stout, plump, chubby, pudgy, obese, oily, fleshy, greasy, fatty, portly, corpulent, paunchy, wide, thick, rotund. (ANT.) slim, gaunt, emaciated, thin, slender.

fatal (SYN.) killing, lethal, doomed, disastrous, deadly, fateful, mortal. (ANT.) nonfatal.

fate (SYN.) end, fortune, doom, issue, destiny, necessity, portion, result, lot, chance, luck, outcome, consequence, kismet.

father (SYN.) cause, sire, breed, originate, founder, inventor.

fatherly (SYN.) protective, paternal, kind, paternalistic.

fathom (SYN.) penetrate, understand, interpret, comprehend.

fatigue (SYN.) weariness, lassitude, exhaustion, enervation, languor, tiredness. (ANT.) vivacity, rejuvenation, energy, vigor.

fault (SYN.) defect, flaw, mistake, imperfection, shortcoming, error, weakness, responsibility, omission, blemish, blame, failure. (ANT.) perfection, completeness.

faultfinding (SYN.) carping, censorious, critical, caviling, nitpicking.

faulty (SYN.) imperfect, broken, defective,

damaged, impaired. (ANT.) flawless, perfect, whole.

favor (SYN.) resemble, liking, service, prefer, approval, like, support, patronize, benefit. (ANT.) deplore, disapprove.

favorite (SYN.) prized, pet, choice, darling, treasured, preferred.

favoritism (SYN.) prejudice, bias, partiality. (ANT.) fairness, impartiality.

fear (SYN.) horror, terror, fright, trepidation, alarm, consternation, dismay, cowardice, panic, anxiety, dread, scare, apprehension. (ANT.) fearlessness, boldness, courage, assurance.

fearless (SYN.) bold, brave, courageous, gallant, dauntless, confident. (ANT.) timid, fearful, cowardly.

feast (SYN.) dinner, banquet, barbecue.

feat (SYN.) performance, act, operation, accomplishment, achievement, doing, transaction, deed. (ANT.) intention, deliberation, cessation.

feature (SYN.) trait, quality, characteristic, highlight, attribute.

fee (SYN.) payment, pay, remuneration, charge, recompense.

feeble (SYN.) faint, puny, exhausted, delicate, weak, enervated, frail, powerless, forceless, sickly, decrepit, ailing. (ANT.) strong, forceful, powerful, vigorous, stout.

feed (SYN.) satisfy, nourish, food, fodder, forage.

feel (SYN.) sense, experience, perceive.

feeling (SYN.) opinion, sensibility, tenderness, affection, impression, belief, sensation, sympathy, thought, passion, sentiment, attitude, emotion. (ANT.) fact, imperturbability, anesthesia, insensibility.

fellowship (SYN.) clan, society, brotherhood, fraternity, camaraderie, companionship, comradeship, association. (ANT.) dislike, discord, distrust, enmity, strife, acrimony.

felonious (SYN.) murderous, criminal, larcenous.

feminine (SYN.) womanly, girlish, ladylike, female, maidenly, womanish. (ANT.) masculine, male, virile.

rocious *(SYN.)* savage, fierce, wild, blood-thirsty, brutal. *(ANT.) playful, gentle, harmless, calm.*

rtile *(SYN.)* rich, fruitful, teeming, plenteous, bountiful, prolific, luxuriant, productive, fecund. *(ANT.) unproductive, barren, sterile.*

stival *(SYN.)* feast, banquet, regalement, celebration.

stive *(SYN.)* joyful, gay, joyous, merry, gala, jovial, jubilant. *(ANT.) sad, gloomy, mournful, morose.*

tching *(SYN.)* charming, attractive, pleasing, captivating, winsome.

ud *(SYN.)* dispute, quarrel, strife, argument, conflict, controversy. *(ANT.) amity, understanding, harmony, peace.*

ber *(SYN.)* line, strand, thread, string.

ckle *(SYN.)* unstable, capricious, restless, changeable, inconstant, variable. *(ANT.) stable, constant, steady, reliable, dependable.*

ction *(SYN.)* fabrication, romance, falsehood, tale, allegory, narrative, fable, novel, story, invention. *(ANT.) verity, reality, fact, truth.*

ctitious *(SYN.)* invented, make-believe, imaginary, fabricated, unreal, counterfeit, feigned. *(ANT.) real, true, genuine, actual.*

delity *(SYN.)* fealty, devotion, precision, allegiance, exactness, constancy, accuracy, faithfulness, loyalty. *(ANT.) treachery, disloyalty.*

dget *(SYN.)* squirm, twitch, wriggle.

endish *(SYN.)* devilish, demonic, diabolical, savage, satanic.

rce *(SYN.)* furious, wild, savage, violent, ferocious, vehement. *(ANT.) calm, meek, mild, gentle, placid.*

ght *(SYN.)* contend, scuffle, struggle, battle, wrangle, combat, brawl, quarrel, dispute, war, skirmish, conflict.

gure *(SYN.)* design, pattern, mold, shape, form, frame, reckon, calculate, compute, determine.

l *(SYN.)* glut, furnish, store, stuff, occupy, gorge, pervade, content, stock, fill up, supply, sate, replenish, satisfy. *(ANT.) void, drain, exhaust, deplete, empty.*

filter *(SYN.)* screen, strainer, sieve.

filth *(SYN.)* pollution, dirt, sewage, foulness. *(ANT.) cleanliness, innocence, purity.*

filthy *(SYN.)* foul, polluted, dirty, stained, unwashed, squalid. *(ANT.) pure, clean, unspoiled.*

final *(SYN.)* ultimate, decisive, concluding, ending, terminal, last, conclusive, eventual, latest. *(ANT.) inaugural, rudimentary, beginning, initial, incipient, first, original.*

finally *(SYN.)* at last, eventually, ultimately.

find *(SYN.)* observe, detect, discover, locate.

fine *(SYN.)* thin, pure, choice, small, elegant, dainty, splendid, handsome, delicate, nice, powdered, beautiful, minute, exquisite, subtle, pretty, refined. *(ANT.) thick, coarse, rough, blunt, large.*

finicky *(SYN.)* fussy, meticulous, finical, fastidious, prim.

finish *(SYN.)* consummate, close, get done, terminate, accomplish, conclude, execute, perform, complete, end, achieve, fulfill, do, perfect. *(ANT.) open, begin, start, beginning.*

fire *(SYN.)* vigor, glow, combustion, passion, burning, conflagration, ardor, flame, blaze, intensity, fervor. *(ANT.) apathy, cold.*

firm *(SYN.)* solid, rigid, inflexible, stiff, unchanging, steadfast, dense, hard, unshakable, compact, business, company, corporation, partnership. *(ANT.) weak, limp, soft, drooping.*

first *(SYN.)* chief, primary, initial, pristine, beginning, foremost, primeval, earliest, prime, primitive, original. *(ANT.) subordinate, last, least, hindmost, latest.*

fishy *(SYN.)* suspicious, questionable, doubtful. *(ANT.) believable, credible.*

fit *(SYN.)* adjust, suit, suitable, accommodate, conform, robust, harmonize, belong, seizure, spasm, attack, suited, appropriate, healthy, agree, adapt. *(ANT.) misfit, disturb, improper.*

fitful *(SYN.)* variable, restless, fickle, capricious, unstable, changeable. *(ANT.) trustworthy, stable, constant, steady.*

fitting *(SYN.)* apt, due, suitable, proper. *(ANT.) improper, unsuitable, inappropriate.*

fix

fix *(SYN.)* mend, regulate, affix, set, tie, repair, attach, settle, link, bind, determine, establish, define, place, rectify, stick, limit, adjust, fasten. *(ANT.)* *damage, change, mistreat, displace, alter, disturb, mutilate.*

fixation *(SYN.)* fetish, obsession, infatuation, compulsion.

flair *(SYN.)* style, dash, flamboyance, drama, gift, knack, aptitude.

flamboyant *(SYN.)* showy, flashy, gaudy, ostentatious.

flame *(SYN.)* blaze, fire.

flash *(SYN.)* flare, flame, wink, twinkling, instant, gleam.

flashy *(SYN.)* tawdry, tasteless, pretentious, garish, flamboyant.

flat *(SYN.)* vapid, stale, even, smooth, tasteless, horizontal, dull, level, insipid, uninteresting, lifeless, boring. *(ANT.)* *tasty, racy, hilly, savory, stimulating, interesting, broken, sloping.*

flattery *(SYN.)* compliment, praise, applause, blarney, acclaim.

flaunt *(SYN.)* exhibit, show off, display, parade. *(ANT.)* *conceal, hide, disguise.*

flavor *(SYN.)* tang, taste, savor, essence, quality, character, season, spice.

flaw *(SYN.)* spot, imperfection, blemish, fault, deformity, blotch.

flee *(SYN.)* fly, abscond, hasten, escape, run away, decamp, evade. *(ANT.)* *remain, appear, stay, arrive.*

fleece *(SYN.)* filch, rob, purloin, swindle, defraud, pilfer, cheat.

fleet *(SYN.)* rapid, swift, quick, fast. *(ANT.)* *unhurried, sluggish, slow.*

fleeting *(SYN.)* brief, swift, passing, temporary. *(ANT.)* *stable, fixed, lasting, permanent.*

fleshy *(SYN.)* overweight, chubby, stocky, plump, obese, stout. *(ANT.)* *spare, underweight, skinny.*

flexible *(SYN.)* lithe, resilient, pliable, tractable, complaint, elastic, yielding, adaptable, agreeable, supple, pliant, easy, ductile. *(ANT.)* *hard, unbending, firm, brittle, inflexible, rigid, fired.*

flighty *(SYN.)* giddy, light-headed, frivolous, irresponsible. *(ANT.)* *sol responsible, steady.*

flimsy *(SYN.)* wobbly, weak, frail, fragi unsteady, delicate, thin. *(ANT.)* *durab stable, firm, strong.*

fling *(SYN.)* pitch, throw, toss, fun, celebr tion, party.

flippant *(SYN.)* disrespectful, sassy, i solent, brazen, rude, impertinent. *(AN courteous, polite, mannerly.*

flit *(SYN.)* flutter, scurry, hasten, dart, ski

flock *(SYN.)* gathering, group, fligl swarm, herd, school.

flog *(SYN.)* thrash, lash, switch, strike, pa dle.

flood *(SYN.)* overflow, deluge, inunda cascade.

florid *(SYN.)* gaudy, fancy, ornate, er bellished. *(ANT.)* *spare, simple, plain.*

flourish *(SYN.)* succeed, grow, prosp wave, thrive, bloom. *(ANT.)* *wither, wa die, decline.*

flout *(SYN.)* disdain, scorn, spurn, igno taunt, ridicule, mock.

flow *(SYN.)* proceed, abound, spout, con stream, run, originate, emanate, resu pour, squirt, issue, gush, spurt.

fluctuate *(SYN.)* vary, oscillate, chang waver, hesitate, vacillate. *(ANT.)* *pers stick, adhere, resolve.*

fluent *(SYN.)* graceful, glib, flowing.

fluid *(SYN.)* liquid, running, liquefied.

flush *(SYN.)* abundant, flat, even, level.

fluster *(SYN.)* rattle, flurry, agitate, ups perturb, quiver, vibrate.

fly *(SYN.)* flee, mount, shoot, decan hover, soar, flit, flutter, sail, escape, ru spring, glide, abscond, dart, float. *(AN sink, descend, plummet.*

foam *(SYN.)* suds, froth, lather.

foe *(SYN.)* opponent, enemy, antagonist, adv sary. *(ANT.)* *associate, ally, friend, comrade.*

fog *(SYN.)* haze, mist, cloud, daze, con sion, stupor, vapor, smog.

foible *(SYN.)* frailty, weakness, faili shortcoming, kink.

foist *(SYN.)* misrepresent, insinuate, fals

fold *(SYN.)* lap, double, overlap, clasp, ple

tuck.

llow *(SYN.)* trail, observe, succeed, ensue, obey, chase, comply, accompany, copy, result, imitate, heed, adopt. *(ANT.)* elude, cause, precede, avoid, flee.

llower *(SYN.)* supporter, devotee, henchman, adherent, partisan, votary, attendant, disciple, successor. *(ANT.)* master, head, chief, dissenter.

llowing *(SYN.)* public, disciples, supporters, clientele, customers.

lly *(SYN.)* silliness, foolishness, indiscretion, absurdity, imprudence, imbecility, stupidity, extravagance. *(ANT.)* reasonableness, judgment, sense, prudence, wisdom.

nd *(SYN.)* affectionate, loving, attached, tender, devoted. *(ANT.)* hostile, cool, distant, unfriendly.

ndness *(SYN.)* partiality, liking, affection. *(ANT.)* hostility, unfriendliness.

od *(SYN.)* viands, edibles, feed, repast, nutriment, sustenance, diet, bread, provisions, meal, rations, victuals, fare. *(ANT.)* want, hunger, drink, starvation.

ol *(SYN.)* dunce, jester, idiot, simpleton, buffoon, harlequin, dolt, blockhead, numskull, clown, dope, trick, deceive, nincompoop. *(ANT.)* scholar, genius, sage.

olish *(SYN.)* senseless, irrational, crazy, silly, brainless, idiotic, simple, nonsensical, stupid, preposterous, asinine. *(ANT.)* sane, sound, sensible, rational, judicious, wise, reasonable, prudent.

oting *(SYN.)* base, basis, foundation.

otloose *(SYN.)* uncommitted, free, detached, independent. *(ANT.)* engaged, rooted, involved.

rbearance *(SYN.)* moderation, abstinence, abstention, continence. *(ANT.)* greed, excess, intoxication.

rbid *(SYN.)* disallow, prevent, ban, prohibit, taboo, outlaw. *(ANT.)* approve, let, allow, permit.

rbidding *(SYN.)* evil, hostile, unfriendly, sinister, scary, repulsive. *(ANT.)* pleasant, beneficent, friendly.

rce *(SYN.)* energy, might, violence, vigor, intensity, dint, power, constraint, coercion, compel, compulsion, oblige, make, coerce, strength. *(ANT.)* weakness, frailty, persuasion, feebleness, impotence, ineffectiveness.

forceful *(SYN.)* dynamic, vigorous, energetic, potent, drastic, intense. *(ANT.)* lackadaisical, insipid, weak.

foreboding *(SYN.)* misgiving, suspicion, apprehension, presage, intuition.

forecast *(SYN.)* prophesy, predict.

foregoing *(SYN.)* above, former, preceding, previous, prior. *(ANT.)* later, coming, below, follow.

foreign *(SYN.)* alien, strange, exotic, different, unfamiliar. *(ANT.)* commonplace, ordinary, familiar.

foreigner *(SYN.)* outsider, alien, newcomer, stranger. *(ANT.)* native.

foreman *(SYN.)* super, boss, overseer, supervisor.

forerunner *(SYN.)* harbinger, proclaimer, informant.

foresee *(SYN.)* forecast, expect, anticipate, surmise, envisage.

forest *(SYN.)* grove, woodland, wood, copse, woods.

forestall *(SYN.)* hinder, thwart, prevent, obstruct, repel.

foretell *(SYN.)* soothsay, divine, predict.

forever *(SYN.)* evermore, always, everlasting, hereafter, endlessly. *(ANT.)* fleeting, temporarily.

forfeit *(SYN.)* yield, resign, lose, sacrifice.

forgive *(SYN.)* exonerate, clear, excuse, pardon. *(ANT.)* impeach, accuse, blame, censure.

forgo *(SYN.)* relinquish, release, surrender, waive, abandon. *(ANT.)* keep, retain.

forlorn *(SYN.)* pitiable, desolate, dejected, woeful, wretched. *(ANT.)* optimistic, cherished, cheerful.

form *(SYN.)* frame, compose, fashion, arrange, construct, make up, devise, create, invent, mold, shape, forge, organize, produce, constitute, make. *(ANT.)* wreck, dismantle, destroy, misshape.

formal *(SYN.)* exact, stiff, correct, outward, conformist, conventional, affected, regular, proper, ceremonious, decorous, methodical, precise, solemn, external,

former

perfunctory. (*ANT.*) *heartfelt, uncon-strained, easy, unconventional.*

former (*SYN.*) earlier, previous, erstwhile, prior.

formidable (*SYN.*) alarming, frightful, imposing, terrible, terrifying, dire, fearful, forbidding. (*ANT.*) *weak, unimpressive, ordinary.*

forsake (*SYN.*) abandon, desert, forgo, quit, discard, neglect.

forte (*SYN.*) gift, capability, talent, specialty, aptitude, bulwark.

forth (*SYN.*) out, onward, forward.

forthright (*SYN.*) honest, direct, candid, outspoken, blunt, sincere, plain, explicit.

forthwith (*SYN.*) instantly, promptly, immediately. (*ANT.*) *afterward, later, ultimately, slowly.*

fortify (*SYN.*) bolster, strengthen, buttress, barricade, defend.

fortuitous (*SYN.*) successful, benign, lucky, advantageous, propitious, happy, favored, chance. (*ANT.*) *unlucky, condemned.*

fortunate (*SYN.*) happy, auspicious, fortuitous, successful, favored, advantageous, benign, charmed, lucky, felicitous, blessed, propitious, blissful. (*ANT.*) *ill-fated, cheerless, unlucky, unfortunate, cursed, condemned.*

fortune (*SYN.*) chance, fate, lot, luck, riches, wealth, kismet, destiny.

fortuneteller (*SYN.*) soothsayer, clairvoyant, forecaster, oracle, medium.

forward (*SYN.*) leading, front, promote, elevate, advance, first, ahead, onward, further, foremost, aggrandize. (*ANT.*) *withhold, retard, hinder, retreat, oppose.*

foul (*SYN.*) base, soiled, dirty, mean, unclean, polluted, impure, vile, evil, muddy, wicked, rainy, stormy, despicable, filthy. (*ANT.*) *pure, neat, wholesome, clean.*

found (*SYN.*) organize, establish.

foundation (*SYN.*) support, root, base, underpinning, groundwork, bottom, establishment, substructure, basis. (*ANT.*) *top, cover, building.*

foxy (*SYN.*) cunning, sly, artful, crafty, wily, sharp, shrewd, slick.

fraction (*SYN.*) fragment, part, section, morsel, share, piece.

fracture (*SYN.*) crack, break, rupture.

fragile (*SYN.*) delicate, frail, weak, breakable, infirm, brittle, feeble. (*ANT.*) *tough, hardy, sturdy, strong, stout, durable.*

fragment (*SYN.*) scrap, piece, bit, remnant, part, splinter, segment.

fragrance (*SYN.*) odor, smell, scent, perfume, aroma.

fragrant (*SYN.*) aromatic, scented, perfumed.

frail (*SYN.*) feeble, weak, delicate, breakable, fragile. (*ANT.*) *sturdy, strong, powerful.*

frame (*SYN.*) support, framework, skeleton, molding, border, mount.

frank (*SYN.*) honest, candid, open, unreserved, direct, sincere, straight-forward. (*ANT.*) *tricky, dishonest.*

frantic (*SYN.*) frenzied, crazed, raving, panicky. (*ANT.*) *composed, stoic.*

fraud (*SYN.*) deception, guile, swindle, deceit, artifice, imposture, trick, cheat, imposition, duplicity, chicanery. (*ANT.*) *sincerity, fairness, integrity.*

fraudulent (*SYN.*) tricky, fake, dishonest, deceitful.

fray (*SYN.*) strife, fight, battle, struggle, tussle, combat, brawl, melee, skirmish. (*ANT.*) *truce, agreement, peace, concord.*

freak (*SYN.*) curiosity, abnormality, monster, oddity.

free (*SYN.*) munificent, clear, autonomous, immune, open, freed, bountiful, liberated, unfastened, emancipate, unconfined, unobstructed, easy, artless, loose, familiar, bounteous, unrestricted, liberal, independent, careless, frank, exempt. (*ANT.*) *stingy, clogged, illiberal, confined, parsimonious.*

freedom (*SYN.*) independence, privilege, familiarity, unrestraint, liberty, exemption, liberation, immunity, license. (*ANT.*) *servitude, constraint, bondage, slavery, necessity.*

freely (*SYN.*) liberally, generous, unstintingly.

fuzzy

freight *(SYN.)* shipping, cargo, load, shipment.

frenzy *(SYN.)* craze, agitation, excitement.

frequent *(SYN.)* usual, habitual, common, often, customary, general. *(ANT.)* unique, rare, solitary, uncommon, exceptional, infrequent, scanty.

fresh *(SYN.)* recent, new, additional, modern, further, refreshing, natural, brisk, novel, inexperienced, late, current, sweet, pure, cool. *(ANT.)* stagnant, decayed, musty, faded.

fret *(SYN.)* torment, worry, grieve, anguish.

fretful *(SYN.)* testy, irritable, touchy, peevish, short-tempered. *(ANT.)* calm.

friend *(SYN.)* crony, supporter, ally, companion, intimate, associate, comrade, mate, patron, acquaintance, chum, defender. *(ANT.)* stranger, adversary.

friendly *(SYN.)* sociable, kindly, affable, genial, companionable, social, neighborly, amicable. *(ANT.)* hostile, antagonistic, reserved.

friendship *(SYN.)* knowledge, familiarity, fraternity, acquaintance, intimacy, fellowship, comradeship, cognizance. *(ANT.)* unfamiliarity, ignorance.

fright *(SYN.)* alarm, fear, panic, terror.

frighten *(SYN.)* scare, horrify, daunt, affright, appall, terrify, alarm, terrorize, astound, dismay, startle, panic. *(ANT.)* soothe, embolden, compose, reassure.

frigid *(SYN.)* cold, wintry, icy, glacial, arctic, freezing.

fringe *(SYN.)* hem, edge, border, trimming, edging.

frisky *(SYN.)* animated, lively, peppy, vivacious.

frolic *(SYN.)* play, cavort, romp, frisk.

front *(SYN.)* facade, face, start, beginning, border, head. *(ANT.)* rear, back.

frontier *(SYN.)* border, boundary.

frugal *(SYN.)* parsimonious, saving, stingy, provident, temperate, economical, sparing. *(ANT.)* extravagant, wasteful, self-indulgent, intemperate.

fruitful *(SYN.)* fertile, rich, bountiful, teeming, fecund, productive, luxuriant. *(ANT.)* lean, barren, sterile.

fruitless *(SYN.)* barren, futile, vain, sterile, unproductive. *(ANT.)* fertile, productive.

frustrate *(SYN.)* hinder, defeat, thwart, circumvent, outwit, foil, baffle, disappoint, balk, discourage, prevent. *(ANT.)* promote, accomplish, further.

fulfill *(SYN.)* do, effect, complete, accomplish, realize.

full *(SYN.)* baggy, crammed, entire, satiated, flowing, perfect, gorged, soaked, complete, filled, packed, extensive. *(ANT.)* lacking, partial, empty, depleted.

full-grown *(SYN.)* ripe, adult, mature, developed, grown-up, complete. *(ANT.)* green, young, unripe, adolescent.

fulsome *(SYN.)* disgusting, repulsive, nauseating, repellent, revolting.

fume *(SYN.)* gas, steam, smoke, rage, rave, vapor.

fun *(SYN.)* merriment, pleasure, enjoyment, piety, sport, amusement.

function *(SYN.)* operation, activity, affair, ceremony, gathering, party.

fundamental *(SYN.)* basic, essential, primary, elementary.

funny *(SYN.)* odd, droll, ridiculous, farcical, laughable, comic, curious, amusing. *(ANT.)* solemn, sad, sober, melancholy.

furious *(SYN.)* angry, enraged. *(ANT.)* serene, calm.

furnish *(SYN.)* yield, give, endow, fit, produce, equip, afford, decorate, supply. *(ANT.)* divest, denude, strip.

furor *(SYN.)* commotion, tumult, turmoil.

furtive *(SYN.)* surreptitious, secret, hidden, clandestine. *(ANT.)* honest, open.

fury *(SYN.)* wrath, anger, frenzy, rage, violence, fierceness. *(ANT.)* calmness, serenity.

fuss *(SYN.)* commotion, bother, pester, annoy, irritate.

futile *(SYN.)* pointless, idle, vain, useless, worthless, minor. *(ANT.)* weighty, important, worthwhile, serious, valuable.

future *(SYN.)* approaching, imminent, coming, impending. *(ANT.)* former, past.

fuzzy (SYN.) indistinct, blurred. (ANT.) lucid, clear.

G

gab *(SYN.)* jabber, babble, chatter, prattle, gossip.

gabble *(SYN.)* chatter, babble, jabber, blab, prate, gaggle, prattle, gibberish.

gabby *(SYN.)* chatty, talkative, wordy, verbose.

gad *(SYN.)* wander, roam, rove, ramble, meander, cruise.

gadget *(SYN.)* contrivance, device, doodad, jigger, thing, contraption.

gaffe *(SYN.)* blunder, boner, mistake, gaucherie, error, howler.

gag *(SYN.)* witticism, crack, jest, joke.

gaiety *(SYN.)* joyousness, cheerfulness, joyfulness, light-heartedness. *(ANT.)* melancholy, sadness, depression.

gain *(SYN.)* acquire, avail, account, good, interest, attain, favor, achieve, get, secure, advantage, earn, profit, procure. *(ANT.)* trouble, lose, calamity, forfeit, handicap, lose, distress.

gainful *(SYN.)* lucrative, rewarding, profitable, beneficial, payable, productive. *(ANT.)* unprofitable, unrewarding.

gainsay *(SYN.)* refute, contradict, controvert, deny, refuse, impugn, contravene, disavow, differ. *(ANT.)* aver, affirm, asseverate.

gait *(SYN.)* stride, walk, tread, step.

gala *(SYN.)* ball, party, carnival, festival.

gale *(SYN.)* burst, surge, outburst.

gall *(SYN.)* nerve, audacity, impudence, annoy, vex, anger, provoke, irritate.

gallant *(SYN.)* bold, brave, courageous, valorous, valiant, noble, polite, fearless, heroic, chivalrous.

gallantry *(SYN.)* valor, daring, courage, prowess, heroism, manliness, dauntlessness, graciousness, attentiveness. *(ANT.)* poltroonery, timidity, cowardice, cravenness, cloddishness.

gallery *(SYN.)* passageway, hall, aisle, hallway, passage, corridor.

galling *(SYN.)* vexing, irritating, annoying, distressful, irksome.

galore *(SYN.)* abounding, plentiful, profuse, rich, overflowing.

gamble *(SYN.)* game, wager, bet, hazard, risk, venture, chance.

gambol *(SYN.)* romp, dance, cavort, frolic.

game *(SYN.)* fun, contest, merriment, pastime, match, play, amusement, recreation, diversion, entertainment. *(ANT.)* labor, hardship, work, business.

gamut *(SYN.)* extent, scope, sweep, horizon, range.

gang *(SYN.)* group, troop, band, company, horde, crew.

gangling *(SYN.)* rangy, lean, skinny, tall, lanky.

gangster *(SYN.)* crook, hoodlum, gunman, criminal.

gap *(SYN.)* cavity, chasm, pore, gulf, aperture, abyss, interval, space, hole, void, pore, break, opening.

gape *(SYN.)* ogle, stare, gawk.

garb *(SYN.)* clothing, dress, vesture, array, attire, clothes, drapery, apparel, garment, costume, raiment.

garbage *(SYN.)* refuse, waste, trash, rubbish.

gargantuan *(SYN.)* colossal, monumental, giant, huge, large, enormous.

garments *(SYN.)* drapery, dress, garb, apparel, array, attire, clothes, vesture. *(ANT.)* nakedness, nudity.

garnish *(SYN.)* decorate, embellish, trim, adorn, enrich, beautify, deck, ornament. *(ANT.)* expose, strip, debase, uncover, defame.

garrulous *(SYN.)* chatty, glib, verbose, talkative, communicative, voluble. *(ANT.)* silent, uncommunicative, laconic, reticent, taciturn.

gash *(SYN.)* lacerate, slash, pierce, cut, hew, slice.

gasp *(SYN.)* pant, puff, wheeze.

gather *(SYN.)* assemble, collect, garner, harvest, reap, deduce, judge, amass, congregate, muster, cull, glean, accumulate, convene. *(ANT.)* scatter, disperse, distribute, disband, separate.

gathering *(SYN.)* meeting, crowd, throng, company, assembly.

gaudy *(SYN.)* showy, flashy, loud, bold, ostentatious.

gaunt *(SYN.)* lank, flimsy, gauzy, narrow, rare, scanty, meager, gossamer, emaciated, scrawny, tenuous, thin, fine, lean, skinny, spare, slim, slight, slender, diluted. *(ANT.)* wide, fat, thick, broad, bulky.

gay *(SYN.)* merry, lighthearted, joyful, cheerful, sprightly, jolly, happy, joyous, gleeful, jovial, colorful, bright, glad. *(ANT.)* glum, mournful, sad, depressed, sorrowful, somber, sullen.

gaze *(SYN.)* look, stare, view, watch, examine, observe, glance, behold, discern, seem, see, survey, witness, inspect, goggle, appear. *(ANT.)* hide, overlook, avert, miss.

geld *(SYN.)* neuter, alter, spay, castrate.

gem *(SYN.)* jewel, semiprecious stone.

general *(SYN.)* ordinary, universal, usual, common, customary, regular, vague, miscellaneous, indefinite, inexact. *(ANT.)* definite, particular, exceptional, singular, rare, precise, exact, specific.

generally *(SYN.)* ordinarily, usually, customarily, normally, mainly. *(ANT.)* seldom, infrequently, rare.

generate *(SYN.)* produce, bestow, impart, concede, permit, acquiesce, cede, relent, succumb, surrender, pay, supply, grant, bear, afford, submit, waive, allow, breed, accord, accede, abdicate, resign, relinquish, surrender, quit. *(ANT.)* assert, refuse, smuggle, resist, dissent, oppose, deny, strive.

generation *(SYN.)* age, date, era, period, seniority, senescence, senility, time, epoch, dotage. *(ANT.)* infancy, youth, childhood.

generosity *(SYN.)* magnanimity, benevolence, humanity, kindness, philanthropy, tenderness, altruism, liberality, charity, beneficence. *(ANT.)* selfishness, malevolence, cruelty, inhumanity, unkindness.

generous *(SYN.)* giving, liberal, unselfish, magnanimous, bountiful, munificent, charitable, big, noble, beneficent. *(ANT.)* greedy, stingy, selfish, covetous, mew, miserly.

genesis *(SYN.)* birth, root, creation, source, origin, beginning.

genius *(SYN.)* intellect, adept, intellectual, sagacity, proficient, creativity, ability, inspiration, faculty, originality, aptitude, brain, gift, prodigy, talent. *(ANT.)* dullard, stupidity, dolt, shallowness, moron, ineptitude, obtuseness.

genre *(SYN.)* chaste, order, set, elegance, class, excellence, kind, caste, denomination, grade.

genteel *(SYN.)* cultured, polished, polite, refined, elegant. *(ANT.)* discourteous, churlish, common.

gentle *(SYN.)* peaceful, placid, tame, serene, relaxed, docile, benign, soothing, calm, soft, mild, amiable, friendly, kindly, cultivated. *(ANT.)* nasty, harsh, rough, fierce, mew, violent, savage.

genuine *(SYN.)* real, true, unaffected, authentic, sincere, bona fide, unadulterated, legitimate, actual, veritable, definite, proven. *(ANT.)* false, sham, artificial, fake, counterfeit, bogus, pretended, insincere.

genus *(SYN.)* kind, race, species, type, variety, character, family, breed, sort.

germ *(SYN.)* pest, virus, contamination, disease, pollution, taint, infection, contagion, poison, ailment.

germinate *(SYN.)* vegetate, pullulate, sprout, develop, grow.

gesture *(SYN.)* omen, signal, symbol, emblem, indication, note, token, symptom, movement, sign, motion.

get *(SYN.)* obtain, receive, attain, gain, achieve, acquire, procure, earn, fetch, carry, remove, prepare, take, ready, urge, induce, secure. *(ANT.)* lose, surrender, forfeit, leave, renounce.

ghastly *(SYN.)* frightful, horrible, horrifying, frightening, grisly, hideous, dreadful.

ghost *(SYN.)* phantom, spook, apparition, specter, trace, hint, vestige, spirit.

ghoulish *(SYN.)* weird, eerie, horrifying, gruesome, sinister, scary.

giant *(SYN.)* monster, colossus, mammoth, superman, gigantic. *(ANT.)* small, tiny, dwarf, runt, midget, infinitesimal.

gibe *(SYN.)* sneer, jeer, mock, scoff, boo, hoot, hiss. *(ANT.)* approve.

giddy *(SYN.)* reeling, dizzy, flighty, silly, scatterbrained. *(ANT.)* serious.

gift *(SYN.)* endowment, favor, gratuity, bequest, talent, charity, present, largess, donation, grant, aptitude, boon, offering, faculty, genius, benefaction. *(ANT.)* purchase, loss, ineptitude, deprivation, earnings.

gigantic *(SYN.)* huge, colossal, immense, large, vast, elephantine, gargantuan, prodigious, mammoth, monumental, enormous. *(ANT.)* small, tiny, minute, diminutive, little.

giggle *(SYN.)* chuckle, jeer, laugh, roar, snicker, titter, cackle, guffaw, mock.

gild *(SYN.)* cover, coat, paint, embellish, sweeten, retouch, camouflage.

gingerly *(SYN.)* gentle, cautiously, carefully, gently. *(ANT.)* roughly.

gird *(SYN.)* wrap, tie, bind, belt, encircle, surround, get set, prepare.

girl *(SYN.)* female, lass, miss, maiden, damsel.

girth *(SYN.)* measure, size, width, dimensions, expanse, proportions.

gist *(SYN.)* connotation, explanation, purpose, significance, acceptation, implication, interpretation, meaning. *(ANT.)* redundancy.

give *(SYN.)* bestow, contribute, grant, impart, provide, donate, confer, deliver, present, furnish, yield, develop, offer, produce, hand over, award, allot, deal out, mete out, bend, sacrifice, supply. *(ANT.)* withdraw, take, retain, keep, seize.

given *(SYN.)* handed over, presented, supposed, stated, disposed, assumed, inclined.

glacier *(SYN.)* frigid, icy, iceberg.

glad *(SYN.)* happy, cheerful, gratified, delighted, joyous, merry, pleased, exulting, charmed, thrilled, satisfied, tickled, gay, bright. *(ANT.)* sad, depressed, dejected, melancholy, unhappy, morose, somber, despondent.

glade *(SYN.)* clearing.

gladiator *(SYN.)* battler, fighter, competitor, combatant, contender, contestant.

gladness *(SYN.)* bliss, contentment, happiness, pleasure, well-being, beatitude, delight, satisfaction, blessedness. *(ANT.)* sadness, sorrow, despair, misery, grief.

glamorous *(SYN.)* spellbinding, fascinating, alluring, charming, bewitching, entrancing, captivating, enchanting, attractive, appealing, enticing, enthralling.

glamour *(SYN.)* charm, allure, attraction, magnetism, fascination.

glance *(SYN.)* eye, gaze, survey, view, examine, inspect, discern, look, see, witness, peek, regard, skim, reflect, glimpse, behold, observe. *(ANT.)* miss, overlook.

glare *(SYN.)* flash, dazzle, stare, glower, glow, shine, glaze, burn, brilliance, flare, blind, scowl.

glaring *(SYN.)* flagrant, obvious, blatant, prominent, dazzling.

glass *(SYN.)* cup, tumbler, goblet, pane, crystal.

glassy *(SYN.)* blank, empty, emotionless, vacant, fixed, expressionless.

glaze *(SYN.)* buff, luster, cover, wax, gloss, coat, polish, shellac.

gleam *(SYN.)* flash, glimmer, glisten, shimmer, sparkle, twinkle, glare, beam, glow, radiate, glimmering, shine, burn, reflection, blaze.

glean *(SYN.)* reap, gather, select, harvest, pick, separate, cull.

glee *(SYN.)* mirth, joy, gladness, enchantment, delight, cheer, bliss, elation, merriment. *(ANT.)* depression, misery, dejection.

glen *(SYN.)* ravine, valley.

glib *(SYN.)* smooth, suave, flat, plain, polished, sleek, urbane. *(ANT.)* rough, rugged, blunt, harsh, bluff.

glide *(SYN.)* sweep, sail, fly, flow, slip, coast, cruise, move easily, skim, slide.

glimmer *(SYN.)* blink, shimmer, flicker, indication, hint, clue, suggestion.

glimpse *(SYN.)* notice, glance, peek, see, impression, look, flash.

glint *(SYN.)* flash, gleam, peek, glance, glimpse, sparkle, glitter.

glisten *(SYN.)* shimmer, shine, glimmer, twinkle, glitter, glister, sparkle.

glitch (SYN.) mishap, snag, hitch, malfunction.

glitter (SYN.) glisten, glimmer, sparkle, shine, twinkle.

gloat (SYN.) triumph, exult, glory, rejoice, revel.

global (SYN.) universal, international, worldwide.

globe (SYN.) orb, ball, world, earth, map, universe, sphere.

gloom (SYN.) bleakness, despondency, misery, sadness, woe, darkness, dejection, obscurity, blackness, shadow, shade, dimness, shadows, melancholy. (ANT.) joy, mirth, exultation, cheerfulness, light, happiness, brightness, frivolity.

gloomy (SYN.) despondent, dismal, glum, somber, sorrowful, sad, dejected, disconsolate, dim, dark, morose, dispirited, moody, grave, pensive. (ANT.) happy, merry, cheerful, high-spirited, bright, sunny, joyous.

glorify (SYN.) enthrone, exalt, honor, revere, adore, dignify, enshrine, consecrate, praise, worship, laud, venerate. (ANT.) mock, dishonor, debase, abuse, degrade.

glorious (SYN.) exalted, high, noble, splendid, supreme, elevated, lofty, raised, majestic, famous, noted, stately, distinguished, celebrated, renowned, famed, magnificent, grand, proud, impressive, elegant, sublime. (ANT.) ridiculous, low, base, ignoble, terrible, ordinary.

glory (SYN.) esteem, praise, respect, reverence, admiration, honor, dignity, worship, eminence, homage, deference. (ANT.) dishonor, disgrace, contempt, reproach, derision.

gloss (SYN.) luster, shine, glow, sheen.

glossary (SYN.) dictionary, thesaurus, wordbook, lexicon.

glossy (SYN.) smooth, glistening, shiny, sleek, polished. (ANT.) matte, dull.

glow (SYN.) beam, glisten, radiate, shimmer, sparkle, glare, blaze, scintillate, shine, light, gleam, burn, flare, flame, dazzle, blush, redden, heat, warmth, flicker.

glower (SYN.) scowl, stare, frown, glare. (ANT.) beam, grin, smile.

glowing (SYN.) fiery, intense, passionate, zealous, enthusiastic, ardent, eager, fervent, favorable, impassioned, keen, complimentary, vehement. (ANT.) cool, indifferent, apathetic, nonchalant.

glue (SYN.) bind, fasten, cement, paste.

glum (SYN.) morose, sulky, fretful, crabbed, sullen, dismal, dour, moody. (ANT.) joyous, merry, amiable, gay, pleasant.

glut (SYN.) gorge, sate, content, furnish, fill, pervade, satiate, stuff, replenish, fill up, satisfy, stock. (ANT.) empty, exhaust, deplete, void, drain.

glutton (SYN.) pig, hog, greedy eater.

gluttony (SYN.) ravenousness, piggishness, devouring, hoggishness, insatiability, voraciousness. (ANT.) satisfaction, fullness.

gnarled (SYN.) twisted, knotted, rugged, knobby, nodular.

gnash (SYN.) gnaw, crunch, grind.

gnaw (SYN.) chew, eat, gnash, grind, erode.

go (SYN.) proceed, depart, flee, move, vanish, exit, walk, quit, fade, progress, travel, become, fit, agree, leave, suit, harmonize, pass, travel, function, operate, withdraw. (ANT.) stay, arrive, enter, stand, come.

goad (SYN.) incite, prod, drive, urge, push, shove, jab, provoke, stimulate.

goal (SYN.) craving, destination, desire, longing, objective, finish, end, passion, aim, object, aspiration.

gobble (SYN.) devour, eat fast, gorge, gulp, stuff.

goblet (SYN.) cup, glass.

goblin (SYN.) troll, elf, dwarf, spirit.

godlike (SYN.) holy, supernatural, heavenly, celestial, divine, transcendent. (ANT.) profane, wicked, blasphemous, diabolical, mundane.

godly (SYN.) pious, religious, holy, pure, divine, spiritual, righteous, saintly.

golden (SYN.) shining, metallic, bright, fine, superior, nice, excellent, valuable. (ANT.) dull, inferior.

gong (SYN.) chimes, bells.

good (SYN.) honest, sound, valid, cheerful, honorable, worthy, conscientious, moral, genuine, humane, kind, fair, useful, skilful, adequate, friendly, genial, proficient, pleasant, exemplary, admirable, virtuous, reliable, precious, benevolent, excellent, pure, agreeable, gracious, safe, commendable. (*ANT.*) *bad, imperfect, vicious, undesirable, unfriendly, unkind, evil.*

good-bye *(SYN.)* so long, farewell.

good-hearted *(SYN.)* good, kind, thoughtful, kindhearted, considerate. (*ANT.*) *evil-hearted.*

good-humored *(SYN.)* pleasant, good-natured, cheerful, sunny, amiable. (*ANT.*) *petulant, cranky.*

goodness *(SYN.)* good, honesty, integrity, virtue, righteousness. (*ANT.*) *sin, evil, dishonesty, corruption.*

goods *(SYN.)* property, belongings, holdings, possessions, merchandise, wares.

good will *(SYN.)* harmony, willingness, readiness.

gore *(SYN.)* impale, penetrate, puncture, gouge.

gorge *(SYN.)* ravine, devour, stuff, gobble, valley, defile, pass, cram, fill.

gorgeous *(SYN.)* grand, ravishing, glorious, stunning, brilliant, divine, splendid, dazzling, beautiful, magnificent. (*ANT.*) *homely, ugly, squalid.*

gory *(SYN.)* bloody.

gossamer *(SYN.)* dainty, fine, filmy, delicate, sheer, transparent.

gossip *(SYN.)* prate, rumor, prattle, hearsay, meddler, tattler, chatter, talk, chat, blabbermouth.

gouge *(SYN.)* scoop, dig, carve, burrow, excavate, chisel, notch.

gourmet *(SYN.)* gourmand, gastronome, connoisseur.

govern *(SYN.)* manage, oversee, reign, preside over, supervise, direct, command, sway, administer, control, regulate, determine, influence, guide, lead, head, rule. (*ANT.*) *assent, submit, acquiesce, obey, yield.*

government *(SYN.)* control, direction, rule, command, authority.

governor *(SYN.)* controller, administrator, director, leader, manager.

gown *(SYN.)* garment, robe, frock, dress, costume, attire.

grab *(SYN.)* snatch, grip, clutch, seize, grasp, capture, pluck.

grace *(SYN.)* charm, beauty, handsomeness, loveliness, dignify, fairness, honor, distinguish, sympathy, attractiveness, elegance, clemency, excuse, pardon, thanks, blessing, prayer, pulchritude. (*ANT.*) *eyesore, homeliness, deformity, ugliness.*

graceful *(SYN.)* elegant, fluid, natural, supple, beautiful, comely, flowing, lithe. (*ANT.*) *clumsy, awkward, gawky, ungainly, deformed.*

gracious *(SYN.)* warm-hearted, pleasing, friendly, engaging, agreeable, kind, amiable, kindly, nice, good, courteous, polite, generous, good-natured. (*ANT.*) *surly, hateful, churlish, rude, disagreeable, impolite, thoughtless, discourteous, ill-natured.*

grade *(SYN.)* kind, rank, elegance, denomination, sort, arrange, category, classify, rate, group, place, mark, incline, slope, excellence, caste, order.

gradual *(SYN.)* deliberate, sluggish, dawdling, laggard, slow, leisurely, moderate, easy, delaying. (*ANT.*) *quick, swift, fast, speedy, raid.*

graduate *(SYN.)* pass, finish, advance.

graft *(SYN.)* fraud, theft, cheating, bribery, dishonesty, transplant, corruption.

grain *(SYN.)* speck, particle, plant, bit, seed, temper, fiber, character, texture, markings, nature, tendency.

grand *(SYN.)* great, elaborate, splendid, royal, stately, noble, considerable, outstanding, distinguished, impressive, prominent, majestic, fine, dignified, large, main, principal. (*ANT.*) *unassuming, modest, insignificant, unimportant, humble.*

grandeur *(SYN.)* resplendence, majesty, distinction, glory.

grandiose *(SYN.)* grand, lofty, magnificent, stately, noble, pompous, dignified, imposing, sublime, majestic. (*ANT.*) *lowly, ordinary, common, undignified, humble.*

grandstand *(SYN.)* bleachers, gallery.

granite *(SYN.)* stone, rock.

grant *(SYN.)* confer, allocate, deal, divide, mete, appropriation, assign, benefaction, distribute, allowance, donate, award, mete out, deal out, consent, bestow, give, measure. *(ANT.)* refuse, withhold, confiscate, keep, retain.

granular *(SYN.)* grainy, sandy, crumbly, rough, gritty.

graph *(SYN.)* design, plan, stratagem, draw up, chart, sketch, cabal, machination, outline, plot, scheme, diagram.

graphic *(SYN.)* vivid, lifelike, significant, meaningful, pictorial, descriptive, representative.

grapple *(SYN.)* grip, seize, clutch, clasp, grasp, fight, struggle.

grasp *(SYN.)* clutch, grip, seize, apprehend, capture, snare, hold, clasp, comprehend, reach, grab, understand, grapple, possession, control, domination, command, perceive, trap. *(ANT.)* release, lose, throw, liberate.

grasping *(SYN.)* possessive, greedy, selfish, acquisitive, mercenary. *(ANT.)* liberal, unselfish, generous.

grate *(SYN.)* file, pulverize, grind, scrape, scratch, annoy, irritate.

grateful *(SYN.)* beholden, obliged, appreciative, thankful, indebted. *(ANT.)* ungrateful, unappreciative, grudging.

gratify *(SYN.)* charm, gladden, please, satisfy. *(ANT.)* frustrate.

gratifying *(SYN.)* contentment, solace, relief, comfort, ease, succor, consolation, enjoyment. *(ANT.)* suffering, torment, affliction, discomfort, torture, misery.

grating *(SYN.)* harsh, rugged, severe, stringent, coarse, gruff, jarring, rigorous, strict. *(ANT.)* smooth, melodious, mild, gentle, soft.

gratis *(SYN.)* complimentary, free.

gratitude *(SYN.)* gratefulness, thankfulness, appreciation. *(ANT.)* ungratefulness.

gratuity *(SYN.)* tip, bonus, gift, donation.

grave *(SYN.)* sober, grim, earnest, serious, important, momentous, sedate, solemn, somber, imposing, vital, essential, staid, consequential, thoughtful. *(ANT.)* light, flighty, trivial, insignificant, unimportant, trifling, merry, gay, cheery, frivolous.

gravel *(SYN.)* stones, pebbles, grain.

gravitate *(SYN.)* incline, tend, lean, approach, toward.

gravity *(SYN.)* concern, importance, seriousness, pull. *(ANT.)* triviality.

graze *(SYN.)* scrape, feed, rub, brush, contact, skim.

grease *(SYN.)* fat, oil, lubrication.

greasy *(SYN.)* messy, buttery, waxy, fatty.

great *(SYN.)* large, numerous, eminent, illustrious, big, gigantic, enormous, immense, vast, weighty, fine, important, countless, prominent, vital, huge, momentous, serious, famed, dignified, excellent, critical, renowned, majestic, august, elevated, noble, grand. *(ANT.)* minute, common, menial, ordinary, diminutive, small, paltry, unknown.

greed *(SYN.)* piggishness, lust, desire, greediness, avarice, covetousness. *(ANT.)* unselfishness, selflessness, generosity.

greedy *(SYN.)* selfish, devouring, ravenous, avaricious, covetous, rapacious, gluttonous, insatiable, voracious. *(ANT.)* full, generous, munificent, giving, satisfied.

green *(SYN.)* inexperienced, modern, novel, recent, further, naive, fresh, natural, raw, unsophisticated, undeveloped, immature, unripe, additional, brisk, artless. *(ANT.)* hackneyed, musty, decayed, faded, stagnant.

greenhorn *(SYN.)* tenderfoot, beginner, apprentice, amateur, novice.

greenhouse *(SYN.)* hothouse.

greet *(SYN.)* hail, accost, meet, address, talk to, speak to, welcome, approach. *(ANT.)* pass by, avoid.

gregarious *(SYN.)* outgoing, civil, affable, communicative, hospitable, sociable. *(ANT.)* inhospitable, antisocial, disagreeable, hermitic.

grief *(SYN.)* misery, sadness, tribulation, affliction, heartache, woe, trial, anguish, mourning, distress, lamentation. *(ANT.)* happiness, solace, consolation, comfort, joy.

grief-stricken *(SYN.)* heartsick, ravaged, devastated, wretched, forlorn, desolate,

grievance

wretched. (*ANT.*) *joyous, blissful, content.*

grievance *(SYN.)* injury, wrong, injustice, detriment, complaint, damage, prejudice, evil, objection, protest, accusation, harm. (*ANT.*) *improvement, benefit, repair.*

grieve *(SYN.)* lament, brood over, mourn, weep, wail, sorrow, distress, bemoan, hurt, deplore. (*ANT.*) *revel, carouse, celebrate, rejoice, gladden, soothe.*

grieved *(SYN.)* contrite, remorseful, beggarly, mean, pitiful, shabby, vile, sorrowful, pained, hurt, sorry, contemptible, worthless. (*ANT.*) *splendid, delighted, cheerful, impenitent, unrepentant.*

grievous *(SYN.)* gross, awful, outrageous, shameful, lamentable, regrettable. (*ANT.*) *agreeable, comforting, pleasurable.*

grill *(SYN.)* cook, broil, question, interrogate, barbecue, grating, gridiron, cross-examine.

grim *(SYN.)* severe, harsh, strict, merciless, fierce, horrible, inflexible, adamant, ghastly, frightful, unyielding, rigid, stern. (*ANT.*) *pleasant, lenient, relaxed, amiable, congenial, smiling.*

grimace *(SYN.)* expression, sneer, scowl.

grimy *(SYN.)* unclean, grubby, soiled.

grin *(SYN.)* beam, smile, smirk.

grind *(SYN.)* mill, mash, powder, crush, crumble, pulverize, smooth, grate, sharpen, even.

grip *(SYN.)* catch, clutch, apprehend, trap, arrest, grasp, hold, bag, suitcase, lay hold of, clench, command, control, possession, domination, comprehension, understanding, seize. (*ANT.*) *release, liberate, lose, throw.*

gripe *(SYN.)* protest, lament, complaint, grumbling.

grit *(SYN.)* rub, grind, grate, sand, gravel, pluck, courage, stamina.

groan *(SYN.)* sob, wail, howl, moan, whimper, wail, complain.

groggy *(SYN.)* dazed, dopey, stupefied, stunned, drugged, unsteady. (*ANT.*) *alert.*

groom *(SYN.)* tend, tidy, preen, curry, spouse, consort.

groove *(SYN.)* furrow, channel, track, routine, slot, scratch.

groovy *(SYN.)* marvelous, delightful, wonderful.

grope *(SYN.)* fumble, feel around.

gross *(SYN.)* glaring, coarse, indelicate, obscene, bulky, great, total, whole, brutal, grievous, aggregate, earthy, rude, vulgar, entire, enormous, plain, crass, rough, large. (*ANT.*) *appealing, delicate, refined, proper, polite, cultivated, slight, comely, trivial, decent.*

grotesque *(SYN.)* strange, weird, odd, incredible, fantastic, monstrous, absurd, freakish, bizarre, peculiar, deformed, disfigured, unnatural, queer.

grotto *(SYN.)* tunnel, cave, hole, cavern.

grouch *(SYN.)* protest, remonstrate, whine, complain, grumble, murmur, mope, mutter, repine. (*ANT.*) *praise, applaud, rejoice.*

grouchy *(SYN.)* cantankerous, grumpy, surly. (*ANT.*) *cheerful, contented, agreeable, pleasant.*

ground *(SYN.)* foundation, presumption, surface, principle, underpinning, premise, base, bottom, fix, basis, soil, land, earth, set, root, support, establish, dirt, presupposition. (*ANT.*) *implication, superstructure, trimming, derivative.*

groundless *(SYN.)* baseless, unfounded, unwarranted, needless.

grounds *(SYN.)* garden, lawns, dregs, foundation, leftovers, reason, sediment, cause, basis, premise, motive.

groundwork *(SYN.)* support, bottom, base, underpinning, premise, presupposition, principle, basis. (*ANT.*) *trimming, implication, derivative, superstructure.*

group *(SYN.)* crowd, clock, party, troupe, swarm, bunch, brook, assembly, herd, band, mob, brood, class, throng, cluster, flock, lot, collection, pack, horde, gathering, aggregation. (*ANT.*) *disassemble.*

grouse *(SYN.)* mutter, grumble, gripe, scold, growl, complain.

grovel *(SYN.)* creep, crawl, cower, cringe, slouch, stoop, scramble.

groveling *(SYN.)* dishonorable, lowly,

sordid, vile, mean, abject, despicable, ignoble, menial, servile, vulgar, ignominious. *(ANT.) lofty, noble, esteemed, exalted.*

grow *(SYN.)* extend, swell, advance, develop, enlarge, germinate, mature, expand, flower, raise, become, cultivate, increase, distend. *(ANT.) wane, shrink, atrophy, decay, diminish, contract.*

growl *(SYN.)* complain, snarl, grumble, gnarl, roar, clamor, bellow.

grown-up *(SYN.)* full-grown, adult, of age, mature, big, senior. *(ANT.) little, childish, budding, junior, juvenile.*

growth *(SYN.)* expansion, development, unfolding, maturing, progress, elaboration, evolution. *(ANT.) degeneration, deterioration, curtailment, abbreviation, compression.*

grub *(SYN.)* gouge, dig, scoop out, burrow, tunnel, excavate, plod, toil, drudge.

grubby *(SYN.)* unkempt, grimy, slovenly, dirty. *(ANT.) tidy, spruce, neat, clean, well-groomed.*

grudge *(SYN.)* malevolence, malice, resentment, bitterness, spite, animosity, enmity, rancor, ill will. *(ANT.) kindness, love, benevolence, affection, good will, friendliness, toleration.*

grudgingly *(SYN.)* reluctantly, unwillingly, under protest, involuntarily.

grueling *(SYN.)* taxing, exhausting, excruciating, trying, arduous, grinding, crushing. *(ANT.) effortless, easy, light, simple.*

gruesome *(SYN.)* hideous, frightful, horrible, loathsome, ghastly, horrifying, grisly. *(ANT.) agreeable, soothing, delightful, charming.*

gruff *(SYN.)* scratchy, crude, incomplete, unpolished, stormy, brusque, rude, rough, uncivil, churlish, violent, harsh, imperfect, craggy, irregular, deep, husky, approximate, tempestuous, blunt. *(ANT.) civil, courteous, polished, calm, even, sleek, smooth, finished, gentle, placid, pleasant, tranquil.*

grumble *(SYN.)* protest, mutter, complain.

grumpy *(SYN.)* ill-tempered, cranky, grouchy, surly, cross-gained, crabbed, fractious, pettish, disgruntled, moody. *(ANT.)* winsome, amiable, pleasant, cheery.

guarantee *(SYN.)* bond, pledge, token, warrant, earnest, surety, bail, commitment, promise, secure, swear, assure, sponsor, certify, warranty, insure, endorse, security.

guarantor *(SYN.)* voucher, sponsor, warrantor, signatory, underwriter, surety.

guaranty *(SYN.)* warranty, token, deposit, earnest, pledge, gage, collateral, stake.

guard *(SYN.)* protect, shield, veil, cloak, conceal, disguise, envelop, preserve, hide, defend, cover, sentry, protector, shroud, curtain. *(ANT.) unveil, expose, ignore, neglect, bare, reveal, disregard, divulge.*

guarded *(SYN.)* discreet, cautious, careful. *(ANT.) audacious, reckless, indiscreet, careless.*

guardian *(SYN.)* curator, keeper, protector, custodian, patron, champion.

guess *(SYN.)* estimate, suppose, think, assume, reason, believe, reckon, speculate, notion, surmise, hypothesis, imagine, consider, opinion, conjecture. *(ANT.) know.*

guest *(SYN.)* caller, client, customer, patient, visitor, company. *(ANT.) host.*

guide *(SYN.)* manage, supervise, conduct, direct, lead, steer, escort, pilot, show, squire, usher, control, affect, influence, regulate. *(ANT.) follower, follow.*

guild *(SYN.)* association, union, society.

guile *(SYN.)* deceitfulness, fraud, wiliness, trick, deceit, chicanery, cunning, deception, craftiness, sham, sneakiness, cheat. *(ANT.) sincerity, openness, honesty, truthfulness, candor, frankness.*

guilt *(SYN.)* sin, blame, fault, offense.

guilty *(SYN.)* culpable, to blame, responsible, at fault, criminal, blameworthy. *(ANT.) blameless, innocent, guileless.*

guise *(SYN.)* aspect, pretense, mien, look, air, advent, apparition, appearance.

gulch *(SYN.)* gorge, valley, gully, ravine.

gullible *(SYN.)* trustful, naive, innocent, deceivable, unsuspicious, believing, *(ANT.) skeptical, sophisticated.*

gully *(SYN.)* ditch, gorge, ravine, valley, gulch, gulf.

gulp *(SYN.)* devour, swallow, gasp,

repress, choke.

gun *(SYN.)* fire, shoot, weapon, discharge, pistol, firearm, revolver.

gust *(SYN.)* blast, wind, outbreak, outburst, eruption.

gutter *(SYN.)* ditch, groove, drain, channel, trench, sewer, trough.

gymnasium *(SYN.)* playground, arena, court, athletic field.

gymnastics *(SYN.)* drill, exercise, acrobatics, calisthenics.

gyp *(SYN.)* swindle, cheat, defraud.

gypsy *(SYN.)* nomad.

gyrate *(SYN.)* spin, whirl, rotate, revolve.

H

habit *(SYN.)* usage, routine, compulsion, use, wont, custom, disposition, practice, addiction, fashion.

habitation *(SYN.)* abode, domicile, lodgings, dwelling, home.

habitual *(SYN.)* general, usual, common, typical, frequent, persistent, customary, routine, regular, often. *(ANT.)* solitary, unique, exceptional, occasional, unusual, scanty, rare.

habituated *(SYN.)* used, accustomed, adapted, acclimated, comfortable, familiarized, addicted, settled.

hack *(SYN.)* cleave, chop, slash, hew, slice, pick, sever, mangle.

hag *(SYN.)* beldam, crone, vixen, granny, ogress, harridan, visage.

haggard *(SYN.)* drawn, careworn, debilitated, spent, gaunt, worn. *(ANT.)* bright, fresh, animated.

haggle *(SYN.)* dicker, bargain.

hail *(SYN.)* welcome, approach, accost, speak to, address, greet. *(ANT.)* pass by, avoid.

hair-do *(SYN.)* hairstyle, coiffure, haircut.

hairdresser *(SYN.)* beautician, barber.

hairless *(SYN.)* shorn, glabrous, bald, depilated. *(ANT.)* hirsute, hairy, unshaven.

hairy *(SYN.)* bearded, shaggy, hirsute, bewhiskered.

hale *(SYN.)* robust, well, wholesome, hearty, healthy, sound, strong, vigorous, salubrious. *(ANT.)* noxious, frail, diseased, delicate, infirm, injurious.

half-baked *(SYN.)* crude, premature, makeshift, illogical, shallow.

half-hearted *(SYN.)* uncaring, indifferent, unenthusiastic, cool. *(ANT.)* eager, enthusiastic, earnest.

half-wit *(SYN.)* dope, simpleton, nitwit, dunce, idiot, fool.

hall *(SYN.)* corridor, lobby, passage, hallway, vestibule, foyer.

hallow *(SYN.)* glorify, exalt, dignify, aggrandize, consecrate, elevate, ennoble, raise, erect. *(ANT.)* dishonor, humiliate, debase, degrade.

hallowed *(SYN.)* holy, sacred, sacrosanct, blessed, divine.

hallucination *(SYN.)* fantasy, mirage, dream, vision, phantasm, appearance, aberration, illusion.

halt *(SYN.)* impede, obstruct, terminate, stop, hinder, desist, check, arrest, abstain, discontinue, hold, end, cork, interrupt, bar, cease. *(ANT.)* start, begin, proceed, speed, beginning, promote.

halting *(SYN.)* imperfect, awkward, stuttering, faltering, hobbling, doubtful, limping, wavering. *(ANT.)* decisive, confident, smooth, graceful, facile.

hammer *(SYN.)* beat, bang, whack, pound, batter, drive, tap, cudgel.

hamper *(SYN.)* prevent, impede, thwart, restrain, hinder, obstruct. *(ANT.)* help, assist, expedite, encourage, facilitate.

hamstrung *(SYN.)* disabled, helpless, paralyzed.

hand *(SYN.)* assistant, helper, support, aid, farmhand, laborer.

handicap *(SYN.)* retribution, penalty, disadvantage, forfeiture, hindrance, chastisement. *(ANT.)* reward, pardon, compensation, remuneration.

handily *(SYN.)* readily, skillfully, easily, dexterously, smoothly, adroitly, deftly.

handkerchief *(SYN.)* bandanna, kerchief.

handle *(SYN.)* hold, touch, finger, clutch,

grip, manipulate, feel, grasp, control, oversee, direct, steer, supervise, run, regulate.

hand out *(SYN.)* disburse, distribute, deal, mete, circulate.

hand over *(SYN.)* release, surrender, deliver, yield, present, fork over.

handsome *(SYN.)* lovely, pretty, fair, comely, beautiful, charming, elegant, good-looking, large, generous, liberal, beauteous, fine. *(ANT.)* repulsive, ugly, unattractive, stingy, small, mean, petty, unsightly, meager, homely, foul, hideous.

handy *(SYN.)* suitable, adapted, appropriate, favorable, fitting, near, ready, close, nearby, clever, helpful, useful, timely, accessible. *(ANT.)* inopportune, troublesome, awkward, inconvenient.

hang *(SYN.)* drape, hover, dangle, suspend, kill, sag, execute, lynch.

hang in *(SYN.)* continue, endure, remain, persevere, resist, persist.

hang-up *(SYN.)* inhibition, difficulty, snag, hindrance, block.

hanker *(SYN.)* wish, yearn, long, desire, pine, thirst, covet.

haphazard *(SYN.)* aimless, random, purposeless, casual, indiscriminate, accidental. *(ANT.)* determined, planned, designed, deliberate.

hapless *(SYN.)* ill-fated, unfortunate, jinxed, luckless, wretched.

happen *(SYN.)* occur, take place, bechance, betide, transpire, come to pass, chance, befall.

happening *(SYN.)* episode, event, scene, incident, affair, experience, phenomenon, transaction.

happiness *(SYN.)* pleasure, gladness, delight, beatitude, bliss, contentment, satisfaction, joy, joyousness, blessedness, joyfulness, felicity, elation. *(ANT.)* sadness, sorrow, despair, misery, grief.

happy *(SYN.)* gay, joyous, cheerful, fortunate, glad, merry, contented, satisfied, lucky, blessed, pleased, opportune, delighted. *(ANT.)* gloomy, morose, sad, sorrowful, miserable, inconvenient, unlucky, depressed, blue.

happy-go-lucky *(SYN.)* easygoing, carefree, unconcerned. *(ANT.)* prudent, responsible, concerned.

harangue *(SYN.)* oration, diatribe, lecture, tirade, exhortation.

harass *(SYN.)* badger, irritate, molest, pester, taunt, torment, provoke, tantalize, worry, aggravate, annoy, nag, plague, vex. *(ANT.)* please, soothe, comfort, delight, gratify.

harbinger *(SYN.)* sign, messenger, proclaim, forerunner, herald.

harbor *(SYN.)* haven, port, anchorage, cherish, entertain, protect, shelter.

hard *(SYN.)* difficult, burdensome, arduous, rigid, puzzling, cruel, strict, unfeeling, severe, stern, impenetrable, compact, tough, solid, onerous, rigorous, firm, intricate, harsh, perplexing. *(ANT.)* fluid, effortless, gentle, tender, easy, simple, plastic, soft, lenient, flabby, elastic.

hard-boiled *(SYN.)* unsympathetic, tough, harsh, unsentimental.

harden *(SYN.)* petrify, solidify. *(ANT.)* loose, soften.

hardheaded *(SYN.)* stubborn, obstinate, unyielding, headstrong.

hard-hearted *(SYN.)* merciless, hard, unmerciful, callous, pitiless, ruthless.

hardly *(SYN.)* barely, scarcely.

hard-nosed *(SYN.)* shrewd, tough, practical.

hardship *(SYN.)* ordeal, test, effort, affliction, misfortune, trouble, experiment, proof, essay, misery, examination, difficulty, tribulation.

hardy *(SYN.)* sturdy, strong, tough, vigorous. *(ANT.)* frail, decrepit, feeble, weak, fragile.

harm *(SYN.)* hurt, mischief, misfortune, mishap, damage, wickedness, cripple, injury, evil, detriment, ill, infliction, wrong. *(ANT.)* favor, kindness, benefit, boon.

harmful *(SYN.)* damaging, injurious, mischievous, detrimental, hurtful, deleterious. *(ANT.)* helpful, salutary, profitable, advantageous, beneficial.

harmless

harmless *(SYN.)* protected, secure, snag, dependable, certain, painless, innocent, trustworthy. *(ANT.) perilous, hazardous, insecure, dangerous, unsafe.*

harmonious *(SYN.)* tuneful, melodious, congenial, amicable. *(ANT.) dissonant, discordant, disagreeable.*

harmony *(SYN.)* unison, bargain, contract, stipulation, pact, agreement, accordance, concord, accord, understanding, unity, coincidence. *(ANT.) discord, dissension, difference, variance, disagreement.*

harness *(SYN.)* control, yoke.

harry *(SYN.)* vex, pester, harass, bother, plague.

harsh *(SYN.)* jarring, gruff, rugged, severe, stringent, blunt, grating, unpleasant, tough, stern, strict, unkind, rigorous, cruel, coarse. *(ANT.) smooth, soft, gentle, melodious, soothing, easy, mild.*

harvest *(SYN.)* reap, gather, produce, yield, crop, gain, acquire, fruit, result, reaping, product, proceeds, glean, garner. *(ANT.) plant, squander, lose, sow.*

haste *(SYN.)* speed, hurry, rush, rapidity, flurry, scramble. *(ANT.) sloth, sluggishness.*

hasten *(SYN.)* hurry, sprint, quicken, rush, precipitate, accelerate, scurry, run, scamper, dispatch, press, urge, dash, expedite, speed. *(ANT.) retard, tarry, detain, linger, dawdle, delay, hinder.*

hasty *(SYN.)* quick, swift, irascible, lively, nimble, brisk, active, speedy, impatient, testy, sharp, fast, rapid. *(ANT.) slow, dull, sluggish.*

hat *(SYN.)* helmet, bonnet, cap.

hatch *(SYN.)* breed, incubate, brood.

hate *(SYN.)* loathe, detest, despise, disfavor, hatred, abhorrence, abominate, abhor, dislike. *(ANT.) love, cherish, approve, admire, like.*

hateful *(SYN.)* loathsome, detestable, offensive. *(ANT.) likable, loving, admirable.*

hatred *(SYN.)* detestation, dislike, malevolence, enmity, rancor, ill will, loathing, hate, hostility, abhorrence, aversion, animosity. *(ANT.) friendship, love, affection, attraction.*

haughty *(SYN.)* proud, stately, vainglorious, arrogant, disdainful, overbearing, supercilious, vain. *(ANT.) meek, ashamed, lowly, humble.*

haul *(SYN.)* draw, pull, drag, tow.

have *(SYN.)* own, possess, seize, hold, control, occupy, acquire, undergo, maintain, experience, receive, gain, affect, include, contain, get, take, obtain. *(ANT.) surrender, abandon, renounce, lose.*

havoc *(SYN.)* devastation, ruin, destruction.

hazard *(SYN.)* peril, chance, dare, risk, offer, conjecture, jeopardy, danger. *(ANT.) safety, defense, protection, immunity.*

hazardous *(SYN.)* perilous, precarious, threatening, unsafe, dangerous, critical, menacing, risky. *(ANT.) protected, secure, safe.*

hazy *(SYN.)* uncertain, unclear, ambiguous, dim, obscure, undetermined, vague, unsettled, indefinite. *(ANT.) specific, clear, lucid, precise, explicit.*

head *(SYN.)* leader, summit, top, culmination, director, chief, master, commander, supervisor, start, source, crest, beginning, crisis. *(ANT.) foot, base, bottom, follower, subordinate, underling.*

headstrong *(SYN.)* obstinate, stubborn, willful. *(ANT.) easygoing, amenable.*

headway *(SYN.)* movement, progress.

heady *(SYN.)* thrilling, intoxicating, exciting, electrifying.

heal *(SYN.)* restore, cure.

healthy *(SYN.)* wholesome, hale, robust, sound, well, vigorous, strong, hearty, healthful, hygienic, salubrious, salutary. *(ANT.) noxious, diseased, unhealthy, delicate, frail, infirm, injurious.*

heap *(SYN.)* collection, mound, increase, store, stack, pile, gather, accumulate, amass, accrue, accumulation, collect. *(ANT.) dissipate, scatter, waste, disperse.*

hear *(SYN.)* heed, listen, detect, hearken, perceive, regard.

heart *(SYN.)* middle, center, sympathy, nucleus, midpoint, sentiment, core, feeling, midst. *(ANT.) outskirts, periphery,* *border, rim, boundary.*

heartache *(SYN.)* anguish, mourning, sadness, sorrow, affliction, distress, grief, lamentation, tribulation. *(ANT.) happiness, joy, solace, comfort, consolation.*

heartbroken *(SYN.)* distressed, forlorn, mean, paltry, worthless, contemptible, wretched, crestfallen, disconsolate, downhearted, comfortless, brokenhearted, low. *(ANT.) noble, fortunate, contented, significant.*

hearten *(SYN.)* encourage, favor, impel, urge, promote, sanction, animate, cheer, exhilarate. *(ANT.) deter, dissuade, deject, discourage, dispirit.*

heartless

heartrending *(SYN.)* heartbreaking, depressing, agonizing.

hearty *(SYN.)* warm, earnest, ardent, cordial, sincere, gracious, sociable. *(ANT.) taciturn, aloof, cool, reserved.*

heat *(SYN.)* hotness, warmth, temperature, passion, ardor, zeal, inflame, cook, excitement, warm. *(ANT.) cool, chill, coolness, freeze, coldness, chilliness, iciness, cold.*

heated *(SYN.)* vehement, fiery, intense, passionate.

heave *(SYN.)* boost, hoist, raise.

heaven *(SYN.)* empyrean, paradise.

heavenly *(SYN.)* superhuman, godlike, blissful, saintly, holy, divine, celestial, angelic, blessed. *(ANT.) wicked, mundane, profane, blasphemous, diabolical.*

heavy *(SYN.)* weighty, massive, gloomy, serious, ponderous, cumbersome, trying, burdensome, harsh, grave, intense, dull, grievous, concentrated, severe, oppressive, sluggish. *(ANT.) brisk, light, animated.*

heckle *(SYN.)* torment, harass, tease, hector, harry.

heed *(SYN.)* care, alertness, circumspection, mindfulness, consider, watchfulness, reflection, study, attention, notice, regard, obey, ponder, respect, meditate, mind, observe, deliberate, examine, contemplate, weigh, esteem, application. *(ANT.) negligence, oversight, overlook, neglect, ignore, disregard, indifference, omission.*

heedless *(SYN.)* sightless, headlong, rash, unmindful, deaf, unseeing, oblivious, ignorant, inattentive, disregardful, blind. *(ANT.) perceiving, sensible, aware, calculated, discerning.*

height *(SYN.)* zenith, peak, summit, tallness, mountain, acme, apex, elevation, altitude, prominence, maximum, pinnacle, culmination. *(ANT.) base, depth.*

heighten *(SYN.)* increase, magnify, annoy, chafe, intensify, amplify, aggravate, provoke, irritate, concentrate, nettle. *(ANT.) soothe, mitigate, palliate, soften, appease.*

heinous *(SYN.)* abominable, grievous, atrocious.

hello *(SYN.)* greeting, good evening, good afternoon, good morning. *(ANT.) farewell, good-bye, so long.*

help *(SYN.)* assist, support, promote, relieve, abet, succor, back, uphold, further, remedy, encourage, aid, facilitate, mitigate. *(ANT.) afflict, thwart, resist, hinder, impede.*

helper *(SYN.)* aide, assistant, supporter.

helpful *(SYN.)* beneficial, serviceable, wholesome, useful, profitable, advantageous, good, salutary. *(ANT.) harmful, injurious, useless, worthless, destructive, deleterious, detrimental.*

helpfulness *(SYN.)* assistance, cooperation, usefulness, serviceability, kindness, neighborliness, willingness, collaboration, supportiveness, readiness. *(ANT.) antagonism, hostility, opposition.*

helpless *(SYN.)* weak, feeble, dependent, disabled, inept, unresourceful, incapable, incompetent. *(ANT.) resourceful, competent, enterprising.*

helplessness *(SYN.)* impotence, feebleness, weakness, incapacity, ineptitude, invalidism, shiftless, awkwardness. *(ANT.) power, strength, might, potency.*

helter-skelter *(SYN.)* haphazardly, chaotically, irregularly.

hem *(SYN.)* bottom, border, edge, rim, margin, pale, verge, flounce, boundary, fringe, brim, fence, hedge, frame.

hem in *(SYN.)* enclose, shut in, confine, restrict, limit.

hence *(SYN.)* consequently, thence, therefore, so, accordingly.

herald *(SYN.)* harbinger, crier, envoy, forerunner, precursor, augury, forecast.

herculean *(SYN.)* demanding, heroic, titanic, mighty, prodigious, laborious, arduous, overwhelming, backbreaking.

herd *(SYN.)* group, pack, drove, crowd, flock, gather.

heretic *(SYN.)* nonconformist, sectarian, unbeliever, sectary, schismatic, apostate, dissenter.

heritage *(SYN.)* birthright, legacy, patrimony, inheritance.

hermit *(SYN.)* recluse, anchorite, eremite.

hero *(SYN.)* paladin, champion, idol.

heroic *(SYN.)* bold, courageous, fearless, gallant, valiant, valorous, brave, chivalrous, adventurous, dauntless, intrepid, magnanimous. *(ANT.)* fearful, weak, cringing, timid, cowardly.

heroism *(SYN.)* valor, bravery, gallant, dauntless, bold, courageous, fearless.

hesitant *(SYN.)* reluctant, unwilling, disinclined, loath, slow, averse. *(ANT.)* willing, inclined, eager, ready, disposed.

hesitate *(SYN.)* falter, waver, pause, doubt, demur, delay, vacillate, wait, stammer, stutter, scruple. *(ANT.)* proceed, resolve, continue, decide, persevere.

hesitation *(SYN.)* distrust, scruple, suspense, uncertainty, unbelief, doubt, incredulity, skepticism. *(ANT.)* determination, belief, certainty, faith, conviction.

hidden *(SYN.)* undeveloped, unseen, dormant, concealed, quiescent, latent, potential, inactive. *(ANT.)* visible, explicit, conspicuous, evident.

hide *(SYN.)* disguise, mask, suppress, withhold, veil, cloak, conceal, screen, camouflage, shroud, pelt, skin, leather, cover. *(ANT.)* reveal, show, expose, disclose, uncover, divulge.

hideous *(SYN.)* frightful, ugly, shocking, frightening, horrible, terrible, horrifying, terrifying, grisly, gross. *(ANT.)* lovely, beautiful, beauteous.

high *(SYN.)* tall, eminent, exalted, elevated, high-pitched, sharp, lofty, proud, shrill, raised, strident, prominent, important, powerful, expensive, dear, high-priced, costly, grave, serious, extreme, towering. *(ANT.)* low, mean, tiny, short, base, lowly, deep, insignificant, unimportant, inexpensive, reasonable, trivial, petty, small.

highly *(SYN.)* extremely, very, extraordinarily, exceedingly.

high-minded *(SYN.)* lofty, noble, honorable. *(ANT.)* dishonorable, base.

high-priced *(SYN.)* dear, expensive, costly. *(ANT.)* economical, cheap.

high-strung *(SYN.)* nervous, tense, wrought-up, intense. *(ANT.)* calm.

highway *(SYN.)* parkway, speedway, turnpike, superhighway, freeway.

hilarious *(SYN.)* funny, side-splitting, hysterical. *(ANT.)* depressing, sad.

hinder *(SYN.)* hamper, impede, block, retard, stop, resist, thwart, obstruct, check, prevent, interrupt, delay, slow, restrain. *(ANT.)* promote, further, assist, expedite, advance, facilitate.

hindrance *(SYN.)* interruption, delay, interference, obstruction, obstacle, barrier.

hinge *(SYN.)* rely, depend, pivot.

hint *(SYN.)* reminder, allusion, suggestion, clue, tip, taste, whisper, implication, intimate, suspicion, mention, insinuation. *(ANT.)* declaration, affirmation, statement.

hire *(SYN.)* employ, occupy, devote, apply, enlist, lease, rent, charter, rental, busy, engage, utilize, retain, let, avail. *(ANT.)* reject, banish, discard, fire, dismiss, discharge.

history *(SYN.)* narration, relation, computation, record, account, chronicle, detail, description, narrative, annal, tale, recital. *(ANT.)* confusion, misrepresentation, distortion, caricature.

hit *(SYN.)* knock, pound, strike, hurt, pummel, beat, come upon, find, discover, blow, smite.

hitch *(SYN.)* tether, fasten, harness, interruption, hindrance, interference.

hoard *(SYN.)* amass, increase, accumulate, gather, save, secret, cache, store, accrue, heap. *(ANT.)* dissipate, scatter, waste, *diminish, squander, spend, disperse.*

hoarse *(SYN.)* deep, rough, husky, raucous, grating, harsh. *(ANT.) clear.*

hoax *(SYN.)* ploy, ruse, wile, device, cheat, deception, antic, imposture, stratagem, stunt, guile, fraud. *(ANT.) openness, sincerity, candor, exposure, honesty.*

hobbling *(SYN.)* deformed, crippled, lame, unconvincing, unsatisfactory, defective, feeble, disabled, maimed, weak. *(ANT.) robust, vigorous, agile, sound, athletic.*

hobby *(SYN.)* diversion, pastime, avocation. *(ANT.) vocation, profession.*

hobo *(SYN.)* derelict, vagrant, vagabond, tramp.

hoist *(SYN.)* heave, lift, elevate, raise, crane, elevator, derrick.

hold *(SYN.)* grasp, occupy, possess, curb, contain, stow, carry, adhere, have, clutch, keep, maintain, clasp, grip, retain, detain, accommodate, restrain, observe, conduct, check, support. *(ANT.) vacate, relinquish, surrender, abandon.*

holdup *(SYN.)* heist, robbery, stickup, delay, interruption, slowdown.

hole *(SYN.)* cavity, void, pore, opening, abyss, chasm, gulf, aperture, tear, pit, burrow, lair, den, gap.

hollow *(SYN.)* unfilled, vacant, vain, meaningless, flimsy, false, hole, cavity, depression, hypocritical, depressed, empty, pit, insincere. *(ANT.) sound, solid, genuine, sincere, full.*

holocaust *(SYN.)* fire, burning, extermination, butchery, disaster, massacre.

holy *(SYN.)* devout, divine, blessed, consecrated, sacred, spiritual, pious, sainted, religious, saintly, hallowed. *(ANT.) worldly, sacrilegious, unconsecrated, evil, profane, secular.*

homage *(SYN.)* reverence, honor, respect.

home *(SYN.)* dwelling, abode, residence, seat, quarters, hearth, domicile, family, house, habitat.

homely *(SYN.)* uncommonly, disagreeable, ill-natured, ugly, vicious, plain, hideous, unattractive, deformed, surly, repellent, spiteful. *(ANT.) fair, handsome, pretty,* *attractive, comely, beautiful.*

homesick *(SYN.)* lonely, nostalgic.

honest *(SYN.)* sincere, trustworthy, truthful, fair, ingenuous, candid, conscientious, moral, upright, open, frank, forthright, honorable, just, straightforward. *(ANT.) fraudulent, tricky, deceitful, dishonest, lying.*

honesty *(SYN.)* frankness, openness, fairness, sincerity, trustworthiness, justice, candor, honor, integrity, responsibility, uprightness. *(ANT.) deceit, dishonesty, trickery, fraud, cheating.*

honor *(SYN.)* esteem, praise, worship, admiration, homage, glory, respect, admire, heed, dignity, revere, value, deference, venerate, reverence, consider, distinction, character, principle, uprightness, honesty, adoration. *(ANT.) scorn, dishonor, despise, neglect, abuse, shame, reproach, disdain, contempt, derision, disgrace.*

honorable *(SYN.)* fair, noble, creditable, proper, reputable, honest, admirable, true, trusty, eminent, respectable, esteemed, just, famed, illustrious, noble, virtuous, upright. *(ANT.) infamous, disgraceful, shameful, dishonorable, ignominious.*

honorary *(SYN.)* gratuitous, complimentary.

hoodlum *(SYN.)* crook, gangster, criminal, hooligan, mobster.

hop *(SYN.)* jump, leap.

hope *(SYN.)* expectation, faith, optimism, anticipation, expectancy, confidence, desire, trust. *(ANT.) pessimism, despair, despondency.*

hopeful *(SYN.)* optimistic, confident. *(ANT.) despairing, hopeless.*

hopeless *(SYN.)* desperate, despairing, forlorn, fatal, incurable, disastrous. *(ANT.) promising, hopeful.*

hopelessness *(SYN.)* gloom, discouragement, depression, pessimism, despondency. *(ANT.) hope, optimism, confidence, elation.*

horde *(SYN.)* host, masses, press, rabble, swarm, throng, bevy, crush, mob, multitude, crowd, populace.

horizontal *(SYN.)* even, level, plane, flat,

straight, sideways. *(ANT.) upright, vertical.*

horrendous *(SYN.)* awful, horrifying, terrible, dreadful, horrid, ghastly. *(ANT.) splendid, wonderful.*

horrible *(SYN.)* awful, dire, ghastly, horrid, terrible, repulsive, frightful, appalling, horrifying, dreadful, ghastly, fearful. *(ANT.) enjoyable, enchanting, beautiful, lovely, fascinating.*

horrid *(SYN.)* repulsive, terrible, appalling, dire, awful, frightful, fearful, shocking, horrible, horrifying, ghastly, dreadful, revolting, hideous. *(ANT.) fascinating, enchanting, enjoyable, lovely, beautiful.*

horror *(SYN.)* dread, awe, hatred, loathing, foreboding, alarm, apprehension, aversion, terror. *(ANT.) courage, boldness, assurance, confidence.*

horseplay *(SYN.)* tomfoolery, clowning, shenanigans.

hospital *(SYN.)* infirmary, clinic, sanatorium, rest home, sanitarium.

hospitality *(SYN.)* warmth, liberality, generosity, graciousness, welcome.

hostile *(SYN.)* unfriendly, opposed, antagonistic, inimical, adverse, warlike. *(ANT.) friendly, favorable, amicable, cordial.*

hostility *(SYN.)* grudge, hatred, rancor, spite, bitterness, enmity, malevolence. *(ANT.) love, friendliness, goodwill.*

hot *(SYN.)* scorching, fervent, hot-blooded, passionate, peppery, ardent, burning, fiery, impetuous, scalding, heated, sizzling, blazing, frying, roasting, warm, intense, torrid, pungent. *(ANT.) indifferent, apathetic, impassive, passionless, bland, frigid, cold, freezing, cool, phlegmatic.*

hot air *(SYN.)* bombast, blather, jabber, gabble.

hotbed *(SYN.)* sink, nest, well, den, nursery, cradle, source, incubator, seedbed.

hot-blooded *(SYN.)* passionate, ardent, excitable, wild, fervent, fiery, impetuous, rash, brash, intense, impulsive. *(ANT.) stolid, impassive, cold, staid.*

hotel *(SYN.)* hostel, motel, inn, hostelry.

hotheaded *(SYN.)* rash, touchy, short-tempered, reckless, unruly. *(ANT.)*

levelheaded, cool-headed, calm.

hound *(SYN.)* harry, pursue, pester, harass.

hourly *(SYN.)* frequently, steadily, constantly, unfailingly, periodically, perpetually, ceaselessly, continually, incessantly. *(ANT.) occasionally, seldom.*

house *(SYN.)* building, residence, abode, dwelling.

housebreaker *(SYN.)* robber, thief, prowler, cracksman, burglar.

household *(SYN.)* manage, family, home.

householder *(SYN.)* homeowner, occupant.

housing *(SYN.)* lodgings, shelter, dwelling, lodgment, case, casing, quarters, domicile, enclosure, console, bracket.

hovel *(SYN.)* cabin, hut, sty, shack, hole, shed.

hover *(SYN.)* hang, drift, poise, stand by, linger, impend, waver, hand around.

however *(SYN.)* notwithstanding, still, nevertheless, but, yet.

howl *(SYN.)* bellow, yowl, wail, yell, cry.

hub *(SYN.)* pivot, center, core, heart, axis, basis, focus, nucleus.

hubbub *(SYN.)* uproar, tumult, commotion, clamor, bustle, turmoil, racket, confusion. *(ANT.) peacefulness, stillness, silence, quiet, quiescence.*

huckster *(SYN.)* peddler, adman, hawker, salesman, pitchman.

huddle *(SYN.)* mass, herd, bunch, crowd, cram, gather, shove, pack, flock, ball, conglomeration, knot, clump, medley, scrum.

hue *(SYN.)* pigment, tint, shade, dye, complexion, paint, stain, color, tone, tincture. *(ANT.) transparency, achromatism, paleness.*

huffy *(SYN.)* sensitive, vulnerable, testy, offended, thin-skinned, touchy, irascible, cross, offended. *(ANT.) tough, placid, stolid, impassive.*

hug *(SYN.)* embrace, coddle, caress, kiss, pet, press, clasp, fondle, cuddle. *(ANT.) tease, vex, spurn, buffet, annoy.*

huge *(SYN.)* great, immense, vast, ample, big, capacious, extensive, gigantic, enormous, tremendous, large, wide, colossal. *(ANT.) short, small, mean, little, tiny.*

husk

hulking *(SYN.)* massive, awkward, bulky, ponderous, unwieldy, overgrown, lumpish, oafish.

hullabaloo *(SYN.)* clamor, uproar, din, racket, tumult, hubbub, commotion, noise, blare. *(ANT.)* calm, peace, silence.

hum *(SYN.)* whir, buzz, whiz, purr, croon, murmur, intone, vibrate.

human *(SYN.)* manlike, hominid, mortal, fleshly, individual, person, tellurian.

humane *(SYN.)* lenient, tender, tolerant, compassionate, clement, forgiving, kind, forbearing, thoughtful, kindhearted, kindly, gentle, merciful. *(ANT.)* remorseless, cruel, heartless, pitiless, unfeeling, brutal.

humanist *(SYN.)* scholar, sage, classicist, savant.

humanitarian *(SYN.)* benefactor, philanthropist.

humanitarianism *(SYN.)* goodwill, beneficence, philanthropy, welfarism, humanism.

humanity *(SYN.)* generosity, magnanimity, tenderness, altruism, beneficence, kindness, charity, philanthropy. *(ANT.)* selfishness, unkindness, cruelty, inhumanity.

humble *(SYN.)* modest, crush, mortify, simple, shame, subdue, meek, abase, break, plain, submissive, compliant, unpretentious, unassuming, abash, unostentatious, lowly, polite, courteous, unpretending, degrade. *(ANT.)* praise, arrogant, exalt, illustrious, boastful, honor, elevate.

humbly *(SYN.)* deferentially, meekly, respectfully, unassumingly, diffidently, modestly, subserviently, submissively. *(ANT.)* insolently, proudly, grandly, arrogantly.

humbug *(SYN.)* drivel, gammon, bosh, nonsense, rubbish, inanity.

humdrum *(SYN.)* commonplace, prosy, mundane, insipid, tedious, routine, dull, boring. *(ANT.)* interesting, stimulating, arresting, striking, exciting.

humid *(SYN.)* moist, damp, misty, muggy, wet, watery, vaporous. *(ANT.)* parched, dry, desiccated.

humiliate *(SYN.)* corrupt, defile, depress, pervert, abase, degrade, disgrace, adulterate, humble, shame, lower, impair, deprave, depress. *(ANT.)* restore, raise, enhance, improve, vitalize.

humiliation *(SYN.)* chagrin, dishonor, ignominy, scandal, abasement, mortification, disrepute, odium, disgrace, shame. *(ANT.)* honor, praise, glory, dignity, renown.

humor *(SYN.)* jocularity, wit, temperament, sarcasm, irony, joking, amusement, facetiousness, joke, disposition, waggery, fun, clowning, satire, mood. *(ANT.)* sorrow, gravity, seriousness.

humorous *(SYN.)* funny, ludicrous, witty, curious, queer, amusing, comical, farcical, laughable, droll. *(ANT.)* sober, unfunny, melancholy, serious, sad, solemn.

hunger *(SYN.)* desire, longing, inclination, relish, stomach, zest, craving, liking, passion. *(ANT.)* satiety, repugnance, disgust, distaste, renunciation.

hungry *(SYN.)* famished, thirsting, craving, avid, longing, starved, ravenous. *(ANT.)* gorged, satisfied, full, sated.

hunt *(SYN.)* pursuit, investigation, examination, inquiry, pursue, track. *(ANT.)* cession, abandonment.

hurl *(SYN.)* throw, cast, propel, fling, toss, pitch, thrust. *(ANT.)* retain, pull, draw, haul, hold.

hurried *(SYN.)* rushed, hasty, swift, headlong, slipshod, careless, impulsive, superficial. *(ANT.)* deliberate, slow, dilatory, thorough, prolonged.

hurry *(SYN.)* quicken, speed, ado, rush, accelerate, run, hasten, race, urge, bustle, expedite, precipitate. *(ANT.)* retard, tarry, hinder, linger, dawdle, delay.

hurt *(SYN.)* damage, harm, grievance, detriment, pain, injustice, injure, abuse, distress, disfigured, mar, afflict, spoil, affront, insult. *(ANT.)* improvement, repair, compliment, help, praise, benefit.

hurtle *(SYN.)* charge, collide, rush, crash, lunge, bump, fling.

husband *(SYN.)* spouse, mate.

hush *(SYN.)* quiet, silence, still.

husk *(SYN.)* shell, hull, pod, skin, covering,

husky

crust, bark.

husky *(SYN.)* strong, brawny, strapping, muscular. *(ANT.) feeble, weak.*

hustle *(SYN.)* hasten, run, race, hurry, speed.

hut *(SYN.)* cottage, shanty, cabin, shed.

hutch *(SYN.)* box, chest, locker, trunk, coffer, bin.

hybrid *(SYN.)* mule, mixture, crossbreed, cross, mongrel, mutt.

hygiene *(SYN.)* cleanliness, sanitation, health, prophylaxis.

hygienic *(SYN.)* robust, strong, clean, well, wholesome, hale, healthy, sound. *(ANT.) frail, noxious, infirm, delicate, diseased.*

hyperbole *(SYN.)* puffery, exaggeration, embellishment, overstatement.

hypercritical *(SYN.)* faultfinding, captious, censorious, finicky, exacting, carping, querulous, nagging, finical, hairsplitting. *(ANT.) lax, easygoing, indulgent, lenient, tolerant.*

hypnotic *(SYN.)* soothing, opiate, sedative, soporific, entrancing, spellbinding, arresting, charming.

hypnotize *(SYN.)* entrance, dazzle, mesmerize, fascinate, spellbind.

hypocrisy *(SYN.)* pretense, deceit, dissembling, fakery, feigning, sanctimony, cant. *(ANT.) openness, candor, truth, directness, honesty, frankness.*

hypocrite *(SYN.)* cheat, deceiver, pretender, dissembler, fake, fraud.

hypothesis *(SYN.)* law, theory, supposition, conjecture. *(ANT.) proof, fact, certainty.*

hypothetical *(SYN.)* conjectural, speculative, theoretical. *(ANT.) actual.*

I

idea *(SYN.)* conception, image, opinion, sentiment, concept, fancy, notion, thought, impression. *(ANT.) thing, matter, entity, object, substance.*

ideal *(SYN.)* imaginary, supreme, unreal, visionary, perfect, faultless, fancied, exemplary, utopian. *(ANT.) imperfect, actual, material, real, faulty.*

idealistic *(SYN.)* extravagant, dreamy, fantastic, fanciful, ideal, maudlin, imaginative, mawkish, sentimental, poetic, picturesque. *(ANT.) practical, literal, factual, prosaic.*

identify *(SYN.)* recollect, apprehend, perceive, remember, confess, acknowledge, name, describe, classify. *(ANT.) ignore, forget, overlook, renounce, disown, repudiate.*

identity *(SYN.)* uniqueness, personality, character, individuality.

ideology *(SYN.)* credo, principles, belief.

idiom *(SYN.)* language, speech, vernacular, lingo, dialect, jargon, slang, tongue. *(ANT.) babble, gibberish, drivel, nonsense.*

idiot *(SYN.)* buffoon, harlequin, dolt, jester, dunce, blockhead, imbecile, numbskull, simpleton, oaf, nincompoop, fool, moron. *(ANT.) philosopher, genius, scholar, sage.*

idiotic *(SYN.)* asinine, absurd, brainless, irrational, crazy, nonsensical, senseless, preposterous, silly, ridiculous, simple, stupid, foolish, inane, moronic, half-witted, simpleminded, dimwitted. *(ANT.) prudent, wise, sagacious, judicious, sane, intelligent, bright, brilliant, smart.*

idle *(SYN.)* unemployed, dormant, lazy, inactive, unoccupied, indolent, slothful, inert, unused. *(ANT.) occupied, working, employed, active, industrious, busy, engaged.*

idolize *(SYN.)* revere, worship, adore. *(ANT.) despise.*

ignoble *(SYN.)* dishonorable, ignominious, lowly, menial, vile, sordid, vulgar, abject, base, despicable, groveling, mean. *(ANT.) righteous, lofty, honored, esteemed, noble, exalted.*

ignominious *(SYN.)* contemptible, abject, despicable, groveling, dishonorable, ignoble, lowly, low, menial, mean, sordid, servile, vulgar, vile. *(ANT.) lofty, noble, esteemed, righteous, exalted.*

ignorant *(SYN.)* uneducated, untaught, uncultured, illiterate, uninformed, unlearned, unlettered, untrained, unaware,

immaculate

unmindful. *(ANT.) cultured, literate, educated, erudite, informed, cultivated, schooled, learned, lettered.*

ignore *(SYN.)* omit, slight, disregard, overlook, neglect, skip. *(ANT.) notice, regard, include.*

ill *(SYN.)* diseased, ailing, indisposed, morbid, infirm, unwell, sick, unhealthy. *(ANT.) robust, healthy, well, sound, fit.*

ill-advised *(SYN.)* injudicious, ill-considered, imprudent.

ill-at-ease *(SYN.)* nervous, uncomfortable, uneasy. *(ANT.) comfortable.*

illegal *(SYN.)* prohibited, unlawful, criminal, illicit, outlawed, illegitimate. *(ANT.) permitted, lawful, honest, legal, legitimate.*

illiberal *(SYN.)* fanatical, bigoted, intolerant, narrow-minded, dogmatic, prejudiced. *(ANT.) progressive, liberal, radical.*

illicit *(SYN.)* illegitimate, criminal, outlawed, unlawful, prohibited, illegal, unauthorized. *(ANT.) legal, honest, permitted, lawful, licit.*

ill-natured *(SYN.)* crabby, cranky, grouchy, cross, irascible.

illness *(SYN.)* complaint, infirmity, ailment, disorder, malady, sickness. *(ANT.) healthiness, health, soundness, vigor.*

illogical *(SYN.)* absurd, irrational, preposterous.

ill-tempered *(SYN.)* crabby, cranky, cross, grouchy.

ill-treated *(SYN.)* harmed, mistreated, abused, maltreated.

illuminate *(SYN.)* enlighten, clarify, irradiate, illustrate, light, lighten, explain, interpret, elucidate, brighten, illumine. *(ANT.) obscure, confuse, darken, obfuscate, shadow, complicate.*

ill-use *(SYN.)* defame, revile, vilify, misemploy, disparage, abuse, traduce, asperse, misapply, misuse. *(ANT.) protect, cherish, respect, honor, praise.*

illusion *(SYN.)* hallucination, vision, phantom, delusion, fantasy, dream, mirage. *(ANT.) substance, actuality, reality.*

illusive *(SYN.)* fallacious, delusive, false, specious, misleading, deceptive, deceitful, delusory. *(ANT.) real, truthful, authentic,* genuine, honest.

illustrate *(SYN.)* decorate, illuminate, adorn, show, picture, embellish, demonstrate.

illustration *(SYN.)* likeness, painting, picture, print, scene, sketch, view, engraving, drawing, panorama, photograph, cinema, etching, effigy, film, appearance, portrayal, resemblance, image, portrait.

illustrator *(SYN.)* painter, artist.

illustrious *(SYN.)* prominent, eminent, renowned, famed, great, vital, elevated, majestic, noble, excellent, dignified, big, gigantic, enormous, immense, huge, vast, large, countless, numerous, celebrated, critical, momentous, august, weighty, grand, fine, magnificent, serious, important. *(ANT.) menial, common, minute, diminutive, small, obscure, ordinary, little.*

image *(SYN.)* reflection, likeness, idea, representation, notion, picture, conception.

imaginary *(SYN.)* fanciful, fantastic, unreal, whimsical. *(ANT.) actual, real.*

imagination *(SYN.)* creation, invention, fancy, notion, conception, fantasy, idea.

imaginative *(SYN.)* inventive, poetical, fanciful, clever, creative, mystical, visionary. *(ANT.) prosaic, dull, unromantic, literal.*

imagine *(SYN.)* assume, surmise, suppose, conceive, dream, pretend, conjecture, fancy, opine, envisage, think, envision, guess, picture.

imbecile *(SYN.)* idiot, numbskull, simpleton, blockhead, dolt, dunce, jester, buffoon, harlequin, nincompoop, clown, fool, oaf. *(ANT.) scholar, genius, philosopher, sage.*

imbibe *(SYN.)* absorb, consume, assimilate, engulf, engage, occupy, engross. *(ANT.) dispense, discharge, emit.*

imitate *(SYN.)* duplicate, mimic, follow, reproduce, mock, ape, counterfeit, copy, simulate, impersonate. *(ANT.) invent, distort, alter, diverge.*

imitation *(SYN.)* replica, reproduction, copy, duplicate, facsimile, transcript, exemplar. *(ANT.) prototype, original.*

immaculate *(SYN.)* clean, spotless,

immature

unblemished. (*ANT.*) *dirty.*

immature (*SYN.*) young, boyish, childish, youthful, childlike, puerile, girlish, juvenile, callow. (*ANT.*) *old, senile, aged, elderly, mature.*

immeasurable (*SYN.*) unlimited, endless, eternal, immense, interminable, unbounded, boundless, illimitable, infinite. (*ANT.*) *limited, confined, bounded, finite, circumscribed.*

immediate (*SYN.*) present, instant, instantaneous, near, close, next, prompt, direct. (*ANT.*) *distant, future.*

immediately (*SYN.*) now, presently, instantly, promptly, straightway, directly, instantaneously, forthwith. (*ANT.*) *sometime, hereafter, later, shortly, distantly.*

immense (*SYN.*) enormous, large, gigantic, huge, colossal, elephantine, great, gargantuan, vast. (*ANT.*) *small, diminutive, little, minuscule, minute, petite, tiny.*

immensity (*SYN.*) hugeness, enormousness, vastness.

immerse (*SYN.*) plunge, dip, dunk, sink, submerge, engage, absorb, engross, douse. (*ANT.*) *uplift, elevate, recover.*

immigration (*SYN.*) settlement, colonization. (*ANT.*) *exodus, emigration.*

imminent (*SYN.*) nigh, impending, overhanging, approaching, menacing, threatening. (*ANT.*) *retreating, afar, distant, improbable, remote.*

immoderation (*SYN.*) profusion, surplus, extravagance, excess, intemperance, superabundance. (*ANT.*) *lack, want, deficiency, dearth, paucity.*

immoral (*SYN.*) sinful, wicked, corrupt, bad, indecent, profligate, unprincipled, antisocial, dissolute. (*ANT.*) *pure, highminded, chaste, virtuous, noble.*

immortal (*SYN.*) infinite, eternal, timeless, undying, perpetual, ceaseless, endless, deathless, everlasting. (*ANT.*) *mortal, transient, finite, ephemeral, temporal.*

immune (*SYN.*) easy, open, autonomous, unobstructed, free, emancipated, clear, independent, unrestricted, exempt, liberated, familiar, loose, unconfined, frank, unfastened, careless, freed. (*ANT.*) *confined, impeded, restricted, subject.*

immutable (*SYN.*) constant, faithful, invariant, persistent, unchanging, unalterable, continual, ceaseless, enduring, fixed, permanent, abiding, perpetual, unwavering. (*ANT.*) *mutable, vacillating, wavering, fickle.*

impact (*SYN.*) striking, contact, collision.

impair (*SYN.*) harm, injure, spoil, deface, destroy, hurt, damage, mar. (*ANT.*) *repair, mend, ameliorate, enhance, benefit.*

impart (*SYN.*) convey, disclose, inform, tell, reveal, transmit, notify, confer, divulge, communicate, relate. (*ANT.*) *hide, withhold, conceal.*

impartial (*SYN.*) unbiased, just, honest, fair, reasonable, equitable. (*ANT.*) *fraudulent, dishonorable, partial.*

impartiality (*SYN.*) indifference, unconcern, neutrality, disinterestedness, apathy, insensibility. (*ANT.*) *passion, ardor, fervor.*

impasse (*SYN.*) standstill, deadlock, stalemate.

impede (*SYN.*) hamper, hinder, retard, thwart, check, encumber, interrupt, bar, clog, delay, obstruct, block, frustrate, restrain, stop. (*ANT.*) *assist, promote, help, advance, further.*

impediment (*SYN.*) barrier, bar, block, difficulty, check, hindrance, snag, obstruction. (*ANT.*) *assistance, help, aid.*

impel (*SYN.*) oblige, enforce, drive, coerce, force, constrain. (*ANT.*) *induce, prevent, convince, persuade.*

impending (*SYN.*) imminent, nigh, threatening, overhanging, approaching, menacing. (*ANT.*) *remote, improbable, afar, distant, retreating.*

impenetrable (*SYN.*) rigid, tough, harsh, strict, unfeeling, rigorous, intricate, arduous, penetrable, cruel, difficult, severe, stem, firm, hard, compact. (*ANT.*) *soft, simple, gentle, tender, brittle, fluid, flabby, elastic, lenient, easy, effortless.*

imperative (*SYN.*) critical, instant, important, necessary, serious, urgent, cogent, compelling, crucial, pressing, impelling, importunate, exigent, insistent. *(ANT.) trivial, insignificant, unimportant, petty.*

imperceptible *(SYN.)* invisible, indiscernible, unseen, indistinguishable. *(ANT.) seen, evident, visible, perceptible.*

imperfection *(SYN.)* flaw, shortcoming, vice, defect, blemish, failure, mistake, omission, fault, error. *(ANT.) correctness, perfection, completeness.*

imperil *(SYN.)* jeopardize, risk, endanger, hazard, risk. *(ANT.) guard, insure.*

impersonal *(SYN.)* objective, detached, disinterested. *(ANT.) personal.*

impersonate *(SYN.)* mock, simulate, imitate, ape, counterfeit, mimic, copy, duplicate. *(ANT.) alter, invent, diverge, distort.*

impertinence *(SYN.)* impudence, presumption, sauciness, effrontery, audacity, rudeness, assurance, boldness, insolence. *(ANT.) truckling, politeness, diffidence, subservience.*

impertinent *(SYN.)* rude, offensive, insolent, disrespectful, arrogant, brazen, impudent, insulting, contemptuous, abusive. *(ANT.) polite, respectful, considerate, courteous.*

impetuous *(SYN.)* rash, heedless, quick, hasty, careless, passionate, impulsive. *(ANT.) cautious, reasoning, careful, prudent, thoughtful, calculating.*

implicate *(SYN.)* reproach, accuse, blame, involve, upbraid, condemn, incriminate, rebuke, censure. *(ANT.) exonerate, absolve.*

implore *(SYN.)* beg, pray, request, solicit, crave, entreat, beseech, ask, importune, supplicate, adjure, appeal, petition. *(ANT.) give, cede, bestow, favor, grant.*

imply *(SYN.)* mean, involve, suggest, connote, hint, mention, indicate, insinuate, signify. *(ANT.) state, assert, declare, express.*

impolite *(SYN.)* rude, unpolished, impudent, boorish, blunt, discourteous, rough, saucy, surly, savage, insolent, gruff, uncivil, coarse, ignorant, crude, illiterate, raw, primitive, vulgar, untaught. *(ANT.) genteel, courteous, courtly, dignified, polite, stately, noble, civil.*

import *(SYN.)* influence, significance, stress, emphasis, importance, value, weight. *(ANT.) triviality, insignificance.*

important *(SYN.)* critical, grave, influential, momentous, well-known, pressing, relevant, prominent, primary, essential, weighty, material, considerable, famous, principle, famed, sequential, notable, significant, illustrious, decisive. *(ANT.) unimportant, trifling, petty, trivial, insignificant, secondary, anonymous, irrelevant.*

impose *(SYN.)* levy, require, demand.

imposing *(SYN.)* lofty, noble, majestic, magnificent, august, dignified, grandiose, high, grand, impressive, pompous, stately. *(ANT.) ordinary, undignified, humble, common, lowly.*

imposition *(SYN.)* load, onus, burden.

impossible *(SYN.)* preposterous.

impregnable *(SYN.)* safe, invulnerable, secure, unassailable. *(ANT.) vulnerable.*

impress *(SYN.)* awe, emboss, affect, mark, imprint, indent, influence.

impression *(SYN.)* influence, indentation, feeling, opinion, mark, effect, depression, guess, thought, belief, dent, sensibility. *(ANT.) fact, insensibility.*

impressive *(SYN.)* arresting, moving, remarkable, splendid, thrilling, striking, majestic, grandiose, imposing, commanding, affecting, exciting, touching, stirring. *(ANT.) regular, unimpressive, commonplace.*

impromptu *(SYN.)* casual, unprepared, offhand, extemporaneous.

improper *(SYN.)* unfit, unsuitable, inappropriate, naughty, indecent, unbecoming. *(ANT.) fitting, proper, appropriate.*

improve *(SYN.)* better, reform, refine, ameliorate, amend, help, upgrade, rectify. *(ANT.) debase, vitiate, impair, corrupt, damage.*

improvement *(SYN.)* growth, advance, progress, betterment, development, advancement, progression. *(ANT.) relapse, regression, decline, retrogression, delay.*

imprudent *(SYN.)* indiscreet, thoughtless, desultory, lax, neglectful, remiss, careless, inattentive, heedless, inconsiderate, reckless, ill-advised, irresponsible. (*ANT.*) careful, meticulous, accurate.

impudence *(SYN.)* boldness, insolence, rudeness, sauciness, assurance, effrontery, impertinence, presumption, audacity. (*ANT.*) politeness, truckling, subservience, diffidence.

impudent *(SYN.)* forward, rude, abrupt, prominent, striking, bold, fresh, impertinent, insolent, pushy, insulting, brazen. (*ANT.*) bashful, flinching, polite, courteous, cowardly, retiring, timid.

impulse *(SYN.)* hunch, whim, fancy, urge, caprice, surge, pulse.

impulsive *(SYN.)* passionate, rash, spontaneous, heedless, careless, hasty, quick, impetuous. (*ANT.*) reasoning, calculating, careful, prudent, cautious.

impure *(SYN.)* dishonest, spoiled, tainted, contaminated, debased, corrupt, profligate, unsound, putrid, corrupted, crooked, depraved, vitiated, venal.

imputation *(SYN.)* diary, incrimination, arraignment, indictment. (*ANT.*) exoneration, pardon, exculpation.

inability *(SYN.)* incompetence, incapacity, handicap, disability, impotence, weakness. (*ANT.*) power, strength, ability, capability.

inaccurate *(SYN.)* false, incorrect, mistaken, untrue, askew, wrong, awry, erroneous, fallacious, imprecise, faulty, amiss. (*ANT.*) right, accurate, true, correct.

inactive *(SYN.)* lazy, unemployed, indolent, motionless, still, inert, dormant, idle, unoccupied. (*ANT.*) employed, working, active, industrious, occupied.

inadequate *(SYN.)* insufficient, lacking, short, incomplete, defective, scanty. (*ANT.*) satisfactory, enough, adequate, ample, sufficient.

inadvertent *(SYN.)* careless, negligent, unthinking, thoughtless.

inane *(SYN.)* trite, insipid, banal, absurd, silly, commonplace, vapid, foolish, stupid, hackneyed. (*ANT.*) stimulating, novel, fresh, original, striking.

inanimate *(SYN.)* deceased, spiritless, lifeless, gone, dull, mineral, departed, dead, insensible, vegetable, unconscious. (*ANT.*) living, stirring, alive, animate.

inattentive *(SYN.)* absent-minded, distracted, abstracted, preoccupied. (*ANT.*) watchful, attending, attentive.

inaugurate *(SYN.)* commence, begin, open, originate, start, arise, launch, enter, initiate. (*ANT.*) end, terminate, close, complete, finish.

incense *(SYN.)* anger, enrage, infuriate.

incentive *(SYN.)* impulse, stimulus, inducement, encouragement. (*ANT.*) discouragement.

inception *(SYN.)* origin, start, source, opening, beginning, outset, commencement. (*ANT.*) end, termination, close, completion, consummation.

incessant *(SYN.)* perennial, uninterrupted, continual, ceaseless, continuous, unremitting, eternal, constant, unceasing, unending, perpetual, everlasting. (*ANT.*) rare, occasional, periodic, interrupted.

incident *(SYN.)* happening, situation, occurrence, circumstance, condition, event.

incidental *(SYN.)* casual, contingent, trivial, undesigned, chance, fortuitous, accidental, secondary, unimportant, unintended. (*ANT.*) intended, fundamental, planned, calculated, willed, decreed.

incidentally *(SYN.)* by the way.

incinerate *(SYN.)* sear, char, blaze, scald, singe, consume, scorch, burn. (*ANT.*) quench, put out, extinguish.

incisive *(SYN.)* neat, succinct, terse, brief, compact, condensed, neat, summary, concise. (*ANT.*) wordy, prolix, verbose, lengthy.

incite *(SYN.)* goad, provoke, urge, arouse, encourage, cause, stimulate, induce, instigate, foment. (*ANT.*) quiet, bore, pacify, soothe.

inclination *(SYN.)* bent, preference, desire, slope, affection, bent, bias, disposition, bending, penchant, incline, attachment, predisposition, predication, tendency, prejudice, slant, lean, leaning. (*ANT.*) nonchalance, apathy, distaste, aversion, reluctance, disinclination, uprightness, *repugnance.*

incline *(SYN.)* slope, nod, lean.

include *(SYN.)* contain, hold, accommodate, embody, encompass, involve, comprise, embrace. *(ANT.)* omit, exclude.

income *(SYN.)* earnings, salary, wages, revenue, pay, return, receipts.

incomparable *(SYN.)* peerless, matchless, unequaled.

incompetency *(SYN.)* inability, weakness, handicap, impotence, disability, incapacity. *(ANT.) strength, ability, power, capability.*

incomprehensible *(SYN.)* unintelligible, indecipherable.

inconceivable *(SYN.)* unbelievable, unimaginable, impossible. *(ANT.) possible, believable.*

incongruous *(SYN.)* inconsistent, contrary, incompatible, irreconcilable, contradictory, unsteady, wavering, paradoxical, vacillating, discrepant, illogical. *(ANT.) consistent, compatible, correspondent.*

inconsiderate *(SYN.)* unthinking, careless, unthoughtful, unmindful. *(ANT.) thoughtful, considerate, kind.*

inconsistency *(SYN.)* discord, variance, contention, conflict, controversy, interference. *(ANT.) harmony, concord, amity, consonance.*

inconsistent *(SYN.)* fickle, wavering, variable, changeable, contrary, unstable, illogical, contradictory, irreconcilable, discrepant, paradoxical, incompatible, self-contradictory, incongruous, unsteady, fitful, shifting. *(ANT.) unchanging, steady, logical, stable, uniform, constant.*

inconspicuous *(SYN.)* retiring, unnoticed, unostentatious. *(ANT.) obvious, conspicuous.*

inconstant *(SYN.)* fickle, shifting, changeable, fitful, vacillating, unstable, wavering. *(ANT.) stable, constant, steady, uniform, unchanging.*

inconvenient *(SYN.)* awkward, inappropriate, untimely, troublesome. *(ANT.) handy, convenient.*

incorrect *(SYN.)* mistaken, wrong, erroneous, inaccurate. *(ANT.) proper, accurate, suitable.*

increase *(SYN.)* amplify, enlarge, grow, magnify, multiply, augment, enhance, expand, intensify, swell, raise, greaten, prolong, broaden, lengthen, expansion, accrue, extend, heighten. *(ANT.) diminish, reduce, atrophy, shrink, shrinkage, decrease, lessening, lessen, contract.*

incredible *(SYN.)* improbable, unbelievable. *(ANT.) plausible, credible, believable.*

incriminate *(SYN.)* charge, accuse, indict, arraign, censure. *(ANT.) release, exonerate, acquit, absolve, vindicate.*

incrimination *(SYN.)* imputation, indictment, accusation, charge, arraignment. *(ANT.) exoneration, pardon, exculpation.*

indebted *(SYN.)* obliged, grateful, beholden, thankful, appreciative. *(ANT.) unappreciative, thankless.*

indecent *(SYN.)* impure, obscene, pornographic, coarse, dirty, filthy, smutty, gross, disgusting. *(ANT.) modest, refined, decent.*

indeed *(SYN.)* truthfully, really, honestly, surely.

indefinite *(SYN.)* unsure, uncertain, vague, confused, unsettled, confusing. *(ANT.) decided, definite, equivocal.*

independence *(SYN.)* liberation, privilege, freedom, immunity, familiarity, liberty, exemption, license. *(ANT.) necessity, constraint, compulsion, reliance, dependence, bondage, servitude.*

independent *(SYN.)* free, unrestrained, voluntary, autonomous, self-reliant, uncontrolled, unrestricted. *(ANT.) enslaved, contingent, dependent, restricted.*

indestructible *(SYN.)* enduring, lasting, permanent, unchangeable, abiding, constant, fixed, stable, changeless. *(ANT.) unstable, temporary, transitory, ephemeral.*

indicate *(SYN.)* imply, denote, signify, specify, intimate, designate, symbolize, show, manifest, disclose, mean, reveal. *(ANT.) mislead, distract, conceal, falsify.*

indication *(SYN.)* proof, emblem, omen, sign, symbol, token, mark, portent, gesture, signal.

indict

indict *(SYN.)* charge, accuse, incriminate, censure, arraign. *(ANT.)* acquit, vindicate, absolve, exonerate.

indictment *(SYN.)* incrimination, arraignment, imputation, charge. *(ANT.)* pardon, exoneration, exculpation.

indifference *(SYN.)* unconcern, apathy, impartiality, disinterestedness, insensibility, neutrality. *(ANT.)* ardor, passion, affection, fervor.

indifferent *(SYN.)* uncaring, insensitive, cool, unconcerned. *(ANT.)* caring, concerned, earnest.

indigence *(SYN.)* necessity, destitution, poverty, want, need, privation, penury. *(ANT.)* wealth, abundance, plenty, riches, affluence.

indigenous *(SYN.)* inborn, native, inherent, domestic, aboriginal, plenty, endemic, innate, natural.

indigent *(SYN.)* destitute, covetous, poor, lacking, requiring, wanting, needy, craving.

indignant *(SYN.)* irritated, irate, angry, aroused, exasperated. *(ANT.)* calm, serene, content.

indignation *(SYN.)* ire, petulance, passion, choler, anger, wrath, temper, irritation, exasperation, animosity, resentment, rage. *(ANT.)* self-control, peace, forbearance, patience.

indignity *(SYN.)* insolence, insult, abuse, affront, offense. *(ANT.)* homage, apology.

indirect *(SYN.)* winding, crooked, devious, roundabout, cunning, tricky, tortuous, circuitous, distorted, erratic, swerving, *(ANT.)* straightforward, direct, straight, honest.

indiscretion *(SYN.)* imprudence, folly, absurdity, extravagance. *(ANT.)* prudence, sense, wisdom, reasonableness, judgment.

indispensable *(SYN.)* necessary, fundamental, basic, essential, important, intrinsic, vital. *(ANT.)* optional, expendable, peripheral, extrinsic.

indistinct *(SYN.)* cloudy, dark, mysterious, vague, blurry, ambiguous, cryptic, dim, obscure, enigmatic, abstruse, hazy, blurred, unintelligible. *(ANT.)* clear, lucid, bright, distinct.

indistinguishable *(SYN.)* identical, like, coincident, equal, same, equivalent. *(ANT.)* dissimilar, opposed, contrary, disparate, distinct.

individual *(SYN.)* singular, specific, unique, distinctive, single, particular, undivided, human, apart, marked, person, different, special, separate. *(ANT.)* universal, common, general, ordinary.

individuality *(SYN.)* symbol, description, mark, kind, character, repute, class, standing, sort, nature, disposition, reputation, sign.

indolent *(SYN.)* slothful, lazy, idle, inactive, slow, sluggish, torpid, supine, inert. *(ANT.)* diligent, active, assiduous, vigorous, zesty, alert.

indomitable *(SYN.)* insurmountable, unconquerable, invulnerable, impregnable, unassailable. *(ANT.)* weak, puny, powerless, vulnerable.

induce *(SYN.)* evoke, cause, influence, persuade, effect, make, originate, prompt, incite, create.

inducement *(SYN.)* incentive, motive, purpose, stimulus, reason, impulse, cause, principle, spur, incitement. *(ANT.)* result, attempt, action, effort, deed.

induct *(SYN.)* instate, establish, install. *(ANT.)* eject, oust.

indulge *(SYN.)* humor, satisfy, gratify.

indulgent *(SYN.)* obliging, pampering, tolerant, easy.

indurate *(SYN.)* impenitent, hard, insensible, tough, obdurate, callous, unfeeling. *(ANT.)* soft, compassionate, tender, sensitive.

industrious *(SYN.)* hard-working, perseverant, busy, active, diligent, assiduous, careful, patient. *(ANT.)* unconcerned, indifferent, lethargic, careless, apathetic, lazy, indolent, shiftless.

inebriated *(SYN.)* drunk, tight, drunken, intoxicated, tipsy. *(ANT.)* sober, clearheaded, temperate.

ineffective *(SYN.)* pliant, tender, vague, wavering, defenseless, weak, inadequate, poor, irresolute, frail, decrepit, delicate, vacillating, assailable, exposed, vulnerable. *(ANT.) sturdy, robust, potent, powerful.*

inept *(SYN.)* clumsy, awkward, improper, inappropriate. *(ANT.) adroit, dexterous, adept, appropriate, proper, apt, fitting.*

inequity *(SYN.)* wrong, injustice, unfairness, grievance, injury. *(ANT.) righteousness, lawfulness, equity, justice.*

inert *(SYN.)* lazy, dormant, slothful, inactive, idle, indolent, motionless, unmoving, fixed, static. *(ANT.) working, active, industrious, occupied.*

inertia *(SYN.)* indolence, torpidity, idleness, slothfulness, sluggishness. *(ANT.) assiduousness, activity, alertness, diligence.*

inevitable *(SYN.)* definite, fixed, positive, sure, undeniable, indubitable, certain, assured, unquestionable, secure. *(ANT.) uncertain, probable, doubtful, questionable.*

inexpensive *(SYN.)* low-priced, cheap, inferior, mean, beggarly, common, poor, shabby, modest, economical. *(ANT.) expensive, costly, dear.*

inexperienced *(SYN.)* naive, untrained, uninformed, green. *(ANT.) experienced, skilled, sophisticated, trained, seasoned.*

inexplicable *(SYN.)* hidden, mysterious, obscure, secret, dark, cryptic, enigmatical, incomprehensible, occult, recondite, inscrutable, dim. *(ANT.) plain, simple, clear, obvious, explained.*

infamous *(SYN.)* shocking, shameful, scandalous.

infantile *(SYN.)* babyish, naive, immature, childish. *(ANT.) mature, grownup, adult.*

infect *(SYN.)* pollute, poison, contaminate, defile, sully, taint. *(ANT.) purify, disinfect.*

infection *(SYN.)* virus, poison, ailment, disease, pollution, pest, germ, taint, contamination, contagion.

infectious *(SYN.)* contagious, virulent, catching, communicable, pestilential, transferable. *(ANT.) noncommunicable, hygienic, healthful.*

infer *(SYN.)* understand, deduce, extract.

inference *(SYN.)* consequence, result, conclusion, corollary, judgment, deduction.

(ANT.) preconception, foreknowledge, assumption, presupposition.

inferior *(SYN.)* secondary, lower, poorer, minor, subordinate, mediocre. *(ANT.) greater, superior, better, higher.*

infinite *(SYN.)* immeasurable, interminable, unlimited, unbounded, eternal, boundless, illimitable, immense, endless, vast, innumerable, numberless, limitless. *(ANT.) confined, limited, bounded, circumscribed, finite.*

infinitesimal *(SYN.)* minute, microscopic, tiny, submicroscopic. *(ANT.) gigantic, huge, enormous.*

infirm *(SYN.)* feeble, impaired, decrepit, forceless, languid, puny, powerless, enervated, weak, exhausted. *(ANT.) stout, vigorous, forceful, lusty, strong.*

infirmity *(SYN.)* disease, illness, malady, ailment, sickness, disorder, complaint. *(ANT.) soundness, health, vigor, healthiness.*

inflame *(SYN.)* fire, incite, excite, arouse. *(ANT.) soothe, calm.*

inflammation *(SYN.)* infection, soreness, irritation.

inflammatory *(SYN.)* instigating, inciting, provocative.

inflate *(SYN.)* expand, swell, distend. *(ANT.) collapse, deflate.*

inflexible *(SYN.)* firm, stubborn, headstrong, immovable, uncompromising, dogged, contumacious, determined, obstinate, rigid, unbending, unyielding, steadfast. *(ANT.) submissive, compliant, docile, amenable, yielding, flexible, giving, elastic.*

inflict *(SYN.)* deliver, deal, give, impose, apply.

influence *(SYN.)* weight, control, effect, sway.

influenced *(SYN.)* sway, affect, bias, control, actuate, impel, stir, incite.

influential *(SYN.)* important, weighty, prominent, significant, critical, decisive, momentous, relevant, material, pressing, consequential, grave. *(ANT.) petty, irrelevant, mean, trivial, insignificant.*

inform *(SYN.)* apprise, instruct, tell, notify, advise, acquaint, enlighten, impart, warn, teach, advise, relate. (*ANT.*) *delude, mislead, distract, conceal.*

informal (*SYN.*) simple, easy, natural, unofficial, familiar. (*ANT.*) *formal, distant, reserved, proper.*

informality (*SYN.*) friendship, frankness, liberty, acquaintance, sociability, intimacy, unreserved. (*ANT.*) *presumption, constraint, reserve, distance, haughtiness.*

information (*SYN.*) knowledge, data, intelligence, facts.

informative (*SYN.*) educational, enlightening, instructive.

informer (*SYN.*) tattler, traitor, betrayer.

infrequent (*SYN.*) unusual, rare, occasional, strange. (*ANT.*) *commonplace, abundant, usual, ordinary, customary, frequent, numerous.*

ingenious (*SYN.*) clever, skillful, talented, adroit, dexterous, quick-witted, bright, smart, witty, sharp, apt, resourceful, imaginative, inventive, creative. (*ANT.*) *dull, slow, awkward, bungling, unskilled, stupid.*

ingenuity (*SYN.*) cunning, inventiveness, resourcefulness, aptitude, faculty, cleverness, ingenuousness. (*ANT.*) *ineptitude, clumsiness, dullness, stupidity.*

ingenuous (*SYN.*) open, sincere, honest, candid, straightforward, plain, frank, truthful, free, naive, simple, innocent, unsophisticated. (*ANT.*) *scheming, sly, contrived, wily.*

ingredient (*SYN.*) component, element, constituent.

inhabit (*SYN.*) fill, possess, absorb, dwell, occupy, live. (*ANT.*) *relinquish, abandon, release.*

inherent (*SYN.*) innate, native, congenital, intrinsic, inborn, inbred, natural, real. (*ANT.*) *extraneous, acquired, external, extrinsic.*

inhibit (*SYN.*) curb, constrain, hold back, restrain, bridle, hinder, repress, suppress, stop, limit. (*ANT.*) *loosen, aid, incite, encourage.*

inhuman (*SYN.*) merciless, cruel, brutal, ferocious, savage, ruthless, malignant, barbarous, barbaric, bestial. (*ANT.*) *kind, benevolent, forbearing, gentle, compassionate,* merciful, humane.

inimical (*SYN.*) hostile, warlike, adverse, antagonistic, opposed, unfriendly. (*ANT.*) *favorable, amicable, cordial.*

iniquitous (*SYN.*) baleful, immoral, pernicious, sinful, wicked, base, bad, evil, noxious, unsound, villainous, unwholesome. (*ANT.*) *moral, good, excellent, honorable, reputable.*

iniquity (*SYN.*) injustice, wrong, grievance, unfairness, injury. (*ANT.*) *lawful, equity, righteousness, justice.*

initial (*SYN.*) original, first, prime, beginning, earliest, pristine, chief, primeval, primary, foremost, basic, elementary. (*ANT.*) *latest, subordinate, last, least, hindmost, final, terminal.*

initiate (*SYN.*) institute, enter, arise, inaugurate, commence, originate, start, open, begin. (*ANT.*) *terminate, complete, end, finish, close, stop.*

initiative (*SYN.*) enthusiasm, energy, vigor, enterprise.

injure (*SYN.*) harm, wound, abuse, dishonor, damage, hurt, impair, spoil, disfigure, affront, insult, mar. (*ANT.*) *praise, ameliorate, help, preserve, compliment, benefit.*

injurious (*SYN.*) detrimental, harmful, mischievous, damaging, hurtful, deleterious, harmful, destructive. (*ANT.*) *profitable, helpful, advantageous, salutary, beneficial, useful.*

injury (*SYN.*) harm, detriment, damage, injustice, wrong, prejudice, grievance, mischief. (*ANT.*) *repair, benefit, improvement.*

injustice (*SYN.*) unfairness, grievance, iniquity, wrong, injury. (*ANT.*) *righteousness, justice, equity, lawfulness.*

inmate (*SYN.*) patient, prisoner.

inn (*SYN.*) motel, lodge, hotel.

innate (*SYN.*) native, inherent, congenital, real, inborn, natural, intrinsic, inbred. (*ANT.*) *extraneous, acquired, external, extrinsic.*

innocent (*SYN.*) pure, sinless, blameless, innocuous, lawful, naive, faultless, virtuous, not guilty. (*ANT.*) *guilty, corrupt, sinful, culpable, sophisticated, wise, worldly.*

innocuous *(SYN.)* naive, pure, innocent, blameless, virtuous, lawful, faultless, sinless. *(ANT.) sinful, corrupt, unrighteous, culpable, guilty.*

inquire *(SYN.)* ask, solicit, invite, demand, claim, entreat, interrogate, query, beg, request, question, investigate, examine. *(ANT.) dictate, insist, reply, command, order.*

inquiring *(SYN.)* prying, searching, curious, inquisitive, peering, snoopy, peeping, meddling, interrogative. *(ANT.) unconcerned, indifferent, uninterested, incurious.*

inquiry *(SYN.)* investigation, quest, research, examination, interrogation, exploration, query, question, scrutiny, study. *(ANT.) inattention, inactivity, disregard, negligence.*

inquisitive *(SYN.)* meddling, peeping, nosy, interrogative, peering, searching, prying, snoopy, inquiring, curious. *(ANT.) unconcerned, indifferent, uninterested.*

insane *(SYN.)* deranged, mad, foolish, idiotic, demented, crazy, delirious, maniacal, lunatic. *(ANT.) sane, rational, reasonable, sensible, coherent.*

insanity *(SYN.)* delirium, aberration, dementia, psychosis, lunacy, madness, frenzy, mania, craziness, derangement. *(ANT.) stability, rationality, sanity.*

insecure *(SYN.)* uneasy, nervous, uncertain, shaky. *(ANT.) secure.*

insensitive *(SYN.)* unfeeling, impenitent, callous, hard, indurate, obdurate, tough. *(ANT.) soft, compassionate, tender, sensitive.*

insight *(SYN.)* intuition, acumen, penetration, discernment, perspicuity. *(ANT.) obtuseness.*

insignificant *(SYN.)* trivial, paltry, petty, small, frivolous, unimportant, insignificant, trifling. *(ANT.) momentous, serious, important, weighty.*

insincere *(SYN.)* false, dishonest, deceitful. *(ANT.) honest, sincere.*

insinuate *(SYN.)* imply, mean, suggest, connote, signify, involve. *(ANT.) express, state, assert.*

insipid *(SYN.)* tasteless, dull, stale, flat, vapid. *(ANT.) racy, tasty, savory, exciting.*

insist *(SYN.)* command, demand, require.

insolence *(SYN.)* boldness, presumption, sauciness, effrontery, audacity, assurance, impertinence, rudeness. *(ANT.) politeness, truckling, diffidence, subservience.*

insolent *(SYN.)* arrogant, impertinent, insulting, rude, brazen, contemptuous, abusive, offensive, disrespectful. *(ANT.) respectful, courteous, polite, considerate.*

inspect *(SYN.)* observe, discern, survey, view, watch, witness, examine, investigate. *(ANT.) overlook, miss, ignore, skip.*

inspection *(SYN.)* examination, retrospect, survey, revision, reconsideration, critique, criticism, review.

inspiration *(SYN.)* creativity, aptitude, genius, originality, ability, faculty, sagacity, talent, proficient, master, gift, adept, intellectual, thought, impulse, idea, notion, hunch. *(ANT.) dullard, moron, shallowness, ineptitude, stupidity, obtuseness, dolt.*

install *(SYN.)* establish.

instance *(SYN.)* occasion, illustration, occurrence, example, case.

instant *(SYN.)* flash, moment.

instantaneous *(SYN.)* hasty, sudden, unexpected, rapid, abrupt, immediate. *(ANT.) slowly, anticipated, gradual.*

instantly *(SYN.)* now, presently, directly, forthwith, immediately, rapidly, straightaway, at once, instantaneously. *(ANT.) sometime, distantly, hereafter, later, shortly.*

instinct *(SYN.)* intuition, feeling.

instinctive *(SYN.)* offhand, voluntary, willing, spontaneous, automatic, impulsive, extemporaneous. *(ANT.) rehearsed, planned, compulsory, prepared, forced.*

institute *(SYN.)* ordain, establish, raise, form, organize, sanction, fix, found, launch, begin, initiate. *(ANT.) overthrow, upset, demolish, abolish, unsettle.*

instruct *(SYN.)* teach, tutor, educate, inform, school, instill, train, inculcate, drill. *(ANT.) misinform, misguide.*

instruction *(SYN.)* advise, warning, information, exhortation, notification, admonition, caution, recommendation, counsel, suggestion, teaching, training,

instrument

education, command, order.

instrument *(SYN.)* channel, device, utensil, tool, agent, apparatus, means, vehicle, medium, agent, implement. *(ANT.) obstruction, hindrance, preventive, impediment.*

insubordinate *(SYN.)* rebellious, unruly, defiant, disorderly, disobedient, undutiful, refractory, intractable, mutinous. *(ANT.) obedient, compliant, submissive, dutiful.*

insufficient *(SYN.)* limited, lacking, deficient, short, inadequate. *(ANT.) ample, protracted, abundant, big, extended.*

insulation *(SYN.)* quarantine, segregation, seclusion, withdrawal, isolation, loneliness, alienation, solitude. *(ANT.) union, communion, association, connection.*

insult *(SYN.)* insolence, offense, abuse, dishonor, affront, indignity, offend, humiliate, outrage. *(ANT.) compliment, homage, apology, salutation, flatter, praise.*

integrated *(SYN.)* mingled, mixed, combined, interspersed, desegregated, non-sectarian, interracial. *(ANT.) separated, divided, segregated.*

integrity *(SYN.)* honesty, openness, trustworthiness, fairness, candor, justice, rectitude, sincerity, uprightness, soundness, wholeness, honor, principle, virtue. *(ANT.) fraud, deceit, cheating, trickery, dishonesty.*

intellect *(SYN.)* understanding, judgment.

intellectual *(SYN.)* intelligent.

intelligence *(SYN.)* reason, sense, intellect, understanding, mind, ability, skill, aptitude. *(ANT.) feeling, passion, emotion.*

intelligent *(SYN.)* clever, smart, knowledgeable, well-informed, alert, discerning, astute, quick, enlightened, smart, bright, wise. *(ANT.) insipid, obtuse, dull, stupid, slow, foolish, unintelligent, dumb.*

intend *(SYN.)* plan, prepare, scheme, contrive, outline, design, sketch, plot, project.

intense *(SYN.)* brilliant, animated, graphic, lucid, bright, expressive, vivid, deep, profound, concentrated, serious, earnest. *(ANT.) dull, vague, dusky, dim, dreary.*

intensify *(SYN.)* accrue, augment, amplify, enlarge, enhance, extend, expand, heighten, grow, magnify, raise, multiply. *(ANT.)*

reduce, decrease, contract, diminish.

intensity *(SYN.)* force, potency, power, toughness, activity, durability, fortitude, vigor, stamina. *(ANT.) weakness, feebleness, infirmity, frailty.*

intent *(SYN.)* purpose, design, objective, intention, aim. *(ANT.) accidental, result, chance.*

intention *(SYN.)* intent, purpose, objective, plan, expectation, aim, object. *(ANT.) chance, accident.*

intentional *(SYN.)* deliberate, intended, studied, willful, contemplated, premeditated, designed, voluntary, purposeful, planned. *(ANT.) fortuitous, accidental, chance.*

intentionally *(SYN.)* purposefully, deliberately, maliciously. *(ANT.) accidentally.*

interest *(SYN.)* attention, concern, care, advantage, benefit, profit, ownership, credit, attract, engage, amuse, entertain. *(ANT.) apathy, weary, disinterest.*

interested *(SYN.)* affected, concerned. *(ANT.) unconcerned, indifferent, uninterested.*

interesting *(SYN.)* engaging, inviting, fascinating, attractive. *(ANT.) boring, tedious, uninteresting, wearisome.*

interfere *(SYN.)* meddle, monkey, interpose, interrupt, tamper, butt in, intervene.

interference *(SYN.)* prying, intrusion, meddling, obstacle, obstruction.

interior (SYN.) internal, inmost, inner, inward, inside, center. *(ANT.) outer, adjacent, exterior, external, outside.*

interject *(SYN.)* intrude, introduce, insert, inject, interpose.

interminable *(SYN.)* immense, endless, immeasurable, unlimited, vast, unbounded, boundless, eternal, infinite. *(ANT.) limited, bounded, circumscribed, confined.*

internal *(SYN.)* inner, interior, inside, intimate, private. *(ANT.) outer, external, surface.*

interpose *(SYN.)* arbitrate, inject, intervene, meddle, insert, interject, introduce, intercede, intrude, interfere. *(ANT.)*

overlook, avoid, disregard.

interpret *(SYN.)* explain, solve, translate, construe, elucidate, decode, explicate, render, unravel, define, understand. *(ANT.) misinterpret, falsify, confuse, distort, misconstrue.*

interrogate *(SYN.)* quiz, analyze, inquire, audit, question, contemplate, assess, dissect, notice, scan, review, view, check, survey, scrutinize, examine. *(ANT.) overlook, omit, neglect, disregard.*

interrupt *(SYN.)* suspend, delay, postpone, defer, adjourn, stay, discontinue, intrude, interfere. *(ANT.) prolong, persist, continue, maintain, proceed.*

interval *(SYN.)* pause, gap.

intervene *(SYN.)* insert, intercede, meddle, inject, introduce, interpose, mediate, interfere, interrupt, intrude. *(ANT.) overlook, avoid, disregard.*

intimacy *(SYN.)* fellowship, friendship, acquaintance, frankness, familiarity, unreserved, liberty. *(ANT.) presumption, distance, haughtiness, constraint, reserve.*

intimate *(SYN.)* chummy, confidential, friendly, loving, affectionate, close, familiar, near, personal, private, secret. *(ANT.) conventional, formal, ceremonious, distant.*

intimation *(SYN.)* reminder, implication, allusion, hint, insinuation. *(ANT.) declaration, statement, affirmation.*

intolerant *(SYN.)* fanatical, narrow-minded, prejudiced, bigoted, illiberal, dogmatic, biased. *(ANT.) tolerant, radical, liberal, progressive, broad-minded, fair.*

intoxicated *(SYN.)* inebriated, tipsy, drunk, tight, drunken, high. *(ANT.) sober, temperate, clearheaded.*

intrepid *(SYN.)* brave, fearless, insolent, abrupt, rude, pushy, adventurous, daring, courageous, prominent, striking, forward, imprudent. *(ANT.) timid, bashful, flinching, cowardly, retiring.*

intricate *(SYN.)* compound, perplexing, complex, involved, complicated. *(ANT.) simple, plain, uncompounded.*

intrigue *(SYN.)* design, plot, cabal, machination, stratagem, scheme, attract, charm,

interest, captivate.

intrinsic *(SYN.)* natural, inherent, inbred, congenital, inborn, native. *(ANT.) extraneous, acquired, external, extrinsic.*

introduce *(SYN.)* acquaint, present, submit, present, offer, propose.

introduction *(SYN.)* preamble, prelude, beginning, prologue, start, preface. *(ANT.) finale, conclusion, end, epilogue, completion.*

intrude *(SYN.)* invade, attack, encroach, trespass, penetrate, infringe, interrupt. *(ANT.) vacate, evacuate, abandon.*

intruder *(SYN.)* trespasser, thief, prowler, robber.

intuition *(SYN.)* insight, acumen, perspicuity, penetration, discernment, instinct, clairvoyance.

invade *(SYN.)* intrude, violate, infringe, attack, penetrate, encroach, trespass. *(ANT.) vacate, abandon, evacuate, relinquish.*

invalidate *(SYN.)* annul, cancel, abolish, revoke, abrogate. *(ANT.) promote, restore, sustain, establish, continue.*

invaluable *(SYN.)* priceless, precious, valuable. *(ANT.) worthless.*

invasion *(SYN.)* assault, onslaught, aggression, attack, intrusion. *(ANT.) surrender, opposition, resistance, defense.*

invective *(SYN.)* insult, abuse, disparagement, upbraiding, reproach, defamation, aspersion. *(ANT.) laudation, plaudit, commendation.*

invent *(SYN.)* devise, fabricate, design, concoct, frame, conceive, contrive, create, originate, devise. *(ANT.) reproduce, copy, imitate.*

inventive *(SYN.)* fanciful, imaginative, visionary, poetical, clever, creative. *(ANT.) unromantic, literal, dull, prosaic.*

inventiveness *(SYN.)* cunning, cleverness, ingeniousness, aptitude. *(ANT.) ineptitude, clumsiness, dullness, stupidity.*

invert *(SYN.)* upset, turn about, transpose, countermand, revoke, reverse. *(ANT.) maintain, stabilize, endorse.*

investigate *(SYN.)* look, probe, ransack, scrutinize, ferret, examine, seek, explore, search, scour, inspect, study.

investigation *(SYN.)* exploration, interrogation, quest, question, scrutiny, inquiry, query, examination, study, research. *(ANT.)* inattention, disregard, inactivity, negligence.

invigorating *(SYN.)* bracing, fortifying, vitalizing, stimulating.

invincible *(SYN.)* insurmountable, unconquerable, impregnable, indomitable, invulnerable, unassailable. *(ANT.)* powerless, weak, vulnerable.

invisible *(SYN.)* indistinguishable, unseen, imperceptible, indiscernible. *(ANT.)* evident, visible, seen, perceptible.

invite *(SYN.)* bid, ask, encourage, request, urge.

inviting *(SYN.)* appealing, attractive, tempting, luring, alluring. *(ANT.)* unattractive, uninviting.

involuntary *(SYN.)* reflex, uncontrolled, automatic, unintentional. *(ANT.)* voluntary, willful.

involve *(SYN.)* include, embrace, entangle, envelop, incriminate, embroil, implicate, contain, complicate, confuse. *(ANT.)* separate, extricate, disengage.

involved *(SYN.)* compound, intricate, complicated, complex, perplexing. *(ANT.)* plain, uncompounded, simple.

invulnerable *(SYN.)* indomitable, unassailable, invincible, unconquerable, insurmountable, impregnable. *(ANT.)* weak, puny, powerless, vulnerable.

irate *(SYN.)* incensed, enraged, angry.

ire *(SYN.)* indignation, irritation, wrath, anger, animosity, fury, passion, temper, exasperation, petulance, rage. *(ANT.)* peace, patience, self-control, forbearance.

irk *(SYN.)* irritate, bother, disturb, pester, trouble, vex, tease, chafe, annoy. *(ANT.)* console, accommodate, gratify.

irrational *(SYN.)* inconsistent, preposterous, unreasonable, absurd, foolish, nonsensical, ridiculous. *(ANT.)* sensible, sound, rational, consistent, reasonable.

irregular *(SYN.)* eccentric, unusual, aberrant, devious, abnormal, unnatural. *(ANT.)* regular, methodical, fixed, usual, ordinary, even.

irrelevant *(SYN.)* foreign, unconnected, remote, alien, strange. *(ANT.)* germane, relevant, akin, kindred.

irresolute *(SYN.)* frail, pliant, vacillating, ineffective, wavering, weak, yielding, fragile, pliable. *(ANT.)* robust, potent, sturdy, strong, powerful.

irresponsible *(SYN.)* unreliable.

irritable *(SYN.)* hasty, hot, peevish, testy, irascible, fiery, snappish, petulant. *(ANT.)* composed, tranquil, calm.

irritate *(SYN.)* irk, molest, bother, annoy, tease, disturb, inconvenience, vex, trouble, pester, inflame, chafe. *(ANT.)* console, gratify, accommodate, soothe, pacify, calm.

irritation *(SYN.)* chagrin, mortification, vexation, annoyance, exasperation, pique. *(ANT.)* pleasure, comfort, gratification, appeasement.

isolate *(SYN.)* detach, segregate, separate, disconnect. *(ANT.)* happy, cheerful.

isolated *(SYN.)* lone, single, alone, desolate, secluded, solitary, deserted, sole. *(ANT.)* surrounded, accompanied.

isolation *(SYN.)* quarantine, seclusion, separation, solitude, alienation, retirement, segregation, detachment. *(ANT.)* fellowship, union, association, communion, connection.

issue *(SYN.)* flow, proceed, result, come, emanate, originate, abound, copy, number, edition, problem, question.

itemize *(SYN.)* register, detail, record. *(ANT.)* generalize, include, summarize.

J

jab *(SYN.)* thrust, poke, nudge, prod, shove, jolt, boost, tap, slap, rap, thwack, push.

jabber *(SYN.)* mumble, gossip, prattle, chatter, gab, palaver.

jacent *(SYN.)* level, flatness, plane, proneness, recline.

jacinth *(SYN.)* decoration, ornament, embellishment.

jack *(SYN.)* fellow, boy, toiler, guy, man, worker.

jackal *(SYN.)* puppet, drone, slave, legman, flunky, slavery, tool, servility, vassal.

jackass *(SYN.)* fool, idiot, dope, dunce, ignoramus, imbecile, ninny, simpleton, blockhead.

jacket *(SYN.)* wrapper, envelope, coat, sheath, cover, casing, folder, enclosure.

jack-of-all-trades *(SYN.)* man friday, expert, proficient, amateur, adept, handyman, dab, master, specialist, mastermind, generalist.

jade *(SYN.)* hussy, wanton, trollop, harlot, common, whore, ignoble, wench, hag, shrew.

jaded *(SYN.)* exhausted, bored, tired, fatigued, satiated, weary, hardened.

jag *(SYN.)* notch, snag, protuberance, barb, dent, cut, nick, serration, indentation, point.

jagged *(SYN.)* crooked, bent, ragged, pointy, notched, aquiline, furcated, serrated. *(ANT.) smooth.*

jail *(SYN.)* stockade, prison, reformatory, penitentiary, keep, dungeon, brig, confine, lock up, detain, imprison, hold captive, coop, cage, house of detention, incarcerate.

jailbird *(SYN.)* convict, parolee, con, inmate, prisoner.

jailer *(SYN.)* guard, keeper, turnkey, warden.

jam *(SYN.)* force, pack, ram, crowd, push, wedge, squeeze, stuff, load, cram, press, crush, marmalade, jelly, conserve, preserve.

jamboree *(SYN.)* celebration, fete, spree, festival, festivity, carousal.

jangle *(SYN.)* rattle, vibrate, clank, clatter, dissonance, discord, quarrel, din, discord.

janitor *(SYN.)* custodian, doorkeeper, caretaker, superintendent, gatekeeper.

jape *(SYN.)* lampoon, banter, joke, jest, tease, ridicule.

jar *(SYN.)* rattle, shake, bounce, jolt.

jargon *(SYN.)* speech, idiom, dialect, vernacular, diction, argot, phraseology, language, patois, parlance, slang. *(ANT.) gibberish, babble, nonsense, drivel.*

jaundiced *(SYN.)* biased, prejudiced. *(ANT.) fair.*

jaunt *(SYN.)* journey, trip, tour, excursion, outing, voyage, expedition.

jaunty *(SYN.)* lively, vivacious, buoyant, winsome, frisky, showy, dapper, breezy.

jazzy *(SYN.)* garish, vivacious, loud, splashy, exaggerated, flashy.

jealous *(SYN.)* covetous, desirous of, envious.

jealousy *(SYN.)* suspicion, envy, resentfulness, greed, covetousness. *(ANT.) tolerance, indifference, geniality, liberality.*

jeer *(SYN.)* taunt, mock, scoff, deride, make fun of, gibe, sneer. *(ANT.) flatter, praise, compliment, laud.*

jeering *(SYN.)* mockery, sneering, derision, sarcasm, irony, ridicule.

jell *(SYN.)* finalize, congeal, set, solidify, shape up, take form.

jeopardize *(SYN.)* risk, dare, expose, imperil, chance, venture, conjecture, hazard, endanger. *(ANT.) know, guard, determine.*

jerk *(SYN.)* quiver, twitch, shake, spasm, jolt, yank, fool.

jerkwater *(SYN.)* remote, hick, backwoods, unimportant, one-horse.

jest *(SYN.)* mock, joke, tease, fun, witticism, quip.

jester *(SYN.)* fool, buffoon, harlequin, clown. *(ANT.) sage, genius, scholar.*

jet *(SYN.)* squirt, spurt, gush, inky, coal-black, nozzle.

jettison *(SYN.)* heave, discharge, throw, eject, cast off, dismiss.

jetty *(SYN.)* pier, breakwater, bulwark, buttress.

jewel *(SYN.)* ornament, gemstone, gem, bauble, stone.

jib *(SYN.)* shrink, shy, dodge, retreat, balk.

jig *(SYN.)* caper, prance, jiggle, leap, skip.

jiggle *(SYN.)* shimmy, agitate, jerk, twitch, wiggle.

jilt *(SYN.)* abandon, get rid of, reject, desert, forsake, leave.

jingle *(SYN.)* chime, ring, tinkle.

jinx *(SYN.)* hex, whammy, nemesis, curse, evil eye.

jittery *(SYN.)* jumpy, nervous, quivering, shaky, skittish.

job *(SYN.)* toil, business, occupation, post, chore, stint, career, duty, employment, profession, trade, work, situation, labor, assignment, position, undertaking, calling, task.

jobless *(SYN.)* idle, unoccupied, inactive, unemployed.

jocularity *(SYN.)* humor, wit, joke, facetiousness, waggery. *(ANT.)* sorrow, gravity.

jocund *(SYN.)* mirthful, elated, pleasant, cheerful, merry, gay, jovial, frolicsome.

jog *(SYN.)* gait, trot, sprint, run, lope.

join *(SYN.)* conjoin, unite, attach, accompany, associate, assemble, fit, couple, combine, fasten, unite, clasp, put together, go with, adjoin, link, connect. *(ANT.)* separate, disconnect, split, sunder, part, divide, detach.

joint *(SYN.)* link, union, connection, junction, coupling, common, combined, mutual, connected. *(ANT.)* divided, separate.

joke *(SYN.)* game, jest, caper, prank, anecdote, quip, tease, antic, banter, laugh.

joker *(SYN.)* wisecracker, humorist, comedian, trickster, comic, jester, wit, punster.

jolly *(SYN.)* merry, joyful, gay, happy, sprightly, pleasant, jovial, gleeful, spirited, cheerful, glad. *(ANT.)* mournful, depressed, sullen, glum.

jolt *(SYN.)* sway, waver, startle, rock, jar, totter, jerk, bounce, quake, bump, shake.

josh *(SYN.)* poke fun at, kid, tease, ridicule.

jostle *(SYN.)* shove, push, bump, thrust, jar, shake.

jot *(SYN.)* note, write, record.

jounce *(SYN.)* bounce, jolt, bump, jostle.

journey *(SYN.)* tour, passage, cruise, voyage, pilgrimage, jaunt, trip, outing, expedition, junket, excursion, travel.

joust *(SYN.)* tournament, contest, skirmish, competition, fight.

jovial *(SYN.)* good-natured, kindly, merry, good-humored, good-hearted, joyful, jolly, gleeful. *(ANT.)* solemn, sad, serious, grim.

joy *(SYN.)* pleasure, glee, bliss, elation, mirth, felicity, rapture, delight, transport, exultation, gladness, happiness, festivity, satisfaction, merriment, ecstasy. *(ANT.)* grief, depression, unhappiness, sorrow, misery, gloom, sadness, affliction.

joyful *(SYN.)* gay, lucky, opportune, cheerful, happy, blissful, jovial, merry, gleeful, delighted, glad, contented, fortunate. *(ANT.)* gloomy, sad, blue, solemn, serious, grim, morose, glum, depressed.

joyous *(SYN.)* jolly, gay, blithe, merry, gleeful, cheerful, jovial. *(ANT.)* sad, gloomy, sorrowful, melancholy.

jubilant *(SYN.)* exulting, rejoicing, overjoyed, triumphant, gay, elated, delighted. *(ANT.)* dejected.

jubilee *(SYN.)* gala, holiday, celebration, festival, fete.

judge *(SYN.)* umpire, think, estimate, decide, arbitrator, condemn, decree, critic, appreciate, adjudicator, determine, arbiter, magistrate, arbitrate, justice, consider, mediate, referee, evaluate.

judgment *(SYN.)* wisdom, perspicacity, discernment, decision, common sense, estimation, verdict, understanding, intelligence, discretion, opinion, sense, discrimination. *(ANT.)* thoughtlessness, senselessness, arbitrariness.

judicial *(SYN.)* legal, judicatory, forensic.

judicious *(SYN.)* sensible, wise, well-advised, thoughtful. *(ANT.)* ignorant.

jug *(SYN.)* bottle, jar, flask, flagon, pitcher.

juice *(SYN.)* broth, liquid, sap, distillation, serum, fluid.

jumble *(SYN.)* disarrangement, tumult, agitation, ferment, turmoil, commotion, confuse, mix, muddle, scramble, disorder. *(ANT.)* peace, arrange, compose, certainty, tranquillity.

jumbo *(SYN.)* huge, big, immense, enormous, giant, colossal, monstrous, mammoth, gigantic, tremendous. *(ANT.)* miniature, midget, dwarf, small, tiny.

jump *(SYN.)* leap, caper, skip, bound, jerk,

vault, hop, spring.

jumpy *(SYN.)* touchy, excitable, nervous, sensitive. *(ANT.)* tranquil, calm, unruffled.

junction *(SYN.)* coupling, joining, union, crossroads, intersection, weld, connection, linking, meeting, tie-up, seam, joint. *(ANT.)* separation.

jungle *(SYN.)* woods, thicket, undergrowth, forest, bush.

junior *(SYN.)* secondary, inferior, minor, lower, younger.

junk *(SYN.)* rubbish, scraps, trash, waste, dump, discard, castoffs, debris.

junky *(SYN.)* tawdry, ramshackle, tattered, tacky, shoddy.

jurisdiction *(SYN.)* power, commission, warrant, authority, authorization, sovereignty.

just *(SYN.)* fair, trustworthy, precise, exact, candid, upright, honest, impartial, lawful, rightful, proper, legal, truthful, merely, only, conscientious. *(ANT.)* tricky, dishonest, unjust, corrupt, lying, deceitful.

justice *(SYN.)* justness, rectitude, equity, law, fairness, impartiality, right. *(ANT.)* inequity, wrong, partiality.

justifiable *(SYN.)* allowable, tolerable, admissible, warranted. *(ANT.)* unsuitable, inadmissible.

justify *(SYN.)* uphold, excuse, defend, acquit, exonerate, absolve, clear, vindicate.

jut *(SYN.)* project, protrude, stick out.

juvenile *(SYN.)* puerile, youthful, childish, youngster, youth, young, child. *(ANT.)* old, aged, adult, mature.

K

kaiser *(SYN.)* czar, caesar, caliph, mogul, padishah, tycoon, khan.

kavass *(SYN.)* badel, macebearer, constable.

keck *(SYN.)* vomit, belch, retch.

keen *(SYN.)* clever, cunning, acute, penetrating, exact, severe, shrewd, wily, astute, sharp, bright, intelligent, smart, sharp-witted, witty, cutting, fine, quick. *(ANT.)* stupid, shallow, dull, blunted, slow, bland, gentle, obtuse, blunt.

keep *(SYN.)* maintain, retain, observe, protect, confine, sustain, continue, preserve, save, guard, restrain, reserve, obey, support, honor, execute, celebrate, conserve, have, tend, detain, commemorate, hold. *(ANT.)* abandon, disobey, dismiss, discard, ignore, neglect, lose, reject, relinquish.

keeper *(SYN.)* warden, jailer, ranger, guard, turnkey, watchman, escort, custodian.

keeping *(SYN.)* congeniality, uniformity, consentaneousness, conformance, congruity, union.

keepsake *(SYN.)* reminder, memorial, relic, souvenir, memento, hint, remembrance.

keg *(SYN.)* container, drum, tub, barrel, receptacle, reservatory, capsule, cask, tank.

kelpie *(SYN.)* sprite, nixie, naiad, pixy.

kelson *(SYN.)* bottom, sole, toe, foot, root, keel.

kempt *(SYN.)* neat, trim, tidy, spruce, cleaned.

ken *(SYN.)* field, view, vision, range, scope.

kennel *(SYN.)* swarm, flock, covy, drove, herd, pound, doghouse.

kerchief *(SYN.)* neckcloth, handkerchief, scarf, headpiece, babushka.

kern *(SYN.)* peasant, carle, serf, tike, tyke, countryman.

kernel *(SYN.)* marrow, pith, backbone, soul, heart, core, nucleus.

ketch *(SYN.)* lugger, cutter, clipper, ship, barge, sloop.

kettle *(SYN.)* pan, caldron, vat, pot, teapot, vessel, receptacle, receiver, tureen.

key *(SYN.)* opener, explanation, tone, lead, cause, source, note, pitch, answer, clue.

keynote *(SYN.)* core, model, theme, pattern, standard, gist.

keystone *(SYN.)* backbone, support.

khan *(SYN.)* master, czar, kaiser, padishah, caesar.

kick *(SYN.)* punt, remonstrate, boot.

kickback *(SYN.)* repercussion, backfire, rebound.

kickoff *(SYN.)* beginning, opening,

commencement, outset, start.

kid *(SYN.)* joke, tease, fool, jest, tot, child.

kidnap *(SYN.)* abduct, snatch, shanghai.

kill *(SYN.)* execute, put to death, slay, butcher, assassinate, murder, cancel, destroy, slaughter, finish, end, annihilate, massacre. *(ANT.)* save, protect, animate, resuscitate, vivify.

killing *(SYN.)* massacre, genocide, slaughter, carnage, butchery, bloodshed.

killjoy *(SYN.)* wet blanket, sourpuss, party-pooper.

kin *(SYN.)* relatives, family, folks, relations.

kind *(SYN.)* humane, affable, compassionate, benevolent, merciful, tender, sympathetic, breed, indulgent, forbearing, kindly, race, good, thoughtful, character, benign, family, sort, species, variety, class, type, gentle. *(ANT.)* unkind, cruel, merciless, severe, mean, inhuman.

kindle *(SYN.)* fire, ignite, light, arouse, excite, set afire, stir up, trigger, move, provoke, inflame. *(ANT.)* extinguish, calm.

kindly *(SYN.)* warm, kind-hearted, kind, warm-hearted. *(ANT.)* mean, cruel.

kindred *(SYN.)* family, relations, relatives, consanguinity, kinsfolk, affinity. *(ANT.)* strangers, disconnection.

kinetic *(SYN.)* vigorous, active, dynamic, energetic, mobile, forceful.

king *(SYN.)* sovereign, ruler, chief, monarch, potentate.

kingdom *(SYN.)* realm, empire, monarchy, domain.

kingly *(SYN.)* kinglike, imperial, regal, royal, majestic.

kink *(SYN.)* twist, curl, quirk, complication.

kinship *(SYN.)* lineage, blood, family, stock, relationship.

kismet *(SYN.)* fate, end, fortune, destiny.

kiss *(SYN.)* pet, caress, fondle, cuddle, osculate, embrace. *(ANT.)* vex, spurn, annoy, tease, buffet.

kit *(SYN.)* outfit, collection, furnishings, equipment, rig, gear, set.

knack *(SYN.)* cleverness, readiness, deftness, ability, ingenuity, skill, talent, aptitude, know-how, art, adroitness, skillfulness. *(ANT.)* inability, clumsiness, awkwardness, ineptitude.

knave *(SYN.)* rogue, rascal, villain, scoundrel.

knead *(SYN.)* combine, massage, blend.

knickknack *(SYN.)* trinket, bric-a-brac, trifle.

knife *(SYN.)* sword, blade.

knightly *(SYN.)* valiant, courageous, gallant, chivalrous, noble.

knit *(SYN.)* unite, join, mend, fasten, connect, combine, heal.

knob *(SYN.)* doorknob, handle, protuberance, bump.

knock *(SYN.)* thump, tap, rap, strike, hit, jab, punch, beat, pound, bang, hammer.

knoll *(SYN.)* hill, elevation, hump, mound, butte.

knot *(SYN.)* cluster, gathering, collection, group, crowd, twist, snarl, tangle.

know *(SYN.)* perceive, comprehend, apprehend, recognize, understand, discern, discriminate, ascertain, identify, be aware, distinguish. *(ANT.)* doubt, suspect, dispute.

knowing *(SYN.)* sage, smart, wise, clever, sagacious, shrewd.

knowledge *(SYN.)* information, wisdom, erudition, learning, apprehension, scholarship, lore, cognizance. *(ANT.)* misunderstanding, ignorance, stupidity, illiteracy.

knurl *(SYN.)* gnarl, knot, projection, burl, node, lump.

kosher *(SYN.)* permitted, okay, fit, proper, acceptable.

kowtow *(SYN.)* stoop, bend, kneel, genuflect, bow.

kudos *(SYN.)* acclaim, praise, approbation, approval.

L

label *(SYN.)* mark, tag, title, name, marker, stamp, sticker, ticket, docket, identity.

labor *(SYN.)* toil, travail, effort, task, childbirth, work, parturition, striving, workers, effort, industry, workingmen, strive, exertion, employment, drudgery, endeavor.

(*ANT.*) *recreation, indolence, idleness, leisure.*

laboratory *(SYN.)* lab, workroom, workshop.

laborer *(SYN.)* wage earner, helper, worker, toiler, coolie, blue-collar worker.

laborious *(SYN.)* tiring, difficult, hard, burdensome, industrious, painstaking. (*ANT.*) *simple, easy, relaxing, restful.*

labyrinth *(SYN.)* complex, maze, tangle.

lace *(SYN.)* openwork, fancywork, embroidery, edging.

lacerate *(SYN.)* mangle, tear roughly.

laceration *(SYN.)* cut, wound, puncture, gash, lesion, injury.

lack *(SYN.)* want, need, shortage, dearth, scarcity, require. (*ANT.*) *profusion, quantity, plentifulness.*

lackey *(SYN.)* yes-man, stooge, flatterer, flunky.

lacking *(SYN.)* insufficient, short, deficient, incomplete, defective, scanty. (*ANT.*) *satisfactory, enough, ample, sufficient, adequate.*

lackluster *(SYN.)* dull, pallid, flat, lifeless, drab, dim.

laconic *(SYN.)* short, terse, compact, brief, curt, succinct, concise.

lacquer *(SYN.)* polish, varnish, gild.

lad *(SYN.)* youth, boy, fellow, stripling.

laden *(SYN.)* burdened, loaded, weighted.

ladle *(SYN.)* scoop, dipper.

lady *(SYN.)* matron, woman, dame, gentlewoman.

ladylike *(SYN.)* feminine, womanly, maidenly, womanish, female. (*ANT.*) *masculine, male, virile, mannish, manly.*

lag *(SYN.)* dawdle, loiter, linger, poke, dillydally, straggle, delay, tarry, slowdown.

laggard *(SYN.)* idler, lingerer, slowpoke, dawdler.

lair *(SYN.)* retreat, burrow, den, nest, mew, hole.

lambaste *(SYN.)* berate, castigate, scold, censure.

lame *(SYN.)* feeble, maimed, disabled, crippled, deformed, hobbling, unconvincing, weak, poor, inadequate, halt, defective, limping. (*ANT.*) *vigorous, convincing, plau-*

sible, athletic, robust, agile, sound.

lament *(SYN.)* deplore, wail, bemoan, bewail, regret, grieve, mourning, lamentation, moaning, wailing, weep, mourn, sorrow. (*ANT.*) *celebrate, rejoice.*

lamentable *(SYN.)* unfortunate, deplorable.

lamp *(SYN.)* light, beam, illumination, shine, insight, knowledge, understanding, radiance, luminosity, incandescence. (*ANT.*) *shadow, darkness, obscurity, gloom.*

lampoon *(SYN.)* skit, tirade, burlesque, parody, satire.

lance *(SYN.)* cut, pierce, perforate, stab, puncture, impale, knife.

land *(SYN.)* earth, continent, ground, soil, domain, estate, field, realm, plain, surface, arrive, descend, country, island, region, alight, shore, sod, tract, farm.

landlord *(SYN.)* owner, landholder, landowner, proprietor.

landmark *(SYN.)* keystone, monument, milestone, point, cornerstone.

landscape *(SYN.)* panorama, environs, countryside, scenery, scene.

landslide *(SYN.)* rockfall, glissade, avalanche.

lane *(SYN.)* alley, way, road, path, aisle, pass, channel, avenue, artery, passage.

language *(SYN.)* dialect, tongue, speech, lingo, jargon, cant, diction, idiom, patter, phraseology, vernacular, words, lingo, talk, slang. (*ANT.*) *gibberish, nonsense, babble, drivel.*

languid *(SYN.)* feeble, drooping, irresolute, debilitated, dull, lethargic, weak, faint, listless, wearied. (*ANT.*) *forceful, strong, vigorous.*

languish *(SYN.)* decline, sink, droop, wither, waste, fail, wilt, weaken. (*ANT.*) *revive, rejuvenate, refresh, renew.*

languor *(SYN.)* weariness, depression, torpor, inertia, apathy.

lanky *(SYN.)* skinny, gaunt, lean, scrawny, slender, thin. (*ANT.*) *chunky, stocky, obese.*

lantern *(SYN.)* torch, light, lamp, flashlight.

lap *(SYN.)* drink, lick, fold over.

lapse *(SYN.)* decline, sink, go down, slump.

larceny *(SYN.)* pillage, robbery, stealing, theft, burglary, plunder.

lard *(SYN.)* grease, fat.

large *(SYN.)* great, vast, colossal, ample, extensive, capacious, sizable, broad, massive, grand, immense, big, enormous, huge, giant, mammoth, wide. *(ANT.)* tiny, little, short, small.

largely *(SYN.)* chiefly, mainly, principally, mostly.

lariat *(SYN.)* lasso, rope.

lark *(SYN.)* fling, frolic, play, fun, spree, joke, revel, celebration.

lascivious *(SYN.)* lecherous, raunchy, lustful, wanton, lewd.

lash *(SYN.)* thong, whip, rod, cane, blow, strike, hit, beat, knout.

lass *(SYN.)* maiden, girl, damsel. *(ANT.)* woman, lad.

lasso *(SYN.)* lariat, rope, noose, snare.

last *(SYN.)* terminal, final, ultimate, remain, endure, concluding, latest, utmost, end, conclusive, hindmost, continue, extreme. *(ANT.)* first, initial, beginning, opening, starring, foremost.

latch *(SYN.)* clasp, hook, fastener, lock, closing, seal, catch.

late *(SYN.)* overdue, tardy, behind, advanced, delayed, new, slow, recent. *(ANT.)* timely, early.

lately *(SYN.)* recently, yesterday.

latent *(SYN.)* potential, undeveloped, unseen, dormant, secret, concealed, inactive, hidden, obscured, covered, quiescent. *(ANT.)* visible, evident, conspicuous, explicit, manifest.

lateral *(SYN.)* sideways, glancing, tangential, marginal, skirting, side.

lather *(SYN.)* suds, foam, froth.

latitude *(SYN.)* range, scope, freedom, extent.

latter *(SYN.)* more recent, later.

lattice *(SYN.)* grating, screen, frame, trellis, openwork, framework, grid.

laud *(SYN.)* commend, praise, extol, glorify, compliment. *(ANT.)* criticize, belittle.

laudable *(SYN.)* creditable, praiseworthy, commendable, admirable.

laudation *(SYN.)* applause, compliment, flattery, praise, commendation, acclaim, extolling, glorification. *(ANT.)* criticizing, condemnation, reproach, disparagement, censure.

laugh *(SYN.)* chuckle, giggle, snicker, cackle, titter, grin, smile, roar, guffaw, jeer, mock.

laughable *(SYN.)* funny, amusing, comical, humorous, ridiculous.

launch *(SYN.)* drive, fire, propel, start, begin, originate, set afloat, initiate. *(ANT.)* finish, stop, terminate.

launder *(SYN.)* bathe, wash, scrub, scour.

laurels *(SYN.)* glory, distinction, recognition, award, commendation, reward, honor.

lavatory *(SYN.)* toilet, washroom, bathroom, latrine.

lavish *(SYN.)* squander, waste, dissipate, scatter, abundant, free, plentiful, liberal, extravagant, ample, wear out, prodigal, generous, spend. *(ANT.)* economize, save, conserve, accumulate, sparing, stingy, preserve.

law *(SYN.)* decree, formula, statute, act, rule, ruling, standard, principle, ordinance, proclamation, regulation, order, edict.

lawful *(SYN.)* legal, permissible, allowable, legitimate, authorized, constitutional, rightful. *(ANT.)* prohibited, criminal, illicit, illegal, illegitimate.

lawless *(SYN.)* uncivilized, uncontrolled, wild, savage, untamed, violent. *(ANT.)* obedient, law-abiding, tame.

lawlessness *(SYN.)* chaos, anarchy.

lawn *(SYN.)* grass, meadow, turf.

lawyer *(SYN.)* counsel, attorney, counselor.

lax *(SYN.)* slack, loose, careless, vague, lenient, lazy. *(ANT.)* firm, rigid.

lay *(SYN.)* mundane, worldly, temporal, place, dispose, bet, wager, hazard, risk, stake, site, earthly, profane, laic, arrange, location, put, set, ballad, deposit, position, song, secular. *(ANT.)* spiritual, unworldly, remove, misplace, disturb, mislay, disarrange, ecclesiastical, religious.

lay off *(SYN.)* discharge, bounce, fire, dismiss.

layout (*SYN.*) plan, arrangement, design.

lazy (*SYN.*) slothful, supine, idle, inactive, sluggish, inert, indolent, torpid. (*ANT.*) alert, ambitious, forceful, diligent, active, assiduous.

lea (*SYN.*) pasture, meadow.

leach (*SYN.*) remove, extract, seep, dilute, wash out.

lead (*SYN.*) regulate, conduct, guide, escort, direct, supervise, command, come first, steer, control. (*ANT.*) follow.

leader (*SYN.*) master, ruler, captain, chief, commander, principal, director, head, chieftain. (*ANT.*) follower, servant, disciple, subordinate, attendant.

leading (*SYN.*) dominant, foremost, principal, first, main, primary.

league (*SYN.*) entente, partnership, association, confederacy, coalition, society, alliance, federation, union. (*ANT.*) separation, schism.

leak (*SYN.*) dribble, flow, drip, opening, perforation.

lean (*SYN.*) rely, tilt, slim, slender, slope, incline, tend, trust, bend, tendency, slant, depend, spare, scant, lanky, thin, meager, inclination, narrow, sag. (*ANT.*) rise, heavy, fat, erect, straighten, portly, raise.

leaning (*SYN.*) trend, proclivity, bias, tendency, bent, predisposition, proneness. (*ANT.*) disinclination, aversion.

leap (*SYN.*) vault, skip, caper, dive, hurdle, jump, bound, start, hop, plunge, spring.

learn (*SYN.*) gain, find out, memorize, acquire, determine.

learned (*SYN.*) erudite, knowing, enlightened, deep, wise, discerning, scholarly, intelligent, educated, sagacious. (*ANT.*) simple, uneducated, ignorant, illiterate, unlettered, foolish.

learning (*SYN.*) science, education, lore, apprehension, wisdom, knowledge, scholarship, erudition. (*ANT.*) misunderstanding, ignorance, stupidity.

lease (*SYN.*) charter, let, rent, engage.

leash (*SYN.*) chain, strap, shackle, collar.

least (*SYN.*) minutest, smallest, tiniest, minimum, fewest, slightest. (*ANT.*) most.

leave (*SYN.*) give up, retire, desert, abandon, withdraw, relinquish, will, depart, quit, liberty, renounce, go, bequeath, consent, allowance, permission, freedom, forsake. (*ANT.*) come, stay, arrive, tarry, remain, abide.

lecherous (*SYN.*) lustful, sensual, carnal, lascivious.

lecture (*SYN.*) talk, discussion, lesson, instruct, speech, conference, sermon, report, recitation, address, oration, discourse. (*ANT.*) writing, meditation, correspondence.

ledge (*SYN.*) eaves, ridge, shelf, rim, edge.

lee (*SYN.*) shelter, asylum, sanctuary, haven.

leech (*SYN.*) barnacle, bloodsucker, parasite.

leer (*SYN.*) eye, grimace, ogle, wink, squint.

leeway (*SYN.*) reserve, allowance, elbowroom, slack, clearance.

leftovers (*SYN.*) scraps, remains, residue, remainder.

legacy (*SYN.*) bequest, inheritance, heirloom.

legal (*SYN.*) legitimate, rightful, honest, allowable, allowed, permissible, lawful, permitted, authorized. (*ANT.*) illicit, illegal, prohibited, illegitimate.

legalize (*SYN.*) authorize, ordain, approve, sanction.

legate (*SYN.*) envoy, agent, representative, emissary.

legend (*SYN.*) saga, fable, allegory, myth, parable, tale, story, folklore, fiction, chronicle. (*ANT.*) history, facts.

legendary (*SYN.*) fictitious, traditional, mythical, imaginary, fanciful.

legible (*SYN.*) plain, readable, clear, distinct. (*ANT.*) illegible.

legion (*SYN.*) outfit, unit, troop, regiment, company, battalion, force, army, team, division.

legislation (*SYN.*) resolution, ruling, lawmaking, regulation, enactment, statute, decree.

legislator (*SYN.*) statesman, congressman, senator, politician, lawmaker.

legitimate (*SYN.*) true, real, bonafide, lawful, proper, right, valid, correct, unadulterated, authentic, rightful, legal, sincere. (*ANT.*) *sham, counterfeit, artificial, false.*

leisure (*SYN.*) respite, intermission, ease, relaxation, rest, calm, tranquillity, recreation, peace, pause. (*ANT.*) *motion, commotion, tumult, agitation, disturbance.*

leisurely (*SYN.*) sluggish, laggard, unhurried, relaxed, casual, dawdling, slow, deliberate. (*ANT.*) *hurried, swift, pressed, rushed, forced, fast, speedy, quick.*

lend (*SYN.*) entrust, advance, confer.

length (*SYN.*) reach, measure, extent, distance, span, longness, stretch.

lengthen (*SYN.*) stretch, prolong, draw, reach, increase, grow, protract, extend. (*ANT.*) *shrink, contract, shorten.*

leniency (*SYN.*) grace, pity, compassion, mildness, charity, mercy, clemency. (*ANT.*) *vengeance, punishment, cruelty.*

lenient (*SYN.*) tender, humane, clement, tolerant, compassionate, merciful, relaxed, forgiving, gentle, mild, lax, kind. (*ANT.*) *unfeeling, pitiless, brutal, remorseless.*

leprechaun (*SYN.*) gnome, imp, goblin, fairy, elf, sprite, banshee.

lesion (*SYN.*) wound, blemish, sore, trauma, injury.

less (*SYN.*) fewer, smaller, reduced, negative, stinted. (*ANT.*) *more.*

lessen (*SYN.*) shorten, reduce, deduct, subtract, curtail, diminish, shrink, dwindle, decline, instruction, teaching, remove, decrease. (*ANT.*) *swell, grow, enlarge, increase, expand, multiply, amplify.*

lesson (*SYN.*) exercise, session, class, assignment, section, recitation.

let (*SYN.*) admit, hire out, contract, allow, permit, consent, leave, grant, rent. (*ANT.*) *deny.*

letdown (*SYN.*) disillusionment, disappointment.

lethal (*SYN.*) mortal, dangerous, deadly, fatal, devastating.

lethargic (*SYN.*) sluggish, logy, slow, listless, phlegmatic, lazy. (*ANT.*) *vivacious, energetic.*

lethargy (*SYN.*) numbness, stupor, daze, insensibility, torpor. (*ANT.*) *wakefulness, liveliness, activity, readiness.*

letter (*SYN.*) note, mark, message, character, symbol, sign, memorandum.

letup (*SYN.*) slowdown, slackening, lessening, abatement, reduction.

levee (*SYN.*) dike, breakwater, dam, embankment.

level (*SYN.*) smooth, even, plane, equivalent, uniform, horizontal, equal, flatten, equalize, raze, demolish, flat. (*ANT.*) *uneven, sloping, hilly, broken.*

level-headed (*SYN.*) reasonable, sensible, calm, collected, cool.

leverage (*SYN.*) clout, power, influence, weight, rank.

levity (*SYN.*) humor, triviality, giddiness, hilarity, fun, frivolity.

levy (*SYN.*) tax, duty, tribute, rate, assessment, exaction, charge, custom. (*ANT.*) *wages, remuneration, gift.*

lewd (*SYN.*) indecent, smutty, course, gross, disgusting, impure. (*ANT.*) *pure, decent, refined.*

liability (*SYN.*) indebtedness, answerability, obligation, vulnerability.

liable (*SYN.*) answerable, responsible, likely, exposed to, subject, amenable, probable, accountable. (*ANT.*) *immune, exempt, independent.*

liaison (*SYN.*) union, coupling, link, connection, alliance.

liar (*SYN.*) fibber, falsifier, storyteller, fabricator, prevaricator.

libel (*SYN.*) slander, calumny, vilification, aspersion, defamation. (*ANT.*) *defense, praise, applause, flattery.*

liberal (*SYN.*) large, generous, unselfish, openhanded, broad, tolerant, kind, unprejudiced, open-minded, lavish, plentiful, ample, abundant, extravagant, extensive. (*ANT.*) *restricted, conservative, stingy.*

liberality (*SYN.*) kindness, philanthropy, beneficence, humanity, altruism, benevolence, generosity, charity. (*ANT.*) *selfishness, cruelty, malevolence.*

liberate (*SYN.*) emancipate, loose, release, let go, deliver, free, discharge. (*ANT.*) *subjugate, oppress, jail, confine, restrict, imprison.*

liberated *(SYN.)* loose, frank, emancipated, careless, liberal, freed, autonomous, exempt, familiar. *(ANT.) subject, clogged, restricted, impeded.*

liberty *(SYN.)* permission, independence, autonomy, license, privilege, emancipation, self-government, freedom. *(ANT.) constraint, imprisonment, bondage, captivity.*

license *(SYN.)* liberty, freedom, liberation, permission, exemption, authorization, warrant, allow, consent, permit, sanction, approval, unrestraint. *(ANT.) servitude, constraint, bondage, necessity.*

lick *(SYN.)* taste, lap, lave.

lid *(SYN.)* top, cover, cap, plug, cork, stopper.

lie *(SYN.)* untruth, fib, illusion, delusion, falsehood, fiction, equivocation, prevarication, repose, location, perjury, misinform, site, recline, similitude. *(ANT.) variance, truth, difference.*

life *(SYN.)* sparkle, being, spirit, vivacity, animation, buoyancy, vitality, existence, biography, energy, liveliness, vigor. *(ANT.) demise, lethargy, death, languor.*

lift *(SYN.)* hoist, pick up, elevate, raise, heft.

light *(SYN.)* brightness, illumination, beam, gleam, lamp, knowledge, brilliance, fixture, bulb, candle, fire, ignite, burn, dawn, incandescence, flame, airy, unsubstantial, dainty, luminosity, shine, radiance, giddy, weightless. *(ANT.) darkness, gloom, shadow, extinguish, darken.*

lighten *(SYN.)* diminish, unburden, reduce, brighten.

light-headed *(SYN.)* giddy, silly, dizzy, frivolous. *(ANT.) sober, clear-headed, rational.*

lighthearted *(SYN.)* carefree, merry, gay, cheerful, happy, glad. *(ANT.) somber, sad, serious, melancholy.*

like *(SYN.)* fancy, esteem, adore, love, admire, care for, prefer, cherish. *(ANT.) disapprove, loathes, hate, dislike.*

likely *(SYN.)* liable, reasonable, probable, possible.

likeness *(SYN.)* similarity, resemblance, representation, image, portrait. *(ANT.) difference.*

likewise *(SYN.)* besides, as well, also, too, similarly.

liking *(SYN.)* fondness, affection, partiality. *(ANT.) antipathy, dislike.*

limb *(SYN.)* arm, leg, member, appendage, part, bough.

limber *(SYN.)* bending, flexible, elastic, pliable. *(ANT.) inflexible, stiff.*

limbo *(SYN.)* exile, banishment, purgatory.

limelight *(SYN.)* spotlight, notice, notoriety, fame, prominence.

limerick *(SYN.)* jingle, rhyme.

limit *(SYN.)* terminus, bound, extent, confine, border, restriction, boundary, restraint, edge, frontier, check, end, limitation. *(ANT.) endlessness, vastness, boundlessness.*

limn *(SYN.)* depict, portray, sketch, paint, illustrate.

limp *(SYN.)* soft, flabby, drooping, walk, limber, supple, flexible, hobble, stagger. *(ANT.) stiff.*

limpid *(SYN.)* clear, open, transparent, unobstructed. *(ANT.) cloudy.*

line *(SYN.)* row, file, series, array, sequence, wire, seam, wrinkle, crease, boundary, arrangement, kind, type, division.

lineage *(SYN.)* race, family, tribe, nation, strain, folk, people, ancestry, clan.

linger *(SYN.)* wait, rest, bide, delay, dawdle, stay, loiter, remain, dilly-dally, tarry. *(ANT.) leave, expedite.*

lingo *(SYN.)* vernacular, dialect, language, jargon, speech.

link *(SYN.)* unite, connector, loop, couple, attach, connective, connection, coupling, juncture, bond. *(ANT.) separate, disconnect, split.*

lip *(SYN.)* edge, brim, rim.

liquid *(SYN.)* watery, fluent, fluid, flowing. *(ANT.) solid, congealed.*

liquidate *(SYN.)* pay off, settle, defray.

liquor *(SYN.)* spirits, alcohol, drink, booze.

lissome *(SYN.)* nimble, quick, lively, flexible, agile.

list

list *(SYN.)* roll, register, slate, series.

listen *(SYN.)* overhear, attend to, heed, hear, list, hearken. *(ANT.)* ignore, scorn, disregard, reject.

listless *(SYN.)* uninterested, tired, lethargic, unconcerned, apathetic. *(ANT.)* active.

literal *(SYN.)* exact, verbatim, precise, strict, faithful.

literally *(SYN.)* actually, exactly, really.

literate *(SYN.)* informed, educated, learned, intelligent, versed, knowledgeable. *(ANT.)* unread, illiterate, ignorant, unlettered.

literature *(SYN.)* books, writings, publications.

lithe *(SYN.)* supple, flexible, bending, limber, pliable. *(ANT.)* stiff.

litigious *(SYN.)* quarrelsome, disputatious, argumentative.

litter *(SYN.)* rubbish, trash, scatter, clutter, strew, debris, rubble, disorder.

little *(SYN.)* tiny, petty, miniature, diminutive, puny, wee, significant, small, short, brief, bit, trivial. *(ANT.)* huge, large, big, long, immense.

liturgy *(SYN.)* ritual, sacrament, worship, service.

live *(SYN.)* dwell, reside, abide, survive, exist, alive, occupy, stay, active, surviving. *(ANT.)* die.

livelihood *(SYN.)* keep, sustenance, support, subsistence, job, trade, profession, vocation.

lively *(SYN.)* blithe, vivaciousness, clear, vivid, active, frolicsome, brisk, fresh, animated, energetic, live, spry, vigorous, quick, nimble, bright, exciting, supple. *(ANT.)* stale, dull, listless, slow, vapid.

livestock *(SYN.)* animals, cattle.

livid *(SYN.)* grayish, furious, pale, enraged.

living *(SYN.)* support, livelihood, existent, alive.

load *(SYN.)* oppress, trouble, burden, weight, freight, afflict, encumber, pack, shipment, cargo, lade, tax. *(ANT.)* lighten, console, unload, mitigate, empty, ease.

loafer *(SYN.)* loiterer, bum, idler, sponger, deadbeat.

loan *(SYN.)* credit, advance, lend.

loath *(SYN.)* reluctant, unwilling, opposed.

loathe *(SYN.)* dislike, despise, hate, abhor, detest, abominate. *(ANT.)* love, approve, like, admire.

loathsome *(SYN.)* foul, vile, detestable, revolting, abominable, atrocious, offensive, odious. *(ANT.)* pleasant, commendable, alluring, agreeable, delightful.

lob *(SYN.)* toss, hurl, pitch, throw, heave.

lobby *(SYN.)* foyer, entry, entrance, vestibule, passageway, entryway.

local *(SYN.)* limited, regional, restricted.

locality *(SYN.)* nearness, neighborhood, district, vicinity. *(ANT.)* remoteness.

locate *(SYN.)* discover, find, unearth, site, situate, place.

located *(SYN.)* found, residing, positioned, situated, placed.

location *(SYN.)* spot, locale, station, locality, situation, place, area, site, vicinity, position, zone, region.

lock *(SYN.)* curl, hook, bolt, braid, ringlet, plait, close, latch, tuft, fastening, bar, hasp, fasten, tress. *(ANT.)* open.

locker *(SYN.)* wardrobe, closet, cabinet, chest.

locket *(SYN.)* case, lavaliere, pendant.

locomotion *(SYN.)* movement, travel, transit, motion.

locution *(SYN.)* discourse, cadence, manner, accent.

lodge *(SYN.)* cabin, cottage, hut, club, chalet, society, room, reside, dwell, live, occupy, inhabit, abide, board, fix, settle.

lodger *(SYN.)* guest, tenant, boarder, occupant.

lofty *(SYN.)* high, stately, grandiose, towering, elevated, exalted, sublime, majestic, proud, grand, tall, pompous. *(ANT.)* undignified, lowly, common, ordinary.

log *(SYN.)* lumber, wood, board, register, record, album, account, journal, timber.

logical *(SYN.)* strong, effective, telling, convincing, reasonable, sensible, rational, sane, sound, cogent. *(ANT.)* crazy, illogical, irrational, unreasonable, weak.

logy *(SYN.)* tired, inactive, lethargic, sleepy,

weary.

loiter *(SYN.)* idle, linger, wait, stay, tarry, dilly-dally, dawdle.

loll *(SYN.)* hang, droop, recline, repose, relax.

lone *(SYN.)* lonely, sole, unaided, single, deserted, isolated, secluded, apart, alone, solitary. *(ANT.)* *surrounded, accompanied.*

loneliness *(SYN.)* solitude, isolation, seclusion, alienation.

lonely *(SYN.)* unaided, isolated, single, solitary, lonesome, unaccompanied, deserted, alone, desolate. *(ANT.)* *surrounded, attended.*

loner *(SYN.)* recluse, maverick, outsider, hermit.

lonesome *(SYN.)* secluded, remote, unpopulated, barren, empty, desolate.

long *(SYN.)* lengthy, prolonged, wordy, elongated, lingering, drawn out, lasting, protracted, extensive, length, prolix, far-reaching, extended. *(ANT.)* *terse, concise, abridged, short.*

long-standing *(SYN.)* persistent, established.

long-winded *(SYN.)* boring, dull, wordy. *(ANT.)* *curt, terse.*

look *(SYN.)* gaze, witness, seem, eye, behold, see, watch, scan, view, appear, stare, discern, glance, examine, examination, peep, expression, appearance, regard, study, contemplation, survey. *(ANT.)* *overlook, hide, avert, miss.*

loom *(SYN.)* emerge, appear, show up.

loop *(SYN.)* ringlet, noose, spiral, fastener.

loose *(SYN.)* untied, unbound, lax, vague, unrestrained, dissolute, limp, undone, baggy, disengaged, indefinite, slack, careless, heedless, unfastened, free, wanton. *(ANT.)* *restrained, steady, fastened, secure, tied, firm, fast, definite, inhibited.*

loosen *(SYN.)* untie, undo, loose, unchain. *(ANT.)* *tie, tighten, secure.*

loot *(SYN.)* booty, plunder, take, steal, rob, sack, rifle, pillage, ravage, devastate.

lope *(SYN.)* run, race, bound, gallop.

lopsided *(SYN.)* unequal, twisted, uneven, askew, distorted.

loquacious *(SYN.)* garrulous, wordy, profuse, chatty, verbose.

lord *(SYN.)* peer, ruler, proprietor, nobleman, master, owner, boss, governor.

lore *(SYN.)* learning, knowledge, wisdom, stories, legends, beliefs, teachings.

lose *(SYN.)* misplace, flop, fail, sacrifice, forfeit, mislay, vanish, surrender. *(ANT.)* *succeed, locate, place, win, discover, find.*

loss *(SYN.)* injury, damage, want, hurt, need, bereavement, trouble, death, failure, deficiency.

lost *(SYN.)* dazed, wasted, astray, forfeited, preoccupied, used, adrift, bewildered, missing, distracted, consumed, misspent, absorbed, confused, mislaid, gone, destroyed. *(ANT.)* *found, anchored.*

lot *(SYN.)* result, destiny, bunch, many, amount, fate, cluster, group, sum, portion, outcome, number, doom, issue.

lotion *(SYN.)* cosmetic, salve, balm, cream.

lottery *(SYN.)* wager, chance, drawing, raffle.

loud *(SYN.)* vociferous, noisy, resounding, stentorian, clamorous, sonorous, thunderous, shrill, blaring, roaring, deafening. *(ANT.)* *soft, inaudible, murmuring, subdued, quiet, dulcet.*

lounge *(SYN.)* idle, loaf, laze, sofa, couch, davenport, relax, rest, lobby, salon, divan.

louse *(SYN.)* scoundrel, knave, cad, rat.

lousy *(SYN.)* revolting, grimy, rotten, dirty, disgusting.

lovable *(SYN.)* charming, attractive, delightful, amiable, sweet, cuddly, likeable.

love *(SYN.)* attachment, endearment, affection, adoration, liking, devotion, warmth, tenderness, friendliness, adore, worship, like, cherish, fondness. *(ANT.)* *loathing, detest, indifference, dislike, hate, hatred.*

loveliness *(SYN.)* grace, pulchritude, elegance, charm, attractiveness, comeliness, fairness, beauty. *(ANT.)* *ugliness, eyesore, disfigurement, deformity.*

lovely *(SYN.)* handsome, fair, charming, pretty, attractive, delightful, beautiful, beauteous, exquisite, comely. *(ANT.)* *ugly, unsightly, homely, foul, hideous, repulsive.*

lover

lover *(SYN.)* fiancé, suitor, courter, sweetheart, beau.

loving *(SYN.)* close, intimate, confidential, affectionate, friendly. *(ANT.)* *formal, conventional, ceremonious, distant.*

low *(SYN.)* mean, vile, despicable, vulgar, abject, groveling, contemptible, lesser, menial. *(ANT.)* *righteous, lofty, esteemed, noble.*

lower *(SYN.)* subordinate, minor, secondary, quiet, soften, disgrace, degrade, decrease, reduce, diminish, inferior. *(ANT.)* *greater, superior, increase, better.*

loyal *(SYN.)* earnest, ardent, addicted, inclined, faithful, devoted, affectionate, prone, fond, patriotic, dependable, true. *(ANT.)* *indisposed, detached, disloyal, traitorous, untrammeled.*

loyalty *(SYN.)* devotion, steadfastness, constancy, faithfulness, fidelity, patriotism, allegiance. *(ANT.)* *treachery, falseness, disloyalty.*

lubricate *(SYN.)* oil, grease, anoint.

lucent *(SYN.)* radiant, beaming, vivid, illuminated, lustrous.

lucid *(SYN.)* plain, visible, clear, intelligible, unmistakable, transparent, limpid, translucent, open, shining, light. *(ANT.)* *unclear, vague, obscure.*

luck *(SYN.)* chance, fortunate, fortune, lot, fate, fluke, destiny, karma. *(ANT.)* *misfortune.*

lucrative *(SYN.)* well-paying, profitable, high-paying, productive, beneficial.

ludicrous *(SYN.)* absurd, ridiculous, preposterous.

lug *(SYN.)* pull, haul, drag, tug.

luggage *(SYN.)* bags, valises, baggage, suitcases, trunks.

lugubrious *(SYN.)* mournful, sad, gloomy, somber, melancholy.

lukewarm *(SYN.)* unenthusiastic, tepid, spiritless, detached, apathetic, mild.

lull *(SYN.)* quiet, calm, soothe, rest, hush, stillness, pause, break, intermission.

lumber *(SYN.)* logs, timber, wood.

luminous *(SYN.)* beaming, lustrous, shining, glowing, gleaming, bright, light.

(ANT.) *murky, dull, dark.*

lummox *(SYN.)* yokel, oaf, bumpkin, clown, klutz.

lump *(SYN.)* swelling, protuberance, mass, chunk, hunk, bump.

lunacy *(SYN.)* derangement, madness, aberration, psychosis, craziness. *(ANT.)* *stability, rationality.*

lunge *(SYN.)* charge, stab, attack, thrust, push.

lurch *(SYN.)* topple, sway, toss, roll, rock, tip, pitch.

lure *(SYN.)* draw, tug, drag, entice, attraction, haul, attract, temptation, persuade, pull, draw on, allure. *(ANT.)* *drive, alienate, propel.*

lurid *(SYN.)* sensational, terrible, melodramatic, startling.

lurk *(SYN.)* sneak, hide, prowl, slink, creep.

luscious *(SYN.)* savory, delightful, juicy, sweet, pleasing, delectable, palatable, delicious, tasty. *(ANT.)* *unsavory, nauseous, acrid.*

lush *(SYN.)* tender, succulent, ripe, juicy. *(ANT.)* *dry, arrid, barren.*

lust *(SYN.)* longing, desire, passion, appetite, craving, aspiration, urge.

lusty *(SYN.)* healthy, strong, mighty, powerful, sturdy, strapping, hale, hardy. *(ANT.)* *weak.*

luxuriant *(SYN.)* abundant, flourishing, dense, lush, rich.

luxurious *(SYN.)* rich, lavish, deluxe, elaborate, fancy, opulent, splendid. *(ANT.)* *simple, crude, sparse.*

luxury *(SYN.)* frills, comfort, extravagance, elegance, splendor. *(ANT.)* *poverty.*

lyric *(SYN.)* musical, text, words, libretto.

lyrical *(SYN.)* poetic, musical.

luster *(SYN.)* shine, gleam, gloss, sparkle, reflection.

macabre *(SYN.)* ghastly, grim, horrible, gruesome.

macala *(SYN.)* mole, patch, freckle, spot.

maceration *(SYN.)* dilution, washing.

machination *(SYN.)* hoax, swindle, card-sharking, cunning, plot, cabal, conspiracy.

machinator *(SYN.)* strategist, schemer.

machine *(SYN.)* motor, mechanism, device, contrivance.

machinist *(SYN.)* engineer.

macilent *(SYN.)* gaunt, lean, lank, meager, emaciated.

mactation *(SYN.)* immolation, self-immolation, infanticide.

maculate *(SYN.)* bespot, stipple.

maculation *(SYN.)* irritation, striae, iridescence, spottiness.

mad *(SYN.)* incensed, crazy, insane, angry, furious, delirious, provoked, enraged, demented, maniacal, exasperated, wrathful, crazy, deranged. *(ANT.) sane, calm, healthy, rational, lucid, cheerful, happy.*

madam *(SYN.)* dame, woman, lady, matron, mistress.

madden *(SYN.)* anger, annoy, infuriate, enrage, provoke, aspirate, outrage. *(ANT.) please, mollify, calm.*

madness *(SYN.)* derangement, delirium, aberration, mania, insanity, craziness, frenzy, psychosis.

maelstrom *(SYN.)* surge, rapids, eddy, white water, riptide.

magazine *(SYN.)* journal, periodical, arsenal, armory.

magic *(SYN.)* sorcery, wizardry, charm, legerdemain, enchantment, black art, necromancy, conjuring.

magical *(SYN.)* mystical, marvelous, magic, miraculous, bewitching, spellbinding.

magician *(SYN.)* conjuror, sorcerer, wizard, witch, artist, trickster.

magistrate *(SYN.)* judge, adjudicator.

magnanimous *(SYN.)* giving, bountiful, beneficent, unselfish. *(ANT.) stingy, greedy, selfish.*

magnate *(SYN.)* leader, bigwig, tycoon, chief, giant.

magnet *(SYN.)* enticer, enticement, lure, temptation.

magnetic *(SYN.)* pulling, attractive, alluring, drawing, enthralling, seductive.

magnetism *(SYN.)* allure, irresistibility, attraction, appeal.

magnificence *(SYN.)* luxury, grandeur, splendor, majesty, dynamic, mesmerizing.

magnificent *(SYN.)* rich, lavish, luxurious, splendid, wonderful, extraordinary, impressive. *(ANT.) simple, plain.*

magnify *(SYN.)* heighten, exaggerate, amplify, expand, stretch, caricature, increase, enhance. *(ANT.) compress, understate, depreciate, belittle.*

magnitude *(SYN.)* mass, bigness, size, area, volume, dimensions, greatness, extent, measure, importance, consequence, significance.

maid *(SYN.)* chambermaid, servant, maidservant.

maiden *(SYN.)* original, foremost, first, damsel, lass, miss.

mail *(SYN.)* dispatch, send, letters, post, correspondence.

maim *(SYN.)* disable, cripple, hurt, wound, injure, mangle, mutilate, incapacitate.

main *(SYN.)* essential, chief, highest, principal, first, leading, cardinal, supreme, foremost. *(ANT.) supplemental, subordinate, auxiliary.*

mainstay *(SYN.)* buttress, pillar, refuge, reinforcement, support, backbone.

maintain *(SYN.)* claim, support, uphold, defend, vindicate, sustain, continue, allege, contend, preserve, affirm, keep, justify, keep up. *(ANT.) neglect, oppose, discontinue, resist, deny.*

maintenance *(SYN.)* subsistence, livelihood, living, support, preservation, upkeep.

majestic *(SYN.)* magnificent, stately, noble, august, grand, imposing, sublime, lofty, high, grandiose, dignified, royal, kingly, princely, regal. *(ANT.) humble, lowly, undignified, common, ordinary.*

majesty *(SYN.)* grandeur, dignity, nobility, splendor, distinction, eminence.

major *(SYN.)* important, superior, larger, chief, greater, uppermost. *(ANT.) inconsequential, minor.*

make

make *(SYN.)* execute, cause, produce, establish, assemble, create, shape, compel, fashion, construct, build, fabricate, manufacture, form, become. *(ANT.) unmake, break, undo, demolish.*

make-believe *(SYN.)* pretend, imagined, simulated, false, fake, unreal.

maker *(SYN.)* inventor, creator, producer, builder, manufacturer, originator.

makeshift *(SYN.)* proxy, deputy, understudy, expedient, agent, lieutenant, alternate, substitute, equivalent. *(ANT.) sovereign, head, principal.*

make-up *(SYN.)* composition, formation, structure, cosmetics.

malady *(SYN.)* disease, illness, sickness, ailment, infirmity, disorder, affliction. *(ANT.) vigor, healthiness, health.*

malaise *(SYN.)* anxiety, apprehension, dissatisfaction, uneasiness, nervousness, disquiet, discontent.

malcontent *(SYN.)* displeased, ill-humored, querulous, discontented, quarrelsome.

male *(SYN.)* masculine, virile. *(ANT.) female, womanly, feminine.*

malefactor *(SYN.)* perpetrator, gangster, hoodlum, wrongdoer, troublemaker, criminal, scoundrel, evildoer, lawbreaker.

malevolence *(SYN.)* spite, malice, enmity, rancor, animosity. *(ANT.) love, affection, toleration, kindness.*

malfunction *(SYN.)* flaw, breakdown, snag, glitch, failure.

malice *(SYN.)* spite, grudge, enmity, ill will, malignity, animosity, rancor, resentment, viciousness, grudge, bitterness. *(ANT.) love, affection, toleration, benevolence, charity.*

malicious *(SYN.)* hostile, malignant, virulent, bitter, rancorous, evil-minded, malevolent, spiteful, wicked. *(ANT.) kind, benevolent, affectionate.*

malign *(SYN.)* misuse, defame, revile, abuse, traduce, asperse, misapply, disparage. *(ANT.) praise, cherish, protect, minor.*

malignant *(SYN.)* harmful, deadly, killing, lethal, mortal, destructive, hurtful, malicious. *(ANT.) benign, harmless.*

malingerer *(SYN.)* quitter, idler, goldbrick.

malleable *(SYN.)* meek, tender, soft, lenient, flexible, mild, compassionate, supple. *(ANT.) tough, rigid, unyielding, hard.*

malodorous *(SYN.)* reeking, fetid, smelly, noxious, vile, rancid, offensive.

malpractice *(SYN.)* wrongdoing, misdeed, abuse, malfeasance, error, mismanagement, dereliction, fault, sin, misconduct.

maltreat *(SYN.)* mistreat, ill-treatment, abuse.

maltreatment *(SYN.)* disparagement, perversion, aspersion, invective, defamation, profanation. *(ANT.) respect, approval, laudation, commendation.*

mammoth *(SYN.)* enormous, immense, huge, colossal, gigantic, gargantuan, ponderous. *(ANT.) minuscule, tiny, small.*

man *(SYN.)* person, human being, society, folk, soul, individual, mortal, fellow, male, gentleman. *(ANT.) woman.*

manacle *(SYN.)* chain, shackle, cuff, handcuff, bond.

manage *(SYN.)* curb, govern, direct, bridle, command, regulate, repress, check, restrain, dominate, guide, lead, supervise, superintend, control, rule. *(ANT.) forsake, submit, abandon, mismanage, bungle.*

manageable *(SYN.)* willing, obedient, docile, controllable, tractable, submissive, governable, wieldy, untroublesome. *(ANT.) recalcitrant, unmanageable, wild.*

management *(SYN.)* regulation, administration, supervision, direction, control.

manager *(SYN.)* overseer, superintendent, supervisor, director, boss, executive.

mandate *(SYN.)* order, injunction, command, referendum, dictate, writ, directive, commission.

mandatory *(SYN.)* compulsory, required, obligatory, imperative, necessary. *(ANT.) optional.*

maneuver *(SYN.)* execution, effort, proceeding, enterprise, working, action, operation, agency, instrumentality. *(ANT.) rest, inaction, cessation.*

mangle *(SYN.)* tear apart, cut, maim,

wound, mutilate, injure, break, demolish.

mangy *(SYN.)* shoddy, frazzled, seedy, threadbare, shabby, ragged, sordid.

manhandle *(SYN.)* maltreat, maul, abuse, ill-treat.

manhood *(SYN.)* maturity, manliness. *(ANT.) youth.*

mania *(SYN.)* insanity, enthusiasm, craze, desire, madness.

manic *(SYN.)* excited, hyped up, agitated.

manifest *(SYN.)* open, evident, lucid, clear, distinct, unobstructed, cloudless, apparent, intelligible, apparent. *(ANT.) vague, overcast, unclear, cloudy, hidden, concealed.*

manifesto *(SYN.)* pronouncement, edict, proclamation, statement, declaration.

manifold *(SYN.)* various, many, multiple, numerous, abundant, copious, profuse. *(ANT.) few.*

manipulate *(SYN.)* manage, feel, work, operate, handle, touch, maneuver.

manly *(SYN.)* strong, brave, masculine, manful, courageous, stalwart.

man-made *(SYN.)* artificial. *(ANT.) natural.*

manner *(SYN.)* air, demeanor, custom, style, method, deportment, mode, habit, practice, way, behavior, fashion.

mannerism *(SYN.)* eccentricity, quirk, habit, peculiarity, idiosyncrasy, trait.

mannerly *(SYN.)* well-bred, gentlemanly, courteous, suave, polite, genteel.

manor *(SYN.)* land, mansion, estate, domain, villa, castle, property, palace.

manslaughter *(SYN.)* murder, killing, assassination, homicide, elimination.

mantle *(SYN.)* serape, garment, overgarment, cover, cloak, wrap.

manual *(SYN.)* directory, guidebook, handbook, physical, laborious, menial.

manufacture *(SYN.)* construct, make, assemble, fabricate, produce, fashion, build.

manure *(SYN.)* fertilizer, droppings, waste, compost.

manuscript *(SYN.)* copy, writing, work, paper, composition, document.

many *(SYN.)* numerous, various, diverse, multitudinous, sundry, multifarious, manifold, abundant, plentiful. *(ANT.) infrequent, meager, few, scanty.*

map *(SYN.)* sketch, plan, chart, graph.

mar *(SYN.)* spoil, hurt, damage, impair, harm, deface, injure. *(ANT.) repair, benefit, mend.*

marathon *(SYN.)* relay, race, contest.

maraud *(SYN.)* invade, plunder, loot, ransack, ravage, raid.

march *(SYN.)* promenade, parade, pace, hike, walk, tramp.

margin *(SYN.)* boundary, border, rim, edge.

marginal *(SYN.)* unnecessary, nonessential, borderline, noncritical. *(ANT.) essential.*

marine *(SYN.)* naval, oceanic, nautical, ocean, maritime.

mariner *(SYN.)* seafarer, gob, seaman, sailor.

marionette *(SYN.)* doll, puppet.

maritime *(SYN.)* shore, coastal, nautical.

mark *(SYN.)* stain, badge, stigma, vestige, sign, feature, label, characteristic, trace, brand, trait, scar, indication, impression, effect, imprint, stamp, brand.

marked *(SYN.)* plain, apparent, noticeable, evident, decided, noted, special, noteworthy.

market *(SYN.)* supermarket, store, bazaar, mart, stall, marketplace, plaza, emporium.

maroon *(SYN.)* desert, leave behind, forsake, abandon, jettison.

marriage *(SYN.)* wedding, matrimony, nuptials, espousal, union, alliance, association. *(ANT.) divorce, celibacy, separation.*

marrow *(SYN.)* center, core, gist, essential.

marry *(SYN.)* wed, espouse, betroth.

marsh *(SYN.)* bog, swamp, mire, everglade, estuary.

marshal *(SYN.)* adjutant, officer, order, arrange, rank.

mart *(SYN.)* shop, market, store.

martial *(SYN.)* warlike, combative, militant, belligerent. *(ANT.) peaceful.*

martyr *(SYN.)* victim, sufferer, tortured, torment, plague, harass, persecute.

marvel *(SYN.)* phenomenon, wonder, miracle, astonishment, sensation.

marvelous *(SYN.)* rare, wonderful, extraordinary, unusual, exceptional, miraculous, wondrous, amazing, astonishing, astounding. *(ANT.) usual, common, ordinary.*

mascot *(SYN.)* pet, amulet, charm.

masculine *(SYN.)* robust, manly, virile, strong, bold, male, lusty, vigorous, hardy, mannish. *(ANT.) weak, emasculated, feminine, effeminate, womanish, female.*

mash *(SYN.)* mix, pulverize, crush, grind, crumble, granulate.

mask *(SYN.)* veil, disguise, cloak, secrete, withhold, hide, cover, protection, protector, camouflage, conceal, screen. *(ANT.) uncover, reveal, disclose, show, expose.*

masquerade *(SYN.)* pretend, disguise, pose, impersonate, costume party.

mass *(SYN.)* society, torso, body, remains, association, carcass, bulk, company, pile, heap, quantity, aggregation. *(ANT.) spirit, mind, intellect.*

massacre *(SYN.)* butcher, murder, carnage, slaughter, execute, slay, genocide, killing, butchery, extermination. *(ANT.) save, protect, vivify, animate.*

massage *(SYN.)* knead, rub, stroke.

masses *(SYN.)* populace, crowd, multitude, people.

massive *(SYN.)* grave, cumbersome, heavy, sluggish, ponderous, serious, burdensome, huge, immense, tremendous, gigantic. *(ANT.) light, animated, small, tiny, little.*

mast *(SYN.)* pole, post.

master *(SYN.)* owner, employer, leader, ruler, chief, head, lord, teacher, manager, holder, commander, overseer, expert, maestro, genius, captain, director, boss. *(ANT.) slave, servant.*

masterful *(SYN.)* commanding, bossy, domineering, dictatorial, cunning, wise, accomplished, skillful, sharp.

masterly *(SYN.)* adroit, superb, skillful, expert. *(ANT.) awkward, clumsy.*

mastermind *(SYN.)* prodigy, sage, guru.

masterpiece *(SYN.)* prizewinner, classic, perfection, model.

mastery *(SYN.)* sway, sovereignty, domination, transcendence, ascendancy, influence, jurisdiction, prestige.

masticate *(SYN.)* chew.

mat *(SYN.)* cover, rug, pallet, bedding, pad.

match *(SYN.)* equivalent, equal, contest, balance, resemble, peer, mate.

matchless *(SYN.)* peerless, incomparable, unequaled, unrivaled, excellent. *(ANT.) ordinary, unimpressive.*

mate *(SYN.)* friend, colleague, associate, partner, companion, comrade. *(ANT.) stranger, adversary.*

material *(SYN.)* sensible, momentous, germane, bodily, palpable, important, physical, essential, corporeal, tangible, substance, matter, fabric. *(ANT.) metaphysical, spiritual, insignificant, mental, immaterial, irrelevant, intangible.*

materialize *(SYN.)* take shape, finalize, embody, incarnate, emerge, appear.

maternal *(SYN.)* motherly. *(ANT.) fatherly.*

mathematics *(SYN.)* measurements, computations, numbers, calculation, figures.

matrimony *(SYN.)* marriage, wedding, espousal, union. *(ANT.) virginity, divorce.*

matrix *(SYN.)* template, stamp, negative, stencil, mold, form, die, cutout.

matron *(SYN.)* lady.

matted *(SYN.)* tangled, clustered, rumpled, shaggy, knotted, gnarled, tousled.

matter *(SYN.)* cause, thing, substance, occasion, material, moment, topic, stuff, concern, theme, subject, consequence, affair, business, interest. *(ANT.) spirit, immateriality.*

mature *(SYN.)* ready, matured, complete, ripe, consummate, mellow, aged, seasoned, full-grown. *(ANT.) raw, crude, undeveloped, young, immature, innocent.*

maudlin *(SYN.)* emotional, mushy, sentimental, mawkish.

maul *(SYN.)* pummel, mistreat, manhandle, beat, batter, bruise, abuse.

mausoleum *(SYN.)* shrine, tomb, vault.

maverick *(SYN.)* nonconformist, oddball, outsider, dissenter, loner.

mawkish *(SYN.)* sentimental, emotional, nostalgic.

maxim *(SYN.)* rule, code, law, proverb,

principle, saying, adage, motto.

maximum *(SYN.)* highest, largest, head, greatest, climax. *(ANT.) minimum.*

may *(SYN.)* can, be able.

maybe *(SYN.)* feasibly, perchance, perhaps, possibly. *(ANT.) definitely.*

mayhem *(SYN.)* brutality, viciousness, ruthlessness.

maze *(SYN.)* complex, labyrinth, network, muddle, confusion, snarl, tangle.

meadow *(SYN.)* field, pasture, lea, range, grassland.

meager *(SYN.)* sparse, scanty, mean, frugal, slight, paltry, inadequate. *(ANT.) ample, plentiful, abundant, bountiful.*

meal *(SYN.)* refreshment, dinner, lunch, repast, breakfast.

mean *(SYN.)* sordid, base, intend, plan, propose, expect, indicate, denote, say, signify, suggest, express, average, nasty, middle, contemptible, offensive, vulgar, unkind, cruel, despicable, vile, low, medium. *(ANT.) dignified, noble, exalted, thoughtful, gentle, openhanded, kind, generous, admirable.*

meander *(SYN.)* wind, stray, wander, twist.

meaning *(SYN.)* gist, connotation, intent, purport, drift, acceptation, implication, sense, import, interpretation, denotation, signification, explanation, purpose, significance.

meaningful *(SYN.)* profound, deep, expressive, important, crucial.

meaningless *(SYN.)* nonsensical, senseless, unreasonable, preposterous.

means *(SYN.)* utensil, channel, agent, money, riches, vehicle, apparatus, device, wealth, support, medium, instrument. *(ANT.) preventive, impediment, hindrance.*

measly *(SYN.)* scanty, puny, skimpy, meager, petty.

measure *(SYN.)* law, bulk, rule, criterion, size, volume, weight, standard, dimension, breadth, depth, test, touchstone, trial, length, extent, gauge.

measureless *(SYN.)* immeasurable, immense, boundless, limitless, infinite, vast. *(ANT.) figurable, ascertainable, measurable.*

meat *(SYN.)* lean, flesh, food.

mecca *(SYN.)* target, shrine, goal, sanctuary, destination.

mechanic *(SYN.)* repairman, machinist.

mechanism *(SYN.)* device, contrivance, tool, machine, machinery.

medal *(SYN.)* decoration, award, badge, medallion, reward, ribbon, prize, honor.

meddle *(SYN.)* tamper, interpose, pry, snoop, intrude, interrupt, interfere, monkey.

meddlesome *(SYN.)* forward, bothersome, intrusive, obtrusive.

mediate *(SYN.)* settle, intercede, umpire, intervene, negotiate, arbitrate, referee.

medicinal *(SYN.)* helping, healing, remedial, therapeutic, corrective.

medicine *(SYN.)* drug, medication, remedy, cure, prescription, potion.

mediocre *(SYN.)* medium, mean, average, moderate, fair, ordinary. *(ANT.) outstanding, exceptional.*

meditate *(SYN.)* remember, muse, think, judge, mean, conceive, contemplate, deem, suppose, purpose, consider, picture, reflect, believe, plan, reckon.

medium *(SYN.)* modicum, average, middling, median. *(ANT.) extreme.*

medley *(SYN.)* hodgepodge, mixture, assortment, conglomeration, mishmash, miscellany.

meek *(SYN.)* subdued, dull, tedious, flat, docile, domesticated, tame, insipid, domestic. *(ANT.) spirited, exciting, savage, wild.*

meet *(SYN.)* fulfill, suffer, find, collide, gratify, engage, connect, converge, encounter, unite, join, satisfy, settle, greet, answer, undergo, meeting, contest, match, assemble, discharge, gather, convene, congregate, confront, intersect. *(ANT.) scatter, disperse, separate, cleave.*

melancholy *(SYN.)* disconsolate, dejected, despondent, glum, somber, pensive, moody, dispirited, depressed, gloomy, dismal, doleful, depression, downcast, gloom, sadness, sad, grave, downhearted, sorrowful. *(ANT.) happy, cheerful, merry.*

meld

meld *(SYN.)* unite, mix, combine, fuse, merge, blend, commingle, amalgamate.

melee *(SYN.)* battle royal, fight, brawl, free-for-all, fracas.

mellow *(SYN.)* mature, ripe, aged, cured, full-flavored, sweet, smooth, melodious, develop, soften. *(ANT.)* unripened, immature.

melodious *(SYN.)* lilting, musical, lyric, dulcet, mellifluous, tuneful, melodic.

melodramatic *(SYN.)* dramatic, ceremonious, affected, stagy, histrionic, overwrought, sensational, stagy. *(ANT.)* unemotional, subdued, modest.

melody *(SYN.)* strand, concord, music, air, song, tune, harmony.

melt *(SYN.)* dissolve, liquefy, blend, fade out, vanish, dwindle, disappear, thaw. *(ANT.)* freeze, harden, solidify.

member *(SYN.)* share, part, allotment, moiety, element, concern, interest, lines, faction, role, apportionment.

membrane *(SYN.)* layer, sheath, tissue, covering.

memento *(SYN.)* keepsake, token, reminder, trophy, sign, souvenir, remembrance.

memoirs *(SYN.)* diary, reflections, experiences, autobiography, journal, confessions.

memorable *(SYN.)* important, historic, significant, unforgettable, noteworthy, momentous, crucial, impressive. *(ANT.)* passing, forgettable, transitory, commonplace.

memorandum *(SYN.)* letter, mark, token, note, indication, remark, message.

memorial *(SYN.)* monument, souvenir, memento, remembrance, commemoration, reminiscent, ritual, testimonial.

memorize *(SYN.)* study, remember.

memory *(SYN.)* renown, remembrance, reminiscence, fame, retrospection, recollection, reputation. *(ANT.)* oblivion.

menace *(SYN.)* warning, threat, intimidation, warn, threaten, imperil, forebode.

menagerie *(SYN.)* collection, zoo, kennel.

mend *(SYN.)* restore, better, refit, sew, remedy, patch, correct, repair, rectify, ameliorate, improve, reform, recover, fix. *(ANT.)* hurt, deface, rend, destroy.

mendacious *(SYN.)* dishonest, false, lying, deceitful, deceptive, tricky. *(ANT.)* honest, truthful, sincere, creditable.

mendicant *(SYN.)* ragamuffin, vagabond, beggar.

menial *(SYN.)* unskilled, lowly, degrading, tedious, humble, routine.

mental *(SYN.)* reasoning, intellectual, rational, thinking, conscious, reflective, thoughtful. *(ANT.)* physical.

mentality *(SYN.)* intellect, reason, understanding, liking, disposition, judgment, brain, inclination, faculties, outlook. *(ANT.)* materiality, corporeality.

mention *(SYN.)* introduce, refer to, reference, allude, enumerate, speak of.

mentor *(SYN.)* advisor, tutor, sponsor, guru, teacher, counselor, master, coach.

mercenary *(SYN.)* sordid, corrupt, venal, covetous, grasping, avaricious, greedy. *(ANT.)* liberal, generous.

merchandise *(SYN.)* stock, wares, goods, sell, commodities, promote, staples, products.

merchant *(SYN.)* retailer, dealer, trader, storekeeper, salesman, businessman.

merciful *(SYN.)* humane, kindhearted, tender, clement, sympathetic, forgiving, tolerant, forbearing, lenient, compassionate, tenderhearted, kind. *(ANT.)* remorseless, cruel, unjust, mean, harsh, unforgiving, vengeful, brutal, unfeeling, pitiless.

merciless *(SYN.)* carnal, ferocious, brute, barbarous, gross, ruthless, cruel, remorseless, bestial, savage, rough, pitiless, inhuman. *(ANT.)* humane, courteous, merciful, openhearted, kind, civilized.

mercurial *(SYN.)* fickle, unstable, volatile, changeable, inconstant, capricious, flighty.

mercy *(SYN.)* grace, consideration, kindness, clemency, mildness, forgiveness, pity, charity, sympathy, leniency, compassion. *(ANT.)* punishment, retribution, ruthlessness, cruelty, vengeance.

mere *(SYN.)* only, simple, scant, bare. *(ANT.)* substantial, considerable.

merely *(SYN.)* only, barely, simply, hardly.

meretricious *(SYN.)* gaudy, sham, bogus, tawdry, flashy.

merge *(SYN.)* unify, fuse, combine, amalgamate, unite, blend, commingle. *(ANT.) separate, decompose, analyze.*

merger *(SYN.)* cartel, union, conglomerate, trust, incorporation, combine, pool.

meridian *(SYN.)* climax, summit, pinnacle, zenith, peak, acme, apex, culmination.

merit *(SYN.)* worthiness, earn, goodness, effectiveness, power, value, virtue, goodness, quality, deserve, excellence, worth. *(ANT.) sin, fault, lose, consume.*

merited *(SYN.)* proper, deserved, suitable, adequate, earned. *(ANT.) unmerited, improper.*

meritorious *(SYN.)* laudable, excellent, commendable, good, praiseworthy, deserving.

merry *(SYN.)* hilarious, lively, festive, joyous, sprightly, mirthful, blithe, gay, cheery, joyful, jolly, happy, gleeful, jovial, cheerful. *(ANT.) sorrowful, doleful, morose, gloomy, sad, melancholy.*

mesh *(SYN.)* grid, screen, net, complex.

mesmerize *(SYN.)* enthrall, transfix, spellbind, bewitch, charm, fascinate, hypnotize.

mess *(SYN.)* dirtiness, untidiness, disorder, confusion, muddle, trouble, jumble, difficulty, predicament, confuse, dirty.

message *(SYN.)* letter, annotation, memo, symbol, indication, sign, note, communication, memorandum, observation, token.

messenger *(SYN.)* bearer, agent, runner, courier, liaison, delegate, page.

messy *(SYN.)* disorderly, dirty, confusing, confused, disordered, sloppy, untidy, slovenly. *(ANT.) orderly, neat, tidy.*

metallic *(SYN.)* grating, harsh, clanging, brassy, brazen.

metamorphosis *(SYN.)* transfiguration, change, alteration, rebirth, mutation.

mete *(SYN.)* deal, assign, apportion, divide, give, allocate, allot, measure. *(ANT.) withhold, keep, retain.*

meteoric *(SYN.)* flashing, blazing, swift, brilliant, spectacular, remarkable.

meter *(SYN.)* record, measure, gauge.

method *(SYN.)* order, manner, plan, way, mode, technique, fashion, approach, design, procedure. *(ANT.) disorder.*

methodical *(SYN.)* exact, definite, ceremonious, stiff, accurate, distinct, unequivocal. *(ANT.) easy, loose, informal.*

meticulous *(SYN.)* precise, careful, exacting, fastidious, fussy, perfectionist.

metropolitan *(SYN.)* civic, city, municipal.

mettle *(SYN.)* intrepidity, resolution, boldness, prowess, bravery, fearlessness. *(ANT.) fear, timidity, cowardice.*

microscopic *(SYN.)* tiny, precise, fine, detailed, minute, infinitesimal, minimal. *(ANT.) general, huge, enormous.*

middle *(SYN.)* midpoint, nucleus, center, midst, median, central, intermediate, core. *(ANT.) end, rim, outskirts, beginning, border, periphery.*

middleman *(SYN.)* dealer, agent, distributor, broker, representative, intermediary.

midget *(SYN.)* gnome, shrimp, pygmy, runt, dwarf. *(ANT.) giant.*

midst *(SYN.)* center, heart, middle, thick.

midway *(SYN.)* halfway, midmost, inside, central, middle.

mien *(SYN.)* way, semblance, manner, behavior, demeanor, expression, deportment.

miff *(SYN.)* provoke, rile, chagrin, irk, irritate, affront, offend, annoy, exasperate.

might *(SYN.)* force, power, vigor, potency, ability, strength. *(ANT.) frailty, vulnerability, weakness.*

mighty *(SYN.)* firm, fortified, powerful, athletic, potent, muscular, robust, strong, cogent. *(ANT.) feeble, weak, brittle, insipid, frail, delicate.*

migrant *(SYN.)* traveling, roaming, straying, roving, rambling, transient, meandering. *(ANT.) stationary.*

migrate *(SYN.)* resettle, move, emigrate, immigrate, relocate, journey. *(ANT.) stay, remain, settle.*

migratory *(SYN.)* itinerant, roving, mobile, vagabond, unsettled, nomadic, wandering.

mild

mild *(SYN.)* soothing, moderate, gentle, tender, bland, pleasant, kind, meek, calm, amiable, compassionate, temperate, peaceful, soft. *(ANT.) severe, turbulent, stormy, excitable, violent, harsh, bitter.*

milieu *(SYN.)* environment, background, locale, setting, scene, circumstances.

militant *(SYN.)* warlike, belligerent, hostile, fighting, pugnacious, aggressive, combative. *(ANT.) peaceful.*

military *(SYN.)* troops, army, service, soldiers.

milksop *(SYN.)* namby-pamby, weakling, sissy, coward.

mill *(SYN.)* foundry, shop, plant, factory, manufactory.

millstone *(SYN.)* load, impediment, burden, encumbrance, hindrance.

mimic *(SYN.)* simulate, duplicate, copy, imitate, mock, counterfeit, simulate. *(ANT.) invent, distort, alter.*

mince *(SYN.)* shatter, fragment, chop, smash.

mind *(SYN.)* intelligence, psyche, disposition, intention, understanding, intellect, spirit, brain, inclination, mentality, soul, wit, liking, brain, sense, watch, faculties, judgment, reason.

mindful *(SYN.)* alert, aware, cognizant, watchful, sensible, heedful.

mine *(SYN.)* shaft, lode, pit, excavation, drill, dig, quarry, source.

mingle *(SYN.)* unite, coalesce, fuse, merge, combine, amalgamate, unify, conjoin, mix, blend, commingle. *(ANT.) separate, analyze, sort, disintegrate.*

miniature *(SYN.)* small, little, tiny, midget, minute, minuscule, wee, petite, diminutive. *(ANT.) outsize.*

minimize *(SYN.)* shorten, deduct, belittle, decrease, reduce, curtail, lessen, diminish, subtract. *(ANT.) enlarge, increase, amplify.*

minimum *(SYN.)* lowest, least, smallest, slightest. *(ANT.) maximum.*

minister *(SYN.)* pastor, clergyman, vicar, parson, curate, preacher, prelate, chaplain, cleric, deacon, reverend.

minor *(SYN.)* poorer, lesser, petty, youth, inferior, secondary, smaller, unimportant, lower. *(ANT.) higher, superior, major, greater.*

minority *(SYN.)* youth, childhood, immaturity.

minstrel *(SYN.)* bard, musician.

mint *(SYN.)* stamp, coin, strike, punch.

minus *(SYN.)* lacking, missing, less, absent, without.

minute *(SYN.)* tiny, particular, fine, precise, jiffy, instant, moment, wee, exact, detailed, microscopic. *(ANT.) large, huge, enormous.*

miraculous *(SYN.)* spiritual, supernatural, wonderful, marvelous, incredible, preternatural. *(ANT.) commonplace, natural, common, plain, everyday, human.*

mirage *(SYN.)* vision, illusion, fantasy, dream, phantom. *(ANT.) reality, actuality.*

mire *(SYN.)* marsh, slush, slime, mud.

mirror *(SYN.)* glass, reflector, reflect.

mirth *(SYN.)* joy, glee, jollity, joyousness, gaiety, joyfulness, laughter, merriment. *(ANT.) sadness, gloom, seriousness.*

misadventure *(SYN.)* accident, adversity, reverse, calamity, catastrophe, hardship, mischance, setback.

misappropriate *(SYN.)* embezzle, steal, purloin, plunder, cheat, filch, defraud.

misbehave *(SYN.)* trespass, act badly. *(ANT.) behave.*

miscalculate *(SYN.)* miscount, blunder, confuse, err, mistake, misconstrue.

miscarriage *(SYN.)* omission, want, decay, fiasco, default, deficiency, loss, abortion, prematurity. *(ANT.) success, sufficiency, achievement.*

miscarry *(SYN.)* flounder, fall short, falter, go wrong, fail. *(ANT.) succeed.*

miscellaneous *(SYN.)* diverse, motley, indiscriminate, assorted, sundry, heterogeneous, mixed, varied. *(ANT.) classified, selected, homogeneous, alike, ordered.*

miscellany *(SYN.)* medley, gallimaufry, jumble, potpourri, mixture, collection.

mischief *(SYN.)* injury, harm, damage, evil, prankishness, rascality, roguishness, playfulness, wrong, detriment, hurt. *(ANT.) kindness, boon, benefit.*

mischievous *(SYN.)* roguish, prankish, naughty, playful. *(ANT.)* *well-behaved, good.*

misconduct *(SYN.)* transgression, delinquency, wrongdoing, negligence.

miscreant *(SYN.)* rascal, wretch, rogue, sinner, criminal, villain, scoundrel.

miscue *(SYN.)* blunder, fluff, mistake, error, lapse.

misdemeanor *(SYN.)* infringement, transgression, violation, offense, wrong.

miser *(SYN.)* cheapskate, tightwad, skinflint. *(ANT.)* *philanthropist.*

miserable *(SYN.)* abject, forlorn, comfortless, low, worthless, pitiable, distressed, heartbroken, disconsolate, despicable, wretched, uncomfortable, unhappy, poor, unlucky, paltry, contemptible, mean. *(ANT.)* *fortunate, happy, contented, joyful, content, wealthy, honorable, lucky, noble.*

miserly *(SYN.)* stingy, greedy, acquisitive, tight, tightfisted, cheap, mean, parsimonious, avaricious. *(ANT.)* *bountiful, generous, spendthrift, munificent, extravagant, openhanded, altruistic.*

misery *(SYN.)* suffering, woe, evil, agony, torment, trouble, distress, anguish, grief, unhappiness, tribulation, calamity, sorrow. *(ANT.)* *fun, pleasure, delight, joy.*

misfit *(SYN.)* crank, loner, deviate, fifth wheel, individualist.

misfortune *(SYN.)* adversity, distress, mishap, calamity, accident, catastrophe, hardship, ruin, disaster, affliction. *(ANT.)* *success, blessing, prosperity.*

misgiving *(SYN.)* suspicion, doubt, mistrust, hesitation, uncertainty.

misguided *(SYN.)* misdirected, misled.

misinformed *(SYN.)* wrong, unwise, foolish, erroneous, unwarranted, ill-advised, misguided.

mishap *(SYN.)* misfortune, casualty, accident, disaster, adversity, reverse. *(ANT.)* *intention, calculation, purpose.*

mishmash *(SYN.)* medley, muddle, gallimaufry, hodge-podge, hash.

misjudge *(SYN.)* err, mistake, miscalculate.

mislay *(SYN.)* misplace, lose. *(ANT.)* *discover, find.*

mislead *(SYN.)* misdirect, misinform, deceive, delude.

misleading *(SYN.)* fallacious, delusive, deceitful, false, deceptive, illusive. *(ANT.)* *real, genuine, truthful, honest.*

mismatched *(SYN.)* unfit, unsuitable, incompatible, unsuited.

misplace *(SYN.)* lose, mislay, miss. *(ANT.)* *find.*

misrepresent *(SYN.)* misstate, distort, falsify, twist, belie, garble, disguise.

miss *(SYN.)* lose, want, crave, yearn for, fumble, drop, error, slip, default, omit, lack, need, desire, fail. *(ANT.)* *suffice, have, achieve, succeed.*

misshapen *(SYN.)* disfigured, deformed, grotesque, malformed, ungainly, gnarled, contorted.

missile *(SYN.)* grenade, shot, projectile.

missing *(SYN.)* wanting, lacking, absent, lost, gone, vanished.

mission *(SYN.)* business, task, job, stint, work, errand, assignment, delegation.

missionary *(SYN.)* publicist, evangelist, propagandist.

mist *(SYN.)* cloud, fog, haze, steam, haze.

mistake *(SYN.)* slip, misjudge, fault, blunder, misunderstand, confuse, inaccuracy, misinterpret, error. *(ANT.)* *truth, accuracy.*

mistaken *(SYN.)* false, amiss, incorrect, awry, wrong, misinformed, confused, inaccurate, askew. *(ANT.)* *true, correct, suitable, right.*

mister *(SYN.)* young man, gentleman, esquire, fellow, buddy.

mistreat *(SYN.)* wrong, pervert, oppress, harm, maltreat, abuse.

mistrust *(SYN.)* suspect, doubt, distrust, dispute, question, skepticism, apprehension. *(ANT.)* *trust.*

misunderstand *(SYN.)* misjudge, misinterpret, jumble, confuse, mistake. *(ANT.)* *perceive, comprehend.*

misunderstanding *(SYN.)* clash, disagreement, dispute, conflict, misinterpretation.

misuse *(SYN.)* defame, malign, abuse, misapply, traduce, asperse, revile, vilify.

mite

(ANT.) protect, honor, respect, cherish.

mite *(SYN.)* particle, mote, smidgen, trifle, iota, corpuscle.

mitigate *(SYN.)* soften, soothe, abate, assuage, relieve, allay, diminish. *(ANT.) irritate, agitate, increase.*

mix *(SYN.)* mingle, blend, consort, fuse, alloy, combine, jumble, fraternize, associate, concoct, commingle, amalgamate, confound, compound, join. *(ANT.) divide, sort, segregate, dissociate, separate.*

mixture *(SYN.)* diversity, variety, strain, change, kind, confusion, heterogeneity, jumble, mess, assortment, breed, mix, hodge-podge, subspecies. *(ANT.) likeness, sameness, homogeneity, monotony.*

moan *(SYN.)* wail, groan, cry, lament.

moat *(SYN.)* fortification, ditch, trench, entrenchment.

mob *(SYN.)* crowd, host, populace, swarm, rot, bevy, horde, rabble, throng, multitude.

mobile *(SYN.)* free, movable, portable. *(ANT.) stationary, immobile, fixed.*

mock *(SYN.)* taunt, jeer, deride, scoff, scorn, ridicule, tease, fake, imitation, sham, gibe, sneer, fraudulent, flout. *(ANT.) praise, applaud, real, genuine, honor, authentic, compliment.*

mockery *(SYN.)* gibe, ridicule, satire, derision, sham, banter, irony, sneering, scorn, travesty, jeering. *(ANT.) admiration, praise.*

mode *(SYN.)* method, fashion, procedure, design, manner, technique, way, style, practice, plan. *(ANT.) disorder, confusion.*

model *(SYN.)* copy, prototype, type, example, ideal, imitation, version, facsimile, design, style, archetype, pattern, standard, mold. *(ANT.) reproduction, imitation.*

moderate *(SYN.)* lower, decrease, average, fair, reasonable, abate, medium, conservative, referee, umpire, suppress, judge, lessen, assuage. *(ANT.) intensify, enlarge, amplify.*

moderation *(SYN.)* sobriety, forbearance, self-control, restraint, continence, temperance. *(ANT.) greed, excess, intoxication.*

moderator *(SYN.)* referee, leader, arbitrator, chairman, chairperson, master of ceremonies, emcee.

modern *(SYN.)* modish, current, recent, novel, fresh, contemporary, new. *(ANT.) old, antiquated, past, bygone, ancient.*

modernize *(SYN.)* refurnish, refurbish, improve, rebuild, renew, renovate.

modest *(SYN.)* unassuming, virtuous, bashful, meek, shy, humble, decent, demure, unpretentious, prudish, moderate, reserved. *(ANT.) forward, bold, ostentatious, conceited, immodest, arrogant.*

modesty *(SYN.)* decency, humility, propriety, simplicity, shyness. *(ANT.) conceit, vanity, pride.*

modicum *(SYN.)* particle, fragment, grain, trifle, smidgen, bit.

modification *(SYN.)* alternation, substitution, variety, change, alteration. *(ANT.) uniformity, monotony.*

modify *(SYN.)* shift, vary, alter, change, convert, adjust, temper, moderate, curb, exchange, transform, veer. *(ANT.) settle, establish, retain, stabilize.*

modish *(SYN.)* current, fashionable, chick, stylish, voguish.

modulate *(SYN.)* temper, align, balance, correct, regulate, adjust, modify.

module *(SYN.)* unit, measure, norm, dimension, component, gauge.

modus operandi *(SYN.)* method, technique, system, means, process, workings, procedure.

mogul *(SYN.)* bigwig, personage, figure, tycoon, magnate, potentate.

moiety *(SYN.)* part, scrap, share, allotment, piece, division, portion.

moist *(SYN.)* damp, humid, dank, muggy, clammy.

moisten *(SYN.)* wet, dampen, sponge. *(ANT.) dry.*

moisture *(SYN.)* wetness, mist, dampness, condensation, evaporation, vapor, humidity. *(ANT.) aridity, dryness.*

mold *(SYN.)* make, fashion, organize, produce, forge, constitute, create, combine, construct, form, pattern, format. *(ANT.) wreck, dismantle, destroy, misshape.*

moldy *(SYN.)* dusty, crumbling, dank, old,

deteriorating.

molest *(SYN.)* irk, disturb, trouble, annoy, pester, bother, vex, inconvenience. *(ANT.)* *console, accommodate.*

mollify *(SYN.)* soothe, compose, quiet, humor, appease, tranquilize, pacify.

molt *(SYN.)* slough off, shed, cast off.

molten *(SYN.)* fusible, melted, smelted, redhot.

moment *(SYN.)* flash, jiffy, instant, twinkling, gravity, importance, consequence, seriousness.

momentary *(SYN.)* concise, pithy, brief, curt, terse, laconic, compendious. *(ANT.)* *long, extended, prolonged.*

momentous *(SYN.)* critical, serious, essential, grave, material, weighty, consequential, decisive, important. *(ANT.)* *unimportant, trifling, mean, trivial, insignificant.*

momentum *(SYN.)* impetus, push, thrust, force, impulse, drive, vigor, propulsion, energy.

monarch *(SYN.)* ruler, king, queen, empress, emperor, sovereign.

monastery *(SYN.)* convent, priory, abbey, hermitage, cloister.

monastic *(SYN.)* withdrawn, dedicated, austere, unworldly, celibate, abstinent, ascetic.

money *(SYN.)* cash, bills, coin, notes, currency, funds, specie, capital.

monger *(SYN.)* seller, hawker, huckster, trader, merchant, shopkeeper, retailer, vendor.

mongrel *(SYN.)* mixed-breed, hybrid, mutt.

monitor *(SYN.)* director, supervisor, advisor, observe, watch, control.

monkey *(SYN.)* tamper, interfere, interrupt, interpose.

monogram *(SYN.)* mark, stamp, signature.

monograph *(SYN.)* publication, report, thesis, biography, treatise, paper, dissertation.

monologue *(SYN.)* discourse, lecture, sermon, talk, speech, address, soliloquy, oration.

monomania *(SYN.)* obsessiveness, passion, single-mindedness, extremism.

monopoly *(SYN.)* corner, control, possession.

monotonous *(SYN.)* dull, slow, tiresome, boring, humdrum, dilatory, tiring, irksome, tedious, burdensome, wearisome. *(ANT.)* *interesting, riveting, quick, fascinating, exciting, amusing.*

monsoon *(SYN.)* storm, rains.

monster *(SYN.)* brute, beast, villain, demon, fiend, wretch.

monstrous *(SYN.)* tremendous, huge, gigantic, immense, enormous, revolting, repulsive, shocking, horrible, hideous, terrible. *(ANT.)* *diminutive, tiny, miniature, small.*

monument *(SYN.)* remembrance, memento, commemoration, souvenir, statue, shrine.

monumental *(SYN.)* enormous, huge, colossal, immense, gigantic, important, significant. *(ANT.)* *trivial, insignificant, tiny, miniature.*

mood *(SYN.)* joke, irony, waggery, temper, disposition, temperament, sarcasm. *(ANT.)* *sorrow, gravity.*

moody *(SYN.)* morose, fretful, crabbed, changeable, sulky, dour, short-tempered, testy, temperamental, irritable, peevish, glum. *(ANT.)* *good-natured, even-tempered, merry, gay, pleasant, joyous.*

moor *(SYN.)* tether, fasten, tie, dock, anchor, bind.

moorings *(SYN.)* marina, slip, harbor, basin, landing, dock, wharf, pier, anchorage.

moot *(SYN.)* unsettled, questionable, problematical, controversial, contestable.

mop *(SYN.)* wash, wipe, swab, scrub.

mope *(SYN.)* gloom, pout, whine, grumble, grieve, sulk, fret. *(ANT.)* *rejoice.*

moral *(SYN.)* just, right, chaste, good, virtuous, pure, decent, honest, upright, ethical, righteous, honorable, scrupulous. *(ANT.)* *libertine, immoral, unethical, licentious, amoral, sinful.*

morale *(SYN.)* confidence, spirit, assurance.

morality

morality *(SYN.)* virtue, strength, worth, chastity, probity, force, merit. *(ANT.) fault, sin, corruption, vice.*

morals *(SYN.)* conduct, scruples, guidelines, behavior, life style, standards.

morass *(SYN.)* fen, march, swamp, mire.

morbid *(SYN.)* sickly, unwholesome, unhealthy, ghastly, awful, horrible, shocking. *(ANT.) pleasant, healthy.*

more *(SYN.)* further, greater, farther, extra, another. *(ANT.) less.*

moreover *(SYN.)* further, in addition, also, furthermore, besides.

mores *(SYN.)* standards, rituals, rules, customs, conventions, traditions.

moron *(SYN.)* subnormal, dunce, blockhead, imbecile, retardate, simpleton.

morose *(SYN.)* gloomy, moody, fretful, crabbed, sulky, glum, dour, surly, downcast, sad, unhappy. *(ANT.) merry, gay, amiable, joyous, pleasant.*

morsel *(SYN.)* portion, fragment, bite, bit, scrap, amount, piece, taste, tidbit. *(ANT.) whole, all, sum.*

mortal *(SYN.)* fatal, destructive, human, perishable, deadly, temporary, momentary, final. *(ANT.) superficial, immortal.*

mortgage *(SYN.)* stake, post, promise, pledge.

mortician *(SYN.)* funeral director, embalmer.

mortified *(SYN.)* embarrassed, humiliated, abashed, ashamed.

mortify *(SYN.)* humiliate, crush, subdue, abase, degrade, shame. *(ANT.) praise, exalt, elevate.*

mortuary *(SYN.)* morgue, crematory, funeral parlor.

most *(SYN.)* extreme, highest, supreme, greatest, majority. *(ANT.) least.*

mostly *(SYN.)* chiefly, generally, largely, mainly, principally, especially, primarily.

mother *(SYN.)* bring about, produce, breed, mom, mama, watch, foster, mind, nurse, originate, nurture. *(ANT.) father.*

motif *(SYN.)* keynote, topic, subject, theme.

motion *(SYN.)* change, activity, movement, proposition, action, signal, gesture, move, proposal. *(ANT.) stability, immobility, equilibrium, stillness.*

motionless *(SYN.)* still, undisturbed, rigid, fixed, stationary, unresponsive, immobilized.

motivate *(SYN.)* move, prompt, stimulate, induce, activate, propel, arouse.

motive *(SYN.)* inducement, purpose, cause, incentive, reason, incitement, idea, ground, principle, stimulus, impulse, spur. *(ANT.) deed, result, attempt, effort.*

motley *(SYN.)* heterogeneous, mixed, assorted, sundry, diverse, miscellaneous. *(ANT.) ordered, classified.*

motor *(SYN.)* engine, generator, machine.

mottled *(SYN.)* streaked, flecked, dappled, spotted, speckled.

motto *(SYN.)* proverb, saying, adage, byword, saw, slogan, catchword, aphorism.

mound *(SYN.)* hillock, hill, heap, pile, stack, knoll, accumulation, dune.

mount *(SYN.)* scale, climb, increase, rise, prepare, ready, steed, horse, tower. *(ANT.) sink, descend.*

mountain *(SYN.)* alp, mount, pike, peak, ridge, height, range.

mountebank *(SYN.)* faker, rascal, swindler, cheat, fraud.

mounting *(SYN.)* backing, pedestal, easel, support, framework, background.

mourn *(SYN.)* suffer, grieve, bemoan, sorrow, lament, weep, bewail. *(ANT.) revel, celebrate, carouse.*

mournful *(SYN.)* gloomy, sorrowful, sad, melancholy, woeful, disconsolate. *(ANT.) joyful, cheerful, happy.*

mourning *(SYN.)* misery, trial, distress, affliction, tribulation, sorrow, woe. *(ANT.) happiness, solace, comfort, joy.*

mousy *(SYN.)* quiet, reserved, dull, colorless, withdrawn, shy, bashful.

move *(SYN.)* impel, agitate, persuade, induce, push, instigate, advance, stir, progress, propel, shift, drive, retreat, proceed, stir, transfer, budge, actuate. *(ANT.) halt, stop, deter, rest.*

moving *(SYN.)* stirring, touching.

mow *(SYN.)* prune, cut, shave, crop, clip.

much *(SYN.)* abundance, quantity, mass, ample, plenty, sufficient, substantial.

mucilage *(SYN.)* adhesive, glue, paste.

muck *(SYN.)* filth, mire, dirt, rot, sludge.

muddle *(SYN.)* disorder, chaos, mess.

muddled *(SYN.)* disconcerted, confused, mixed, bewildered, perplexed. *(ANT.)* plain, lucid, organized.

muff *(SYN.)* blunder, spoil, mess, fumble.

muffle *(SYN.)* soften, deaden, mute, quiet, drape, shroud, veil, cover. *(ANT.)* louden, amplify.

mug *(SYN.)* cup, stein, goblet, tankard.

muggy *(SYN.)* damp, warm, humid, stuffy, sticky, dank.

mulct *(SYN.)* amerce, punish, penalize.

mulish *(SYN.)* obstinate, stubborn, headstrong, rigid, tenacious, willful.

multifarious *(SYN.)* various, many, numerous, diversified, several, manifold. *(ANT.)* scanty, infrequent, scarce, few.

multiply *(SYN.)* double, treble, increase, triple, propagate, spread, expand. *(ANT.)* lessen, decrease.

multitude *(SYN.)* crowd, throng, mass, swarm, host, mob, army, legion. *(ANT.)* scarcity, handful.

mumble *(SYN.)* stammer, whisper, hesitate, mutter. *(ANT.)* shout, yell.

mundane *(SYN.)* temporal, earthly, profane, worldly, lay, secular, common. *(ANT.)* unworldly, religious.

municipal *(SYN.)* urban, metropolitan.

munificent *(SYN.)* bountiful, full, generous, forthcoming, satisfied. *(ANT.)* voracious, insatiable, grasping, ravenous.

murder *(SYN.)* homicide, kill, slay, slaughter, butcher, killing, massacre, assassinate, execute. *(ANT.)* save, protect, vivify, animate.

murky *(SYN.)* gloomy, dark, obscure, unclear, impenetrable. *(ANT.)* cheerful, light.

murmur *(SYN.)* mumble, whine, grumble, whimper, lament, mutter. *(ANT.)* praise, applaud, rejoice.

muscle *(SYN.)* brawn, strength, power, fitness, vigor, vim, stamina, robustness.

muse *(SYN.)* ponder, brood, think, meditate, ruminate, reflect.

museum *(SYN.)* exhibit hall, treasure house, gallery, repository.

mushroom *(SYN.)* multiply, proliferate, flourish, spread, grow, pullulate.

musical *(SYN.)* tuneful, melodious, dulcet, lyrical, harmonious.

muss *(SYN.)* mess, disarray, rumple, litter, clutter, disarrange. *(ANT.)* fix, arrange.

must *(SYN.)* ought to, should, duty, obligation, ultimatum.

muster *(SYN.)* cull, pick, collect, harvest, accumulate, garner, reap, deduce. *(ANT.)* separate, disband, scatter.

musty *(SYN.)* mildewed, rancid, airless, dank, stale, decayed, rotten, funky.

mute *(SYN.)* quiet, noiseless, dumb, taciturn, hushed, peaceful, speechless, uncommunicative, silent. *(ANT.)* raucous, clamorous, noisy.

mutilate *(SYN.)* tear, cut, clip, amputate, lacerate, dismember, deform, castrate.

mutinous *(SYN.)* revolutionary, rebellious, unruly, turbulent, riotous. *(ANT.)* dutiful, obedient, complaint.

mutiny *(SYN.)* revolt, overthrow, rebellion, rebel, coup, uprising, insurrection.

mutter *(SYN.)* complain, mumble, whisper, grumble, murmur.

mutual *(SYN.)* correlative, interchangeable, shared, alternate, joint, common. *(ANT.)* unshared, unrequited, separate, dissociated.

muzzle *(SYN.)* restrain, silence, bridle, bind, curb, suppress, gag, stifle, censor.

myopia *(SYN.)* incomprehension, folly, shortsightedness, obtuseness.

myriad *(SYN.)* considerable, many.

mysterious *(SYN.)* hidden, mystical, secret, cryptic, incomprehensible, occult, dim, dark, inexplicable, enigmatical. *(ANT.)* simple, obvious, clear, plain.

mystery *(SYN.)* riddle, difficulty, enigma, puzzle, strangeness, conundrum. *(ANT.)* solution, key, answer, resolution.

mystical *(SYN.)* secret, cryptic, hidden, dim, obscure, dark, cabalistic. *(ANT.)* simple, explained, plain, clear.

mystify *(SYN.)* puzzle, confound, bewilder, stick, get, bamboozle.

myth *(SYN.)* fable, parable, allegory, fiction, tradition, lie, saga, legend. *(ANT.)* history.

N

nag *(SYN.)* badger, harry, provoke, tease, bother, annoy, molest, taunt, vex, torment, worry, annoy, pester, irritate, pick on, horse. *(ANT.)* please, comfort, soothe.

nail *(SYN.)* hold, fasten, secure, fix, seize, catch, snare, hook, capture. *(ANT.)* release.

naive *(SYN.)* frank, unsophisticated, natural, artless, ingenuous, simple, candid, open, innocent. *(ANT.)* worldly, cunning, crafty.

naked *(SYN.)* uncovered, unfinished, nude, bare, open, unclad, stripped, exposed, plain, mere, simple, barren, unprotected, bald, defenseless, unclothed. *(ANT.)* covered, protected, dressed, clothed, concealed.

name *(SYN.)* title, reputation, appellation, style, fame, repute, renown, denomination, appoint, character, designation, surname, distinction, christen, denominate, mention, specify, epithet, entitle, call, label. *(ANT.)* anonymity, hint, misname.

nap *(SYN.)* nod, doze, sleep, snooze, catnap, slumber, drowse.

narcissistic *(SYN.)* egotistical, egocentric, self-centered, egotistic.

narcotics *(SYN.)* opiates, drugs, sedatives, tranquilizers, barbiturates.

narrate *(SYN.)* recite, relate, declaim, detail, rehearse, deliver, review, tell, describe, recount.

narrative *(SYN.)* history, relation, account, record, chronicle, detail, recital, description, story, tale. *(ANT.)* distortion, caricature, misrepresentation.

narrow *(SYN.)* narrow-minded, illiberal, bigoted, fanatical, prejudiced, close, restricted, slender, cramped, confined, meager, thin, tapering, tight. *(ANT.)* progressive, liberal, wide.

narrow-minded *(SYN.)* close-minded, intolerant, partisan, arbitrary, bigoted. *(ANT.)* tolerant, liberal, broad-minded.

nascent *(SYN.)* prime, introductory, emerging, elementary.

nasty *(SYN.)* offensive, malicious, selfish, mean, disagreeable, unpleasant, foul, dirty, filthy, loathsome, disgusting, polluted, obscene, indecent, sickening, nauseating, obnoxious, revolting. *(ANT.)* generous, dignified, noble, admirable, pleasant.

nation *(SYN.)* state, community, realm, nationality, commonwealth, kingdom, country, republic, land, society, tribe.

native *(SYN.)* domestic, inborn, inherent, natural, aboriginal, endemic, innate, inbred, indigenous, hereditary. *(ANT.)* alien, stranger, foreigner, outsider, foreign.

natty *(SYN.)* chic, well-dressed, sharp, dapper.

natural *(SYN.)* innate, genuine, real, unaffected, characteristic, native, normal, regular, inherent, original, simple, inbred, inborn, hereditary, typical, authentic, honest, legitimate, pure, customary. *(ANT.)* irregular, false, unnatural, formal, abnormal.

naturally *(SYN.)* typically, ordinarily, usually, indeed, normally, plainly, of course, surely, certainly. *(ANT.)* artificially.

nature *(SYN.)* kind, disposition, reputation, character, repute, world, quality, universe, essence, variety, features, traits.

naught *(SYN.)* zero, nothing.

naughty *(SYN.)* unmanageable, insubordinate, disobedient, mischievous, unruly, bad, misbehaving, disorderly, wrong, evil, rude, improper, indecent. *(ANT.)* obedient, good, well-behaved.

nausea *(SYN.)* sickness, vomiting, upset, queasiness, seasickness.

nauseated *(SYN.)* unwell, sick, queasy, squeamish.

nautical *(SYN.)* naval, oceanic, marine.

naval *(SYN.)* oceanic, marine, nautical, maritime.

navigate *(SYN.)* sail, cruise, pilot, guide, steer.

near *(SYN.)* close, nigh, dear, adjacent, familiar, at hand, neighboring, approaching, impending, proximate, imminent, bordering. *(ANT.)* removed, distant, far, remote.

neutralize

nearly *(SYN.)* practically, close to, approximately, almost.

neat *(SYN.)* trim, orderly, precise, clear, spruce, nice, clean, well-kept, clever, skillful, adept, apt, dapper, smart, proficient, expert, handy, well-done, shipshape, elegant, well-organized. *(ANT.)* unkempt, sloppy, dirty, slovenly, messy, sloppy, disorganized.

nebulous *(SYN.)* fuzzy, indistinct, indefinite, clouded, hazy. *(ANT.)* definite, distinct, clear.

necessary *(SYN.)* needed, expedient, unavoidable, required, essential, indispensable, urgent, imperative, inevitable, compelling, compulsory, obligatory, needed, exigent. *(ANT.)* optional, nonessential, contingent, casual, accidental, unnecessary, dispensable, unneeded.

necessity *(SYN.)* requirement, fate, destiny, constraint, requisite, poverty, exigency, compulsion, want, essential, prerequisite. *(ANT.)* option, luxury, freedom, choice, uncertainty.

necromancy *(SYN.)* witchcraft, charm, sorcery, conjuring, wizardry.

need *(SYN.)* crave, want, demand, claim, desire, covet, wish, lack, necessity, requirement, poverty, require, pennilessness.

needed *(SYN.)* necessary, indispensable, essential, requisite. *(ANT.)* optional, contingent.

needle *(SYN.)* goad, badger, tease, nag, prod, provoke.

needless *(SYN.)* nonessential, unnecessary, superfluous, useless, purposeless.

needy *(SYN.)* poor, indigent, impoverished, penniless, destitute. *(ANT.)* affluent, well-off, wealthy, well-to-do.

nefarious *(SYN.)* detestable, vicious, wicked, atrocious, horrible, vile.

negate *(SYN.)* revoke, void, cancel, nullify.

neglect *(SYN.)* omission, default, heedlessness, carelessness, thoughtlessness, disregard, negligence, oversight, omission, ignore, slight, failure, overlook, omit, skip, pass over, be inattentive, miss. *(ANT.)* diligence, do, protect, watchfulness, care, attention, careful, attend, regard, concern.

negligent *(SYN.)* imprudent, thoughtless, lax, careless, inattentive, indifferent, remiss, neglectful. *(ANT.)* careful, nice, accurate, meticulous.

negligible *(SYN.)* trifling, insignificant, trivial, inconsiderable. *(ANT.)* major, vital, important.

negotiate *(SYN.)* intervene, talk over, mediate, transact, umpire, referee, arbitrate, arrange, settle, bargain.

neighborhood *(SYN.)* environs, nearness, district, vicinity, area, section, locality. *(ANT.)* remoteness.

neighboring *(SYN.)* bordering, near, adjacent, next to, surrounding, adjoining.

neighborly *(SYN.)* friendly, sociable, amiable, affable, companionable, congenial, kind, cordial, amicable. *(ANT.)* distant, reserved, cool, unfriendly, hostile.

neophyte *(SYN.)* greenhorn, rookie, amateur, beginner, apprentice, tyro, student.

nepotism *(SYN.)* bias, prejudice, patronage, favoritism.

nerve *(SYN.)* bravery, spirit, courage, boldness, rudeness, strength, stamina, bravado, daring, impudence, mettle, impertinence. *(ANT.)* frailty, cowardice, weakness.

nervous *(SYN.)* agitated, restless, excited, shy, timid, upset, disturbed, shaken, rattle, high-strung, flustered, tense, jittery, strained, edgy, perturbed, fearful. *(ANT.)* placid, courageous, confident, calm, tranquil, composed, bold.

nest *(SYN.)* den, refuge, hideaway.

nestle *(SYN.)* cuddle, snuggle.

net *(SYN.)* snare, trap, mesh, earn, gain, web, get, acquire, secure, obtain.

nettle *(SYN.)* irritate, vex, provoke, annoy, disturb, irk, needle, pester.

neurotic *(SYN.)* disturbed, psychoneurotic.

neutral *(SYN.)* nonpartisan, uninvolved, detached, impartial, cool, unprejudiced, indifferent, inactive. *(ANT.)* involved, biased, partisan.

neutralize *(SYN.)* offset, counteract, nullify, negate.

nevertheless *(SYN.)* notwithstanding, however, although, anyway, but, regardless.

new *(SYN.)* modem, original, newfangled, late, recent, novel, young, firsthand, fresh, unique, unusual. *(ANT.)* antiquated, old, ancient, obsolete, outmoded.

newborn *(SYN.)* baby, infant, cub, suckling.

news *(SYN.)* report, intelligence, information, copy, message, advice, tidings, knowledge, word, story, data.

next *(SYN.)* nearest, following, closest, successive, succeeding, subsequent.

nibble *(SYN.)* munch, chew, bit.

nice *(SYN.)* pleasing, pleasant, agreeable, thoughtful, satisfactory, friendly, enjoyable, gratifying, desirable, fine, good, cordial. *(ANT.)* nasty, unpleasant, disagreeable, unkind, inexact, careless, thoughtless.

niche *(SYN.)* corner, nook, alcove, cranny, recess.

nick *(SYN.)* cut, notch, indentation, dash, score, mark.

nickname *(SYN.)* byname, sobriquet.

nigh *(SYN.)* close, imminent, near, adjacent, approaching, bordering, neighboring, impending. *(ANT.)* removed, distant.

nightmare *(SYN.)* calamity, horror, torment, bad dream.

nil *(SYN.)* zero, none, naught, nothing.

nimble *(SYN.)* brisk, quick, active, supple, alert, lively, spry, light, fast, speedy, swift, agile. *(ANT.)* slow, heavy, sluggish, clumsy.

nincompoop *(SYN.)* nitwit, idiot, fool, moron, blockhead, ninny, idiot, simpleton.

nip *(SYN.)* bite, pinch, chill, cold, squeeze, crispness, sip, small.

nippy *(SYN.)* chilly, sharp, bitter, cold, penetrating.

nit-picker *(SYN.)* fussbudget, precise, purist, perfectionist.

nitty-gritty *(SYN.)* essentials, substance, essence.

noble *(SYN.)* illustrious, exalted, dignified, stately, eminent, lofty, grand, elevated, honorable, honest, virtuous, great, distinguished, majestic, important, prominent, magnificent, grandiose, aristocratic, upright, well-born. *(ANT.)* vile, low, base, mean, dishonest, common, ignoble.

nod *(SYN.)* bob, bow, bend, tip, signal.

node *(SYN.)* protuberance, growth, nodule, cyst, lump, wen.

noise *(SYN.)* cry, sound, din, babel, racket, uproar, clamor, outcry, tumult, sounds, hubbub, bedlam, commotion, rumpus, clatter. *(ANT.)* quiet, stillness, hush, silence, peace.

noisome *(SYN.)* repulsive, disgusting, revolting, obnoxious, malodorous, rotten, rancid.

noisy *(SYN.)* resounding, loud, clamorous, vociferous, stentorian, tumultuous. *(ANT.)* soft, dulcet, subdued, quiet, silent, peaceful.

nomad *(SYN.)* gypsy, rover, traveler, roamer, migrant, vagrant, wanderer.

nominate *(SYN.)* propose, choose, select.

nomination *(SYN.)* appointment, naming, choice, selection, designation.

nominee *(SYN.)* contestant, candidate.

nonbeliever *(SYN.)* skeptic, infidel, atheist, heathen.

nonchalant *(SYN.)* unconcerned, indifferent, cool, casual, easygoing.

noncommittal *(SYN.)* neutral, tepid, undecided, cautious, guarded, uncommunicative.

nonconformist *(SYN.)* protester, rebel, radical, dissenter, renegade, dissident, eccentric.

nondescript *(SYN.)* unclassifiable, indescribable, indefinite.

nonentity *(SYN.)* nothing, menial, nullity.

nonessential *(SYN.)* needless, unnecessary.

nonpareil *(SYN.)* unsurpassed, exceptional, paramount, unrivaled.

nonplus *(SYN.)* confuse, perplex, dumfound, mystify, confound, puzzle, baffle, bewilder. *(ANT.)* illumine, clarify, salve, explain.

nonsense *(SYN.)* balderdash, rubbish, foolishness, folly, ridiculousness, stupidity, absurdity, poppycock, trash.

nonsensical *(SYN.)* silly, preposterous, absurd, unreasonable, foolish, irrational, ridiculous, stupid, senseless. (*ANT.*) *sound, consistent, reasonable.*

nonstop *(SYN.)* constant, continuous, unceasing, endless.

nook *(SYN.)* niche, corner, recess, cranny.

noose *(SYN.)* snare, rope, lasso, loop.

normal *(SYN.)* ordinary, uniform, natural, unvaried, customary, regular, healthy, sound, whole, usual, typical, characteristic, routine, standard. (*ANT.*) *rare, erratic, unusual, abnormal.*

normally *(SYN.)* regularly, frequently, usually, customarily.

nosy *(SYN.)* inquisitive, meddling, peering, searching, prying, snooping. (*ANT.*) *unconcerned, incurious, uninterested.*

notable *(SYN.)* noted, unusual, uncommon, noteworthy, remarkable, conspicuous, distinguished, distinctive, celebrity, starts, important, striking, special, memorable, extraordinary, rare, exceptional, personality. (*ANT.*) *commonplace, ordinary, usual.*

notch *(SYN.)* cut, nick, indentation, gash.

note *(SYN.)* sign, annotation, letter, indication, observation, mark, symbol, comment, remark, token, message, memorandum, record, memo, write, list, inscribe, notice.

noted *(SYN.)* renowned, glorious, celebrated, famous, illustrious, well-known, distinguished, famed, notable. (*ANT.*) *unknown, hidden, infamous, ignominious.*

noteworthy *(SYN.)* consequential, celebrated, exceptional, prominent.

notice *(SYN.)* heed, perceive, hold, mark, behold, descry, recognize, observe, attend to, remark, note, regard, see, sign, announcement, poster, advertisement, observation, warning. (*ANT.*) *overlook, disregard, skip.*

notify *(SYN.)* apprise, acquaint, instruct, tell, advise, warn, teach, inform, report, remind, announce, mention, reveal. (*ANT.*) *mislead, delude, conceal.*

notion *(SYN.)* image, conception, sentiment, abstraction, thought, idea, impression, fancy, understanding, view, opin-ion, concept. (*ANT.*) *thing, matter, substance, entity.*

notorious *(SYN.)* celebrated, renowned, famous, well-known, popular, infamous.

nourish *(SYN.)* strengthen, nurse, feed, supply, nurture, sustain, support.

nourishment *(SYN.)* nutriment, food, sustenance, support. (*ANT.*) *starvation, deprivation.*

novel *(SYN.)* fiction, narrative, allegory, tale, fable, story, romance, invention, different, unusual, strange, original. (*ANT.*) *verity, history, truth, fact.*

novice *(SYN.)* beginner, amateur, newcomer, greenhorn, learner, apprentice, freshman, dilettante. (*ANT.*) *expert, professional, adept, master.*

now *(SYN.)* today, at once, right away, immediately, at this time, present. (*ANT.*) *later.*

noxious *(SYN.)* poisonous, harmful, damaging, toxic, detrimental. (*ANT.*) *harmless.*

nucleus *(SYN.)* core, middle, heart, focus, hub, kernel.

nude *(SYN.)* naked, unclad, plain, open, defenseless, mere, bare, exposed, unprotected, simple, stripped, uncovered. (*ANT.*) *dressed, protected, clothed, covered.*

nudge *(SYN.)* prod, push, jab, shove, poke, prompt.

nugget *(SYN.)* clump, mass, lump, wad, chunk, hunk.

nuisance *(SYN.)* annoyance, bother, irritation, pest.

nullify *(SYN.)* abolish, cross out, delete, invalidate, obliterate, cancel, expunge, repeal, annul, revoke, quash, rescind. (*ANT.*) *perpetuate, confirm, enforce.*

numb *(SYN.)* unfeeling, dull, insensitive, deadened, anesthetized, stupefied.

numeral *(SYN.)* figure, symbol, digit.

numerous *(SYN.)* many, several, manifold, multifarious, various, multitudinous, diverse, abundant, sundry. (*ANT.*) *infrequent, meager, few, scarce.*

nuptials *(SYN.)* marriage, wedding, espousal, wedlock, matrimony. (*ANT.*) *virginity, divorce, celibacy.*

nurse *(SYN.)* tend, care for, nourish, nurture, feed, train, mind, attend.

nurture *(SYN.)* hold dear, foster, sustain, appreciate, prize, rear, value, treasure. *(ANT.)* dislike, disregard, abandon.

nutriment *(SYN.)* food, diet, sustenance, repast, meal, fare, edibles. *(ANT.)* hunger, want, starvation.

nutrition *(SYN.)* nourishment, sustenance, food, nutriment.

oaf *(SYN.)* boor, clod, clown, lummox, fool, lout, dunce, bogtrotter.

oasis *(SYN.)* shelter, haven, retreat, refuge.

oath *(SYN.)* promise, pledge, vow, profanity, curse, agreement, commitment.

obdurate *(SYN.)* insensible, callous, hard, rough, unfeeling, insensitive. *(ANT.)* soft, compassionate, tender.

obedience *(SYN.)* docility, submission, subservience, compliance. *(ANT.)* rebelliousness, disobedience.

obedient *(SYN.)* dutiful, yielding, tractable, compliant, submissive. *(ANT.)* rebellious, intractable, insubordinate, obstinate.

obese *(SYN.)* portly, fat, pudgy, chubby, plump, rotund, stout, thickset, corpulent, stocky. *(ANT.)* slim, lean, thin, slender.

obey *(SYN.)* submit, yield, mind, comply, listen to, conform. *(ANT.)* resist, disobey.

obfuscate *(SYN.)* bewilder, complicate, fluster, confuse.

object *(SYN.)* thing, aim, intention, design, end, objective, particular, mark, purpose, goal, target, article. *(ANT.)* assent, agree, concur, approve, acquiesce.

objection *(SYN.)* disagreement, protest, rejection, dissent, challenge, noncompliance, difference, nonconformity, recusancy, disapproval, criticism. *(ANT.)* acceptance, compliance, agreement, assent.

objectionable *(SYN.)* improper, offensive, unbecoming, deplorable.

objective *(SYN.)* aspiration, goal, passion, desire, aim, hope, purpose, drift, design, ambition, end, object, intention, intent, longing, craving. *(ANT.)* biased, subjective.

objectivity *(SYN.)* disinterest, neutrality, impartiality.

obligate *(SYN.)* oblige, require, pledge, bind, force, compel.

obligation *(SYN.)* duty, bond, engagement, compulsion, account, contract, ability, debt. *(ANT.)* freedom, choice, exemption.

oblige *(SYN.)* constrain, force, impel, enforce, coerce, drive, gratify. *(ANT.)* persuade, convince, allure, free, induce, disoblige, prevent.

obliging *(SYN.)* considerate, helpful, thoughtful, well-meaning, accommodating. *(ANT.)* discourteous.

obliterate *(SYN.)* terminate, destroy, eradicate, raze, extinguish, exterminate, annihilate, devastate, wipe out, ravage. *(ANT.)* make, save, construct, establish, preserve.

oblivious *(SYN.)* sightless, unmindful, headlong, rash, blind, senseless, ignorant, forgetful, undiscerning, preoccupied, unconscious, heedless. *(ANT.)* sensible, aware, calculated, perceiving, discerning.

obloquy *(SYN.)* defamation, rebuke, censure.

obnoxious *(SYN.)* hateful, offensive, nasty, disagreeable, repulsive, loathsome, vile, disgusting, detestable, wretched, terrible, despicable, dreadful.

obscene *(SYN.)* indecent, filthy, impure, dirty, gross, lewd, pornographic, coarse, disgusting, bawdy, offensive, smutty. *(ANT.)* modest, pure, decent, refined.

obscure *SYN.)* cloudy, enigmatic, mysterious, abstruse, cryptic, dim, dusky, ambiguous, dark, indistinct, unintelligible, unclear, shadowy, fuzzy, blurred, vague. *(ANT.)* clear, famous, distinguished, noted, illumined, lucid, bright, distinct.

obsequious *(SYN.)* fawning, flattering.

observance *(SYN.)* protocol, ritual, ceremony, rite, parade, pomp, solemnity. *(ANT.)* omission.

observant *(SYN.)* aware, alert, mindful, watchful, heedful, considerate, attentive, anxious, circumspect, cautious, wary.

(*ANT.*) unaware, indifferent, oblivious.

observation (*SYN.*) attention, watching, comment, opinion, remark, notice.

observe (*SYN.*) note, behold, discover, notice, perceive, eye, detect, inspect, keep, commemorate, mention, utter, watch, examine, mark, view, express, see, celebrate. (*ANT.*) neglect, overlook, disregard, ignore.

observer (*SYN.*) examiner, overseer, lookout, spectator, bystander, witness, watcher.

obsession (*SYN.*) preoccupation, mania, compulsion, passion, fetish, infatuation.

obsolete (*SYN.*) old, out-of-date, ancient, archaic, extinct, old-fashioned, discontinued, obsolescent, venerable, dated, antiquated. (*ANT.*) modern, stylish, current, recent, fashionable, extant.

obstacle (*SYN.*) block, hindrance, barrier, impediment, snag, check, deterrent, stoppage, hitch, bar, difficulty, obstruction. (*ANT.*) help, aid, assistance, encouragement.

obstinate (*SYN.*) firm, headstrong, immovable, stubborn, determined, dogged, intractable, uncompromising, inflexible, willful, bullheaded, contumacious, obdurate, unbending, unyielding, pertinacious. (*ANT.*) yielding, docile, amenable, submissive, pliable, flexible, compliant.

obstruct (*SYN.*) clog, barricade, impede, block, delay, hinder, stop, close, bar. (*ANT.*) promote, clear, aid, help, open, further.

obstruction (*SYN.*) block, obstacle, barrier, blockage, interference.

obtain (*SYN.*) get, acquire, secure, win, procure, attain, earn, gain, receive, assimilate. (*ANT.*) surrender, forfeit, lose, forego, miss.

obtrusive (*SYN.*) blatant, garish, conspicuous.

obtuse (*SYN.*) blunt, dull, slow-witted, unsharpened, stupid, dense, slow. (*ANT.*) clear, interesting, lively, bright, animated, sharp.

obviate (*SYN.*) prevent, obstruct, forestall, preclude, intercept, avert, evade.

obvious (*SYN.*) plain, clear, evident, palpable, patent, self-evident, apparent, distinct, understandable, manifest, unmistakable. (*ANT.*) concealed, hidden, abstruse, obscure.

obviously (*SYN.*) plainly, clearly, surely, evidently, certainly.

occasion (*SYN.*) occurrence, time, happening, excuse, opportunity, chance.

occasional (*SYN.*) random, irregular, sporadic, infrequent, periodically, spasmodic. (*ANT.*) chronic, regular, constant.

occasionally (*SYN.*) seldom, now and then, infrequently, sometimes, irregularly. (*ANT.*) regularly, often.

occlude (*SYN.*) clog, obstruct, choke, throttle.

occupant (*SYN.*) tenant, lodger, boarder, dweller, resident, inhabitant.

occupation (*SYN.*) employment, business, enterprise, job, trade, vocation, work, profession, matter, interest, concern, affair, activity, commerce, trading, engagement. (*ANT.*) hobby, pastime, avocation.

occupy (*SYN.*) dwell, have, inhabit, absorb, hold, possess, fill, busy, keep. (*ANT.*) relinquish, abandon, release.

occur (*SYN.*) take place, bechance, come about, befall, chance, transpire, betide, happen.

occurrence (*SYN.*) episode, event, issue, end, result, consequence, happening, circumstance, outcome.

ocean (*SYN.*) deep, sea, main, briny.

odd (*SYN.*) strange, bizarre, eccentric, unusual, single, uneven, unique, queer, quaint, peculiar, curious, unmatched, remaining, singular. (*ANT.*) matched, common, typical, normal, familiar, even, usual.

odious (*SYN.*) obscene, depraved, vulgar, despicable, mean, wicked, sordid, foul, base, loathsome, vicious, displeasing, hateful, revolting, offensive, repulsive, horrible, obnoxious, vile. (*ANT.*) decent, upright, laudable, attractive, honorable.

odor (*SYN.*) fume, aroma, fragrance, redolence, smell, stink, scent, essence, stench.

odorous (*SYN.*) scented, aromatic, fragrant.

odyssey *(SYN.)* crusade, quest, journey, voyage.

offbeat *(SYN.)* uncommon, eccentric, strange, unconventional, peculiar.

off-color *(SYN.)* rude, improper, earthy, suggestive, salty.

offend *(SYN.)* annoy, anger, vex, irritate, displease, provoke, hurt, grieve, pain, disgust, wound, horrify, stricken, insult, outrage. *(ANT.)* flatter, please, delight.

offender *(SYN.)* criminal, culprit, lawbreaker, miscreant.

offense *(SYN.)* indignity, injustice, transgression, affront, outrage, misdeed, sin, insult, atrocity, aggression, crime. *(ANT.)* morality, gentleness, innocence, right.

offensive *(SYN.)* attacking, aggressive, unpleasant, revolting, disagreeable, nauseous, disgusting. *(ANT.)* pleasing, defending, defensive, pleasant, attractive, agreeable.

offer *(SYN.)* suggestion, overture, proposal, present, suggest, propose, try, submit, attempt, tender. *(ANT.)* withdrawal, denial, rejection.

offhand *(SYN.)* informal, unprepared, casual, impromptu, spontaneous. *(ANT.)* considered, planned, calculated.

office *(SYN.)* position, job, situation, studio, berth, incumbency, capacity, headquarters, duty, task, function, work, post.

officiate *(SYN.)* regulate, administer, superintend, oversee, emcee.

offset *(SYN.)* compensate, counterbalance, cushion, counteract, neutralize, soften, balance.

offshoot *(SYN.)* outgrowth, addition, byproduct, supplement, appendage, accessory, branch.

offspring *(SYN.)* issue, children, progeny, descendants.

often *(SYN.)* frequently, repeatedly, commonly, generally, many times, recurrently. *(ANT.)* seldom, infrequently, rarely, occasionally, sporadically.

ogle *(SYN.)* gaze, stare, eye, leer.

ogre *(SYN.)* fiend, monster, devil, demon.

ointment *(SYN.)* lotion, pomade, balm, emollient.

old *(SYN.)* antique, senile, ancient, archaic, old-fashioned, superannuated, obsolete, venerable, antiquated, elderly, discontinued, abandoned, aged. *(ANT.)* new, youthful, recent, modern, young.

old-fashioned *(SYN.)* outmoded, old, dated, ancient. *(ANT.)* modern, fashionable, current, new.

olio *(SYN.)* potpourri, variety, mixture, jumble.

omen *(SYN.)* sign, gesture, indication, proof, portent, symbol, token, emblem, signal.

ominous *(SYN.)* unfavorable, threatening, sinister, menacing.

omission *(SYN.)* failure, neglect, oversight, default. *(ANT.)* inclusion, notice, insertion.

omit *(SYN.)* exclude, delete, cancel, eliminate, ignore, neglect, skip, leave out, drop, miss, bar, overlook, disregard. *(ANT.)* insert, notice, enter, include, introduce.

omnipotent *(SYN.)* all-powerful, almighty, divine.

oncoming *(SYN.)* imminent, approaching, arriving, nearing.

onerous *(SYN.)* intricate, arduous, hard, perplexing, difficult, burdensome, puzzling. *(ANT.)* simple, easy, facile, effortless.

one-sided *(SYN.)* unfair, partial, biased, prejudiced. *(ANT.)* impartial, neutral.

ongoing *(SYN.)* advancing, developing, continuing, progressive.

onlooker *(SYN.)* witness, spectator, observer, bystander.

only *(SYN.)* lone, sole, solitary, single, merely, but, just.

onset *(SYN.)* commencement, beginning, opening, start, assault, attack, charge, offense, onslaught. *(ANT.)* end.

onslaught *(SYN.)* invasion, aggression, attack, assault, offense, drive, criticism, onset, charge, denunciation. *(ANT.)* vindication, defense, surrender, opposition, resistance.

onus *(SYN.)* load, weight, burden, duty.

onward *(SYN.)* ahead, forward, frontward. *(ANT.)* backward.

ooze *(SYN.)* seep, leak, drip, flow, filter.

opacity *(SYN.)* obscurity, thickness, imperviousness.

opaque *(SYN.)* murky, dull, cloudy, filmy, unilluminated, dim, obtuse, indistinct, shadowy, dark, obscure. *(ANT.)* light, clear, bright.

open *(SYN.)* uncovered, overt, agape, unlocked, passable, accessible, unrestricted, candid, plain, clear, exposed, unclosed, unobstructed, free, disengaged, frank, unoccupied, public, honest, ajar, available.

open *(SYN.)* unbar, unfold, exhibit, spread, unseal, expand, unfasten. *(ANT.)* close, shut, conceal, hide.

open-handed *(SYN.)* kind, generous, charitable, lavish, extravagant, bountiful. *(ANT.)* mean, stingy.

openhearted *(SYN.)* frank, honest, candid, sincere, ingenuous, straightforward. *(ANT.)* insincere, devious.

opening *(SYN.)* cavity, hole, void, abyss, aperture, chasm, pore, gap, loophole.

openly *(SYN.)* sincerely, frankly, freely. *(ANT.)* secretly.

open-minded *(SYN.)* tolerant, fair, just, liberal, impartial, reasonable, unprejudiced. *(ANT.)* prejudiced, bigoted.

operate *(SYN.)* comport, avail, behave, interact, apply, manage, utilize, demean, run, manipulate, employ, act, exploit, exert, exercise, practice, conduct. *(ANT.)* neglect, waste.

operation *(SYN.)* effort, enterprise, mentality, maneuver, action, instrumentality, performance, working, proceeding, agency. *(ANT.)* inaction, cessation, rest, inactivity.

operative *(SYN.)* busy, active, industrious, working, effective, functional. *(ANT.)* inactive, dormant.

opiate *(SYN.)* hypnotic, tranquilizer, narcotic.

opinion *(SYN.)* decision, feeling, notion, view, idea, conviction, belief, judgment, sentiment, persuasion, impression. *(ANT.)* knowledge, fact, misgiving, skepticism.

opinionated *(SYN.)* domineering, over-bearing, arrogant, dogmatic, positive, magisterial, obstinate, pertinacious. *(ANT.)* questioning, fluctuating, indecisive, skeptical, open-minded, indecisive.

opponent *(SYN.)* competitor, foe, adversary, contestant, enemy, rival, contender, combatant, antagonist. *(ANT.)* comrade, team, ally, confederate.

opportune *(SYN.)* fitting, suitable, appropriate, proper, favorable, felicitous.

opportunity *(SYN.)* possibility, chance, occasion, time, contingency, opening. *(ANT.)* obstacle, disadvantage, hindrance.

oppose *(SYN.)* defy, resist, withstand, combat, bar, counteract, confront, thwart, struggle, fight, contradict, hinder, obstruct. *(ANT.)* submit, support, agree, cooperate, succumb.

opposed *(SYN.)* opposite, contrary, hostile, adverse, counteractive, unlucky, antagonistic, unfavorable, disastrous. *(ANT.)* lucky, benign, propitious, fortunate, favorable.

opposite *(SYN.)* reverse, contrary, different, unlike, opposed. *(ANT.)* like, same, similar.

opposition *(SYN.)* combat, struggle, discord, collision, conflict, battle, fight, encounter, discord, controversy, inconsistency, variance. *(ANT.)* harmony, amity, concord, consonance.

oppress *(SYN.)* harass, torment, vex, afflict, annoy, harry, pester, hound, worry, persecute. *(ANT.)* encourage, support, comfort, assist, aid.

oppression *(SYN.)* cruelty, tyranny, persecution, injustice, despotism, brutality, abuse. *(ANT.)* liberty, freedom.

oppressive *(SYN.)* difficult, stifling, burdensome, severe, domineering, harsh, unjust, overbearing, overwhelming.

oppressor *(SYN.)* bully, scourge, slave-driver.

opprobrium *(SYN.)* disgrace, contempt, reproach, shame, discredit.

opt *(SYN.)* choose, prefer, pick, select.

optical *(SYN.)* seeing, visual.

optimism *(SYN.)* faith, expectation, optimism, anticipation, trust, expectancy,

optimistic

confidence, hope. (*ANT.*) *despair, pessimism, despondency.*

optimistic *(SYN.)* happy, cheerful, bright, glad, pleasant, radiant, lighthearted. (*ANT.*) *pessimistic.*

option *(SYN.)* preference, choice, selection, alternative, election, self-determination.

optional *(SYN.)* selective, elective, voluntary. (*ANT.*) *required.*

opulence *(SYN.)* luxury, abundance, fortune, riches, wealth, plenty, affluence. (*ANT.*) *need, indigence, want, poverty.*

opulent *(SYN.)* wealthy, rich, prosperous, well-off, affluent, well-heeled.

oracle *(SYN.)* authority, forecaster, wizard, seer, mastermind, clairvoyant.

oral *(SYN.)* voiced, sounded, vocalized, said, uttered, verbal, vocal, spoken. (*ANT.*) *recorded, written, documentary.*

orate *(SYN.)* preach, lecture, sermonize.

oration *(SYN.)* address, lecture, speech, sermon, discourse, recital, declamation.

orb *(SYN.)* globe, sphere, ball, moon.

orbit *(SYN.)* path, lap, course, circuit, revolution, revolve, circle.

orchestra *(SYN.)* ensemble, band.

orchestrate *(SYN.)* coordinate, direct, synchronize, organize.

ordain *(SYN.)* constitute, create, order, decree, decide, dictate, command, rule, bid, sanction, appoint. (*ANT.*) *terminate, disband.*

ordeal *(SYN.)* hardship, suffering, test, affliction, trouble, fortune, proof, examination, trial, experiment, tribulation, misery. (*ANT.*) *consolation, alleviation.*

order *(SYN.)* plan, series, decree, instruction, command, system, method, aim, arrangement, class, injunction, mandate, instruct, requirement, dictate, guide, rule, direct, govern, manage, regulate, bid, conduct (*ANT.*) *consent, license, confusion, disarray, irregularity, permission.*

orderly *(SYN.)* regulated, neat, well-organized, disciplined, methodical, shipshape. (*ANT.*) *sloppy, messy, haphazard, disorganized.*

ordinarily *(SYN.)* commonly, usually, generally, mostly, customarily, normally.

ordinary *(SYN.)* common, habitual, normal, typical, usual, conventional, familiar, accustomed, customary, average, standard, everyday, inferior, mediocre, regular, vulgar, plain. (*ANT.*) *uncommon, marvelous, extraordinary, remarkable, strange.*

ordnance *(SYN.)* munitions, artillery.

organ *(SYN.)* instrument, journal, voice.

organic *(SYN.)* living, biological, animate.

organism *(SYN.)* creature, plant, micro organism.

organization *(SYN.)* order, rule, system, arrangement, method, plan, regularity, scheme, mode, process. (*ANT.*) *irregularity, chaos, disarrangement, chance, disorder.*

organize *(SYN.)* assort, arrange, plan, regulate, systematize, devise, categorize, classify, prepare. (*ANT.*) *jumble, disorder, disturb, confuse, scatter.*

organized *(SYN.)* planned, neat, orderly, arranged.

orient *(SYN.)* align, fit, accustom, adjust.

orifice *(SYN.)* vent, slot, opening, hole.

origin *(SYN.)* birth, foundation, source, start, commencement, inception, beginning, derivation, infancy, parentage, spring, cradle. (*ANT.*) *product, issue, outcome, end.*

original *(SYN.)* primary, fresh, new, initial, pristine, creative, first, primordial, inventive, primeval, novel, introductory. (*ANT.* *banal, trite, subsequent, derivative, late, modern, terminal.*

originality *(SYN.)* unconventionality, genius, novelty, creativity, imagination.

originate *(SYN.)* fashion, invent, cause, create, make, initiate, inaugurate, organize, institute, produce, engender, commence, found, establish, form, begin, arise, generate, formulate. (*ANT.*) *demolish, terminate, annihilate, disband, destroy.*

originator *(SYN.)* creator, inventor, discoverer. (*ANT.*) *follower, imitator.*

ornament *(SYN.)* decoration, ornamentation, adornment, embellishment, trimming, garnish.

ornamental *(SYN.)* ornate, decorative.

ornate *(SYN.)* florid, overdone, elaborate, showy, flowery, pretentious.

ornery *(SYN.)* disobedient, firm, unruly, stiff, rebellious, stubborn, headstrong, willful, contrary, rigid, mean, difficult, malicious, cross, disagreeable. *(ANT.)* pleasant.

orthodox *(SYN.)* customary, usual, conventional, correct, proper, accepted. *(ANT.)* different, unorthodox.

oscillate *(SYN.)* vary, change, hesitate, waver, undulate, fluctuate, vacillate. *(ANT.)* persist, resolve, adhere, stick, decide.

ostentation *(SYN.)* parade, show, boasting, pageantry, vaunting, pomp, display, flourish. *(ANT.)* reserve, humility, unobtrusiveness, modesty.

ostentatious *(SYN.)* flashy, showy, overdone, fancy, pretentious, garish.

ostracize *(SYN.)* hinder, omit, bar, exclude, blackball, expel, prohibit, shout out, prevent, except. *(ANT.)* welcome, accept, include, admit.

other *(SYN.)* distinct, different, extra, further, new, additional, supplementary.

ought *(SYN.)* must, should, be obliged.

oust *(SYN.)* eject, banish, exclude, expatriate, ostracize, dismiss, exile, expel. *(ANT.)* shelter, accept, receive, admit, harbor.

ouster *(SYN.)* expulsion, banishment, ejection, overthrow.

outbreak *(SYN.)* riot, revolt, uprising, disturbance, torrent, eruption, outburst.

outburst *(SYN.)* outbreak, eruption, torrent, ejection, discharge.

outcast *(SYN.)* friendless, homeless, deserted, abandoned, forsaken, disowned, derelict, forlorn, rejected.

outclass *(SYN.)* outshine, surpass.

outcome *(SYN.)* fate, destiny, necessity, doom, portion, consequence, result, end, fortune, effect, issue, aftermath.

outcry *(SYN.)* scream, protest, clamor, noise, uproar.

outdated *(SYN.)* old-fashioned, unfashionable, old, outmoded. *(ANT.)* stylish.

outdo *(SYN.)* outshine, defeat, excel, beat, surpass.

outer *(SYN.)* remote, exterior, external.

outfit *(SYN.)* garb, kit, gear, furnish, equip, rig, clothing, provisions.

outgoing *(SYN.)* leaving, departing, friendly, congenial, amicable. *(ANT.)* unfriendly, incoming.

outgrowth *(SYN.)* effect, outcome, upshot, fruit, result, consequence, product.

outing *(SYN.)* journey, trip, excursion, jaunt, expedition, junket.

outlandish *(SYN.)* peculiar, odd, weird, curious, strange, queer, exotic, bazaar. *(ANT.)* ordinary, common.

outlast *(SYN.)* survive, endure, outlive.

outlaw *(SYN.)* exile, bandit, outcast, badman, convict, criminal, fugitive, desperado.

outlay *(SYN.)* expense, costs, spending, disbursement, expenditure, charge.

outlet *(SYN.)* spout, opening, passage.

outline *(SYN.)* form, sketch, brief, draft, figure, profile, contour, chart, diagram, skeleton, delineation, plan, silhouette.

outlook *(SYN.)* viewpoint, view, prospect, opportunity, position, attitude, future.

outlying *(SYN.)* external, remote, outer, out-of-the-way, suburban, rural.

outmoded *(SYN.)* unfashionable, oldfashioned. *(ANT.)* up-to-date, modern.

outnumber *(SYN.)* exceed.

output *(SYN.)* yield, crop, harvest, proceeds, productivity, production.

outrage *(SYN.)* aggression, transgression, vice, affront, offense, insult, indignity, atrocity, misdeed, trespass, wrong. *(ANT.)* morality, right, gentleness, innocence.

outrageous *(SYN.)* shameful, shocking, disgraceful, insulting, nonsensical, absurd, foolish, crazy, excessive, ridiculous, bizarre, preposterous, offensive. *(ANT.)* prudent, reasonable, sensible.

outright *(SYN.)* entirely, altogether, completely, quite, fully, thoroughly.

outset *(SYN.)* inception, origin, start, commencement, opening, source. *(ANT.)* end, completion, termination, consummation, close.

outside *(SYN.)* covering, exterior, surface,

outsider

facade, externals, appearance. *(ANT.)* intimate, insider.

outsider *(SYN.)* immigrant, stranger, foreigner, alien, newcomer, bystander. *(ANT.)* countryman, friend, acquaintance, neighbor, associate.

outsmart *(SYN.)* outmaneuver, outwit.

outspoken *(SYN.)* rude, impolite, unceremonious, brusque, unrestrained, vocal, open, straight-forward, blunt, unreserved, frank, forthright, rough. *(ANT.)* suave, tactful, shy, polished, polite, subtle.

outstanding *(SYN.)* well-known, important, prominent, leading, eminent, distinguished, significant, conspicuous. *(ANT.)* insignificant, unimportant.

outward *(SYN.)* apparent, outside, exterior, visible.

outweigh *(SYN.)* predominate, supersede, counteract, dwarf.

outwit *(SYN.)* baffle, trick, outsmart, bewilder, outdo, outmaneuver, confuse.

oval *(SYN.)* egg-shaped, elliptical, ovular.

ovation *(SYN.)* fanfare, homage, applause, tribute, cheers, acclamation.

overall *(SYN.)* comprehensive, complete, general, extensive, wide-spread, entire.

overbearing *(SYN.)* domineering, masterful, autocratic, dictatorial, arrogant, bossy, imperious, haughty. *(ANT.)* humble.

overcast *(SYN.)* dim, shadowy, cloudy, murky, dark, mysterious, gloomy, somber, dismal, hazy, indistinct. *(ANT.)* sunny, bright, limpid, clear.

overcome *(SYN.)* quell, beat, crush, surmount, rout, humble, conquer, subjugate, defeat, subdue, upset, vanquish. *(ANT.)* retreat, surrender, capitulate, cede, lose.

overconfident *(SYN.)* egotistical, presumptuous, arrogant, conceited.

overdo *(SYN.)* stretch, exaggerate, enlarge, magnify, exhaust, overexert.

overdue *(SYN.)* tardy, advanced, slow, delayed, new. *(ANT.)* timely, early, beforehand.

overflow *(SYN.)* run over, flood, spill, cascade, inundate.

overflowing *(SYN.)* ample, plentiful, teeming, abundant, copious, profuse *(ANT.)* insufficient, deficient, scarce.

overhang *(SYN.)* protrude, extend.

overhaul *(SYN.)* recondition, rebuild, service, repair, condition, revamp.

overhead *(SYN.)* high, above, aloft, expenses, costs.

overjoyed *(SYN.)* enchanted, delighted ecstatic, enraptured, elated, blissful *(ANT.)* depressed.

overlap *(SYN.)* overhang, extend, superimpose.

overload *(SYN.)* burden, weight, oppress afflict, weigh, trouble, encumber, tax *(ANT.)* ease, lighten, console, alleviate.

overlook *(SYN.)* miss, disregard, exclude cancel, omit, skip, ignore, drop, delete neglect, exclude, watch, eliminate. *(ANT.* notice, include, introduce, inset.

overly *(SYN.)* exceedingly, unreasonably.

overpass *(SYN.)* span, bridge, viaduct.

overpower *(SYN.)* overcome, conquer defeat, surmount, vanquish, overwhelm *(ANT.)* surrender.

overrule *(SYN.)* disallow, nullify, cancel override, repeal, revoke.

overrun *(SYN.)* spread, exceed, beset, infest, flood, abound.

oversee *(SYN.)* direct, run, operate, administer, boss, manage, supervise.

overseer *(SYN.)* leader, ruler, master teacher, chief, commander, lord, employer manager, head. *(ANT.)* slave, servant.

overshadow *(SYN.)* dominate, control outclass, surpass, domineer.

oversight *(SYN.)* omission, charge superintendence, surveillance, inattention error, inadvertence, neglect, mistake, inspection, control, slip, management *(ANT.)* scrutiny, attention, observation.

overstep *(SYN.)* surpass, exceed, trespass transcend, impinge, violate, intrude.

overt *(SYN.)* honest, candid, frank, plain open, apparent, straightforward.

overtake *(SYN.)* outdistance, reach, catch pass.

overthrow *(SYN.)* defeat, demolish overcome, destroy, ruin, rout, vanquish

parsimonious

subvert, reverse, supplant, overturn, over-power, upset. *(ANT.)* *revive, restore, construct, regenerate, reinstate.*

overturn *(SYN.)* demolish, overcome, vanquish, upset, supplant, destroy. *(ANT.)* *uphold, construct, build, preserve, conserve.*

overweight *(SYN.)* pudgy, stout, heavy, obese, fat.

overwhelm *(SYN.)* crush, surmount, vanquish, conquer, astonish, surprise, bewilder, astound, startle, overcome.

overwrought *(SYN.)* distraught, hysterical.

owe *(SYN.)* be liable, be indebted.

own *(SYN.)* monopolize, hold, possess, maintain, have.

owner *(SYN.)* landholder, partner, proprietor, possessor.

P

pace *(SYN.)* rate, gait, step.

pacify *(SYN.)* appease, lull, relieve, quell, soothe, allay, assuage, calm, satisfy, compose, placate, alleviate. *(ANT.)* *incense, inflame, arouse, excite.*

pack *(SYN.)* prepare, stow, crowd, stuff, bundle, parcel, load, crowd, gang, mob.

package *(SYN.)* parcel, packet, load, bundle, box, bottle, crate.

packed *(SYN.)* filled, complete, plentiful, crammed, fall, replete, gorged, satiated. *(ANT.)* *lacking, depleted, devoid, vacant, insufficient, partial, empty.*

pageant *(SYN.)* show, display, spectacle.

pain *(SYN.)* twinge, ache, pang, agony, distress, grief, anguish, throe, paroxysm. *(ANT.)* *happiness, pleasure, comfort, relief, solace, ease, delight, joy.*

painful *(SYN.)* hurting, galling, poignant, bitter, grievous, agonizing, aching. *(ANT.)* *sweet, pleasant, soothing.*

painting *(SYN.)* image, picture, portrayal, scene, view, sketch, illustration, panorama, likeness, representation.

pair *(SYN.)* team, couple, mate, match.

palatial *(SYN.)* majestic, magnificent, sumptuous, luxurious.

pale *(SYN.)* colorless, white, pallid, dim, faint, whiten, blanch. *(ANT.)* *flushed, ruddy, bright, dark.*

pamphlet *(SYN.)* leaflet, brochure.

pang *(SYN.)* throb, pain, hurt.

panic *(SYN.)* fear, terror, fright, alarm, apprehension, trembling, horror, dread. *(ANT.)* *tranquillity, composure, calmness, serenity, calm, soothe.*

pant *(SYN.)* wheeze, puff, gasp.

pantry *(SYN.)* cupboard, storeroom.

paper *(SYN.)* journal, newspaper, document, article, essay.

parable *(SYN.)* fable, saga, legend, myth, allegory, chronicle, fiction.

parade *(SYN.)* procession, cavalcade, succession, train, file, cortege, retinue, sequence, march, review, pageant, strut.

paradise *(SYN.)* utopia, heaven.

paradoxical *(SYN.)* unsteady, contradictory, discrepant, incompatible, inconsistent, vacillating, wavering, illogical. *(ANT.)* *correspondent, compatible, congruous, consistent.*

parallel *(SYN.)* allied, analogous, comparable, corresponding, akin, similar, correlative, alike, like, resembling, equal, counterpart, likeness, correspondence, resemble, equal, match. *(ANT.)* *opposed, different, incongruous.*

paralyze *(SYN.)* numb, deaden.

paraphernalia *(SYN.)* effect, gear, belonging, equipment.

parcel *(SYN.)* packet, package, bundle.

parched *(SYN.)* dry, arid, thirsty, drained, dehydrated, desiccated. *(ANT.)* *moist, damp.*

pardon *(SYN.)* absolution, amnesty, excuse, exoneration, forgive, acquit, condone, overlook, absolve, remit. *(ANT.)* *punish, chastise, accuse, sentence, penalty, conviction, condemn, convict.*

pare *(SYN.)* skin, peel, reduce, trim, shave.

parley *(SYN.)* interview, talk, conference, chat, dialogue, colloquy.

paroxysm *(SYN.)* twinge, pang, ache, pain. *(ANT.)* *ease, relief, comfort.*

parsimonious *(SYN.)* avaricious, miserly,

penurious, stingy, acquisitive, greedy. (*ANT.*) *munificent, extravagant, bountiful, altruistic, generous.*

part (*SYN.*) piece, section, allotment, portion, segment, element, member, concern, side, interest, lines, role, apportionment, division, share, fragment, ingredient, organ, party, moiety, section, fraction, participation, divide, separate, sever, sunder. (*ANT.*) *whole, entirety, join, combine, unite, convene.*

partake (*SYN.*) dispense, parcel, allot, assign, distribute, partition, appropriate, divide, portion, share. (*ANT.*) *condense, aggregate, combine.*

partial (*SYN.*) unfinished, undone, incomplete, prejudiced, unfair. (*ANT.*) *comprehensive, complete.*

partiality (*SYN.*) preconception, bias, predisposition, bigotry. (*ANT.*) *reason, fairness, impartiality.*

participant (*SYN.*) associate, colleague, partner, shareholder.

participate (*SYN.*) join, share, partake.

participation (*SYN.*) communion, sacrament, union, intercourse, association, fellowship. (*ANT.*) *nonparticipation, alienation.*

particle (*SYN.*) mite, crumb, scrap, atom, corpuscle, grain, iota, shred, smidgen, grain, speck, bit, spot. (*ANT.*) *quantity, bulk, mass.*

particular (*SYN.*) peculiar, unusual, detailed, specific, fastidious, individual, distinctive, singular, circumstantial, exact, careful, squeamish, special. (*ANT.*) *general, rough, universal, comprehensive, undiscriminating.*

partisan (*SYN.*) follower, successor, adherent, attendant, henchman, devotee, disciple, votary. (*ANT.*) *leader, chief, master, head.*

partition (*SYN.*) distribution, division, separation, screen, barrier, separator, divider, wall. (*ANT.*) *unification, joining.*

partly (*SYN.*) comparatively, partially, somewhat.

partner (*SYN.*) colleague, comrade, friend, crony, consort, associate, companion, mate, participant. (*ANT.*) *stranger, enemy, adversary.*

party (*SYN.*) company, gathering, crowd, group.

pass (*SYN.*) proceed, continue, move, go, disregard, ignore, exceed, gap, permit, permission, admission, throw, toss. (*ANT.*) *note, consider, notice.*

passable (*SYN.*) fair, average, mediocre, acceptable, adequate, satisfactory. (*ANT.*) *worst, excellent, first-rate, exceptional, extraordinary, superior.*

passage (*SYN.*) section, passageway, corridor, section, voyage, tour, crossing.

passenger (*SYN.*) traveler, tourist, rider, voyager, commuter.

passion (*SYN.*) feeling, affection, turmoil, sentiment, perturbation, agitation, emotion, trepidation, zeal, rapture, excitement, desire, love, liking, fondness, enthusiasm. (*ANT.*) *tranquillity, indifference, calm, restraint, dispassion, apathy, coolness.*

passionate (*SYN.*) fiery, ardent, burning, glowing, irascible, fervid, excitable, hot, impetuous, emotional, impulsive, excited, zealous, enthusiastic, earnest, sincere. (*ANT.*) *calm, cool, apathetic, deliberate.*

passive (*SYN.*) relaxed, idle, stoical, enduring, inert, inactive, patient, submissive. (*ANT.*) *dynamic, active, aggressive.*

password (*SYN.*) code word.

past (*SYN.*) done, finished, gone, over, former. (*ANT.*) *future, present, ahead.*

pastime (*SYN.*) match, amusement, diversion, fun, play, sport, contest, merriment, recreation, entertainment, hobby. (*ANT.*) *quiescence, labor, apathy, business.*

patch (*SYN.*) restore, fix, repair, ameliorate, correct, rectify, remedy, sew, mend, better. (*ANT.*) *rend, deface, destroy, hurt, injure.*

patent (*SYN.*) conspicuous, apparent, obvious, clear, evident, unmistakable, open, overt, manifest, indubitable, protection, control, copyright, permit. (*ANT.*) *hidden, concealed, obscure, coven.*

path (*SYN.*) avenue, street, trail, walk, course, route, thoroughfare, channel, way,

peninsula

track, lane, footpath, pathway, walkway.

pathetic *(SYN.)* piteous, sad, affecting, moving, poignant, pitiable, touching, pitiful, touching. *(ANT.)* funny, comical.

patience *(SYN.)* perseverance, composure, endurance, fortitude, long-suffering, forbearance, calmness, passiveness, serenity, courage, persistence. *(ANT.)* restlessness, nervousness, impatience, impetuosity.

patient *(SYN.)* indulgent, stoical, forbearing, composed, assiduous, passive, uncomplaining, resigned, persistent, untiring, persevering, submissive, resigned, serene, calm, quiet, unexcited, unruffled. *(ANT.)* turbulent, high-strung, chafing, clamorous, hysterical.

patrol *(SYN.)* inspect, watch, guard.

patron *(SYN.)* purchaser, buyer, client, customer.

patronize *(SYN.)* support.

pattern *(SYN.)* guide, example, original, model, design, figure, decoration.

paunchy *(SYN.)* fat, pudgy, stout, plump, portly, rotund, corpulent, obese, stocky. *(ANT.)* slim, slender, gaunt, lean, thin.

pause *(SYN.)* falter, hesitate, waver, demur, doubt, scruple, delay, vacillate, hesitation, rest, interruption, break, delay, intermission, recess. *(ANT.)* proceed, continue, decide, resolve, persevere, continuity.

pawn *(SYN.)* tool, puppet, stooge.

pay *(SYN.)* earnings, salary, allowance, stipend, wages, payment, compensation, recompense. *(ANT.)* gratuity, present, gift.

payable *(SYN.)* unpaid, due, owed, owing.

peace *(SYN.)* hush, repose, serenity, tranquillity, silence, stillness, calmness, quiescence, calm, quietude, rest, quiet, peacefulness, pact. *(ANT.)* noise, tumult, agitation, disturbance, excitement.

peaceable *(SYN.)* mild, calm, friendly, peaceful, amiable, gentle, pacific. *(ANT.)* aggressive, hostile, warlike.

peaceful *(SYN.)* pacific, calm, undisturbed, quiet, serene, mild, placid, gentle, tranquil, peaceable. *(ANT.)* noisy, violent, agitated, turbulent, disturbed, disrupted, riotous.

peak *(SYN.)* climax, culmination, summit, zenith, height, acme, consummation, apex, top, point, crest. *(ANT.)* depth, floor, base, anticlimax, base, bottom.

peculiar *(SYN.)* odd, eccentric, extraordinary, unusual, individual, particular, striking, rare, exceptional, distinctive, strange, unfamiliar, uncommon, queer, curious, outlandish. *(ANT.)* ordinary, common, normal, general, regular.

peculiarity *(SYN.)* characteristic, feature, mark, trait, quality, attribute, property, distinctiveness.

pedantic *(SYN.)* formal, scholastic, erudite, academic, learned, bookish, theoretical, scholarly. *(ANT.)* simple, commonsense, ignorant, practical, unlearned.

peddle *(SYN.)* sell, vend, hawk.

pedestrian *(SYN.)* stroller, walker.

pedigree *(SYN.)* descent, line, parentage, lineage, ancestry, family.

peek *(SYN.)* glimpse, look, peer, peep.

peel *(SYN.)* rind, skin, peeling.

peep *(SYN.)* squeak, cheep, chirp.

peer *(SYN.)* match, rival, equal, parallel, peep, glimpse, examine, peek, scrutinize.

peeve *(SYN.)* nettle, irk, irritate, annoy.

peevish *(SYN.)* ill-natured, irritable, waspish, touchy, petulant, snappish, fractious, ill-tempered, fretful. *(ANT.)* pleasant, affable, good-tempered, genial, good-natured.

pen *(SYN.)* coop, enclosure, cage.

penalize *(SYN.)* dock, punish.

penalty *(SYN.)* fine, retribution, handicap, punishment, chastisement, disadvantage, forfeiture, forfeit. *(ANT.)* remuneration, compensation, reward, pardon.

penchant *(SYN.)* disposition, propensity, tendency, partiality, inclination, bent, tendency, slant, bias. *(ANT.)* justice, fairness, equity, impartiality.

penetrate *(SYN.)* bore, hole, pierce, enter.

penetrating *(SYN.)* profound, recondite, abstruse, deep, solemn, piercing, puncturing, boring, sharp, acute. *(ANT.)* superficial, trivial, shallow, slight.

peninsula *(SYN.)* spit, headland, neck, point.

penitent

penitent *(SYN.)* remorseful, sorrowful, regretful, contrite, sorry, repentant. *(ANT.)* remorseless, objurgate.

penniless *(SYN.)* poor, destitute, impecunious, poverty-stricken, needy. *(ANT.)* rich, wealthy, affluent, opulent, prosperous, well-off.

pensive *(SYN.)* dreamy, meditative, thoughtful, introspective, reflective, contemplative. *(ANT.)* thoughtless, heedless, inconsiderate, precipitous, rash.

penurious *(SYN.)* avaricious, greedy, parsimonious, miserly, stingy, acquisitive, tight. *(ANT.)* munificent, extravagant, bountiful, generous, altruistic.

penury *(SYN.)* poverty, want, destitution, necessity, indigence, need, privation. *(ANT.)* riches, affluence, abundance, plenty.

people *(SYN.)* humans, person.

perceive *(SYN.)* note, conceive, see, comprehend, understand, discern, recognize, apprehend, notice, observe, distinguish, grasp. *(ANT.)* overlook, ignore, miss.

perceptible *(SYN.)* sensible, appreciable, apprehensible. *(ANT.)* imperceptible, absurd, impalpable.

perception *(SYN.)* understanding, apprehension, conception, insight, comprehension, discernment. *(ANT.)* misconception, ignorance, misapprehension.

perceptive *(SYN.)* informed, observant, apprised, cognizant, aware, conscious, sensible, mindful, discerning, sharp, acute, observant. *(ANT.)* unaware, ignorant, oblivious, insensible.

perfect *(SYN.)* ideal, whole, faultless, immaculate, complete, superlative, absolute, unqualified, utter, sinless, holy, finished, blameless, entire, excellent, pure, flawless, ideal. *(ANT.)* incomplete, defective, imperfect, deficient, blemished, lacking, faulty, flawed.

perfectionist *(SYN.)* purist, pedant.

perform *(SYN.)* impersonate, pretend, act, play, do, accomplish, achieve, complete.

performance *(SYN.)* parade, entertainment, demonstration, movie, show, production, ostentation, spectacle, presentation, offering.

performer *(SYN.)* entertainer, actress, actor.

perfume *(SYN.)* cologne, scent, essence.

perfunctory *(SYN.)* decorous, exact, formal, external, correct, affected, methodical, precise, stiff, outward, proper, solemn. *(ANT.)* unconventional, easy, unconstrained, natural, heartfelt.

perhaps *(SYN.)* conceivable, possible, maybe. *(ANT.)* absolutely, definitely.

peril *(SYN.)* jeopardy, risk, danger, hazard. *(ANT.)* safety, protection, defense, security.

perilous *(SYN.)* menacing, risky, hazardous, critical, dangerous, precarious, unsafe, insecure, threatening. *(ANT.)* safe, firm, protected, secure.

period *(SYN.)* era, age, interval, span, tempo, time, epoch, duration, spell, date.

periodical *(SYN.)* uniform, customary, orderly, systematic, regular, steady. *(ANT.)* exceptional, unusual, abnormal, rare, erratic.

perish *(SYN.)* die, sink, cease, decline, decay, depart, wane, wither, languish, expire, cease, pass away. *(ANT.)* grow, survive, flourish, begin, live.

perishable *(SYN.)* decomposable.

permanent *(SYN.)* constant, durable, enduring, abiding, fixed, changeless, unchangeable, lasting, indestructible, stable, continuing, long-lived, persistent, persisting, everlasting, unchanging, unaltered. *(ANT.)* unstable, transient, ephemeral, temporary, transitory, passing, inconstant, fluctuating.

permeate *(SYN.)* penetrate, pervade, run through, diffuse, fill, saturate, infiltrate.

permissible *(SYN.)* allowable, fair, tolerable, admissible, justifiable, probable, warranted. *(ANT.)* unsuitable, inadmissible.

permission *(SYN.)* authorization, liberty, permit, authority, consent, leave, license, freedom. *(ANT.)* refusal, prohibition, denial, opposition.

permissive *(SYN.)* easy, tolerant, open-minded. *(ANT.)* restrictive.

permit *(SYN.)* let, tolerate, authorize, sanction, allow, grant, give. *(ANT.)* refuse, resist, *forbid, protest, object, prohibit, disallow.*

perpendicular *(SYN.)* standing, upright, vertical. *(ANT.) horizontal.*

perpetrate *(SYN.)* commit, perform, do. *(ANT.) neglect, fail, miscarry.*

perpetual *(SYN.)* everlasting, immortal, ceaseless, endless, timeless, undying, infinite, eternal, unceasing, continuing, continual, continuous, permanent, constant, eternal. *(ANT.) transient, mortal, finite, temporal, ephemeral, inconstant, intermittent, fluctuating.*

perpetually *(SYN.)* continually, ever, incessantly, eternally, forever, always, constantly. *(ANT.) rarely, sometimes, never, occasionally, fitfully.*

perplex *(SYN.)* confuse, dumbfound, mystify, puzzle, bewilder, confound, nonplus. *(ANT.) solve, explain, illumine, instruct, clarify.*

perplexed *(SYN.)* confused, disorganized, mixed, bewildered, deranged, disordered, muddled, disconcerted. *(ANT.) plain, obvious, clear, lucid, organized.*

perplexing *(SYN.)* intricate, complex, involved, compound, complicated. *(ANT.) uncompounded, plain, simple.*

persecute *(SYN.)* harass, hound, torment, worry, vex, torture, harry, afflict, annoy, oppress, pester, ill-treat, victimize, maltreat. *(ANT.) support, comfort, assist, encourage, aid.*

persevere *(SYN.)* remain, abide, endure, last, persist, continue. *(ANT.) vacillate, desist, discontinue, cease, waver, lapse.*

perseverance *(SYN.)* persistency, constancy, pertinacity, steadfastness, tenacity, industry. *(ANT.) sloth, cessation, laziness, idleness, rest.*

persist *(SYN.)* endure, remain, abide, persevere, continue, last. *(ANT.) vacillate, waver, desist, cease, discontinue, stop.*

persistence *(SYN.)* persistency, constancy, perseverance, steadfastness, tenacity. *(ANT.) cessation, rest, sloth, idleness.*

persistent *(SYN.)* lasting, steady, obstinate, stubborn, fixed, enduring, immovable, constant, indefatigable, dogged.

(ANT.) wavering, unsure, hesitant.

person *(SYN.)* human, individual, somebody, someone.

personal *(SYN.)* secret, private. *(ANT.) general, public.*

personality *(SYN.)* make-up, nature, disposition, character.

perspicacity *(SYN.)* intelligence, understanding, discernment, judgment, wisdom, sagacity. *(ANT.) thoughtlessness, stupidity, arbitrariness, senselessness.*

persuade *(SYN.)* entice, coax, exhort, prevail upon, urge, allure, induce, influence, win over, convince. *(ANT.) restrain, deter, compel, dissuade, coerce, discourage.*

persuasion *(SYN.)* decision, feeling, notion, view, sentiment, conviction, belief, opinion. *(ANT.) knowledge, skepticism, fact, misgiving.*

persuasive *(SYN.)* winning, alluring, compelling, convincing, stimulating, influential. *(ANT.) dubious, unconvincing.*

pertain *(SYN.)* refer, relate, apply.

pertinacious *(SYN.)* firm, obstinate, contumacious, head-strong, dogged, inflexible, obdurate, uncompromising, determined, immovable, unyielding. *(ANT.) yielding, docile, amenable, submissive, compliant.*

pertinent *(SYN.)* apt, material, relevant, relating, applicable, to the point, germane, apropos, apposite, appropriate. *(ANT.) unrelated, foreign, alien, extraneous.*

perturbed *(SYN.)* agitated, disturbed, upset, flustered.

pervade *(SYN.)* penetrate, saturate, fill, diffuse, infiltrate, run through, permeate.

perverse *(SYN.)* obstinate, ungovernable, sinful, contrary, fractious, peevish, forward, disobedient, wicked, intractable, petulant. *(ANT.) docile, agreeable, tractable.*

perversion *(SYN.)* maltreatment, outrage, desecration, abuse, profanation, misuse, reviling. *(ANT.) respect.*

pervert *(SYN.)* deprave, humiliate, impair, debase, corrupt, degrade, abase, defile. *(ANT.) improve, raise, enhance.*

perverted *(SYN.)* wicked, perverse, sinful.

pest

pest *(SYN.)* annoyance, bother, nuisance, bother, irritant, irritation.

pester *(SYN.)* disturb, annoy, irritate, tease, bother, chafe, inconvenience, molest, trouble, vex, harass, torment, worry. *(ANT.)* console, soothe, accommodate, gratify.

pet *(SYN.)* darling, favorite, caress.

petition *(SYN.)* invocation, prayer, request, appeal, entreaty, supplication, suit, plea, application, solicitation, entreaty.

petty *(SYN.)* paltry, trivial, frivolous, small, unimportant, trifling, insignificant. *(ANT.)* important, serious, weighty, momentous, grand, vital, significant, generous.

petulant *(SYN.)* irritable, ill-natured, fretful, snappish, peevish, ill-tempered, waspish, touchy. *(ANT.)* pleasant, affable, good-tempered, genial, good-natured.

phantom *(SYN.)* apparition, ghost, specter.

phase *(SYN.)* period, stage, view, condition.

phenomenon *(SYN.)* occurrence, fact, happening, incident.

philanthropy *(SYN.)* kindness, benevolence, charity, generosity, tenderness, liberality, humanity, magnanimity, altruism. *(ANT.)* unkindness, inhumanity, cruelty, malevolence, selfishness.

phlegmatic *(SYN.)* unfeeling, passionless, listless, cold, lethargic, sluggish, slow, lazy. *(ANT.)* passionate, ardent, energetic.

phony *(SYN.)* counterfeit, artificial, ersatz, fake, synthetic, unreal, spurious, feigned, assumed, bogus, sham, false, forged. *(ANT.)* real, genuine, natural, true.

phrase *(SYN.)* expression, term, word, name.

physical *(SYN.)* material, bodily, carnal, corporeal, natural, somatic, corporal. *(ANT.)* spiritual, mental.

pick *(SYN.)* cull, opt, select, elect, choose. *(ANT.)* reject, refuse.

picture *(SYN.)* etching, image, painting, portrait, print, representation, sketch, appearance, cinema, effigy, engraving, scene, view, illustration, panorama, resemblance, likeness, drawing, photograph.

piece *(SYN.)* portion, bit, fraction, morsel, scrap, fragment, amount, part, quantity, unit, section, portion. *(ANT.)* sum, whole, entirety, all, total.

piecemeal *(SYN.)* gradually, partially. *(ANT.)* whole, complete, entire.

pierce *(SYN.)* puncture, perforate.

pigheaded *(SYN.)* inflexible, stubborn, obstinate.

pigment *(SYN.)* shade, tint, color, dye, hue, complexion, tincture, stain, tinge. *(ANT.)* transparency, paleness.

pile *(SYN.)* accumulation, heap, collection.

pilgrim *(SYN.)* wanderer, traveler.

pilgrimage *(SYN.)* trip, journey, tour, expedition.

pillar *(SYN.)* support, prop, column, shaft.

pillow *(SYN.)* bolster, cushion, pad.

pilot *(SYN.)* helmsman, aviator, steersman.

pin *(SYN.)* clip, fastening, peg, fastener.

pinch *(SYN.)* squeeze, nip.

pinnacle *(SYN.)* crown, zenith, head, summit, chief, apex, crest, top. *(ANT.)* bottom, foundation, base, foot.

pioneer *(SYN.)* guide, pilgrim, pathfinder, explorer.

pious *(SYN.)* devout, religious, spiritual, consecrated, divine, hallowed, holy, saintly, reverent. *(ANT.)* worldly, sacrilegious, evil, secular, profane, irreligious, impious.

pirate *(SYN.)* plunderer, buccaneer, privateer.

pistol *(SYN.)* gun, revolver, weapon, handgun.

pit *(SYN.)* well, cavity, hole, excavation.

pitch *(SYN.)* throw, cast, toss, propel, hurl, fling, thrust, establish. *(ANT.)* retain, draw, hold, pull, haul.

pitcher *(SYN.)* jug.

piteous *(SYN.)* poignant, touching, affecting, moving, pitiable, sad, pathetic. *(ANT.)* funny, ludicrous, comical.

pitfall *(SYN.)* lure, snare, wile, ambush, bait, intrigue, trick, trap, artifice, net, snare.

pitiable *(SYN.)* poignant, touching, moving, affecting, sad. *(ANT.)* ludicrous, funny, comical.

pitiful *(SYN.)* distressing, pathetic, pitiable.

pitiless *(SYN.)* unmerciful, mean, unpitying, merciless, cruel. *(ANT.)* gentle, kind.

pity *(SYN.)* sympathy, commiseration, condolence, mercy, compassion, charity, mercy. *(ANT.)* ruthlessness, hardness, cruelty, inhumanity, brutality, vindictiveness.

pivotal *(SYN.)* crucial, critical, essential, central. *(ANT.)* peripheral, unimportant.

place *(SYN.)* lay, arrange, dispose, put, deposit, space, region, location, plot, area, spot. *(ANT.)* mislay, remove, disarrange, disturb, misplace.

placid *(SYN.)* pacific, serene, tranquil, calm, imperturbable, composed, peaceful, quiet, still, undisturbed, unruffled. *(ANT.)* wild, frantic, turbulent, stormy, excited.

plagiarize *(SYN.)* recite, adduce, cite, quote, paraphrase, repeat, extract. *(ANT.)* retort, contradict, misquote, refute.

plague *(SYN.)* hound, pester, worry, harass, annoy, persecute, torment, vex, afflict, badger, torture, epidemic, trouble. *(ANT.)* encourage, aid, comfort, assist, support.

plain *(SYN.)* candid, simple, flat, smooth, clear, evident, sincere, unpretentious, level, distinct, absolute, visible, open, frank, palpable, undecorated, ordinary, unembellished, unadorned. *(ANT.)* embellished, abstruse, abrupt, rough, insincere, adorned, fancy, elaborate, beautiful, ornamented.

plan *(SYN.)* design, purpose, sketch, devise, invent, contrive, intend, draw, create, scheme, plot, method, procedure.

plane *(SYN.)* level, airplane.

plastic *(SYN.)* pliable, moldable, supple, flexible, synthetic.

platform *(SYN.)* stage, pulpit.

plausible *(SYN.)* likely, practical, credible, feasible, possible, probable. *(ANT.)* impracticable, impossible, visionary.

play *(SYN.)* entertainment, amusement, pastime, sport, game, fun, diversion, recreation, show, performance, drama, theatrical. *(ANT.)* work, labor, boredom, toil.

playful *(SYN.)* sportive, frolicsome, frisky.

plaything *(SYN.)* game, trinket, toy, gadget.

playwright *(SYN.)* scriptwriter, dramatist.

plea *(SYN.)* invocation, request, appeal, entreaty, supplication, petition, suit.

plead *(SYN.)* beseech, defend, rejoin, supplicate, discuss, beg, appeal, ask, implore, argue, entreat. *(ANT.)* deny, refuse.

pleasant *(SYN.)* agreeable, welcome, suitable, charming, pleasing, amiable, gratifying, acceptable, pleasurable, enjoyable, nice, satisfying, satisfactory, acceptable, affable, mild, friendly. *(ANT.)* offensive, disagreeable, obnoxious, unpleasant, horrid, sour, difficult, nasty.

please *(SYN.)* satisfy, suffice, fulfill, content, appease, gratify, satiate, compensate, remunerate. *(ANT.)* dissatisfy, annoy, tantalize, frustrate, displease, vex.

pleasing *(SYN.)* luscious, melodious, sugary, delightful, agreeable, honeyed, mellifluous, engaging, pleasant, charming, engaging. *(ANT.)* repulsive, sour, acrid, bitter, offensive, irritating, annoying.

pleasure *(SYN.)* felicity, delight, amusement, enjoyment, gratification, happiness, joy, satisfaction, gladness, well-being. *(ANT.)* suffering, pain, vexation, trouble, affliction, discomfort, torment.

pledge *(SYN.)* promise, statement, assertion, declaration, assurance, agreement, oath, commitment, agree, vow, swear; bind, obligate, commit. *(ANT.)* renounce, release, neglect, mistrust.

plentiful *(SYN.)* ample, profuse, replete, bountiful, abundant, plenteous, luxurious, fullness, fruitful, copious. *(ANT.)* rare, scanty, deficient, scarce, insufficient.

plenty *(SYN.)* fruitfulness, bounty, fullness, abundance. *(ANT.)* want, scarcity, need.

pliable *(SYN.)* elastic, supple, flexible, compliant, pliant, resilient, ductile. *(ANT.)* rigid, unbending, hard, brittle, stiff.

plight *(SYN.)* dilemma, situation, difficulty, condition, predicament, fix, scrape, state. *(ANT.)* satisfaction, ease, comfort, calmness.

plot *(SYN.)* design, plan, scheme, cabal, conspiracy, diagram, sketch, graph, chart, machination, intrigue.

plotting *(SYN.)* cunning, scheming, objective, artfulness, contrivance, purpose, intent, design. *(ANT.)* accident, chance, result, candor, sincerity.

ploy *(SYN.)* ruse, guile, antic, deception,

pluck

hoax, subterfuge, wile, cheat, artifice, fraud, trick. (*ANT.*) *honesty, sincerity, openness, exposure, candor.*

pluck *(SYN.)* yank, snatch, jerk, pull.

plug *(SYN.)* cork, stopper.

plump *(SYN.)* obese, portly, stout, thickset, rotund, chubby, fat, paunchy, stocky, corpulent, pudgy, fleshy. (*ANT.*) *slim, thin, gaunt, lean, slender, skinny.*

plunder *(SYN.)* ravage, strip, sack, rob, pillage, raid, loot.

plunge *(SYN.)* immerse, dip, submerge.

pocketbook *(SYN.)* purse, handbag.

poem *(SYN.)* lyric, verse, poetry, rhyme.

pogrom *(SYN.)* massacre, carnage, slaughter, butchery.

poignant *(SYN.)* pitiable, touching, affecting, impressive, sad, tender, moving, heart-rending.

point *(SYN.)* direct, level, train, aim, locality, position, spot, location. (*ANT.*) *distract, misguide, deceive, misdirect.*

pointed *(SYN.)* keen, sharp, shrewd, witty, quick, acute, penetrating, cutting, piercing, astute, severe. (*ANT.*) *shallow, stupid, bland, blunt, gentle.*

pointless *(SYN.)* vain, purposeless.

poise *(SYN.)* composure, self-possession, equanimity, equilibrium, carriage, calmness, balance, self-control, assurance, control, dignity. (*ANT.*) *rage, turbulence, agitation, anger, excitement.*

poison *(SYN.)* corrupt, sully, taint, infect, befoul, defile, contaminate, venom, toxin, virus. (*ANT.*) *purify, disinfect.*

poke *(SYN.)* punch, stab, thrust, jab.

policy *(SYN.)* procedure, system, rule, approach, tactic.

polish *(SYN.)* brighten, shine, finish, brightness, gloss. (*ANT.*) *tarnish, dull.*

polished *(SYN.)* glib, diplomatic, urbane, refined, sleek, suave, slick. (*ANT.*) *rough, blunt, bluff, harsh, rugged.*

polite *(SYN.)* civil, refined, well-mannered, accomplished, courteous, genteel, urbane, well-bred, cultivated, considerate, thoughtful, mannerly, respectful. (*ANT.*) *uncouth, impertinent, rude, boorish, uncivil,* discourteous.

pollute *(SYN.)* contaminate, poison, taint, sully, infect, befoul, defile, dirty. (*ANT.*) *purify, disinfect, clean, clarify.*

pomp *(SYN.)* flourish, pageantry, vaunting, show, boasting, ostentation, parade, display. (*ANT.*) *reserve, humility, modesty.*

pompous *(SYN.)* high, magnificent, stately, august, dignified, grandiose, noble, majestic, lofty, imposing, arrogant, vain, pretentious. (*ANT.*) *lowly, undignified, humble, common, ordinary.*

ponder *(SYN.)* examined, study, contemplate, investigate, meditate, muse, scrutinize, cogitate, reflect, weigh, deliberate, consider.

ponderous *(SYN.)* burdensome, trying, gloomy, serious, sluggish, massive, heavy, cumbersome, grievous, grave, dull, weighty. (*ANT.*) *light, animated, brisk.*

poor *(SYN.)* penniless, bad, deficient, destitute, inferior, shabby, wrong, scanty, indigent, needy, poverty-stricken, unfavorable, impoverished. (*ANT.*) *wealthy, prosperous, rich, fortunate, good, excellent.*

poppycock *(SYN.)* rubbish, babble, twaddle, nonsense.

popular *(SYN.)* favorite, general, common, familiar, prevalent, liked, prevailing, well-liked, approved, accepted, celebrated, admired, ordinary. (*ANT.*) *unpopular, esoteric, restricted, exclusive.*

populous *(SYN.)* dense, thronged, crowded.

porch *(SYN.)* patio, veranda.

pornographic *(SYN.)* impure, indecent, obscene, coarse, dirty, filthy, lewd, smutty, offensive, disgusting. (*ANT.*) *refined, modest, pure, decent.*

port *(SYN.)* harbor, refuge, anchorage.

portable *(SYN.)* transportable, movable.

portal *(SYN.)* entry, doorway, opening, inlet, entrance. (*ANT.*) *exit, departure.*

portend *(SYN.)* foreshadow, presage, foretoken.

portentous *(SYN.)* significant, critical, momentous. (*ANT.*) *trivial.*

portion *(SYN.)* share, bit, parcel, part, piece, section, fragment, division, quota, segment, allotment. *(ANT.)* *whole, bulk.*

portly *(SYN.)* majestic, grand, impressive, dignified, stout, fat, heavy, obese. *(ANT.)* *slender, thin, slim.*

portrait *(SYN.)* painting, representation, picture, likeness.

portray *(SYN.)* depict, picture, represent, sketch, describe, delineate, paint. *(ANT.)* *misrepresent, caricature, suggest.*

position *(SYN.)* caste, site, locality, situation, condition, standing, incumbency, office, bearing, posture, berth, place, job, pose, rank, attitude, location, spot, station, situation, occupation.

positive *(SYN.)* sure, definite, fixed, inevitable, undeniable, indubitable, assured, certain, unquestionable, unmistakable. *(ANT.)* *uncertain, doubtful, questionable, unsure, dubious, confused, negative, adverse.*

positively *(SYN.)* unquestionably, surely, certainly, absolutely.

possess *(SYN.)* own, obtain, have, seize, hold, occupy, affect, control. *(ANT.)* *surrender, abandon, lose, renounce.*

possessed *(SYN.)* entranced, obsessed, consumed, haunted, enchanted.

possession *(SYN.)* custody, ownership, occupancy.

possessions *(SYN.)* commodities, effects, goods, property, merchandise, wares, wealth, belongings, stock.

possible *(SYN.)* likely, practical, probable, achievable, feasible, plausible, credible, practicable. *(ANT.)* *implausible, impossible, improbable.*

possibility *(SYN.)* opportunity, chance, contingency, occasion. *(ANT.)* *obstacle, disadvantage, hindrance.*

possibly *(SYN.)* perchance, perhaps, maybe.

post *(SYN.)* position, job, berth, incumbency, situation, shaft, pole, fort, base, station.

postpone *(SYN.)* delay, stay, suspend, discontinue, defer, adjourn, interrupt, put off. *(ANT.)* *persist, maintain, continue, proceed.*

postulate *(SYN.)* principle, adage, saying, proverb, truism, byword, aphorism, axiom,

fundamental, maxim.

potency *(SYN.)* effectiveness, capability, skillfulness, efficiency, competency, ability. *(ANT.)* *wastefulness, inability, ineptitude.*

potent *(SYN.)* mighty, influential, convincing, effective. *(ANT.)* *feeble, weak, powerless, impotent.*

potential *(SYN.)* likely, possible, dormant, hidden, latent.

pouch *(SYN.)* container, bag, sack.

pound *(SYN.)* buffet, beat, punch, strike, thrash, defeat, subdue, pulse, smite, belabor, knock, thump, overpower, palpitate, rout, vanquish. *(ANT.)* *fail, surrender, stroke, defend, shield.*

pour *(SYN.)* flow.

pout *(SYN.)* brood, sulk, mope.

poverty *(SYN.)* necessity, need, want, destitution, privation, indigence, distress. *(ANT.)* *plenty, abundance, wealth, riches, affluence, richness, comfort.*

power *(SYN.)* potency, might, authority, control, predominance, capability, faculty, validity, force, vigor, command, influence, talent, ability, dominion, competency. *(ANT.)* *incapacity, fatigue, weakness, disablement, impotence, ineptitude.*

powerful *(SYN.)* firm, strong, concentrated, enduring, forcible, robust, sturdy, tough, athletic, forceful, hale, impregnable, hardy, mighty, potent. *(ANT.)* *feeble, insipid, brittle, delicate, fragile, weak, ineffectual, powerless.*

practical *(SYN.)* sensible, wise, prudent, reasonable, sagacious, sober, sound, workable, attainable. *(ANT.)* *stupid, unaware, impalpable, absurd, impractical.*

practically *(SYN.)* almost, nearly.

practice *(SYN.)* exercise, habit, custom, manner, wont, usage, drill, tradition, performance, action, repetition. *(ANT.)* *inexperience, theory, disuse, idleness, speculation.*

practiced *(SYN.)* able, expert, skilled, adept. *(ANT.)* *inept.*

prairie *(SYN.)* plain, grassland.

praise *(SYN.)* applaud, compliment, extol, laud, glorify, commend, acclaim, eulogize, flatter, admire, celebrate, commendation,

pray

approval. *(ANT.) criticize, censure, reprove, condemn, disparage, disapprove, criticism.*

pray *(SYN.)* supplicate, importune, beseech, beg.

prayer *(SYN.)* plea, suit, appeal, invocation, supplication, petition, entreaty, request.

preach *(SYN.)* teach, moralize, lecture.

preamble *(SYN.)* overture, prologue, beginning, introduction, prelude, start, foreword, preface. *(ANT.) end, finale, completion, conclusion, epilogue.*

precarious *(SYN.)* dangerous, perilous, threatening, menacing, critical, risky, unsafe, hazardous. *(ANT.) secure, firm, protected, safe.*

precaution *(SYN.)* foresight, forethought, care.

precedence *(SYN.)* preference, priority.

precedent *(SYN.)* model, example.

precept *(SYN.)* doctrine, tenet, belief, creed, teaching, dogma. *(ANT.) practice, conduct, performance, deed.*

precious *(SYN.)* dear, useful, valuable, costly, esteemed, profitable, expensive, priceless, dear. *(ANT.) poor, worthless, cheap, mean, trashy.*

precipice *(SYN.)* bluff, cliff.

precipitate *(SYN.)* speedy, swift, hasty, sudden.

precipitous *(SYN.)* unannounced, sudden, harsh, rough, unexpected, sharp, abrupt, hasty, craggy, steep, precipitate. *(ANT.) expected, smooth, anticipated, gradual.*

precise *(SYN.)* strict, exact, formal, rigid, definite, unequivocal, prim, ceremonious, distinct, accurate, correct. *(ANT.) loose, easy, vague, informal, careless, erroneous.*

precisely *(SYN.)* specifically, exactly.

precision *(SYN.)* correction, accuracy, exactness.

preclude *(SYN.)* hinder, prevent, obstruct, forestall, obviate, thwart, impede. *(ANT.) permit, aid, expedite, encourage, promote.*

preclusion *(SYN.)* omission, exception, exclusion. *(ANT.) standard, rule, inclusion.*

predicament *(SYN.)* dilemma, plight, situation, condition, fix, difficulty, strait, scrape. *(ANT.) satisfaction, comfort, ease.*

predict *(SYN.)* forecast, foretell.

prediction *(SYN.)* forecast, prophecy.

predilection *(SYN.)* attachment, inclination, affection, bent, desire, penchant, disposition, preference. *(ANT.) repugnance, aversion, apathy, distaste, nonchalance.*

predominant *(SYN.)* highest, paramount, cardinal, foremost, main, first, leading, supreme, principal, essential, prevalent, dominant, prevailing. *(ANT.) subsidiary, auxiliary, supplemental, minor, subordinate.*

predominate *(SYN.)* prevail, outweigh, rule.

preface *(SYN.)* foreword, introduction, preliminary, prelude, prologue, preamble.

prefer *(SYN.)* select, favor, elect, fancy.

preference *(SYN.)* election, choice, selection, alternative, option.

prejudice *(SYN.)* bias, favoritism, unfairness, partiality.

prejudiced *(SYN.)* fanatical, narrow-minded, dogmatic, bigoted, illiberal, intolerant. *(ANT.) radical, liberal, tolerant, progressive.*

preliminary *(SYN.)* introductory, preparatory, prelude, preface.

premature *(SYN.)* early, untimely, unexpected. *(ANT.) timely.*

premeditated *(SYN.)* intended, voluntary, contemplated, designed, intentional, willful, deliberate, studied. *(ANT.) fortuitous, accidental.*

premeditation *(SYN.)* intention, deliberation, forethought, forecast. *(ANT.) hazard, accident, impromptu, extemporization.*

premise *(SYN.)* basis, presupposition, assumption, postulate, principle, presumption. *(ANT.) superstructure, derivative, trimming, implication.*

preoccupied *(SYN.)* abstracted, distracted, absorbed, meditative, inattentive, absent, absent-minded. *(ANT.) attentive, alert, conscious, present, attending, watchful.*

prepare *(SYN.)* contrive, furnish, ready, predispose, condition, fit, arrange, plan, qualify, make ready, get ready.

preposterous *(SYN.)* foolish, nonsensical, silly, contradictory, unreasonable, absurd, inconsistent, irrational, self-contradictory. (*ANT.*) *sensible, rational, consistent, sound.*

prerequisite (*SYN.*) essential, requirement, necessity, condition, demand.

prerogative (*SYN.*) grant, right, license, authority, privilege. (*ANT.*) *violation, encroachment, wrong, injustice.*

prescribe (*SYN.*) order, direct, designate.

presence (*SYN.*) nearness, attendance, closeness, vicinity, appearance, bearing, personality.

present (*SYN.*) donation, gift, today, now, existing, current, largess, donate, acquaint, introduce, being, give, gratuity, boon, grant. (*ANT.*) *reject, spurn, accept, retain, receive.*

presentable (*SYN.*) polite, well-bred, respectable, well-mannered.

presently (*SYN.*) shortly, soon, directly, immediately.

preserve (*SYN.*) protect, save, conserve, maintain, secure, rescue, uphold, spare, keep, can, safeguard, defend, rescue. (*ANT.*) *impair, abolish, destroy, abandon, squander, injure.*

preside (*SYN.*) officiate, direct, administrate.

press (*SYN.*) impel, shove, urge, hasten, push, compress, squeeze, hug, crowd, propel, force, drive, embrace, smooth, iron, insist on, pressure, promote, urgency, jostle. (*ANT.*) *oppose, pull, falter, drag, retreat.*

pressing (*SYN.*) impelling, insistent, necessary, urgent, compelling, imperative, instant, serious, important, cogent, exigent, importunate. (*ANT.*) *unimportant, trifling, insignificant, petty, trivial.*

pressure (*SYN.*) force, influence, stress, press, compulsion, urgency, constraint, compression. (*ANT.*) *relaxation, leniency, ease, recreation.*

prestige (*SYN.*) importance, reputation, influence, renown, fame, distinction.

presume (*SYN.*) guess, speculate, surmise, imagine, conjecture, apprehend, believe, think, assume, suppose, deduce. (*ANT.*) *prove, ascertain, demonstrate, know.*

presumption (*SYN.*) boldness, impertinence, insolence, rudeness, assurance, effrontery, impudence, assumption, audacity, supposition, sauciness. (*ANT.*) *politeness, diffidence.*

presumptuous (*SYN.*) bold, impertinent, fresh, imprudent, rude, forward, arrogant.

presupposition (*SYN.*) basis, principle, premise, assumption, postulate. (*ANT.*) *superstructure, derivative, implication.*

pretend (*SYN.*) feign, stimulate, act, profess, make believe, imagine, fake, sham, affect. (*ANT.*) *expose, reveal, display.*

pretense (*SYN.*) mask, pretext, show, affection, disguise, garb, semblance, simulation, fabrication, lie, excuse, falsification, deceit, subterfuge. (*ANT.*) *sincerity, actuality, truth, fact, reality.*

pretentious (*SYN.*) gaudy, ostentatious. (*ANT.*) *simple, humble.*

pretty (*SYN.*) charming, handsome, lovely, beauteous, fair, comely, attractive, beautiful, elegant. (*ANT.*) *repulsive, foul, unsightly, homely, plain, hideous.*

prevail (*SYN.*) win, succeed, predominate, triumph. (*ANT.*) *yield, lose.*

prevailing (*SYN.*) common, current, general, habitual, steady, regular, universal.

prevalent (*SYN.*) ordinary, usual, common, general, familiar, popular, prevailing, widespread, universal, frequent. (*ANT.*) *odd, scarce, exceptional, extraordinary.*

prevent (*SYN.*) impede, preclude, forestall, stop, block, check, halt, interrupt, deter, slow, obviate, hinder, obstruct, thwart. (*ANT.*) *expedite, help, allow, abet, aid, permit, encourage, promote.*

previous (*SYN.*) former, anterior, preceding, prior, antecedent, earlier, aforesaid, foregoing. (*ANT.*) *subsequent, following, consequent, succeeding, later.*

prey (*SYN.*) raid, seize, victimize.

price (*SYN.*) worth, cost, expense, charge, value.

pride (*SYN.*) self-respect, vanity, glory, superciliousness, haughtiness, conceit, arrogance, self-importance, pretension, egotism, satisfaction, fulfillment, enjoyment, self-esteem.

prim

(*ANT.*) *modesty, shame, humbleness, lowliness, meekness, humility.*

prim *(SYN.)* formal, puritanical, priggish, prudish.

primarily *(SYN.)* mainly, chiefly, firstly, essentially, originally. (*ANT.*) *secondarily.*

primary *(SYN.)* first, principal, primeval, pristine, beginning, original, initial, fundamental, elementary, chief, foremost, earliest, main, prime. (*ANT.*) *subordinate, last, secondary, least, hindmost, latest.*

prime *(SYN.)* first, primary, chief, excellent, best, superior, ready.

primeval *(SYN.)* fresh, primary, novel, inventive, creative, primordial, original, first, new, initial. (*ANT.*) *modern, subsequent, banal, later, terminal, derivative.*

primitive *(SYN.)* antiquated, early, primeval, prehistoric, uncivilized, uncultured, simple, pristine, old, aboriginal, unsophisticated, rude, rough, primary. (*ANT.*) *sophisticated, modish, civilized, cultured, cultivated, late.*

primordial *(SYN.)* pristine, inventive, novel, creative, original, first, initial, new, primary. (*ANT.*) *trite, terminal, banal, modern, derivative, subsequent, later.*

principal *(SYN.)* first, leading, main, supreme, predominant, chief, foremost, highest, prime, primary, leader, headmaster, paramount, essential, cardinal. (*ANT.*) *supplemental, secondary, auxiliary, subsidiary, accessory, minor, subordinate.*

principle *(SYN.)* law, method, axiom, rule, propriety, regulation, maxim, formula, order, statute. (*ANT.*) *exception, hazard, chance, deviation.*

print *(SYN.)* issue, reprint, publish, letter, sign, fingerprint, mark, picture, lithograph, engraving, etching.

prior *(SYN.)* previous, aforesaid, antecedent, sooner, earlier, preceding, former, foregoing. (*ANT.*) *succeeding, following, later, consequent, subsequent.*

prison *(SYN.)* brig, jail, stockade, penitentiary.

pristine *(SYN.)* primordial, creative, first, original, fresh, inventive, novel, primary,

initial. (*ANT.*) *trite, terminal, derivative, modem, banal, subsequent, plagiarized, later.*

private *(SYN.)* concealed, hidden, secret, clandestine, unknown, personal, surreptitious, covert, individual, particular, special, latent. (*ANT.*) *exposed, known, closed, general, public, conspicuous, disclosed.*

privation *(SYN.)* necessity, penury, destitution, need, poverty, want. (*ANT.*) *wealth, affluence, abundance, plenty, riches.*

privilege *(SYN.)* liberty, right, advantage, immunity, freedom, license, favor, sanction. (*ANT.*) *restriction, inhibition, prohibition, disallowance.*

prize *(SYN.)* compensation, bonus, award, premium, remuneration, reward, bounty, esteem, value, rate, recompense, requital. (*ANT.*) *charge, punishment, wages, earnings, assessment.*

probable *(SYN.)* presumable, likely.

probe *(SYN.)* stretch, reach, investigate, examine, examination, scrutiny, scrutinize, inquire, explore, inquiry, investigation, extend. (*ANT.*) *miss, short.*

problem *(SYN.)* dilemma, question, predicament, riddle, difficulty, puzzle.

procedure *(SYN.)* process, way, fashion, form, mode, conduct, practice, manner, habit, system, operation, management, plan.

proceed *(SYN.)* progress, continue, issue, result, spring, thrive, improve, advance, emanate, rise. (*ANT.*) *retard, withhold, withdraw, hinder, retreat, oppose.*

proceeding *(SYN.)* occurrence, business, affair, deal, negotiation, transaction, deed.

proceedings *(SYN.)* account, record, document.

proceeds *(SYN.)* result, produce, income, reward, intake, fruit, profit, store, yield, product, return, harvest, crop.

process *(SYN.)* method, course, system, procedure, operation, prepare, treat.

procession *(SYN.)* cortege, parade, sequence, train, cavalcade, file, retinue, succession.

proclaim *(SYN.)* declare, assert, make known, promulgate, state, assert, broadcast, express, announce, aver, advertise, tell, publish, profess.

roclamation *(SYN.)* declaration, announcement, promulgation.

rocrastinate *(SYN.)* waver, vacillate, defer, hesitate, delay, postpone.

rocreate *(SYN.)* generate, produce, beget, engender, originate, propagate, sire, create, father. *(ANT.) murder, destroy, abort, kill, extinguish.*

rocure *(SYN.)* secure, gain, win, attain, obtain, get, acquire, earn. *(ANT.) lose.*

rod *(SYN.)* goad, nudge, jab, push.

rodigious *(SYN.)* astonishing, enormous, immense, monstrous, remarkable, marvelous, huge, amazing, astounding, stupendous, monumental. *(ANT.) insignificant, commonplace, small.*

roduce *(SYN.)* harvest, reaping, bear, result, originate, bring about, store, supply, make, create, crop, proceeds, bring forth, occasion, breed, generate, cause, exhibit, show, demonstrate, fabricate, hatch, display, manufacture, exhibit, give, yield. *(ANT.) conceal, reduce, destroy, consume, waste, hide.*

roduct *(SYN.)* outcome, result, output, produce, goods, commodity, stock, merchandise.

roductive *(SYN.)* fertile, luxuriant, rich, bountiful, fruitful, creative, fecund, teeming, plenteous, prolific. *(ANT.) wasteful, unproductive, barren, useless, sterile.*

rofanation *(SYN.)* dishonor, insult, outrage, aspersion, defamation, invective, misuse, abuse, reviling, maltreatment, desecration, perversion. *(ANT.) plaudit, commendation, laudation, respect, approval.*

rofane *(SYN.)* deflower, violate, desecrate, pollute, dishonor, ravish, debauch.

rofess *(SYN.)* declare, assert, make known, state, protest, announce, aver, express, broadcast, avow, tell. *(ANT.) suppress, conceal, repress, withhold.*

rofession *(SYN.)* calling, occupation, vocation, employment. *(ANT.) hobby, avocation, pastime.*

roffer *(SYN.)* extend, tender, volunteer, propose, advance. *(ANT.) reject, spurn,* accept, receive, retain.

proficient *(SYN.)* competent, adept, clever, able, cunning, practiced, skilled, versed, ingenious, accomplished, skillful, expert. *(ANT.) untrained, inexpert, bungling, awkward, clumsy.*

profit *(SYN.)* gain, service, advantage, return, earnings, emolument, improvement, benefit, better, improve, use, avail. *(ANT.) waste, loss, detriment, debit, lose, damage, mum.*

profitable *(SYN.)* beneficial, advantageous, helpful, wholesome, useful, gainful, favorable, beneficial, serviceable, salutary, productive, good. *(ANT.) harmful, destructive, injurious, deleterious, detrimental.*

profligate *(SYN.)* corrupt, debased, tainted, unsound, vitiated, contaminated, crooked, depraved, impure, venal.

profound *(SYN.)* deep, serious, knowing, wise, intelligent, knowledgeable, recondite, solemn, abstruse, penetrating. *(ANT.) trivial, slight, shallow, superficial.*

profuse *(SYN.)* lavish, excessive, extravagant, improvident, luxuriant, prodigal, wasteful, exuberant, immoderate, plentiful. *(ANT.) meager, poor, economical, sparse, skimpy.*

profusion *(SYN.)* immoderation, superabundance, surplus, extravagance, intemperance, superfluity. *(ANT.) lack, paucity, death, want, deficiency.*

program *(SYN.)* record, schedule, plan, agenda, calendar.

progress *(SYN.)* advancement, improvement, development, betterment, advance, movement, improve, progression. *(ANT.) regression, relapse, retrogression, decline.*

progression *(SYN.)* gradation, string, train, chain, arrangement, following, arrangement, order.

prohibit *(SYN.)* hinder, forbid, disallow, obstruct, prevent, stop, ban, interdict, debar. *(ANT.) help, tolerate, allow, sanction, encourage, permit.*

prohibition *(SYN.)* prevention, ban, embargo, restriction. *(ANT.) allowance, permission.*

prohibitive

prohibitive *(SYN.)* forbidding, restrictive.

project *(SYN.)* design, proposal, scheme, contrivance, outline, homework, activity, purpose, bulge, protrude, throw, cast, device, plan. *(ANT.)* production, accomplishment, performance.

prolific *(SYN.)* fertile, rich, fruitful, teeming, fecund, bountiful, luxuriant, productive, plenteous. *(ANT.)* unproductive, barren, sterile, impotent.

prolong *(SYN.)* extend, increase, protract, draw, stretch, lengthen. *(ANT.)* shorten.

prominent *(SYN.)* distinguished, illustrious, outstanding, renowned, influential, famous, well-known, noted, notable, important, conspicuous, eminent, leading, celebrated. *(ANT.)* low, vulgar, ordinary, common.

promise *(SYN.)* assurance, guarantee, pledge, undertaking, agreement, bestowal, word, contract, oath, vow.

promote *(SYN.)* advance, foster, encourage, assist, support, further, aid, help, elevate, raise, facilitate, forward. *(ANT.)* obstruct, demote, hinder, impede.

prompt *(SYN.)* punctual, timely, exact, arouse, evoke, occasion, induce, urge, effect, cite, suggest, hint, cause, mention, propose, make, precise, originate. *(ANT.)* laggardly, slow, tardy, dilatory.

promptly *(SYN.)* immediately, instantly, straightaway, forthwith, directly, instantaneously, presently. *(ANT.)* later, sometime, hereafter, distantly, shortly.

promulgate *(SYN.)* declare, known, protest, affirm, broadcast, profess, assert, proclaim, state, aver, tell. *(ANT.)* repress, conceal, withhold.

prone *(SYN.)* apt, inclined, disposed, likely, predisposed.

pronounce *(SYN.)* proclaim, utter, announce, articulate, enunciate.

pronounced *(SYN.)* clear, definite. *(ANT.)* minor, unnoticeable.

proof *(SYN.)* evidence, verification, confirmation, experiment, demonstration, testimony, trial, protected, impenetrable, corroboration, test. *(ANT.)* fallacy, inva-

lidity, failure.

propagate *(SYN.)* create, procreate, sire, beget, breed, father, originate, produce. *(ANT.)* extinguish, kill, abort, destroy.

propel *(SYN.)* drive, push, transfer, actuate, induce, shift, persuade, move. *(ANT.)* sta... deter, halt, rest, stop.

propensity *(SYN.)* leaning, proneness, trend, drift, aim, inclination, bias, proclivity, tendency, predisposition. *(ANT.)* disin... clination, aversion.

proper *(SYN.)* correct, suitable, decent, peculiar, legitimate, right, conventional.

property *(SYN.)* real estate, effects, possessions, quality, characteristic, merchandise, stock, possession, land. *(ANT.)* poverty, destitution, want, deprivation.

prophecy *(SYN.)* augury, prediction.

prophesy *(SYN.)* foretell, predict, augur.

prophet *(SYN.)* fortuneteller, oracle, seer, soothsayer, clairvoyant.

propitious *(SYN.)* lucky, opportune, advantageous, favorable, fortunate, promising, happy.

proportion *(SYN.)* steadiness, poise, composure, relation, balance, equilibrium. *(ANT.)* unsteadiness, imbalance, fall.

proposal *(SYN.)* plan, proposition, tender, scheme, program, offer, suggestion, overture. *(ANT.)* rejection, acceptance, denial.

propose *(SYN.)* offer, proffer, recommend, plan, mean, expect, move, design, propound, present, tender. *(ANT.)* fulfill, perform, effect.

proposition *(SYN.)* proposal, motion.

propound *(SYN.)* bring forward, offer, advance, allege, propose, assign. *(ANT.)* retreat, hinder, withhold, retard.

proprietor *(SYN.)* master, owner. *(ANT.)* slave, servant.

prosaic *(SYN.)* commonplace, common, everyday, ordinary, routine. *(ANT.)* exciting, different, extraordinary.

proscribe *(SYN.)* forbid, ban, prohibit. *(ANT.)* permit, allow.

prospect *(SYN.)* anticipation, expectation, candidate, buyer, explore, search.

rospective *(SYN.)* planned, proposed.

rosper *(SYN.)* succeed, win, achieve, gain, rise, prevail, flourish, thrive. *(ANT.)* miscarry, wane, miss, fail.

rosperous *(SYN.)* rich, wealthy, affluent, well-to-do, sumptuous, well-off, flourishing, thriving, opulent, luxurious. *(ANT.)* impoverished, indigent, beggarly, needy, destitute, poor.

rostrate *(SYN.)* prone, supine, overcome, recumbent, crushed.

rotect *(SYN.)* defend, preserve, save, keep, conserve, safeguard, maintain, guard, shield, secure. *(ANT.)* impair, abandon, destroy, abolish, injure.

rotest *(SYN.)* dissent, noncompliance, disagree, objection, disagreement, challenge, difference, complaint, nonconformity, variance, opposition. *(ANT.)* acquiesce, assent, compliance, concur, comply, acceptance, approval.

ototype *(SYN.)* model, archetype, specimen, instance, illustration, example, pattern, sample. *(ANT.)* rule, concept, precept.

otract *(SYN.)* extend, strain, distend, expand, spread, stretch, elongate, distort, lengthen. *(ANT.)* tighten, contract, loosen.

otuberance *(SYN.)* prominence, projection, bulge, protrusion, swelling.

oud *(SYN.)* overbearing, vain, arrogant, haughty, stately, vain, glorious, disdainful, prideful, conceited, egotistical, self-important, supercilious. *(ANT.)* humble, meek, ashamed, lowly.

ove *(SYN.)* manifest, verify, confirm, demonstrate, establish, show, affirm, examine, corroborate, try, test. *(ANT.)* contradict, refute, disprove.

overb *(SYN.)* maxim, byword, saying, adage, saw, motto, apothegm.

overbial *(SYN.)* common, well-known.

ovide *(SYN.)* supply, endow, afford, produce, yield, give, fit, equip, furnish. *(ANT.)* strip, denude, divest, despoil.

ovident *(SYN.)* saving, thrifty, economical, frugal, sparing. *(ANT.)* wasteful, lavish, extravagant.

ovision *(SYN.)* supply, fund, condition, arrangement, accumulation, reserve, store.

provisions *(SYN.)* stock, supplies, store.

provoke *(SYN.)* excite, stimulate, agitate, arouse, incite, stir up, vex, bother, disquiet, excite, irritate, annoy, anger. *(ANT.)* quell, allay, pacify, calm, quiet.

prowess *(SYN.)* fortitude, mettle, boldness, fearlessness, courage, chivalry, bravery. *(ANT.)* fear, cowardice, timidity.

prowl *(SYN.)* sneak, slink, lurk.

proximate *(SYN.)* nigh, imminent, adjacent, neighboring, bordering, close. *(ANT.)* removed, distant, far.

proximity *(SYN.)* vicinity, nearness.

proxy *(SYN.)* representative, equivalent, makeshift, alternate, deputy, substitute. *(ANT.)* sovereign, head, principal, master.

prudence *(SYN.)* watchfulness, care, heed, vigilance, wariness, carefulness, tact, judgment, wisdom, common, foresight, caution. *(ANT.)* rashness, recklessness, abandon, foolishness, carelessness.

prudent *(SYN.)* reasonable, sensible, sound, discreet, practical, judicious. *(ANT.)* stupid, unaware, absurd.

pry *(SYN.)* peer, peep, meddle, peek.

prying *(SYN.)* inquisitive, meddling, curious, inquiring, nosy, peering, searching, interrogative, snoopy. *(ANT.)* unconcerned, incurious, indifferent, uninterested.

psyche *(SYN.)* judgment, reason, understanding, brain, intellect, mentality, soul, mind, faculties, spirit. *(ANT.)* materiality, body, matter, corporeality.

psychosis *(SYN.)* derangement, insanity, madness, delirium, dementia, frenzy, lunacy, mania, aberration. *(ANT.)* stability, rationality, sanity.

public *(SYN.)* common, civil, governmental, federal, unrestricted, people, society, open.

publish *(SYN.)* distribute, issue, declare, announce, reveal, proclaim, publicize.

pull *(SYN.)* attract, induce, prolong, draw, tow, drag, remove, take out, persuade, allure, entice, extract. *(ANT.)* shorten, alienate, drive, propel.

pulsate *(SYN.)* beat, throb, palpitate.

pummel

pummel *(SYN.)* punish, correct, castigate, discipline, chastise, strike. *(ANT.)* release, acquit, free, exonerate.

pump *(SYN.)* interrogate, question, ask, inquire, quiz, examine, query. *(ANT.)* state, answer, respond, reply.

punctual *(SYN.)* timely, prompt, exact, ready, precise. *(ANT.)* laggardly, tardy, dilatory, late.

punish *(SYN.)* correct, pummel, chasten, reprove, strike, castigate, chastise. *(ANT.)* release, exonerate, reward, pardon, acquit, free.

puny *(SYN.)* feeble, impaired, exhausted, infirm, unimportant, weak, decrepit. *(ANT.)* strong, forceful, lusty, vigorous.

purchase *(SYN.)* get, procure, buy, acquire, obtain. *(ANT.)* sell, dispose of, vend.

pure *(SYN.)* chaste, absolute, clean, immaculate, untainted, spotless, guiltless, modest, virgin, bare, unmixed, simple. *(ANT.)* corrupt, mixed, defiled, foul, tainted, adulterated, polluted, tarnished.

puritanical *(SYN.)* prim, stiff. *(ANT.)* permissive.

purport *(SYN.)* import, meaning, explanation, acceptation, drift, sense, significance, purpose, intent, gist.

purpose *(SYN.)* intention, end, goal, aim, objective, application, use, drift, object. *(ANT.)* hazard, accident, fate.

pursue *(SYN.)* persist, track, follow, hunt, hound, chase, trail. *(ANT.)* evade, abandon, flee, elude.

pursuit *(SYN.)* hunt, chase.

push *(SYN.)* jostle, urge, press, thrust, force, drive, crowd, hasten, shove, propel, promote. *(ANT.)* ignore, falter, halt, drag, oppose.

pushy *(SYN.)* impudent, abrupt, prominent, insolent, forward, brazen, conspicuous, bold, striking. *(ANT.)* retiring, timid, cowardly, bashful.

put *(SYN.)* set, place, state, express, say, assign, attach, establish.

putrefy *(SYN.)* disintegrate, decay, rot, waste, spoil, decompose. *(ANT.)* grow, increase, luxuriate.

putrid *(SYN.)* decayed, rotten, mold⟨ decomposed.

puzzle *(SYN.)* mystery, mystify, confoun⟨ perplex, riddle, conundrum, confusio⟩ bewilder, enigma, dilemma. *(ANT.)* ke⟨ solution, solve, explain, answer, resolutio⟩ illumine, clue.

quack *(SYN.)* faker, fake, fraud, gagg⟨ clack, gabble, bluffer, cackle, dissemble⟨ charlatan, impostor.

quackery *(SYN.)* charlatanism, decei⟨ make-believe, fakery, duplicity, di⟨ simulation, pretense, fraudulence, sha⟨ counterfeiting, show. *(ANT.)* integri⟨ probity, veracity, sincerity, honesty.

quaff *(SYN.)* swig, swill, swallow, lap u⟨ sip, drink, ingurgitate, guzzle, imbibe.

quagmire *(SYN.)* swamp, bog, fen, ooz⟨ morass, slough, marsh, plight, predic⟨ ment, dilemma, impasse, fix, entangl⟨ ment, quicksand, hole, quandary.

quail *(SYN.)* recoil, cower, flinch, blen⟨ wince, falter, shrink, shake, hesitate, fai⟨ droop. *(ANT.)* brave, resist, defy, withstan⟨

quaint *(SYN.)* odd, uncommon, old-fas⟨ ioned, antique, antiquated, queer, unusu⟨ curious, eccentric, peculiar, picturesqu⟨ singular, whimsical, droll, charming, fa⟨ ciful, strange. *(ANT.)* usual, normal, co⟨ mon, navel, ordinary, modern, curre⟨ commonplace, familiar.

quake *(SYN.)* shake, tremble, shudd⟨ quiver, pulsate, stagger, shiver, tembl⟨ vibrate, quaver, throb, earthquake.

qualification *(SYN.)* efficiency, adapt⟨ tion, restriction, aptness, skill, ability, fa⟨ ulty, talent, power, aptitude, competen⟨ suitability, capability, fitness, conditi⟨ dexterity. *(ANT.)* unreadiness, incapaci⟨ disability.

qualified *(SYN.)* clever, skillful, efficie⟨ suitable, able, capable, fit, fitted, suite⟨ bounded, limited, contingent, eligib⟨ delimited, adept, circumscribed, equippe⟨ modified, competent. *(ANT.)* deficie⟨

inept, impotent, categorical, unlimited, unfitted, unfit, incapable, unsuitable, inadequate.

qualify *(SYN.)* fit, suit, befit, ready, prepare, empower, lessen, moderate, soften, capacitate, condition, adapt, label, designate, name, call, equip, train, restrict, limit, change. *(ANT.)* unfit, incapacitate, disable, disqualify, enlarge, reinforce, aggravate.

quality *(SYN.)* trait, feature, attribute, value, peculiarity, grade, caliber, character, distinction, rank, condition, status, characteristic, kind, nature, constitution, mark, type, property. *(ANT.)* nature, inferiority, mediocrity, triviality, indifference, inferior, shoddy, second-rate, being, substance, essence.

qualm *(SYN.)* doubt, uneasiness, anxiety, suspicion, skepticism, question, pang, compunction, twinge, regret, uncertainty, demur, fear, remorse, misgiving. *(ANT.)* security, comfort, confidence, easiness, invulnerability, firmness.

quandary *(SYN.)* predicament, perplexity, confusion, uncertainty, puzzle, plight, bewilderment, fix, difficulty, entanglement, impasse, doubt, dilemma. *(ANT.)* ease, relief, certainty, assurance.

quantity *(SYN.)* sum, measure, volume, content, aggregate, bulk, mass, portion, amount, number, multitude, extent. *(ANT.)* zero, nothing.

quarantine *(SYN.)* segregate, separate, confine, isolate, seclude.

quarrel *(SYN.)* contention, argument, affray, dispute, altercation, squabble, feud, difference, disagree, bicker, differ, spar, fight, bickering, tiff, argue, disagreement, spat. *(ANT.)* peace, friendliness, reconciliation, amity, agreement, sympathy, accord, concur, support, agree, unity, harmony.

quarrelsome *(SYN.)* testy, contentious, edgy, peevish, irritable, snappish, argumentative, disputatious, cranky, belligerent, combative, disagreeable. *(ANT.)* genial, friendly, peaceful, easygoing, peaceable, tempered.

quarry *(SYN.)* prey, quest, game, victim, goal, aim, prize, objective.

quarter *(SYN.)* place, source, fount, well,

origin, mainspring, mercy, pity, compassion, clemency, spring, benevolence, forbearance. *(ANT.)* ruthlessness, brutality, cruelty, barbarity, harshness, ferocity.

quarters *(SYN.)* residence, rooms, lodgings, dwelling, flat, billets, chambers, accommodations.

quash *(SYN.)* void, annul, overthrow, nullify, suppress, cancel, quench, quell, repress, invalidate. *(ANT.)* reinforce, sustain, authorize, sanction, validate, incite.

quasi *(SYN.)* would-be, partial, synthetic, nominal, imitation, bogus, counterfeit, mock. *(ANT.)* certified, real, legitimate.

quaver *(SYN.)* tremble, shake, hesitate, trill, oscillate, waver, vibrate, shiver, quiver, falter, quake.

quay *(SYN.)* dock, wharf, pier, jetty, bank.

queasy *(SYN.)* sick, squeamish, nauseated, uneasy, queer, restless, nauseous, uncomfortable. *(ANT.)* untroubled, comfortable, easy, relaxed.

queen *(SYN.)* empress, diva, goddess, star.

queer *(SYN.)* odd, quaint, curious, unusual, droll, strange, peculiar, extraordinary, singular, uncommon, eccentric, weird, funny, nutty, screwy, wacky, deviant, whimsical. *(ANT.)* familiar, usual, normal, common, commonplace, plain, patent, ordinary.

queerness *(SYN.)* oddity, oddness, freakishness, strangeness, singularity, outlandishness, weirdness. *(ANT.)* normality, familiarity, commonness, standardization.

quell *(SYN.)* subdue, calm, pacify, quiet, cool, hush, appease, lull, mollify, reduce, crush, smother, suppress, stifle, extinguish. *(ANT.)* foment, arouse, foster, incite.

quench *(SYN.)* extinguish, stop, suppress, sate, allay, abate, stifle, slacken, put out, slake, satisfy *(ANT.)* set, light, begin, start, kindle.

querulous *(SYN.)* faultfinding, fretful, carping, critical, complaining, censorious, captious, petulant. *(ANT.)* pleased, easygoing, contented, carefree.

query *(SYN.)* inquire, interrogate, demand, investigate, probe, examine, question, inquiry, ask. *(ANT.)* answer.

quest *(SYN.)* investigation, interrogation, research, examination, search, question, exploration, seek, pursue, journey, hunt, pursuit, explore, query. *(ANT.)* negligence, inactivity, disregard.

question *(SYN.)* interrogate, quiz, doubt, ask, pump, challenge, inquiry, uncertainty, interview, suspect, inquire, dispute, demand, examine, query. *(ANT.)* accept, solution, reply, assurance, rejoinder, state, answer, result, response, attest, avow, confidence, respond.

questionable *(SYN.)* uncertain, doubtful, dubious, implausible, debatable, hypothetical, unlikely. *(ANT.)* obvious, assured, indubitable, proper, unimpeachable, seemly, conventional, sure, certain.

queue *(SYN.)* file, row, line, series, chain, tier, sequence, string.

quibble *(SYN.)* cavil, shift, evasion, equivocation, dodge, sophism, prevaricate.

quick *(SYN.)* rapid, touchy, shrewd, active, hasty, testy, nimble, irascible, discerning, fast, swift, precipitate, excitable, speedy, sharp, impatient, acute, abrupt, curt, brisk, clever, keen, sensitive, lively. *(ANT.)* inattentive, dull, gradual, patient, slow, unhurried, backward, deliberate, sluggish.

quicken *(SYN.)* expedite, forward, rush, hurry, accelerate, push, hasten, dispatch, facilitate, speed. *(ANT.)* slow, impede, hinder, hamper, delay, kill, deaden, retard, block.

quickly *(SYN.)* soon, rapidly, fast, at once, promptly, presently, swiftly, hastily, fleetly, headlong. *(ANT.)* deliberately, gradually.

quickness *(SYN.)* energy, vigor, intensity, action, movement, briskness, exercise, motion, rapidity, agility, enterprise. *(ANT.)* sloth, idleness, inertia, dullness.

quick-witted *(SYN.)* astute, shrewd, alert, keen, penetrating, quick, intelligent. *(ANT.)* slow, dull, unintelligent, plodding.

quiescent *(SYN.)* latent, resting, silent, tranquil, undeveloped, still, quiet, dormant, secret, unseen, inactive. *(ANT.)* visible, aroused, evident, active, patent, astir, manifest.

quiet *(SYN.)* meek, passive, hushed, peaceful, calm, patient, quiescent, motionless, tranquil, gentle, undisturbed, mild, peace, silent, quiescence, hush, modest, quietude, rest, tranquillity. *(ANT.)* disturbed, agitation, excitement, loud, disturbance, restless, noisy, boisterous, perturbed, noise, agitated.

quietness *(SYN.)* tranquillity, repose, calm, silence, quietude, stillness. *(ANT.)* flurry, disturbance, fuss, turbulence, agitation, uproar, tumult.

quintessence *(SYN.)* heart, soul, extract, essence, distillation, core. *(ANT.)* contingency, adjunct, excrescence, nonessential.

quip *(SYN.)* jest, sally, wisecrack, witticism, joke, jibe, pleasantry.

quirk *(SYN.)* mannerism, idiosyncrasy, foible, peculiarity, oddity, quiddity, vagary, habit, trait, eccentricity.

quirky *(SYN.)* odd, weird, whimsical, peculiar, pixilated, erratic, kinky. *(ANT.)* normal, conventional, steady.

quisling *(SYN.)* collaborationist, traitor, subversive, betrayer. *(ANT.)* partisan, loyalist.

quit *(SYN.)* leave, stop, desist, depart, abandon, resign, withdraw, refrain, retreat, cease, vacate, end, relinquish, discontinue, halt, lay off, surrender. *(ANT.)* persevere, remain, stay, endure, persist, abide, continue.

quite *(SYN.)* somewhat, rather, completely, truly, absolutely, really, entirely. *(ANT.)* hardly, merely, barely, somewhat.

quitter *(SYN.)* shirker, dropout, defeatist, piker, loser, malingerer.

quiver *(SYN.)* quake, shake, shudder, tremble, vibrate, shiver.

quixotic *(SYN.)* unrealistic, romantic, visionary, impractical, idealistic, chimerical, lofty, fantastic, fey. *(ANT.)* pragmatic, realistic, practical.

quiz *(SYN.)* challenge, interrogate, inquire, pump, doubt, question, ask, dispute, test, query, examine. *(ANT.)* reply, say, inform, respond, accept, answer, state.

quizzical *(SYN.)* teasing, coy, mocking, derisive, insolent, arch, bantering, puzzled, questioning, baffled. *(ANT.)* respectful, obsequious, uninterested, normal, usual, serious, attentive.

quota *(SYN.)* share, portion, apportionment, ratio, proportion, allotment.

quotation *(SYN.)* quote, selection, excerpt, repetition, cutting, reference.

quote *(SYN.)* refer to, recite, paraphrase, adduce, repeat, illustrate, cite, echo. *(ANT.)* retort, contradict, refute.

R

rabble *(SYN.)* throng, mob, horde, crowd.

rabid *(SYN.)* frantic, frenzied, violent, raging, raving, zealous, fanatical. *(ANT.)* normal, sound, sober, moderate.

race *(SYN.)* meet, run, clan, stock, lineage, strain, match, course, stream, hasten, compete, folk, competition. *(ANT.)* linger, dawdle, dwell.

rack *(SYN.)* frame, framework, bracket, scaffold, skeleton.

racket *(SYN.)* sound, cry, babel, noise, uproar, hubbub, clamor, fuss, disturbance, din, tumult, fracas, clatter. *(ANT.)* stillness, hush, silence, quiet, tranquillity, peace.

racy *(SYN.)* interesting, vigorous, lively, bawdy, lewd, shameless, spirited, animated, entertaining.

radiance *(SYN.)* luster, brilliancy, brightness, splendor, effulgence, glowing. *(ANT.)* gloom, darkness, obscurity.

radiant *(SYN.)* showy, superb, brilliant, illustrious, dazzling, grand, shining, bright, effulgent, beaming, sumptuous. *(ANT.)* dark, unimpressive, dull, dim, lusterless, ordinary.

radiate *(SYN.)* spread, emit, diffuse, shed, irradiate, shine, gleam, illuminate.

radical *(SYN.)* ultra, innate, essential, organic, complete, revolutionary, insurgent, natural, total, fundamental, extreme, basic, original, thorough. *(ANT.)* extraneous, moderate, conservative, superficial, shallow, established.

radius *(SYN.)* orbit, reach, extent, scope, sphere, range, sweep.

raft *(SYN.)* pontoon, platform, float.

rag *(SYN.)* dishcloth, dishrag, cloth.

rage *(SYN.)* passion, ire, exasperation, fashion, fad, vogue, craze, anger, temper, fury, irritation, mania, rave, rant, storm, fume, wrath. *(ANT.)* peace, forbearance, patience.

ragged *(SYN.)* tattered, torn, worn, shredded, seedy, threadbare, shabby.

raging *(SYN.)* raving, severe, boisterous, violent, fierce, wild, passionate, acute, intense, powerful. *(ANT.)* feeble, soft, calm, quiet.

raid *(SYN.)* assault, attack, invasion, arrest, invade, seizure, maraud, foray.

rail *(SYN.)* railing, fence, bar.

railing *(SYN.)* balustrade, banister, barrier, fence.

rain *(SYN.)* shower, drizzle, rainstorm, sprinkle, deluge, downpour.

raise *(SYN.)* grow, muster, elevate, heave, cultivate, awake, rouse, excite, enlarge, increase, rise, breed, hoist, bring up. *(ANT.)* destroy, decrease, lessen, cut, depreciate, lower, abase, debase, drop, demolish.

rakish *(SYN.)* dapper, dashing, smart, debonair, natty, swanky, showy.

rally *(SYN.)* muster, convoke, summon, convene, convention, assemblage.

ramble *(SYN.)* amble, wander, roam, saunter, walk, deviate. *(ANT.)* stop, linger, stay, halt, settle.

rambling *(SYN.)* incoherent, erratic. *(ANT.)* straightforward, coherent.

rambunctious *(SYN.)* stubborn, defiant, unruly, aggressive, contrary.

ramification *(SYN.)* aftermath, extension, branch, offshoot, result, consequence.

rampage *(SYN.)* tumult, outbreak, uproar, rage, frenzy, ebullition, storm.

rampant *(SYN.)* excessive, flagrant, boisterous, menacing. *(ANT.)* bland, calm, mild.

ramshackle *(SYN.)* rickety, decrepit, flimsy, dilapidated, shaky.

rancid *(SYN.)* spoiled, rank, tainted, sour, musty, putrid, rotten, putrescent. *(ANT.)* pure, fresh, wholesome, fragrant.

rancor *(SYN.)* spite, grudge, malice, animosity, malevolence, hostility. *(ANT.)* kindness, toleration, affection.

random

random *(SYN.)* haphazard, chance, unscheduled, unplanned, casual. *(ANT.)* intentional, specific, particular.

range *(SYN.)* expanse, extent, limit, area, grassland, pasture, plain, change, wander, roam, travel, rove.

ransack *(SYN.)* pillage, loot, rummage, plunder, despoil, ravish, search.

ransom *(SYN.)* release, deliverance, compensation, redeem.

rant *(SYN.)* declaim, rave, harangue.

rap *(SYN.)* thump, knock, blow, whack.

rapacious *(SYN.)* greedy, wolfish, avaricious, ravenous, grasping, predatory.

rapid *(SYN.)* speedy, quick, swift, fast. *(ANT.)* deliberate, halting, sluggish, slow.

rapine *(SYN.)* destruction, pillage, robbery, marauding, spoiling.

rapport *(SYN.)* harmony, fellowship, agreement, mutuality, accord, empathy.

rapture *(SYN.)* joy, gladness, ecstasy, bliss, transport, exultation, delight, happiness, enchantment, ravishment. *(ANT.)* woe, misery, wretch, depression.

rare *(SYN.)* unique, strange, precious, uncommon, infrequent, choice, singular, occasional, unusual, fine, matchless. *(ANT.)* worthless, common, commonplace, usual, everyday, customary.

rarely *(SYN.)* scarcely, hardly, infrequently, occasionally, sparingly, barely. *(ANT.)* usually, continually, often.

rascal *(SYN.)* scoundrel, villain, trickster, rogue, scamp, swindler, imp, prankster.

rash *(SYN.)* quick, careless, passionate, thoughtless, hotheaded, reckless, foolhardy, eruption, dermatitis, heedless. *(ANT.)* thoughtful, considered, prudent, reasoning, calculating, careful.

raspy *(SYN.)* gruff, harsh, dissonant, grinding, hoarse, grating, strident.

rate *(SYN.)* try, adjudicate, consider, decide, condemn, decree, estimate, speed, pace, measure, judge, arbitrate.

ratify *(SYN.)* validate, certify, confirm, establish, support, endorse, uphold.

rating *(SYN.)* assessment, position, assignment, status, classification.

ration *(SYN.)* portion, allowance, distribute, measure, allotment, share, percentage.

rational *(SYN.)* sound, wise, sane, intelligent, sober, sensible, judicious, sober. *(ANT.)* irrational, absurd, insane.

rationality *(SYN.)* cause, aim, intelligence, reason, basis, understanding, ground, argument, mind, sense.

raucous *(SYN.)* raspy, harsh, grating, hoarse, discordant, rowdy. *(ANT.)* pleasant, sweet.

ravage *(SYN.)* ruin, despoil, strip, waste, destroy, pillage, plunder, sack, havoc. *(ANT.)* conserve, save, accumulate.

rave *(SYN.)* rage, storm, laud, praise.

ravenous *(SYN.)* hungry, voracious, craving, starved, gluttonous, famished. *(ANT.)* replete, gorged, satiated, full.

ravine *(SYN.)* chasm, gorge, crevasse, canyon, abyss.

ravish *(SYN.)* violate, debauch.

ravishing *(SYN.)* enchanting, captivating, bewitching, fascinating, alluring. *(ANT.)* loathsome, disgusting, repulsive.

raw *(SYN.)* harsh, rough, coarse, unrefined, undone, uncooked, unprocessed, crude, unpolished, natural. *(ANT.)* finished, refined, processed.

ray *(SYN.)* beam.

raze *(SYN.)* ravage, wreck, destroy, flatten, annihilate, obliterate, demolish. *(ANT.)* erect, construct, preserve, establish, save.

reach *(SYN.)* overtake, arrive at, extent, distance, scope, range, extend, attain, stretch. *(ANT.)* fail, miss.

react *(SYN.)* result, reply, respond. *(ANT.)* overlook, disregard.

reaction *(SYN.)* result, response, reception, repercussion.

readable *(SYN.)* understandable, distinct, legible, plain, clear, comprehensible. *(ANT.)* obliterated, illegible, defaced.

readily *(SYN.)* quickly, promptly, easily.

ready *(SYN.)* mature, ripe, complete, seasonable, done, arrange, prompt, prepared, completed, quick, mellow. *(ANT.)* undeveloped, immature, green.

real *(SYN.)* true, actual, positive, authentic, genuine, veritable. *(ANT.)* counterfeit, unreal, fictitious, false, sham, supposed.

realization *(SYN.)* completion, achievement, performance, accomplishment, comprehension, insight. *(ANT.)* failure.

realize *(SYN.)* discern, learn, comprehend, appreciate, perfect, actualize, understand, apprehend, know, see. *(ANT.)* misunderstand, misapprehend.

really *(SYN.)* truly, actually, honestly, undoubtedly, positively, genuinely. *(ANT.)* questionably, possibly, doubtfully.

realm *(SYN.)* land, domain, farm, kingdom, sphere, department, estate, world.

reap *(SYN.)* gather, harvest, gain, glean, produce, cut, pick, acquire, garner. *(ANT.)* plant, seed, sow, lose, squander.

reaping *(SYN.)* proceeds, result, crop, yield, fruit, produce.

rear *(SYN.)* posterior, raise, lift, train, nurture, rump, back, elevate, construct, build.

reason *(SYN.)* intelligence, objective, understanding, mind, aim, argument, cause, judgment, common sense, sanity, gather, assume, sake, motive.

reasonable *(SYN.)* prudent, rational, logical, sage, sound, moderate, intelligent, sensible, discreet. *(ANT.)* unaware, insane, absurd, stupid, illogical, irrational.

rebel *(SYN.)* revolutionary, traitor, mutineer, mutiny, revolt, disobey.

rebellion *(SYN.)* revolt, uprising, coup, overthrow, insurrection, revolution. *(ANT.)* submission, obedience, repression, peace.

rebellious *(SYN.)* unruly, forward, defiant, undutiful, disobedient. *(ANT.)* obedient, compliant, submissive.

rebirth *(SYN.)* renascence, renaissance, revival.

rebuff *(SYN.)* snub, oppose, resist, reject, refuse, slight, opposition. *(ANT.)* welcome, encourage, support.

rebuild *(SYN.)* restore, renew, refresh, reconstruct, renovate.

rebuke *(SYN.)* chide, scold, reproach, censure, upbraid, scolding, condemn. *(ANT.)* praise, exonerate, absolve.

rebuttal *(SYN.)* contradiction, defense, answer. *(ANT.)* argument, validation, corroboration.

recall *(SYN.)* recollect, remembrance, withdraw, retract, remember, recollection. reminisce, mind, memory, remind. *(ANT.)* forget, overlook, ignore.

recede *(SYN.)* withdraw, ebb, retire, retreat.

receive *(SYN.)* entertain, acquire, admit, accept, shelter, greet, obtain, welcome. *(ANT.)* reject, offer, give, bestow, discharge.

recent *(SYN.)* novel, original, late, new, newfangled, fresh, modern, current. *(ANT.)* old, antiquated, ancient.

reception *(SYN.)* gathering, party.

recess *(SYN.)* hollow, opening, nook, cranny, dent, respite, rest, break, pause. *(ANT.)* gather, convene.

recession *(SYN.)* slump, depression.

recipe *(SYN.)* instructions, formula, prescriptions, procedure, method.

recital *(SYN.)* history, account, relation, chronicle, narrative, detail, narration. *(ANT.)* distortion, confusion, misrepresentation.

recite *(SYN.)* describe, narrate, declaim, rehearse, tell, mention, repeat, detail, recapitulate, report, list, relate, deliver.

reckless *(SYN.)* thoughtless, inconsiderate, careless, imprudent, rash, indiscreet, unconcerned. *(ANT.)* careful, nice, accurate.

reclaim *(SYN.)* reform, rescue, reinstate, regenerate, recycle.

recline *(SYN.)* stretch, sprawl, repose, rest, lounge, loll, incline.

recluse *(SYN.)* hermit, eremite, loner, anchorite.

recognize *(SYN.)* remember, avow, own, know, admit, apprehend, recollect, recall, concede, acknowledge, confess. *(ANT.)* disown, ignore, renounce.

recollect *(SYN.)* recall, remember, memory, reflect, call to mind, reminisce. *(ANT.)* forget.

recollection *(SYN.)* remembrance, retrospection, impression, recall. *(ANT.)* forgetfulness, oblivion.

recommend

recommend *(SYN.)* hind, refer, advise, commend, suggest, counsel, allude, praise, approve, intimate, advocate. *(ANT.)* disapprove, declare, insist.

recommendation *(SYN.)* instruction, justice, trustworthiness, counsel, admonition, caution, integrity, uprightness. *(ANT.)* fraud, deceit, trickery, cheating.

reconcile *(SYN.)* meditate, unite, adapt, adjust, settle, reunite, appease.

recondition *(SYN.)* rebuild, overhaul, restore, service.

reconsider *(SYN.)* ponder, reevaluate, mull over, reflect, reassess.

record *(SYN.)* enter, write, register, chronicle, history, account, document.

recount *(SYN.)* report, convey, narrate, tell, detail, recite, describe, repeat.

recoup *(SYN.)* regain, recover, repay, retrieve.

recover *(SYN.)* regain, redeem, recapture, retrieve, salvage, better, improve, mend, heal. *(ANT.)* debilitate, succumb, worsen.

recreation *(SYN.)* entertainment, amusement, enjoyment, diversion, fun.

recrimination *(SYN.)* vindication, reproach, dissension, accusation, countercharge.

recruit *(SYN.)* trainee, beginner, volunteer, draftee, select, enlist, novice.

recuperate *(SYN.)* regain, retrieve, cure, recapture, redeem, rally, convalesce, recover, repossess, restore. *(ANT.)* sicker, weaken, lose, regress, forfeit.

redeem *(SYN.)* claim, recover, repossess, regain, reclaim, cash in, retrieve.

reduce *(SYN.)* lessen, decrease, lower, downgrade, degrade, suppress, abate, diminish. *(ANT.)* enlarge, swell, raise, elevate, revive, increase, amplify.

reduction *(SYN.)* shortening, abridgment, abbreviation. *(ANT.)* amplification, extension, enlargement.

reek *(SYN.)* odor, stench, stink, smell.

refer *(SYN.)* recommend, direct, commend, regard, concern, relate, suggest, mention.

referee *(SYN.)* judge, arbitrator, umpire, arbiter, moderator, mediator.

reference *(SYN.)* allusion, direction, mention, concern, respect, referral.

refine *(SYN.)* purify, clarify, improve, clean. *(ANT.)* pollute, debase, muddy, downgrade.

refined *(SYN.)* purified, cultured, cultivated, courteous, courtly. *(ANT.)* rude, coarse, crude, vulgar.

refinement *(SYN.)* culture, enlightenment, education, civilization. *(ANT.)* vulgarity, ignorance, boorishness.

reflect *(SYN.)* muse, mirror, deliberate, cogitate, think, reproduce, ponder, consider, reason, meditate, contemplate.

reflection *(SYN.)* warning, conception, intelligence, appearance, likeness, image, cogitation, notification.

reform *(SYN.)* right, improve, correction, change, amend, improvement, better, betterment, correct, rectify. *(ANT.)* spoil, damage, aggravate, vitiate.

refresh *(SYN.)* exhilarate, renew, invigorate. *(ANT.)* exhaust, tire.

refreshing *(SYN.)* bracing, cool, brisk, fresh.

refreshment *(SYN.)* food, snack, drink, nourishment, exhilaration, stimulation.

refuge *(SYN.)* safety, retreat, shelter, asylum, sanctuary, harbor. *(ANT.)* peril, exposure, jeopardy, danger.

refuse *(SYN.)* spurn, rebuff, decline, reject, trash, rubbish, withhold, disallow, waste, garbage, deny, demur. *(ANT.)* allow, accept, welcome, grant.

refute *(SYN.)* rebut, disprove, confute, falsify, controvert, contradict. *(ANT.)* prove, confirm, accept, establish.

regain *(SYN.)* redeem, retrieve, recover, repossess, recapture. *(ANT.)* lose.

regalement *(SYN.)* feast, dinner, celebration, entertainment.

regard *(SYN.)* estimate, value, honor, affection, notice, care, consideration, consider, relation, respect, attend, thought, reference, care, attention, esteem, concern, liking. *(ANT.)* neglect, disgust, antipathy.

regards *(SYN.)* salutation, greetings, good wishes, respects, remembrances.

regenerate *(SYN.)* improve, reconstruct,

remedy, reestablish, rebuild.

regime *(SYN.)* direction, government, administration, management, dynasty, command, leadership.

regimented *(SYN.)* ordered, directed, controlled, orderly, rigid, disciplined. *(ANT.)* loose, free, unstructured.

region *(SYN.)* belt, place, spot, territory, climate, area, zone, locality, station, locale.

register *(SYN.)* catalog, record, book, list, roll, enter, roster, chronicle.

regressive *(SYN.)* revisionist, retrograde. *(ANT.)* progressive, civilized, advanced.

regret *(SYN.)* sorrow, qualm, lament, grief, compunction, bemoan, concern, scruple, misgiving, remorse, contrition. *(ANT.)* obduracy, complacency.

regular *(SYN.)* steady, orderly, natural, normal, customary, usual, habitual, even, uniform, systematic, unvaried, methodical, symmetrical. *(ANT.)* odd, exceptional, unusual, irregular, abnormal, rare.

regulate *(SYN.)* control, manage, govern, direct, legislate, set, adjust, systematize.

regulation *(SYN.)* method, rule, axiom, guide, control, standard, canon, precept, restraint, requirement. *(ANT.)* chaos, deviation, hazard, turbulence, confusion.

rehabilitate *(SYN.)* renew, restore, rebuild, reestablish, repair, reconstruct.

rehearse *(SYN.)* repeat, practice, train, learn, coach, prepare, perfect, direct.

reign *(SYN.)* dominion, power, rule, sovereignty, govern, domination.

reimburse *(SYN.)* recompense, remunerate, compensate, remit.

rein *(SYN.)* restriction, bridle, check, deterrent, curb, restraint, barrier, control.

reinforce *(SYN.)* brace, strengthen, fortify, intensify, support.

reiterate *(SYN.)* reproduce, recapitulate, duplicate, repeat, rephrase.

reject *(SYN.)* spurn, rebuff, decline, renounce, expel, discard, deny, refuse. *(ANT.)* endorse, grant, welcome, accept.

rejection *(SYN.)* dissent, nonconformity, variance, challenge, remonstrance, difference, noncompliance. *(ANT.)* assent, acceptance, compliance.

rejoice *(SYN.)* celebrate, delight, enjoy, revel, exhilarate, elate.

rejuvenate *(SYN.)* refresh, rekindle, overhaul, revitalize, animate, invigorate. *(ANT.)* deplete, weaken, exhaust.

relapse *(SYN.)* worsen, deteriorate, regress, weaken, fade, sink, fail. *(ANT.)* strengthen, progress, advance, get well.

relate *(SYN.)* refer, beat, report, describe, tell, correlate, narrate, recount, compare, connect.

relation *(SYN.)* entente, compact, coalition, alliance, connection, relationship, association, partnership, similarity, kinsman, treaty, marriage. *(ANT.)* separation, divorce.

relationship *(SYN.)* link, tie, alliance, connection, union, bond, affinity, conjunction. *(ANT.)* separation, disunion.

relative *(SYN.)* dependent, proportional, about, pertinent, regarding.

relax *(SYN.)* slacken, loosen, repose, rest, recline, unwind. *(ANT.)* increase, tighten, intensify.

relaxation *(SYN.)* comfort, ease, rest, enjoyment, lull, recess, breather, loafing.

relaxed *(SYN.)* welcome, pleasing, casual, acceptable, informal, restful, agreeable. *(ANT.)* formal, planned, wretched, distressing, troubling.

release *(SYN.)* liberate, emancipate, relinquish, proclaim, publish, liberation, announce, deliver, free, discharge. *(ANT.)* restrict, imprison, subjugate.

relegate *(SYN.)* entrust, authorize, remand, refer, assign.

relent *(SYN.)* cede, yield, surrender, give, relax, abdicate, relinquish, waive. *(ANT.)* strive, assert, struggle.

relentless *(SYN.)* eternal, stubborn, tenacious, dogged, ceaseless, incessant, persistent, determined.

relevant *(SYN.)* related, material, apt, applicable, fit, relating, germane. *(ANT.)* foreign, alien, unrelated.

reliable *(SYN.)* trusty, tried, certain, secure, trustworthy, dependable. *(ANT.)*

reliance

unreliable, eccentric, questionable, erratic, dubious.

reliance *(SYN.)* faith, confidence, trust. *(ANT.)* mistrust, doubt, skepticism.

relic *(SYN.)* remains, fossil, throwback, souvenir, keepsake, heirloom.

relief *(SYN.)* help, aid, comfort, ease, backing, patronage, alms, support. *(ANT.)* hostility, defiance, antagonism, resistance.

relieve *(SYN.)* diminish, soothe, calm, abate, pacify, ease, lessen, replace, spell, lighten, comfort, alleviate. *(ANT.)* disturb, irritate, agitate, trouble, aggravate, worry.

religion *(SYN.)* tenet, belief, dogma, faith, creed, persuasion.

religious *(SYN.)* godly, reverent, faithful, devout, zeal, pious, divine, holy, devoted, sacred, theological. *(ANT.)* profane, irreligious, skeptical, impious, lax, atheistic.

religiousness *(SYN.)* love, zeal, affection, devoutness, fidelity, ardor. *(ANT.)* indifference, apathy, unfaithfulness.

relinquish *(SYN.)* capitulate, submit, yield, abandon, cede, sacrifice, disclaim. *(ANT.)* overcome, conquer, rout, resist.

relish *(SYN.)* enjoyment, satisfaction, delight, gusto, appreciation, condiment, like, enjoy, enthusiasm. *(ANT.)* distaste, antipathy, disfavor, dislike.

reluctance *(SYN.)* disgust, hatred, repulsion, abhorrence, distaste, repugnance, aversion. *(ANT.)* enthusiasm, affection.

reluctant *(SYN.)* slow, averse, hesitant, unwilling, loath, disinclined, balky. *(ANT.)* ready, eager, willing, disposed.

rely *(SYN.)* confide, trust, lean, depend. *(ANT.)* mistrust, disbelieve, question, distrust.

remain *(SYN.)* survive, rest, stay, abide, halt, endure, dwell, tarry, continue, linger. *(ANT.)* finish, leave, terminate, dissipate.

remainder *(SYN.)* leftover, residue, rest, surplus, balance, excess.

remains *(SYN.)* residue, balance, rest, remnants, relics, discards, waste, junk.

remark *(SYN.)* comment, state, utterance, mention, note, observe, observation, annotation, declaration, statement.

remarkable *(SYN.)* exciting, impressive, overpowering, unusual, affecting, thrilling, splendid, special, noteworthy, extraordinary, touching, august. *(ANT.)* ordinary, unimpressive, commonplace, average.

remedy *(SYN.)* redress, help, cure, relief, medicine, restorative, rectify, alleviate, medication, correct, reparation.

remember *(SYN.)* recollect, reminisce, recall, memorize, mind, retain, remind. *(ANT.)* forget, overlook, disregard.

remembrance *(SYN.)* monument, memory, recollection, memento, recall, keepsake, souvenir, retrospection.

remiss *(SYN.)* delinquent, lax, careless, negligent, oblivious, forgetful, absentminded, sloppy, irresponsible.

remit *(SYN.)* send, pay, forward, forgive, pardon, overlook, excuse, reimburse.

remittance *(SYN.)* payment.

remnant *(SYN.)* remains, remainder, rest, residue, trace, relic.

remodel *(SYN.)* remake, reshape, rebuild, redecorate, renovate, modify, change, alter, convert, refurbish, update.

remonstrate *(SYN.)* grouch, protest, complain, grumble, murmur, repine, dispute. *(ANT.)* rejoice, applaud, praise.

remorse *(SYN.)* sorrow, qualm, contrition, regret, compunction, repentance. *(ANT.)* obduracy, complacency.

remorseless *(SYN.)* savage, unrelenting, crude, barbaric, merciless, cruel, fiendish, brutal, callous. *(ANT.)* kind, refined, polite, civilized.

remote *(SYN.)* inconsiderable, removed, slight, far, unlikely, distant, inaccessible, unreachable, isolated, sequestered. *(ANT.)* visible, nearby, current, near, close.

remove *(SYN.)* transport, eject, move, vacate, withdraw, dislodge, transfer, doff, displace, eliminate, murder, kill, oust, extract. *(ANT.)* insert, retain, stay, keep.

removed *(SYN.)* aloof, distant, cool, remote.

remuneration *(SYN.)* wages, pay, salary, compensation, reimbursement, reward.

render *(SYN.)* become, make, perform, do,

offer, present, give, submit.

rendition *(SYN.)* interpretation, version, depiction, expression, characterization.

renegade *(SYN.)* defector, insurgent, dissenter, rebel, maverick, mutineer, betrayer.

renege *(SYN.)* let down, doublecross, deceive.

renew *(SYN.)* restore, renovate, overhaul, revise, modernize, reshape, redo.

renounce *(SYN.)* resign, disown, revoke, abandon, quit, retract, forgo, leave, forsake, abdicate, reject, relinquish, deny. *(ANT.)* assert, uphold, recognize, maintain.

renovate *(SYN.)* restore, rehabilitate, rebuild, refresh, renew, overhaul, redesign.

renown *(SYN.)* honor, reputation, eminence, acclaim, glory, repute, luster, fame, notability. *(ANT.)* obscurity, anonymity.

renowned *(SYN.)* noted, famous, distinguished, well-known, glorious, celebrated. *(ANT.)* unknown, infamous, hidden, obscure.

rent *(SYN.)* payment, rental, let, lease, hire.

repair *(SYN.)* rebuilding, mend, renew, linker, correct, patch, restore, adjust, reconstruction, remedy, amend, rehabilitation, retrieve. *(ANT.)* harm, break.

repartee *(SYN.)* badinage, banter.

repast *(SYN.)* feast, banquet, meal, refreshment, snack.

repeal *(SYN.)* end, cancel, nullify, annul, quash, abolish, cancellation, rescind, abolition, abrogate.

repeat *(SYN.)* reiterate, restate, redo, rehearse, quote, remake, relate, iterate, reproduce.

repel *(SYN.)* check, repulse, rebuff, reject, decline, discourage. *(ANT.)* lure, attract.

repellent *(SYN.)* sickening, offensive, disgusting, nauseating, repugnant, obnoxious.

repent *(SYN.)* deplore, regret, rue, lament.

repentance *(SYN.)* penitence, remorse, sorrow, compunction, qualm, grief. *(ANT.)* obduracy, complacency.

repentant *(SYN.)* regretful, sorrowful, contrite, sorry, penitent. *(ANT.)* remorseless, obdurate.

repented *(SYN.)* continuous, frequent, recurrent, continual.

repetitious *(SYN.)* repeated, monotonous, boring, tiresome, humdrum.

repine *(SYN.)* protest, lament, complain, whine, regret, grouch, murmur, grumble. *(ANT.)* rejoice, applaud, praise.

replace *(SYN.)* alternate, return, reinstate.

replacement *(SYN.)* understudy, proxy, second, alternate, substitute, replica, surrogate.

replenish *(SYN.)* store, pervade, fill, stock, occupy, supply. *(ANT.)* empty, void, deplete, exhaust.

replica *(SYN.)* reproduction, copy, exemplar, imitation, duplicate, facsimile. *(ANT.)* prototype.

reply *(SYN.)* retort, rejoinder, answer, retaliate, respond, confirmation. *(ANT.)* summoning, inquiry.

report *(SYN.)* declare, herald, publish, announce, summary, publish, advertise. *(ANT.)* suppress, conceal, withhold, bury.

reporter *(SYN.)* journalist.

repose *(SYN.)* hush, quiet, tranquillity, rest, peace, slumber, calm, stillness, sleep, calmness. *(ANT.)* tumult, excitement, agitation.

reprehensible *(SYN.)* criminal, immoral, damnable, culpable, wrong, wicked.

represent *(SYN.)* picture, draw, delineate, portray, depict, denote, symbolize. *(ANT.)* misrepresent, caricature.

representation *(SYN.)* effigy, film, likeness, portrait, print, scene, appearance, drawing, scene, view, cinema.

representative *(SYN.)* delegate, agent, substitute, surrogate.

repress *(SYN.)* limit, stop, check, bridle, curb, restrain, constrain, suppress. *(ANT.)* loosen, aid, incite, liberate, encourage.

reprimand *(SYN.)* rate, scold, vituperate, berate, lecture, blame, admonish, upbraid. *(ANT.)* praise, approve.

reproach *(SYN.)* defamation, dishonor, insult, profanation, abuse, disparagement, misuse, reviling. *(ANT.)* respect, laudation, approval, plaudit.

reproduction *(SYN.)* replica, copy, exemplar, transcript, duplicate, photocopy.

reproof *(SYN.)* rebuke, punishment, blame, censure, disapproval, scorn, disdain, admonition.

repugnance *(SYN.)* disgust, hatred, reluctance, abhorrence, aversion, loathing, antipathy, distaste, repulsion. *(ANT.) devotion, affection, enthusiasm, attachment.*

repulsive *(SYN.)* repellent, ugly, homely, deformed, horrid, offensive, plain, uncomely. *(ANT.) fair, pretty, attractive.*

reputable *(SYN.)* honest, upstanding, trustworthy, straightforward, upright, reliable. *(ANT.) notorious, corrupt, disreputable.*

reputation *(SYN.)* class, nature, standing, name, fame, kind, renown, prominence, character, distinction, disposition, repute.

repute *(SYN.)* class, nature, standing, kind, character, reputation, disposition, sort.

request *(SYN.)* sue, implore, petition, desire, appeal, question, entreaty, beseech, ask, pray, supplicate. *(ANT.) require.*

require *(SYN.)* exact, need, order, command, order, lack, claim, demand, want.

requirement *(SYN.)* demand, need, necessity, condition, provision, prerequisite.

requisite *(SYN.)* vital, necessary, basic, fundamental, indispensable, essential, needed. *(ANT.) casual, nonessential, peripheral.*

rescind *(SYN.)* annul, quash, revoke, abolish, invalidate, abrogate, withdraw.

rescue *(SYN.)* liberate, ransom, release, deliver, deliverance, liberation.

research *(SYN.)* exploration, quest, scrutiny, exploration, interrogation, query, examination, study, investigation. *(ANT.) inattention, disregard, negligence.*

resemblance *(SYN.)* parity, similitude, analogy, likeness, correspondence. *(ANT.) distinction, difference.*

resemble *(SYN.)* duplicate, mirror, look like.

resentfulness *(SYN.)* envy, jealousy, covetousness, suspicion. *(ANT.) liberality, geniality, tolerance, difference.*

resentment *(SYN.)* displeasure, bitterness, indignation, rancor, outrage, hostility. *(ANT.) complacency, understanding, good will.*

reservation *(SYN.)* skepticism, restriction, objection, limitation, doubt.

reserve *(SYN.)* fund, hold, keep, store, accumulation, save, stock, maintain, supply. *(ANT.) waste, squander.*

reserved *(SYN.)* cautious, fearful, timorous, wary, aloof, chary, sheepish, restrained, proper, unfriendly, bashful, diffident. *(ANT.) forward, bold, wild, immodest, brazen, abandoned, friendly.*

reside *(SYN.)* inhabit, dwell, abide, live, lie.

residence *(SYN.)* home, dwelling, stay, seat, abode, quarters, domicile, living quarters.

residue *(SYN.)* balance, remainder, rest, ashes, remnants, dregs, leftovers, ends.

resign *(SYN.)* vacate, withdraw, leave, surrender, quit.

resignation *(SYN.)* withdrawal, surrender, quitting, abdication, acquiescence. *(ANT.) recalcitrance, defiance, resistance.*

resigned *(SYN.)* forbearing, stoical, assiduous, passive, accepting, composed, uncomplaining, *(ANT.) turbulent, chafing.*

resilience *(SYN.)* rubbery, springy, buoyant, elasticity. *(ANT.) unresponsive, fixed, stolid.*

resist *(SYN.)* defy, attack, withstand, hinder, confront, oppose. *(ANT.) relent, allow, yield, accede.*

resolute *(SYN.)* firm, resolved, set, determined, decided. *(ANT.) irresolute, wavering, vacillating.*

resolution *(SYN.)* resolve, courage, determination, persistence, statement, verdict, recommendation, decision, steadfastness, dedication, perseverance. *(ANT.) indecision, inconstancy.*

resolve *(SYN.)* determination, resolution, courage, settle, decide, persistence, determine, confirm, decision, steadfastness. *(ANT.) integrate, indecision, inconstancy.*

resort *(SYN.)* motel, lodge, hotel, solve.

resound *(SYN.)* echo, ring, reverberate.

resource *(SYN.)* store, source, supply, reserve.

resourceful *(SYN.)* inventive, ingenious, creative, clever, imaginative, skillful.

respect *(SYN.)* honor, approval, revere, heed, value, admire, esteem, point, detail, admiration, reverence, regard, feature, particular, venerate, consider. *(ANT.)* neglect, abuse, scorn, disregard, despise.

respectable *(SYN.)* becoming, respected, proper, seemly, tolerable, decent, acceptable, fair, adequate, passable, suitable, honorable, valuable. *(ANT.)* unsavory, vulgar, gross, disputable, reprehensible.

respectful *(SYN.)* courteous, polite, well-behaved, well-bred, compliant, submissive. *(ANT.)* disobedient, impertinent, rude.

respite *(SYN.)* deferment, adjournment, suspension.

respond *(SYN.)* rejoin, answer, reply, acknowledge, retort. *(ANT.)* overlook, disregard.

response *(SYN.)* reply, acknowledgment, answer, retort, rejoinder. *(ANT.)* summoning, inquiry.

responsibility *(SYN.)* duty, obligation, accountability, trustworthiness, trust, liability, commitment.

responsible *(SYN.)* answerable, chargeable, trustworthy, liable, accountable, able, capable, upstanding, reliable, solid, indebted, creditable. *(ANT.)* careless, free, negligent.

rest *(SYN.)* ease, intermission, calm, quiet, balance, surplus, repose, lounge, inactivity, motionlessness, immobility, standstill, relax, remainder, excess, relaxation, slumber, peace, tranquillity, leisure. *(ANT.)* tumult, commotion, motion, agitation.

restful *(SYN.)* peaceful, quiet, tranquil, calm. *(ANT.)* tumultuous, upsetting, agitated, disturbed.

restitution *(SYN.)* recompense, satisfaction, refund, amends, retrieval.

restive *(SYN.)* balky, disobedient, fractious, impatient, unruly, fidgety, uneasy.

restless *(SYN.)* sleepless, unquiet, transient, active, agitated, disturbed, jumpy, nervous, uneasy, disquieted, irresolute. *(ANT.)* quiet, tranquil, calm, peaceable.

restore *(SYN.)* repair, recover, rebuild, reestablish, renovate, return, renew, mend, reinstall, revive, rehabilitate, replace.

restrain *(SYN.)* limit, curb, constraint, stop, bridle, control, constrain, repress, check, suppress, hinder. *(ANT.)* incite, aid, loosen.

restraint *(SYN.)* order, self-control, reserve, control, regulation, limitation, confinement. *(ANT.)* freedom, liberty.

restrict *(SYN.)* fetter, restrain, confine, limit, engage, attach, connect, link, tie, bind. *(ANT.)* broaden, enlarge, untie, loose, free.

restriction *(SYN.)* curb, handicap, check, boundary, ban, limitation, control, deterrent.

result *(SYN.)* effect, issue, outcome, resolve, end, consequence, happen, determination, conclusion, reward, aftermath. *(ANT.)* cause, beginning, origin.

resume *(SYN.)* restart, continue, recommence, reassume.

resurgence *(SYN.)* rebirth, comeback, recovery, revival, resuscitation, rejuvenation, renewal.

resuscitate *(SYN.)* restore, revive.

retain *(SYN.)* keep, hold, recall, remember, employ, hire, engage.

retainer *(SYN.)* aide, assistant, lackey, attendant, servant.

retaliate *(SYN.)* repay, revenge, return, avenge. *(ANT.)* condone, forgive, overlook, excuse, forget.

retard *(SYN.)* detain, slacken, defer, impede, hold back, delay, postpone. *(ANT.)* accelerate, speed, hasten, rush.

retention *(SYN.)* reservation, acquisition, holding, tenacity, possession.

reticent *(SYN.)* reserved, subdued, quiet, shy, withdrawn, restrained, bashful, silent. *(ANT.)* outspoken, forward, opinionated.

retire *(SYN.)* resign, quit, abdicate, depart, vacate.

retiring *(SYN.)* timid, bashful, withdrawn, modest, reticent, quiet, reserved. *(ANT.)* gregarious, assertive, bold.

retort *(SYN.)* reply, answer, response, respond, rejoin, rejoinder, retaliate. *(ANT.)* summoning, inquiry.

retreat *(SYN.)* leave, depart, retire, withdraw,

retirement, withdrawal, departure, shelter, refuge. (*ANT.*) *advanced.*

retrench (*SYN.*) reduce, scrape, curtail.

retribution (*SYN.*) justice, vengeance, reprisal, punishment, comeuppance, vindictiveness, revenge, retaliation.

retrieve (*SYN.*) regain, recover, recapture, repossess, reclaim, salvage, recoup.

retrograde (*SYN.*) regressive, backward, declining, deteriorating, worsening. (*ANT.*) *onward, progression, advanced.*

return (*SYN.*) restoration, replace, revert, recur, restore, retreat. (*ANT.*) *keep, take, retain.*

reveal (*SYN.*) discover, publish, communicate, impart, uncover, tell, betray, divulge, disclose. (*ANT.*) *conceal, cover, obscure, cloak, hide.*

revel (*SYN.*) rejoice, wallow, bask, enjoy, delight, savor, gloat, luxuriate, relish.

revelation (*SYN.*) hallucination, dream, prophecy, apparition, ghost, mirage, discovery, daydream, surprise, shocker.

revelry (*SYN.*) merriment, merry-making, carousal, feasting, gala, festival.

revenge (*SYN.*) vindictiveness, reprisal, requital, vengeance, repayment, repay, retribution, reparation. (*ANT.*) *reconcile, forgive, pity.*

revenue (*SYN.*) take, proceeds, income, profit, return.

revere (*SYN.*) admire, honor, worship, respect, venerate, adore. (*ANT.*) *ignore, despise.*

reverence (*SYN.*) glory, worship, homage, admiration, dignity, renown, respect, esteem, veneration, adoration, honor. (*ANT.*) *dishonor, derision, reproach.*

reverent (*SYN.*) honoring, respectful, adoring, pious, devout, humble. (*ANT.*) *silent, disrespectful.*

reverse (*SYN.*) overthrow, unmake, rescind, opposite, invert, contrary, rear, back, misfortune, defeat, upset, countermand, revoke. (*ANT.*) *vouch, stabilize, endorse, affirm.*

revert (*SYN.*) return, relapse, backslide, reverse, retreat, recur, go back. (*ANT.*)

keep, take, appropriate.

review (*SYN.*) reconsideration, examination, commentary, retrospection, restudy, journal, synopsis, study, reexamine, critique, inspection.

revile (*SYN.*) defame, malign, vilify, abuse, traduce, asperse, scandalize, smear. (*ANT.*) *honor, respect, cherish, protect.*

revise (*SYN.*) change, alter, improve, correct, amend, update, rewrite, polish.

revision (*SYN.*) inspection, survey, retrospection, commentary, critique.

revival (*SYN.*) renaissance, exhumation, resurgence, renewal, revitalization.

revive (*SYN.*) refresh, lessen, decrease, renew, reduce, lower, abate, reanimate, diminish, reawaken, rejuvenate, suppress. (*ANT.*) *increase, amplify, intensify.*

revoke (*SYN.*) nullify, cancel, abolish, quash, rescind, abrogate.

revolt (*SYN.*) mutiny, rebel, disgust, revolution, uprising, rebellion, upheaval, takeover, insurgence, abolish.

revolting (*SYN.*) hateful, odious, abominable, foul, vile, detestable, loathsome, repugnant, obnoxious, sickening. (*ANT.*) *delightful, agreeable, pleasant.*

revolution (*SYN.*) rebellion, mutiny, turn, coup, revolt, overthrow, cycle, spin, uprising.

revolutionary (*SYN.*) insurgent, extremist, radical, subversive, mutinous.

revolve (*SYN.*) spin, wheel, rotate, circle, turn, whirl, gyrate.

revolver (*SYN.*) gun, pistol.

revulsion (*SYN.*) dislike, distaste, aversion, repugnance, disgust. (*ANT.*) attraction, desire, fondness, preference.

reward (*SYN.*) bounty, premium, award, compensation, prize, recompense, bonus, remuneration, accolade. (*ANT.*) punishment, penalty, chastisement.

rewarding (*SYN.*) pleasing, productive, fruitful, profitable, favorable, satisfying, gratifying, fulfilling.

rhetoric (*SYN.*) style, verbosity, expressiveness, eloquence, fluency, flamboyance.

rhyme (*SYN.*) poem, verse, poetry, ballad, ditty, rhapsody, sonnet.

ribald *(SYN.)* suggestive, off-color, indecent, spicy, rude, vulgar.

rich *(SYN.)* ample, costly, wealthy, fruitful, prolific, abundant, well-off, affluent, plentiful, fertile, bountiful, luxuriant. *(ANT.) poor, unfruitful, beggarly, barren, impoverished, scarce, scanty, unproductive, destitute.*

rickety *(SYN.)* unsound, unsteady, flimsy, unstable, shaky, decrepit, wobbly. *(ANT.) steady, solid, sturdy.*

ricochet *(SYN.)* recoil, backfire, rebound, bounce, deviate, boomerang.

rid *(SYN.)* free, clear, shed, delivered, eliminate, disperse, unload, purge.

riddle *(SYN.)* puzzle, mystery, conundrum, problem, question, enigma. *(ANT.) key, solution, answer, resolution.*

ride *(SYN.)* tour, journey, motor, manage, drive, control, guide.

ridge *(SYN.)* hillock, backbone, spine, crest, mound, hump.

ridicule *(SYN.)* gibe, banter, mock, jeering, deride, tease, taunt, satire, mockery, derision. *(ANT.) praise.*

ridiculous *(SYN.)* silly, nonsensical, absurd, accurate, inconsistent, farcical, proper, laughable, apt, preposterous, foolish. *(ANT.) sound, reasonable, consistent.*

rife *(SYN.)* widespread, abundant, innumerable, rampant, teeming.

rifle *(SYN.)* plunder, pillage, rummage, ransack, rob, steal.

rift *(SYN.)* crevice, fault, crack, flaw, fissure, split, breach, opening.

right *(SYN.)* correct, appropriate, suitable, ethical, fit, real, legitimate, justice, factual, just, directly, virtue, true, definite, straight, honorably, seemly. *(ANT.) immoral, unfair, wrong, bad, improper.*

righteous *(SYN.)* ethical, chaste, honorable, good, virtuous, noble. *(ANT.) sinful, libertine, amoral, licentious.*

rigid *(SYN.)* strict, unyielding, stiff, stern, austere, rigorous, inflexible, stringent, unbendable, severe, harsh, unbending. *(ANT.) supple, flexible, mild, compassionate, pliable, limp, relaxed.*

rigorous *(SYN.)* unfeeling, rough, strict, blunt, cruel, hard, severe, grating, coarse, jarring, stern, stringent. *(ANT.) soft, mild, tender, gentle, smooth.*

rile *(SYN.)* irritate, nettle, hector, exasperate, provoke, gripe.

rim *(SYN.)* verge, frontier, border, outskirts, edge, brink, lip, limit, termination, boundary, fringe, brim, margin. *(ANT.) core, mainland, center.*

rind *(SYN.)* layer, cover, skin, hide, peel, crust, bark.

ring *(SYN.)* fillet, band, loop, circlet, circle, surround, encircle, peal, sound, resound, jingle, tinkle.

ringleader *(SYN.)* provoker, troublemaker, leader, instigator, chief, inciter, agitator.

rinse *(SYN.)* launder, cleanse, wash, soak, immerse, laundering, rinsing, bathe, clean.

riot *(SYN.)* disturbance, disorder, outburst, commotion, insurgence, uproar, panic, boisterousness, lark, hoot, sensation, caper, roister, frolic, eruption, confusion, tumult, revolt.

riotous *(SYN.)* boisterous, wild, rambunctious, tumultuous, turbulent, noisy, loud, rowdy, rollicking,

rip *(SYN.)* tear, rend, wound, rive, cleave, cut, slit, slash, lacerate, shred, scramble, dart, dash, split, disunite. *(ANT.) mend, join, repair.*

ripe *(SYN.)* ready, finished, mature, complete, full-grown, develop, mellow, seasonable, full-fledged, primed, disposed, keen, avid, consummate. *(ANT.) raw, crude, undeveloped, premature, unprepared, unripe.*

ripen *(SYN.)* grow, season, age, mature, mellow, develop, progress, maturate.

rip into *(SYN.)* assail, lash out at, attack, charge.

rip-off *(SYN.)* fraud, dishonesty, gyp, racket, swindle, exploitation, heist, theft, extortion, thievery, larceny, shakedown.

riposte *(SYN.)* rejoinder, comeback, quip, retort, response, reply, wisecrack.

ripple *(SYN.)* wave, ruffle, wavelet, gurgle, undulate, corrugation, rumple, crumple, dribble, bubble.

rise *(SYN.)* thrive, awaken, ascend, climb,

risk

mount, tower, arise, wake, scale, flourish, prosper, advance, proceed, soar. (*ANT.*) *fail, drop, plunge, fade, slump, decline, sinking, depression, waning, comedown, setback, retrogression, descend.*

risk (*SYN.*) hazard, peril, danger, endanger, chance, jeopardy, threat, vulnerability, contingency, precariousness, shakiness. (*ANT.*) *protection, safety, immunity, defense.*

risky (*SYN.*) menacing, chancy, threatening, critical, perilous, insecure, unsafe, dicey, unsound, dangerous. (*ANT.*) *guarded, safe, certain, firm, secure.*

rite (*SYN.*) pomp, solemnity, ceremony, observance, ceremonial, formality.

ritual (*SYN.*) pomp, solemnity, ceremony, parade, rite, ritualism, prescription, routine, custom, tradition.

rival (*SYN.*) enemy, opponent, contestant, compete, foe, adversary, oppose, competitor, contest, antagonist. (*ANT.*) *colleague, confederate, allay, collaborator, helpmate, teammate.*

rivalry (*SYN.*) contest, struggle, duel, race, vying, opposition, contention, competition. (*ANT.*) *alliance, collaboration, partnership, teamwork, coalition.*

river (*SYN.*) brook, stream, headstream, watercourse, tributary, creek.

rivet (*SYN.*) weld, bolt, fasten, attach, secure, bind, join, staple, nail, couple.

road (*SYN.*) street, way, highway, pike, drive, expressway, boulevard.

roam (*SYN.*) err, saunter, deviate, rove, range, wander, digress, ramble, stroll. (*ANT.*) *stop, linger, stay, halt, settle.*

roar (*SYN.*) cry, bellow, yell, shout, yowl, howl, bawl, hoot, bang, boom, blast, blare, scream, whoop, holler, yelp.

roast (*SYN.*) deride, ridicule, kid, ride, mock, tease, twit, parody, burlesque.

rob (*SYN.*) fleece, steal, despoil, pilfer, pillage, sack, loot, plunder, burglarize, ransack, hold up, rip off, thieve.

robbery (*SYN.*) larceny, plundering, thievery, stealing, theft, pillage, swiping, caper, snatching, burglary, plunder.

robe (*SYN.*) housecoat, bathrobe, dressing gown, caftan, muumuu, smock, cape.

robot (*SYN.*) computer, android, automaton, pawn, workhorse, drudge, laborer.

robust (*SYN.*) well, hearty, hale, sound, healthy, strong, able-bodied, stalwart. (*ANT.*) *fragile, feeble, debilitated, reserved, refined, puny, frail, delicate, infirm.*

rock (*SYN.*) pebble, boulder, stone, gravel, granite, roll, sway, swagger, limestone.

rocky (*SYN.*) unstable, faint, rock-like, stony, pebbly, gravelly, rough, bumpy, formidable, quavering, challenging, unsteady, dizzy. (*ANT.*) *effortless, easy, slight, simple, sound, rugged, stout, hardy, strong, robust.*

rod (*SYN.*) bar, pole, wand, stick, pike, staff, billy, baton.

rogue (*SYN.*) criminal, rascal, outlaw, scoundrel, scamp, good-for-nothing, villain.

roguish (*SYN.*) prankish, playful, mischievous, elfish, waggish, devilish, tricky. (*ANT.*) *grave, humorless, solemn, staid.*

roil (*SYN.*) muddy, rile, mire, disturb.

roister (*SYN.*) bluster, swagger, swashbuckle, vaunt, bluff, flourish, rollick.

role (*SYN.*) task, part, function, characterization, portrayal, face, character.

roll (*SYN.*) revolve, rotate, whirl, swing, rock, waver, reel, lumber, swagger, stagger, progress, proceed, turn, spin.

rollicking (*SYN.*) spirited, animated, frolicsome, exuberant, lighthearted, carefree.

roll up (*SYN.*) amass, collect, accumulate, gather.

romance (*SYN.*) affair, enchantment, novel, tale, adventure, enterprise, story.

romantic (*SYN.*) poetic, mental, dreamy, fanciful, imaginative, extravagant, impractical, exaggerated, wild, idealistic, mawkish, ideal, maudlin. (*ANT.*) *homely, faint-hearted, familiar, unromantic, pessimistic, unemotional, cynical, literal, prosaic.*

romp (*SYN.*) caper, gambol, frolic, play, conquer, triumph, horseplay, frisk. (*ANT.*) *defeat, rout.*

room (*SYN.*) enclosure, cell, chamber, space, stay, lodge, cubicle, reside.

roomy (*SYN.*) broad, large, wide, sizable,

generous, capacious, ample, spacious, extensive, commodious, vast. (*ANT.*) *tight, limited, crowded, confined, narrow.*

roost *(SYN.)* coop, hen house, perch, hutch, residence, abode, hearth, lodgings.

root *(SYN.)* reason, bottom, groundwork, cause, support, base, underpinning, beginning, mainspring, source, basis. (*ANT.*) *cover, top, building.*

rooted *(SYN.)* fixed, fast, firm, steadfast, immovable, stationary.

root for *(SYN.)* back, support, boost, promote, bolster, encourage, hail, cheer.

root out *(SYN.)* dispose of, uproot, cut out, pluck out.

rope *(SYN.)* string, wire, cord, cable, line, strand, rigging, ropework, cordage.

ropy *(SYN.)* wiry, stringy, viscous, threadlike, viscoid.

roster *(SYN.)* list, census, muster, enrollment, listing, register.

rosy *(SYN.)* reddish, pink, healthy, fresh, cheerful, bright, happy, glowing, flushed, promising, favorable. (*ANT.*) *pale, pallid, gray, wan, disheartening, ashen, unfavorable, gloomy.*

rot *(SYN.)* putrefy, waste, decay, mold, decompose, dwindle, spoil, decline, decomposition, wane, rotting, ebb. (*ANT.*) *increase, rise, grow.*

rotary *(SYN.)* axial, rotating, turning, gyrate, revolving, rolling, whirling, rotational.

rotate *(SYN.)* spin, twirl, wheel, circle, twist, orbit, invert, swivel, gyrate, wind, alternate, recur, intermit, pivot. (*ANT.*) *stop, arrest, stand.*

rote *(SYN.)* repetition, system, convention, routine, mechanization, habitude, habit, custom.

rough *(SYN.)* jagged, scratchy, crude, incomplete, severe, craggy, stormy, rugged, unpolished, approximate, uneven, irregular, bumpy, coarse. (*ANT.*) *calm, polished, civil, mild, refined, placid, gentle, smooth, sleek, sophisticated, suave.*

round *(SYN.)* rotund, chubby, curved, bulbous, entire, complete, spherical, circular, bowed. (*ANT.*) *slender, trim, slim, thin, lean.*

rouse *(SYN.)* waken, awaken, stimulate, excite, summon, arise, stir. (*ANT.*) *rest, calm, sleep, restrain, sedate.*

rousing *(SYN.)* exciting, galvanic, stimulating, electric, moving, exhilarating, stirring, breathtaking, inciting. (*ANT.*) *flat, uninteresting, drab, monotonous, boring, tiresome, slow, dull.*

rout *(SYN.)* defeat, beat, quell, vanquish, conquer, humble, subdue, scatter. (*ANT.*) *cede, retreat, surrender.*

route *(SYN.)* street, course, trail, way, avenue, passage, thoroughfare, track.

routine *(SYN.)* way, habit, use, custom, practice, fashion, method, system. (*ANT.*) *unusual, rate, uncommon.*

rover *(SYN.)* traveler, adventurer, wanderer, voyager.

row *(SYN.)* file, order, series, rank, progression, sequence, arrangement.

rowdy *(SYN.)* disorderly, unruly, brawling, roughneck, scrapper.

royal *(SYN.)* lordly, regal, noble, courtly, ruling, stately, dignified, supreme, majestic, sovereign, imperial, kingly. (*ANT.*) *servile, common, low, humble, vulgar.*

rub *(SYN.)* shine, polish, scour, scrape.

rubbish *(SYN.)* debris, garbage, trash, waste, junk, clutter.

ruddy *(SYN.)* rosy, reddish, healthy, robust, blushing, sanguine.

rude *(SYN.)* gruff, impudent, blunt, impolite, boorish, insolent, saucy, rough, crude, unmannerly, coarse, impertinent. (*ANT.*) *courtly, civil, stately, calm, dignified, polished, courteous, cultivated, polite.*

rudimentary *(SYN.)* essential, primary, fundamental, original, imperfect.

rue *(SYN.)* lament, repine, sorrow, deplore, regret, bemoan.

ruffian *(SYN.)* crook, hoodlum, thug.

ruffle *(SYN.)* rumple, disarrange, disorder, disturb, trimming, frill.

rug *(SYN.)* floorcovering, carpet.

rugged *(SYN.)* jagged, craw, scratchy, irregular, uneven, harsh, severe, tough. (*ANT.*)

ruin

smooth, level, even.

ruin *(SYN.)* wreck, exterminate, devastate, annihilate, raze, demolish, spoil. *(ANT.)* save, establish, preserve.

rule *(SYN.)* law, guide, order, regulation, dominion, sovereignty, control.

ruler *(SYN.)* commander, chief, leader, governor, yardstick.

ruling *(SYN.)* judgment, decision, decree.

ruminate *(SYN.)* brood, reflect, meditate, ponder, consider, speculate.

rummage *(SYN.)* root, scour, ransack.

rumor *(SYN.)* innuendo, hearsay, gossip.

rumple *(SYN.)* tousle, furrow, crease, wrinkle, dishevel.

run *(SYN.)* race, hurry, speed, hasten, sprint, dart, scamper, dash.

runaway *(SYN.)* refugee, deserter, fugitive.

run-down *(SYN.)* ramshackle, dilapidated, tumble-down, weakened.

rupture *(SYN.)* fracture, fissure, cleft, break, split, gash.

rural *(SYN.)* country, farm, rustic, backwoods. *(ANT.)* citified, urban.

rush *(SYN.)* dash, speed, hurry, hasten, run, scoot, hustle, scurry. *(ANT.)* tarry, linger.

rut *(SYN.)* routine, habit, groove, track.

S

sabotage *(SYN.)* subversion, undermine, treason, treachery, damage, disable, subvert.

sack *(SYN.)* pouch, bag.

sacrament *(SYN.)* communion, fellowship, rite, association, participation, union. *(ANT.)* nonparticipation, alienation.

sacred *(SYN.)* consecrated, blessed, devout, divine, holy, hallowed, pious, religious, spiritual, saintly. *(ANT.)* profane, evil, sacrilegious, worldly, secular, blasphemous, impious.

sad *(SYN.)* dejected, cheerless, despondent, depressed, disconsolate, doleful, downhearted, downcast, dismal, melancholy, somber, glum, saddening. *(ANT.)* happy, cheerful, glad, merry.

safe *(SYN.)* dependable, certain, harmless, secure, snug, trustworthy. *(ANT.)* hazardous, dangerous, unsafe, insecure, perilous.

sag *(SYN.)* incline, bend, lean, slant, tend, depend, rely, trust, fail. *(ANT.)* rise, raise, erect, straighten.

sagacity *(SYN.)* erudition, discretion, foresight, insight, information, judgment, intelligence, knowledge, learning. *(ANT.)* foolishness, imprudence, stupidity, nonsense.

sage *(SYN.)* intellectual, disciple, learner, savant, scholar, pupil, student, wise, judicious, sagacious, rational, logical. *(ANT.)* dunce, fool, dolt, idiot.

saintly *(SYN.)* virtuous, moral, holy, devout, righteous, good.

sake *(SYN.)* motive, reason, purpose, benefit, advantage, welfare.

salary *(SYN.)* compensation, allowance, earnings, pay, fee, payment, recompense, wages. *(ANT.)* gratuity, present, gift.

saloon *(SYN.)* pub, bar.

salubrious *(SYN.)* healthy, hale, sound, robust, strong, well, hygienic, wholesome, salutary. *(ANT.)* diseased, delicate, frail, injurious.

salutary *(SYN.)* beneficial, advantageous, profitable, useful, wholesome. *(ANT.)* destructive, deleterious, detrimental, injurious, harmful.

salute *(SYN.)* receive, greet.

salvage *(SYN.)* retrieve, rescue, recover.

salvation *(SYN.)* release, rescue, deliverance.

same *(SYN.)* equal, coincident, equivalent, like, indistinguishable. *(ANT.)* disparate, contrary, dissimilar, opposed, distinct.

sample *(SYN.)* example, case, illustration, model, instance, pattern, prototype, specimen, token.

sanction *(SYN.)* approval, approbation, authorization, authority, let, permit. *(ANT.)* reproach, reprimand, stricture, censure, object, forbid, refuse, resist.

sanctuary *(SYN.)* harbor, haven, asylum, refuge, retreat, shelter. *(ANT.)* danger, hazard, exposure, jeopardy, peril.

sane *(SYN.)* balanced, rational, normal,

• •

sound, reasonable. (*ANT.*) crazy, insane, irrational.

sanitary (*SYN.*) purified, clean, hygienic, disinfected. (*ANT.*) soiled, fouled, unclean, dirty.

sap (*SYN.*) exhausted, drain, weaken.

sarcastic (*SYN.*) biting, acrimonious, cutting, caustic, derisive, sardonic, satirical, ironic, sneering. (*ANT.*) agreeable, affable, pleasant.

sardonic (*SYN.*) bitter, caustic, acrimonious, severe, harsh. (*ANT.*) mellow, pleasant, sweet.

satanic (*SYN.*) demonic, fiendish, diabolic.

sate (*SYN.*) fill up, fill, occupy, furnish, pervade, stock, replenish, store, supply, content, gorge, satiate, stuff, satisfy. (*ANT.*) empty, drain, deplete, void.

satire (*SYN.*) cleverness, fun, banter, humor, irony, raillery, pleasantry. (*ANT.*) platitude, sobriety, commonplace, solemnity.

satirical (*SYN.*) biting, caustic, acrimonious, cutting, ironic, derisive, sarcastic, sneering, sardonic, taunting. (*ANT.*) agreeable, affable, pleasant.

satisfactory (*SYN.*) ample, capable, adequate, commensurate, enough, sufficient, fitting, suitable, okay. (*ANT.*) scant, lacking, deficient, unsatisfactory, poor.

satisfy (*SYN.*) compensate, appease, content, gratify, fulfill, suitable. (*ANT.*) displease, dissatisfy, annoy, tantalize.

saturate (*SYN.*) fill, diffuse, infiltrate, penetrate, permeate, run through.

saucy (*SYN.*) insolent, bold, impudent, impertinent. (*ANT.*) shy, demure.

savage (*SYN.*) brutal, cruel, barbarous, ferocious, inhuman, merciless. (*ANT.*) compassionate, gentle, humane, kind, merciful, tame, cultivated.

save (*SYN.*) defend, conserve, keep, maintain, guard, preserve, protect, safeguard, rescue, secure, uphold, spare. (*ANT.*) abolish, destroy, abandon, impale, injure.

savory (*SYN.*) delectable, delightful, delicious, palatable, luscious, tasty. (*ANT.*) distasteful, nauseous, acrid, unpalatable, unsavory.

say (*SYN.*) converse, articulate, declare, express, discourse, harangue, talk, speak, tell, utter, remark, state. (*ANT.*) hush, refrain, be silent.

saying (*SYN.*) aphorism, adage, byword, maxim, proverb, motto.

scalding (*SYN.*) hot, scorching, burning, torrid, warm, fervent, ardent, fiery. (*ANT.*) cool, cold, freezing, passionless, frigid, bland.

scale (*SYN.*) balance, proportion, ration, range, climb, mount.

scamp (*SYN.*) troublemaker, rascal.

scan (*SYN.*) examine, study.

scandal (*SYN.*) chagrin, humiliation, abashment, mortification, dishonor, disgrace, disrepute, odium. (*ANT.*) glory, honor, dignity, praise.

scandalize (*SYN.*) asperse, defame, abuse, disparage, revile, vilify, traduce. (*ANT.*) honor, respect, cherish.

scandalous (*SYN.*) disgraceful, discreditable, dishonorable, ignominious, disreputable, shameful. (*ANT.*) honorable, renowned, esteemed.

scant (*SYN.*) succinct, concise, terse, inadequate, deficient, insufficient. (*ANT.*) ample, big, extended, abundant, protracted.

scarce (*SYN.*) occasional, choice, infrequent, exceptional, incomparable, precious, singular, rare, uncommon. (*ANT.*) frequent, ordinary, usual, customary, abundant, numerous, worthless.

scarcely (*SYN.*) barely, hardly.

scarcity (*SYN.*) want, insufficiency, lack, need, dearth. (*ANT.*) abundance.

scare (*SYN.*) alarm, papal, affright, astound, dismay, daunt, frighten, intimidate, horrify, terrorize, shock. (*ANT.*) compose, reassure, soothe.

scared (*SYN.*) apprehensive, afraid, fainthearted, frightened, fearful, timid. (*ANT.*) bold, assured, courageous, composed, sanguine.

scarf (*SYN.*) kerchief.

scatter (*SYN.*) dispel, disperse, diffuse, disseminate, separate, dissipate, spread. (*ANT.*) assemble, accumulate, amass, gather, collect.

scene (*SYN.*) exhibition, view, display.

scent (*SYN.*) fragrance, fume, aroma,

schedule

incense, perfume, odor, redolence, stench, stink, smell.

schedule *(SYN.)* program, timetable.

scheme *(SYN.)* conspiracy, cabal, design, machination, intrigue, plot, plan, chart.

scholar *(SYN.)* intellectual, pupil, learner, disciple, sage, student, savant, teacher. *(ANT.)* dunce, idiot, fool, ignoramus.

scholarly *(SYN.)* bookish, erudite, formal, academic, learned, pedantic, theoretical, scholastic. *(ANT.)* practical, simple.

scholarship *(SYN.)* cognizance, erudition, apprehension, information, learning, knowledge, science, wisdom. *(ANT.)* illiteracy, stupidity, ignorance, misunderstanding.

science *(SYN.)* enlightenment, discipline, knowledge, scholarship. *(ANT.)* superstition, ignorance.

scoff *(SYN.)* ridicule, belittle, mock.

scold *(SYN.)* berate, blame, lecture, rebuke, censure, admonish, reprehend, upbraid, reprimand, criticize. *(ANT.)* commend, praise, approve.

scope *(SYN.)* area, compass, expanse, amount, extent, magnitude, degree, measure, reach, size, range.

scorch *(SYN.)* burn, char, consume, blaze, incinerate, sear, singe, scald. *(ANT.)* put out, quench, extinguish.

score *(SYN.)* reckoning, tally, record, mark, rating.

scorn *(SYN.)* contumely, derision, contempt, detestation, hatred, disdain, despise, hate, spurn, refuse, reject. *(ANT.)* esteem, respect, awe.

scornful *(SYN.)* disdainful, contemptuous.

scoundrel *(SYN.)* rogue, villain, cad.

scour *(SYN.)* wash, clean, scrub.

scourge *(SYN.)* affliction, lash, whip.

scowl *(SYN.)* glower, frown, glare.

scramble *(SYN.)* combine, mix, blend, hasten, clamber, climb.

scrap *(SYN.)* fragment, rag, apportionment, part, portion, piece, section, share, segment, crumb, junk. *(ANT.)* whole, entirety.

scrape *(SYN.)* difficulty, dilemma, condition, fix, predicament, plight, situation,

strait, scour, rub, scratch. *(ANT.)* comfort, ease, calmness.

scratch *(SYN.)* scrape, scar.

scrawny *(SYN.)* gaunt, skinny, spindly. *(ANT.)* husky, burly.

scream *(SYN.)* screech, shriek, yell.

screech *(SYN.)* yell, cry, scream, shriek.

screen *(SYN.)* partition, cover, separation, protection.

scrimp *(SYN.)* skimp, save, economize, conserve.

script *(SYN.)* penmanship, hand, handwriting, text, lines.

scrounge *(SYN.)* sponge, borrow.

scrub *(SYN.)* cleanse, mop, purify, clean, sweep, wash, scour. *(ANT.)* pollute, dirty, stain, sully.

scrupulous *(SYN.)* conscientious, candid, honest, honorable, fair, just, sincere, truthful, upright, painstaking, critical. *(ANT.)* dishonest, fraudulent, lying, deceitful, tricky.

scrutinize *(SYN.)* criticize, appraise, evaluate, examine, inspect, analyze. *(ANT.)* neglect, overlook, approve.

scurrilous *(SYN.)* insulting, outrageous.

scurry *(SYN.)* scamper, scramble, hasten, hustle, hurry.

scuttle *(SYN.)* swamp, ditch, sink.

seal *(SYN.)* emblem, stamp, symbol, crest, signet.

search *(SYN.)* exploration, examination, investigation, inquiry, pursuit, quest, explore, scrutinize, investigate, hunt, probe, rummage, ransack, seek, scour. *(ANT.)* resignation, abandonment.

searching *(SYN.)* inquiring, inquisitive, interrogative, nosy, curious, peeping, peering, snoopy, prying. *(ANT.)* indifferent, unconcerned, incurious, uninterested.

season *(SYN.)* mature, perfect, ripen, develop, age.

seasoned *(SYN.)* veteran, skilled.

secede *(SYN.)* quit, withdraw, resign.

secluded *(SYN.)* deserted, desolate, isolated, alone, lonely, lone, unaided, only, sole, solitary, single, separate, sheltered, hidden, secret. *(ANT.)* surrounded, accompanied.

sensation

seclusion *(SYN.)* insulation, isolation, loneliness, alienation, quarantine, segregation, separation, retirement. *(ANT.)* fellowship, union, connection, association, communion.

secondary *(SYN.)* minor, poorer, inferior, lower, subordinate. *(ANT.)* greater, higher, superior.

secret *(SYN.)* concealed, hidden, latent, covert, private, surreptitious, unknown. *(ANT.)* disclosed, exposed, known, obvious, conspicuous, open, public.

secrete *(SYN.)* clothe, conceal, cover, cloak, curtain, envelop, disguise, hide, mask, guard, protect, shroud, veil. *(ANT.)* divulge, reveal, expose, unveil.

sect *(SYN.)* segment, denomination, faction, group.

section *(SYN.)* district, country, domain, dominion, division, land, place, province, territory, subdivision.

secular *(SYN.)* lay, earthly, laic, mundane, temporal, profane, worldly, temporal. *(ANT.)* religious, spiritual, unworldly, ecclesiastical.

secure *(SYN.)* certain, definite, fixed, assured, indubitable, positive, inevitable, undeniable, sure, unquestionable, firm, *(ANT.)* probable, questionable, uncertain, doubtful, loose, endangered, free.

security *(SYN.)* bond, earnest, pawn, bail, guaranty, pledge, token, surety.

sedate *(SYN.)* controlled, serene, calm, composed, unruffled.

sediment *(SYN.)* residue, lees, dregs, grounds.

see *(SYN.)* contemplate, descry, behold, discern, espy, distinguish, glimpse, inspect, look at, observe, perceive, scan, watch, view, witness, regard, examine, study, notice, eye.

seek *(SYN.)* explore, hunt, examine, look, investigate, probe, ransack, search, scour, rummage, scrutinize.

seem (SYN) look, appear, assume, suggest, resemble, pretend. *(ANT.)* exist, be, disappear, withdraw, vanish.

segment *(SYN.)* apportionment, division, fragment, moiety, allotment, part, portion, piece, scrap, share, section, element, faction, ingredient, interest, side. *(ANT.)* whole, entirety.

segregate *(SYN.)* exclude, separate. *(ANT.)* include, combine.

seize *(SYN.)* check, detain, hinder, apprehend, arrest, obstruct, stop, restrain, withhold, grab, grasp, clutch. *(ANT.)* free, liberate, release, activate, discharge, loosen.

seldom *(SYN.)* infrequently, scarcely, rarely.

select *(SYN.)* cull, opt, pick, choose, elect, prefer. *(ANT.)* reject, refuse.

selection *(SYN.)* election, choice, alternative, option, preference.

self-denial *(SYN.)* abstinence, continence, abstention, forbearance, fasting, sobriety, moderation, temperance. *(ANT.)* gluttony, excess, greed, intoxication, self-indulgence.

self-important *(SYN.)* egotistical, proud, conceited, egocentric.

self-indulgence *(SYN.)* egotism, narrowness, self-centeredness, self-seeking, stinginess. *(ANT.)* charity, magnanimity, altruism, liberality.

selfish *(SYN.)* narrow, self-centered, self-seeking, mercenary, stingy, ungenerous, greedy, mean, miserly. *(ANT.)* charitable.

self-satisfied *(SYN.)* smug, complacent.

sell *(SYN.)* market, retail, merchandise, vend, trade, barter.

send *(SYN.)* discharge, emit, dispatch, cast, propel, impel, throw, transmit, forward, ship, convey, mail. *(ANT.)* get, hold, retain, receive, bring.

senescence *(SYN.)* dotage, senility, age, seniority. *(ANT.)* infancy, youth, childhood.

senile *(SYN.)* antiquated, antique, aged, ancient, archaic, obsolete, old, elderly, old-fashioned, venerable. *(ANT.)* new, youthful, young, modern.

senior *(SYN.)* superior, older, elder. *(ANT.)* minor, junior.

sensation *(SYN.)* feeling, image, impression, apprehension, sense, sensibility, perception, sensitiveness. *(ANT.)*

sensational

insensibility, torpor, stupor, apathy.

sensational *(SYN.)* exciting, marvelous, superb, thrilling, startling, spectacular.

sense *(SYN.)* drift, connotation, explanation, gist, implication, intent, import, interpretation, purport, meaning, purpose, signification, significance, sensation, perception, feeling, awareness, insight, consciousness, appreciate, discern, perceive.

senseless *(SYN.)* dense, dull, crass, brainless, dumb, obtuse, foolish, stupid. *(ANT.)* discerning, intelligent, alert, clever, bright.

sensibility *(SYN.)* sensation, emotion, feeling, passion, tenderness, sentiment. *(ANT.) coldness, imperturbability, anesthesia, insensibility, fact.*

sensible *(SYN.)* apprehensible, perceptible, appreciable, alive, aware, awake, cognizant, comprehending, perceiving, conscious, sentient, intelligent, discreet, practical, judicious, prudent, sagacious, reasonable, sage, sober, wise, sound. *(ANT.) impalpable, imperceptible, absurd, stupid, unaware, foolish.*

sensitive *(SYN.)* perceptive, prone, impressionable, responsive, susceptible, sentient, tender, sore, delicate, tender, tense, touchy, nervous, keen. *(ANT.) dull, hard, callous, insensitive.*

sensual *(SYN.)* lascivious, earthy, lecherous, carnal, sensory, voluptuous, wanton, erotic, lustful, sexual, indecent. *(ANT.) chaste, ascetic, abstemious, virtuous, continent.*

sentence *(SYN.)* convict, condemn. *(ANT.) acquit, pardon, absolve.*

sentiment *(SYN.)* affection, emotion, sensation, feeling, sensibility, passion, tenderness, impression, opinion, attitude. *(ANT.) coldness, imperturbability, insensibility, fact.*

sentimental *(SYN.)* extravagant, fanciful, fantastic, dreamy, fictitious, idealistic, ideal, maudlin, imaginative, mawkish, poetic, romantic, picturesque. *(ANT.) literal, practical, prosaic.*

separate *(SYN.)* part, sever, sunder, divide, allot, dispense, share, distribute, disconnect, split, isolate, segregate, different, distinct, independent. *(ANT.) convene, join, gather, combine.*

separation *(SYN.)* insulation, isolation, loneliness, alienation, quarantine, seclusion, retirement, solitude, segregation, withdrawal. *(ANT.) communion, fellowship, union, association, connection.*

sequence *(SYN.)* chain, graduation, order, progression, arrangement, following, series, succession, train, string.

serene *(SYN.)* composed, imperturbable, calm, dispassionate, pacific, placid, peaceful, quiet, tranquil, still, undisturbed, unruffled. *(ANT.) frantic, turbulent, wild, excited, stormy, agitated, turbulent.*

serenity *(SYN.)* calmness, hush, calm, quiet, peace, quiescence, quietude, rest, repose, stillness, silence, tranquillity. *(ANT.) tumult, excitement, noise, agitation.*

series *(SYN.)* following, chain, arrangement, graduation, progression, order, sequence, train, string.

serious *(SYN.)* important, momentous, great, earnest, grave, sedate, sober, staid, alarming, solemn, critical, dangerous, risky, solemn. *(ANT.) trivial, informal, relaxed, small.*

servant *(SYN.)* attendant, butler, domestic, valet, manservant, maid.

serve *(SYN.)* assist, attend, help, succor, advance, benefit, forward, answer, promote, content, satisfy, suffice, supply, distribute, wait on, aid. *(ANT.) command, direct, dictate, mule.*

service *(SYN.)* advantage, account, avail, benefit, behalf, favor, good, gain, profit, interest. *(ANT.) distress, calamity, trouble, handicap.*

serviceable *(SYN.)* beneficial, good, helpful, advantageous, profitable, salutary, wholesome, useful. *(ANT.) destructive, deleterious, detrimental, injurious, harmful.*

servile *(SYN.)* base, contemptible, despicable, abject, groveling, dishonorable, ignominious, ignoble, lowly, low, menial, mean, sordid, vulgar, vile. *(ANT.) honored, exalted, lofty, esteemed, righteous, noble.*

servitude *(SYN.)* confinement, captivity, bondage, imprisonment, slavery. *(ANT.)* liberation, freedom.

set *(SYN.)* deposit, dispose, lay, arrange, place, put, position, pose, station, appoint, fix, assign, settle, establish. *(ANT.)* mislay, misplace, disturb, remove, disarrange.

settle *(SYN.)* close, conclude, adjudicate, decide, end, resolve, agree upon, establish, satisfy, pay, lodge, locate, reside, determine, abide, terminate. *(ANT.)* suspend, hesitate, doubt, vacillate, waver.

settlement *(SYN.)* completion, close, end, finale, issue, conclusion, termination, deduction, decision, inference. *(ANT.)* commencement, prelude, start, inception, beginning.

sever *(SYN.)* part, divide, sunder, split, cut, separate. *(ANT.)* convene, connect, gather, join, unite, combine.

several *(SYN.)* some, few, a handful.

severe *(SYN.)* arduous, distressing, acute, exacting, hard, harsh, intense, relentless, rigorous, sharp, stem, rigid, stringent, strict, cruel, firm, unyielding, unmitigated, difficult, unpleasant, dangerous, violent. *(ANT.)* genial, indulgent, lenient, yielding, merciful, considerate.

sew *(SYN.)* mend, patch, fix, stitch, refit, restore, repair.

shabby *(SYN.)* indigent, impecunious, needy, penniless, worn, ragged, destitute, poor, threadbare, deficient, inferior, scanty. *(ANT.)* rich, wealthy, ample, affluent, opulent, right, sufficient, good.

shack *(SYN.)* hovel, hut, shanty, shed.

shackle *(SYN.)* chain, fetter, handcuff.

shade *(SYN.)* complexion, dye, hue, paint, color, stain, pigment, darkness, shadow, tincture, dusk, gloom, blacken, darken, conceal, screen, tint, tinge. *(ANT.)* transparency, paleness.

shadowy *(SYN.)* dark, dim, gloomy, murky, black, obscure, dusky, unilluminated, dismal, evil, gloomy, sinister, indistinct, hidden, vague, undefined, wicked, indefinite, mystic, secret, occult. *(ANT.)* bright, clear, light, pleasant, lucid.

shady *(SYN.)* shifty, shaded, questionable, doubtful, devious.

shaggy *(SYN.)* hairy, unkempt, uncombed, woolly.

shake *(SYN.)* flutter, jar, jolt, quake, agitate, quiver, shiver, shudder, rock, totter, sway, tremble, vibrate, waver.

shaky *(SYN.)* questionable, uncertain, iffy, faltering, unsteady. *(ANT.)* sure, definite, positive, certain.

shallow *(SYN.)* exterior, cursory, flimsy, frivolous, slight, imperfect, superficial. *(ANT.)* complete, deep, abstruse, profound, thorough.

sham *(SYN.)* affect, act, feign, assume, pretend, simulate, profess. *(ANT.)* exhibit, display, reveal, expose.

shame *(SYN.)* chagrin, humiliation, abashment, disgrace, mortification, dishonor, ignominy, embarrassment, disrepute, odium, mortify, humiliate, abash, humble, opprobrium, scandal. *(ANT.)* pride, glory, praise, honor.

shameful *(SYN.)* disgraceful, dishonorable, disreputable, discreditable, humiliating, ignominious, scandalous. *(ANT.)* honorable, renowned, respectable, esteemed.

shameless *(SYN.)* unembarrassed, unashamed, brazen, bold, impudent. *(ANT.)* demure, modest.

shape *(SYN.)* create, construct, forge, fashion, form, make, produce, mold, constitute, compose, arrange, combine, organize, frame, outline, figure, invent, appearance, pattern, cast, model, devise. *(ANT.)* disfigure, misshape, dismantle, wreck.

shapeless *(SYN.)* rough, amorphous, vague.

shapely *(SYN.)* attractive, well-formed, curvy, alluring. *(ANT.)* shapeless.

share *(SYN.)* parcel, bit, part, division, portion, ration, piece, fragment, allotment, partake, apportion, participate, divide, section. *(ANT.)* whole.

shared *(SYN.)* joint, common, reciprocal, correlative, mutual.

sharp *(SYN.)* biting, pointed, cunning, acute, keen, rough, fine, cutting, shrill,

sharpen

pungent, witty, acrid, blunt, steep, shrewd. (*ANT.*) *gentle, bland, shallow, smooth, blunt.*

sharpen (*SYN.*) whet, hone, strop.

shatter (*SYN.*) crack, rend, break, pound, smash, burst, demolish, shiver, infringe. (*ANT.*) *renovate, join, repair, mend.*

shattered (*SYN.*) fractured, destroyed, reduced, separated, broken, smashed, flattened, rent, wrecked. (*ANT.*) *united, integral, whole.*

shawl (*SYN.*) stole, scarf.

sheepish (*SYN.*) coy, embarrassed, shy, humble, abashed, diffident, timid, modest, timorous. (*ANT.*) *daring, outgoing, adventurous, gregarious.*

sheer (*SYN.*) thin, transparent, clear, simple, utter, absolute, abrupt, steep, see-through.

sheet (*SYN.*) leaf, layer, coating, film.

shelter (*SYN.*) retreat, safety, cover, asylum, protection, sanctuary, harbor, guard, haven, security. (*ANT.*) *unveil, expose, bare.*

shield (*SYN.*) envelop, cover, clothe, curtain, protest, protection, cloak, guard, conceal, defense, shelter, hide, screen, veil, shroud. (*ANT.*) *unveil, divulge, reveal, bare.*

shift (*SYN.*) move, modify, transfer, substitute, vary, change, alter, spell, turn, transfigure. (*ANT.*) *settle, establish.*

shifting (*SYN.*) wavering, inconstant, changeable, fitful, variable, fickle. (*ANT.*) *uniform, stable, unchanging.*

shiftless (*SYN.*) idle, lazy, slothful. (*ANT.*) *energetic.*

shifty (*SYN.*) shrewd, crafty, tricky.

shilly-shally (*SYN.*) fluctuate, waver, hesitate, vacillate.

shimmer (*SYN.*) glimmer, shine, gleam. (*ANT.*) *dull.*

shine (*SYN.*) flicker, glisten, glow, blaze, glare, flash, beam, shimmer, glimmer, radiate, brush, polish, twinkle, buff, luster, gloss, scintillate, radiance, gleam.

shining (*SYN.*) dazzling, illustrious, showy, superb, brilliant, effulgent, magnificent, splendid, bright. (*ANT.*) *ordinary, dull.*

shiny (*SYN.*) bright, glossy, polished, glistening. (*ANT.*) *lusterless, dull.*

shipshape (*SYN.*) clean, neat. (*ANT.*) *sloppy, messy.*

shiver (*SYN.*) quiver, quake, quaver, tremble, shudder, shake, break, shatter.

shock (*SYN.*) disconcert, astonish, surprise, astound, amaze, clash, disturbance, bewilder, outrage, horrify, revolt, agitation, stagger, blow, impact, collision, surprise, startle, upset, stun.

shocking (*SYN.*) hideous, frightful, severe, appalling, horrible, awful, terrible, dire, fearful. (*ANT.*) *safe, happy, secure, joyous.*

shore (*SYN.*) seaside, beach, coast. (*ANT.*) *inland.*

short (*SYN.*) abrupt, squat, concise, brief, low, curtailed, dumpy, terse, inadequate, succinct, dwarfed, small, abbreviated, lacking, abridge, condensed, undersized, slight, little. (*ANT.*) *extended, protracted.*

shortage (*SYN.*) deficiency, deficit, shortfall. (*ANT.*) *surplus, enough.*

shortcoming (*SYN.*) error, vice, blemish, failure, flaw, omission, failing. (*ANT.*) *perfection, completeness.*

shorten (*SYN.*) curtail, limit, cut, abbreviate, reduce, abridge, lessen, restrict. (*ANT.*) *lengthen, elongate.*

shortening (*SYN.*) reduction, abridgment, abbreviation. (*ANT.*) *enlargement, amplification.*

short-handed (*SYN.*) understaffed.

shortly (*SYN.*) soon, directly, presently.

shortsighted (*SYN.*) myopic, nearsighted, unimaginative, unthinking, thoughtless.

shout (*SYN.*) ejaculate, cry, yell, roar, vociferate, bellow, exclaim. (*ANT.*) *whisper.*

shove (*SYN.*) propel, drive, urge, crowd, jostle, force, push, promote. (*ANT.*) *retreat, falter, oppose, drag, halt.*

shovel (*SYN.*) spade.

show (*SYN.*) flourish, parade, point, reveal, explain, array, movie, production, display, exhibit, note, spectacle, demonstrate, entertainment, tell, usher, guide, prove, indicate, present, lead, demonstration.

showy (*SYN.*) ceremonious, stagy, affected, theatrical, artificial. (*ANT.*) *unaffected, modest, unemotional, subdued.*

shred *(SYN.)* particle, speck, iota, mite, bit, smidgen, tear, slit, cleave, rip, disunite, wound, rend, mince, tatter, lacerate. *(ANT.)* bulk, unite, quantity, mend, aggregate, repair.

shrewd *(SYN.)* cunning, covert, artful, stealthy, foxy, astute, ingenious, guileful, crafty, sly, surreptitious, wily, tricky, clever, intelligent, clandestine. *(ANT.)* frank, sincere, candid, open.

shriek *(SYN.)* screech, scream, howl, yell.

shrill *(SYN.)* keen, penetrating, sharp, acute, piercing, severe. *(ANT.)* gentle, bland, shallow.

shrink *(SYN.)* diminish, shrivel, dwindle.

shrivel *(SYN.)* wizen, waste, droop, decline, sink, dry, languish, wither. *(ANT.)* renew, refresh, revive, rejuvenate.

shun *(SYN.)* escape, avert, forestall, avoid, forbear, evade, ward, elude, dodge, free. *(ANT.)* encounter, confront, meet.

shut *(SYN.)* seal, finish, stop, close, terminate, conclude, clog, end, obstruct. *(ANT.)* begin, open, start, unbar, inaugurate, unlock, commence.

shy *(SYN.)* reserved, fearful, bashful, retiring, cautious, demure, timid, shrinking, wary, chary. *(ANT.)* brazen, bold, immodest, self-confident, audacious.

sick *(SYN.)* ill, morbid, ailing, unhealthy, diseased, unwell, infirm. *(ANT.)* sound, well, robust, strong.

sickness *(SYN.)* illness, ailment, disease, complaint, disorder. *(ANT.)* soundness, healthiness, vigor.

side *(SYN.)* surface, face, foe, opponent, rival, indirect, secondary, unimportant.

siege *(SYN.)* blockade.

sieve *(SYN.)* screen, strainer, colander.

sight *(SYN.)* eyesight, vision, scene, view, display, spectacle, eyesore.

sightless *(SYN.)* unmindful, oblivious, blind, unseeing, heedless, ignorant. *(ANT.)* sensible, discerning, aware, perceiving.

sign *(SYN.)* omen, mark, emblem, token, suggestion, indication, clue, hint, approve, authorize, signal, gesture, symbol, portent.

signal *(SYN.)* beacon, sign, alarm.

significance *(SYN.)* connotation, drift, acceptation, explanation, implication, gist, importance, interpretation, intent, weight, meaning, purpose, purport, sense.

significant *(SYN.)* grave, important, critical, material, indicative, meaningful, crucial, momentous, telling, vital, weighty. *(ANT.)* irrelevant, insignificant, meaningless, unimportant, negligible.

signify *(SYN.)* designate, imply, denote, intimate, reveal, indicate, manifest, mean, communicate, show, specify. *(ANT.)* distract, divert, mislead, conceal.

silence *(SYN.)* motionless, peaceful, placid, hushed, stillness, quiescent, still, soundlessness, quiet, tranquil, noiselessness, hush, muteness, undisturbed. *(ANT.)* strident, loud, racket, disturbed, clamor, agitated.

silent *(SYN.)* dumb, hushed, mute, calm, noiseless, quiet, peaceful, still, soundless, speechless, tranquil, uncommunicative, taciturn. *(ANT.)* communicative, loud, noisy, raucous, talkative, clamorous.

silhouette *(SYN.)* contour, delineation, brief, draft, form, figure, outline, profile, plan, sketch.

silly *(SYN.)* asinine, brainless, crazy, absurd, foolish, irrational, witless, nonsensical, simple, ridiculous, stupid. *(ANT.)* sane, wise, judicious, prudent.

similar *(SYN.)* alike, akin, allied, comparable, analogous, correlative, corresponding, correspondent, parallel, resembling, like. *(ANT.)* dissimilar, divergent, opposed, different, incongruous.

similarity *(SYN.)* likeness, parity, analogy, correspondence, resemblance, similitude. *(ANT.)* distinction, variance, difference.

simple *(SYN.)* effortless, elementary, pure, easy, facile, mere, single, uncompounded, homely, humble, unmixed, plain, artless, naive, frank, natural, unsophisticated, open, asinine, foolish, credulous, silly. *(ANT.)* artful, complex, intricate, adorned.

simpleton *(SYN.)* idiot, fool, ignoramus.

simulate *(SYN.)* copy, counterfeit, duplicate, ape, imitate, impersonate, mock, mimic. (*ANT.*) *distort, diverge, alter, invent.*

sin (*SYN.*) evil, crime, iniquity, transgress, guilt, offense, ungodliness, trespass, vice, transgression, wickedness, wrong. (*ANT.*) *goodness, purity, virtue, righteousness.*

sincere (*SYN.*) earnest, frank, heartfelt, genuine, candid, honest, open, true, straightforward, faithful, truthful, upright, trustworthy, unfeigned. (*ANT.*) *hypocritical, insincere, affected, dishonest, untruthful.*

sincerity (*SYN.*) fairness, frankness, honesty, justice, candor, integrity, openness, responsibility, rectitude, uprightness. (*ANT.*) *deceit, dishonesty, cheating.*

sinful (*SYN.*) bad, corrupt, dissolute, antisocial, immoral, licentious, profligate, evil, indecent, unprincipled, vicious. (*ANT.*) *pure, noble, virtuous.*

sing (*SYN.*) chant, croon, hum, carol, intone, lilt, warble.

singe (*SYN.*) burn, char, consume, blaze, incinerate, scorch, sear, scald. (*ANT.*) *put out, quench, extinguish.*

single (*SYN.*) individual, marked, particular, distinctive, separate, special, specific, lone, one, solitary, sole, unwed, unmarried, singular, unique. (*ANT.*) *ordinary, universal, general.*

singular (*SYN.*) exceptional, eccentric, odd, peculiar, rate, extraordinary, strange, unusual, striking, characteristic, remarkable, rare, individual, distinctive, uncommon, special. (*ANT.*) *normal, ordinary.*

sink (*SYN.*) diminish, droop, subside, hang, decline, fall, extend, downward, drop, descend. (*ANT.*) *mount, climb, soar, arise.*

sinless (*SYN.*) faultless, holy, immaculate, perfect, blameless, holy, consummate, ideal, excellent, superlative, supreme. (*ANT.*) *defective, faulty, imperfect.*

sip (*SYN.*) drink, taste, swallow.

sire (*SYN.*) breed, create, father, engender, beget, generate, procreate, originate, produce, propagate. (*ANT.*) *destroy, ill, extinguish, murder, abort.*

site (*SYN.*) place, position, location, situation, station, locality.

situation (*SYN.*) circumstance, plight, state, site, location, placement, locale, predicament, position, state, condition.

size (*SYN.*) bigness, bulk, dimensions, expanse, amplitude, measurement, area, extent, largeness, magnitude, mass, greatness, volume.

skeptic (*SYN.*) doubter, infidel, agnostic, deist, questioner, unbeliever. (*ANT.*) *believer, worshiper, adorer.*

skepticism (*SYN.*) hesitation, questioning, wavering, doubting, distrust, mistrust, suspicion. (*ANT.*) *confidence, reliance, trust.*

sketch (*SYN.*) draft, figure, form, outline, contour, delineation, drawing, picture, represent, silhouette, draw, profile.

sketchy (*SYN.*) indefinite, vague, incomplete, indistinct. (*ANT.*) *definite, detailed, complete.*

skill (*SYN.*) cunning, deftness, dexterity, ability, adroitness, cleverness, talent, readiness, skillfulness. (*ANT.*) *ineptitude, inability.*

skillful (*SYN.*) adept, clever, able, accomplished, competent, expert, ingenious, cunning, proficient, practiced, versed, skilled. (*ANT.*) *untrained, inept, clumsy, inexpert, bungling, awkward.*

skimpy (*SYN.*) cheap, scanty, meager. (*ANT.*) *abundant, generous.*

skin (*SYN.*) outside, covering, peel, rind, shell, pare.

skinny (*SYN.*) gaunt, thin, raw-boned. (*ANT.*) *fat, hefty, heavy.*

skip (*SYN.*) drop, eliminate, ignore, exclude, cancel, delete, disregard, omit, overlook, neglect, miss. (*ANT.*) *notice, introduce, include, insert.*

skirmish (*SYN.*) brawl, battle, conflict, combat, dispute, encounter, contend, quarrel, squabble, scuffle, wrangle.

slack (*SYN.*) lax, limp, indefinite, free, disengaged, unbound, untied, unfastened, vague, dissolute, heedless, careless, unrestrained, limp, lazy, loose, inactive, sluggish, wanton. (*ANT.*) *restrained, tied, right, stiff, taunt, rigid, fast, inhibited.*

slander (*SYN.*) libel, calumny, backbiting,

aspersion, scandal, vilification. (*ANT.*) *praise, flattery, commendation, defense.*

slang (*SYN.*) jargon, dialect.

slant (*SYN.*) disposition, inclination, bias, bent, partiality, slope, tilt, pitch, penchant, prejudice, proneness, proclivity, turn, incline, lean, tendency. (*ANT.*) *justice, fairness, impartiality, equity.*

slash (*SYN.*) gash, cut, slit, lower, reduce.

slaughter (*SYN.*) butcher, kill, massacre, slay, butchering, killing.

slave (*SYN.*) bondservant, serf.

slavery (*SYN.*) captivity, imprisonment, serfdom, confinement, bondage, thralldom, servitude, enslavement. (*ANT.*) *freedom, liberation.*

slay (*SYN.*) assassinate, kill, murder.

sleek (*SYN.*) smooth, polished, slick. (*ANT.*) *blunt, harsh, rough, rugged.*

sleep (*SYN.*) drowse, nap, nod, catnap, repose, doze, rest, slumber, snooze.

sleepy (*SYN.*) tired, drowsy, nodding.

slender (*SYN.*) lank, lean, meager, emaciated, gaunt, scanty, rare, skinny, scrawny, slight, spare, trim, slim, tenuous, thin. (*ANT.*) *fat, broad, overweight, thick, wide, bulky.*

slide (*SYN.*) glide, slip, skim, skid.

slight (*SYN.*) lank, lean, meager, emaciated, gaunt, fine, narrow, scanty, scrawny, skinny, sparse, small, rare, slender, spare, insignificant, tenuous, unimportant, slim, thin. (*ANT.*) *regarded, notice, enormous, large, major, huge, include.*

slim (*SYN.*) thin, slender, lank, slight, weak, insignificant, unimportant.

slip (*SYN.*) error, fault, inaccuracy, shift, err, slide, mistake, glide, blunder. (*ANT.*) *precision, truth, accuracy.*

slipshod (*SYN.*) sloppy, careless. (*ANT.*) *careful.*

slit (*SYN.*) slash, cut, tear, slot.

slogan (*SYN.*) catchword, motto.

slope (*SYN.*) incline, leaning, inclination, bending, slant.

sloth (*SYN.*) indolence, idleness, inactivity, inertia, sluggishness, torpidity. (*ANT.*) *alertness, assiduousness, diligence, activity.*

slothful (*SYN.*) indolent, idle, inactive, lazy, inert, supine, sluggish, torpid. (*ANT.*) *alert, diligent, active, assiduous.*

slovenly (*SYN.*) sloppy, bedraggled, unkempt, messy. (*ANT.*) *meticulous, neat.*

slow (*SYN.*) deliberate, dull, delaying, dawdling, gradual, leisurely, tired, sluggish, unhurried, behindhand, delayed. (*ANT.*) *rapid, quick, swift, speedy, fast.*

sluggish (*SYN.*) dull, deliberate, dawdling, delaying, laggard, gradual, leisurely, tired, slow, lethargic. (*ANT.*) *quick, raid, fast, speedy, swift, energetic, vivacious.*

slumber (*SYN.*) drowse, catnap, nod, doze, repose, sleep, rest, snooze.

slump (*SYN.*) drop, decline, descent.

sly (*SYN.*) covert, artful, astute, crafty, clandestine, foxy, furtive, cunning, insidious, guileful, stealthy, subtle, shrewd, tricky, surreptitious, underhand, wily, secretive. (*ANT.*) *sincere, ingenuous, open, candid.*

small (*SYN.*) little, minute, petty, diminutive, puny, wee, tiny, trivial, slight, miniature. (*ANT.*) *immense, enormous, large, huge.*

smart (*SYN.*) dexterous, quick, skillful, adroit, apt, clever, bright, witty, ingenious, sharp, intelligent. (*ANT.*) *foolish, stupid, unskilled, awkward, clumsy, bungling, slow, dumb.*

smash (*SYN.*) burst, crush, demolish, destroy, break, crack, fracture, pound, fringe, rack, rupture, shatter, rend. (*ANT.*) *mend, renovate, restore, repair.*

smear (*SYN.*) wipe, rub, spread.

smell (*SYN.*) fragrance, fume, odor, perfume, incense, aroma, fetidness, stench, stink, scent, sniff, detect, bouquet.

smidgen (*SYN.*) crumb, mite, small, bit, particle, shred, speck, scrap. (*ANT.*) *bulk, mass, quantity, aggregate.*

smile (*SYN.*) grin. (*ANT.*) *frown.*

smite (*SYN.*) knock, hit, dash, beat, belabor, buffet, pound, punch, pummel, thrash, thump, defeat, overthrow, overpower, subdue, vanquish, rout. (*ANT.*) *surrender, fail, defend, shield, stroke.*

smooth

smooth *(SYN.)* polished, sleek, slick, glib, diplomatic, flat, level, plain, suave, urbane, even, unwrinkled. *(ANT.) rugged, harsh, rough, blunt, bluff, uneven.*

smother *(SYN.)* suffocate, asphyxiate, stifle.

smutty *(SYN.)* disgusting, filthy, impure, coarse, dirty, lewd, offensive, obscene, pornographic. *(ANT.) modest, refined, decent, pure.*

snag *(SYN.)* difficulty, bar, barrier, check, hindrance, obstruction. *(ANT.) assistance, help, encouragement.*

snappish *(SYN.)* ill-natured, ill-tempered, fractious, irritable, fretful, peevish, testy, touchy, petulant. *(ANT.) good-tempered, pleasant, good-natured, affable, genial.*

snappy *(SYN.)* quick, stylish, chic.

snare *(SYN.)* capture, catch, arrest, clutch, grasp, grip, lay, apprehend, seize, trap, net. *(ANT.) throw, release, lose, liberate.*

snarl *(SYN.)* growl.

snatch *(SYN.)* grasp, seize, grab.

sneak *(SYN.)* steal, skulk, slink.

sneer *(SYN.)* flout, jeer, mock, gibe, deride, taunt, scoff, scorn. *(ANT.) laud, flatter, praise, compliment.*

sneering *(SYN.)* derision, gibe, banter, jeering, mockery, raillery, sarcasm, ridicule, satire.

sniveling *(SYN.)* whimpering, sniffling, weepy, whining, blubbering.

snobbish *(SYN.)* uppity, conceited, snobby, snotty.

snoopy *(SYN.)* inquisitive, interrogative, curious, inquiring, meddling, peeping, prying, peering. *(ANT.) uninterested, incurious, unconcerned, indifferent.*

snub *(SYN.)* rebuke, insult, slight.

snug *(SYN.)* constricted, close, contracted, compact, firm, narrow, taut, tense, stretched, tight, cozy, comfortable, sheltered. *(ANT.) loose, lax, slack, relaxed, open.*

soak *(SYN.)* saturate, drench, steep, wet.

soar *(SYN.)* flutter, fly, flit, float, glide, sail, hover. *(ANT.) plummet, sink, fall, descend.*

sob *(SYN.)* weep, cry, lament.

sober *(SYN.)* sedate, serious, staid, earnest, grave, solemn, moderate. *(ANT.) ordinary, joyful, informal, boisterous, drunk, fuddled, inebriated.*

sobriety *(SYN.)* forbearance, abstinence, abstention, self-denial, moderation, temperance. *(ANT.) self-indulgence, excess, intoxication.*

social *(SYN.)* friendly, civil, gregarious, affable, communicative, hospitable, sociable, group, common, genial, polite. *(ANT.) inhospitable, hermitic, antisocial, disagreeable.*

society *(SYN.)* nation, community, civilization, organization, club, association, fraternity, circle, association, company, companionship.

soft *(SYN.)* gentle, lenient, flexible, compassionate, malleable, meek, mellow, subdued, mild, tender, supple, yielding, pliable, elastic, pliant. *(ANT.) unyielding, rough, hard, tough, rigid.*

soften *(SYN.)* assuage, diminish, abate, allay, alleviate, mitigate, relieve, soothe. *(ANT.) irritate, increase, aggravate, agitate.*

soil *(SYN.)* defile, discolor, spot, befoul, blemish, blight, stain, sully, earth, dirt, loam, dirty. *(ANT.) purify, honor, cleanse, bleach, decorate.*

solace *(SYN.)* contentment, ease, enjoyment, comfort, consolation, relief, succor. *(ANT.) torture, torment, misery, affliction, discomfort.*

sole *(SYN.)* isolated, desolate, deserted, secluded, unaided, lone, alone, only, single, solitary. *(ANT.) surrounded, accompanied, attended.*

solemn *(SYN.)* ceremonious, imposing, formal, impressive, reverential, ritualistic, grave, sedate, earnest, sober, staid, serious, dignified. *(ANT.) ordinary, joyful, informal, boisterous, cheerful, gay, happy.*

solicit *(SYN.)* beg, beseech, request, seek, pray.

solicitous *(SYN.)* anxious, concerned.

solicitude *(SYN.)* concern, worry, anxiety, care, attention, regard, vigilance, caution, wariness. *(ANT.) indifference, disregard, neglect, negligence.*

solid *(SYN.)* hard, dense, compact, firm. *(ANT.)* loose.

solitary *(SYN.)* isolated, alone, lonely, deserted, unaided, secluded, only, single, lone, sole. *(ANT.)* surrounded, attended, accompanied.

solitude *(SYN.)* loneliness, privacy, refuge, retirement, seclusion, retreat, alienation, asylum, concealment. *(ANT.)* publicity, exposure, notoriety.

solution *(SYN.)* explanation, answer.

solve *(SYN.)* explain, answer, unravel.

somatic *(SYN.)* corporeal, corporal, natural, material, bodily, physical. *(ANT.)* spiritual, mental.

somber *(SYN.)* dismal, dark, bleak, doleful, cheerless, natural, physical, serious, sober, gloomy, grave. *(ANT.)* lively, joyous, cheerful, happy.

sometimes *(SYN.)* occasionally. *(ANT.)* invariably, always.

soon *(SYN.)* shortly, early, betimes, beforehand. *(ANT.)* tardy, late, overdue, belated.

soothe *(SYN.)* encourage, console, solace, comfort, cheer, gladden, sympathize, calm, pacify. *(ANT.)* dishearten, depress, antagonize, aggravate, disquiet, upset, unnerve.

soothing *(SYN.)* gentle, benign, docile, calm, mild, placid, peaceful, serene, soft, relaxed, tractable, tame. *(ANT.)* violent, savage, fierce, harsh.

sophisticated *(SYN.)* cultured, worldly, blase, cultivated, urbane, cosmopolitan, suave, intricate, complex, advanced. *(ANT.)* uncouth, ingenuous, simple, naive, crude.

sorcery *(SYN.)* enchantment, conjuring, art, charm, black magic, voodoo, witchcraft, wizardry.

sordid *(SYN.)* vicious, odious, revolting, obscene, foul, loathsome, base, depraved, debased, vile, vulgar, abject, wicked, ignoble, despicable, mean, low, worthless, wretched, dirty, unclean. *(ANT.)* upright, decent, honorable.

sore *(SYN.)* tender, sensitive, aching, hurting, painful.

sorrow *(SYN.)* grief, distress, heartache, anguish, misery, sadness, mourning, trial, tribulation, gloom, depression. *(ANT.)* consolation, solace, joy, happiness, comfort.

sorrowful *(SYN.)* dismal, doleful, dejected, despondent, depressed, disconsolate, gloomy, melancholy, glum, moody, somber, sad, grave, aggrieved. *(ANT.)* merry, happy, cheerful, joyous.

sorry *(SYN.)* hurt, pained, sorrowful, afflicted, grieved, contrite, repentant, paltry, poor, wretched, remorseful, mean, shabby, contemptible, worthless, vile, regretful, apologetic. *(ANT.)* delighted, impenitent, cheerful, unrepentant, splendid.

sort *(SYN.)* class, stamp, category, description, nature, character, kind, type, variety. *(ANT.)* peculiarity, deviation.

sound *(SYN.)* effective, logical, telling, binding, powerful, weighty, legal, strong, conclusive, valid. *(ANT.)* weak, null, counterfeit.

sour *(SYN.)* glum, sullen, bitter, peevish, acid, rancid, tart, acrimonious, sharp, bad-tempered, unpleasant, cranky. *(ANT.)* wholesome, kindly, genial, benevolent, sweet.

source *(SYN.)* birth, foundation, agent, determinant, reason, origin, cause, start, incentive, motive, spring, inducement, principle, beginning. *(ANT.)* product, harvest, outcome, issue, consequence, end.

souvenir *(SYN.)* memento, monument, commemoration, remembrance.

sovereign *(SYN.)* monarch, king, emperor, queen, empress.

sovereignty *(SYN.)* command, influence, authority, predominance, control, sway. *(ANT.)* debility, incapacity, disablement, ineptitude, impotence.

space *(SYN.)* room, area, location.

spacious *(SYN.)* capacious, large, vast, ample, extensive, wide, roomy, large. *(ANT.)* limited, narrow, small, cramped.

span *(SYN.)* spread, extent.

spare *(SYN.)* preserve, safeguard, uphold, conserve, protect, defend, rescue, reserve, additional, unoccupied. *(ANT.)* impair, abolish, injure, abandon.

sparing

sparing *(SYN.)* economical, thrifty, frugal. *(ANT.)* lavish.

sparkle *(SYN.)* gleam, glitter, twinkle, beam, glisten, radiate, shine, blaze.

spat *(SYN.)* quarrel, dispute, affray, wrangle, altercation. *(ANT.)* peace, friendliness, agreement, reconciliation.

spawn *(SYN.)* yield, bear.

speak *(SYN.)* declare, express, say, articulate, harangue, converse, talk, utter. *(ANT.)* refrain, hush, quiet.

special *(SYN.)* individual, uncommon, distinctive, peculiar, exceptional, unusual, extraordinary, different, particular. *(ANT.) general, widespread, broad, prevailing, average, ordinary.*

specialist *(SYN.)* authority, expert.

species *(SYN.)* variety, type, kind, class, sort.

specific *(SYN.)* limited, characteristic, definite, peculiar, explicit, categorical, particular, distinct, precise. *(ANT.) generic, general, nonspecific.*

specify *(SYN.)* name, call, mention, appoint, denominate, designate, define. *(ANT.) miscall, hint.*

specimen *(SYN.)* prototype, example, sample, model, pattern, type.

speck *(SYN.)* scrap, jot, bit, mite, smidgen, crumb, iota, particle, spot. *(ANT.) quantity, bulk, aggregate.*

spectacle *(SYN.)* demonstration, ostentation, movie, array, exhibition, show, display, performance, parade, splurge.

spectator *(SYN.)* viewer, observer.

speculate *(SYN.)* assume, deduce, surmise, apprehend, imagine, consider, view, think, guess, suppose, conjecture. *(ANT.) prove, demonstrate, conclude.*

speech *(SYN.)* gossip, discourse, talk, chatter, lecture, conference, discussion, address, dialogue, articulation, accent. *(ANT.) silence, correspondence, writing, meditation.*

speed *(SYN.)* forward, push, accelerate, hasten, rapidity, dispatch, swiftness. *(ANT.) impede, slow, block, retard.*

spellbound *(SYN.)* fascinated, entranced, hypnotized, mesmerized, rapt.

spend *(SYN.)* pay, disburse, consume. *(ANT.) hoard, save.*

spendthrift *(SYN.)* squanderer, profligate.

sphere *(SYN.)* globe, orb, ball, environment, area, domain.

spherical *(SYN.)* round, curved, globular.

spicy *(SYN.)* hot, indecent, off-color, suggestive, indelicate.

spin *(SYN.)* revolve, turn, rotate, whirl, twirl, tell, narrate, relate.

spine *(SYN.)* vertebrae, backbone.

spineless *(SYN.)* weak, limp, cowardly. *(ANT.) brave, strong, courageous.*

spirit *(SYN.)* courage, phantom, verve, fortitude, apparition, mood, soul, ghost. *(ANT.) listlessness, substance, languor.*

spirited *(SYN.)* excited, animated, lively, active, vigorous, energetic. *(ANT.) indolent, lazy, sleepy.*

spiritless *(SYN.)* gone, lifeless, departed, dead, insensible, deceased, unconscious. *(ANT.) stirring, alive, living.*

spiritual *(SYN.)* sacred, unearthly, holy, divine, immaterial, supernatural. *(ANT.) material, physical, corporeal.*

spite *(SYN.)* grudge, rancor, malice, animosity, malevolence, malignity. *(ANT.) kindness, toleration, affection.*

spiteful *(SYN.)* vicious, disagreeable, surly, ill-natured. *(ANT.) pretty, beautiful, attractive, fair.*

splendid *(SYN.)* glorious, illustrious, radiant, brilliant, showy, superb, bright. *(ANT.) ordinary, mediocre, dull.*

splendor *(SYN.)* effulgence, radiance, brightness, luster, magnificence, display. *(ANT.) darkness, obscurity, dullness.*

splinter *(SYN.)* fragment, piece, sliver, chip, shiver.

split *(SYN.)* rend, shred, cleave, disunite, sever, break, divide, opening, lacerate. *(ANT.) repair, unite, join, sew.*

spoil *(SYN.)* rot, disintegrate, waste, decay, ruin, damage, mold, destroy. *(ANT.) luxuriate, grow, flourish.*

spoken *(SYN.)* verbal, pronounced, articulated, vocal, uttered, oral. *(ANT.)*

written, documentary.

spokesman *(SYN.)* agent, representative.

spontaneous *(SYN.)* impulsive, voluntary, automatic, instinctive, willing, extemporaneous, natural, unconscious. *(ANT.) planned, rehearsed, forced, studied, prepared.*

sport *(SYN.)* match, play, amusement, fun, pastime, entertainment, athletics.

sporting *(SYN.)* considerate, fair, sportsmanlike.

spot *(SYN.)* blemish, mark, stain, flaw, blot, location, place, site, splatter.

spotty *(SYN.)* erratic, uneven, irregular, inconsistent. *(ANT.) regular, even.*

spout *(SYN.)* spurt, squirt, tube, nozzle.

spray *(SYN.)* splash, spatter, sprinkle.

spread *(SYN.)* unfold, distribute, open, disperse, unroll, unfurl, scatter, jelly. *(ANT.) shut, close, hide, conceal.*

sprightly *(SYN.)* blithe, hopeful, vivacious, buoyant, lively, light, nimble. *(ANT.) hopeless, depressed, sullen, dejected, despondent.*

spring *(SYN.)* commencement, foundation, start, beginning, inception, jump, cradle, begin, birth, bound, originate. *(ANT.) issue, product, end.*

sprinkle *(SYN.)* strew, spread, scatter, rain.

spruce *(SYN.)* orderly, neat, trim, clear, nice. *(ANT.) unkempt, sloppy, dirty.*

spry *(SYN.)* brisk, quick, agile, nimble, energetic, supple, alert, active, lively. *(ANT.) heavy, sluggish, inert, clumsy.*

spur *(SYN.)* inducement, purpose, cause, motive, impulse, reason, incitement. *(ANT.) effort, action, result, attempt.*

squabble *(SYN.)* bicker, debate, altercate, contend, discuss, argue, quarrel. *(ANT.) concede, agree, assent.*

squalid *(SYN.)* base, indecent, grimy, dirty, pitiful, filthy, muddy, nasty. *(ANT.) wholesome, clean, pure.*

squander *(SYN.)* scatter, lavish, consume, dissipate, misuse. *(ANT.) preserve, conserve, save, accumulate.*

squeamish *(SYN.)* particular, careful.

stab *(SYN.)* stick, gore, pierce, knife, spear, bayonet.

stability *(SYN.)* steadiness, balance, proportion, composure, symmetry. *(ANT.) imbalance, fall, unsteadiness.*

stable *(SYN.)* firm, enduring, constant, fixed, unwavering, steadfast, steady. *(ANT.) irresolute, variable, changeable.*

stack *(SYN.)* mass, pile, mound, heap, accumulate.

staff *(SYN.)* pole, stick, club, personnel, crew, employees.

stage *(SYN.)* frame, platform, boards, theater, scaffold, period, phase, step, direct, produce, present.

stagger *(SYN.)* totter, sway, reel, vary, falter, alternate.

staid *(SYN.)* solemn, sedate, earnest, sober, grave. *(ANT.) joyful, informal, ordinary.*

stain *(SYN.)* blight, dye, tint, befoul, spot, defile, mark, dishonor, disgrace, smirch, blot, tint, blemish, discolor, color, tinge. *(ANT.) honor, bleach, decorate, purify.*

stair *(SYN.)* staircase, stairway, steps.

stake *(SYN.)* rod, pole, picket, post, pale, bet, wager, concern, interest.

stale *(SYN.)* tasteless, spoiled, old, inedible, dry, uninteresting, trite, flat, dull, vapid, insipid. *(ANT.) new, fresh, tasty.*

stalk *(SYN.)* dog, follow, track, shadow, hunt.

stall *(SYN.)* hesitate, stop, delay, postpone.

stammer *(SYN.)* falter, stutter.

stamp *(SYN.)* crush, trample, imprint, mark, brand, block, seal, die.

stand *(SYN.)* tolerate, suffer, stay, stand up, endure, bear, abide, halt, arise, rise, remain, sustain, rest. *(ANT.) run, yield, advance.*

standard *(SYN.)* law, proof, pennant, emblem, touchstone, measure, example, gauge, model, banner, symbol, test. *(ANT.) guess, chance, irregular, unusual, supposition.*

standing *(SYN.)* rank, position, station, status.

standpoint *(SYN.)* position, viewpoint, attitude.

staple *(SYN.)* main, principal, chief, essential, necessary.

stare *(SYN.)* gaze.

stark *(SYN.)* utter, absolute, sheer, complete,

start

rough, severe, harsh, grim.

start *(SYN.)* opening, source, commence, onset, surprise, shock, beginning, origin, begin, initiate, jerk, jump, advantage, lead, commencement, outset. *(ANT.)* end, completion, termination, close.

startle *(SYN.)* astonish, disconcert, aback, alarm, shock, agitate, surprise, astound, amaze, stun. *(ANT.)* caution, prepare, admonish, forewarn.

starved *(SYN.)* longing, voracious, hungry, craving, avid, famished. *(ANT.)* satisfied, sated, gouged, full.

state *(SYN.)* circumstance, predicament, case, situation, condition, affirm, declare, express, nation, country, status, assert, recite, tell, recount. *(ANT.)* imply, conceal, retract.

stately *(SYN.)* lordly, elegant, regal, sovereign, impressive, magnificent, courtly, grand, imposing, majestic, noble, supreme, dignified. *(ANT.)* low, common, mean, servile, humble, vulgar.

statement *(SYN.)* announcement, mention, allegation, declaration, thesis, assertion, report.

station *(SYN.)* post, depot, terminal, position, place.

statuesque *(SYN.)* imposing, stately, regal, majestic, dignified.

status *(SYN.)* place, caste, standing, condition, state, rank, position.

statute *(SYN.)* law, ruling, decree, rule. *(ANT.)* intention, deliberation.

staunch *(SYN.)* faithful, true, constant, reliable, loyal, devoted. *(ANT.)* treacherous, untrustworthy.

stay *(SYN.)* delay, continue, hinder, check, hold, hindrance, support, brace, line, rope, linger, sojourn, abide, halt, stand, rest, remain, tarry, arrest, wait. *(ANT.)* hasten, progress, go, depart, advance, leave.

stead *(SYN.)* place.

steadfast *(SYN.)* solid, inflexible, constant, stable, unyielding, secure. *(ANT.)* unstable, insecure, unsteady.

steadfastness *(SYN.)* persistence, industry, tenacity, constancy, persistency.

(ANT.) laziness, sloth, cessation.

steady *(SYN.)* regular, even, unremitting, stable, steadfast, firm, reliable, solid.

steal *(SYN.)* rob, swipe, burglarize, pilfer, shoplift, embezzle, snitch. *(ANT.)* restore, buy, return, refund.

stealthy *(SYN.)* sly, secret, furtive. *(ANT.)* direct, open, obvious.

steep *(SYN.)* sharp, hilly, sheer, abrupt, perpendicular, precipitous. *(ANT.)* gradual, level, flat.

steer *(SYN.)* manage, guide, conduct, lead, supervise, navigate, drive, control, direct.

stem *(SYN.)* stalk, trunk, arise, check, stop, originate, hinder.

stench *(SYN.)* odor, fetor, fetidness, stink, aroma, smell, fume, scent.

step *(SYN.)* stride, pace, stage, move, action, measure, come, go, walk.

stern *(SYN.)* harsh, rigid, exacting, rigorous, sharp, severe, strict, hard, unyielding, unmitigated, stringent. *(ANT.)* indulgent, forgiving, yielding, lenient, considerate.

stew *(SYN.)* ragout, goulash, boil, simmer.

stick *(SYN.)* stalk, twig, rod, staff, pole, pierce, spear, stab, puncture, gore, cling, adhere, hold, catch, abide, remain, persist.

stickler *(SYN.)* nitpicker, perfectionist, disciplinarian.

sticky *(SYN.)* tricky, delicate, awkward.

stiff *(SYN.)* severe, unbendable, unyielding, harsh, inflexible, unbending, rigid, firm, hard, solid, rigorous. *(ANT.)* supple, yielding, compassionate, mild, lenient, resilient.

stifle *(SYN.)* choke, strangle, suffocate.

stigma *(SYN.)* trace, scar, blot, stain, mark, vestige.

still *(SYN.)* peaceful, undisturbed, but, mild, hushed, calm, patient, modest, nevertheless, motionless, meek, quiescent, stationary, besides, however, quiet, hush, tranquil, serene, placid. *(ANT.)* agitated, loud.

stimulate *(SYN.)* irritate, excite, arouse, disquiet, rouse, activate, urge, invigorate, animate, provoke. *(ANT.)* quell, calm, quiet.

stimulus *(SYN.)* motive, goad, arousal, provocation, encouragement. *(ANT.)* discouragement, depressant.

stingy *(SYN.)* greedy, penurious, avaricious, mean, penny-pinching, cheap, selfish, miserly, tight, tightfisted. *(ANT.)* munificent, generous, giving, extravagant, openhanded, bountiful.

stipend *(SYN.)* payment, earnings, salary, allowance, pay, compensation, wages. *(ANT.)* gratuity, gift.

stipulate *(SYN.)* require, demand.

stir *(SYN.)* instigate, impel, push, agitate, induce, mix, rouse, move, propel. *(ANT.)* halt, stop, deter.

stock *(SYN.)* hoard, store, strain, accumulation, supply, carry, keep, provision, fund, breed, sort. *(ANT.)* sameness, likeness, homogeneity, uniformity.

stoical *(SYN.)* passive, forbearing, uncomplaining, composed, patient. *(ANT.)* turbulent, chafing, hysterical.

stolid *(SYN.)* obtuse, unsharpened, dull, blunt, edgeless. *(ANT.)* suave, tactful, polished, subtle.

stone *(SYN.)* pebble, gravel, rock.

stony *(SYN.)* insensitive, unsentimental, cold.

stoop *(SYN.)* bow, bend, lean, crouch.

stop *(SYN.)* terminate, check, abstain, hinder, arrest, close, bar, cork, halt, end, conclude, obstruct, finish, quit, pause, discontinue, stay, impede, cease. *(ANT.)* start, proceed, speed, begin.

store *(SYN.)* amass, hoard, collect, market, shop, reserve, supply, deposit, bank, save, accrue, increase, stock. *(ANT.)* dissipate, waste, disperse.

storm *(SYN.)* gale, tempest, tornado, thunderstorm, hurricane, rage, rant, assault, besiege.

stormy *(SYN.)* rough, inclement, windy, blustery, roaring, tempestuous. *(ANT.)* quiet, calm, tranquil, peaceful.

story *(SYN.)* yarn, novel, history, tale, falsehood, account, fable, anecdote, narrative, fabrication, lie, level, floor, fiction, report.

stout *(SYN.)* plump, obese, chubby, fat, paunchy, overweight, portly, heavy, sturdy, strong, pudgy, thickset. *(ANT.)* thin, slender, flimsy, gaunt, slim.

straight *(SYN.)* erect, honorable, square, just, direct, undeviating, unbent, right, upright, honest, uncurving, directly, moral, correct, orderly, vertical. *(ANT.)* dishonest, bent, circuitous, twisted, crooked.

straightforward *(SYN.)* forthright, direct, open, candid, aboveboard. *(ANT.)* devious.

strain *(SYN.)* stock, kind, variety, stretch, breed, tighten, harm, injure, screen, filter, sprain, sort.

strainer *(SYN.)* colander, sieve, filter.

strait *(SYN.)* fix, situation, passage, condition, dilemma, channel, trouble, predicament, difficulty, distress, crisis. *(ANT.)* ease, calmness, satisfaction, comfort.

strange *(SYN.)* bizarre, peculiar, odd, abnormal, irregular, unusual, curious, uncommon, singular, extraordinary, foreign, eccentric, unfamiliar, queer. *(ANT.)* regular, common, familiar, conventional.

stranger *(SYN.)* foreigner, outsider, newcomer, alien, outlander, immigrant. *(ANT.)* friend, associate, acquaintance.

strap *(SYN.)* strip, belt, thong, band.

stratagem *(SYN.)* design, ruse, cabal, plot, machination, subterfuge, trick, wile, conspiracy.

strategy *(SYN.)* technique, management, tactics, approach.

stray *(SYN.)* ramble, rove, deviate, lost, strayed, wander, digress, roam, stroll. *(ANT.)* linger, stop, halt, settle.

stream *(SYN.)* issue, proceed, flow, come, abound, spout, run, brook.

street *(SYN.)* way, road, boulevard, avenue.

strength *(SYN.)* power, might, toughness, durability, soundness, vigor, potency. *(ANT.)* weakness, frailty, feebleness.

strengthen *(SYN.)* verify, assure, confirm, fix, sanction, ratify, substantiate.

strenuous *(SYN.)* forceful, energetic, active, vigorous, determined.

stress *(SYN.)* urgency, press, emphasize, accentuate, accent, weight, strain, importance, compulsion, pressure. *(ANT.)* relaxation, lenience, ease.

stretch *(SYN.)* strain, expand, elongate, extend, lengthen, spread, distend, protract,

strict

distort. *(ANT.)* tighten, loosen, slacken, contract.

strict *(SYN.)* rough, stiff, stringent, harsh, unbending, severe, rigorous. *(ANT.)* easygoing, lenient, mild.

strife *(SYN.)* disagreement, conflict, discord, quarrel, difference, unrest. *(ANT.)* tranquillity, peace, concord.

strike *(SYN.)* pound, hit, smite, beat, assault, attack, affect, impress, overwhelm, sit down, walkout, slowdown.

striking *(SYN.)* arresting, imposing, splendid, august, impressive, thrilling, stirring, awesome, awe-inspiring. *(ANT.)* ordinary, unimpressive, commonplace, regular.

stringent *(SYN.)* harsh, rugged, grating, severe, gruff.

strip *(SYN.)* disrobe, undress, remove, uncover, peel, ribbon, band, piece.

stripped *(SYN.)* open, simple, bare, nude, uncovered, exposed, bald, plain, naked, barren, defenseless. *(ANT.)* protected, dressed, concealed.

strive *(SYN.)* aim, struggle, attempt, undertake, design, endeavor, try. *(ANT.)* omit, abandon, neglect, decline.

stroke *(SYN.)* rap, blow, tap, knock, feat, achievement, accomplishment, caress.

stroll *(SYN.)* amble, walk, ramble.

strong *(SYN.)* potent, hale, athletic, mighty, sturdy, impregnable, resistant. *(ANT.)* feeble, insipid, brittle, weak, bland, fragile.

structure *(SYN.)* construction, framework, arrangement.

struggle *(SYN.)* fray, strive, fight, contest, battle, skirmish, oppose, clash. *(ANT.)* peace, agreement, truce.

stubborn *(SYN.)* obstinate, firm, determined, inflexible, obdurate, uncompromising, pigheaded, contumacious, rigid, unbending, intractable. *(ANT.)* docile, yielding, amenable, submissive.

student *(SYN.)* pupil, observer, disciple, scholar, learner.

studio *(SYN.)* workroom, workshop.

study *(SYN.)* weigh, muse, master, contemplate, reflect, examination, examine.

stuff *(SYN.)* thing, subject, material, theme, matter, substance, fill, ram, cram, pack, textile, cloth, topic.

stumble *(SYN.)* sink, collapse, tumble, drop, topple, lurch, trip, fall. *(ANT.)* steady, climb, soar, arise.

stun *(SYN.)* shock, knock out, dumbfound, take, amaze, alarm. *(ANT.)* forewarn, caution, prepare.

stunning *(SYN.)* brilliant, dazzling, exquisite, ravishing. *(ANT.)* drab, ugly.

stunt *(SYN.)* check, restrict, hinder.

stupid *(SYN.)* dull, obtuse, half-witted, brainless, foolish, dumb, witless, idiotic. *(ANT.)* smart, intelligent, clever, quick, bright, alert, discerning.

stupor *(SYN.)* lethargy, torpor, daze, languor, drowsiness, numbness. *(ANT.)* wakefulness, liveliness, activity.

sturdy *(SYN.)* hale, strong, rugged, stout, mighty, enduring, hardy, well-built. *(ANT.)* fragile, brittle, insipid, delicate.

style *(SYN.)* sort, type, kind, chic, smartness, elegance.

subdue *(SYN.)* crush, overcome, rout, beat, reduce, lower, defeat, vanquish. *(ANT.)* retreat, cede, surrender.

subject *(SYN.)* subordinate, theme, case, topic, dependent, citizen, matter.

sublime *(SYN.)* lofty, raised, elevated, supreme, exalted, splendid, grand. *(ANT.)* ordinary, vase, low, ridiculous.

submerge *(SYN.)* submerse, dunk, sink, dip, immerse, engage, douse, engross. *(ANT.)* surface, rise, uplift, elevate.

submissive *(SYN.)* deferential, yielding, dutiful, compliant. *(ANT.)* rebellious, intractable, insubordinate.

submit *(SYN.)* quit, resign, waive, yield, tender, offer, abdicate, cede, surrender. *(ANT.)* fight, oppose, resist, struggle, deny.

subordinate *(SYN.)* demean, reduce, inferior, assistant, citizen. *(ANT.)* superior.

subsequent *(SYN.)* later, following. *(ANT.)* preceding, previous.

subside *(SYN.)* decrease, lower, sink, droop, hang, collapse, downward. *(ANT.)* mount, steady, arise, climb.

subsidy *(SYN.)* support, aid, grant.

substance *(SYN.)* stuff, essence, importance, material, moment, matter. *(ANT.)* spirit, immaterial.

substantial *(SYN.)* large, considerable, sizable, actual, real, tangible, influential. *(ANT.)* unimportant, trivial.

substantiate *(SYN.)* strengthen, corroborate, confirm.

substitute *(SYN.)* proxy, expedient, deputy, makeshift, replacement, alternate, lieutenant, representative, surrogate, displace, exchange, equivalent. *(ANT.)* sovereign, master, head.

substitution *(SYN.)* change, mutation, vicissitude, alteration, modification. *(ANT.)* uniformity, monotony.

subterfuge *(SYN.)* pretext, excuse, cloak, simulation, disguise, garb, pretension. *(ANT.)* reality, truth, actuality, sincerity.

subtle *(SYN.)* suggestive, indirect. *(ANT.)* overt, obvious.

subtract *(SYN.)* decrease, reduce, curtail, deduct, diminish, remove, lessen. *(ANT.)* expand, increase, add, enlarge, grow.

succeed *(SYN.)* thrive, follow, replace, achieve, win, flourish, prevail, inherit. *(ANT.)* flop, miscarry, anticipate, fail, precede.

success *(SYN.)* advance, prosperity, luck. *(ANT.)* failure.

successful *(SYN.)* fortunate, favorable, lucky, triumphant.

succession *(SYN.)* chain, course, series, order, string, arrangement, progression, train, following.

successive *(SYN.)* serial, sequential.

succinct *(SYN.)* pithy, curt, brief, short, compendious, terse. *(ANT.)* prolonged, extended, long, protracted.

succor *(SYN.)* ease, solace, comfort, enjoyment, consolation. *(ANT.)* suffering, discomfort, torture, affliction, torment.

sudden *(SYN.)* rapid, swift, immediate, abrupt, unexpected, unforeseen, hasty. *(ANT.)* slowly, anticipated.

suffer *(SYN.)* stand, experience, endure, bear, feel, allow, let, permit, sustain. *(ANT.)* exclude, banish, overcome.

suffering *(SYN.)* distress, ache, anguish, pain, woe, misery, torment. *(ANT.)* ease, relief, comfort.

sufficient *(SYN.)* fitting, enough, adequate, satisfactory. *(ANT.)* scant, deficient.

suffix *(SYN.)* ending. *(ANT.)* prefix.

suggest *(SYN.)* propose, offer, refer, advise, hint, insinuate, recommend, allude. *(ANT.)* dictate, declare, insist.

suggestion *(SYN.)* exhortation, recommendation, intelligence, caution, admonition, warning, advice.

suit *(SYN.)* conform, accommodate, fit. *(ANT.)* misapply, disturb.

suitable *(SYN.)* welcome, agreeable, acceptable, gratifying. *(ANT.)* offensive, disagreeable.

sullen *(SYN.)* fretful, morose, dismal, silent, sulky, bitter, sad, somber, glum, gloomy, dour, moody. *(ANT.)* pleasant, joyous, merry.

sultry *(SYN.)* close, hot, stifling.

sum *(SYN.)* amount, total, aggregate, whole, increase, append, add. *(ANT.)* sample, fraction, reduce, deduct.

summarize *(SYN.)* abstract, abridge. *(ANT.)* restore, add, unite, return.

summary *(SYN.)* digest, outline, abstract, synopsis, concise, brief, short, compact.

summit *(SYN.)* peak, top, head, crest, zenith, apex, crown, pinnacle. *(ANT.)* bottom, foundation, base, foot.

summon *(SYN.)* invoke, call, invite. *(ANT.)* dismiss.

sundry *(SYN.)* miscellaneous, several, different, various, divers. *(ANT.)* similar, identical, alike, same, congruous.

sunny *(SYN.)* cheery, cheerful, fair, joyful, happy, cloudless. *(ANT.)* overcast, cloudy.

superannuated *(SYN.)* old, archaic, aged, senile, ancient, venerable, elderly. *(ANT.)* youthful, modern, young.

superb *(SYN.)* splendid, wonderful, extraordinary, marvelous.

supercilious *(SYN.)* contemptuous, snobbish, overbearing, vainglorious, arrogant, haughty. *(ANT.)* meek, ashamed, lowly.

superficial *(SYN.)* flimsy, shallow, cursory,

superintend

slight, exterior. (*ANT.*) *thorough, deep, abstruse, profound.*

superintend *(SYN.)* control, govern, rule, command, manage, direct, regulate. (*ANT.*) *ignore, follow, submit, abandon.*

superintendence *(SYN.)* control, oversight, surveillance, management.

superintendent *(SYN.)* manager, supervisor, overseer, director, administrator.

superiority *(SYN.)* profit, mastery, advantage, good, service, edge, utility. (*ANT.*) *harm, detriment, impediment.*

superlative *(SYN.)* pure, consummate, sinless, blameless, holy, perfect, faultless, ideal, unqualified, immaculate. (*ANT.*) *lacking, defective, imperfect, deficient.*

supernatural *(SYN.)* unearthly, preternatural, marvelous, miraculous. (*ANT.*) *plain, human, physical, common.*

supervise *(SYN.)* rule, oversee, govern, command, direct, superintend, manage. (*ANT.*) *submit, forsake, abandon.*

supervision *(SYN.)* oversight, inspection, surveillance, charge, management.

supervisor *(SYN.)* manager, boss, foreman, director.

supplant *(SYN.)* overturn, overcome. (*ANT.*) *uphold, conserve.*

supple *(SYN.)* lithe, pliant, flexible, limber, elastic, pliable. (*ANT.*) *stiff, brittle, rigid.*

supplement *(SYN.)* extension, complement, addition, extend, add.

supplicate *(SYN.)* beg, petition, solicit, adjure, beseech, entreat, ask, pray, crave. (*ANT.*) *cede, give, bestow, grant.*

supplication *(SYN.)* invocation, plea, appeal, request, entreaty.

supply *(SYN.)* provide, inventory, hoard, reserve, store, accumulation, stock, furnish, endow, give.

support *(SYN.)* groundwork, aid, favor, base, prop, assistance, comfort, basis, succor, living, subsistence, encouragement, backing, livelihood, help. (*ANT.*) *discourage, abandon, oppose, opposition, attack.*

supporter *(SYN.)* follower, devotee, adherent, henchman, attendant, disciple, votary. (*ANT.*) *master, head, chief.*

suppose *(SYN.)* believe, presume, deduce, apprehend, think, assume, imagine, speculate, guess, conjecture. (*ANT.*) *prove, demonstrate, ascertain.*

supposition *(SYN.)* theory, conjecture. (*ANT.*) *proof, fact.*

suppress *(SYN.)* diminish, reduce, overpower, abate, lessen, decrease, subdue. (*ANT.*) *revive, amplify, intensify, enlarge.*

supremacy *(SYN.)* domination, predominance, ascendancy, sovereignty.

supreme *(SYN.)* greatest, best, highest, main, principal, cardinal, first, chief, foremost, paramount. (*ANT.*) *supplemental, minor, subsidiary, auxiliary.*

sure *(SYN.)* confident, fixed, inevitable, certain, positive, trustworthy, reliable, unquestionable, convinced, steady. (*ANT.*) *probable, uncertain, doubtful.*

surface *(SYN.)* outside, exterior, cover, covering.

surge *(SYN.)* heave, swell, grow. (*ANT.*) *wane, ebb, diminish.*

surly *(SYN.)* disagreeable, hostile, unfriendly, ugly, antagonistic.

surmise *(SYN.)* judge, think, believe, assume, suppose, presume, guess.

surpass *(SYN.)* pass, exceed, excel, outstrip, outdo.

surplus *(SYN.)* extravagance, intemperance, superabundance, excess, immoderation, remainder, extra, profusion, superfluity. (*ANT.*) *want, lack, dearth.*

surprise *(SYN.)* miracle, prodigy, wonder, awe, phenomenon, marvel, bewilderment, wonderment, rarity. (*ANT.*) *expectation, triviality, indifference, familiarity.*

surrender *(SYN.)* relinquish, resign, yield, abandon, sacrifice, submit, cede. (*ANT.*) *overcome, rout, conquer.*

surreptitious *(SYN.)* sneaky, sneaking, underhand, sly, furtive. (*ANT.*) *openhanded, open, straightforward.*

surround *(SYN.)* confine, encompass, circle, encircle, girdle, fence, circumscribe, limit, envelop. (*ANT.*) *open, distend, expose, enlarge.*

surveillance *(SYN.)* inspection, oversight,

supervision, management, control.

survey *(SYN.)* scan, inspect, view, examine, inspection, examination.

survive *(SYN.)* live, remain, continue, persist. *(ANT.)* die, fail, succumb.

suspect *(SYN.)* waver, disbelieve, presume, suppose, mistrust, distrust.

suspend *(SYN.)* delay, hang, withhold, interrupt, postpone, dangle, adjourn, poise. *(ANT.)* persist, proceed, maintain.

suspicion *(SYN.)* unbelief, distrust, suspense, uncertainty, doubt. *(ANT.)* determination, conviction, faith, belief.

sustain *(SYN.)* bear, carry, undergo, foster, keep, prop, help, advocate, back. *(ANT.)* discourage, oppose, destroy.

sustenance *(SYN.)* fare, food, diet, rations, nutriment, edibles, victuals. *(ANT.)* hunger, want, drink.

swallow *(SYN.)* gorge, eat, mouthful.

swallow up *(SYN.)* consume, absorb, engulf, assimilate. *(ANT.)* exude, dispense, expel, discharge.

swarm *(SYN.)* throng, horde, crowd.

swarthy *(SYN.)* sable, dark. *(ANT.)* bright, light.

swear *(SYN.)* declare, state, affirm, vouchsafe, curse, maintain. *(ANT.)* demur, oppose, deny, contradict.

sweat *(SYN.)* perspiration, perspire.

sweeping *(SYN.)* extensive, wide, general, broad, tolerant, comprehensive, vast. *(ANT.)* restricted, confined.

sweet *(SYN.)* engaging, luscious, pure, clean, fresh, melodious, pleasant. *(ANT.)* bitter, harsh, nasty, irascible, discordant, irritable, acrid.

swell *(SYN.)* increase, grow, expand, enlarge. *(ANT.)* diminish, shrink.

swift *(SYN.)* quick, fast, fleet, speedy, rapid, expeditious.

swindle *(SYN.)* bilk, defraud, con, deceive, cheat, guile, deception, deceit. *(ANT.)* sincerity, honesty, fairness.

swing *(SYN.)* rock, sway, wave.

switch *(SYN.)* shift, change, turn.

swoon *(SYN.)* faint.

symbol *(SYN.)* sign, character.

sympathetic *(SYN.)* considerate, compassionate, gentle, benevolent, good, tender, affable, merciful, thoughtful. *(ANT.)* unkind, merciless, unsympathetic, indifferent, intolerant, cruel.

sympathy *(SYN.)* compassion, agreement, tenderness, commiseration, pity. *(ANT.)* indifference, unconcern, antipathy.

symptom *(SYN.)* indication, sign.

synopsis *(SYN.)* outline, digest.

synthetic *(SYN.)* counterfeit, artificial, phony, unreal, bogus, sham. *(ANT.)* natural, true, genuine.

system *(SYN.)* organization, procedure, regularity, arrangement, mode, order. *(ANT.)* confusion, chance, disorder.

systematic (SYN.) orderly, organized. *(ANT.)* irregular, random.

T

table *(SYN.)* catalog, list, schedule, postpone, chart, index, shelve, delay, put off.

tablet *(SYN.)* pad, notebook, capsule, sketchpad, pill, lozenge.

taboo *(SYN.)* banned, prohibited, forbidden, restriction. *(ANT.)* accepted, allowed.

tacit *(SYN.)* understood, assumed, implied.

taciturn *(SYN.)* quiet, withdrawn, reserved.

tack *(SYN.)* add, join, attach, clasp, fasten.

tackle *(SYN.)* rigging, gear, apparatus, equipment, grab, seize, catch, down, throw, try, undertake.

tacky *(SYN.)* gummy, sticky, gooey.

tact *(SYN.)* dexterity, poise, diplomacy, judgment, savior-faire, skill, finesse, sense, prudence, adroitness, address. *(ANT.)* incompetence, vulgarity, blunder, rudeness, insensitivity, grossness.

tactical *(SYN.)* foxy, cunning, proficient, deft, adroit, clever, expert. *(ANT.)* blundering, gauche, clumsy, inept.

tactics *(SYN.)* plan, strategy, approach, maneuver, course, scheme.

tag *(SYN.)* sticker, label, mark, identification, marker, name.

tail *(SYN.)* rear, back, follow, end, shadow,

tailor

pursue, trail, heel.

tailor *(SYN.)* modest, couturier, modify, redo, shape, fashion.

taint *(SYN.)* spot, stain, tarnish, soil, mark, discolor. *(ANT.) cleanse, disinfect, clean.*

tainted *(SYN.)* crooked, impure, vitiated, profligate, debased, spoiled, corrupted, depraved, dishonest, contaminated, putrid, unsound.

take *(SYN.)* accept, grasp, catch, confiscate, clutch, adopt, assume, receive, bring, attract, claim, necessitate, steal, ensnare, capture, demand, select, appropriate, obtain, captivate, hold, seize, win, escort, note, record, rob, shoplift, get, remove, gain, choose.

taking *(SYN.)* charming, captivating, winning, attractive.

takeover *(SYN.)* revolution, merger, usurpation, confiscation.

tale *(SYN.)* falsehood, history, yarn, chronicle, account, fable, fiction, narration, story, narrative, anecdote.

talent *(SYN.)* capability, knack, skill, endowment, gift, cleverness, aptitude, ability, genius. *(ANT.) ineptitude, incompetence.*

talented *(SYN.)* skillful, smart, adroit, dexterous, clever, apt, quick-witted, witty, ingenious. *(ANT.) dull, clumsy, awkward, unskilled, stupid, slow.*

talk *(SYN.)* conversation, gossip, report, speech, communicate, discuss, confer, chatter, conference, preach, dialogue, reason, jabber, discourse, lecture, communication, consul, plead, argue, converse, rant, chat, mutter, speak, rumor, deliberate, discussion. *(ANT.) silence, correspondence, meditation, writing.*

talkative *(SYN.)* glib, communicative, chattering, loquacious, voluble, garrulous, chatty. *(ANT.) uncommunicative, laconic, reticent, silent.*

tall *(SYN.)* elevated, high, towering, big, lofty, imposing, gigantic. *(ANT.) tiny, low, short, small, stunted.*

tally *(SYN.)* score, count, compute, reckon, calculate, estimate, list, figure, correspond, agree, match, check.

tame *(SYN.)* domesticated, dull, insipid, docile, broken, uninteresting, gentle, subdued, insipid, flat, unexciting, boring, break, domesticate, mild, tedious, domestic, submissive. *(ANT.) spirited, savage, wild, exciting, animated, undomesticated.*

tamper *(SYN.)* mix in, interrupt, interfere, meddle, interpose.

tang *(SYN.)* zest, sharpness, tartness, taste.

tangible *(SYN.)* material, sensible, palpable, corporeal, bodily. *(ANT.) metaphysical, mental, spiritual.*

tangle *(SYN.)* confuse, knot, snarl, twist, ensnare, embroil, implicate.

tangy *(SYN.)* pungent, peppery, seasoned, sharp, tart.

tantalize *(SYN.)* lease, tempt, entice, titillate, stimulate, frustrate.

tantrum *(SYN.)* outburst, fit, fury, flare-up, conniption, rampage.

tap *(SYN.)* pat, rap, hit, strike, blow, faucet, spout, spigot, bunghole.

tape *(SYN.)* ribbon, strip, fasten, bandage, bind, record, tie.

taper *(SYN.)* narrow, candle, decrease.

tardy *(SYN.)* slow, delayed, overdue, late, belated. *(ANT.) prompt, timely, punctual, early.*

target *(SYN.)* aim, goal, object, objective.

tariff *(SYN.)* duty, tax, levy, rate.

tarnish *(SYN.)* discolor, blight, defile, sully, spot, befoul, disgrace, stain. *(ANT.) honor, purify, cleanse, bleach, shine, gleam, sparkle.*

tarry *(SYN.)* dawdle, loiter, linger, dally, remain, delay, procrastinate.

tart *(SYN.)* sour, acrid, pungent, acid, sharp, distasteful, bitter. *(ANT.) mellow, sweet, delicious, pleasant.*

task *(SYN.)* work, job, undertaking, labor, chore, duty, stint.

taste *(SYN.)* tang, inclination, liking, sensibility, flavor, savor, try, sip, sample, zest, experience, undergo, appreciation, relish, discrimination, discernment, judgment. *(ANT.) indelicacy, disinclination, antipathy.*

tasteful *(SYN.)* elegant, choice, refined, suitable, artistic. *(ANT.) offensive, unbecoming.*

tasteless *(SYN.)* flavorless, insipid, unpalatable, rude, unrefined, uncultivated, boorish, uninteresting.

tasty *(SYN.)* delectable, delicious, luscious, palatable, tempting.

tattered *(SYN.)* ragged, torn, shoddy, shabby, frazzled, frayed, tacky, seedy.

tattle *(SYN.)* inform, divulge, disclose, blab, reveal.

taunt *(SYN.)* tease, deride, flout, scoff, sneer, mock, annoy, pester, bother, ridicule, jeer. *(ANT.)* praise, compliment, laud, flatter.

taunting *(SYN.)* ironic, caustic, cutting, sardonic, derisive, biting, acrimonious, sarcastic, satirical, sneering. *(ANT.)* pleasant, agreeable, affable, amiable.

taut *(SYN.)* tight, constricted, firm, stretched, snug, tense, extended. *(ANT.)* slack, loose, relaxed, open, lax.

tavern *(SYN.)* pub, bar, cocktail lounge.

tawdry *(SYN.)* pretentious, showy, vulgar, tasteless, sordid, garish.

tax *(SYN.)* duty, assessment, excise, levy, toll, burden, strain, tribute, tariff, assess, encumber, overload, impost, custom, exaction, rate. *(ANT.)* reward, gift, remuneration, wages.

taxi *(SYN.)* cab, taxicab.

teach *(SYN.)* inform, school, educate, train, inculcate, instruct, instill, tutor. *(ANT.)* misinform, misguide.

teacher *(SYN.)* tutor, instructor, professor, lecturer.

team *(SYN.)* company, band, party, crew, gang, group.

teamwork *(SYN.)* collaboration, co-operation.

tear *(SYN.)* rend, shred, sunder, cleave, rip, lacerate, teardrop, disunite, divide, drop, wound, split, slit, sever. *(ANT.)* mend, repair, join, unite, sew.

tearful *(SYN.)* sad, weeping, crying, sobbing, weepy, lachrymose.

tease *(SYN.)* badger, harry, bother, irritate, nag, pester, taunt, vex, annoy, disturb, harass, worry, tantalize, plague, aggravate, provoke, torment. *(ANT.)* please, delight, soothe, comfort, gratify.

technical *(SYN.)* industrial, technological, specialized, mechanical.

technique *(SYN.)* system, method, routine, approach, procedure.

tedious *(SYN.)* boring, dilatory, humdrum, sluggish, monotonous, irksome, dreary, dull, tiring, burdensome, tiresome, wearisome, tardy. *(ANT.)* interesting, entertaining, engaging, exciting, amusing, quick.

teem *(SYN.)* abound, swarm.

teeming *(SYN.)* overflowing, bountiful, abundant, ample, profuse, plenteous, rich, copious. *(ANT.)* scant, scarce, deficient, insufficient.

teeter *(SYN.)* sway, hesitate, hem and haw, waver.

telecast *(SYN.)* broadcast.

televise *(SYN.)* telecast.

tell *(SYN.)* report, mention, state, betray, announce, recount, relate, narrate, rehearse, mention, utter, confess, disclose, direct, request, acquaint, instruct, notify, inform, determine, reveal, divulge.

telling *(SYN.)* persuasive, convincing, forceful, effective.

telltale *(SYN.)* revealing, informative, suggestive, meaningful.

temerity *(SYN.)* rashness, foolhardiness, audacity, boldness, recklessness, precipitancy. *(ANT.)* prudence, wariness, caution, hesitation, timidity.

temper *(SYN.)* fury, choler, exasperation, anger, passion, petulance, disposition, nature, rage, soothe, soften, wrath, indignation, irritation, pacify, animosity, mood, resentment. *(ANT.)* peace, self-control, forbearance, conciliation.

temperament *(SYN.)* humor, mood, temper, nature, disposition.

temperamental *(SYN.)* testy, moody, touchy, sensitive, irritable. *(ANT.)* calm, unruffled, serene.

temperance *(SYN.)* abstinence, sobriety, self-denial, forbearance, abstention. *(ANT.)* intoxication, excess, self-indulgence, gluttony, wantonness.

temperate *(SYN.)* controlled, moderate,

tempest

cool, calm, restrained. (*ANT.*) *excessive, extreme, prodigal.*

tempest (*SYN.*) draft, squall, wind, blast, gust, storm, hurricane, commotion, tumult, zephyr. (*ANT.*) *calm, tranquillity.*

tempo (*SYN.*) measure, beat, cadence, rhythm.

temporal (*SYN.*) mundane, earthly, lay, profane, worldly, terrestrial, laic. (*ANT.*) *spiritual, ecclesiastical, unworldly, religious, heavenly.*

temporary (*SYN.*) brief, momentary, short-lived, fleeting, ephemeral, passing, short, transient. (*ANT.*) *lasting, permanent, immortal, everlasting, timeless, abiding.*

tempt (*SYN.*) entice, allure, lure, attract, seduce, invite, magnetize.

tenacious (*SYN.*) persistent, determined, unchanging, unyielding.

tenable (*SYN.*) correct, practical, rational, reasonable, sensible, defensible.

tenacity (*SYN.*) perseverance, steadfastness, industry, constancy, persistence, pertinacity. (*ANT.*) *laziness, rest, cessation, idleness, sloth.*

tenant (*SYN.*) renter, lessee, lodger, leaseholder, dweller, resident.

tend (*SYN.*) escort, follow, care for, lackey, watch, protect, take care of, attend, guard, serve.

tendency (*SYN.*) drift, inclination, proneness, leaning, bias, aim, disposition, predisposition, propensity, trend, impulse. (*ANT.*) *disinclination, aversion, deviation.*

tender (*SYN.*) sympathetic, sore, sensitive, painful, gentle, meek, delicate, fragile, proffer, bland, mild, loving, offer, affectionate, soothing, propose, moderate, soft. (*ANT.*) *rough, severe, fierce, chewy, tough, cruel, unfeeling, harsh.*

tenderfoot (*SYN.*) novice, apprentice, beginner, amateur.

tenderhearted (*SYN.*) kind, sympathetic, merciful, softhearted, understanding, sentimental, affectionate, gentle, sensitive.

tenderness (*SYN.*) attachment, kindness, love, affection, endearment. (*ANT.*) *repugnance, indifference, aversion, hatred.*

tenet (*SYN.*) dogma, belief, precept, doctrine, creed, opinion. (*ANT.*) *deed, conduct, practice, performance.*

tense (*SYN.*) strained, stretched, excited, tight, nervous. (*ANT.*) *loose, placid, lax, relaxed.*

tension (*SYN.*) stress, strain, pressure, anxiety, apprehension, distress.

tentative (*SYN.*) hypothetical, indefinite, probationary, conditional.

tenure (*SYN.*) administration, time, regime, term.

tepid (*SYN.*) temperate, mild, lukewarm. (*ANT.*) *boiling, scalding, passionate, hot.*

term (*SYN.*) period, limit, time, boundary, duration, name, phrase, interval, session, semester, expression, word.

terminal (*SYN.*) eventual, final, concluding, decisive, ending, fatal, latest, last, ultimate, conclusive. (*ANT.*) *original, first, rudimentary, incipient, inaugural.*

terminate (*SYN.*) close, end, finish, abolish, complete, cease, stop, conclude, expire, culminate. (*ANT.*) *establish, begin, initiate, start, commence.*

terminology (*SYN.*) vocabulary, nomenclature, terms, phraseology.

terms (*SYN.*) stipulations, agreement, conditions, provisions.

terrible (*SYN.*) frightful, dire, awful, gruesome, horrible, shocking, horrifying, terrifying, horrid, hideous, appalling. (*ANT.*) *secure, happy, joyous, pleasing, safe.*

terrific (*SYN.*) superb, wonderful, glorious, great, magnificent, divine, colossal, sensational, marvelous.

terrify (*SYN.*) dismay, intimidate, startle, terrorize, appall, frighten, petrify, astound, alarm, affright, horrify, scare. (*ANT.*) *soothe, allay, reassure, compose, embolden.*

territory (*SYN.*) dominion, province, quarter, section, country, division, region, domain, area, place, district.

terror (*SYN.*) fear, alarm, dismay, horror, dread, consternation, fright, panic. (*ANT.*) *calm, security, assurance, peace.*

terse (*SYN.*) concise, incisive, succinct, summary, condensed, compact, neat, pithy, summary. (*ANT.*) *verbose, wordy,* *lengthy, prolix.*

test *(SYN.)* exam, examination, trial, quiz, analyze, verify, validate.

testify *(SYN.)* depose, warrant, witness, state, attest, swear.

testimony *(SYN.)* evidence, attestation, declaration, proof, witness, confirmation. *(ANT.)* refutation, argument, disproof, contradiction.

testy *(SYN.)* ill-natured, irritable, snappish, waspish, fractious, fretful, touchy, ill-tempered, peevish, petulant. *(ANT.)* pleasant, affable, good-tempered, genial, good-natured.

tether *(SYN.)* tie, hamper, restraint, bridle.

text *(SYN.)* textbook, book, manual.

textile *(SYN.)* material, cloth, goods, fabric.

texture *(SYN.)* construction, structure, make-up, composition, grain, finish.

thankful *(SYN.)* obliged, grateful, appreciative. *(ANT.)* thankless, ungrateful, resenting.

thaw *(SYN.)* liquefy, melt, dissolve. *(ANT.)* solidify, freeze.

theater *(SYN.)* arena, playhouse, battlefield, stadium, hall.

theatrical *(SYN.)* ceremonious, melodramatic, stagy, artificial, affected, dramatic, showy, compelling. *(ANT.)* unemotional, subdued, unaffected.

theft *(SYN.)* larceny, robbery, stealing, plunder, burglary, pillage, thievery.

theme *(SYN.)* motive, topic, argument, subject, thesis, text, point, paper, essay, composition.

theoretical *(SYN.)* bookish, learned, scholarly, pedantic, academic, formal, erudite, scholastic. *(ANT.)* practical, ignorant, commonsense, simple.

theory *(SYN.)* doctrine, guess, presupposition, postulate, assumption, hypothesis, speculation. *(ANT.)* practice, verity, fact, proof.

therefore *(SYN.)* consequently, thence so, accordingly, hence, then.

thick *(SYN.)* compressed, heavy, compact, viscous, close, concentrated, crowded, syrupy, dense. *(ANT.)* watery, slim, thin, sparse, dispersed, dissipated.

thief *(SYN.)* burglar, robber, criminal.

thin *(SYN.)* diluted, flimsy, lean, narrow, spare, emaciated, diaphanous, gauzy, meager, slender, tenuous, slim, rare, sparse, scanty, lank, gossamer, slight. *(ANT.)* fat, wide, broad, thick, bulky.

think *(SYN.)* picture, contemplate, ponder, esteem, intend, mean, imagine, deliberate, recall, speculate, recollect, deem, apprehend, consider, devise, plan, judge, reflect, suppose, assume, meditate, muse. *(ANT.)* forget, conjecture, guess.

thirst *(SYN.)* appetite, desire, craving.

thirsty *(SYN.)* arid, dry, dehydrated, parched, craving, desirous. *(ANT.)* satisfied.

thorn *(SYN.)* spine, barb, prickle, nettle, bramble.

thorough *(SYN.)* entire, complete, perfect, total, finished, unbroken, careful, thoroughgoing, consummate, undivided. *(ANT.)* unfinished, careless, slapdash, imperfect, haphazard, lacking.

thoroughfare *(SYN.)* avenue, street, parkway, highway, boulevard. *(ANT.)* byway.

though *(SYN.)* in any case, notwithstanding, however, nevertheless.

thought *(SYN.)* consideration, pensive, attentive, heedful, prudent, dreamy, reflective, introspective, meditation, notion, view, deliberation, sentiment, fancy, idea, impression, reasoning, contemplation, judgment, regard. *(ANT.)* thoughtlessness.

thoughtful *(SYN.)* considerate, attentive, dreamy, pensive, provident, introspective, meditative, cautious, heedful, kind, courteous, friendly. *(ANT.)* thoughtless, heedless, inconsiderate, rash, precipitous, selfish.

thoughtless *(SYN.)* inattentive, unconcerned, negligent, lax, desultory, inconsiderate, careless, imprudent, inaccurate, neglectful, indiscreet, remiss. *(ANT.)* meticulous, accurate, nice, careful.

thrash *(SYN.)* whip, beat, defeat, flog, punish, strap, thresh.

thread *(SYN.)* yarn, strand, filament, fiber, string, cord.

threadbare

threadbare *(SYN.)* shabby, tacky, worn, ragged, frayed.

threat *(SYN.)* menace, warning, danger, hazard, jeopardy, omen.

threaten *(SYN.)* caution, warning, forewarn, menace, intimidate, loom.

threatening *(SYN.)* imminent, nigh, approaching, impending, overhanging, sinister, foreboding. *(ANT.)* improbable, retreating, afar, distant, remote.

threshold *(SYN.)* edge, verge, start, beginning, doorsill, commencement.

thrift *(SYN.)* prudence, conservation, saving, economy.

thrifty *(SYN.)* saving, economical, sparing, frugal, provident, stingy, saving, parsimonious. *(ANT.)* wasteful, spendthrift, intemperate, self-indulgent, extravagant.

thrill *(SYN.)* arouse, rouse, excite, stimulation, excitement, tingle. *(ANT.)* bore.

thrive *(SYN.)* succeed, flourish, grow, prosper. *(ANT.)* expire, fade, shrivel, die, fail.

throb *(SYN.)* pound, pulsate, palpitate, beat, pulse.

throe *(SYN.)* pang, twinge, distress, suffering, pain, ache, grief, agony. *(ANT.)* pleasure, relief, ease, solace, comfort.

throng *(SYN.)* masses, press, crowd, bevy, populace, swarm, rabble, horde, host, mass, teem, mob, multitude.

throttle *(SYN.)* smother, choke, strangle.

through *(SYN.)* completed, done, finished, over.

throughout *(SYN.)* all over, everywhere, during.

throw *(SYN.)* propel, cast, pitch, toss, hurl, send, thrust, fling. *(ANT.)* retain, pull, draw, haul, hold.

thrust *(SYN.)* jostle, push, promote, crowd, force, drive, hasten, press, shove, urge. *(ANT.)* ignore, falter, retreat, drag, oppose, halt.

thug *(SYN.)* mobster, hoodlum, mugger, gangster, assassin, gunman.

thump *(SYN.)* blow, strike, knock, jab, poke, pound, beat, clout, bat, rap, bang.

thunderstruck *(SYN.)* amazed, astounded, astonished, awed, flabbergasted, surprised, dumbfounded, bewildered, spellbound.

thus *(SYN.)* hence, therefore, accordingly, so, consequently.

thwart *(SYN.)* defeat, frustrate, prevent, foil, stop, baffle, circumvent, hinder, obstruct, disappoint, balk, outwit. *(ANT.)* promote, accomplish, fulfill, help, further.

ticket *(SYN.)* stamp, label, tag, seal, token, pass, summons, certificate, ballot, sticker, slate, citation.

tickle *(SYN.)* delight, entertain, thrill, amuse, titillate, excite.

ticklish *(SYN.)* fragile, delicate, tough, difficult.

tidings *(SYN.)* message, report, information, word, intelligence, news.

tidy *(SYN.)* trim, clear, neat, precise, spruce, orderly, shipshape. *(ANT.)* disheveled, unkempt, sloppy, dirty, slovenly.

tie *(SYN.)* bond, join, relationship, bind, restrict, fetter, connect, conjunction, association, alliance, union, fasten, engage, attach, restrain, oblige, link, affinity. *(ANT.)* separation, disunion, unfasten, open, loose, untie, free, isolation.

tier *(SYN.)* line, row, level, deck, layer.

tiff *(SYN.)* bicker, squabble, argue, row, clash, dispute, altercation.

tight *(SYN.)* firm, taut, penny-pinching, constricted, snug, taut, parsimonious, secure, fast, strong, sealed, fastened, watertight, locked, close, compact, stingy. *(ANT.)* slack, lax, open, relaxed, loose.

till *(SYN.)* plow, work, moneybox, depository, cultivate, vault.

tilt *(SYN.)* slant, slope, incline, tip, lean.

timber *(SYN.)* lumber, wood, logs.

time *(SYN.)* epoch, span, term, age, duration, interim, period, tempo, interval, space, spell, season.

timeless *(SYN.)* unending, lasting, perpetual, endless, immemorial. *(ANT.)* temporary, mortal, temporal.

timely *(SYN.)* prompt, exact, punctual, ready, precise. *(ANT.)* slow, tardy, late.

timepiece *(SYN.)* clock, watch.

timetable *(SYN.)* list, schedule.

timid *(SYN.)* coy, humble, sheepish,

torrid

abashed, embarrassed, modest, bashful, diffident, shamefaced, retiring, fearful, faint-hearted, shy, timorous. *(ANT.)* *gregarious, bold, daring, adventurous, fearless.*

inge *(SYN.)* color, tint, dye, stain, flavor, imbue, season, impregnate.

ingle *(SYN.)* shiver, chime, prickle.

inker *(SYN.)* potter, putter, fiddle with, dawdle, dally, dabble.

inkle *(SYN.)* sound, peal, ring, jingle, chime, toll.

int *(SYN.)* color, tinge, dye, stain, hue, tone, shade.

iny *(SYN.)* minute, little, petty, wee, slight, diminutive, miniature, small, insignificant, trivial, puny. *(ANT.)* *huge, large, immense, big, enormous.*

ip *(SYN.)* point, end, top, peak, upset, tilt, reward, gift, gratuity, clue, hint, suggestion, inkling.

irade *(SYN.)* outburst, harangue, scolding.

ire *(SYN.)* jade, tucker, bore, weary, exhaust, weaken, wear out, fatigue. *(ANT.)* *restore, revive, exhilarate, invigorate, refresh.*

ired *(SYN.)* weary, exhausted, fatigued, run-down, sleepy, faint, spent, wearied, worn, jaded. *(ANT.)* *rested, fresh, hearty, invigorated, energetic, tireless, eager.*

ireless *(SYN.)* active, enthusiastic, energetic, strenuous. *(ANT.)* *exhausted, wearied, fatigued.*

iresome *(SYN.)* dull, boring, monotonous, tedious. *(ANT.)* *interesting.*

itan *(SYN.)* colossus, powerhouse, mammoth.

itle *(SYN.)* epithet, privilege, name, appellation, claim, denomination, due, heading, ownership, right, deed, designation.

oast *(SYN.)* salutation, pledge, celebration.

oddle *(SYN.)* stumble, wobble, shuffle.

oil *(SYN.)* labor, drudgery, work, travail, performance, business, achievement, employment, occupation, slave, sweat, effort. *(ANT.)* *recreation, ease, vacation, relax, loll, play, leisure, repose.*

oken *(SYN.)* mark, sign, sample, indication, evidence, symbol.

olerant *(SYN.)* extensive, vast, considerate, broad, patient, large, sweeping, liberal, wide. *(ANT.)* *intolerant, bigoted, biased, restricted, narrow, confined.*

tolerate *(SYN.)* endure, allow, bear, authorize, permit, brook, stand, abide. *(ANT.)* *forbid, protest, prohibit, discriminating.*

toll *(SYN.)* impost, burden, rate, assessment, duty, custom, excise, tribute, levy, burden, strain. *(ANT.)* *reward, wages, gift, remuneration.*

tomb *(SYN.)* vault, monument, catacomb, grave, mausoleum.

tone *(SYN.)* noise, sound, mood, manner, expression, cadence.

tongs *(SYN.)* tweezers, hook, grapnel, forceps.

tongue *(SYN.)* diction, lingo, cant, jargon, vernacular, dialect, idiom, speech, phraseology. *(ANT.)* *nonsense, drivel, babble.*

too *(SYN.)* furthermore, moreover, similarly, also, in addition, besides, likewise.

tool *(SYN.)* devise, medium, apparatus, agent, implement, utensil, agent, vehicle, instrument. *(ANT.)* *preventive, hindrance, impediment, obstruction.*

top *(SYN.)* crown, pinnacle, peak, tip, cover, cap, zenith, apex, crest, chief, head, summit. *(ANT.)* *bottom, foundation, base, foot.*

topic *(SYN.)* subject, thesis, issue, argument, matter, theme, point.

topple *(SYN.)* collapse, sink, fall, tumble.

torrent *(SYN.)* pain, woe, pester, ache, distress, misery, harass, throe, annoy, vex, torture, anguish, suffering, misery. *(ANT.)* *relief, comfort, ease, gratify, delight.*

torpid *(SYN.)* sluggish, idle, lazy, inert, inactive, supine, slothful, indolent, motionless, lethargic. *(ANT.)* *alert, assiduous, diligent, active.*

torpor *(SYN.)* lethargy, daze, numbness, stupor, drowsiness, insensibility, languor. *(ANT.)* *wakefulness, liveliness, activity, alertness, readiness.*

torrent *(SYN.)* flood, downpour, deluge.

torrid *(SYN.)* scorching, ardent, impetuous, passionate, scalding, warm, fiery, hot-blooded, sultry, tropical, intense, sweltering, burning, hot. *(ANT.)* *passionless,*

torso

impassive, cold, frigid, apathetic, freezing, phlegmatic, indifferent, temperate.

torso *(SYN.)* form, frame, body. *(ANT.) soul, mind, spirit, intellect.*

torture *(SYN.)* anguish, badger, plague, distress, ache, torment, pester, pain, hound, agony, woe, worry, vex, persecute, suffering, throe, afflict, misery. *(ANT.) aid, relief, comfort, ease, support, encourage, mitigation.*

toss *(SYN.)* throw, cast, hurl, pitch, tumble, thrust, fling, propel. *(ANT.) retain, pull, draw, haul, hold.*

total *(SYN.)* entire, complete, concluded, finished, thorough, whole, entirely, collection, aggregate, conglomeration, unbroken, perfect, undivided, consummate, full. *(ANT.) part, element, imperfect, unfinished, ingredient, particular, lacking.*

tote *(SYN.)* move, transfer, convey, drag, carry.

totter *(SYN.)* falter, stagger, reel, sway, waver, stumble, wobble.

touch *(SYN.)* finger, feel, handle, move, affect, concern, mention, hint, trace, suggestion, knack, skill, ability, talent.

touch-and-go *(SYN.)* dangerous, risky, perilous, hazardous.

touching *(SYN.)* pitiable, affecting, moving, sad, adjunct, bordering, tangent, poignant, tender, effective, impressive, adjacent. *(ANT.) removed, enlivening, animated, exhilarating.*

touchy *(SYN.)* snappish, irritable, fiery, choleric, testy, hot, irascible, nervous, excitable, petulant, sensitive, short-tempered, jumpy, peevish. *(ANT.) composed, agreeable, tranquil, calm, serene, stolid, cool.*

tough *(SYN.)* sturdy, difficult, trying, incorrigible, troublesome, hard, stout, leathery, strong, laborious, inedible, sinewy, cohesive, firm, callous, obdurate, vicious. *(ANT.) vulnerable, submissive, easy, brittle, facile, weak, fragile, compliant, tender, frail.*

toughness *(SYN.)* stamina, fortitude, durability, intensity, force, might, stoutness, power, sturdiness, vigor. *(ANT.) weakness, feebleness, infirmity, frailty.*

tour *(SYN.)* rove, travel, go, visit, excursion, ramble, journey, roam. *(ANT.) stop, stay.*

tourist *(SYN.)* traveler, sightseer, vagabond, voyager.

tournament *(SYN.)* tourney, match, contest, competition.

tout *(SYN.)* vend, importune, peddle, solicit, sell, hawk.

tow *(SYN.)* tug, take out, unsheathe, haul, draw, remove, extract, pull, drag. *(ANT.) propel, drive.*

towering *(SYN.)* elevated, exalted, high, lofty, tall, proud, eminent. *(ANT.) base, mean, stunted, small, tiny, low.*

town *(SYN.)* hamlet, village, community, municipality.

toxic *(SYN.)* deadly, poisonous, fatal, lethal, harmful. *(ANT.) beneficial.*

toy *(SYN.)* play, romp, frolic, gamble, stake, caper, plaything, wager, revel.

trace *(SYN.)* stigma, feature, indication, trait, mark, stain, scar, sign, trial, trace, suggestion, characteristic, vestige.

track *(SYN.)* persist, pursue, follow, sign, mark, spoor, trace, path, route, road, carry, hunt, chase. *(ANT.) escape, evade, abandon, flee, elude.*

tract *(SYN.)* area, region, territory, district, expanse, domain.

tractable *(SYN.)* yielding, deferential, submissive, dutiful, compliant, obedient. *(ANT.) rebellious, intractable, insubordinate.*

trade *(SYN.)* business, traffic, commerce, dealing, craft, occupation, profession, livelihood, swap, barter, exchange.

trademark *(SYN.)* logo, brand name, identification, emblem, insignia, monogram.

tradition *(SYN.)* custom, legend, folklore, belief, rite, practice.

traduce *(SYN.)* defame, malign, vilify, revile, abuse, asperse, scandalize, disparage. *(ANT.) protect, honor, cherish, praise, respect, support, extol.*

tragedy *(SYN.)* unhappiness, misfortune, misery, adversity, catastrophe.

tragic *(SYN.)* miserable, unfortunate, depressing, melancholy, mournful. *(ANT.) happy, cheerful, comic.*

trail *(SYN.)* persist, pursue, chase, follow, drag, draw, hunt, track. *(ANT.)* evade, flee, abandon, elude, escape.

train *(SYN.)* direct, prepare, aim, point, level, teach, drill, tutor, bid, instruct, order, command. *(ANT.)* distract, deceive, misguide, misdirect.

traipse *(SYN.)* roam, wander, saunter, meander.

trait *(SYN.)* characteristic, feature, attribute, peculiarity, mark, quality, property.

traitor *(SYN.)* turncoat, betrayer, spy, double-dealer, conspirator.

traitorous *(SYN.)* disloyal, faithless, apostate, false, recreant, perfidious, treasonable, treacherous. *(ANT.)* devoted, trite, loyal, constant.

tramp *(SYN.)* bum, beggar, rover, hobo, march, stamp, stomp, vagabond, wanderer, vagrant. *(ANT.)* laborer, worker, gentleman.

trample *(SYN.)* crush, stomp, squash.

tranquil *(SYN.)* composed, calm, dispassionate, imperturbable, peaceful, pacific, placid, quiet, still, serene, undisturbed, unruffled. *(ANT.)* frantic, stormy, excited, disturbed, upset, turbulent, wild.

tranquillity *(SYN.)* calmness, calm, hush, peace, quiet, quiescence, quietude, repose, serenity, rest, stillness, silence, placid. *(ANT.)* disturbance, agitation, excitement, tumult, noise.

transact *(SYN.)* conduct, manage, execute, treat, perform.

transaction *(SYN.)* business, deal, affair, deed, settlement, occurrence, negotiation, proceeding.

transcend *(SYN.)* overstep, overshadow, exceed.

transcribe *(SYN.)* write, copy, rewrite, record.

transfer *(SYN.)* dispatch, send, transmit, remove, transport, transplant, consign, move, shift, reassign, assign, relegate.

transform *(SYN.)* change, convert, alter, modify, transfigure, shift, vary, veer. *(ANT.)* continue, settle, preserve, stabilize.

transgression *(SYN.)* atrocity, indignity, offense, insult, outrage, aggression, injustice, crime, misdeed, trespass, sin, wrong, vice. *(ANT.)* innocence, morality, gentleness, right.

transient *(SYN.)* ephemeral, evanescent, brief, fleeting, momentary, temporary, short-lived. *(ANT.)* immortal, abiding, permanent, lasting, timeless, established.

transition *(SYN.)* change, variation, modification.

translate *(SYN.)* decipher, construe, decode, elucidate, explicate, explain, interpret, solve, render, unravel. *(ANT.)* distort, falsify, misinterpret, misconstrue.

transmit *(SYN.)* confer, convey, communicate, divulge, disclose, impart, send, inform, relate, notify, reveal, dispatch, tell. *(ANT.)* withhold, hide, conceal.

transparent *(SYN.)* crystalline, clear, limpid, lucid, translucent, thin, evident, manifest, plain, evident, explicit, obvious, open. *(ANT.)* opaque, muddy, turbid, thick, questionable, ambiguous.

transpire *(SYN.)* befall, bechance, betide, happen, chance, occur.

transport *(SYN.)* carry, bear, convey, remove, move, shift, enrapture, transfer, lift, entrance, ravish, stimulate.

transpose *(SYN.)* change, switch, reverse.

trap *(SYN.)* artifice, bait, ambush, intrigue, net, lure, pitfall, ensnare, deadfall, snare, ruse, entrap, bag, trick, stratagem, wile.

trash *(SYN.)* refuse, garbage, rubbish, waste.

trashy *(SYN.)* insignificant, worthless.

trauma *(SYN.)* ordeal, upheaval, jolt, shock, disturbance.

travail *(SYN.)* suffering, torment, anxiety, distress, anguish, misery, ordeal.

travel *(SYN.)* journey, go, touring, ramble, rove, voyage, cruise, tour, roam. *(ANT.)* stop, stay, remain, hibernate.

travesty *(SYN.)* farce, joke, misrepresentation, counterfeit, mimicry.

treachery *(SYN.)* collusion, cabal, combination, intrigue, conspiracy, machination, disloyalty, betrayal, treason, plot. *(ANT.)* allegiance, steadfastness, loyalty.

treason *(SYN.)* cabal, combination,

treasure

betrayal, sedition, collusion, intrigue, conspiracy, machination, disloyalty, treachery, plot.

treasure *(SYN.)* cherish, hold dear, abundance, guard, prize, appreciate, value, riches, wealth, foster, sustain, nurture. *(ANT.) disregard, neglect, dislike, abandon, reject.*

treat *(SYN.)* employ, avail, manipulate, exploit, operate, utilize, exert, act, exercise, practice, handle, manage, deal, entertain, indulge, host, negotiate, tend, attend, heal, use. *(ANT.) neglect, overlook, ignore, waste.*

treaty *(SYN.)* compact, agreement, pact, bargain, covenant, alliance, marriage. *(ANT.) schism, separation, divorce.*

trek *(SYN.)* tramp, hike, plod, trudge.

tremble *(SYN.)* flutter, jolt, jar, agitate, quake, quiver, quaver, rock, shake, shudder, shiver, totter, sway, vibrate, waver.

trembling *(SYN.)* apprehension, alarm, dread, fright, fear, horror, terror, panic. *(ANT.) composure, calmness, tranquillity.*

tremendous *(SYN.)* enormous, huge, colossal, gigantic, great, large.

tremor *(SYN.)* flutter, vibration, palpitation.

trench *(SYN.)* gully, gorge, ditch, gulch, moat, dugout, trough.

trenchant *(SYN.)* clear, emphatic, forceful, impressive, meaningful.

trend *(SYN.)* inclination, drift, course, tendency, direction.

trendy *(SYN.)* modish, faddish, stylish, voguish, popular, current.

trepidation *(SYN.)* apprehension, alarm, dread, fright, fear, horror, panic, terror. *(ANT.) boldness, bravery, fearlessness, courage, assurance.*

trespass *(SYN.)* atrocity, indignity, affront, insult, outrage, offense, aggression, crime, misdeed, injustice, vice, wrong, sin. *(ANT.) evacuate, vacate, relinquish, abandon.*

trespasser *(SYN.)* invader, intruder, encroacher.

trial *(SYN.)* experiment, ordeal, proof, test, examination, attempt, effort, endeavor, essay, affliction, misery, hardship,

suffering, difficulty, misfortune, tribulation, trouble. *(ANT.) consolation, alleviation.*

tribe *(SYN.)* group, race, clan, bunch.

tribulation *(SYN.)* anguish, distress, agony, grief, misery, sorrow, torment, suffering, woe, disaster, calamity, evil, trouble, misfortune. *(ANT.) elation, delight, joy, fun.*

tribunal *(SYN.)* arbitrators, judges, decision makers, judiciary.

trick *(SYN.)* artifice, antic, deception, device, cheat, fraud, hoax, guile, imposture, ruse, ploy, stratagem, trickery, deceit, jest, joke, prank, defraud, subterfuge, wile, stunt. *(ANT.) exposure, candor, openness, honesty, sincerity.*

trickle *(SYN.)* drip, drop, dribble, leak, seep.

tricky *(SYN.)* artifice, antic, covert, cunning, foxy, crafty, furtive, guileful, insidious, sly, shrews, stealthy, surreptitious, subtle, underhand, wily. *(ANT.) frank, candid, ingenuous, sincere, open.*

trifling *(SYN.)* insignificant, frivolous, paltry, petty, trivial, small, unimportant. *(ANT.) momentous, serious, important.*

trigger *(SYN.)* generate, provoke, prompt, motivate, activate.

trim *(SYN.)* nice, clear, orderly, precise, tidy, spruce, adorn, bedeck, clip, shave, prune, cut, shear, compact, neat, decorate, embellish, garnish. *(ANT.) deface, deform, spoil, mar, serious, momentous.*

trimmings *(SYN.)* accessories, adornments, decorations, garnish, ornaments.

trinket *(SYN.)* bead, token, memento, bauble, charm, knickknack.

trio *(SYN.)* threesome, triad, triple.

trip *(SYN.)* expedition, cruise, stumble, err, journey, jaunt, passage, blunder, bungle, slip, excursion, tour, pilgrimage, voyage, travel.

trite *(SYN.)* common, banal, hackneyed, ordinary, stereotyped, stale. *(ANT.) modern, fresh, momentous, stimulating, novel, new.*

triumph *(SYN.)* conquest, achievement, success, prevail, win, jubilation, victory, ovation. *(ANT.) succumb, failure, defeat.*

triumphant *(SYN.)* celebrating, exultant, joyful, exhilarated, smug.

trivial *(SYN.)* insignificant, frivolous, paltry, petty, trifling, small, unimportant. *(ANT.) momentous, important, weighty, serious.*

troops *(SYN.)* militia, troopers, recruits, soldiers, enlisted men.

trophy *(SYN.)* award, memento, honor, testimonial, prize.

tropical *(SYN.)* sultry, sweltering, humid, torrid.

trouble *(SYN.)* anxiety, affliction, calamity, distress, hardship, grief, pain, misery, sorrow, woe, bother, annoyance, care, embarrassment, irritation, torment, pains, worry, disorder, problem, disturbance, effort, exertion, toil, inconvenience, misfortune, labor. *(ANT.) console, accommodate, gratify, soothe, joy, peace.*

troublemaker *(SYN.)* rebel, scamp, agitator, demon, devil, ruffian.

troublesome *(SYN.)* bothersome, annoying, distressing, irksome, disturbing, trying, arduous, vexatious, arduous, difficult, burdensome, laborious, tedious. *(ANT.) accommodating, gratifying, easy, pleasant.*

trounce *(SYN.)* lash, flog, switch, whack, punish, whip, stomp.

truant *(SYN.)* delinquent, absentee, vagrant, malingerer.

truce *(SYN.)* armistice, cease-fire, interval, break, intermission, respite.

trudge *(SYN.)* march, trek, lumber, hike.

true *(SYN.)* actual, authentic, accurate, correct, exact, genuine, real, veracious, veritable, constant, honest, faithful, loyal, reliable, valid, legitimate, steadfast, sincere. *(ANT.) erroneous, counterfeit, false, spurious, fictitious, faithless, inconstant, fickle.*

truly *(SYN.)* indeed, actually, precisely, literally, really, factually.

truncate *(SYN.)* prune, clip, pare, shorten.

truss *(SYN.)* girder, brace, framework, shoring.

trust *(SYN.)* credence, confidence, dependence, reliance, faith, trust, depend on, rely on, reckon on, believe, hope, credit, commit, entrust, confide. *(ANT.) incredulity, doubt, skepticism, mistrust.*

trusted *(SYN.)* trustworthy, reliable, true, loyal, staunch, devoted.

trustworthy *(SYN.)* dependable, certain, reliable, secure, safe, sure, tried, trust. *(ANT.) fallible, dubious, questionable, unreliable, uncertain.*

truth *(SYN.)* actuality, authenticity, accuracy, correctness, exactness, honesty, fact, rightness, truthfulness, veracity, verisimilitude, verity. *(ANT.) falsity, fiction, lie, untruth.*

truthful *(SYN.)* frank, candid, honest, sincere, open, veracious, accurate, correct. *(ANT.) misleading, sly, deceitful.*

try *(SYN.)* endeavor, attempt, strive, struggle, undertake, afflict, test, prove, torment, trouble, essay, examine, analyze, investigate, effort, aim, design, aspire, intend, mean. *(ANT.) decline, ignore, abandon, omit, neglect, comfort, console.*

trying *(SYN.)* bothersome, annoying, distressing, disturbing, troublesome, arduous, vexatious, difficult, tedious. *(ANT.) easy, accommodating, pleasant, gratifying.*

tryout *(SYN.)* audition, trial, chance, test.

tryst *(SYN.)* rendezvous, meeting, appointment.

tub *(SYN.)* basin, vessel, sink, bowl.

tube *(SYN.)* hose, pipe, reed.

tubular *(SYN.)* hollow, cylindrical.

tuck *(SYN.)* crease, fold, gather, bend.

tuft *(SYN.)* bunch, group, cluster.

tug *(SYN.)* pull, wrench, tow, haul, jerk.

tuition *(SYN.)* instruction, schooling, teaching, education.

tumble *(SYN.)* toss, trip, fall, sprawl, wallow, lurch, flounder, plunge, topple.

tumult *(SYN.)* chaos, agitation, commotion, confusion, disarray, disarrangement, disorder, noise, hubbub, ferment. *(ANT.) peacefulness, order, peace, tranquillity.*

tune *(SYN.)* song, concord, harmony, air, melody, strain. *(ANT.) aversion, discord.*

tunnel *(SYN.)* passage, grotto, cave.

turbid *(SYN.)* dark, cloudy, thick, muddy, murky.

turf *(SYN.)* lawn, grassland, sod, grass.

turmoil *(SYN.)* chaos, agitation, commotion, confusion, disarray, disorder. *(ANT.)*

turn

order, peace, certainty, quiet, tranquillity.

turn *(SYN.)* circulate, circle, invert, rotate, revolve, spin, twist, twirl, whirl, wheel, avert, reverse, become, sour. *(ANT.) fix, stand, arrest, stop, continue, endure, proceed.*

turncoat *(SYN.)* renegade, defector, deserter, rat, betrayer, traitor. *(ANT.) loyalist.*

turret *(SYN.)* watchtower, belfry, steeple, tower, cupola, lookout.

tussle *(SYN.)* wrestle, struggle, contend, battle, fight, scuffle.

tutor *(SYN.)* instruct, prime, school, teach, train, prepare, drill.

tweak *(SYN.)* squeeze, pinch, nip.

twig *(SYN.)* sprig, branch, shoot, stem.

twilight *(SYN.)* sunset, sundown, nightfall, eventide, dusk.

twin *(SYN.)* lookalike, imitation, copy, double, replica.

twine *(SYN.)* string, cordage, rope, cord.

twinge *(SYN.)* smart, pang, pain.

twinkle *(SYN.)* shine, gleam, glisten, sparkle, glitter, shimmer, scintillate.

twirl *(SYN.)* rotate, spin, wind, turn, pivot, wheel, swivel, whirl.

twist *(SYN.)* bow, bend, crook, intertwine, curve, incline, deflect, lean, braid, distort, contort, warp, interweave, stoop, turn. *(ANT.) resist, break, straighten, stiffen.*

twitch *(SYN.)* fidget, shudder, jerk.

two-faced *(SYN.)* deceitful, insincere, hypocritical, false, untrustworthy. *(ANT.) straightforward, honest.*

tycoon *(SYN.)* millionaire, industrialist, businessman.

tyke *(SYN.)* rascal, urchin, brat, ragamuffin, imp.

typhoon *(SYN.)* hurricane, cyclone, storm, tornado, whirlwind, twister.

typical *(SYN.)* common, accustomed, conventional, familiar, customary. *(ANT.) marvelous, extraordinary, odd, atypical, uncommon, strange.*

typify *(SYN.)* symbolize, illustrate, signify, represent, incarnate, indicate.

tyrannize *(SYN.)* oppress, victimize, threaten, brutalize, coerce.

tyrannous *(SYN.)* arbitrary, absolute, authoritative, despotic. *(ANT.) conditional, accountable, contingent, qualified, dependent.*

tyrant *(SYN.)* dictator, autocrat, despot, oppressor, slave driver, martinet, disciplinarian, persecutor.

U

ugly *(SYN.)* hideous, homely, plain, deformed, repellent, uncomely, repulsive, ill-natured, unsightly, nasty, unpleasant, wicked, disagreeable, spiteful, surly, vicious. *(ANT.) beautiful, fair, pretty, attractive, handsome, comely, good.*

ultimate *(SYN.)* extreme, latest, final, concluding, decisive, hindmost, last, terminal, utmost, greatest, maximum. *(ANT.) foremost, opening, first, beginning, initial.*

umbrage *(SYN.)* anger, displeasure.

umpire *(SYN.)* judge, referee, arbitrator.

unadulterated *(SYN.)* genuine, clear, clean, immaculate, spotless, pure, absolute, untainted, sheer, bare. *(ANT.) foul, sullied, corrupt, tainted, polluted, tarnished, defiled.*

unalterable *(SYN.)* fixed, unchangeable, steadfast, inflexible.

unanimity *(SYN.)* accord, unity, agreement.

unannounced *(SYN.)* hasty, precipitate, abrupt, unexpected. *(ANT.) courteous, expected, anticipated.*

unassuming *(SYN.)* humble, lowly, compliant, modest, plain, meek, simple, unostentatious, retiring, submissive, unpretentious. *(ANT.) haughty, showy, pompous, proud, vain, arrogant, boastful.*

unattached *(SYN.)* apart, separate, unmarried, single, free, independent. *(ANT.) committed, involved, entangled.*

unavoidable *(SYN.)* inescapable, certain, inevitable, unpreventible.

unawares *(SYN.)* abruptly, suddenly, unexpectedly, off guard.

unbalanced *(SYN.)* crazy, mad, insane, deranged.

unbearable *(SYN.)* insufferable, intolerable. *(ANT.) tolerable, acceptable.*

unbeliever *(SYN.)* dissenter, apostate,

understanding

heretic, schismatic, nonconformist, sectary, sectarian.

unbending *(SYN.)* firm, inflexible, determined, obstinate. *(ANT.)* flexible.

unbiased *(SYN.)* honest, equitable, fair, impartial, reasonable, unprejudiced, just. *(ANT.)* partial, fraudulent, dishonorable.

unbroken *(SYN.)* complete, uninterrupted, continuous, whole.

unburden *(SYN.)* clear, disentangle, divest, free.

uncanny *(SYN.)* amazing, remarkable, extraordinary, strange.

uncertain *(SYN.)* dim, hazy, indefinite, obscure, indistinct, unclear, undetermined, unsettled, ambiguous, unsure, doubtful, questionable, dubious, vague. *(ANT.)* explicit, lucid, specific, certain, unmistakable, precise, clear.

uncertainty *(SYN.)* distrust, doubt, hesitation, incredulity, scruple, ambiguity, skepticism, suspense, suspicion, unbelief. *(ANT.)* faith, belief, certainty, conviction, determination.

uncivil *(SYN.)* impolite, rude, discourteous. *(ANT.)* polite.

uncivilized *(SYN.)* barbaric, barbarous, barbarian, brutal, crude, inhuman, cruel, merciless, rude, remorseless, uncultured, savage, unrelenting. *(ANT.)* humane, kind, polite, civilized, refined.

unclad *(SYN.)* exposed, nude, naked, bare, stripped, defenseless, uncovered, open, unprotected. *(ANT.)* concealed, protected, clothed, covered, dressed.

uncommon *(SYN.)* unusual, rare, odd, scarce, strange, peculiar, queer, exceptional, remarkable. *(ANT.)* ordinary, usual.

uncompromising *(SYN.)* determined, dogged, firm, immovable, contumacious, headstrong, inflexible, obdurate, intractable, obstinate, pertinacious, stubborn, unyielding. *(ANT.)* docile, compliant, amenable, yielding, submissive, pliable.

unconcern *(SYN.)* disinterestedness, impartiality, indifference, apathy, insensibility, neutrality. *(ANT.)* affection, fervor, passion, ardor.

unconditional *(SYN.)* unqualified, unrestricted, arbitrary, absolute, pure, complete, actual, authoritative, perfect, entire, ultimate, tyrannous. *(ANT.)* conditional, contingent, accountable, dependent, qualified.

unconscious *(SYN.)* lethargic, numb, comatose.

uncouth *(SYN.)* green, harsh, crude, coarse, ill-prepared, rough, raw, unfinished, unrefined, vulgar, rude, impolite, discourteous, unpolished, ill-mannered, crass. *(ANT.)* well-prepared, cultivated, refined, civilized, finished.

uncover *(SYN.)* disclose, discover, betray, divulge, expose, reveal, impart, show. *(ANT.)* conceal, hide, cover, obscure, cloak.

undependable *(SYN.)* changeable, unstable, uncertain, shifty, irresponsible. *(ANT.)* stable, dependable, trustworthy.

under *(SYN.)* beneath, underneath, following, below, lower, downward. *(ANT.)* over, above, up, higher.

undercover *(SYN.)* hidden, secret.

undergo *(SYN.)* endure, feel, stand, bear, indulge, suffer, sustain, experience, let, allow, permit, tolerate. *(ANT.)* overcome, discard, exclude, banish.

underhand *(SYN.)* sly, secret, sneaky, secretive, stealthy, crafty. *(ANT.)* honest, open, direct, frank.

undermine *(SYN.)* demoralize, thwart, erode, weaken, subvert, sabotage.

underscore *(SYN.)* emphasize, stress.

undersigned *(SYN.)* casual, chance, contingent, accidental, fortuitous, incidental, unintended. *(ANT.)* decreed, planned, willed, calculated.

understand *(SYN.)* apprehend, comprehend, appreciate, conceive, discern, know, grasp, hear, learn, realize, see, perceive. *(ANT.)* misunderstand, mistake, misapprehend, ignore.

understanding *(SYN.)* agreement, coincidence, concord, accordance, concurrence, harmony, unison, compact, contract, arrangement, bargain, covenant, stipulation. *(ANT.)* variance, difference, discord, dissension, disagreement.

underststudy

understudy *(SYN.)* deputy, agent, proxy, representative, agent, alternate, lieutenant, substitute. *(ANT.)* head, principal, sovereign, master.

undertake *(SYN.)* venture, attempt.

undertaking *(SYN.)* effort, endeavor, attempt, experiment, trial, essay. *(ANT.)* laziness, neglect, inaction.

undesirable *(SYN.)* obnoxious, distasteful, objectionable, repugnant. *(ANT.)* appealing, inviting, attractive.

undivided *(SYN.)* complete, intact, entire, integral, total, perfect, unimpaired, whole. *(ANT.)* partial, incomplete.

undoing *(SYN.)* ruin, downfall, destruction, failure, disgrace.

undying *(SYN.)* endless, deathless, eternal, everlasting, ceaseless, immortal, infinite, perpetual, timeless. *(ANT.)* transient, mortal, temporal, ephemeral, impermanent.

unearthly *(SYN.)* metaphysical, ghostly, miraculous, marvelous, preternatural, superhuman, spiritual, foreign, strange, weird, supernatural. *(ANT.)* physical, plain, human, natural, common, mundane.

uneducated *(SYN.)* uncultured, ignorant, illiterate, uninformed, unlearned, untaught, unlettered. *(ANT.)* erudite, cultured, educated, literate, formed.

unemployed *(SYN.)* inert, inactive, idle, jobless, unoccupied. *(ANT.)* working, occupied, active, industrious, employed.

uneven *(SYN.)* remaining, single, odd, unmatched, rugged, gnarled, irregular. *(ANT.)* matched, even, flat, smooth.

unexceptional *(SYN.)* commonplace, trivial, customary.

unexpected *(SYN.)* immediate, hasty, surprising, instantaneous, unforeseen, abrupt, rapid, startling, sudden. *(ANT.)* expected, gradual, predicted, anticipated, planned.

unfaithful *(SYN.)* treacherous, disloyal, deceitful, capricious. *(ANT.)* true, loyal, steadfast, faithful.

unfasten *(SYN.)* open, expand, spread, exhibit, unbar, unlock, unfold, unseal. *(ANT.)* shut, hide, conceal, close.

unfavorable *(SYN.)* antagonistic, contrary, adverse, opposed, opposite, disastrous, counteractive, unlucky. *(ANT.)* benign, fortunate, lucky, propitious.

unfeeling *(SYN.)* hard, rigorous, cruel, stern, callous, numb, strict, unsympathetic, severe. *(ANT.)* tender, gentle, lenient, humane.

unfold *(SYN.)* develop, create, elaborate, amplify, evolve, mature, expand. *(ANT.)* wither, restrict, contract, stunt, compress.

unfurnished *(SYN.)* naked, mere, bare, exposed, stripped, plain, open, simple. *(ANT.)* concealed, protected, covered.

ungainly *(SYN.)* clumsy, awkward, bungling, clownish, gawky. *(ANT.)* dexterous, graceful, elegant.

unhappy *(SYN.)* sad, miserable, wretched, melancholy, distressed, depressed. *(ANT.)* joyful, happy, cheerful.

unhealthy *(SYN.)* infirm, sick, diseased, sickly. *(ANT.)* vigorous, well, healthy, hale.

uniform *(SYN.)* methodical, natural, customary, orderly, normal, consistent, ordinary, regular, unvarying, unchanging, systematic, steady, unvaried. *(ANT.)* rare, unusual, erratic, abnormal, exceptional.

unimportant *(SYN.)* petty, trivial, paltry, trifling, insignificant, indifferent, minor.

uninformed *(SYN.)* illiterate, uncultured, uneducated, ignorant, unlearned, untaught, unlettered. *(ANT.)* informed, literate, erudite, cultured, educated.

uninhibited *(SYN.)* loose, open, liberated, free. *(ANT.)* constrained, tense, suppressed.

unintelligible *(SYN.)* ambiguous, cryptic, dark, cloudy, abstruse, dusky, mysterious, indistinct, obscure, vague. *(ANT.)* lucid, distinct, bright, clear.

uninteresting *(SYN.)* burdensome, dilatory, dreary, dull, boring, slow, humdrum, monotonous, sluggish, tedious, tardy, wearisome, tiresome. *(ANT.)* entertaining, exciting, quick, amusing.

union *(SYN.)* fusion, incorporation, combination, joining, concurrence, solidarity, agreement, unification, concord, harmony, alliance, unanimity, coalition, confederacy, amalgamation, league, concert, marriage.

(*ANT.*) *disagreement, separation, discord.*

unique *(SYN.)* exceptional, matchless, distinctive, choice, peculiar, singular, rare, sole, single, incomparable, uncommon, solitary, unequaled. (*ANT.*) *typical, ordinary, commonplace, frequent, common.*

unison *(SYN.)* harmony, concurrence, understanding, accordance, concord, agreeable, coincidence. (*ANT.*) *disagreement, difference, discord, variance.*

unite *(SYN.)* attach, blend, amalgamate, combine, conjoin, associate, connect, embody, consolidate, join, link, fuse, unify, merge. (*ANT.*) *sever, divide, separate, disrupt, disconnect.*

universal *(SYN.)* frequent, general, popular, common, familiar, prevailing, prevalent, usual. (*ANT.*) *scarce, odd, regional, local, extraordinary, exceptional.*

unkempt *(SYN.)* sloppy, rumpled, untidy, messy, bedraggled. (*ANT.*) *presentable, well-groomed, tidy, neat.*

unkind *(SYN.)* unfeeling, unsympathetic, unpleasant, cruel, harsh. (*ANT.*) *considerate, sympathetic, amiable, kind.*

unlawful *(SYN.)* illegitimate, illicit, illegal, outlawed, criminal, prohibited. (*ANT.*) *permitted, honest, legal, legitimate.*

unlike *(SYN.)* dissimilar, different, distinct, contrary, diverse, divergent, opposite, incongruous, variant, miscellaneous, divers. (*ANT.*) *conditional, accountable, contingent, qualified, dependent.*

unlucky *(SYN.)* cursed, inauspicious, unfortunate. (*ANT.*) *fortunate, blessed.*

unmerciful *(SYN.)* cruel, merciless, heartless, brutal.

unmistakable *(SYN.)* clear, patent, plain, visible, obvious.

unnecessary *(SYN.)* pointless, needless, superfluous, purposeless.

unoccupied *(SYN.)* empty, vacant, uninhabited.

unparalleled *(SYN.)* peerless, unequaled, rare, unique, unmatched.

unpleasant *(SYN.)* offensive, disagreeable, repulsive, obnoxious, unpleasing.

unqualified *(SYN.)* inept, unfit, incapable, incompetent, unquestioned, absolute.

unreasonable *(SYN.)* foolish, absurd, irrational, inconsistent, nonsensical, ridiculous, silly. (*ANT.*) *reasonable, sensible, sound, consistent, rational.*

unruffled *(SYN.)* calm, smooth, serene, unperturbed.

unruly *(SYN.)* unmanageable, disorganized, disorderly, disobedient. (*ANT.*) *orderly.*

unsafe *(SYN.)* hazardous, insecure, critical, dangerous, perilous, menacing, risky, precarious, threatening, (*ANT.*) *protected, secure, firm, safe.*

unselfish *(SYN.)* bountiful, generous, liberal, giving, beneficent, magnanimous, openhanded, munificent. (*ANT.*) *miserly, stingy, greedy, selfish, covetous.*

unsightly *(SYN.)* ugly, unattractive, hideous.

unsophisticated *(SYN.)* frank, candid, artless, ingenuous, naive, open, simple, natural. (*ANT.*) *sophisticated, worldly, cunning, crafty.*

unsound *(SYN.)* feeble, flimsy, weak, fragile, sick, unhealthy, diseased, invalid, faulty, false.

unstable *(SYN.)* fickle, fitful, inconstant, capricious, changeable, restless, variable. (*ANT.*) *steady, stable, trustworthy, constant.*

unswerving *(SYN.)* fast, firm, inflexible, constant, secure, stable, solid, steady, steadfast, unyielding. (*ANT.*) *sluggish, insecure, unsteady, unstable, loose, slow.*

untainted *(SYN.)* genuine, pure, spotless, clean, clear, unadulterated, guiltless, innocent, chaste, modest, undefiled, sincere, virgin. (*ANT.*) *polluted, tainted, sullied, tarnished, defiled, corrupt, foul.*

untamed *(SYN.)* fierce, savage, uncivilized, barbarous, outlandish, rude, undomesticated, wild, frenzied, mad, turbulent, impetuous, wanton, boisterous, wayward, stormy, extravagant, tempestuous, foolish, rash, giddy, reckless. (*ANT.*) *quiet, gentle, calm, civilized, placid.*

untidy

untidy *(SYN.)* messy, sloppy, disorderly, slovenly.

untoward *(SYN.)* disobedient, contrary, peevish, fractious, forward, petulant, obstinate, intractable, stubborn, perverse, ungovernable. *(ANT.) docile, tractable, obliging, agreeable.*

unusual *(SYN.)* capricious, abnormal, devious, eccentric, aberrant, irregular, variable, remarkable, extraordinary, odd, peculiar, uncommon, strange, exceptional, unnatural. *(ANT.) regular, usual, fixed, ordinary.*

unyielding *(SYN.)* fast, firm, inflexible, constant, solid, secure, stable, steadfast, unswerving, steady. *(ANT.) sluggish, slow, insecure, loose, unsteady, unstable.*

upbraid *(SYN.)* blame, censure, berate, admonish, rate, lecture, rebuke, reprimand, reprehend, scold, vituperate. *(ANT.) praise, commend, approve.*

uphold *(SYN.)* justify, espouse, assert, defend, maintain, vindicate. *(ANT.) oppose, submit, assault, deny, attack.*

upright *(SYN.)* undeviating, right, unswerving, direct, erect, unbent, straight, fair, vertical. *(ANT.) bent, dishonest, crooked, circuitous, winding.*

uprising *(SYN.)* revolution, mutiny, revolt, rebellion.

uproar *(SYN.)* noise, disorder, commotion, tumult, disturbance.

upset *(SYN.)* disturb, harass, bother, annoy, haunt, molest, inconvenience, perplex, pester, tease, plague, trouble, worry, overturn, topple, upend, capsize, fluster, agitate. *(ANT.) soothe, relieve, gratify.*

urbane *(SYN.)* civil, considerate, cultivated, courteous, genteel, polite, accomplished, refined, well-mannered. *(ANT.) rude, uncouth, boorish, uncivil.*

urge *(SYN.)* craving, desire, longing, lust, appetite, aspiration, yearning, incite, coax, entice, force, drive, prod, press, plead, coerce, persuade, implore, beg, recommend, advise. *(ANT.) loathing, hate, distaste, aversion, deter, dissuade, discourage.*

urgency *(SYN.)* emergency, exigency, pass, pinch, strait, crisis.

urgent *(SYN.)* critical, crucial, exigent, imperative, impelling, insistent, necessary, instant, serious, pressing, cogent, important, importunate, immediate. *(ANT.) trivial, unimportant, insignificant.*

usage *(SYN.)* use, treatment, custom, practice, tradition.

use *(SYN.)* custom, practice, habit, training, usage, manner, apply, avail, employ, operate, utilize, exert, exhaust, handle, manage, accustom, inure, exploit, manipulate, spend, expend, consume. *(ANT.) disuse, neglect, waste, ignore, overlook, idleness.*

useful *(SYN.)* beneficial, helpful, good, serviceable, wholesome, advantageous. *(ANT.) harmful, injurious, deleterious, destructive, detrimental.*

usefulness *(SYN.)* price, merit, utility, excellence, virtue, worth, worthiness. *(ANT.) cheapness, valueless, uselessness.*

useless *(SYN.)* bootless, empty, idle, pointless, vain, valueless, worthless, abortive, fruitless, unavailing, ineffectual, vapid. *(ANT.) profitable, potent, effective.*

usher *(SYN.)* guide, lead.

usual *(SYN.)* customary, common, familiar, general, normal, habitual, accustomed, everyday, ordinary, regular. *(ANT.) irregular, exceptional, rare, extraordinary, abnormal.*

utensil *(SYN.)* instrument, tool, vehicle, apparatus, device, implement. *(ANT.) preventive, obstruction.*

utilize *(SYN.)* use, apply, devote, busy, employ, occupy, avail. *(ANT.) reject, banish, discharge, discard.*

utopian *(SYN.)* perfect, ideal, faultless, exemplary, supreme, visionary, unreal. *(ANT.) real, imperfect, actual, faulty.*

utter *(SYN.)* full, perfect, whole, finished, entire, speak, say, complete, superlative. *(ANT.) imperfect, deficient, lacking, faulty, incomplete.*

V

vacancy *(SYN.)* void, emptiness, vacuum, hollowness, blankness, vacuity, depletion, nothingness. *(ANT.) plenitude, fullness, profusion, completeness.*

vacant *(SYN.)* barren, empty, blank, bare, unoccupied, void, vacuous. *(ANT.) filled, packed, employed, full, replete, busy, engaged.*

vacate *(SYN.)* abjure, relinquish, abdicate, renounce, abandon, resign, surrender, desert, waive, quit, leave. *(ANT.) stay, support, uphold, maintain.*

vacation *(SYN.)* rest, holiday, recess, break. *(ANT.) labor, work, routine.*

vacillate *(SYN.)* hesitate, oscillate, undulate, change, fluctuate, vary, waver. *(ANT.) adhere, persist, stick, decide.*

vacillating *(SYN.)* contrary, illogical, contradictory, inconsistent, incongruous, incompatible, paradoxical, irreconcilable, unsteady, wavering. *(ANT.) correspondent, congruous, consistent, compatible.*

vacuity *(SYN.)* space, emptiness, vacuum, void, blank, nothingness, ignorance, unawareness, senselessness, mindlessness, chatter, nonsense, froth, absurdity. *(ANT.) matter, fullness, content, substance, knowledge, intelligence.*

vacuous *(SYN.)* dull, blank, uncomprehending, imbecilic, foolish, thoughtless, distracted, absent-minded. *(ANT.) responsive, alert, attentive, bright, intelligent, aware.*

vacuum *(SYN.)* void, gap, emptiness, hole, chasm, nothingness, abyss.

vagabond *(SYN.)* pauper, ragamuffin, scrub, beggar, mendicant, starveling, wretch, tatterdemalion, hobo, tramp. *(ANT.) responsible, established, rooted, installed, reliable.*

vagary *(SYN.)* notion, whim, fantasy, fancy, daydream, caprice, conceit, quirk, whimsy, impulse.

vagrant *(SYN.)* hobo, rover, tramp, beggar, bum, wanderer, vagabond. *(ANT.) settled, worker, laborer, rooted, ambitious, gentleman.*

vague *(SYN.)* indefinite, hazy, dim, indistinct, ambiguous, obscure, undetermined, unclear, unsure, unsettled. *(ANT.) certain, spelled out, specific, lucid, clear, definite, distinct, explicit, precise, unequivocal.*

vain *(SYN.)* fruitless, empty, bootless, futile, idle, abortive, ineffectual, unavailing, vapid, pointless, valueless, useless, trivial, unfruitful, worthless, unsuccessful, proud, conceited. *(ANT.) meek, modest, potent, rewarding, self-effacing, diffident, profitable, effective, humble.*

vainglory *(SYN.)* conceit, pride, self-esteem, arrogance, self-respect, superciliousness, haughtiness, vanity. *(ANT.) shame, modesty, meekness, humility, lowliness.*

valet *(SYN.)* groom, dresser, attendant, manservant.

valiant *(SYN.)* bold, brave, courageous, adventurous, audacious, chivalrous, daring, fearless, heroic, gallant, magnanimous, intrepid, unafraid, valorous, dauntless. *(ANT.) weak, fearful, cowardly, timid.*

valid *(SYN.)* cogent, conclusive, effective, convincing, binding, efficacious, logical, powerful, legal, sound, weighty, well-founded, real, genuine, actual, true, trustworthy, strong, telling, authentic. *(ANT.) weak, unconvincing, void, unproved, null, spurious, counterfeit.*

validate *(SYN.)* corroborate, substantiate, support, confirm, prove, uphold, sustain, authenticate. *(ANT.) disprove, contradict, cancel.*

valise *(SYN.)* satchel, bag, baggage.

valley *(SYN.)* dale, dell, lowland, basin, gully, vale, ravine. *(ANT.) highland, hill, upland, headland.*

valor *(SYN.)* courage, heroism, bravery, boldness, intrepidity, fearlessness.

valuable *(SYN.)* profitable, useful, costly, precious, dear, expensive, worthy, important, high-priced, esteemed. *(ANT.) trashy, poor, cheap, worthless.*

value *(SYN.)* price, merit, usefulness, value, virtue, utility, appreciate, prize, hold dear,

vanish

treasure, excellence, benefit, cost, rate, evaluate, appraise, esteem, importance, worth, worthiness. (*ANT.*) *valueless, uselessness, cheapness.*

vanish *(SYN.)* evaporate, disappear. (*ANT.*) *appear.*

vanity *(SYN.)* complacency, egotism, pride, self-esteem, conceit, caprice, fancy, idea, conception, notion, haughtiness, self-respect, whim, smugness, vainglory, arrogance, imagination. (*ANT.*) *meekness, humility, diffidence.*

vanquish *(SYN.)* defeat, crush, humble, surmount, master, beat, conquer, overcome, rout, quell, subjugate, subdue. (*ANT.*) *surrender, cede, lose, retreat, capitulate.*

vapid *(SYN.)* hackneyed, inane, insipid, trite, banal, commonplace. (*ANT.*) *striking, novel, fresh, original, stimulating.*

vapor *(SYN.)* steam, fog, mist, smog, haze, steam.

variable *(SYN.)* fickle, fitful, inconstant, unstable, shifting, changeable, unsteady, wavering, vacillating. (*ANT.*) *unchanging, uniform, stable, unwavering, steady, constant.*

variant *(SYN.)* dissimilar, different, distinct, contrary, diverse, divergent, opposite, unlike, incongruous, divers, sundry, various, miscellaneous. (*ANT.*) *similar, same, congruous, identical, alike.*

variation *(SYN.)* change, alternation, alteration, substitution, variety, substitute, mutation, exchange, vicissitude. (*ANT.*) *uniformity, stability, monotony.*

variety *(SYN.)* dissimilarity, diversity, heterogeneity, assortment, change, difference, medley, mixture, miscellany, form, type, class, breed, sort, kind, strain, stock. (*ANT.*) *likeness, monotony, uniformity, sameness, homogeneity.*

various *(SYN.)* miscellaneous, sundry, divers, several, contrary, distinct, dissimilar, divergent, unlike, incongruous, opposite, different. (*ANT.*) *identical, similar, same, alike, congruous.*

vary *(SYN.)* exchange, substitute, alter,

change, modify, shift, convert, transform, transfigure, diversify, veer. (*ANT.*) *settle, stabilize, continue, establish, preserve.*

vassalage *(SYN.)* confinement, captivity, imprisonment, slavery, thralldom. (*ANT.*) *liberation, freedom.*

vast *(SYN.)* big, capacious, extensive, huge, great, ample, immense, wide, unlimited, enormous, measureless, large. (*ANT.*) *tiny, small, short, little.*

vault *(SYN.)* caper, jerk, jump, leap, bound, crypt, sepulcher, hop, spring, safe, start, tomb, grave, catacomb, skip.

vaunt *(SYN.)* crow, flaunt, glory, boast. (*ANT.*) *minimize, humble, deprecate, apologize.*

vaunting *(SYN.)* flourish, display, ostentation, parade, show, pomp. (*ANT.*) *modesty, reserve, humility.*

vehement *(SYN.)* excitable, fervent, ardent, burning, fiery, glowing, impetuous, hot, irascible, passionate. (*ANT.*) *calm, quiet, cool, apathetic, deliberate.*

veil *(SYN.)* clothe, conceal, cover, cloak, web, hide, curtain, disguise, gauze, envelop, screen, mask, shield, film. (*ANT.*) *reveal, unveil, bare, divulge.*

velocity *(SYN.)* quickness, rapidity, speed, swiftness.

venal *(SYN.)* greedy, mercenary, sordid, corrupt. (*ANT.*) *liberal, honorable, generous.*

venerable *(SYN.)* antiquated, aged, antique, ancient, elderly, old, superannuated, old-fashion. (*ANT.*) *young, new, youthful, modern.*

venerate *(SYN.)* approve, esteem, admire, appreciate, wonder, respect. (*ANT.*) *dislike, despise.*

vengeance *(SYN.)* requital, reprisal, reparation, retribution, revenge. (*ANT.*) *forgiveness, remission, pardon, mercy.*

venom *(SYN.)* toxin, poison, bitterness, spite, hate.

vent *(SYN.)* eject, emit, expel, shoot, spurt, emanate, hurl, shed, belch, discharge, breathe.

venture *(SYN.)* speculate, attempt, test, dare, hazard, gamble, chance, risk. (*ANT.*)

insure, secure, protect.

verbal *(SYN.)* oral, spoken, literal, unwritten, vocal. *(ANT.)* printed, written, recorded.

verbose *(SYN.)* communicative, glib, chattering, chatty, garrulous, loquacious, talkative. *(ANT.)* uncommunicative, silent.

verbosity *(SYN.)* long-windedness, verboseness, redundancy, wordiness. *(ANT.)* terseness, laconic, conciseness.

verdict *(SYN.)* judgment, finding, opinion, decision.

verge *(SYN.)* lip, rim, edge, margin, brink, brim.

verification *(SYN.)* confirmation, demonstration, evidence, proof, test, experiment, testimony, trial.

verify *(SYN.)* confirm, substantiate, acknowledge, determine, assure, establish, approve, fix, settle, ratify, strengthen, corroborate, affirm, sanction.

veritable *(SYN.)* authentic, correct, genuine, real, true, accurate, actual. *(ANT.)* false, fictitious, spurious, erroneous, counterfeit.

versed *(SYN.)* conversant, familiar, intimate, knowing, acquainted, aware. *(ANT.)* untrained, unaccomplished.

version *(SYN.)* interpretation, rendition.

vertical *(SYN.)* erect, perpendicular, upright. *(ANT.)* horizontal.

very *(SYN.)* exceedingly, extremely, greatly, considerably.

vessel *(SYN.)* craft, boat, ship.

vestige *(SYN.)* stain, scar, mark, brand, stigma, characteristic, trace, feature, trait, symptom, hint, token, suggestion, indication.

veto *(SYN.)* refusal, denial, refuse, deny, negate, forbid, prohibit. *(ANT.)* approve, approval.

vex *(SYN.)* embitter, exasperate, aggravate, annoy, chafe, bother, provoke, pester, plague, anger, nettle. *(ANT.)* soften, soothe, palliate, mitigate.

vexation *(SYN.)* chagrin, irritation, annoyance, mortification, irritation, pique. *(ANT.)* comfort, pleasure, appeasement, gratification.

vibrate *(SYN.)* flutter, jar, quake, jolt, quaver, agitate, transgression, wickedness, ungodliness, tremble.

vice *(SYN.)* iniquity, crime, offense, evil, guilt, sin, ungodliness, wickedness, depravity, corruption, wrong. *(ANT.)* righteousness, virtue, goodness, innocence, purity.

vicinity *(SYN.)* district, area, locality, neighborhood, environs, proximity, nearness, adjacency. *(ANT.)* remoteness, distance.

vicious *(SYN.)* bad, evil, wicked, sinful, corrupt, cruel, savage, dangerous.

victimize *(SYN.)* cheat, dupe, swindle, deceive, take advantage of.

victor *(SYN.)* champion, winner. *(ANT.)* loser.

victory *(SYN.)* conquest, jubilation, triumph, success, achievement, ovation. *(ANT.)* defeat, failure.

view *(SYN.)* discern, gaze, glance, behold, eye, stare, watch, examine, witness, prospect, vision, vista, sight, look, panorama, opinion, judgment, belief, impression, perspective, range, regard, thought, observation, survey, scene, conception, outlook, inspect, observe. *(ANT.)* miss, overlook, avert, hide.

viewpoint *(SYN.)* attitude, standpoint, aspect, pose, disposition, position, stand, posture.

vigilant *(SYN.)* anxious, attentive, careful, alert, circumspect, cautious, observant, wary, watchful, wakeful. *(ANT.)* inattentive, neglectful, careless.

vigor *(SYN.)* spirit, verve, energy, zeal, fortitude, vitality, strength, liveliness. *(ANT.)* listlessness.

vigorous *(SYN.)* brisk, energetic, active, blithe, animated, frolicsome, strong, spirited, lively, forceful, sprightly, vivacious, powerful, supple. *(ANT.)* vapid, dull, listless, insipid.

vile *(SYN.)* foul, loathsome, base, depraved, debased, sordid, vulgar, wicked, abject, ignoble, mean, worthless, sinful, bad, low,

vilify

wretched, evil, offensive, objectionable, disgusting. (*ANT.*) *honorable, upright, decent, laudable, attractive.*

vilify (*SYN.*) asperse, defame, disparage, abuse, malign, revile, scandalize. (*ANT.*) *protect, honor, praise, cherish.*

village (*SYN.*) hamlet, town. (*ANT.*) *metropolis, city.*

villain (*SYN.*) rascal, rogue, cad, brute, scoundrel, devil, scamp.

villainous (*SYN.*) deleterious, evil, bad, base, iniquitous, unsound, sinful, unwholesome, wicked. (*ANT.*) *honorable, reputable, moral, good, excellent.*

vindicate (*SYN.*) clear, assert, defend, absolve, excuse, acquit, uphold, support. (*ANT.*) *accuse, convict, abandon.*

violate (*SYN.*) disobey, invade, defile, break, desecrate, pollute, dishonor, debauch, profane, deflower, ravish.

violence (*SYN.*) constraint, force, compulsion, coercion. (*ANT.*) *weakness, persuasion, feebleness, impotence, frailty.*

violent (*SYN.*) strong, forceful, powerful, forcible, angry, fierce, savage, passionate, furious. (*ANT.*) *gentle.*

virgin (*SYN.*) immaculate, genuine, spotless, clean, clear, unadulterated, chaste, untainted, innocent, guiltless, untouched, modest, maid, maiden, sincere, unused, undefiled, pure. (*ANT.*) *foul, tainted, defiled, sullied, polluted, corrupt.*

virile (*SYN.*) hardy, male, mannish, lusty, bold, masculine, strong, vigorous. (*ANT.*) *feminine, unmanly, weak, effeminate, womanish, emasculated.*

virtue (*SYN.*) integrity, probity, purity, chastity, goodness, rectitude, effectiveness, force, honor, power, efficacy, quality, strength, merit, righteousness. (*ANT.*) *fault, vice, lewdness, corruption.*

virtuous (*SYN.*) good, ethical, chaste, honorable, moral, just, pure, righteous, upstanding, upright, scrupulous. (*ANT.*) *licentious, unethical, amoral, sinful, libertine, immoral.*

virulent (*SYN.*) hostile, malevolent, malignant, bitter, spiteful, wicked. (*ANT.*)

kind, affectionate, benevolent.

vision (*SYN.*) dream, hallucination, mirage, eyesight, sight, fantasy, illusion, specter, revelation, phantom, spook. (*ANT.*) *verity, reality.*

visionary (*SYN.*) faultless, ideal, perfect, unreal, supreme. (*ANT.*) *real, actual, imperfect, faulty.*

visit (*SYN.*) attend, see, appointment.

visitor (*SYN.*) caller, guest.

vista (*SYN.*) view, scene, aspect.

vital (*SYN.*) cardinal, living, paramount, alive, essential, critical, basic, indispensable, urgent, life-and-death. (*ANT.*) *lifeless, unimportant, inanimate, nonessential.*

vitality (*SYN.*) buoyancy, being, life, liveliness, existence, spirit, vigor. (*ANT.*) *death, lethargy, dullness, demise.*

vitiate (*SYN.*) allay, abase, corrupt, adulterate, debase, defile, depress, deprave, degrade, impair, humiliate, pervert.

vivacious (*SYN.*) lively, spirited.

vivid (*SYN.*) brilliant, striking, clear, bright, intense, lively, strong, graphic. (*ANT.*) *dim, dusky, vague, dull, dreary.*

vocal (*SYN.*) said, uttered, oral, spoken, definite, outspoken, specific.

vocation (*SYN.*) commerce, employment, business, art, job, profession, trade, occupation, career, calling, work, trading. (*ANT.*) *pastime, hobby, avocation.*

void (*SYN.*) barren, emptiness, space, annul, cancel, empty, bare, unoccupied, meaningless, invalid, useless, invalidate, worthless, vacant, barren. (*ANT.*) *employed, full, replete, engaged.*

volatile (*SYN.*) effervescent, resilient, buoyant, animated, cheerful, hopeful, lively, sprightly, spirited, vivacious. (*ANT.*) *depressed, sullen, hopeless, dejected, despondent.*

volition (*SYN.*) desire, intention, pleasure, preference, choice, decision, resolution, testament, wish, will. (*ANT.*) *disinterest, compulsion, indifference.*

voluble (*SYN.*) glib, communicative, verbose, loquacious, chatty, chattering. (*ANT.*) *uncommunicative, laconic, taciturn,* *silent.*

volume *(SYN.)* capacity, loudness, sound, magnitude, mass, book, dimensions, quantity, amount, size.

voluntary *(SYN.)* extemporaneous, free, automatic, spontaneous, offhand. *(ANT.) forced, planned, required, rehearsed, compulsory, prepared.*

volunteer *(SYN.)* extend, offer, present, advance, propose, tender, sacrifice. *(ANT.) receive, spurn, reject, accept, retain.*

voracious *(SYN.)* insatiable, ravenous.

vow *(SYN.)* oath, pledge, swear, promise.

voyage *(SYN.)* tour, journey, excursion.

vulgar *(SYN.)* ordinary, popular, common, general, crude, coarse, low, rude. *(ANT.) polite, refined, select, aristocratic.*

vulnerable *(SYN.)* unguarded, defenseless, unprotected.

W

wacky *(SYN.)* strange, crazy, peculiar.

wad *(SYN.)* hunk, clump, chunk.

wafer *(SYN.)* cracker, lozenge.

waft *(SYN.)* convey, glide, sail, float.

wage *(SYN.)* conduct, pursue, make.

wager *(SYN.)* stake, bet, play, gamble, speculate, risk, chance.

wages *(SYN.)* payment, compensation, fee, allowance, pay, salary, earnings, rate, recompense.

wagon *(SYN.)* carriage, buggy, cart, surrey, stagecoach.

waif *(SYN.)* guttersnipe, ragamuffin, tramp, vagrant, urchin.

wail *(SYN.)* mourn, moan, cry, bewail, lament, bemoan, sorrow.

wait *(SYN.)* linger, tarry, attend, bide, watch, delay, await, abide, stay, serve, pause, remain, rest, minister, expect. *(ANT.) hasten, act, leave, expedite.*

waive *(SYN.)* renounce, abandon, surrender, relinquish, forgo. *(ANT.) uphold, maintain.*

wake *(SYN.)* awaken, rouse, waken, arouse, stimulate, activate. *(ANT.) doze, sleep.*

waken *(SYN.)* wake, arouse, rouse, awaken, stimulate, activate. *(ANT.) doze, sleep.*

walk *(SYN.)* step, stroll, march, amble, saunter, hike, lane, path, passage.

wall *(SYN.)* barricade, divider, partition, panel, stockade.

wallow *(SYN.)* plunge, roll, flounder, grovel.

wan *(SYN.)* colorless, haggard, gaunt, pallid, pasty, pale.

wander *(SYN.)* rove, stroll, deviate, ramble, digress, roam, traipse, range, err, meander, saunter. *(ANT.) linger, stop, settle.*

wane *(SYN.)* abate, weaken, fade, ebb, decrease, wither, subside.

want *(SYN.)* penury, destitution, crave, desire, requirement, poverty, wish, require, need, privation. *(ANT.) wealth, plenty, abundance.*

wanton *(SYN.)* lecherous, immoral, loose, lewd, salacious, lustful.

war *(SYN.)* battle, hostility, combat, fight, strife, contention. *(ANT.) peace, calm, friendship, harmony.*

warble *(SYN.)* sing, trill, chirp.

ward *(SYN.)* annex, wing, section.

warden *(SYN.)* custodian, guard, guardian, keeper, turnkey, jailer, curator.

wares *(SYN.)* merchandise, staples, inventory, commodities, goods.

wariness *(SYN.)* heed, care, watchfulness, caution, vigilance. *(ANT.) carelessness, abandon.*

warlike *(SYN.)* hostile, unfriendly, combative, belligerent, antagonistic, pugnacious, bellicose, opposed, aggressive. *(ANT.) cordial, peaceful, amicable.*

warm *(SYN.)* sincere, cordial, hearty, earnest, sympathetic, ardent, heated, gracious, temperate, enthusiastic, lukewarm, tepid, eager, sociable. *(ANT.) cool, aloof, taciturn, brisk, indifferent.*

warmhearted *(SYN.)* loving, kind, kindhearted, friendly, generous.

warmth *(SYN.)* friendliness, cordiality, geniality, understanding, compassion.

warn *(SYN.)* apprise, notify, admonish, caution, advise, inform.

warning

warning *(SYN.)* advice, information, caution, portent, admonition, indication, notice, sign.

warp *(SYN.)* turn, bend, twist, distort, deprave.

warrant *(SYN.)* pledge, assurance, warranty, guarantee, authorize, approve, mandate, sanction.

warrior *(SYN.)* combatant, fighter, soldier, mercenary, guerrilla.

wary *(SYN.)* careful, awake, watchful, heedful, attentive, alive, mindful, cautious, thoughtful. *(ANT.)* unaware, indifferent, careless, apathetic.

wash *(SYN.)* launder, cleanse, rub, wet, clean, scrub, bathe. *(ANT.)* soil, dirty, stain.

washed-out *(SYN.)* bleached, dull, faded, pale, discolored, pallid.

waspish *(SYN.)* irritable, petulant, fractious, ill-tempered, testy, snappish, touchy. *(ANT.)* pleasant, genial.

waste *(SYN.)* forlorn, bleak, wild, solitary, dissipate, abandoned, spend, deserted, bare, consume, dwindle, decay, misspend, decrease, wither, wear, effluent, useless, unused, garbage, rubbish, refuse, trash, squander, uninhabited. *(ANT.)* cultivated, attended.

wasteful *(SYN.)* wanton, costly, lavish, extravagant.

watch *(SYN.)* inspect, descry, behold, distinguish, guard, attend, observe, contemplate, espy, perceive, look at, protect, chronometer, timepiece, patrol, vigil, duty, shift, regard, note, view, scan, sentinel, watchman, sentry, discern.

watchdog *(SYN.)* lookout, guard, sentinel, sentry.

watchful *(SYN.)* alert, careful, attentive, vigilant, wary, cautious.

waterfall *(SYN.)* cascade, cataract.

watertight *(SYN.)* impregnable, firm, solid.

wave *(SYN.)* ripple, whitecap, undulation, breaker, surf, swell, sea, surge, tide, flow, roll.

waver *(SYN.)* question, suspect, flicker, deliberate, doubt, distrust, hesitate, falter, stagger. *(ANT.)* confide, trust, believe, decide.

wavering *(SYN.)* fickle, shifting, variable, changeable, vacillating, fitful. *(ANT.)* unchanging, constant, uniform.

wavy *(SYN.)* rippling, serpentine, curly.

wax *(SYN.)* raise, heighten, expand, accrue, enhance, extend, multiply, enlarge, augment, amplify. *(ANT.)* contract, reduce, atrophy, diminish.

way *(SYN.)* habit, road, course, avenue, route, mode, system, channel, track, fashion, method, walk, approach, manner, technique, means, procedure, trail, proceed, progress, path, style.

waylay *(SYN.)* surprise, accost, ambush, attack, pounce, intercept.

wayward *(SYN.)* stubborn, headstrong, contrary, obstinate, naughty, disobedient, rebellious, refractory.

weak *(SYN.)* frail, debilitated, delicate, poor, wavering, infirm, bending, lame, defenseless, vulnerable, fragile, pliant, feeble, watery, diluted, undecided, assailable, irresolute, unsteady, yielding, tender. *(ANT.)* strong, potent, sturdy, powerful.

weaken *(SYN.)* exhaust, sap, disable, devitalize.

weakling *(SYN.)* sissy, namby-pamby, milksop, milquetoast.

weakness *(SYN.)* incompetence, inability, impotence, handicap, fondness, liking, affection, disability, incapacity, feebleness. *(ANT.)* strength, ability, power.

wealth *(SYN.)* fortune, money, riches, possessions, means, abundance, opulence, affluence, property, quantity, profession, luxury. *(ANT.)* want, need.

wealthy *(SYN.)* rich, exorbitant, prosperous, affluent, successful. *(ANT.)* poverty-stricken, poor, indigent, impoverished, beggarly, destitute, needy.

wear *(SYN.)* erode, fray, grind, apparel, clothes, garb, attire.

wearied *(SYN.)* weak, languid, faint, irresolute, feeble, timid. *(ANT.)* brave, vigorous.

weary *(SYN.)* faint, spent, worn, tired, fatigued, exhausted, tiresome, bored, wearied, tedious, jaded. *(ANT.)* rested, hearty, fresh.

weasel *(SYN.)* cheat, traitor, betrayer.

weave *(SYN.)* lace, interlace, plait, intertwine, braid, knit.

web *(SYN.)* netting, network, net, cobweb, trap, entanglement.

wed *(SYN.)* espouse, marry.

wedge *(SYN.)* chock, jam, lodge.

wedlock *(SYN.)* marriage, union, espousal, wedding, matrimony.

wee *(SYN.)* small, tiny, miniature, petite, microscopic, minute.

weep *(SYN.)* mourn, sob, bemoan, cry, lament, whimper, wail.

weigh *(SYN.)* heed, deliberate, consider, study, ponder, contemplate, reflect, evaluate. *(ANT.)* neglect, ignore.

weight *(SYN.)* importance, emphasis, load, burden, import, stress, influence, heaviness, pressure, value, gravity, significance. *(ANT.)* triviality, levity, insignificance, lightness, buoyancy.

weird *(SYN.)* odd, eerie, strange, unnatural, peculiar, spooky.

welcome *(SYN.)* entertain, greet, accept, receive, reception, gain, greeting, shelter. *(ANT.)* reject, bestow, impart, discharge.

weld *(SYN.)* solder, connect, fuse, bond.

welfare *(SYN.)* good, well-being, prosperity.

well *(SYN.)* hearty, happy, sound, hale, beneficial, good, convenient, expedient, healthy, favorably, fully, thoroughly, surely, adequately, satisfactorily, competently, certainly, completely, trim, undoubtedly, fit, profitable. *(ANT.)* infirm, depressed, weak.

well-being *(SYN.)* delight, happiness, satisfaction, contentment, gladness. *(ANT.)* sorrow, grief, sadness, despair.

well-bred *(SYN.)* cultured, polite, genteel, courtly, refined, cultivated. *(ANT.)* crude, vulgar, boorish, rude.

well-known *(SYN.)* famous, illustrious, celebrated, noted, eminent, renowned. *(ANT.)* unknown, ignominious, obscure, hidden.

wet *(SYN.)* moist, dank, soaked, damp, drenched, dampen, moisten. *(ANT.)* arid, dry, parched.

wharf *(SYN.)* pier, dock.

wheedle *(SYN.)* coax, cajole, persuade.

whim *(SYN.)* fancy, notion, humor, quirk, caprice, whimsy, inclination, vagary.

whimsical *(SYN.)* quaint, strange, curious, odd, unusual, droll, queer, eccentric, peculiar. *(ANT.)* normal, common, usual, familiar.

whine *(SYN.)* whimper, cry, moan, complain.

whip *(SYN.)* scourge, thrash, beat, lash.

whirl *(SYN.)* rotate, twirl, spin, revolve, reel.

whole *(SYN.)* total, sound, all, intact, complete, well, hale, integral, unimpaired, healed, entire, uncut, undivided, unbroken, undamaged, perfect. *(ANT.)* partial, defective, imperfect, deficient.

wholesome *(SYN.)* robust, well, hale, healthy, sound, salubrious, good, hygienic, salutary, nourishing, healthful, strong, nutritious, hearty. *(ANT.)* frail, noxious, infirm, delicate, injurious, diseased.

wicked *(SYN.)* deleterious, iniquitous, immoral, bad, evil, base, ungodly, unsound, sinful, bitter, blasphemous, malicious, evil-minded, profane, baleful, hostile, rancorous, unwholesome. *(ANT.)* moral, good, reputable, honorable.

wide *(SYN.)* large, broad, sweeping, extensive, vast, expanded. *(ANT.)* restricted, narrow.

width *(SYN.)* wideness, extensiveness, breadth.

wield *(SYN.)* handle, brandish.

wild *(SYN.)* outlandish, uncivilized, untamed, irregular, wanton, foolish, mad, barbarous, rough, waste, desert, uncultivated, boisterous, unruly, savage, primitive, giddy, unrestrained, silly, wayward, uncontrolled, impetuous, crazy, ferocious, undomesticated, desolate. *(ANT.)* quiet, gentle, placid, tame, restrained, civilized.

will *(SYN.)* intention, desire, volition, decision, resolution, wish, resoluteness, choice, determination, pleasure. *(ANT.)*

willful

disinterest, coercion, indifference.

willful *(SYN.)* intentional, designed, contemplated, studied, premeditated. *(ANT.)* fortuitous.

willing *(SYN.)* agreeing, energetic, enthusiastic, consenting, agreeable, eager.

wilt *(SYN.)* sag, droop, weaken.

wily *(SYN.)* cunning, foxy, sly, crafty.

win *(SYN.)* gain, succeed, prevail, achieve, thrive, obtain, get, acquire, earn, flourish. *(ANT.)* lose, miss, forfeit, fail.

wind *(SYN.)* gale, breeze, storm, gust, blast, air, breath, flurry, puff, blow, hurricane, typhoon, cyclone, tornado, suggestion, hint, clue, zephyr, squall, coil, crank, screw, meander, wander, twist, weave, draft.

winsome *(SYN.)* winning, charming, agreeable.

wisdom *(SYN.)* insight, judgment, learning, sense, discretion, reason, prudence, erudition, foresight, intelligence, knowledge, information, sagacity. *(ANT.)* nonsense, foolishness, stupidity, ignorance.

wise *(SYN.)* informed, sagacious, learned, penetrating, enlightened, advisable, prudent, profound, deep, erudite, scholarly, knowing, sound, intelligent, expedient, discerning. *(ANT.)* simple, shallow, foolish.

wish *(SYN.)* crave, hanker, long, hunger, yearning, lust, craving, yearn, want, appetite, covet, longing, desire, urge. *(ANT.)* hate, aversion, loathing, distaste.

wit *(SYN.)* sense, humor, pleasantry, satire, intelligence, comprehension, understanding, banter, mind, wisdom, intellect, wittiness, fun, drollery, humorist, wag, comedian, raillery, irony, witticism. *(ANT.)* solemnity, commonplace, sobriety.

witch *(SYN.)* magician, sorcerer, enchanter, sorceress, enchantress, warlock.

witchcraft *(SYN.)* enchantment, magic, wizardry, conjuring, voodoo.

withdraw *(SYN.)* renounce, leave, abandon, recall, retreat, go, secede, desert, quit, retire, depart, retract, remove, forsake. *(ANT.)* enter, tarry, abide, place, stay.

wither *(SYN.)* wilt, languish, dry, shrivel, decline, fade, decay, sear, waste, wizen,

weaken, droop, sink, fail, shrink. *(ANT.)* renew, refresh, revive.

withhold *(SYN.)* forbear, abstain, repress, check, refrain. *(ANT.)* persist, continue.

witness *(SYN.)* perceive, proof, spectator, confirmation, see, attestation, watch, observe, eyewitness, notice, testimony. *(ANT.)* refutation, contradiction, argument.

witty *(SYN.)* funny, talented, apt, bright, adroit, sharp, clever. *(ANT.)* foolish, slow, dull, clumsy, awkward.

wizard *(SYN.)* magician, conjuror, sorcerer.

wizardry *(SYN.)* voodoo, legerdemain, conjuring, witchcraft, charm.

woe *(SYN.)* sorrow, disaster, trouble, evil, agony, suffering, anguish, sadness, grief, distress, misery, torment, misfortune. *(ANT.)* pleasure, delight, fun.

womanly *(SYN.)* girlish, womanish, female, ladylike. *(ANT.)* mannish, virile, male, masculine.

wonder (SYN.) awe, curiosity, miracle, admiration, surprise, wonderment. *(ANT.)* expectation, familiarity, indifference, apathy, triviality.

wonderful *(SYN.)* extraordinary, marvelous, astonishing, amazing, remarkable, astounding.

wont *(SYN.)* practice, use, custom, training, habit, usage, manner. *(ANT.)* inexperience, disuse.

word *(SYN.)* phrase, term, utterance, expression, articulate.

wordy *(SYN.)* talkative, verbose, garrulous.

work *(SYN.)* opus, employment, achievement, performance, toil, business, exertion, occupation, labor, job, product. *(ANT.)* recreation, leisure, vacation, ease.

working *(SYN.)* busy, active, industrious. *(ANT.)* lazy, dormant, passive, inactive.

world *(SYN.)* globe, earth, universe.

worn *(SYN.)* tired, jaded, exhausted, wearied, faint, weary. *(ANT.)* invigorated, fresh, rested.

worry *(SYN.)* concern, trouble, disquiet, anxiety, fear, pain, harry, gall, grieve. *(ANT.)* console, comfort, contentment, satisfaction, peace.

worship *(SYN.)* honor, revere, adore, idolize, reverence, glorify, respect. *(ANT.)* curse, scorn, blaspheme, despise.

worth *(SYN.)* value, price, deserving, excellence, usefulness, utility, worthiness. *(ANT.)* uselessness, valueless, cheapness.

worthless *(SYN.)* empty, idle, abortive, ineffectual, bootless, vain, unavailing. *(ANT.)* effective, valuable, potent.

wound *(SYN.)* mar, harm, damage, hurt, dishonor, injure, injury, spoil, wrong. *(ANT.)* compliment, preserve, help.

wrap *(SYN.)* cover, protect, shield, cloak, mask, clothe, curtain, guard, conceal. *(ANT.)* reveal, bare, unveil, expose.

wrath *(SYN.)* fury, anger, irritation, rage, animosity, passion, temper, petulance. *(ANT.)* patience, conciliation, peace.

wreck *(SYN.)* ravage, devastation, extinguish, destroy, annihilate, damage, raze. *(ANT.)* construct, preserve, establish.

wrench *(SYN.)* tug, jerk, twist.

wrestle *(SYN.)* fight, tussle, grapple.

wretch *(SYN.)* cad, scoundrel, rogue.

wretched *(SYN.)* forlorn, miserable, comfortless, despicable, paltry, low. *(ANT.)* contented, happy, significant.

wring *(SYN.)* twist, extract.

writer *(SYN.)* creator, maker, author, composer.

writhe *(SYN.)* twist, squirm.

wrong *(SYN.)* awry, incorrect, improper, amiss, naughty, inappropriate, criminal, faulty, erroneous, bad, evil, imprecise. *(ANT.)* proper, true, correct, suitable.

wry *(SYN.)* amusing, witty, dry, droll.

Y

yacht *(SYN.)* sailboat, boat, cruiser.

yank *(SYN.)* pull, wrest, draw, haul, tug, jerk, wrench, heave, extract.

yap *(SYN.)* howl, bark.

yard *(SYN.)* pen, confine, court, enclosure, compound, garden.

yardstick *(SYN.)* measure, criterion, gauge.

yarn *(SYN.)* wool, tale, narrative, thread, story, fiber, anecdote.

yaw *(SYN.)* tack, change course, pitch, toss, roll.

yawn *(SYN.)* open, gape.

yearly *(SYN.)* annually.

yearn *(SYN.)* pine, long for, want, desire, crave, wish.

yearning *(SYN.)* hungering, craving, desire, longing, appetite, lust, urge, aspiration, wish. *(ANT.)* distaste, loathing, abomination, hate.

yell *(SYN.)* call, scream, shout, whoop, howl, roar, holler, wail, bawl.

yellow *(SYN.)* fearful, cowardly, chicken. *(ANT.)* bold, brave.

yelp *(SYN.)* screech, squeal, howl, bark.

yen *(SYN.)* longing, craving, fancy, appetite, desire, lust, hunger.

yet *(SYN.)* moreover, also, additionally, besides.

yield *(SYN.)* produce, afford, breed, grant, accord, cede, relent, succumb, bestow, allow, permit, give way, submit, bear, surrender, supply, fruits, give up, abdicate, return, impart, harvest, permit, accede, acquiesce, crop, capitulate, pay, concede, generate, relinquish. *(ANT.)* assert, deny, refuse, resist, struggle, oppose, strive.

yielding *(SYN.)* dutiful, submissive, compliant, obedient, tractable. *(ANT.)* rebellious, intractable, insubordinate.

yoke *(SYN.)* tether, leash, bridle, harness.

yokel *(SYN.)* hick, peasant, hayseed, innocent.

young *(SYN.)* immature, undeveloped, youthful, underdeveloped, juvenile, junior, underage. *(ANT.)* old, mature, elderly.

youngster *(SYN.)* kid, lad, stripling, minor, youth, child, fledgling. *(ANT.)* adult, elder.

youthful *(SYN.)* childish, immature, young, boyish, childlike, callow, girlish, puerile. *(ANT.)* old, elderly, senile, aged, mature.

yowl *(SYN.)* yell, shriek, cry, wail, whoop, howl, scream.

Z

zany *(SYN.)* clownish, comical, foolish, silly, scatterbrained.

zap *(SYN.)* drive, vim, pep, determination.

zeal *(SYN.)* fervor, eagerness, passion, vehemence, devotion, intensity, excitement, earnestness, inspiration, warmth, ardor, fanaticism, enthusiasm. *(ANT.)* unconcern, *ennui, apathy, indifference.*

zealot *(SYN.)* champion, crank, fanatic, bigot.

zealous *(SYN.)* enthusiastic, fiery, keen, eager, fervid, ardent, intense, vehement, fervent, glowing, hot, impassioned, passionate. *(ANT.) cool, nonchalant, apathetic.*

zenith *(SYN.)* culmination, apex, height, acme, consummation, top, summit, pinnacle, climax, peak. *(ANT.) floor, nadir, depth, anticlimax.*

zero *(SYN.)* nonexistent, nil, nothing, none.

zest *(SYN.)* enjoyment, savor, eagerness, relish, satisfaction, gusto, spice, tang, pleasure, exhilaration.

zestful *(SYN.)* delightful, thrilling, exciting, stimulating, enjoyable.

zip *(SYN.)* vigor, vim, energy, vitality, spirited, animation, provocative.

zone *(SYN.)* region, climate, tract, belt, sector, section, district, locality, precinct, territory.

zoo *(SYN.)* menagerie.

zoom *(SYN.)* zip, fly, speed, whiz, roar, race.